CONTEMPORARY AMERICAN RELIGION

WADE CLARK ROOF
Editor in Chief

VOLUME 2

MACMILLAN REFERENCE USA
An Imprint of The Gale Group
NEW YORK

Copyright © 2000 by Macmillan Reference USA

Macmillan Reference USA
1633 Broadway
New York, NY 10019

PRINTED IN THE UNITED STATES OF AMERICA

Printing Number

1 2 3 4 5 6 7 8 9 10

LIBRARY OF CONGRESS CATALOGING-IN-PUBLICATION DATA

       p. cm.
   Includes bibliographical references and index.
   ISBN 0-02-864926-5 (v. 1 : alk. paper)—ISBN 0-02-864927-3 v. 2 : alk. paper)—
ISBN 0-02-864928-1 (2 v. set : alk. paper)
     1. United States—Religion—Encyclopedias. I. Roof, Wade Clark.

BL2525 .C65 1999
200'.973'03—dc21

                                    99-046712

This paper meets the requirements of ANSI/NISO Z39.48-1992 (Permanence of Paper).

M

Macrobiotics

Macrobiotics (from the Greek words *makro* and *bios*, meaning "the great art of life") is a health-oriented movement that began in Japan about a hundred years ago. Introduced into the United States in the late 1950s, macrobiotics flourished from the 1960s through the late 1980s as a diet and health movement and greatly affected how Americans think about food and health and how they eat.

One may question whether macrobiotics can be called a religion. For many or most of the people influenced by it, macrobiotics is primarily an approach to health and to diet. Yet macrobiotics does have a cosmology and a view of the nature and destiny of the human being. Also, it claims to be a means by which one can transcend the limitations of human existence and reestablish a connection with the spiritual and eternal dimension of reality. As such it fulfills the basic definition of a religion as a means of reconnecting (*religare*) the human and the divine. Since macrobiotics came to the United States, a small though committed group of persons have found in it a worldview, set of values, way of life, and spiritual practice. Thus macrobiotics can also be accurately designated as a "religious movement."

The modern founder of macrobiotics is Ishitsuka Sagen (1850–1910), a physician in Japan. Inspired by traditional Oriental thought (*The Yellow Emperor's Classic of Internal Medicine*, a work of the Japanese physician and philosopher Kaibara Ekken et al.) and using modern scientific analysis and experimentation, Ishitsuka developed what he called *shoku-yoo* or "cur-

ing through food." Shoku-yoo was based on the following ideas:

- Human health—the harmonious functioning of the body and of the whole organism—is based on the proper balance among mineral salts within the body, particularly the balance between sodium and potassium.
- What one eats and drinks is paramount in creating this balance and hence in creating human health and illness.
- Food, then, is the primary determinant of health. Proper diet can prevent illness and can cure existing disease.
- Generally speaking, the optimal diet for human beings is one based on whole grains supplemented by beans, locally produced vegetables, and perhaps animal food in small amounts. This is most likely to provide the proper balance of minerals and nutrients. The human being is by nature an eater of grains. Our dentition and digestive system suggest this. Grains are the most abundant food crop in most climates. In extreme climates, where grains do not grow, a proper diet would be based on the local foods available.
- A balanced diet leads to physical, emotional, mental, and spiritual health—the last including a sense of oneness with the universe.

The leading proponent of Shoku-yoo after Ishitsuka was Sakurazawa Jyoichi (1893–1966), who was known in America as George Ohsawa. Ohsawa introduced a Taoist cosmology as a basis of macrobiotics, teaching that the multiplicity of phenomena are all expressions of an Absolute Unity—the Tao—which has bifurcated into the opposing, complementary, and creative forces of yin and yang. He applied the yin-yang classifications to diet, designating foods as yin or yang. Ohsawa also clearly presented macrobiotics as a means of achieving spiritual development. He maintained that the true basis of spiritual practice is proper diet and cited Zen Buddhism as an example, holding that the critical factor in Zen is its vegetarian, grain-based diet. For a time Ohsawa referred to his teachings as "Zen macrobiotics." He also called macrobiotics *shoku-doo*—the "Tao (or path) of eating." In so doing, he tried to place macrobiotics on a level with *cha-do* (the Tao of tea), *ka-do* (the Tao of flower arrangement), *sho-do* (the Tao of calligraphy) and other Japanese spiritual disciplines that bring the human being into harmony with the Absolute and to an enlightened state of being. Ohsawa also held that human society could be transformed by proper diet and proposed macrobiotics as the basis of a world peace movement.

Starting in about 1950, Ohsawa sent young Japanese students of macrobiotics to other parts of the world. Michio and Aveline Kushi and Herman and Cornellia Aihara came to the United States and were to play an important part in the spread of macrobiotics in American culture. Ohsawa and his wife, Lima, first visited in 1959, and until his death he devoted much time and energy to teaching macrobiotics in America.

In the United States, Kushi and Aihara developed the basic themes of macrobiotics as presented by Ohsawa. Kushi, through his many books, lecture tours, and educational activities, became the symbol of macrobiotics in American and in fact around the world. He was very active in presenting macrobiotics as a prevention and cure for cancer. He also carried on the political agenda of Ohsawa, founding what he called the "One Peaceful World" movement. Kushi also developed macrobiotics as a path of spiritual development. He introduced elements of esoteric Shinto and Buddhist teachings such as chanting and meditation and gave special "spiritual seminars" in America and abroad.

Starting in the late 1960s, macrobiotics became an important factor in American life, particularly in the so-called alternative culture or New Age movement. The number of persons who identified themselves as macrobiotic and who deeply studied macrobiotics has been small, perhaps several thousand. However, the number of persons affected by its teachings about food, diet, and health has been large. Teachers of macrobiotics helped spread the idea that food is a primary factor in health both within and without the alternative culture long before the medical establishment began to do so. The first bona fide natural-foods store—Erewhon of Boston—was founded by the Kushis, and persons promoting macrobiotics have been instrumental in creating that now important part of the food industry.

For the past three decades the macrobiotic diet or some form of it has been the unofficial diet of the broad alternative culture movement. For example, hippies, students of Yoga, Tai chi, and Zen, homesteaders, members of intentional communities, environmental activists, and people interested in alternative medicine typically have used brown rice, and other whole grains, tofu, soy sauce, rice crackers, organically grown vegetables, and so on in their diet. In time this influence has percolated even into the mainstream, so that many of these macrobiotic foods have appeared on supermarket shelves.

The early 1980s were a kind of heyday for macrobiotics in America. A book written by physician Anthony Satillaro recounting his cure of cancer through macrobiotics attracted much attention. Celebrities such as John Denver and actor Dirk Benedict espoused and practiced macrobiotics. Macrobiotic counselors and teachers were in great demand. Macrobiotic centers flourished, and new ones were founded around the country. This boom waned in time, and by the mid-1990s there were only a handful of centers and teachers. Still, in the late 1970s, Kushi Institute-sponsored week-long summer conferences were drawing their largest number of attendees ever, with close to one thousand registering for these annual events.

As a food and health movement macrobiotics has had a major impact on American culture. The Kushis, Aiharas, and many second-generation teachers of macrobiotics have helped to make Americans aware of good food and its relation to health. As a religious movement, though, its influence has been small. While universalistic in theory, the spiritual teachings and practices are largely an amalgam of Taoist, Buddhist, and Shinto elements. Although this blend has appealed to some Americans, mostly young people from the social periphery, within the broader context of American culture it does not have a wide appeal. There are believers in macrobiotics as the "Tao of eating," but their number is not great. Many people, though, combine the macrobiotic diet with other forms of spiritual practice.

The idea that food, physical health, and religious experience are interrelated is not a common one in the history of religion in America. It is not unknown, however. For example, some teachers in the Adventist movement in the middle of the nineteenth century were concerned with the relationships among food, health, and religious life. After the disappointment of the millennial expectation in the Millerite movement of the 1840s, the leaders of the Seventh-Day Adventist movement emphasized good eating and healthful living as means of preparing for the millennial deliverance. The Seventh-Day Adventists do not, of course, maintain that good eating and healthful living alone can effect salvation.

See also BUDDHISM; FOOD; HEALTH; JAPANESE-AMERICAN RELIGIONS; NEW AGE SPIRITUALITY; SEVENTH-DAY ADVENTISM; TAOISM; VEGETARIANISM; YOGA; ZEN.

BIBLIOGRAPHY

Koetzsch, Ronald E. *Macrobiotics Yesterday and Today.* 1985.

Ronald E. Koetzsch

Magazines, Religious.

See Journalism, Religious.

Magic

Magic is the ability to create desirable outcomes with means that seem—in terms of ordinary, everyday logic—to be incapable of producing those results. For example, a magical practitioner may believe that saying a certain sequence of words while dropping oil onto a cloth filled with newspaper clippings of want ads will cause her to succeed in getting a job she might otherwise fail to get.

So defined, magic is extremely common in cultures worldwide. Indeed, it could rightly be called a cross-cultural universal, if all that is meant by magic is the attempt to control events by way of ritual actions that do not have an obvious cause-and-effect relationship with the ends they are trying to produce. Such basic religious practices as prayer could be construed as magic, since a practitioner may believe, for example, that through prayer she can heal an illness that might otherwise yield only to medical interventions.

For such an apparently straightforward concept, the term "magic" has had a tortured history. This is due in part to an inherent difficulty in pinning down the precise differences between magic on the one hand and technology on the other. Both magic and technology aim at producing events through a regular, teachable set of techniques, and in fact what one culture considers magic another may regard as science. Some champions of magic go so far as to claim that magic is merely technology that science has not

yet come to understand. For example, the herbs that a medieval witch tosses onto the fire in a sick person's home to burn the disease out of his body turn out to have healing properties that medical science only later comes to recognize. Thus magic is, according to some, the cutting edge of tomorrow's science. Others—particularly Victorian-era anthropologists such as Edward Tylor and James Frazer, who first turned attention to the "problem" of magic as it appeared cross-culturally—regard magic as simply bad (i.e., inefficacious) science. Magic is what happens when people, desperate to exert some control over events important to them, resort to techniques that have no hope of actually working. Once techniques that work—"scientific" techniques—become available to them, say these commentators, people give up magic as an inferior technology.

And yet most cultures, at whatever level of scientific development, make a distinction between what they regard as magic and what is mere technology, and they treat the two differently. It is not simply a matter of "our" science compared to "their" magic. Even contemporary Americans who believe that magic works know that it is not the same thing as technology. Psychic channelers and psychiatric professionals, for example, are recognized to operate out of different worldviews, and the former are thought of as exotic while the latter are thought of as quotidian. This distinction has led some commentators, such as anthropologist Bronislaw Malinowski, to see magic as being more like religion and less like science. Both religion and magic deal with "suprasensible" or sacred realities, while science, in contrast, is wedded to the profane world.

But here magic runs up against another stumbling block, this one religious in nature. The major religions of the West have generally been eager to disown magic, to contrast it explicitly to approved religious practices such as meditation, prayer, or ritual, which are seen as morally superior. This has been true from the time of ancient Israel, when the Hebrews denounced pagan idolatry. Interestingly, idolatry was not condemned because it was believed that invocations to pagan idols could not produce desirable results, but because such practices were not consistent with the covenantal relationship between God and his people. To practice magic was, in effect, to go behind God's back, to play at being God, and was therefore forbidden. This injunction against magic has persisted to the present in the biblical religions, which often make a loud (if not always clear) distinction between magic, which they regard as coercive and manipulative in nature, and religious ritual, which is seen as a set of intercessionary acts that seek harmony with the divine will. In other words, the faithful religious practitioner wants what God wants for her; she can negotiate, but she must finally submit. The magician, on the other hand, wants whatever she wants and will get it however she can.

Amid all this controversy, it is probably easiest to regard magic, as Ludwig Wittgenstein has, as a way of stating wishes in highly symbolic terms. What relationship these performances bear to the results at which they aim and how they are expected (or not expected) to produce results vary according to the practitioner or observer in question.

From a phenomenological or anthropological viewpoint, magic is everywhere in contemporary American culture, from the purchase and use of face creams purported to reverse the aging process to saying a quick prayer to catch one's train on time. But relatively few Americans of any religious stripe are willing to claim that what they are doing is practicing magic, even when they are quite obviously casting spells, complete with sacred objects and incantations. Those who do make this claim generally do so with the awareness that they are embarking on a bold and potentially dangerous enterprise that will cause other people's eyes to widen in shock or fear. Doing this intentionally, they sacrifice a degree of respectability (which they occasionally try to gain back through careful expositions of what magic "really" is) for power.

Apart from occult or Satanic groups that practice magic but that also value secrecy, the only Americans who practice magic and are vocal about its benefits are neopagans. (Some Afro-Caribbean religions occasionally use the term, but they are more likely to speak of "working the spirits," and reserve the term "magic" for the efforts of people misusing sacred forces to do harm.) Neopagans have a well-developed literature on magic, including both theoretical treatments of the worldview behind it and practical "cookbooks" of magical recipes for every occasion. Neopagan explanations of how magic works vary, but most emphasize the thoughts and intentions of the practitioner to a greater or lesser degree. At one end of the spectrum, magic is held to work simply by changing the consciousness of the practitioner. Doing a spell for financial success changes his feelings about work and money at a deep level, and this in turn changes his behavior. It is through changed behavior, though—hardly something ordinarily thought to be magical—that he eventually achieves financial success. This might be thought of as the "power of positive thinking" version of magic. At the other end of the spectrum, magic is thought to work with lawlike certainty through the manipulation (whether clumsy or clever) of unseen levers that produce specific events in the world. In the middle of the spectrum are those who believe that magic works through a change in consciousness, but that this change is able to affect the universe directly without necessarily changing the practitioner's behavior. Many neopagans, for example, claim that "thoughts are things" and that using magical and symbolic means to focus thoughts makes them especially powerful, especially capable of triggering a desired chain of events completely on their own. Deities also play a role in some neopagan magic. A variety of gods and goddesses can, upon invocation or request, influence change in the desired direction. Neopagans differ on whether these deities exist as discrete entities or as mere symbols for certain types of "energy."

It is quite common for neopagans to conceptualize the world as consisting entirely of energy patterns, of which the magical efforts of the practitioner are only a part. But because this larger network of energy actually exists, the practitioner's ritual efforts, if the correct formula is followed, may be rewarded with success. This result may appear "magical," but it requires nothing apart from a sensitivity to the underlying structure of the universe and a determination to work within it. If neopagan explanations of magic frequently border on the technological, however, they are no less religious for being so. Indeed, neopagans are often as devoted as others to avoiding the implications of selfishness and irresponsibility that the term "magic" often suggests. They want what they want and will use magic to get it, but they go to pains to make sure that their desires are legitimate and that fulfilling them will harm no one. Most are quite scrupulous about not using magic for nefarious purposes. "What you send out returns three times over" is a common neopagan saying, and it expresses the conviction that so-called negative magic will only hurt the practitioner and is thus not worth pursuing. In many neopagan writings, magic is broadened and elevated to the point that the use of specific charms and spells gives way to a program of self-improvement that is indistinguishable from many other programs of spiritual discipline in religions of all types.

See also AFRO-CUBAN RELIGIONS; CHANNELING; GODDESS; LAVEY, ANTON; NEOPAGANISM; OCCULT; PSYCHOLOGY OF RELIGION; RITUAL; WICCA.

BIBLIOGRAPHY

Luhrmann, T. J. *Persuasions of the Witches' Craft.* 1991.
Malinowski, Bronislaw. *Magic, Science and Religion and Other Essays.* 1954.
Starhawk. *The Spiral Dance: A Rebirth of the Ancient Religion of the Great Goddess,* 2nd ed. 1989.
Tambiah, Stanley Jeyaraja. *Magic, Science, Religion, and the Scope of Rationality.* 1990.

Thomas, Keith. *Religion and the Decline of Magic.* 1971.
Weinstein, Marion. *Positive Magic,* rev. ed. 1981.

Cynthia Eller

Maharishi Mahesh Yogi.

See Transcendental Meditation.

Mainline Protestantism

The adjectives "mainline" and "mainstream" are often used interchangeably to distinguish social groups and ideas based on relative power, influence, or acceptability. The origins of the terms are not altogether clear. "Mainline" is often said to refer to the wealthy suburbs of Philadelphia's Main Line and the railroad that serves them or to drug users' attempts to inject substances directly into the blood system. "Mainstream" probably comes from the larger rivers into which tributaries flow. Both terms assume that some groups or ideas are more popular or acceptable than others. In politics, for example, policy positions that are widely held are viewed as mainline or mainstream; positions that deviate from popular consensus or challenge conventional wisdom are seen as nonmainline.

"Mainline" as Establishment

The use of the term "mainline" with reference to Protestant Christianity has a complex history that is peculiar to North America. Early European immigrants to the United States and Canada brought with them a variety of Protestant and Catholic religious traditions. Most immigrant groups were familiar with the Old World pattern of a single dominant faith community functioning as an established church (Anglicanism in England, Lutheranism in Germany, Catholicism in Spain, France, Italy, and elsewhere). Other groups (e.g., Puritans and Quakers) were dissenters and separatists but familiar with the European state-church tradition. The early American pattern resembled that of Europe, with Congregationalism functioning as the *de jure* establishment church in New England, as did Anglicanism in parts of the South.

Religious pluralism came early to the American colonies as new immigrant populations brought their own religious backgrounds and practices. With the passing of the first generation of Puritans, new groups brought challenges to the hegemony of Congregationalism in New England. The established church spawned its own dissenters. The more tolerant colonies of the Mid-Atlantic states, Virginia and the Car-

olinas, were more accepting of religious diversity. Over time, and culminating in the Bill of Rights and disestablishment at the state level, the European pattern of state churches was broken.

What remained for several centuries, however, was a religious culture in which some groups, in some areas, continued to hold more power and influence than others. As William Hutchison (1989) has pointed out, through the early years of the twentieth century, the social networks of Protestant clergy, leaders of business, culture, and government remained very strong. The legal establishment ended, but a fairly small number of Protestant churches and their leaders continued to occupy a special privileged place in American culture.

The first sense in which the term "mainline" is used with reference to Protestantism, therefore, is with respect to the early dominant churches. Mainline Protestant churches are those that once occupied the status of formal and, later, informal power in American society. They included colonial America's "big three" established churches: Congregationalist, Presbyterian, and Episcopalian, joined over time by churches of later waves of European immigrants—the German and Dutch Reformed churches and Lutheran churches of varying ethnic backgrounds—and by Protestant traditions of the expanding frontier, Methodist and the Disciples of Christ.

"Mainline" as Protestant Subcommunity

By the 1920s, it was clear that Protestantism was no longer the only major religious tradition contending for the hearts and souls of an increasingly diverse population. Roman Catholics of various national backgrounds were dominant in several major metropolitan areas, and Jews had come to positions of considerable influence in major centers of influence such as New York City.

Somewhat grudgingly, the religious establishment began to accommodate leaders of these traditions. The "mainline" was changing. By the 1950s Will Herberg could write a book entitled *Protestant Catholic Jew,* which he viewed as the three ways of being an American. The relationship of the historic black churches to the informal religious establishment remained ambiguous. Some African Americans were members of historically white churches, but most were members of major black Baptist and Methodist denominations, denied full participation in the religious as well as in other sectors of American life. Similarly, other faith traditions (e.g., Buddhism, Hinduism, Islam, Sikhism) and indigenous American faith communities (Mormons, Native American religions) occupied a

The Midway Church in Midway, Georgia, was built early in the eighteenth century, serving a Congregationalist community there. The Congregationalist Church in the United States was a forerunner of present-day "mainline" Protestant denominations such as the United Church of Christ. (Credit: CORBIS/Raymond Gehman.)

peripheral role in the emerging American religious system.

Wade Clark Roof and William McKinney, in *American Mainline Religion,* have argued that by the 1960s the notion of an integrated religious establishment had largely succumbed to the influence of religious individualism and true religious pluralism. They point to a new, much more pluralistic situation in which few religious groups may be said to hold lasting cultural power. In such a situation, groups once seen as marginal are granted a legitimate claim to be heard and to share in society's effort to define its core values and practices.

Also clear by the 1920s was the fact that Protestantism itself had come to include considerable internal diversity. Divided into a growing number of denominations, most of which reflected wider cultural divisions along national, regional, racial, and ethnic lines, Protestant Christianity had also become a center of theological and political controversy. The rise of industrialization and urbanization in the nineteenth century and the new "higher criticism" in biblical studies pioneered in Germany presented Protestant churches with major intellectual and strategic challenges. Responding to these challenges gave rise to the theological movement known as Christocentric Liberalism and its institutional counterpart, the Social Gospel movement. In turn, scholars and religious leaders seeing Liberalism, or Modernism, as a challenge to historic orthodoxy would come spawn the

Fundamentalist movement, setting the stage for sustained conflict within Protestantism itself.

The Fundamentalist-Modernist controversy, which continued in various forms throughout the twentieth century, revealed divisions both among and within denominations. These divisions have been the subject of numerous scholarly studies, most of which have reflected what historian Martin E. Marty has called the "two-party system" in American Protestantism. Most scholars agree that Protestant Christianity is too complex to reduce to only two groups or movements; the hundreds of Protestant denominations present in North America have different histories and theological traditions and differ in demographics and polities. Nonetheless, the intra-Protestant fissures that were apparent by the late nineteenth and early twentieth centuries remain evident today. Various labels have been used to describe the two "parties": liberal and conservative, ecumenical and sectarian, public and private, progressivist and orthodox, mainline and evangelical. Each of these pairs of labels refers to something different (theological orientation, stance toward interchurch and interfaith cooperation, openness to engagement of social and political issues, appeal to various sources of religious authority, and so on). Adding further confusion, these labels are attached to different populations: individuals, congregations, denominations, or interchurch organizations such as councils and associations of churches.

The first usage of the term "mainline," discussed above, emphasizes the status of a religious group or idea in relation to others. This second use points to particular religious groups and traditions, usually to distinguish between these groups and others. Mainline Protestantism, in this sense, refers to a substream of Protestant Christianity.

To what precise substream does mainline Protestantism refer? This is a more complicated question than it may appear on the surface. As noted above, the European churches that flourished and dominated during the colonial and frontier periods of American history (Episcopalians, Presbyterians and Congregationalists, followed by Methodists, the Reformed churches, Lutherans, and Disciples of Christ) enjoyed a special role in American culture. These churches also developed special relationships among themselves. The rise of the home missions and Sunday school movements, while strongly denominational in many respects, brought these churches into contact with one another, and in 1867 most of these churches were represented in the U.S. branch of the Evangelical Alliance. The early twentieth century saw the founding of national church women's organizations and federations of churches at the local and state levels. In 1908 most of these churches came together as the Federal Council of Churches. Their leaders were in close contact through a variety of national and international conferences concerning home and foreign missions.

While these churches and their leaders were aware of the presence of other Protestant groups in the United States, they paid them little attention. These other groups, while growing, were seen as little threat to ecumenical Protestantism's numerical and cultural dominance.

There was little expectation that these cooperating churches would unite or achieve full doctrinal consensus. Each church would retain its freedom, identity, and independence, but in the words of German Reformed theologian Philip Schaff in 1893, they would also recognize "one another as sisters with equal rights, and cooperating in general enterprises such as the spread of the Gospel at home and abroad, the defense of the faith against infidels, the elevation of the poor and neglected classes of society, works of philanthropy and charity and moral reform." The activist impulse was strong in the early years of interchurch cooperation and the ecumenical movement became associated with the Social Gospel. While Protestant Christianity remained relatively orthodox and broadly evangelical in its creedal formulations, its cooperative social and religious agenda had a decidedly progressive bent.

By the 1920s, with growing protest movements rising within the ecumenical denominations themselves over what Charles Hodge of Princeton and others described as "creeping liberalism" in the Presbyterian and other churches, it was clear that Protestantism was moving toward schism. Battle lines were drawn within most churches, with Presbyterians and Baptists being especially affected. These conflicts spawned new denominations and gave rise to what are today known as Mainline and Evangelical camps.

Both uses of mainline Protestantism are rather imprecise theologically and sociologically, though widely used by analysts of American religion in dealing with the liberal or modernist wing of Protestant Christianity. This family of churches and sensibilities is distinguished as much by an ethos and series of interrelationships as by doctrine, demographics, or organizational structure. Most of the nation's leading educational institutions and thousands of national and local cultural and social-service institutions were founded by mainline Protestant churches and laity. While most of the official ties between churches and institutions like the Ivy League and liberal arts colleges, or art museums and benevolence agencies and their founding churches are gone, they nonetheless share common origins and values.

The decades since the 1960s have been difficult for the institutions of mainline Protestantism, including denominational structures. Its churches have lost members nearly every year since 1965. These declines have reduced the membership of some denominations by a third or more. David A. Roozen and Kirk Hadaway (1993) report that in 1990 eight leading Mainline Protestant churches included 22.6 million members, down 6.4 million from 1965. Over four decades these churches' share of the U.S. religious "market" fell from 15.9 percent to 9.1 percent.

In addition, membership declines, combined with inflation and the desire on the part of local churches and members to have more choice in allocating mission support dollars, have increased the financial pressure on national and regional church bodies. As denominations have faced financial difficulties they have reduced contributions to regional, national, and worldwide ecumenical agencies.

One response to financial difficulties has been to attempt to reduce the psychological distance between national church settings and local churches. By the 1980s a long-term trend toward locating denominational offices in New York City, in close proximity to the offices of the National Council of Churches at 475 Riverside Drive, was reversed. Presbyterians relocated to Louisville, the new Evangelical Lutheran Church in America to Chicago, and the United Church of Christ to Cleveland (McKinney 1991). The size of the National Council's program and staff was reduced radically as this national symbol of mainline Protestant cooperation struggled to find new direction.

While organized ecumenism has experienced great stress in recent decades interchurch cooperation has continued to flourish. In 1983 the Presbyterian Church (USA) brought together the northern and southern branches of Presbyterianism, which had been divided since Civil War times. The new Evangelical Lutheran Church in America, founded in 1987, united three major Lutheran streams. The United Church of Christ and the Christian Church (Disciples of Christ) have covenanted to share several ministries, including their overseas mission work. Further, these churches have reached important ecumenical agreements leading to mutual recognition of members and ministries.

Diagnosing the Mainline

As public recognition of the changing shape of mainline Protestantism has grown, scholars, foundations, and consultants have given a good deal of attention to its current situation and future prospects. This attention has run the gamut from the analytical (changing birthrates, shifting denominational priorities, and so on), to the angry (who failed to lead the churches and why), and to the prescriptive (what to do next).

From the early seventies (with the publication of Dean M. Kelley's *Why Conservative Churches Are Growing*) through the 1980s these studies tended to be sociological in character. By the 1990s mainline Protestantism was receiving greater attention from historians and theologians. Among the many books that have attempted to understand changes affecting these churches are Roof and Michaelsen (1986), Roof and McKinney (1987), Wuthnow (1988), Hutchison (1989), Hunter (1989), and Roozen and Hadaway (1993). Ammerman's study of congregations and changing communities is an important resource for understanding mainline Protestantism in its congregational form. Miller (1997) looks at this family of churches in relation to Evangelical churches.

What is the future of mainline Protestantism in North America? Several things seem clear. Low internal birth rates, the slow growth of its traditional constituencies, and relatively low priority given to evangelism and membership growth make dramatic changes in its long-term pattern of declining "market share." Recent growth among racial-ethnic and immigrant populations should help stem declines.

Even more interesting than the future of its institutions is the question of the future of mainline Protestantism's ethos and value system. In a more pluralistic, competitive, and adversarial public square, this community's historic impulse to bridge conflicting ideas and movements becomes a greater challenge than was true when these churches enjoyed a privileged position in the society. The idea that these churches have a special responsibility for promoting the ways in which diverse groups can coexist in relation to one another is questioned from within and without. It has been an important component of the history and current identity of mainline Protestantism, and the need for bridging and mediating institutions continues. No question is more important to these churches as some of them enter their fourth century on America's shores.

See also BAPTIST TRADITION; CULTURE WARS; ECUMENICAL MOVEMENT; EPISCOPAL CHURCHES; EVANGELICAL CHRISTIANITY; FUNDAMENTALIST CHRISTIANITY; LUTHERAN CHURCHES; METHODISM; NATIONAL COUNCIL OF CHURCHES OF CHRIST IN THE U.S.A.; PRESBYTERIANISM.

BIBLIOGRAPHY

Ammerman, Nancy T. *Congregations and Community.* 1997.
Hunter, James Davison. *Culture Wars: The Struggle to Define America.* 1989.
Hutchison, William R. *Between the Times: The Travail of the Protestant Establishment in America, 1900–1960.* 1989.
McKinney, William. "Mainline Protestantism 2000." *The Annals* 558 (July 1998).
Miller, Donald E. *Reinventing American Protestantism: Christianity in the New Millennium.* 1997.
Roof, Wade Clark, and Robert Michaelsen, eds. *Liberal Protestantism.* 1986.
Roof, Wade Clark, and William McKinney. *American Mainline Religion: Its Changing Shape and Future.* 1987.
Roozen, David A., and Kirk Hadaway. *Church and Denominational Growth.* 1993.
Wuthnow, Robert. *The Restructuring of American Religion.* 1988.

William McKinney

Makkah.

See Mecca.

Malcolm X

(1925–1965), black Muslim leader.

Malcolm X, national spokesperson for the Nation of Islam in the early 1960s and founder of the Sunni Muslim Mosque, Inc., and the Organization of Afro-American Unity in 1965, was the most important model for African-American Islamic identity in the twentieth century. He was born Malcolm Little in Omaha, Nebraska, on May 19, 1925, to parents who were black-nationalist organizers for Marcus Garvey's Universal Negro Improvement Association. After his father was murdered by white supremacists in 1931 and he and his siblings were dispersed to separate foster homes by the public-relief authorities in Lansing, Michigan, in 1939, Malcolm became a troubled teenager, deeply involved in criminal activities in Boston and New York in the 1940s.

His spiritual transformation from Malcolm Little to Malcolm X occurred in a Massachusetts prison from 1947 to 1952, as he became a self-educated, disciplined convert to the Nation of Islam. Utilizing the Islamic concept of jihad—the struggle for the truth—as an internal struggle with the ego and as an intellectual struggle with knowledge and words, Malcolm X established a powerful role model for African-American Islamic identity that attracted thousands of young converts to the Nation of Islam in the 1950s and 1960s. In this context the surname "X" signified

Malcolm X addressing a rally in Harlem, New York City, on June 29, 1963.   (Credit: AP/Wide World Photos.)

the intellectual and spiritual search for the African identity that was lost during slavery and the recovery of dignity and self-esteem through the discipline and the structures of the Nation of Islam.

After his release from prison in 1952, Malcolm became a traveling minister for the Nation of Islam. He "fished" for new converts and established many new temples in black communities across the United States in the 1950s. The young male membership of the Nation of Islam had been decimated by FBI persecution in the 1940s, and Elijah Muhammad, leader of the Nation of Islam, used Malcolm's youthful charisma and oratory to invigorate the membership of his community. In the early 1960s the Nation of Islam achieved national prominence as the richest black organization in American history as a result of Elijah Muhammad's successful black-nationalist economic programs and Malcolm's militant speeches and television appearances as the national spokesperson for his community.

However, in the wake of President John F. Kennedy's assassination in 1963, a public controversy between Elijah Muhammad and Malcolm X evolved into a permanent separation related to the politics of religious identity in the black Muslim community. Muhammad's conservative political vision for his community, which conflicted with Malcolm X's public image as a militant spokesperson and symbol for black nationalism in the United States, eventually led to the latter's official break with the Nation of Islam in 1964. Establishing a new spiritual and political identity, Malcolm abandoned the heterodox, racial-separatist philosophy of the Nation of Islam and converted to the multiracial Sunni Islam during the last year of his life.

In March 1964 he founded the Sunni Muslim Mosque, Inc., in Harlem, as the base for a spiritual and political program to eliminate economic and social oppression against black Americans. Then Malcolm made the hajj, the Islamic pilgrimage to Mecca, Saudi Arabia, in April 1964. There he changed his name from Malcolm X to El Hajj Malik El-Shabazz, which signified the adoption of a new identity that was linked to mainstream Islam. Malcolm's Sunni Islamic identity became a significant model for many African Americans who have converted to mainstream Islam since the 1960s.

After Mecca, Malcolm traveled extensively through North and West Africa, establishing important religious and political linkages with Third World nations. These profound international experiences deepened his pan-African political identity, which connected African-American Islam to global black unity and West African cultural and political roots. When Malcolm came back to the United States he founded the Organization of Afro-American Unity in New York City on June 29, 1964, to promote his political perspective, which linked the African-American struggle for social justice to global human rights issues in the Third World.

During the last months of his life, as he was stalked by his enemies in the intelligence community, the Nation of Islam, and the New York City Police Department, Malcolm's powerful jihad of words critiqued capitalism, Christianity, imperialism, and worldwide racial oppression. He planned to use his political connections in the Muslim world to bring the case of the American government's human-rights crimes against African Americans before the United Nations. Malcolm X was shot to death during a speech at the Audubon Ballroom in New York City on February 21, 1965.

See also AFRICAN-AMERICAN RELIGIONS; CIVIL RIGHTS MOVEMENT; CONVERSION; ISLAM; JIHAD; MUHAMMAD, ELIJAH; NATION OF ISLAM; PRISON AND RELIGION; PROSELYTIZING.

BIBLIOGRAPHY

Evanzz, Karl. *The Judas Factor: The Plot to Kill Malcolm X.* 1992.

Haley, Alex. *The Autobiography of Malcolm X.* 1965.
Strickland, William, and Cheryll Y. Greene. *Malcolm X: Make It Plain.* 1994.
Turner, Richard Brent. *Islam in the African-American Experience.* 1997.

Richard Brent Turner

Mantra

Mantra, a Sanskrit word that means "mystic utterance," refers to a wide range of ritual incantations that characterize religious traditions of South Asia and their successors. The practice of mantra recitation, best known in Hinduism and Buddhism, stems from the Vedic heritage of India in which sound (in the Sanskrit language) had metaphysical power. Hymns of the Vedas (1500 B.C.E.), believed to be of divine origin, contained "seed syllables" in auspicious combinations of sounds, sequence, and intonation. When these sounds were uttered by ritual specialists, they held the power to create, sustain, and destroy the entire world. Knowledge of these syllables and their utterance was considered magical, joining the spiritual and temporal and opening access to ultimate wisdom.

Mantras (also called *dhāraṇīs*) vary in length from a single Sanskrit letter to hundreds of Sanskrit syllables. The most ancient mantras had no interpretable meaning, but eventually some mantras developed that could be translated into a semblance of conventional meaning. Recitation of mantras was associated in Hinduism and Indian Buddhism with initiations to particular rituals, the invocation of the power of a particular deity or deities, exorcism of obstacles and protection from future ones, and opening spiritually sensitive parts of the subtle Yogic body in meditation. Mantra practices were also assimilated by Sikh and Sufi traditions.

Mantras outside of India

The mantra tradition was disseminated to other parts of Asia with the spread of Buddhism. For example, the popular Sanskrit Heart Sutra (Prajnaparamita-hrdaya-sutra) contains a famous mantra that is fervently intoned in Chinese, Korean, and Japanese versions of Sanskrit. Japanese Pure Land Buddhism sought a single mantra that would contain all others, elevating the recitation of the Nembutsu, the name of the celestial and compassionate Amitabha Buddha (Amida Butsu in Japanese), to to level of a supreme, universal meditation. Esoteric Buddhism (called Shingon in Japan) especially preserved mantra practices throughout Asia, The richest and most vital esoteric Buddhism of Tibet assimilated the Indian mantra tra-

ditions most enthusiastically, identifying them as foundational in tantric ritual life and meditation.

American Mantras

The United States was popularly introduced to mantras by the Hindu guru Maharishi Mahesh Yogi, who propagated a highly Americanized Transcendental Meditation movement in the late 1960s. TM, as it was called, centered on the cultivation of mental calm through concentrated recitation of a special Sanskrit mantra given by the guru. With the growing popularity of Hindu and Buddhist meditation in the last decades of the millennium, Americans have embraced mantra practices from a variety of Asian traditions. Students of the International Society of Krishna Consciousness (ISKCON), founded in India, sing "Hare Krishna, Hare Krishna" and Tibetan Buddhists chant "Om Mani Padme Hum"; students of the Japanese Soka Gakkai repeat the Gohonzon from the Buddhist Lotus Sūtra "Namu Myōhō Renge Kyō." Though these various traditions have different interpretations of the importance of mantras, each embraces their transformative power for focusing and purifying the mind, synchronizing the intention, and opening the heart in meditation practice.

See also BUDDHISM; CHANTING; EXORCISM; HINDUISM; INTERNATIONAL SOCIETY FOR KRISHNA CONSCIOUSNESS; MEDITATION; PRACTICE; RITUAL; SOKA GAKKAI; TIBETAN BUDDHISM; TRANSCENDENTAL MEDITATION; VEDAS.

BIBLIOGRAPHY
Alper, Harvey, ed. *Understanding Mantras.* 1989.
Blofeld, John. *Mantras: Sacred Words of Power.* 1977.
Coward, Harold, and David Goa. *Mantra: Hearing the Divine in India.* 1991.

Judith Simmer-Brown

Marian Devotions

"Devotion" comes from the Latin phrase *de voto,* "from a promise," referring to solemn pledges of service made in honor of a religious personage. In common usage the term refers to a religious cult or to the practice of certain rituals and prayers motivated by an affective commitment toward a religious experience. Marian devotion is rooted in the Christian Scriptures, which depict Mary of Nazareth as the mother of Jesus Christ and a key member of the early Christian Church. The Fourth Gospel, John 2:1–12; 19:25–27, adds a symbolic dimension to Mary's maternity of

Christ, a theme amplified in the apocalyptic language of Revelation. (Revelation 12)

Evolution of Marian Devotion

Iraeneus, bishop of Lyons in 180 C.E., developed the theological concept of Mary as "New Eve," describing her as the woman who reversed the effects of sin brought by the first Eve. Iraeneus was born in Smyrna in Asia Minor, and his writings probably attest to concepts current in Eastern Christianity. Artistic representations of Mary are found in the Roman catacombs, confirming to an abiding appreciation of her role in salvation history in the West. The Annunciation by the Angel Gabriel that Mary had been chosen to be Mother of God is a favored theme, apparently because that episode stressed the free will of Mary, whose acceptance of her mission contradicted pagan myths wherein the birth of a god was the result of a rape. Extracanonical books such as the Protogospel of James offered vivid tales of Mary's interaction with the child Jesus, suggesting that the earliest Christians had much interest in Mary's life.

Athanasius (ca. 293–373 C.E.), who had fled his see in Alexandria to avoid persecution by Arians, attributes to Mary the title Θεotokos, "Parent of God," a concept later celebrated by the faithful at Ephesus in 431 C.E. in opposition to Nestorius, who taught that Mary was mother only of the human nature of Jesus. Completing the development of early Marian doctrine Ambrose of Milan (340–397) asserted that Mary was free from original sin and remained a perpetual virgin, notions reiterated by Jerome (347–420), the translator of the Bible from the original languages into Latin. It has been said that Marian devotion developed as a response to Arianism, since Mary received from orthodox Christianity the status that Arians ascribed to Jesus: she was not divine, but had received all the graces necessary to transform her into the model for all salvation.

Marian Devotion in Popular Practice

Mary had an impact on Christian practice at a popular level. Since the first days of the church, believers have made prayerful promises to undertake some pious practice or make some sacrifice in petition or in thanksgiving for favors. The safe return of a son from war, recovery from a serious illness, or a healthy pregnancy are some individual favors connected to Marian devotions. Entire communities might also contribute to the devotion, as, for instance, if a town was not seriously damaged by a flood. Many of these favors might not qualify as a "miracle," that is, something unexplainable by nature, but they became traditional causes of devotion, with special processions and prayers to commemorate specific events. Christians honored images of Mary with the same reverence as would be shown were she physically present. Gold ornaments, deep bows and genuflections, and candles and flowers before the image became essential elements of the devotion. This was the dynamic of popular religion that created Marian shrines throughout the Christian world, many of which became magnets for pilgrimages, exquisite churches, and inspired art. Throughout the Middle Ages and until the fifteenth century, most Marian devotions were highly localized and were focused on the favors received rather than on apparitions or revelations.

Christian theologians were generally careful to avoid contradicting the scriptural definition of Christ as the only intercessor with God the Father (I Timothy 2:5). While feudalism dominated the social relations in Western Christianity, Mary became "Our Lady," an object of chivalric devotion. This chivalric norm was promoted extensively by Bernard of Clairvaux (1090–1153) and became an essential element of Marian devotion in the West. Thomas Aquinas (ca. 1224–1274) defined Christian devotion to Mary utilizing Greek theological terms: Mary received *dulia* (servanthood) rather than *latria* (worship). This distinction emphasized the fundamental differences between prayers to Mary the creature and Christ the Divine Person.

The sixteenth-century Reformation severely criticized Marian devotion for distorting biblical texts, for its commercialism, and for a frequent vulgarization that approximated superstition. This radical critique of Marian devotion did not displace belief in the Virgin Birth for Luther, Calvin, or Zwingli. Elizabeth I of England did little to suppress the Marian notion of "Virgin Queen," possibly because it benefited her legitimacy on the English throne. But insistence on the primacy of Scripture and an elimination of adornment in many Reformation traditions combined with a rejection of most Catholic traditions to virtually eliminate Marian devotion within Protestantism.

While the Council of Trent (1543–1563) reaffirmed Marian devotion as part of the deposit of faith, it also addressed the legitimate objections of Protestants. By requiring all cults to submit to a rigorous ecclesiastical approval and by composing official prayers, Trent connected exuberant popular religiosity to Vatican orthodoxy. The commercial development of American and Asian colonies had created a global Catholic public, and the printing press facilitated mass diffusion of devotional items such as holy cards with a picture of Mary on one side and a theologically correct prayer on the other. Novenas, popular preaching, and devotional books publicized the favors received through Mary's intercession. The rosary, considered a bouquet of prayers analogous to a wreath of roses (hence the name), was promoted worldwide after the decisive victory over the Turks at Lepanto in 1571. Thus Catholicism acquired a purified and regulated form of devotion that may be called "devotionalism."

Marian Beliefs and Contemporary Religion

Post-Tridentine Marian devotionalism was characterized by interest in the origins of local shrines, such as that of Our Lady of Guadalupe in Mexico. In 1648 its origins were ascribed to a miraculous apparition that was reported to have taken place a century earlier. Similar traditions for Mary under special titles as national protector include: Our Lady of Czestochowa in Poland, Our Lady of Montserrat in Catalonia, Our Lady of Charity in Cuba, and Our Lady of Altagracia in the Dominican Republic.

To these devotions with a nationalist character must be added the two Marian doctrines that have been declared dogmas. The Immaculate Conception (1854) affirms that Mary was conceived without original sin. The dogma of the Assumption (1950) articulates an ancient tradition that Mary was assumed bodily into heaven after death. Both doctrines had been long contested within Catholic theology because they have no clear scriptural basis, despite ample historical evidence of their origins in the traditions of early Christianity.

Wearing the brown wool cloth of the Carmelite scapular is a practice believed to bring Mary's intercession for freedom from Purgatory on the first Saturday after one's death. Connected by legend to the Star of the Sea (stella maris) in many parts of Latin America and the Ibero-Mediterranean world on the feast day of Our Lady of Mount Carmel in July, a statue is adorned with flowers and set adrift in port waters to implore protection for sailors throughout the year. This and similar local customs repeat the oldest patterns of devotions to Mary.

The most famous of Marian apparitions in the modern period are those to St. Catherine Labouré in 1830, which introduced the practice of wearing the Miraculous Medal, proclaiming the Immaculate Conception. Lourdes in France (1858) was the site of the first apparition subjected to rigorous examination with modern science. Claims of miraculous healing in the spring at Lourdes are substantiated with X rays and medical reports by a panel of doctors that includes nonbelievers. The apparitions to children at La Salette in France (1846) and at Fatima in Portugal (1917) portray Mary as requesting repentance from the world to avoid punishments.

In the United States, devotion to Lourdes and Fatima have been the most common among all Catholics. Various ethnic groups maintain particular fervor for Mary under her other titles. The shrine to Mary in Washington, D.C., completed in the 1960s, is distinguished by its many chapels and statues of this rich diversity in Marian devotionalism. The reforms of Vatican Council II curtailed Marian devotionalism, and some feminist Christians repudiated the traditional image of Mary because they contend this image perpetuates a model of a submissive and domesticated woman.

Despite the feminist critique, traditional Marian devotions have experienced a modern revival, often with a new edge reflecting contemporary concerns. For instance, Our Lady of Guadalupe is now presented as a devotion with a message about contemporary race relations. There are frequent manifestations of the depth of attachment to Mary among the faithful. Medjugorje in the former Yugoslavia has become a modern Marian shrine, as has Sábana Grande in Puerto Rico. The materiality of these devotions exercises an appeal to many believers who seek symbols that transcend the rationalistic limitations of institutionalized belief.

See also FEMINIST THEOLOGY; MARY; MIRACLE; ROMAN CATHOLICISM; SHRINES; VIRGIN OF GUADALUPE.

BIBLIOGRAPHY

Christian, William. *Local Religion in Sixteenth-Century Spain.* 1981.

Cruz, Joan Carroll. *Miraculous Images of Our Lady.* 1992.

Elizondo, Virgil. *The Future Is Mestizo.* 1992.

Gebara, Ivone, and María Clara Bingemer. *Mary, Mother of God, Mother of the Poor.* 1989.

Hamington, Maurice. *Hail Mary? The Struggle for the Ultimate Womanhood in Catholicism.* 1995.

Lafaye, Jacques. *Quetzalcoatl and Guadalupe: The Formation of Mexican National Consciousness, 1531–1813.* 1976.

McDannell, Colleen. *Material Christianity: Religion and Popular Culture in America.* 1995.

Orsi, Robert. *The Madonna of 101st Street: Faith and Community in Italian Harlem, 1880–1950.* 1985.

Pelican, Jaroslav. *Mary Through the Centuries: Her Place in the History of Culture.* 1996.

Poole, Stafford, C. M. *Our Lady of Guadalupe: The Origins and Sources of a Mexican National Symbol, 1531–1797.* 1995.

Stevens-Arroyo, Anthony M. "The Evolution of Marian Devotionalism Within Christianity and the Ibero-Mediterranean Polity." *Journal for the Scientific Study of Religion* 37, no. 1 (1998): 50–73.

Stratton, Suzanne L. *The Immaculate Conception in Spanish Art.* 1994.

Tweed, Thomas A. *Our Lady of the Exile: Diasporic Religion at a Cuban Catholic Shrine in Miami.* 1997.

Zimdars Swartz, Sandra J. *Encountering Mary: From La Salette to Medjugorje.* 1991.

Anthony M. Stevens-Arroyo

Marriage, Christian

Like Jewish marriage, Christian marriage is conceived of as a covenantal relationship that mirrors God's relationship with humanity and Christ and his church. For Roman Catholics, marriage is also the sacrament of matrimony. As a sacrament, an outward sign instituted by Christ to give grace, it not only serves the well-being of the spouses and the procreation and education of children, but also represents the perfect communion of life and love between Christ and the Church.

In the Western Catholic Church as well as in other Western Christian traditions, the couple acts as the minister of marriage. Thus the exchange of consent is seen as sealing the sacrament of marriage and the priest or other minister is merely a witness. In the Eastern tradition, the proper minister of the sacrament is the priest or bishop. After receiving the mutual consent of the spouses, he successively crowns the bride and groom as a sign of the marriage covenant.

Until the sixteenth century, Catholics in the West could marry simply by exchanging consent. This was changed by the Council of Trent (1545–1563), which required a public procedure for Catholics to enter into marriage. These changes were made due to concerns about the abuses of "clandestine" marriages, desertions, and denial by one or the other spouse that an exchange of consent had ever actually taken place.

Because marriage is understood as a sacrament instituted by Christ and confirmed by him as an indissoluble bond between man and woman, the Catholic Church has a long-standing tradition of careful, legal judgment (that is, in accordance with the written code of Church law) by which it determines if a marriage was contracted in a state of less-than-free consent or of seriously flawed consent. A freely contracted marriage thus cannot be one that is agreed to under constraint of any kind or is impeded by natural or Church law. In such an instance, a marriage between two baptized Catholics may be declared null (granted an "annulment"), thus declaring that, despite appearances to the contrary, the relationship was not a marriage relationship.

But this declaration of "annulment," which then gives a person the right to contract a sacramental marriage in the Catholic Church, should be understood for what it is not. It is not an indication that a relationship between the two persons never existed, nor is it an indication that it was not necessarily a very loving relationship. An annulment does not even say that a marriage never existed between the parties, but only that the marriage was not a canonically valid one. This refers to the terms of the Code of Canon Law, the official rules for much of the life of the Catholic Church, which is descended from attempts in ancient Roman and Medieval tradition to spell out human and Church relationships on the basis of Gospel teaching. In Church law, a marriage that is declared de facto invalid (and for which an annulment can be issued) is known as a "putative" marriage—but a marriage nonetheless. Finally, an annulment does not declare children born of the union to be illegitimate; rather, Church law clearly states that all children born of either a valid or a putative marriage are to be considered equally legitimate.

Due to the relationship between sexuality and marriage, a marriage where the consent is valid but free consummation open to procreation has been nonexistent may be dissolved. Thus while the medieval theological debate as to what establishes marriage—consent or consummation—has long been resolved in favor of the former, the latter continues to play a role in the understanding of the nature and meaning of marriage. Finally, since only a marriage between baptized persons is regarded as a "sacramental marriage," it is considered possible to dissolve a marriage between a baptized and nonbaptized person for the sake of allowing the baptized person to affirm a life of Christian faith. Thus the Pauline Privilege (based on 1 Corinthians 7) allows for the dissolution of a marriage originally contracted by two nonbaptized persons when one converts to Christianity and finds that the relationship with the nonbaptized party seriously impedes the other's ability to be faithful to Christ. The Petrine Privilege also involves marriages between a baptized person and a nonbaptized person, but the circumstances are broader, although only direct dispensation from the Pope as the successor of Peter dissolves the marriage.

The Rite of Marriage approved by the Catholic Church in 1969 allows for one of three forms: the celebration of the sacrament during Mass, the celebration of the sacrament outside of Mass, and the celebration between a baptized and a nonbaptized Catholic. Regardless, the exchange of consent must be witnessed by a priest or deacon and at least two other witnesses. The exchange of consent involves recognizing three elements of marriage: freedom of choice, fidelity and perpetuity, and the acceptance of children and their Christian formation. At the solemn moment of consent, each spouse-to-be pronounces

A priest stands next to a bride, groom, and best man during a Roman Catholic wedding in San Juan Capistrano, California, in 1994. (Credit: © Spencer Grant/Stock, Boston/PNI.)

words expressing willingness to take the other as husband or wife: "to have and to hold, from this day forward, for better, for worse, for richer, for poorer, in sickness and in health, until death do us part." Marriage thus is held to introduce one into an ecclesial order; that is, it creates rights and duties in the Church between the spouses and toward their children. It is also a "state of life" in the Church and creates a "domestic Church."

The most perfect form of human relationship is that of a marriage, the perfect human relationship of exclusive, deep love and total, unreserved, lifelong intimacy. This has been particularly emphasized in recent statements of Catholic Church teaching such as *Familiaris Consortio,* a pastoral letter of Pope John Paul II and the *Catechism of the Catholic Church.* The Catholic understanding of marriage has clearly changed in important ways over the centuries, however. Many early Christians understood marriage in negative terms—marriage was for those, St. Paul said, who could not do as he did, to allow them to still live virtuously. Up to the Second Vatican Council, the pri-

mary end of marriage was held to be procreation and the upbringing of children; the well-being of the spouses was seen as secondary. Since the Pastoral Constitution on the Church in the Modern World was developed during the Second Vatican Council, however, marriage has been seen as having both purposes intertwined, with no one dimension having primacy over the other. In part this is a development of the personalist worldview that so dominated Catholic thought in the twentieth century and which was itself seen as a culmination of earlier philosophical trends in Christian life.

In the words of the *Catechism of the Catholic Church:* "Thus the marriage bond has been established by God himself in such a way that a marriage concluded and consummated between baptized persons can never be dissolved. This bond, which results from the free human act of the spouses and their consummation of the marriage, is a reality, henceforth irrevocable, and gives rise to a covenant guaranteed by God's fidelity. The Church does not have the power to contravene this disposition of divine wisdom." (1640).

Marriage over the centuries has been come to be seen as part of the divine plan itself to deepen human intimacy and to allow the direct human experience of the relational, trinitarian God. Marriage is seen as a way to deepen community and to strengthen family life. The indissolubility of marriage is thus an essential property of marriage and not a mere separate good unto itself. Therefore, marriage occurs with the publically witnessed consent of the spouses in the presence of a priest, who witnesses the sacrament but does not actually perform the marriage bond itself—since that is based on shared free and public consent and the consummation of their sexual relationship as intimate partners.

The weight given to this rich, emerging understanding of the theology of matrimony has led the Catholic Church to require mandatory marriage preparation. As a result, the Catholic Church has developed pioneering programs in the United States and around the world in recent decades. In the words of Pope John Paul II, "the Church must promote better and more intensive programs of marriage preparation in order to eliminate as far as possible the difficulties that many married couples find themselves in, and even more in order to favor positively the establishing and maturing of successful marriages." The 1993 study of marriage-preparation programs (Michael G. Lawler, Center for Marriage and Family, Creighton University) confirms the usefulness of these programs: A proportional random sample of 40,000 couples married between 1987 and 1993 found that in the first year of marriage, 94 percent found the preparation to have been valuable. Major issues in Catholic marriage preparation today include preexisting sexual relationships, second marriages, and cohabitation—studies show that perhaps as many as 50 percent of all couples married today have been living together before marriage.

Every Catholic diocese in the United States has come to require some form of marriage preparation since the Diocese of Phoenix first made this a requirement for contracting sacramental marriage in the late 1960s. More than 264,000 Catholic sacramental marriages were performed in 1998—184,000 between two Catholics and 80,000 between a Catholic and a non-Catholic, compared to 426,000 in 1970. This is due to demographic changes as well as the greater likelihood for some Catholics to contract exclusively civil marriages not recognized by the Church.

The tradition of separation of church and state in the United States has curiously produced a situation whereby the majority of marriages have been, and continue to be, celebrated in the context of a religious service. The relationship between church and state in the United States is one that recognizes the legal independence of religious officials as part of a private, and completely distinct, sphere with which the state does not interfere. Thus ministers, priests, rabbis, and other religious officials in the United States are recognized as having the civil power to witness marriages. In localities with particular religious traditions, such as Quaker communities in Pennsylvania, legal sanction also exists for a marriage witnessed by the couple themselves, with no specifically recognized religious official being present at all. In other countries, where tensions exist or have existed between the government and a currently or formerly established church, such as Catholicism in certain countries in Latin America, marriage is less likely to be contracted before a religious official and the state is less likely to permit a religious official to act as a witness for the consent for a civilly recognized marriage.

While the Catholic Church and the Eastern Orthodox churches require baptized church members to marry before an authorized priest or deacon, all other Christian churches allow members to "validly" marry before any official recognized by civil law. Marriages of Catholics not in the form prescribed by the Church manner are said to have a "lack of form." Church courts consider these marriages so obviously invalid that declarations of invalidity can be given by a simple procedure without a more involved judicial process. One interesting piece of canonical tradition regarding Catholic marriage tribunals is the custom of the "Defender of the Bond," who is responsible for calling the attention of the Church tribunal to anything that can be considered to positively support a finding of the validity of the marriage. Also, no declaration of invalidity of a sacramental marriage is definitive until a similar second decision has been reached by an appeals court (of the "second instance"), to which all marriage-related cases are automatically referred.

See also ANNULMENT; DIVORCE, CHRISTIAN; DIVORCE, JEWISH; MARRIAGE, JEWISH; SACRAMENTS; SEXUALITY; VATICAN II.

BIBLIOGRAPHY

Bellah, Robert et al. *Habits of the Heart.* 1985.

Davis, Kingsley, and Amyra Grossbard-Schechtman, eds. *Contemporary Marriage: Comparative Perspectives on a Changing Institution.* 1986.

Everett, William Johnson. "Marriage: A Protestant Perspective." In *Religion and Family: A Practical Theology Handbook,* edited by Herbert Anderson et al. 1998.

Harakas, S. *Guidelines for Marriage in the Orthodox Church.* 1980.

Hogan, Richard M. *Covenant of Love: Pope John Paul II on Sexuality, Marriage, and Family in the Modern World.* 1992.

Lawler, Michael G. *Marriage and Sacraments: A Theology of Christian Marriage.* 1993.

Waddell, Paul J. "Marriage: A Catholic Perspective." In *Religion and Family: A Practical Theology Handbook,* edited by Herbert Anderson et al. 1998.

Witte, John, Jr. *From Sacrament to Contract: Marriage, Religion, and Law in the Western Tradition.* 1997.

Bryan Froehle

Marriage, Jewish

The Jewish tradition speaks of marriage in three ways: as a contract between two individuals, as a social phenomenon, and as a sacred status.

The Contractual Element in Jewish Marriage

In biblical society, as in the ancient Near East generally, marriage was an agreement not between two individuals but between two families. The newly married couple usually took up residence in the groom's father's house. The family of the groom thus gained, and the family of the bride lost, a valuable member to tend the flock, draw water from the well, grind flour, bake bread, and assist in household tasks. It is not surprising, therefore, that marriage was viewed as the acquisition of the woman by the groom and his family from the family of the bride. Biblical stories indicate that the consent of the woman to her marriage was sought, but only in a perfunctory way.

Originally the acquisition was instantaneous. The father of the groom paid the father of the bride a bride price, and the groom gave the bride gifts. As time went on, though, Jewish marriage increasingly took the character of a contract, with greater emphasis on the two elements that characterize a contract, in contrast to an acquisition: futurity and consent. During the difficult economic circumstances of the late second century and early first century B.C.E., many Jewish men did not marry because they simply could not afford to. Simeon ben Shetah, head of the Pharisees at that time, devised an ingenious scheme that simultaneously encouraged marriage and discouraged divorce. He transformed the bride price into a lien against the husband's property that would have to be paid to the woman (not her father) in the event he divorced or predeceased her. This made marriage easier, for the man did not need cash on hand for the bride price. It also discouraged divorce, for the lien would become due in the event of divorce.

The gifts that the groom originally gave the bride at the time of marriage were also transformed into a lien against the groom's property. Moreover, by this time the explicit agreement of the woman to the marriage contract was required.

The contractual nature of Jewish marriage has several important implications. First, like any contracting parties, the couple may modify the terms of the standard contract, the *ketubbah.* Second, because marriage is a contract, the parties are free to terminate the contract at will, without showing grounds to any public authority; indeed, only the writ of the husband, not that of the court, can dissolve a marriage (Deuteronomy 24:1–4).

The ketubbah contains clauses indicating the liens on the groom's property mentioned above. It also stipulates that the document is "according to the usage of Moses and the People Israel," thus invoking the social and sacred aspects of Jewish marriage. Among American Jews, the Conservative, Reconstructionist, and Reform movements have altered the language of the standard contract in a variety of ways to make it more egalitarian. In some, both parties acquire each other, but in others, the language of acquisition is dropped altogether. The Conservative movement has also developed language, inserted either in the contract itself or in a separate codicil, to ensure that if the couple divorces in the civil courts, they both will take the steps necessary in Jewish law for each of them to remarry. Jewish communities in other parts of the world rarely use these American innovations.

The Social Element of Jewish Marriage

Marriage is a social institution in several quite different connotations of the word "social." Marriage is social in that it is especially vital to group self-perpetuation. Since Jews have lacked common land and political sovereignty for most of their history, geography could not be the determining factor in Jewish identity, as it is for most nations. The rabbis did not define Jewish identity in terms of ideological convictions either. Instead, one is a Jew by either being born to a Jewish woman or through conversion. Endogamy (i.e., Jews marrying Jews) is thus a crucial element of Jewish group survival. Especially since Jews now number only 0.2 percent of the world's population, the high rate of intermarriage between Jews and non-Jews in recent times demographically threatens the future of Jewry and Judaism. Orthodox and Conservative rabbis will not officiate at the wedding of a Jew to a non-Jew; some Reconstructionist and Reform rabbis will. Even when an intermarriage has occurred, every effort is made to convince the couple to raise their

A bride and groom stand under a canopy as a rabbi officiates at an outdoor Jewish wedding in Brooklyn, New York, in 1994.   (Credit: © Elena Rooraid/PhotoEdit/PNI.)

children as Jews, but only 10 percent of intermarried couples do. That makes endogamy all the more crucial.

Marriage is also social in that it defines social status. It establishes entitlements and obligations regarding the distribution of goods and services among spouses, parents and children, and siblings. Noneconomic forms of social status, such as honor, respect, and position, are also defined at least in part through marriage. Jewish law spells out the expectations that men and women may have of each other in marriage in areas as diverse as food, clothing, shelter, medical expenses, redemption from captivity, household chores, and sex. For example, there are two independent commandments in the Torah regarding sex, indicating that it is both for procreation (Genesis 1:8) and for the mutual enjoyment and bonding of the couple (Exodus 21:10).

Marriage creates a new social unit of husband and wife, a third social dimension of marriage. Indeed, Jewish sources put great emphasis on the importance of marriage, to the point of claiming that without marriage a person is incomplete. The stories of Genesis stand out among nations' foundational literature in the extent to which they depict marital interactions. Another aspect of the social unit in this sense is children, who are seen as a great blessing and who learn the tradition within the family. According to Jewish law, the couple should, if possible, have at least two children, and preferably more. This is especially imperative in contemporary America, where every 2 Jews statistically produce only 1.6 children, far less than the 2.3 rate needed for a population simply to sustain itself.

Finally, weddings are social occasions in yet another sense: They are public occasions. Even Jews who are not particularly religious in other areas of their lives overwhelmingly want to be married in some form of the traditional ceremony to link themselves to Jews of the past, present, and future. Moreover, recitation of the seven blessings that constitute the core of the wedding ceremony requires a communal quorum of ten (a minyan) to help the bride and groom celebrate their marriage and to give communal reinforcement to their marital bond. The rabbis maintained that even God likes to attend weddings!

The Sacred Element in Jewish Marriage

God wants people to marry because marriage enables some forms of divine activity to take place. Marriage advances the work of creation and the fulfillment of the covenant as each couple participates in making new lives and in passing on to their seed the promise and responsibility received from their ancestors. Moreover, in Jewish theology, God works in the world through love: We are to love God (Deuteronomy 6:5), and God loves us by giving us the Torah and entering into a covenant with us. Thus through their experience of love, humans learn about the nature of God. God is so committed to marriage that, according to rabbinic lore, he spends a portion of each day matching husbands to wives! The sacred element of Jewish marriage is clearly evident in the blessings and the theological themes of the Jewish wedding ceremony. God is blessed for creating humanity, the genders, and this particular husband and wife. God is also praised for enabling the bride and groom to rejoice with each other. The blessings link the couple to, and make them symbolic of, ideal times: Adam and Eve in the Garden of Eden, and the messianic future. They are thus an expression of our hope—and God's—for a future, perfected world.

See also BELONGING, RELIGIOUS; DIVORCE, JEWISH; JEWISH IDENTITY; JEWISH OBSERVANCE; JUDAISM; RELIGIOUS COMMUNITIES; RITES OF PASSAGE; RITUAL; SOCIOLOGY OF RELIGION.

BIBLIOGRAPHY

Dorff, Elliot N., and Arthur Rosett. *A Living Tree: The Roots and Growth of Jewish Law.* 1988.
Lamm, Maurice. *The Jewish Way in Love and Marriage.* 1980.

Elliot N. Dorff

Martial Arts

The practice of taiji quan, also known as tai chi chuan, characterized by its slow, almost ritualized movements, in massed groups of old and young, male and female, generally in the early hours of the morning, is familiar to most travelers in China. Yet, for all its traditional aura, it is a phenomenon of the twentieth century. This mass expression of one of China's better-known martial arts emerged at the beginning of the century as part of a response to Western colo-

nialism and the desire to modernize. The humiliation of China by the colonial powers was perceived as the result of a shameful moral and physical weakness of the old society. Shorn of much of its religious associations, this more democratized practice of taiji was advocated by reforming intellectuals as a homegrown means to develop national health. Though characterized as a martial art, no argument was made for its potential to oppose the industrialized warfare of modernity. How then are we to understand this set of practices, characterized as martial, both within their countries of origin and in America?

The term "martial arts" is a direct translation of the Chinese term *wushu* and denotes any of the traditional arts of warfare that demanded a high level of individual skill and mastery, including those in which one's hands are used not only to wield small weapons but also, more commonly, in place of any such weapons. In America the term encompasses not only the Chinese arts of the warrior but the martial arts of Korea (tai kwan do), Japan (judo, karate, kendo, aikido), the Philippines, Burma, Malaysia, and Thailand as well.

An important component of the martial arts in China has been the concept of *qi*, understood as the fundamental energy or life force that permeates the natural world or cosmos, including the human body. It has long been taken for granted in Chinese culture that the cultivation of one's bodily qi is essential for developing any skill as well as for maintaining health and life itself. Qi plays as much a role in traditional Chinese medicine as it does in most aspects of Chinese religion. In Japan the fundamental role of qi is conspicuous in aikido ("The Way of Conjoined Qi"), a martial art form developed in the early part of the twentieth century. The notion of qi has rapidly found its way into contemporary Western understandings of the martial arts and lies at the root of most Western understandings of the "spiritual" nature of these practices.

Native Roots

Taoism, with its emphasis on the cultivation of health and the energies of life that could lead to immortality, offers the clearest precedent to the religious understanding of the martial arts in the contemporary world. Taoist monks and priests often include taiji as part of their training as a method to purify their bodily energies. Buddhism, which arrived in China from India in the first century C.E., appears to have brought no martial forms with it, but its meditative practices, with their focus on the measured circulation of breath, provided an easy bridge to Chinese notions of the circulation of qi.

Throughout much of Chinese history, Confucians regarded military skills as the domain of the less cultivated and the lower classes. Nonetheless, Confucians perceived a strong relationship between the sorts of physical activities that were effective in circulating the qi within the body, and physical health and insight. Only in the early nineteenth century do we see evidence of Confucian gentry figures developing the martially inspired set of exercises that have come to be know as Taiji quan. Popular tradition traces these practices back to the semilegendary Taoist sage Zhang Sanfeng, alleged to have lived from 960 to 1279, but there is no reliable evidence for this assertion. Confucian taiji was probably less concerned with developing techniques of self-defense than with constructing the individual's body as a metaphor for China's cultural values as interpreted by a fiercely nationalistic scholarly minority.

Local village and temple associations have also carried on a vibrant martial arts tradition over the past few centuries. The lion dance, a mandatory component of many village or temple festivities, is generally performed by a trained group of the young men of the village, or in modern Taiwan by a semiprofessional group of traveling performers. Martial arts is a basic component of their training and their performances. These local associations provided the basis for the dispersion of martial arts training throughout China among the masses.

The practice of martial arts in Japan originates in the martial skills associated with the samurai, members of an elite and privileged class within Japanese society. In the twelfth century they affiliated themselves with the religious institution and practices of Zen Buddhism. The 1920s witnessed the introduction of Okinawan fighting skills into the mainstream of Japanese culture, and these have evolved into the modern form known as karate. Modern karate, judo, and kendo still bear the stamp of the Meiji nationalists' attempt to instill in these arts the discipline and spirit of the samurai, understood as the national essence. This spirit formed a core mentality exploited by the architects of Japanese military expansion in the mid-twentieth century.

The martial arts as they developed in Asia over the past millennium can be characterized as being relatively unconcerned with martial effectiveness, but heavily laden with philosophy and symbol, variously deployed in the service of mostly nonmartial goals: maintenance of health, healing, prolonging life, enlightenment, cultural preservation, and nationalism.

They are generally represented as taking place within and on behalf of the social order.

The Martial Arts in America

Various forms of the martial arts had been present in the United States within immigrant Asian communities throughout much of the twentieth century, long before they attracted the attention of the general population. Lion dance associations in American Chinatowns and martial arts clubs associated with Japanese Buddhist temples in the United States carried these traditions to the Americas early in this century. But it was not until the end of World War II and the Allied occupation of Japan that these arts began to attract attention among non-Asians. American GIs began studying these arts and bringing them home to be spread among the non-Asian population. The actual self-defense effectiveness of the martial arts in contemporary America is highly questionable in terms of the ratio of people who have trained in them to those who have actually used them to advantage and given the pervasiveness of high-powered automatic weapons on the streets today. It is perhaps the recognition of this fact that has led to the adaptation of the martial arts by some to the arena of American sports.

An additional and distinct impetus for the development of American martial arts can be found among that portion of the American youth culture of the 1960s who were seeking an alternative to an establishment culture they characterized as materialistic, predatory, and spiritually empty. Many thought they had found it in the religious, medical, and martial traditions of Asia, the "spiritual East." The practice of various forms of Buddhist meditation, the quest for alternative methods of healing, and an increasing variety of "soft" martial forms, though still marginal in American culture at the time, laid the basis for the broad popularity that these Asian imports enjoy today. Out of such aspirations have arisen many of the symbolic and religious aspects that characterize the martial arts in America.

In many respects the American institutions take on a modified or a simulated monastic quality. A common, nonmartial, black or white garb is adopted by many groups. Many of the exercises and practices are highly ritualized and reaffirm hierarchies within the group. There is a strong emphasis on teaching lineages, just as there is in Chan/Zen monasteries. Martial practices of qi circulation are closely assimilated to breathing practices used in meditation, and in many groups there is explicit reference to meditation, however adumbrated or symbolic. In some practice halls there is a small image altar where incense is burned. The image might be a Buddha, an honored teacher, or a piece of Chinese calligraphy. Lectures of a philosophical or religious nature are not uncommon. Great value is placed on discipline and constancy.

In America there is an ever-broadening range of attitudes and practices associated with the martial arts. They extend from defensive or aggressive fighting styles, and their alter ego, the sports forms on one end of the spectrum, to the highly internal meditative forms on the other. In contrast to Asian expressions, they are often taken as idioms by which the established order is rejected or circumvented. The individual with a special, unconventional, or perhaps even mystical identity tends to be idealized, and the interests of the group are relatively marginal.

See also BODY; BUDDHISM; CHINESE-AMERICAN RELIGIONS; CONFUCIANISM; HEALTH; JAPANESE-AMERICAN RELIGIONS; KOREAN-AMERICAN RELIGIONS; MEDITATION; RITUAL; SPIRITUALITY; TAOISM; ZEN.

BIBLIOGRAPHY

Despeux, Catherine. "Gymnastics: The Ancient Tradition." In *Taoist Meditation and Longevity Techniques,* edited by Livia Kohn. 1989.

Donohue, John. *Warrior Dreams: The Martial Arts and the American Imagination.* 1994.

Miura, Kunio. "The Revival of Qi: Qigong in Contemporary China." In *Taoist Meditation and Longevity Techniques,* edited by Livia Kohn. 1989.

Wile, Douglas. *Lost T'ai-chi Classics from the Late Ch'ing Dynasty.* 1996.

William Powell

Marty, Martin

(1928–), author, scholar, and editor.

Martin Marty is Fairfax M. Cone distinguished service professor emeritus of history of modern Christianity at the Divinity School of the University of Chicago. Born and raised in West Point, Nebraska, he was ordained to the ministry in 1952 and served for a decade as a Lutheran pastor. In 1963 he joined the faculty at the University of Chicago Divinity School. From 1956 to 1998 Marty was associate editor and later senior editor for *Christian Century* magazine. He was one of the founders of the Park Ridge Center for the Study of Health, Faith, and Ethics, where he is the George B. Caldwell senior scholar-in-residence.

Possessing a seemingly unlimited amount of energy that is channeled into a hectic but well-organized daily routine, Marty has been able to write fifty books and more than forty-three hundred articles, essays, and reviews. In 1972 he won the National Book Award for *Righteous Empire.* His major work, *Modern American Religion,* is a four-volume study of religion in twentieth-century America. Marty has also written a spiritual classic, *A Cry of Absence: Reflections for the Winter of the Heart,* a meditation occasioned by the death of his first wife, Elsa, in 1981. He has written other spiritual books, illustrated by the photographs of his son, Micah, that reflect on the Christian journey through life. A pastor as well as a scholar, Marty preaches regularly in various houses of worship, mainly in the area around Riverside, Illinois, where he lives with his second wife, Harriet.

In 1986 *Time* magazine called Marty "the most influential living interpreter of religion" in the United States. He is regularly featured in the media as the master analyst of the nation's religious landscape. Marty can best be described as a public intellectual who has a unique ability to popularize historical scholarship in an energetic and polished style. Because of this gift he is in great demand as a speaker, giving as many as one hundred talks a year throughout the country. In these talks he regularly examines a theme central to his thought, religious pluralism and the nation's search for the common good. He has described this as his life quest—to understand and explain the place of religion in the public sphere of the nation.

In addition to his role as a national public voice for religion, Marty has also distinguished himself as an acclaimed scholar. His major work, *Modern American Religion,* evidences a breadth of vision not found in the work of many other historians of American religion. Marty's ecumenical spirit shines through the work as he examines the diverse ways in which the forces of modernity have shaped the nation's three major religions—Protestantism, Judaism, and Roman Catholicism. His gift is the ability to synthesize large amounts of material in a readable narrative that incorporates telling quotes and anecdotes.

From 1988 to 1994 Marty served as the director of the Fundamentalism Project. Sponsored by the American Academy of Arts and Sciences, this was an interdisciplinary public policy study that examined the place of religious fundamentalism in the modern world. The results of this study were published in six volumes, which Marty coedited with R. Scott Appleby. They represent one of the most exhaustive studies of religious fundamentalism ever published. Like all of Marty's work, these volumes of essays, written by scholars from numerous countries throughout the world, offer a balanced and unbiased view of the global resurgence of religious fundamentalism.

Marty's many honors include fifty-nine honorary degrees, the National Humanities Medal (1997), and the Medal of the American Academy of Arts and Sciences (1995).

See also JOURNALISM, RELIGIOUS; PUBLISHING, RELIGIOUS; RELIGIOUS STUDIES.

BIBLIOGRAPHY

Marty, Martin. *Modern American Religion.* 3 vols. to date. 1986–1996. (A fourth, final volume is in preparation.)

Temple, Kerry. "With a Grin and a Prayer." *University of Chicago Magazine* 90, no. 6 (August 1998): 22–27.

Jay P. Dolan

Mary

In pre-Christian Mediterranean cultures the many cosmic goddesses were a background for an early and vigorous diaspora of Christian traditions on Mary. In Europe, important preparations for widespread medieval Marian devotion were made at the ubiquitous prehistoric goddess worship sites at springs, caves, and wooded areas. A strong devotion to Mary accompanied the first Catholic settlers to the Western Hemisphere. They were mostly Spanish (1492), French (1534), and English (1634). In the New World the strength and survival of a great variety of European Marian traditions can often be traced back to ingenious adaptations by the practitioners of indigenous and Afro-Caribbean rituals.

The Marian devotions imported to French territories were mostly limited to a few titles of Mary approved by Rome and universal throughout Europe. There had been no preparation among the hunter-gatherer natives of Canada for an effective grafting of Marian devotions onto an organized goddess-worship system. Nonetheless, Indians were at times deeply moved by the pictures of Mary used by Jesuit missionaries at sites such as Sault Ste. Marie, Immaculate Conception Mission on the Illinois River, and later, in the Northwest.

English Catholic colonists arriving in Maryland in 1634 named their first settlement St. Mary's City. Devotions to Mary under a few general European Marian titles continued but were kept private due to religious struggles with dominant Protestants. The destruction of indigenous societies and the consequent establishment of a secular-commercial civilization preempted a deeply rooted Marian religious culture among future U.S. Catholics. However, upon his consecration as North America's first Roman Catholic bishop in 1790, John Carroll spread an official devotion to the small number of colonial Catholics based on his experiences at the Italian shrine of Our Lady of Loretto. A few religious orders, such as the Sulpicians and the Carmelites, were also beginning to establish limited and generalized Eurocentric Marian titles.

With the conquest of Latin America, more than five hundred separate Spanish Marian cults were introduced. These were the vestiges of a huge number of local Iberian goddess traditions, and each Marian cult had individualized local histories, rituals, and iconographies. Very many of the images preserved legends about their miraculous discovery in Spain's wilderness after eight hundred years of Muslim domination. Most were gradually appropriated by the official church but usually maintained a basic folk ownership. Titles and specific American images such as Nuestra Señora de Altagracia and Nuestra Señora de la Caridad were introduced early into Caribbean settlements. From the beginning, they accumulated additional popular symbolisms and narratives frequently related to struggles of poverty, hunger, sickness, exploitation, racial persecution, and so on. For example, the rediscovery of the Spanish statue of Nuestra Señora de la Caridad in the ocean by three young Cuban slaves—two indigenous and one black—is the root legend for its New World transformation. "Del Cobre" was added to this Virgin's name because the devotion and shrine were developed in the copper mining town of Cobre, which had a large slave population. The trajectory of this devotion among colonial populations reveals a basic paradigm for the development of a great many other Latin American Marian cultures.

Another precondition frequently existed. The Mexica (Aztecs) and the many other civilizations of Central and South America were organized within systems of territories, cities, villages, and neighborhoods called *calpulli*, each with their patron deities. Important areas and sites, and also significant forces of nature, were under the protection and control of goddesses. Individual citizens, households, trades, working tools and activities, trees, hilltops, crossroads, and every single day in the calendar (*tonalamatl*) were each assigned to a specific god within an immense pantheon of at least sixteen hundred deities possessing their own identifying iconographies. Feminine deities were preeminent. Teteoinnan was Mother of all Gods. Toci was Our Grandmother; Atlan, Our Mother; Cihuacoatl, Woman Serpent; Ilamatecuhtli, Old Lady; Tonantzin, Our Mother, Earth Mother, Mother of Fertility, Mother of Flowers (very closely associated later with Our Lady of Guadalupe), and so on.

Spanish missionary practice alternated between efforts to eradicate these indigenous religious cultures and efforts to insert into them an endless variety of Virgin Mary and other saints' traditions. These would

An image resembling the Virgin Mary is seen by a crowd of onlookers on this building in Clearwater, Florida, on Saturday, March 29, 1997. (Credit: AP/Wide World Photos.)

often take the forms of lay fraternities (*cofradías*), through which Indians preserved elements of their own religions. Furthermore, Charles V's New Laws of 1542 attempted to protect Indian property and hence, indirectly, some of the older religious observances. In effect there developed a coexistence of indigenous religious systems with Catholic Virgin Mary and saints' devotions and fiestas. There were frequent Marian titular designations for personal names, lands, temples, natural sites, villages, and lay groups. Native responses to official Catholic religious questionnaires, such as that of royal chronicler Juan Lopez de Velasco in 1577, were based on incomplete indigenous historiographies and native pictographs that were impossible for the Spanish to decipher accurately. Moreover, Catholic images of Mary and the saints afforded direct access to sacred powers the indigenous religions had already possessed in their own ways. The worship of Jesus was largely controlled by ecclesiastical authorities, but the ubiquitous number and variety of cults to

Mary allowed the faithful to frequently bypass official church control, partly due to the absence of an adequate number of priests, especially in outlying areas. Indians and mestizos continued the indigenous custom of dressing goddess effigies in robes appropriate for each feast day. They continued to develop *curanderismo* (folk medicine) systems using titles and images of Mary and the saints, still obvious today in the many *botanica* shops throughout U.S. Latino neighborhoods. The cofradías and their chosen Marian titles were very popular and politically effective among the *castas* (racial mixtures), since official Spanish census lists did not record persons by race or racial mixture. This encouraged a very rich crossfertilization of Marian cofradías that sponsored occupational groups, apprenticeships, artistic expression, public sponsorships for fiestas, neighborhood organizations, and other kinds of services and reputations that enhanced ethnic identities. The profuse racial mixtures of Spanish colonial society must be taken into account to appreciate the fermentation in varieties of Marian devotions. The major divisions of the castas were *españoles* (Spanish born in Spain), *criollos* (Spanish born in the New World), *indios* (well over five hundred cultures), *negros* (slaves and free), *mestizos* (español + indio), *castizos* (español + mestizo), *mulatos* (español + negro), *morisco* (español + mulato), *lobo* (indio + negro), *coyote* (indio + mulato), and *chino* (indio + lobo). The great Mexican mystic and intellectual Sor Juana Ines de la Cruz (1648–1695) composed Christmas carols for these different castas.

An example of casta contribution to New World Marian tradition is the 1695 wilderness discovery by the wood gatherer Juana Pereira of a negroid statuette of Mary, La Negreta. This developed into the national Costa Rican Marian title of Nuestra Señora de los Angeles. Numerous other Latin American Marian cults originated among wood gatherers, wood carvers, fishermen, farm laborers, and pack carriers, such as Nuestra Señora de Ocotlan (Tlaxcala, 1541), Señora de Esperanza (Michoacan, 1685), Nuestra Señora de Quinche (Ecuador, 1585), Nuestra Señora de Copacabana (Bolivia, 1579), and Nuestra Señora de Guadalupe (Tepeyac, 1531). The original images were those of dark-skinned maidens called morenitas.

The hordes of European Catholic immigrants who inundated the United States during the nineteenth century established a pluralistic, ethnic church. They brought with them and established their own Marian devotions, but these were normally under more official titles, such as the Immaculate Conception, which itself frequently split into subsidiary devotions such as the Miraculous Medal, the Sacred Heart of Mary, or Our Lady of Lourdes. For a while the devotions to the Immaculate Mary symbolized a cultural resistance to the dominant secular U.S. civilization and strengthened the ethnic identities of Irish, Italian, German, Polish, Lithuanian, Slovak, and African-American Catholics. A type of Marian melting pot approach soon developed as Catholic ethnic groups assimilated to a consumer culture. However, there remain a few Marian shrines throughout the United States that preserve some of their European ethnic Catholic backgrounds. Because Florida stayed Spanish until 1821 and had retained connections to Catholic slaves in the Caribbean and escaped slaves from the North, Latin American Marian cofradia titles were often inherited among the black Catholic confraternities in St. Augustine (Florida), Baltimore, Mobile, and New Orleans. Today, other U.S. Catholic minorities manage to preserve an energetic Marian spirituality, such as the Vietnamese, who participate in a massive gathering in southwestern Missouri every August 15 for the Feast of the Assumption. Filipinos also observe their own public fiestas, such as that of Nuestra Señora de Antipolo in Chicago.

However, after 1960, for the majority of U.S. Catholics, there was a great erosion in Marian traditions. Earlier ethnic Catholics had assimilated to U.S. secularism, but the Second Vatican Council (1963–1965) reduced Marian tradition almost to an afterthought in its key document *Lumen Gentium* and hence influenced a considerable weakening in U.S. Catholic Marian spirituality. But there had already been a kind of melting pot reduction in North American Marian observances. However, in 1979 the Latin American Bishops' Conference held in Puebla, Mexico, compensated for Vatican II's lack of a strong and multicultural Mariology with a firm support for popular religion and questioned "any universality that is synonymous with uniformity or leveling that fails to respect different cultures by weakening them, absorbing them, or annihilating them." The conference criticized religious universality used as a tool of domination by "some peoples or social strata over other peoples and social strata." The Puebla documents also praise popular religion as a "storehouse of values" and a power for resisting cultures of consumerism among dominant groups.

These Latin American developments supported the ongoing fermentation in Marian popular religion among Latin America's poor—the vast majority of the population. These poor are now streaming into the United States, so that Hispanics will soon be 50 percent of U.S. Catholics. Both legal and undocumented immigrants are rapidly adding to the U.S. Hispanic/Latino population which will number forty million before long. They continue to bring with them a great repertoire of Marian customs. With a few notable exceptions, Catholic parishes usually do not publically

sustain much variety in Latin American Marian observances. Some dioceses have an annual, centralized Marian celebration to which Latino ethnic groups bring their own images of Mary. But the people themselves preserve a rich variety of Marian customs in their homes and in their ever-expanding botanica shops. Each of the many U.S. Latino/Hispanic Marian traditions continues to possess its own unique image and history, with important influences contributed by Latin American Indian and Afro-Caribbean cultures. Great numbers of new immigrants and the many circular migrants reinvigorate many of the second- and third-generation Hispanic Marian practices that might have become submerged or manipulated beneath a more generic Catholicism. Latin American refugees fleeing natural disasters, political persecution, or economic hardship enter the United States highlighting their narratives of exile with miracles of Mary's deliverance. U.S. Latin American ethnic groups continue to support a thriving multiplicity of unique Marian traditions that challenge any kind of arid or sterile uniformity. A few of the most notable Hispanic/Latino Marian devotions in the United States today are: Nuestra Señora de Guadalupe (Mexico), Nuestra Señora de la Caridad del Cobre (Cuba), Nuestra Señora de Providentia (Puerto Rico), and Nuestra Señora de San Juan de Lagos (Mexico).

A Hispanic/Latino multicultural Marian hemispherization is the strongest development in devotion to Mary taking place today in the United States among the people. How this Latino fecundity in the many expressions of its Marian cultures will affect the monocultural Catholicism of the United States remains to be seen.

See also BELONGING, RELIGIOUS; CULT; GODDESS; LATINO TRADITIONS; MARIAN DEVOTIONS; RELIGIOUS COMMUNITIES; RELIGIOUS EXPERIENCE; ROMAN CATHOLICISM; SOCIOLOGY OF RELIGION; VIRGIN OF GUADALUPE.

BIBLIOGRAPHY

Chance, John K. *Race and Class in Colonial Oaxaca.* 1978.

Davis, Cyprian, O. S. B. *The History of Black Catholics in the United States.* 1995.

Deck, Allan Figueroa, S. J., *The Second Wave: Hispanic Minority and the Evangelization of Culture.* 1989.

Díaz-Stevens, Ana María, and Anthony M. Stevens-Arroyo. *Recognizing the Latino Resurgence in U.S. Religion.* 1998.

Gruzinski, Serge. *The Conquest of Mexico: The Incorporation of Indian Societies into the Western World, Sixteenth to Eighteenth Centuries.* 1993.

Holler, Stephen C. "Exploring the Popular Religion of U.S. Hispanic/Latino Ethnic Groups," *Latino Studies Journal* 6 (1995): 3–29.

Holler, Stephen C. *Mary and the Poor in Latin America since Vatican II: Responses of the Church to Marian Popular Religon.* 1992.

Holler, Stephen C. "The Origins of Marian Devotion in Latin American Cultures in the United States." *Marian Studies* 46 (1995): 108–127.

Matibag, Eugenio. *Afro-Cuban Religious Experience.* 1996.

Price, Richard, ed. *Maroon Societies: Rebel Slave Communities in the Americas.* 1996.

Sargent, Daniel. *Our Land and Our Lady.* 1939.

Wauchope, Robert, ed. *Handbook of Middle American Indians,* vol. 10. 1971.

Stephen C. Holler

Masculine Spirituality

As cultural constructs, understandings and practices of masculine spirituality have varied from one social group to another and within any given group over time. They have been postures at once private and public, personal and social, sacred and secular, spiritual and physical. Contemporary American religious life entails many models, all with deep historical roots.

Indigenous American concepts and practices of masculine spirituality have varied widely but generally addressed relationships among bodily experience, group survival, and the environment. Expressed in visions, dances, and other rites of passage, healing, sexuality, hunting, planting, and war, masculine spirituality—particularly that of the male shamans, priests, and secret societies who specialized in ritual—regulated personal and group relations with the spirits, mythic heroes, animals, plants, and people that inhabited and shaped the surrounding world. As Native Americans' physical and cultural environment was altered by white settlement, they infused traditional expressions of masculine spirituality with new meanings. Some have identified male religiosity with a red God of justice. Others have had visions calling for a vigorous physical defense of their communities, territory, natural environment, and traditional values against perceived external threats. Still others have promoted a male spirituality that emphasizes ethical and peaceful living and incorporates such white Christian values as temperance and industry.

Unlike Native Americans, the Protestant Christians who colonized America assumed a dualism between spirit and body in which the former was identified as masculine and dominant and the latter as feminine and requiring control. Seventeenth-century Puritan men therefore defined their pious submission to God as "feminine" while assuming their spiritual superiority and exercising religious authority in church, state, and the family. Male spiritual power was to be demonstrated in stern enforcement of moral law and in practices of piety, humility, self-control, diligent labor, and monogamous procreative sexuality. These practices endure as hallmarks of American male spirituality, but the social, economic, and cultural changes accompanying the growth of commercial capitalism and the modernization of American life rendered masculine spirituality more problematic by the early nineteenth century. Men became separated from the home; new models of manhood portrayed them as sexual and economic aggressors, urging them to the competitive, amoral pursuit of business success in the public sphere and a tightly controlled sexuality while identifying piety, purity, domesticity, and emotional expression as private postures best suited to women. The result was a tension between spirituality and masculinity, between Christian commitment, self-control, and humility on the one hand and material success and personal ambition on the other.

From the Victorian era to the present, American Protestant men have responded to this perceived disjuncture by seeking the meaning of masculine spirituality. Some radical Protestant men of the mid-nineteenth century found it by rejecting emerging gender and sexual constructs in favor of gender equity, communal living, and biblically based sexual practices ranging from those of the Oneida community, where Christian love meant a liberated yet controlled sexuality of multiple partners and male continence, to those of the Shakers, who sublimated male sexuality in celibacy, diligent labor, and ecstatic dance. Millions of liberal Protestant men turned from what they considered "feminized" churches and sentimentalized theology to fraternal orders, where they found Christian male fellowship, a masculinized theology of sin and rebirth, mystical initiation rites, and emotional release. (Though less troubled by a feminization of worship, Jewish and Catholic men likewise found in fraternal ritual an assertion of male spiritual identity.) Evangelical Protestants promoted a "muscular Christianity" that equated spiritual with physical virility and urged men to offset the enervating effects of office work and female sentimentalism with the masculine power of Christ. The Men and Religion Forward Movement of 1911–1912 combined muscular Christianity with male domesticity in all-male religious meetings that identified masculine spirituality with church leadership, businesslike social service, and marital fulfillment.

Muscular Christianity and fraternalism waned in the 1920s, but similar contemporary movements illustrate the continuing effort to articulate a masculine spirituality amid profound technological change, post-industrial downsizing, changing family and workforce demographics, and modern feminism. Self-proclaimed "Wild Men" reject feminist critiques of masculinity, assert a distinctly male spiritual and physical essence, and urge men alienated by modern society to revitalize that essence by seeking mythic warrior-hero models and the bonding and emotional release of all-male shamanistic rituals. In sports stadiums and small groups, the Promise Keepers, led by a football coach, have incorporated feminism by rejecting competitiveness, aggression, and careerism in favor of piety, male friendship, emotionality, and family commitment. Some evangelicals and athletes have revived the hypermasculine spirituality and brawny Jesus of muscular Christianity, while more liberal theologians offer an alternative model of masculine spirituality based on a feminine, feminist Jesus and a concept of God that moves beyond phallic firmness to embrace the realities of male physical desire and frailty.

Middle-class Catholics of the nineteenth and twentieth centuries have joined the Protestant effort to define masculine spirituality but have looked to Catholic thought as well as Protestant models, tried to establish Catholicism in American life, and addressed a working-class culture with limited economic opportunity and strong traditions of male celibacy and homosocial revelry. They and Protestants alike have assumed a tension between manhood and piety and have urged diligence, thrift, sobriety, regular worship, and marital sexuality as male spiritual ideals. But they deemphasized the spiritual benefits of all-male spaces, contrasted a manly Catholicism with a feminized Protestantism, and rejected the perceived Protestant premium on competitiveness, acquisitiveness, and ambition in favor of patience, honesty, humility, family devotion, and the preindustrial Catholic notion of acceptance of station. Much of this ideal endures, particularly among Irish Americans, although it has been counteracted by working-class resistance to middle-class standards and, well into the twentieth century, by resistance to an Irish-dominated church hierarchy among such non-Irish Catholic men as Italian and Mexican Americans. The movement of Catholic ethnic groups to the suburbs after World War II led the church to produce a burst of ethnically neutral literature urging men to seek the spiritual benefits of domestic devotion, but this literature has underscored rather than resolved the problems of male spirituality that Catholics share with other American men. Feminist challenges to the male church hierarchy and a rethinking of traditional gendered concepts of God in the wake of the Second Vatican Council have in-

tensified attempts to develop new models of Catholic male spirituality.

For Jewish-American men, the problem of masculine spirituality has been tied to issues of ethnic identity and social marginality. Spirituality and masculinity are closely identified in traditional Judaism, in which sacred learning is an exclusively male duty, fathers are expected to lead family prayer and ensure their sons' spiritual well-being, and seating in worship is segregated by gender. Orthodox groups in America maintain these aspects of male religiosity, but Reform and Conservative Jewish men have anxiously sought to reconcile the male spirituality of the dominant American culture with that of tradition. Loyalty to the family—traditionally understood as the focus of ethnic and religious identity—is considered a crucial element of male spirituality by all of these groups. But American anti-intellectualism, hypermasculinity, and anti-Semitism have led some to question the Old Testament identification of superior spirituality with physical delicacy and maternal orientation, the male imperative to spiritual study, and the concept of circumcision as a supreme act of masculine piety. Some have also challenged a long influential model of manhood—developed in Europe as a survival mechanism—that rejects ambition, arrogance, and anger in favor of humility, restraint, emotional coolness, and conciliation. Reform men in Victorian America redefined male spirituality to embrace gender-integrated (or "family") worship; Conservatives followed in the early to mid-twentieth century. Many Jewish-American men have also embraced the ethic of achievement, while more recently others have seen in Israeli men a constructive reclamation of anger and a combination of spiritual with physical vigor. The patriarchal elements of male Jewish spirituality have also been challenged in an American setting, most successfully in liberal groups, by female challenges to male religious authority and by secularizing currents that have pulled Jewish men from sacred learning to professional ambition. But the endurance of such masculine spirituality, even in Reform Judaism, is evident in continued paternal leadership of such domestic rituals as the Passover Seder.

Even more than Jewish-American men, African-American men have built models of masculine spirituality on experiences of oppression and marginality. But their models, shaped by a legacy of slavery and resistance to white racism, have emphasized racial pride, dignity, independence, reclamation of the exploited and stereotyped body, and an agenda of social and political liberation. Slave religion idealized Moses the liberator as well as the more gentle Jesus as an appropriate model of black spirituality. The black spokesmen and emerging African-American denominations of the nineteenth century defined male religiosity in terms of strenuous, angry, and sometimes violent resistance to racial oppression and a celebration of physical and cultural blackness. Some urged removal to Africa on the grounds that the African male embodied a spiritual manliness impossible of realization in a white society. These positions remain central to black male spirituality. African-American Christians of the 1950s and 1960s fashioned a theology of liberation that associated masculine spirituality with Christian commitment and a vigorous but nonviolent struggle for respect and social justice. The Nation of Islam, nationally prominent since the 1950s, has offered an alternative definition of spiritual manliness that postulates a black God and black superiority, asserts black power, questions Christian nonviolence, sanctions righteous anger, counsels strict morality, and urges militant and if necessary physical resistance to white dominance. The recent Million Man March, which like the Promise Keepers urged male spiritual fellowship and family commitment, successfully combined both models.

Addressing men's religious, psychic, cultural, and social needs, masculine spiritualities have been and remain as dynamic and plural as American life itself.

See also AFRICAN-AMERICAN RELIGIONS; BELONGING, RELIGIOUS; BODY; CELIBACY; ECSTASY; FEMINIST SPIRITUALITY; FEMINIST THEOLOGY; GENDER ROLES; JUDAISM; LIBERATION THEOLOGY; MAINLINE PROTESTANTISM; NATION OF ISLAM; PROMISE KEEPERS; RITES OF PASSAGE; RITUAL; ROMAN CATHOLICISM; SECRET SOCIETIES; SHAMANISM; SPIRIT; SPIRITUALITY; TEMPERANCE; VATICAN II.

BIBLIOGRAPHY

Becker, William H. "The Black Church: Manhood and Mission." *Journal of the American Academy of Religion* 40 (1972): 316–333.
Boyd, Stephen B., W. Merle Longwood, and Mark W. Muesse, eds. *Redeeming Men: Religion and Masculinities.* 1996.
Brod, Harry, ed. *A Mensch Among Men: Explorations in Jewish Masculinity.* 1988.
Carnes, Mark C. *Secret Ritual and Manhood in Victorian America.* 1989.
Krondorfer, Björn, ed. *Men's Bodies, Men's Gods: Male Identities in a (Post-) Christian Culture.* 1996.
Lippy, Charles H. "Miles to Go: Promise Keepers in Historical and Cultural Context." *Soundings* 80 (1997): 289–304.
McDannell, Colleen. "Catholic Domesticity, 1860–1960." In *Religion and American Culture,* edited by David G. Hackett. 1995.

Bret E. Carroll

Master Fard.

See Fard, W. D.

Material Religion

Material religion refers to the physical objects and practices that play a role in everyday American religious life. The term does not suggest that it is a separate belief system alongside religions such as Christianity, Taoism, and Islam. Instead, it is a sort of scholarly shorthand for a collection of behaviors and beliefs in every religious community. Many Catholics pray using a rosary, a string of beads, each representing a prayer or meditation. Some evangelical Protestants hang pictures of Jesus on their walls. They do not pray to the picture, but it reminds them of Jesus' love. American Muslims center their prayers on a collection of holy places in Mecca. Buddhist homes contain a small shrine, often featuring a figure of the Buddha, that serves as a center of meditation. Most religions have ethical codes to determine behavior concerning the body—including clothing, eating, and interpersonal relations. Almost all institutional religions maintain some kind of building—churches, synagogues, mosques, temples—that serve as worship and community centers. To maintain those buildings—and to pay professional leaders—they have to raise money, through donations or fees. All of these are examples of material religion.

This is a broad definition of "material." It includes obvious things, such as pictures and shrines. But it also includes economic concerns, such as fund-raising and salaries. Finally, it includes the way materiality is understood in a religion, including attitudes toward the body and the rest of the physical world. Material religion involves the relationship between religious belief and life in a material world and recognizes that human beings spend their lives creating, handling, and exchanging material objects.

While material religious practices appear in most, if not all, religious traditions, modern American culture makes those practices a prominent part of contemporary American religious life. Consumer capitalism, with its concentration on the exchange of ideas and products in the free market, provides the context for seeing religious objects as commodities. General prosperity makes possible the support of large religious institutions and buildings. Modern mass production and marketing make possible the broad dissemination of religious material, including images and devotional objects. Finally, the diversity of religion in America presents a rich variety of religious material objects and practices. All these factors give material religion an important place in contemporary America.

Scholars of religion have only recently started paying attention to material religion. They have usually defined religion as an intellectual or spiritual activity, solely engaging the mind or the spirit and scorning the body. This definition sees material beliefs and practices as profane and thus less than religious. Scholars working with this traditional definition tend to ignore material religion. Others may study it but focus on kitsch aspects of religious material, including bumper stickers, pens, key chains, and other inexpensive items with religious images—sometimes dismissed as "Jesus junk."

For many people, however, these objects are essential parts of their religious practice. Through buildings, devotional objects, and food, they connect with their spiritual source and with fellow believers. For these people material religion does not take the place of more spiritual things; the material and the spiritual together form their entire religious worldview. Studying material religion opens a window to understanding the religious life of many average believers. Material religion is all around, even in unexpected places. This all-pervasive nature of material religion helps to question theories of secularization.

Anthropologists have studied material religion for generations, looking at the material culture of "primitive" religions. Only in the past decade or two have scholars turned their approach to Western religions. Historian Colleen McDannell brought much of this work together in her *Material Christianity* (1995). Other scholars of American religion have looked at other religious traditions, including Judaism and Native American religions.

Studying material religion requires asking different questions and using different sources than traditional scholarship uses. In addition to reading theological treatises, scholars have to look at artifacts, cookbooks, budgets, and photographs. In this respect the study of material religion is similar to the study of material culture, focused on things. But understanding material religion also requires looking at peoples' behaviors in relation to those things because things exist to be used. So scholars have to look at practices such as fund-raising, church dinners, and rituals. But these objects have meanings beyond their uses, so a full understanding of material religion requires looking at how those things are understood, which includes theories of materialism and materialization. Historians, sociologists, anthropologists, theologians, and art historians have all developed tools that can be used to study material religion.

Some scholars—especially those with theological commitments—have questioned some of the research regarding material religion. While acknowledging that material practices are important, they argue that religious life is ultimately about spirit, not matter. The relationship between spiritual and material is far more complex than the scholars of material religion admit, they conclude. Other scholars point out that material religion does not exist as a thing or a religious belief; instead, it is a scholarly tool for understanding the material aspects of religious life. As a tool, however, it is helpful for understanding human behavior in a world that is both material and spiritual.

See also ALTAR; CHURCH; IMPLICIT RELIGION; MENORAH; NATURE RELIGION; SECULARIZATION; SPIRITUALITY; SWEAT LODGE; SYNAGOGUE; TEMPLE.

BIBLIOGRAPHY

Hall, David D., ed. *Lived Religion in America: Toward a History of Practice.* 1997.

Joselit, Jenna Weissman. *The Wonders of America: Reinventing Jewish Culture, 1880–1950.* 1994.

McDannell, Colleen. *Material Christianity: Religion and Popular Culture in America.* 1995.

Morgan, David. *Visual Piety: A History and Theory of Popular Religious Images.* 1998.

Daniel Sack

Matriarchal Core

The matriarchal core is a concept derived from analysis of women's roles in the maintenance, transmission, and transformation of religious practice. It is a premise of contemporary feminist studies of religion that, where gender defines distinct modes of religious participation, men generally appropriate to themselves positions they consider to be dominant and allow lesser functions for women. The matriarchal core differs from other feminist interpretations of religion by considering gender differentiation to create a space where women enjoy autonomous decision making. While it may be the intention of clergy-controlled denominations such as Catholicism to relegate women to subordinate roles, in practice the matriarchal core often exceeds these secondary functions and instead subverts and transforms religious production.

Contrary to the view that patriarchal religion is necessarily antagonistic to women, the matriarchal core understands power not as an absolute but as the ability to mobilize resources and to gain influence. Power of this sort often avoids overtly stating its boundaries. Some modern feminist scholars have come to recognize in the convents of medieval Christianity and among contemporary religious orders of women, societies where women possessed total power to shape and interpret their own values. The model of feminine religious practice derived from the practices in the secluded cells of the monasteries have been applied to the protected atmosphere of home life. Women's roles, therefore, while not official and clerical, have often become in both Protestantism and Catholicism the most influential and practical.

The contemporary experience among Latinas in the United States creates the social setting for the matriarchal core. Persons of Latin American heritage in the United States today frequently have experienced migration from agricultural societies into urban ones. Latino males in the new social setting generally have lost the ability to dominate socioeconomic relations, while the traditional roles of women in caring for home, religion, and the education of the children are offered higher status in the United States than in the sending countries. Paradoxically, holding to traditional tasks provides for an increase in social status for Latinas, while the opposite is the result for men. In these circumstances women assumed community leadership, which created a process that extended the responsibilities as communicators of religious values within the home to modes of influence within the wider community. The frequency of minority feminine leadership within social movements is linked by this trend in religion.

The matriarchal core consists of all those practices and rituals that have survived the test of time mainly because of women's role in them. It also applies to the values undergirding these practices and rituals as well as to the specific mode and character imparted to them by women's active and creative participation. To avoid the negative connotations of popular religion as folklore or unsophisticated practice, the product of the matriarchal core is defined as "communitarian spirituality." The emphasis is on the value of social expectations and religious traditions to provide a set of common inspirational symbols for group cohesiveness. This phenomenon is not limited to Latinas and other Christians, since American Jewish women, for example, are described in similar terms.

See also FEMINIST SPIRITUALITY; FEMINIST THEOLOGY; GENDER ROLES; MATRIARCHY; ORDINATION OF WOMEN; PATRIARCHY; PRIESTESS; WOMANIST THEOLOGY; WOMEN'S AGLOW FELLOWSHIP INTERNATIONAL; WOMEN'S STUDIES.

BIBLIOGRAPHY

Arenal, Electa, and Stacey Schlau. *Untold Sisters: Hispanic Nuns in Their Own Works.* 1989.

Davidman, Lynn. *Tradition in a Rootless World: Women Turn to Orthodox Judaism.* 1991.

Díaz-Stevens, Ana María. "Latinas and the Church." In *Hispanic Catholic Culture in the U.S.: Issues and Concerns,* edited by Jay Dolan and Allan Figueroa Deck. 1994.

Díaz-Stevens, Ana María. "The Saving Grace: The Matriarchal Core of Latino Catholicism." *Latino Studies Journal* 4, no. 3 (1993): 60–78.

Kosmin, Barry A., and Ariela Keysar. "The Impact of Religious Identification on Differences in Educational Attainment Among American Women in 1990." *Journal for the Scientific Study of Religion* 34, no. 1 (1995): 49–62.

McDannell, Colleen. *Material Christianity: Religion and Popular Culture in America.* 1995.

Prieto, Yolanda. "Continuity or Change? Two Generations of Cuban American Women." *New Jersey History* 113 (1–2) (1995): 47–60.

Sullivan, Kathleen. "Religious Conversion and the Recreation of Community in an Urban Setting Among the Tzotzil Maya of Highland Chiapas, Mexico." Doctoral diss., City University of New York. 1998.

Ana María Díaz-Stevens

Matriarchy

Matriarchy, or mother rule, refers to female supremacy in a social institution such as a family, state, or religion. Since the vast majority of the world's religions are patriarchal, such institutions are found, if at all, at the margins of contemporary American religion, and even those that have been labeled matriarchal are subject to continued scholarly debate.

Until fairly recently, it was held that some Native American religions may have been matriarchal. Among the Iroquois, for example, families were matrilineal, creation myths centered on a goddess, women called "faith keepers" were in charge of organizing religious rituals, and a woman called the "chief's matron" held the set of wampum beads that gave her the power to depose or install a new chief. However, more recent research suggests that there were significant checks on female power: It was male singers and dancers who actually performed most rituals, women could never be chief, and the matron's decisions could be overridden by a council. The perception that Iroquois religion was matriarchal simply reflected the bias of Victorian scholars, who viewed any system that treated women closer to equally than nineteenth-century Christianity as female-dominated.

Several American Christian sects are labeled matriarchal, including the Shakers (founded by Ann Lee) in the eighteenth century, Christian Science (Mary Baker Eddy) and Spiritualism (the Fox sisters) in the nineteenth century, and various Pentecostal sects (e.g., Aimee S. McPherson's Foursquare Gospel Church) in the twentieth century. Although all of these religions were headed by women, this does not necessarily make them matriarchal. To deserve that label, a religion must institutionalize female supremacy, and there is little evidence that these groups did. Lee and Eddy developed theologies about a mother-father God and used them to justify gender equality, not female rule. A number of local Christian Science churches were led by women, but after Eddy's death the national organization was frequently headed by men. The Shakers required that colonies be governed by male-female pairs, but the division of labor in their settlements maintained conventional gender roles (women in the kitchen, men in the fields). Most spiritualist churches did not last beyond the life of their charismatic founder, and the Foursquare Gospel Church no longer permits women to head a congregation.

Various new religions outside Christianity have taken matriarchal form, including Theosophy (founded by Helena Blavatsky) in the nineteenth century, and more recently Siddha Yoga (currently led by Gurumayi Chidvilasananda) and Vodun (Vodou or Voodoo). Drawing on Eastern philosophy, the first two religions see their leaders as the current incarnation in a long lineage of spiritual leaders who can be either male or female. Matriarchy in this case is temporary, an accident of birth, rather than a religious institution (and, indeed, Blavatsky's successor was male). Female rule is not institutionalized in Vodun either, as many Vodun priests in Haiti are male. Karen McCarthy Brown has written about a Vodun priestess in Brooklyn, New York, who continues in a long family line of female religious leaders. But matriarchy in such cases may arise more from necessity (the absence of men in poor families) than from an ideology of female supremacy.

It is not until the middle of the twentieth century and the birth of the Goddess (or feminist spirituality) movement that we see the emergence of what might be called institutionalized matriarchy. Drawing on Neopagan themes, the theology of these groups emphasizes the centrality of female divinity, and rituals are led by and sometimes are exclusively open to women. The most prominent leaders of this movement (Starhawk, Budapest) seek to restore what they believe was a universal female-dominated religion that preceded and was suppressed by Judeo-Christian patriarchy. This religion, they claim, will liberate all people because, unlike patriarchal religions, which oppress women, the ancient matriarchies treated men and women equally.

These are highly contentious claims, even within feminist circles. First, there is considerable debate over the existence of a universal matriarchal religion that preceded the patriarchal norm. The theory was first suggested by Victorian scholars who found numerous female figurines in India and concluded that this pointed to goddess worship. They also observed that some tribal religions, particularly agricultural ones, had myths in which a goddess creates the world and rituals in which women participate in significant ways. The theory was then expanded by twentieth-century archaeologists who made similar findings in the Middle East and Europe. It posited that goddess-worshiping cultures (e.g., in Mesopotamia or in the Indus valley) were peaceful, agricultural settlements who were overrun by nomadic, warlike tribes (e.g., Hebrews, Arians) who incorporated formerly independent and powerful goddesses as lesser deities into their male pantheon and subordinated human women to men. Yet, as some critics point out, female figurines may not have been goddesses but a form of "Paleolithic pornography." Even if the figurines were goddesses, we cannot assume that worshiping them translated into higher status for human women. Goddesses of love and fertility were important in ancient Greece and Roman; yet most women were the property of men and had few rights beyond those of slaves. Since the medieval period, Mahadevi (the Great Goddess) has been perhaps the most popular divinity in Hinduism, worshiped by millions of men and women; yet women could not become priestesses and, according to the Laws of Manu, were always to be kept under the control of a man. And even if goddess worship was accompanied by female power in some ancient societies, there is simply not enough evidence to suggest that matriarchal religion was universal.

Second, critics have contested the claim that matriarchal religion will liberate all human beings. The claim is based on the assumption that, although patriarchal religions oppress women, matriarchal religion would not oppress men because women are different—more nurturing, cooperative, and flexible. Ann Lee of the Shakers, for example, established gender-balanced—not female-dominated—religious leadership, and in many of today's Goddess groups leadership rotates among all members. Yet, as critics point out, patriarchal religion does not always oppress women. As studies of Christian and Jewish conservatives have indicated, there is a difference between official authority (usually assigned to men) and actual power (sometimes wielded by women). Thus some fundamentalist women feel that patriarchal religion is the best way to protect their interests. Matriarchal religion will not liberate women unless it incorporates a theology that institutionalizes women's power. As the examples of the Shakers and Christian Science illustrate, even with such a theology, old habits die hard.

Finally, and perhaps most importantly, there is still no consensus as to whether characteristics such as nurturing or cooperation come naturally to women or are simply products of patriarchal social conditioning. To assert that women are radically different from men is exactly the kind of essentialism that, for most of human history, has kept women enslaved.

See also CHRISTIAN SCIENCE; FEMINIST SPIRITUALITY; FEMINIST THEOLOGY; GENDER ROLES; GODDESS; HINDUISM; MASCULINE SPIRITUALITY; MATRIARCHAL CORE; ORDINATION OF WOMEN; PATRIARCHY; PENTECOSTAL AND CHARISMATIC CHRISTIANITY; PRIESTESS; SPIRITUALISM; THEOSOPHICAL SOCIETY; VODUN (VOODOO); WOMANIST THEOLOGY; WOMEN'S STUDIES; YOGA.

BIBLIOGRAPHY

Arenal, Electa, and Stacey Schlau. *Untold Sisters: Hispanic Nuns in Their Own Words.* 1989.

Brown, Karen McCarthy. *Mama Lola: A Vodou Priestess in Brooklyn.* 1991.

McNamara, Joann Kay. *Sisters in Arms: Catholic Nuns Through Two Millennia.* 1996.

Sered, Susan S. *Priestess, Mother, Sacred Sister: Religions Dominated by Women.* 1994.

Shimony, Annemarie. "Women of Influence and Prestige Among the Native American Iroquois." In N. Falk and R. Gross, eds., *Unspoken Worlds: Women's Religious Lives.* 1989.

Spretnak, Charlene, ed. *Women's Spirituality: Essays on the Rise of Spiritual Power within the Feminist Movement.* 1982.

Wessinger, Catherine, ed. *Women's Leadership in Marginal Religions.* 1993.

Christel Manning

Mecca

Mecca, also known as Makkah, is a Muslim holy city in Arabia located in Hijāz, some forty-six miles inland from the Red Sea port of Jidda. The holy city surrounds the Ka'bah, a rectangular building called the "House of God" *(bayt allāh)*. The Ka'bah had been known as a sacred sanctuary long before Islam appropriated it as the *qiblah* (the source of orientation in prayer) for its followers. The Qur'an speaks about "the House" *(al-bayt),* "a place of visitation for the people and a sanctuary," and attributes the "raising of the foundations" of the Ka'bah to Abraham and his son Ishmael (Qur'an 2:125–127). The Arab tribes in Mecca traced their genealogy to Ishmael, but their legend connected the city and its sanctuary with Adam, for whom God built the original Ka'bah. Abraham "raised the foundations" of the shrine after its destruction in the Flood. Today the Ka'bah is taller and more firmly built than the original edifice, which was described in early sources as "made of loose stones above a man's height." The Ka'bah determines the ritual direction, the focal point toward which all devotional acts and sacred buildings in Islam are oriented. Today, Muslims in the United States and throughout the world observe this ritual orientation.

Mecca is not situated in an agricultural area. In ancient times it had access to sufficient underground water for its inhabitants and was protected from invasion by surrounding hills. Later it came to possess the respected shrine to which the Arab tribes would make pilgrimage. The generations following Abraham had introduced idolatrous, polytheistic practices in the shrine, contrary to the pure monotheism of Abraham. The annual fairs took the form of pilgrimages, which brought prosperity by combining religious rituals with opportunities for trade. In due course Mecca became the most important trading center in Arabia. Trade routes connected it northward to Syria, northeastward to Iraq, southward to the Yemen, and westward to Tidda, the Red Sea port. Some generations before Muhammad, who died in 632, a tribe called the Quraysh, under the leadership of Qusayy, took over the springs there and the shrine. The Quraysh rebuilt and roofed the Ka'bah, draping it with a black cloth known as *kiswah.* To protect the tribes that came for trade and pilgrimage, the Meccans established four sacred truce months during which fighting was prohibited. Mecca provided a point of convergence for the Arabs, who maintained their solidarity through worship at the Ka'bah. A common cult had emerged to provide the collective practice of circling the Ka'bah a fixed number of times and touching the Black Stone in one corner. In the Ka'bah a great many sacred tokens of all the clans of Mecca were gathered to share in its sacredness. Nearby there was a sacred well, called *zamzam.* The space around the sanctified area, extending all around Mecca, was regarded as *haram,* an area in which fighting was taboo even when it was not a truce month.

Muhammad was born in Mecca in about 570. The Meccan moral, social, and spiritual conditions were ripe for a reformer to make a lasting impact in the region. When he emerged as a prophet in 610, the Meccans initially rejected his monotheism as a challenge to their polytheistic cults, which had made Mecca an important commercial and financial center. But many Meccans, caught up in the materialism and weakening interpersonal relations of the era, found Muhammad's message increasingly relevant. In 622 Muhammad was forced to leave his native city and to migrate to Medina, also known as Madina. This journey was called the *hijra*. In 630 Mecca opened its gates to Muhammad, who was able to take it without bloodshed. The Ka'bah was cleansed of the pre-Islamic sacred objects, but the Black Stone was retained. In 632, just before his death that year, Muhammad performed the *hajj*, in which he established the Islamic rituals that are emulated by Muslims even today. As the spiritual significance of Mecca increased, its commercial and political significance declined. Today all Muslims, in the United States and elsewhere, have a duty to perform the pilgrimage to Mecca at least once in a lifetime if their circumstances permit it.

Mecca has witnessed numerous struggles for supremacy among Muslim rulers of different dynasties, who at one time or another intervened in Meccan affairs to control its growing wealth through endowments and to acquire the prestige of being the protectors of the "House of God." The last in the line of the rulers were the Su'ūd, who gained complete control of Mecca and Medina in December 1925. In Mecca, Wahhābī forces, in accord with their opposition to anything that smacked of idolatry, destroyed a number of domed tombs, the reputed birthplace of the Prophet, and two houses revered as those of Khadīja (Muhammad's first wife) and Abū Bakr (the first caliph). Despite the iconoclastic attitudes of the Su'ūdis, the entire institution of the annual pilgrimage has continued to provide the regime with a religious prestige and acceptance. Maintenance of order and peace during the pilgrimage season has been one of their major achievements. The main mosque and other religious buildings have been expanded and renovated extensively since the Su'ūdis took over Mecca.

The requirement of the pilgrimage and the desire of the pious to live and die near the "House of God" have given Mecca a unique position among the Muslim holy cities. The population is a highly mixed one. Much of the city's life is dominated by the pilgrimage and the ceremonies connected with the various holy sites in or around the city. Religious occasions form part of the rhythm of participation in the life of the city. Besides the proper *hajj* season, there are numerous occasions for the performance of the *'umra* (the lesser pilgrimage) throughout the year, especially during the holy month of Ramadan. The pilgrimage service industry has grown over the centuries and is highly specialized. The guides *(mutawwifūn)* for the intending pilgrims from different parts of the Muslim world work closely with particular ethnic groups through the various arrangements that must be made with great precision to supply the material needs and facilitate the performance of the prescribed rites. Today Mecca has been modernized, and its complex infrastructure has evolved to meet the requirements of a city whose fixed population is three hundred thousand residents but that swells to some two million during the primary pilgrimage period.

To Muslims throughout history, Mecca has furnished a focus in their spiritual quest and has reenacted its symbolic presence in all sacred buildings of Islam—in the United States and throughout the world. The Ka'bah is the center as well as the orientation of Muslim devotion to God, the "Lord of the House."

See also ALLAH; IMAM; ISLAM; MOSQUE; MULLAH; QUR'AN.

BIBLIOGRAPHY

Farāhānī, Muhammad Husayn Husyanī. *A Shī'ite Pilgrimage to Mecca, 1885–1886: The Safarnameh of Mīrzā Muhammad Hosayn Farahani,* edited, translated, and annotated by Hafez Farmayan and Elton L. Daniel. 1990.

Long, David E. *The Hajj Today: A Survey of the Contemporary Makkah Pilgrimage.* 1979.

"Makkah." In *Encylopaedia of Islam,* 2nd ed., vol. VI.

Peters, F. E. *Jerusalem and Mecca: The Typology of the Holy City in the Near East.* 1986.

Peters, F. E. *Mecca and the Hijaz: A Literary History of the Muslim Holy Places.* 1994.

Abdulaziz A. Sachedina

Meditation

Meditation is increasingly becoming a viable practice for working Americans as opposed to being a way of life only for people living in monasteries. No longer viewed exclusively as an exotic import from the East, meditation is being incorporated into traditional religious practices, and numerous meditation groups have formed. The knowledge that meditation yields has just recently been discovered by scientists in the West, which has legitimated it. For instance, research in the field of particle physics confirmed what Buddhist and Hindu meditators have been asserting for three thousand years: the universe is a vast dance of energy rather than solid materiality. The appeal of meditation is its ability to bring attention to what transcends mundane, transient, and material concerns. It is seminal among a variety of practices gripping mainstream Americans who are on a massive search for meaning in order to counter the stresses of modernity that threaten to cast a veil of meaninglessness on life.

The English word "meditate" is etymologically derived from the Latin *meditari*, which connotes deep, continued reflection. The practices and goals of the different meditation traditions in the United States share a family resemblance. Apophatic procedures are those that aim to empty the mind of discursive content. Cataphatic practices in contrast purposefully hold an image, idea, or deity in mind and tend to be more heart-centered or devotionally oriented. Meditation can also be prayerful by focusing on scriptural passages in order to gain inspiration and deepen wisdom.

History

The growth of meditation practice in the United States stems from a number of Eastern teachers who introduced their ideas to the West. In 1893 Swami Vivekananda traveled from India to attend the Worlds Parliament of Religions in Chicago, where he drew considerable attention. Also from India, Paramahansa Yogananda came to Boston for the 1920 International Congress of Religious Liberals, where he spoke about a yogi's ability to attain self-mastery. Arriving in the United States on his first world tour in 1959, Maharishi Mahesh Yogi planned to bring in the Age of Enlightenment by teaching meditative practices. Originally from Tibet, Tarthang Tulku arrived in the United States in 1969 and founded a meditation center. Swami Muktananda came to the West in 1970 to introduce Siddha Yoga and to inspire what he termed a meditation revolution.

In the 1950s and 1960s the phenomenon known as the Beat way of life incorporated ideas from Zen Buddhism and thereby popularized an incipient interest in the nature of consciousness and meditation. Jack Kerouac wrote about Zen in *The Dharma Bums* (1958), and Alan Watts discussed Zen and Eastern culture on Pacifica Radio Network in terms that Westerners could understand. Watts explained how to live in the present moment by practicing meditation, which he said is the art of suspending verbal and symbolic thinking for a time. The whole point is to realize that there is no future and that the real sense of life is an exploration of the eternal now.

Meditation in the United States

Formally known as Siddha Yoga Dham Associates (SYDA), Siddha Yoga was brought to the West in 1970, when Swami Muktananda embarked upon a worldwide mission to inspire a meditation revolution. During the 1970s many residential ashrams and centers for the practice of Siddha Yoga were founded, and currently there are more than six hundred centers worldwide. In 1982, just before Swami Muktananda passed away, he transmitted the full power and knowledge of the Siddha lineage to his disciple, Swami Chidvilasananda, who currently guides Siddha students in their meditation practices. Affectionately called Gurumayi, Swami Chidvilasananda bestows her grace during the sacred initiation known as shaktipat, which awakens the inner kundalini energy and confers a spontaneous ability to meditate. Siddha students use the mantra and breath control to still their minds. Alternatively, they focus on an object or person such as Gurumayi to inspire their meditative practice. Meditation ultimately is said to bring knowledge of the transcendent and eternal Self. Seekers who cultivate yogic discipline may experience a sense of inner freedom and the highest love. The tranquillity acquired during sitting meditation is then to be infused into daily activities. The goal of Siddha Yoga meditation is to become a siddha, a perfected or accomplished human being, and thus realize that God dwells within the Self. Gurumayi has said that meditation is looking within, finding peace, which is a deeply personal treasure.

The vast traditions of Jewish meditation were hidden for centuries because the rabbis feared that meditation was dangerous for uninitiated people and because secularized Jews considered it to be backward and therefore abandoned it. Recently, however, these traditions have been recovered by interested Jews who seek inner silence and equanimity. Practices include sitting silently to empty the mind, focusing on Hebrew letters or words, breath control, chanting, imaging techniques, and contemplating Torah or philosophy. Meditation and prayer complement one another, and the goal is to become closer to God. Chochmat HaLev (Wisdom of the Heart) is a San Francisco Bay area multidenominational center that specializes in Jewish meditation and spirituality training and practice. While balancing the wisdom of the ancient tradition with the insights and demands of modernity, the teachings derive from the belief that the Torah can open the heart and heal the spirit. Founded in 1994 by Dr. Avram Davis, Chochmat HaLev attracts the minority segment of the Jewish population that is drawn to contemplative and meditative practice as a response to the escalation of information flow that leaves people busy but sad, and crowded but lonely. Metivta (from the Aramaic for "academy" and implying spiritual fellowship) is a Los Angeles–based nondenominational center for con-

A group meditation session is held in New York City's Central Park during the annual Change Your Mind Day, on Saturday, June 5, 1999. (Credit: AP/Wide World Photos.)

templative Judaism. Founded by Rabbi Jonathan Omer-Man in the early 1980s, Metivta emphasizes meditative techniques that empty the mind. Guided imagery or kabbalistic theme meditations are not encouraged. International meditation conferences and retreats bring Jews together from various denominations in order to explore the Jewish contemplative tradition.

For seven centuries the Mevlevi Order has taught the principles of Sufism, the mystical tradition of Islam. Adapting itself to changing historical circumstances, the Mevlevi Order has held the light of the religion of love, offering spiritual refuge and enlightenment for those who wished to develop their humanness to the highest level. In North America this order is represented by Dr. Edmund Kabir Helminski, who was appointed to this position by the late Dr. Celaleddin Celebi of Istanbul, Turkey, head of the Mevlevi Tariqu (Order) and direct descendant of the famous Sufi master, Jalāl al-Din Rūmī. In 1994 at a conference in Konya, Turkey, the heads of this order

declared the Threshold Mevlevi Center in Brattleboro, Vermont, as New Konya. The goal of the Mevlevi Order and the Threshold Society is to spread Rumi's message of universal love and to enable people to merge their hearts with the Divine Will. Shaikh Kabir Helminski, who wrote the book *Living Presence: A Sufi Way to Mindfulness and the Essential Self,* introduced the Mevlevi Dervishes of Turkey, a spiritual dance group, to more than twenty thousand people during their 1994 tour of North America. Monthly meetings of the Threshold Society encourage members to pause, reflect on their yearning for God, and then remember the capacity for conscious decision to unite people in their common yearning to know divine reality. Seminars and retreats that include contemplative practice, *dhikr* (remembrance of God), music, dance, and exploration of Rumi's teachings are held at different institutes throughout the United States.

The Nyingma Institute in Berkeley, California, was opened in 1973 under the guidance of Tarthang Tulku, a Tibetan lama of the Nyingma tradition. An institute for Buddhist education, it offers classes, workshops, and retreats where Buddhist teachings that derive from a wisdom tradition more than 2,500 years old meet with modern Western life. Known to his students as Rinpoche, a title earned by exceptionally well-qualified Tibetan lamas, Tarthang Tulku arrived in the United States in 1968. He presented meditation and philosophy not as exotic disciplines but as practical ways to negotiate personal experience. Both sitting for meditation and cultivating awareness at work are presented as opportunities for improving a disciplined lifestyle. The goal of these practices is to develop a spontaneous awareness of reality and directly experience an all-knowing understanding. Rinpoche teaches students to absorb themselves in the process until they, in a sense, become the meditation experience. Proper meditation, he suggests, requires concentration, but no sense of striving or strain. When a state of meditative awareness is attained, experiences occur that are pure, not affected or distorted by prior expectations, disappointments, or disillusionments.

Meditation practice in Roman Catholicism is often described under the rubric of prayer: mental prayer, prayerful time, or centering prayer. A revival of the sense of meditation is occurring within Catholicism, and it is particularly prominent in the growing movement of spirituality among women. Women Church, a group founded for women who believe they are called to ordination, draws women who are interested in many practices, including both individual and communal meditation. In Catholicism discursive techniques such as *lectio divina* (from Latin, "divine reading") and thinking about religious material or devotional reading are common. Focusing one's attention on mental, visual, or auditory objects such as an image of God is another meditative technique, the goal of which is to transform the mind into the object. Deriving from the practice of the Desert Fathers, nondiscursive centering prayer techniques involve repetition of a sacred word in order to develop a loving attitude toward God that leads toward silence. After centering oneself using this method, one might say a prayer. Nonimaging techniques that purify the mind are similar to Theravādan Buddhist vipassana practice. Among the variety of practices, the ultimate goal is to attain union with God, and lesser benefits include the reduction of emotional turmoil and an increased ability to concentrate.

See also BUDDHISM; CENTERING PRAYER; ENLIGHTENMENT; HINDUISM; JUDAISM; PRAYER; TIBETAN BUDDHISM; TORAH; TRANSCENDENTAL MEDITATION; YOGA; ZEN.

BIBLIOGRAPHY

Brooks, Douglas Renfrew, Swami Durgananda, Paul. E. Muller-Ortega, William K. Mahony, Constantina Rhodes Bailly, and S. P. Sabharathnam. *Meditation Revolution: A History and Theology of the Siddha Yoga Lineage.* 1997.

Davis, Avram, ed. *Meditation from the Heart of Judaism.* 1997.

Meadow, Mary Jo, and Kevin Culligan. "Congruent Spiritual Paths: Christian Carmelite and Theravadan Buddhist Vipassana." *Journal of Transpersonal Psychology* 19, no. 2 (1987): 181–195.

Muktananda, Swami. *Meditate.* 1991.

Tulku, Tarthang. *Gesture of Balance: A Guide to Awareness, Self-healing, and Meditation.* 1977.

Underwood, Frederic B., and Winston L. King. "Meditation" In *The Encyclopedia of Religion,* edited by Mircea Eliade. Vol. 9. 1987, pp. 324–336.

Waldman, Anne, ed. *The Beat Book: Poems and Fiction of the Beat Generation.* 1996.

Watts, Alan. *The Way of Liberation: Essays and Lectures on the Transformation of the Self.* 1983.

www.chochmat.org

www.metivta.org

www.nyingma.org

www.siddhayoga.org

www.sufism.org

Marcy Braverman

Megachurch

The term "megachurch" describes very large congregations (memberships from 2,000 to 15,000 are common) but is best applied to a set of characteristics beyond mere size. At latest count there are more than 400 such congregations in the United States, claiming 1.7 million members.

In general, the typical megachurch is a large or growing congregation that stresses outreach and growth through techniques that seem to have been borrowed from the secular world: sophisticated marketing; a "consumer" orientation toward members; a stress on the services to be provided to members; an emphasis on the attractiveness—even the "entertainment" values—of services and public events; and a downplaying of some of the more familiar characteristics of conventional congregations.

Though a number of megachurches are congregations of mainline denominations, most are evangelical. Theologically, most (but not all) are neo-evangelical: on the conservative side of the Protestant spectrum, they eschew the harsh rhetoric of fundamentalism, preferring a softer, evangelical approach that strives to be inviting and inclusive. They emerge from the same neo-evangelical tendencies that produced televangelism and Christian marketing and material culture. A minority are more charismatic in orientation.

Most structure their formal periods of worship and other rites to introduce people through various stages or types of involvement. The best-known of the megachurches, Willow Creek Community Church in suburban Chicago, begins with "seeker services" that are designed to avoid aspects of "traditional church" that prospective members consider a "turnoff." There is no offering, no sermon, no altar call. Those elements are saved for the "believers' services," which take place at another time.

Demographically, the megachurch is a phenomenon of the "baby boom" and "baby bust" generations and a response to the "seeker" or "quester" religiosity typical of those generations. Located in suburban and exurban settings in the Sun Belt and the Northeast, they are integrated into the service marketplace, satisfying market needs through provision of such things as convenient parking, good child care, and upscale food and entertainment services. The religious tastes and desires in these contexts tend toward modes of religious practice that are not typical of traditional Protestantism: rites of passage, a visual approach to aesthetics, drama, music, and direct emotional encounters of various kinds.

Two primary characteristics typify most megachurches: (1) market research (formal and informal), through which prospective members in a given catchment area are probed for insight into their needs and interests; and (2) small groups, through which those needs and interests are addressed. The range of such

The third worship service of the day is held at Calvary Chapel in Albuquerque, New Mexico, on Sunday morning, February 21, 1999. This megachurch has an active membership of about twelve thousand, more than could be accommodated in a single worship service. (Credit: AP/Wide World Photos.)

groups at a typical megachurch is very wide, including the whole range of contemporary therapeutic culture. These groups are the glue that holds the megachurch together. The forces of the cultural divide that have so polarized major denominations (issues such as abortion and homosexuality) are finessed in the megachurch through a careful parsing and focusing of interests into identity groups and through a stress in rites and rituals on the self as opposed to larger social issues.

The most frequent criticisms focus on the megachurch's seeming orientation to superficialities as against theological authority or purity. Leaders in the movement are also vocal in distancing themselves from denominationalism and ecumenism, though several loose confederations of megachurches have formed.

See also BELONGING, RELIGIOUS; CHURCH; EVANGELICAL CHRISTIANITY; NEW RELIGIOUS MOVEMENTS; POPULAR RELIGION; PRACTICE; PSYCHOLOGY OF RELIGION; SOCIOLOGY OF RELIGION; TELEVANGELISM.

BIBLIOGRAPHY

"Big on Religion." *USA Today,* (April 1, 1999): 1D.

Brasher, Brenda. *Godly Women: Fundamentalism and Female Power.* 1999.

Diamond, Sara. *Not By Politics Alone: The Enduring Influence of the Christian Right.* 1999.

Gale, Elaine. "Religion: The Young Leaders of the 1960s Christian Movement Have Grown Up—As Have Their Churches." *Los Angeles Times,* (April 23, 1999): A1.

Roof, Wade Clark. *A Generation of Seekers.* 1993.

Truehart, Charles. "The Next Church," *Atlantic Monthly,* August, 1996, pp. 37–58.

Stewart M. Hoover

Meher Baba

(1894–1969), Indian spiritual master.

Meher Baba claimed to be the most recent "avatar," or God-man. He said that Zoroaster, Rama, Krishna, Buddha, Christ, and Muhammad were all "avatars," incarnations of God whose appearances on earth each signify the beginning of a new spiritual era. Central to Meher Baba's teachings is the theme of God as the underlying unity behind the apparent diversity of the world, expressed in his saying "We are all One." He described a reincarnation/karma pattern of personal development in which individuals progress spiritually through many lifetimes until they finally achieve full consciousness that their souls and God are one. He deemphasized the importance of formal religious principles, precepts, or techniques in achieving such transcendence and emphasized instead the development of individualized inner relationships between each of his followers and himself through love and the heart wherein he functions as an inner guide. He said, "The voice of intuition is my voice."

Baba began keeping silence in 1926 and remained silent until his death. He communicated first through an alphabet board and later through his own sign language. Baba said, "Things that are real are given and received in silence." In India, Baba conducted mass spiritual programs called *darshans,* at which large crowds of people would gather to bow down to him and receive his *prasad* (small gifts of candy or other foods representing spiritual sustenance given to the aspirant from the master). Beginning in the 1930s, a small number of "Baba-lovers" (followers of Meher Baba) began developing in Europe and the United States. After that point Baba made many trips to the West and kept in contact with his Western followers. In 1952 his followers established the "Meher Spiritual Center," a spiritual retreat center in Myrtle Beach, South Carolina, where during the 1950s Baba conducted several "Sahavas" programs (spiritual retreats at which the master lives intimately with his devotees).

Previous to the "hippie" movement, Baba-lovers in the West were middle-aged and relatively few. However, during and following the widespread hippie countercultural trend in the 1960s, Meher Baba's following in the West grew substantially. The initial interest of Western youth in Eastern mysticism was closely tied to the "utopiate" psychedelic scene associated with the hippie movement. It was in fact Richard Alpert (who popularized the use of LSD to achieve a "raised consciousness") and other counterculture figures, such as rock star Peter Townsend (of the rock band The Who), who initially helped spread Baba's message in the West.

Baba, however, did not condone the use of psychedelic or other drugs, saying that they are "harmful physically, mentally, and spiritually." He also said, "If God can be found through the medium of any drug, God is not worthy of being God." So most of those who wished to follow Baba closely found themselves halting drug use and searching for the true "raised consciousness" associated with realizing the oneness of everyone and everything through love and selfless service.

Thus, although Baba set no precepts in the sense of moral absolutes, he generally discouraged a hedonistic lifestyle, encouraging monogamy, freedom from drugs, and attention to normal family and vocational responsibilities. Baba said, "Do not shirk your responsibilities. Attend faithfully to your worldly duties, but keep always in the back of your mind that all this is Baba's." Consequently, today most Baba-lovers lead outwardly conventional lives, and new Baba-lovers do not necessarily have countercultural or bohemian backgrounds.

Long-term observers estimate that there are five thousand to ten thousand devoted Baba-lovers in the United States, although the exact number is hard to pin down with certainty because the relationship between the aspirant and Baba is very individualized. Baba-lovers don't necessarily participate in a Baba group, and furthermore, membership in such groups is very loosely defined. There are no formal criteria of membership in terms of belief or financial obligation, and anyone who expresses "a sincere personal interest in Meher Baba," however he or she defines such interest, may participate fully in the group.

Groups typically meet about once a week and are democratically organized. Meetings are centered around activities designed to facilitate a sense of inner contact with Baba. These include movies, videos, and music focused on him, listening to people who met Baba reminisce about their times with him, and discussions of Baba's discourses and of personal experiences regarding him as well as how best to follow him, remember him, and love him. Pilgrimages to residential Baba centers in both the United States and India, as well as organized retreats celebrating key holidays commemorating important events in Baba's life, play an important role in the lives of most Baba-lovers.

The Baba movement that emerged out of the counterculture of the sixties seems to have become well rooted, and it shows signs of becoming a long-lasting institution. The movement engages in very little explicit proselytization, and most people get involved through low-key personal contact with members. Nevertheless, once individuals "come to Baba," they tend to remain followers for the long term. Their children tend to become Baba-lovers themselves, and there exists a definite Baba youth movement, centralized in the "Youth Sahavas," yearly retreats for teenage second-generation Baba-lovers. (The web site youthsahavas .com serves as a year-'round communication center for teenage Baba-lovers.) A publishing house, Sheriar Press in Myrtle Beach, South Carolina, is devoted to printing and distributing books by or about Meher Baba.

See also BELONGING, RELIGIOUS; DRUGS; HINDUISM; MYSTICISM; REINCARNATION; RELIGIOUS COMMUNITIES; TRANSCENDENCE.

BIBLIOGRAPHY

Anthony, Dick, and Thomas Robbins. "The Meher Baba Movement: Its Effect on Post-Adolescent Social Alienation." In *Religious Movements in Contemporary America,* edited by Irving I. Zaretsky and Mark P. Leone. 1974.

Baba, Meher. *Discourses.* 1995.

Hopkinson, Tom, and Dorothy Hopkinson. *Much Silence: Meher Baba, His Life and Work.* 1975.

Steven Barrie-Anthony

Meidung.

See Shunning.

Mennonites

Mennonites in America, currently numbering 416,000, derive from three main streams of European immigration, augmented by significant numbers of African Americans, Native Americans, Hispanics, and other Americans who have become Mennonites in response to mission endeavors. Vietnamese and Cambodian immigrants have also formed Mennonite congregations in recent decades. The largest concentrations of Mennonites are in eastern Pennsylvania, central Kansas, southern Manitoba, Ontario, Ohio, northern Indiana, and the Mennonite Brethren in California.

Mennonites, from their beginnings in about 1525, stressed that church membership must be a voluntary choice. This is symbolized by baptism of believers (i.e., infants may not be baptized). Baptism may be by sprinkling, pouring, or immersion, depending on the group. Congregational singing, often a cappella (without instrumental accompaniment), has a high priority in group worship.

From their beginnings Mennonites stood apart from the state, largely eschewing political office and extolling humility and service rather than power and empire. This set them apart from dominant religious and cultural emphases. Changes since 1960, both among Mennonites and in the larger culture, have brought segments of each much closer together.

The first stream of Mennonite immigration to America, in about 1700, was from Switzerland and southern Germany. The second wave, from 1830 to 1870, was made up of Amish Mennonites from Alsace and the Palatinate. The third major immigration was of Mennonites of Dutch origin who, fleeing persecution, had immigrated to Prussia and then to Russia, coming to America in 1870. The fourth group was the Mennonite Brethren Church, formed in Russia in response to German Pietism and immigrated after 1920. Already in Russia they had subdivided into several groups, some of which have recently dropped the name "Mennonite," ostensibly in the interest of advancing evangelism. The Mennonite Brethren Church is the third largest Mennonite group in the United States today.

The Amish Mennonites and Mennonites of Swiss origin amalgamated in about 1900 to form the Mennonite Church. The Mennonites from Russia, several congregations from northern Germany, a more liberal group from eastern Pennsylvania, and some Illinois Mennonites formed the General Conference of the Mennonites of North America. These two bodies are now merging. This process has been complicated by contrasting church polities, with the General Conference Mennonites emphasizing autonomy for both

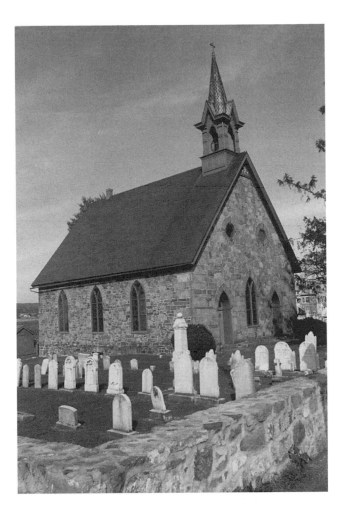

A stone Mennonite church and graveyard in Lancaster, Pennsylvania. (Credit: CORBIS/Lee Snider.)

individuals and congregations, while the Mennonite Church is more group-minded in relation to congregations. The two groups share a common confession of faith. Top denominational leadership for both groups is by election.

Mennonites, like most religious groups immigrating to America, have fragmented into numerous subgroups, reflecting their time of immigration and acculturation. A major schism involved the formation of the Old Order Mennonites following 1872. They rejected institutionalization, including Sunday schools, and continue to be locally organized. Some still drive horses and buggies. Other subgroups include Conservative Mennonites, Fellowship Churches, and others too numerous to mention. Issues for these Mennonites have included the rejection of acculturation as well as increasing institutionalization and bureaucratization in the main bodies and sometimes retention of traditional symbols such as the prayer veiling for women together with variations in biblical interpretation. Frequently these subgroups have objected to the prominence given to war resistance and witness to the state by the main groups as well as to women in ministry and to liberal theology.

Mennonites officially reject participation in warfare, and since the 1960s Mennonites have increasingly emphasized peacemaking, relief, and service. The Mennonite Central Committee (MCC), a relief and service agency that is supported by all branches of the Mennonite Church, was begun in response to famine in Russia, particularly in the Mennonite communities, in 1920. Its volunteers currently serve in programs worldwide. Two of its projects, which have elicited widespread support across lay groups, are relief sales, designed to raise funds to support MCC programs, and the Mennonite Disaster Service, which coordinates volunteer efforts in response to national disasters.

See also BAPTISM; MUSIC; PRACTICE; RELIGIOUS COMMUNITIES; RELIGIOUS PERSECUTION.

BIBLIOGRAPHY

Hostetler, Beulah S. *American Mennonites and Protestant Movements: A Community Paradigm.* 1987.
Mennonite Encyclopedia. 5 vols. 1956–1959, 1990.
The Mennonite Experience in America, 4 vols. 1985–1998.
Mennonite Yearbook. Published biannually.

Beulah S. Hostetler

Menorah

Menorah ("lamp") refers in the Hebrew Bible to the seven-branched candelabrum of the wilderness tabernacle and Jerusalem Temples. As described in Exodus 25:31–40 and 37:17–24, the menorah was hammered from a large piece of pure gold by the craftsman Bezalel. Based on a tripod, three branches curved from both sides of a vertical shaft; these, with the central stem, were decorated with cups carved in the shape of open almond blossoms, the uppermost holding the lamps. According to 1 Kings 7:39 (and 2 Chronicles 4:7), ten pure gold menorot adorned Solomon's Temple (tenth century B.C.E. to sixth century B.C.E.), five on the south side of the main hall and five on the north. The Second Temple (fifth century B.C.E. to first century C.E.), following the priestly directions for the wilderness tabernacle in Exodus, had one golden menorah. According to the first century C.E. Jewish writer Flavius Josephus (*Antiquities* 3.9.199), three of its lamps burned all day; the rest were lit in the evening. The Babylonian Talmud relates that the westernmost lamp, closest to the Holy

An electrically illuminated menorah next to a stained-glass window at Temple Israel synagogue in New York City. (Credit: CORBIS/Lyn Hughes.)

of Holies, was never extinguished. The Temple menorah was removed in 169 B.C.E. by Antiochus Epiphanes IV of Syria during his desecration of the Temple. Judah Maccabee supplied a new menorah when the Temple was cleansed (1 Maccabees 4:49–50; 2 Maccabees 10:3). Josephus recounts that when the Second Temple was destroyed in 70 C.E., the menorah was carried away by the Romans (War 7.5.148–49). The Temple menorah appears to be depicted on the Arch of Titus in Rome, although there is some controversy over this rendition's accuracy, particularly regarding the double octagonal pedestal, since according to all Jewish sources and considerable archaeological evidence, the menorah stood on three legs. Since 70 C.E., the seven-branched Temple menorah has been an enduring Jewish religious and national symbol, frequently appearing in synagogue, domestic, and funerary art; it also appears on the emblem of the State of Israel.

In the United States, the menorah is most popularly associated with the holiday of Chanukah, which commemorates Judah Maccabee's rededication of the Temple. This menorah, more precisely designated a *chanukiah,* has nine lights, one for each of the eight nights of Chanukah and the ninth for the *shamash* (Hebrew for "servant"), which is used to kindle the others. Each night an additional light is added while blessing are recited. A Chanukah menorah has no required shape—originally nine individual oil lamps were used; Judaica collections preserve chanukiot made of clay, porcelain, tin, silver, and brass embellished with historic and decorative symbols and images of all kinds. A talmudic injunction against making chanukiot resemble the Temple menorah was ignored by medieval times, and eight- and nine-branched chanukiot became common. Contemporary artists create chanukiot in all shapes, sizes, and materials; most utilize candles. In recent times some have suggested instituting a menorah for Yom Hashoah, the commemoration of the Nazi murder of almost six million Jews; however, the kindling of six separate yellow memorial candles remains more usual.

See also JEWISH IDENTITY; JEWISH OBSERVANCE; JUDAISM; MATERIAL RELIGION; RITUAL; SYNAGOGUE; TEMPLE.

BIBLIOGRAPHY

Baskin, Judith R. "Menorah." In *The Oxford Companion to the Bible,* edited by Bruce M. Metzger and Michael D. Coogan. 1993.

Dosick, Wayne. *Living Judaism: The Complete Guide to Jewish Belief, Tradition and Practice.* 1995.

Ross, Lesli Koppelman. *Celebrate! The Complete Jewish Holidays Handbook.* 1994.

Judith R. Baskin

Merton, Thomas

(1915–1968), Trappist monk, activist, writer.

There is perhaps no American Catholic who has had more written about him and his spirituality in the past thirty years than Thomas Merton. Superficially this publishing phenomenon might seem strange for a man who spent twenty-seven years in the enclosed Cistercian (Trappist) Abbey of Gethsemani in rural Kentucky. And yet the announcement of his death in 1968, while attending a monastic conference in Bangkok, was reported widely by the press.

During his early years Merton seemed unlikely to choose a life of prayer, work, worship, silence, and solitude in one of the strictest Catholic monastic orders. He was born on December 10, 1915, in France to an American mother, Ruth, and a father, Owen, who was from New Zealand. His parents were not particularly devout and he grew up with little formalized religious education. Merton also experienced great upheavals in his early life. His mother died when he was six. His father then took him from the stable home of his grandparents to live in Bermuda, France, and England, where he spent much of his time in boarding schools. His father died when he was fifteen. In 1933 he entered Cambridge University. His Cambridge education ended because of drinking, the loss of his scholarship, and an accusation that he had fathered a child. He then entered Columbia University, where he received undergraduate and master's degrees in English. He was baptized into the Catholic Church in 1938 and in 1941 entered the monastery.

The public first knew of Merton's writings in 1948, when he published his autobiography *The Seven Storey Mountain.* He continued to write about prayer, spirituality, and monastic life. Then, in the late 1950s, he began to correspond and meet with a diverse number of persons—poets and writers, persons from other religious traditions, including those of Asia, advocates of peace and justice, and ordinary people. These interactions were grounded by a deepening life of prayer. Gradually he began to respond to others, not only with acts of mercy and compassion, which he had practiced previously, but also in written protest against conditions that marginalized and depersonalized human beings. This position was reflected in his writings, in which he advocated the need to feed the hungry, care for the sick, visit prisoners, and welcome strangers. In addition, he stressed the necessity for personal transformation in preparation for changing those institutional structures of the culture, church, and monastery that contributed to injustice, violence,

Trappist monk Thomas Merton sits in the shade on a sunny day in an undated portrait. (Credit: AP/ Wide World Photos.)

and the inability of persons to become responsible members of the human community.

His stances against nuclear weapons, racism, war and violence, consumerism, and materialism were not based on social, political, or economic principles. They were founded in his loving, prayer-filled relationship with God, which overflowed in a love for other persons and a protest against all that diminished their human dignity, freedom, and life itself. Although the specific concerns of our day may be different, Merton's transformative prophetic stance of prayer, protest, and action continues to challenge new generations of his readers who also face the realities of injustice, violence, and the marginalization of human persons.

See also CENTERING PRAYER; CONVERSION; MEDITATION; MYSTICISM; PRAYER; RELIGIOUS COMMUNITIES; SPIRITUALITY.

BIBLIOGRAPHY

Cunningham, Lawrence, ed. *Thomas Merton: Spiritual Master: The Essential Writings.* 1992.

Mott, Michael. *The Seven Mountains of Thomas Merton.* 1984.

Shannon, William, ed. *Passion for Peace: The Social Essays of Thomas Merton.* 1995.

Dorothy J. LeBeau

Mestizo Worship

Mestizo worship as the life-giving blend of ritual traditions of various religions is a concept that has been introduced by Hispanic theologians of the United States to describe, study, and develop the reality of worship among the mestizo peoples of Latin America, a form of worship that has been evolving since the encounter of 1492. It recognizes and celebrates that modern-day Latin American forms of worship are a powerful synthesis of religious elements inherited from a number of sources, especially the religious traditions of the Iberians of the 1500s, various forms of Mesoamerican religions, and elements of African religions.

While traditionally this synthesis has been condemned by Eurocentered Western church leaders as syncretism and even as a form of underdeveloped Christianity, U.S. Hispanic theologians have demonstrated that the synthesis represents the normal evolution of Christianity as it takes root historically in various parts of the world, an evolution called by the Catholic Church "the way of the Incarnation." Furthermore, it is precisely these forms of mestizo worship that give Latin American Christianity its own proper identity, as distinct from Eastern and Western Christianity. Mestizo worship is the very soul, outward manifestation, and chief characteristic of Latin American Christianity.

As we look into the origins of the various contemporary forms of worship, it is easy to recognize that all worship is mestizo! The feasts of the Jewish people are a synthesis of Jewish beliefs with previous religious traditions—that is, those of the peoples they encountered. The Roman liturgy of Western Catholicism is a synthesis that emerged out of synagogue practices coupled with the cultural and religious traditions of Rome and gradually enhanced with elements such as Gothic vestments for the Mass and various forms of church music, architecture, music, art, and rituals. Established religions strive for purity and fear all forms of syncretism, while in effect all forms of worship are amalgamations of previous forms of religious celebration.

In order to address explicitly the subject of mestizo worship, it is necessary to first look deeper into the meaning of "mestizo," for it is not a common or popular word in the English or German language, though it is quite common in Spanish, French, Italian, and Portuguese. Because race mixture was prohibited in the United States, there is no ordinary word for the reality. Derogatory expressions such as "half-breed" or even "bastard" have been commonly used to refer to mestizos.

Mestizos are born out of the mixture of human groups of different genetic characteristics—those determining the color and shape of the eyes, hair and skin pigmentation, and the makeup of the bone structure. As the number of mestizos increases with the passage of time, a mestizo culture begins to emerge that relates to the parent cultures very much like the child relates to the parent. There is no difficulty with the biological and cultural mixing of peoples, but it is a completely different story when it comes to the psychological, social, political, and religious mixing of persons and of peoples. Such a development poses a threat to the established and accepted ways of the parent groups, especially their religious expressions. The biological, cultural, and religious disturbance of the group's life, especially through intermarriage, is so feared that in many places it is still prohibited, and in most others it is deeply frowned upon. Yet it is happening more widely and rapidly than ever before.

The mestizo is born out of various genetic pools, histories, cultures, and religions. In the very consciousness of the mestizo begins a new history, a new culture, and new forms of religious expression. This beginning entails the most devastating suffering for the mestizo, especially in the early stages of *mestizaje*, while at the same time appearing most threatening to both parent groups.

Because the mestizo will be truly a new being, the deepest suffering and insecurity come from what we might call an "unfinished" identity or, better yet, an undefined one, productive of a deep sense of impurity and margination. It produces a profound sense of not belonging fully to either of the parent groups and, most of all, of not being correct by either's standards and norms. From earliest childhood mestizos will struggle with the question, "Who am I?" for they are not regarded as "fully human" by either of the parent groups.

In this "between" or unfinished existence lies the greatest potential for creativity: to pool the cultural and religious genes and chromosomes of both cultures so as to create a new one! The greatest breakthrough comes in moving from the shame of "nonbeing" to the pride and joy of "new-being." In Latin America, this breakthrough, beginning in 1531, came through the mestiza face and heart of Our Lady of Guadalupe and Juan Diego, who was able to combine the Iberian Catholic religion with the Mesoamerican religions in such a way that both were purified and enhanced but no longer opposed!

The difficult passage from nonbeing to new-being is brought about in many ways but is especially affirmed, manifested, and celebrated through ritual. Mestizo worship is resistance and affirmation—resistance to the various cultural forms of Western religions that try to "annihilate" its adherents through conversion to their Western forms of religious expression, which they see as normative for all cultures; affirmation because it is the spontaneous and festive celebration of who the mestizo people are. As such, it is the legitimization of what others considered false but its adherents regard as true and authentic.

Some of the major examples of mestizo worship are the celebration of the Day of the Dead on November 2, the feast of Our Lady of Guadalupe on December 12, Ash Wednesday at the beginning of Lent, Good Friday, and the patronal feast of each Latin American country and even of each municipality, such as the celebrations of the Indian pueblos in New Mexico.

Mestizo worship provides a rootedness and a continuity with the past while enabling people to enter creatively and boldly into uncharted situations of the present and the future. It is a deeply mystical experience that allows the participants—and there are no passive observers or excluded persons—to enter the continuum of time and experience the spiritual energy of the entire people in union with their God. In the moments of celebration, everyone experiences the collective oneness of the group.

See also BRICOLAGE; DAY OF THE DEAD; LATINO TRADITIONS; LENT; LIVED RELIGION; LITURGY AND WORSHIP; PATRON SAINTS AND PATRON-SAINT FEASTS; SYNCRETISM; VIRGIN OF GUADALUPE.

BIBLIOGRAPHY

Elizondo, Virgilio. *Christianity and Culture.* 1999.

Elizondo, Virgilio. *The Future Is Mestizo: Life Where Cultures Meet.* 1998.

Elizondo, Virgilio. *Galilean Journey: The Mexican American Promise.* 1983.

Elizondo, Virgilio. *Guadalupe: Mother of the New Creation.* 1997.

Elizondo, Virgilio, and Timothy Matovina. *Mestizo Worship.* 1998.

Elizondo, Virgilio, and Timothy Matovina. *San Fernando Cathedral: Soul of the City.* 1999.

Espin, Orlando. *Faith of a People: Hispanic Popular Catholicism.* 1997.

Rivera, Alejandro Garcia. *The Community of the Beautiful.* 1999.

Virgilio Elizondo

Methodism

There are more than twenty Methodist denominations in America that trace their origins directly to the movement begun in England by the Anglican priest John Wesley (1703–1791). Wesley was the dominant figure in establishing the beliefs, structure, and practices of American Methodism.

Methodism was organized in America in the 1760s, when immigrant laypeople from Ireland and England began to preach an evangelical message and formed Methodist societies and classes similar to those established by Wesley. At Christmas 1784 in Baltimore, Maryland, American Methodists, with Wesley's blessing, founded the Methodist Episcopal Church. It was the parent church of American Methodism. Several denominations trace their ancestry to the Methodist Episcopal Church, including the African Methodist Episcopal Church (1816), the African Methodist Episcopal Zion Church (1821), the Methodist Protestant Church (1830), the Wesleyan Church (1843), the Methodist Episcopal Church, South (1845), the Free Methodist Church (1860), and the Christian Methodist Episcopal Church (1870). Three of these denominations, the African Methodist Episcopal Church, the African Methodist Episcopal Zion Church, and the Christian Methodist Episcopal Church, have almost entirely African-American memberships. In 1939 the Methodist Episcopal Church, the Methodist Protestant Church, and the Methodist Episcopal Church, South, reunited to form the Methodist Church. In 1968 the Methodist Church united with the Evangel-

The Rev. Cecil Williams leads a service at the Glide Memorial Methodist Church in San Francisco, on Sunday, May 24, 1998. Williams's church is known nationally as a sanctuary for the poor.   (Credit: AP/ Wide World Photos.)

ical United Brethren Church, a denomination with similar polity and theology, to become the United Methodist Church, at the time the largest Protestant denomination in the United States. The churches that are identified with the Holiness and Pentecostal movements in America also share the theological heritage of the Wesleyan/Methodist churches.

United Methodists share a similar connectional polity with the three African-American denominations. Each is divided into geographical annual conferences presided over by elected bishops who serve as their spiritual and administrative leaders. Bishops also perform the important task of appointing the clergy to their ministerial work. Bishops are assisted by episcopally appointed superintendents who advise the bishop and act as liaison between the annual conference and the local churches within its bounds. Each of these denominations has a general conference, with elected representatives from the annual conferences; the general conference meets every four years to set the official policies of the denomination. The structure and policies are set forth in the denom-

ination's Book of Discipline as revised by the general conference.

From its earliest days American Methodism has considered three theological documents of major importance, although it has not always paid much attention to them. They include John Wesley's *Explanatory Notes Upon the New Testament* (first published in 1755), Wesley's *Sermons on Several Occasions* (a series of doctrinal sermons published in 1787–1788), and *Articles of Religion,* sent to America by Wesley in 1784. United Methodism has added *The Confession of Faith of the Evangelical United Brethren Church* (1963) to its collection of documents called *Doctrinal Standards.* In 1972 United Methodism also adopted a document titled *Our Theological Task* (revised in 1988), which sets forth a theological methodology using Scripture, tradition, reason, and experience as bases for understanding and practicing the Christian faith.

Worship is considered important in each of the Methodist denominations, especially the Sunday morning gathering of the congregation. Usually 30 to 40 percent of the membership attends Sunday morning worship. Although worship practices vary considerably among the churches in a denomination, the liturgies employed among Methodists tend to be less formal. The order for worship includes hymns, prayers, perhaps music by a choir, Scripture reading, offering, and a sermon, which is the centerpiece of worship. Two sacraments are observed: the baptism of infants and adults, and the Lord's Supper or Holy Communion.

Theological diversity characterizes the Methodist family, especially United Methodism, where theological controversy has been quite pronounced since the 1960s. One of the parties in this theological dispute has adopted a more liberal theological stance. It is represented by the Methodist Federation for Social Action, founded in 1907. The federation emphasizes a social action agenda, including the elimination of racism, boycotts of corporations that threaten the environment or exploit workers, and acceptance of the homosexual lifestyle. Their views are explicated in their newsletter *Social Questions Bulletin.* Another party, represented by the Good News Movement, founded in 1966, believes that the denomination has drifted too much toward liberalism and theological pluralism. They hold that the church must return to its evangelical roots, reaffirm the primacy and authority of the Bible, and continue its ban on ordaining homosexuals. In 1984 Good News launched its own Mission Society to correct what it judged to be the liberal agenda of the denomination's General Board of Global Ministries. Furthermore, the Good News leaders were instrumental in three theological documents that state Good News views: the Houston Declaration (1984), the DuPage Declaration (1990), and the Louisville Declaration (1990). Much of the disagreement between these two parties concerns the issue of whether the denomination should make evangelism or social action its priority. A large number of United Methodists stand between these two positions, believing that both should be emphases of the denomination.

Another recent theological development has been the rediscovery of the theology of John Wesley. The theologian/ecumenist Albert C. Outler (1908–1989) was the key figure calling attention to the substance and relevance of Wesley's thought for the second half of the twentieth century. Outler's leadership, the publication of the definitive new edition of Wesley's writings, *The Works of John Wesley* (thirty-five volumes when complete), and many books and articles on Wesley's theology have appeared regularly and continue to do so.

Most of the Methodist denominations are members of the World Methodist Council, founded in 1881, with offices at Lake Junaluska, North Carolina. The council sponsors a World Methodist Conference every five years, usually outside the United States. The largest Methodist bodies are also active members of other ecumenical organizations, including the National Council of Churches and the World Council of Churches. The African Methodist Episcopal, African Methodist Episcopal Zion, Christian Methodist Episcopal, and United Methodist denominations are engaged in a Pan-Methodist Movement, which seeks closer relationships and cooperation in common areas of ministry.

A number of critical tensions and controversies have been evident among Methodists in recent years. One of the more serious problems has been declining membership in the largest Methodist denomination.

United Methodism's falling membership, not unlike the drop in some other American Protestant bodies, has caused alarm. In response, some call for new programs of evangelism, the restructure and streamlining of the denomination to make its ministry more effective, and new programs and forms of worship to attract and involve children, youth, and young adults. Declining membership also puts stress on the sources of funding on which the churches rely to perpetuate their ministries.

The United Methodist Church has been at the forefront of a number of internal theological and structural conflicts. Although the racially divided structure created by the Methodist Church in 1939 was formally eliminated in 1968 in the union with the Evangelical United Brethren, much was still required to develop a racially inclusive church. Therefore it established the Commission on Religion and Race in 1968 to ensure racial inclusiveness. Since 1968 racial/ethnic caucuses have also been important forces in drafting legislation and ensuring representation in United Methodist denominational life.

The status and role of women has been another decisive area in Methodism. Laywomen have always been prominent in the life of Methodist congregations, but their role in leadership has been limited until recently. Beginning with the 1960s, women's role in the larger Methodist denominations has expanded. Women are now eligible for ordination in them, and growing numbers of women are voting members of the boards and committees of local churches, annual conferences, the general conference, and denominational agencies. In 1980 the United Methodist Church elected its first female bishop, Marjorie Matthews (1916–1986), and a significant number of women are currently pastors, superintendents, and bishops in the denomination. One noteworthy controversy related to the place of women in the church is the use of inclusive language, especially for God, in which references to God as masculine are eliminated in favor of gender-neutral language.

Other social issues generate controversy at the denominations' policymaking level, such as abortion, homosexuality, war and peace, economic and business matters, criminal justice including the death penalty, and international affairs.

Denomination	1965	1975	1985	1998
United Methodist	10,300,000	10,031,000	9,230,000	8,549,000
African Methodist Episcopal	1,166,000	1,166,000	2,210,000	2,100,000
African Methodist Episcopal Zion	770,000	1,025,000	1,134,00	1,036,000
Christian Methodist Episcopal	444,000	467,000	719,000	719,000

Source: *Yearbook of American and Canadian Churches.*

See also DENOMINATION; EVANGELICAL CHRISTIANITY; HUMAN RIGHTS; MAINLINE PROTESTANTISM; PUBLISHING, RELIGIOUS.

BIBLIOGRAPHY

Campbell, James T. *Songs of Zion: The African Methodist Episcopal Church in the United States and South Africa.* 1995.

Frank, Thomas Edward. *Polity, Practice, and the Mission of the United Methodist Church.* 1997.

Heitzenrater, Richard P. *Wesley and the People Called Methodists.* 1995.

Kirby, James E., Russell E. Richey, and Kenneth E. Rowe. *The Methodist.* 1998.

McEllhenney, John G. *United Methodism in America: A Compact History.* 1992.

Charles Yrigoyen, Jr.

Metropolitan Community Church

The Metropolitan Community Church (MCC), known denominationally as the Universal Fellowship of Metropolitan Community Churches (UFMCC), primarily serves lesbian, gay, bisexual, and transgender (LGBT) Christians. The organization was founded in Los Angeles in October 1968 by former Church of God minister Troy Perry. From an initial group of thirteen, the church grew to add four new congregations across the United States within two years. The denomination held its inaugural General Conference in 1970, and in 1972 it began to make contact with LGBT Christian congregations in other countries. The UFMCC currently claims approximately three hundred churches and more than thirty-two thousand members in eighteen countries.

Although Perry's background was solidly Pentecostal, from the beginning his church has attracted people from a wide variety of Christian backgrounds. Early participants had been raised in a number of different churches, ranging from fundamentalist and Pentecostal to Seventh-Day Adventist, mainline Protestant, and Roman Catholic. Denominational beliefs and practices reflect this mixture; although UFMCC bylaws outline a standard Protestant doctrine and most churches follow similar worship procedures, individual congregations vary widely from conservative to metaphysical to charismatic.

The UFMCC sees itself primarily as an organization that offers religious acceptance to LGBT Christians. However, issues of concern for the denomination as a whole reflect the concerns of both the LGBT and American Protestant communities. Although the UFMCC has been campaigning for admission to the National Council of Churches (NCC) since the early 1980s, it has been denied to date because of the objection of some NCC members to its positive stance on homosexuality and transgender identities.

See also BELONGING, RELIGIOUS; CHURCH; FREEDOM OF RELIGION; LESBIAN AND GAY RIGHTS MOVEMENT; NEW RELIGIOUS MOVEMENTS; RELIGIOUS COMMUNITIES.

BIBLIOGRAPHY

Lukenbill, W. Bernard. "Observations on the Corporate Culture of a Gay and Lesbian Congregation." *Journal for the Scientific Study of Religion* 37 (1998):440–452.

Perry, Troy, as told to Charles L. Lucas. *The Lord Is My Shepherd and He Knows I'm Gay.* 1972.

Perry, Troy, with Thomas L. P. Swicegood. *Don't Be Afraid Anymore.* 1990.

Warner, R. Stephen. "The Metropolitan Community Church and the Gay Agenda: The Power of Pentecostalism and Essentialism." In *Sex, Lies, and Sanctity: Religion and Deviance in Contemporary North America,* edited by Mary Jo Neitz and Marion S. Goldman. 1995.

Wilson, Nancy. *Our Tribe: Queer Folks, God, Jesus, and the Bible.* 1995.

Melissa M. Wilcox

Midrash

Midrash, from the Hebrew root *DRSh* (to search out), refers to the characteristic hermeneutics of the rabbis in the classical age and beyond. The term was first used by Ben Sira (second century B.C.E.) in a compound word meaning "my house of study" (Ben Sira 51:23), but it is employed commonly to refer to a particular hermeneutic posture, only by the rabbis themselves.

Rabbinic midrash begins with the text of Hebrew scripture, assuming scripture to be the product of divine revelation and hence a source of potentially infinite instruction. Legal texts are interpreted, often employing technical hermeneutic methods, to derive or support rabbinic law. Narrative texts are read with creative imagination to yield new models for Jewish piety or conduct, often rendering biblical texts relevant to a new era.

In medieval rabbinic culture, halakhic (legal) study was valued above midrashic discourse. However, despite the lower status of the midrashic enterprise, old midrashim were compiled into new collections, and new midrashim were composed. Some have argued that because midrash had few direct normative consequences, it was the mechanism through which the rabbinic imagination was realized.

The great freedom exhibited by midrashic readings—and midrashic support of multiple readings of the same base text—has allowed midrash to gain surprising popularity in contemporary circles. Literary theorists have turned to midrash as an exemplar of the claim that a text's meaning (even a divine text) is indeterminate and, further, that the author's intent does not control meaning. Because of the evident innovative possibilities of a midrashic approach, many contemporary Jews have returned to the Hebrew Bible to write "modern midrash." Particularly notable as part of this phenomenon are new feminist midrashim.

See also JUDAISM.

BIBLIOGRAPHY
Hartman, Geoffrey H., and Sanford Budick. *Midrash and Literature.* 1986.
Neusner, Jacob. *The Midrash: An Introduction.* 1990.

David Kraemer

Mikveh

The biblical Book of Leviticus describes a number of forms of ritual impurity that require immersion in water to return to a state of ritual purity. The rabbis decreed that such water must either be in a natural body of water, such as a lake, or in a mikveh (literally, "collection of water"), a specially constructed bath that does not use drawn water and thus is similar to a natural pool of water. Since the destruction of the Temple in Jerusalem, though, only the ritual impurity of menstruation may be removed by immersion. By biblical law (Leviticus 18:19; 20:18), married couples may not engage in sexual intercourse during a woman's menses, and the rabbis added an additional period of five "clean days," after which the woman immerses in a mikveh and then they may resume sexual activity. Some American Jews now observe these laws not primarily for reasons of ritual purity but rather to insert a period of sexual abstinence into each month so that neither partner will see the other as merely a sex object. New dishes purchased from non-Jews are also traditionally dipped into the mikveh (in the spirit of Numbers 31:21–23), but that is a practice not widely observed by American Jews. Converts to Judaism immerse in a mikveh as part of the process of rebirth into their new religion (although some Reform rabbis do not require that).

In the United States, the mikveh is also used increasingly by those who want to mark other significant times of transition in their lives. Since the person immerses into the mikveh naked, men and women use the mikveh at different times to preserve modesty, and usually one at a time. The point of all these bathing rituals is not hygiene but rather spiritual purification and renewal.

See also BELONGING, RELIGIOUS; CONVERSION; JEWISH IDENTITY; JEWISH OBSERVANCE; JUDAISM; PRACTICE; RITUAL.

BIBLIOGRAPHY
Kotlar, David. "Mikveh." *Encyclopedia Judaica* 11:1534–1544.

Elliot N. Dorff

Millennialism

Millennialism theoretically refers to a period of one thousand years. In Christian thought, the millennium is associated with the Second Coming or Second Advent of Christ. All expressions of millennialism are linked to adventism, or the return of Christ. Premillennialism holds that Christ will return and reign over the earth for a thousand years after a time of great tribulation. Then the final confrontation between good and evil will occur. Postmillennialism sees the world evolving into an ideal realm; then, after a thousand years of prosperity and happiness, Christ will return. While both premillennial and postmillennial ideas have had advocates in the twentieth century, most Christian religious groups have opted for a less precise understanding called amillennialism. This view sees the millennium more in symbolic terms, emphasizing the presence of Christ's spirit in the church and the efforts of the church to bring human society in harmony with religious ideals. In the popular mind, however, millennialism is inseparable from concerns about the end of the world and Christ's return in judgment.

Premillennialism in the later twentieth century gained fresh currency in the resurgence of fundamentalism. Much of fundamentalism's approach derives from a particular theological understanding called premillennial dispensationalism. That view insists that all history, from creation to final judgment, is divided into time blocks or dispensations. In each God offers humanity a means of salvation, but every age ultimately becomes one of decline and increasing hostility to the ways of God. The present age is the sixth of seven dispensations leading up to Christ's return. Premillennial dispensationalism looks to the apocalyptic books of the Bible, especially Daniel and Revelation, as coded guides to contemporary historical events. Unraveling the code enables believers not only to see the significance in current events but also prepares them for the "rapture" when the faithful will soar through the air to their heavenly reward, and the Antichrist or the embodiment of evil will be revealed.

Premillennial dispensationalism reached millions through the Scofield Reference Bible, first published in 1909. That study Bible contained cross-references and time lines reflecting dispensationalist assumptions. The Scofield Reference Bible remains among the best-selling editions of Christian scriptures at the end of the twentieth century. Evangelist Billy Graham also drew on dispensationalism thinking for much of his critique of modern culture in the early decades of his career as a revivalist. In the 1970s, popular religious writer Hal Lindsey also revived dispensationalist ideas in his best-selling (with Carole C. Carlson) *The Late Great Planet Earth* and its sequel, *Satan Is Alive and Well on Planet Earth.* The former became the basis for a feature film.

If premillennialism was pessimistic about the present, seeing decline in society and ever-growing sin as signs of the nearness of Christ's return, postmillennialism tended to be optimistic. Early in the twentieth century, Social Gospel thinkers such as Walter Rauschenbusch championed technological advance and reform of social structures to transform American society into the millennial kingdom. But the devastation of two world wars, global economic depression in the 1930s, and the seeming inability of humans to use scientific and technological gains to alleviate human suffering undermined that optimism. Many theological thinkers therefore dismissed postmillennialism for its overestimation of human potential.

But from the 1970s on, Christian Reconstructionism revived postmillennialism, albeit with a new twist. Centered on the thinking of Rousas J. Rushdoony, Reconstructionism calls for the reinstitution of biblical law (theonomy) and the refashioning of all elements of society, from government to economics, according to a particular understanding of biblical teaching. A system based on biblical authority, not democracy, would thus pave the way for the millennial age. Reconstructionism attracted some who were dismayed by the presumed moral decay and erosion of religious values in the later decades of the twentieth century, but who saw dispensationalism and the popularized ideas of Hal Lindsey and others as overly simplistic.

Some religious communities have sustained particular versions of millennialism in their own doctrine. Two with roots in adventist thinking in the nineteenth century are the Jehovah's Witnesses and the Seventh-Day Adventists. Both showed significant growth in the second half of the twentieth century not only because of their aggressive proselytizing but also because of the same societal malaise that fueled fundamental-

ism's resurgence. Jehovah's Witnesses once insisted that Christ would return and the world would end in 1917; when such did not occur, the group suffered some problems of plausibility. Seventh-Day Adventists insist that humans must adhere strictly to biblical norms, including worship on the seventh day (Saturday) rather than the first day (Sunday) and Hebrew dietary codes, to pave the way for Christ's return. Both groups tend to see society as fraught with evil and therefore call for high standards of moral and ethical behavior for members by contrast; as a result, they gained currency as other millennialist thinkers likewise dismissed the social order as evil.

As the twenty-first century approached, popular millennialism soared, for the new century would also bring the dawn of the third millennium after the birth of Jesus. Hence speculation about the nearness of the end abounded, most of it ignored or criticized by theologians and religious leaders.

In the last analysis, whether premillennialism, postmillennialism, or amillennialism most accurately reflects biblical teaching matters little. What is significant is how all variations of millennialism see the present as a prelude to a more glorious future. All therefore tend to devalue empirical history, seeing some idealized society coming in the future as the goal of present endeavor. Whether that ideal world issues from gradual social change or follows cataclysmic upheaval or whether its arrival precedes, follows, or has no real relation to the anticipated Second Advent of Christ are really secondary issues. What matters is the conviction that society and its institutions will become what was intended at creation. The end will thus be like the beginning.

See also ESCHATOLOGY; FUNDAMENTALIST CHRISTIANITY; GRAHAM, BILLY; JEHOVAH'S WITNESSES; PREMILLENIALISM; RECONSTRUCTIONIST CHRISTIANITY; SECOND COMING; SEVENTH-DAY ADVENTISTS.

BIBLIOGRAPHY

Boyer, Paul S. *When Time Shall Be No More: Prophecy Belief in Modern American Culture.* 1992.

Carpenter, Joel A. *Revive Us Again: The Reawakening of American Fundamentalism.* 1997.

Clouse, Robert G., ed. *The Meaning of the Millennium: Four Views.* 1977.

Gaustad, Edwin S., ed. *The Rise of Adventism in America.* 1977.

Lindsey, Hal, with Carole C. Carlson. *The Late Great Planet Earth.* 1970.

Lindsey, Hal, with Carole C. Carlson. *Satan Is Alive and Well on Planet Earth.* 1972.

Marsden, George M. *Fundamentalism and American Culture: The Shaping of Twentieth-Century Evangelicalism, 1870–1925.* 1980.

Weber, Timothy P. *Living in the Shadow of the Second Coming: American Premillennialism, 1875–1982.* Enlarged ed., 1983.

Charles H. Lippy

Ministry

Ministry in most U.S. religious traditions refers primarily to religious leadership and acts of service offered for or on behalf of faith communities. The word "ministry" has been used specifically by Christian (particularly Protestant) religious groups, but its meaning and use also include the work of Jewish and other faith traditions. Ministry encompasses at least three levels of meaning: (1) professional religious leadership; (2) acts offered by individual members or groups in service to others; and (3) the relationship of faith communities to the larger world, expressed in acts of service. Ministry describes a broad range of activities of care for those in need, including persons who belong to congregations and persons and groups outside organized religious groups. Such caring has addressed spiritual, emotional, physical, financial, political, and ecological concerns.

During the twentieth century the word "ministry" has most commonly been used to refer to the career or vocation of church or synagogue leaders. Religious traditions have historically identified and prepared individuals for particular leadership roles in congregations and other faith communities. These leaders are variously designated as ministers, pastors, preachers, priests, sisters (nuns), brothers, or rabbis in certain religious groups. The word "clergy" is sometimes used to encompass all religious professionals. Depending on the particular religious community, ministers are ordained, consecrated, or licensed before they are permitted to practice the full range of ministerial duties. In most traditions persons are selected for ministry on the basis of personal qualities of emotional and spiritual maturity, educational ability, and leadership skill. In many religious traditions, persons report experiences of a "call to ministry," either through self-examination of their personal qualities and the needs of ministry or through a deeply personal religious experience.

Many organized religious groups require substantial educational preparation for ministry. U.S. Protestant denominations (e.g., United Methodist, Presbyterian, Episcopal) require a college degree plus three or more years of academic seminary or theological school training before an individual may assume leadership in a congregation or other ministerial setting. Some traditions have few or no academic requirements for professional ministry, relying instead on the candidate's personal and spiritual qualities and experienced sense of call. In virtually all religious traditions, however, persons expecting to enter ministry explore their vocational choices with representatives of the religious community they will represent and serve. Roman Catholic priests, brothers, and sisters are generally required to remain celibate (unmarried), but most other Christian, Jewish, and other religious groups permit or encourage marriage and family life for their ministers.

Functions of Ministry

The functions of ministry vary considerably across religious traditions. However, those functions can be categorized into eight primary areas. Some religious groups will expect all of these functions from ministers, while others will emphasize only one or two. Preaching involves study of the Bible or other sacred texts and the delivery of sermons, usually as part of a worship service. The sermon or homily is usually expected to relate the sacred texts to issues in contemporary living. The worship function includes the preparation and leadership of religious services, including performing the rites and sacraments of the church. Weddings and marriage preparation, funerals, and rituals such as Baptism and Communion are important dimensions of ministry. Through teaching the minister explains the religious beliefs of a particular tradition and helps congregational members apply those teachings to their own experiences.

As a congregational leader the minister oversees the administrative responsibilities for a church or a synagogue. In addition to managing the details of congregational life, the minister often assists congregations in planning for the future. When providing pastoral care, the minister offers the church or synagogue's resources to person at crisis points in life, such as death or other losses, marriage and birth of children, and personal or family difficulty. Care activities include home or hospital visitation, informal conversation, and counseling. Evangelism includes those activities in which persons outside the community are contacted, and often invited into membership or participation in the community of faith. Prophetic witness requires the minister to engage in critical analysis of the society and other institutions. He or she works for justice or advocates on behalf of persons who have been oppressed by those institutions. Mission involves religious communities in specific service to disadvantaged persons outside the congregation, such as the poor, children, victims of violence, and prison inmates. The balance among these functions will depend on the particular emphases of a given religious tradition.

Ministers are often employed by congregations where they serve. In smaller or underprivileged congregations, clergy may serve more than one congregation at the same time or hold an additional full- or part-time job to support themselves. Ministry may occur outside of traditional congregational settings as well. Ministers often serve in community agencies such as counseling centers or advocacy organizations. Others work in larger institutions, such as hospitals, university campuses, or correctional facilities, where they are often designated as chaplains.

In many religious traditions, ministry is not the sole responsibility of professional clergy, but rather it is the work of the whole religious community, including the activities of nonclergy, or laity (from the Greek word for people, *laos*). Clergy perform critical functions for congregations, but ministry is the responsibility of all members of a congregation according to their various gifts and abilities. Professional clergy are often expected to prepare and encourage members for service to God and the world rather than to practice ministry on behalf of the congregation. In this context, all congregational members are understood as the ministers who embody their religious commitments in the world. In these settings members report a stronger sense of ownership of, and responsibility for, the mission of the church or synagogue. Second, the sharp distinctions between clergy and laity have diminished, and a stronger sense of shared service to God and the world has developed.

Twentieth-Century Developments in Ministry

In addition to emphasizing the role of laity in ministry, several other important developments have affected the shape and practice of ministry in the twentieth century. The increasing role of women in professional ministry has resulted in increased opportunities for women and has provided a larger pool of candidates for ministry. Women in ministry have influenced the ways in which ministry is practiced, resulting in more collegial professional relationships and a reduction in hierarchical structures. In some traditions that do not permit full endorsement of women for ministry, such as the Roman Catholic Church and some conservative Protestant denominations, alternative avenues for service have been provided in lieu of ordination, including worship leadership and spiritual care.

For approximately four centuries ministry has been viewed as a profession along with medicine, the law, and teaching. More recently this understanding of ministry has competed with demands for personal spiritual leadership in congregations and in the culture. Many religious traditions continue to expect ministers to master a significant body of knowledge, submit to review by church governing bodies, and follow established professional ethical principles. Other traditions have focused more on the unique spiritual, personal and leadership qualities of ministers and have rejected the notion of professional ministry.

An expanding awareness of cultural and religious differences in the United States and around the world has led most religious leaders to dialogue with persons of other faith traditions to deepen understanding and find ways to work together in ministry. Some congregations have intentionally hired ministers of different cultural backgrounds to sharpen their awareness of the theological issues that a diverse world demands. Some denominations have reached formal agreements so that ministers and congregations can work together more effectively and in some cases even serve each other's congregations.

Technological advances, particularly television and computers, have profoundly affected ministry. In addition to offering new ways to communicate, these media have exposed the public to a variety of images of ministry and have changed congregants' expectations of worship.

The historic exclusion of persons of different sexual orientations from candidacy for ordination has prompted a reexamination of criteria for ministry in some denominations.

Increasing concerns about the environment and its effect on the welfare of persons around the world has prompted many clergy to study, teach, and lead congregations in attempts to understand and respond to the intricate relationship of humanity and the environment as central to ministry.

The word "ministry" describes both the vocation of professional spiritual leadership and the central work of congregations and faith groups, involving all members. The particular tasks of ministry vary from one religious group to another, but the central meaning of ministry is expressed in the notion of service to neighbor and to God.

See also CELIBACY; CLERGY; LITURGY AND WORSHIP; ORDINATION; ORDINATION OF WOMEN; PARISH; PASTORAL COUNSELING; PRAYER; PREACHING; PRIESTHOOD; RABBINATE; RITES OF PASSAGE; RITUAL.

BIBLIOGRAPHY

Cobb, John B. *Lay Theology.* 1994.
Messer, Donald E. *Contemporary Images of Christian Ministry.* 1989.

Niebuhr, H. Richard, and Daniel Day Williams, eds. *The Ministry in Historical Perspectives.* 1956, 1983.

Schneider, Carl J., and Dorothy Schneider. *In Their Own Right: The History of American Clergywomen.* 1997.

Schuller, David S., Merton P. Strommen, and Milo L. Brekke, eds. *Ministry in America.* 1980.

World Council of Churches. *Baptism, Eucharist and Ministry.* 1982.

David Hogue

Miracles

In Clearwater, Florida, crowds gather to pray to an image of the Virgin Mary that is said to have miraculously appeared on the side of a building. In rural churches in Tennessee the faithful believe that God will supernaturally protect them as they handle poisonous snakes during worship. New Age leaders cite theoretical physics to prove that the universe is unpredictable and hence compatible with belief in everything from astrology to out-of-body experiences (OBEs). Literal belief in the Bible's miracle stories is part of the increasingly conservative agenda in the massive Southern Baptist convention. Pentecostal faith healers like Benny Hinn talk without a blush about their repeated trips to Heaven to visit Jesus and announce raisings from the dead in their worldwide crusades.

That American religion is open to the miraculous at the end of the twentieth century is both quite natural and quite surprising. On the one hand, given the Biblical worldview that has informed Jewish, Catholic, and Protestant theology, one would expect many Jews and Christians to retain belief in the wonder-working power of the Creator. This is the especially the case for Hasidic Jews and for followers of Jesus influenced profoundly by the dominance of miracles in the four Gospels, the traditions recorded in the Acts of the Apostles, and stories about the Virgin Mary and other saints.

What is surprising in the vitality of supernatural belief in American religion, Christianity in particular, is the degree to which it has survived centuries of skepticism. Here the shadow of David Hume, following in the footsteps of René Descartes (1596–1650), Baruch Spinoza (1632–1677), and Gottfried Wilhelm Leibniz (1646–1716), looms most significantly. Hume (1711–1776), the famous Scottish philosopher, forever altered discussion of miracles with his brilliant and provocative essay "On Miracles." It has been the subject of hundreds of essays and books and is the key philosophical document in the enormous literature on the subject.

Hume's skepticism about miracles has been interpreted in two main directions. There are some philosophers who believe that he simply thought that miracles were impossible since they were contrary to unalterable laws of nature. This would make the issue of miracles one of logical deduction from scientific certainties. Grant the premise that laws of nature cannot be broken, and there needs to be no historical inquiry about this or that purported miracle.

Other philosophers contend that Hume was not making a scientific point but a historical one. According to these interpreters, Hume's whole essay is largely a work about human experience and historical analysis. In the end, given the fallibility of human testimony, the superstitious core in various contradictory religions, Hume believes that the wise person always remain skeptical about miraculous reports. Hume is not really saying that miracles are impossible but that they are so improbable as to be unworthy of serious consideration.

Whatever interpretation one adopts, Hume's ultimately negative verdict about miracles created an immediate shock wave in European and American thought. Christian apologists attacked his personal integrity and also mounted logical objections to his essay's argument. Hume was also targeted for his lack of clarity, a point that has been seconded even by agnostic philosophers like Antony Flew, one of Hume's best defenders and most careful critics. Is Hume making a logical case against miracles? If so, his openness to historical testimony is absurd. If his argument is largely historical, it is curious that he speaks about the "absolute impossibility" of miracles.

These points aside, despite instant replies from Christian philosophers, Hume's essay dealt a withering blow to supernaturalism. Hume's contempt for Jewish and Christian religion is masked by his professed concern for any religion that seeks to have miracles at its foundation. Hume's allies and enemies knew full well that he meant for his essay to be another blow to religion in the name of rational Enlightenment truth.

Hume's legacy had an immediate impact on biblical study. It became fashionable to reinterpret the miracles of the Bible so that the supernatural elements disappeared. Thus the story of Jesus walking on water was really just about the Nazarene reaching the disciples on a raft (unseen just below the surface of the lake). The feeding of the five thousand was actually about people sharing their hidden lunches. Jesus' resurrection was reduced to faith's encounter with his enduring teaching and example. Miracle became parable in a new liberal paradigm.

The power of Hume has waned in the last half of the twentieth century. This is due in part to mounting philosophical skepticism about the validity of Hume's specific arguments. American philosophy is no longer in the grip of thoroughly rationalistic systems (like the logical positivism of A. J. Ayer), due in part to the creative work of Christian philosophers. Alvin Plantinga, in particular, has constructed a Reformed epistemology that feels no need to build worldviews on Cartesian or Humean skepticism.

As well, science no longer wears its crown so proudly, and its utility is celebrated more than its value as the foundation for all knowledge. This is reflected in such celebrated works as Robert M. Pirsig's *Zen and the Art of Motorcycle Maintenance* or Fritjof Capra's *The Tao of Physics*. As well, the astounding evidence of design in the universe makes the case for miracles of another sort seem more reasonable. Martin Gardner, a theist and critic of all religions, argues for a sense of wonder about the natural world that makes belief in God and immortality seem sensible, if not rationally certain. Finally, the new postmodern mindset has made more room for alternate understandings of the universe, even ones that allow things to go bump in the night.

Of course, the religious landscape of the United States has always been varied, despite powerful unifying trends in philosophy and theology. Even after the triumph of Charles Darwin's naturalism in the last century, many Americans became fascinated with the emerging spiritualist tradition, and its claims about contacting the spirit of dead relatives. While Protestant liberalism was losing all interest in miracles (past or present), Pentecostalism swept the nation, with astounding tales of healings and supernatural visions. After midcentury, the emergence of Billy Graham and a new evangelicalism led to greater assent to the reality of miracles, especially about the core miracles in the Biblical narrative.

The arrival of other world religions to the United States has meant new worlds of supernatural discourse. The stories of Buddha (his special birth, his powers over nature, his ultimate enlightenment) combine with the traditions about Krishna (or other Hindu gods) to rival the stories of Jesus and also unite in opposition to a secular mindset. In orthodox Islam the great miracle is its holy book (the Qur'an), delivered from heaven to the prophet Muhammad. In folk Islam, legends about Muhammad combine with animistic traditions to create a world where Allah's infinite powers extend to every aspect of nature and daily life.

The United States is also home to many new religions that have no worries about Hume and his legacy. Sun Myung Moon, the founder of the Unification Church, alleges that he has been to heaven to converse with God directly. The Mormon Church is built on reports of angelic visits to their prophet Joseph Smith. Scientology's therapy program is rooted in phenomenal stories about humanity's cycles of reincarnation. Shirley MacLaine's miracle-laden New Age life got repeated national coverage in the mid-1980s. In the 1990s angel stories circulate freely, creating a whole new market for books, trinkets, and television shows.

Hume's arguments still have enormous power in American intellectual life or in religious traditions as they subject other religions to his skeptical thrusts. On the whole, however, Hume would be disappointed that his Enlightenment skepticism held power so briefly and has virtually no impact on the lives of millions of Americans who believe that with God (or Buddha or the Force or your inner self, and so on) that "all things are possible."

See also GRAHAM, BILLY; HEALING; MAGIC; MYTH; NEW AGE SPIRITUALITY; SNAKE HANDLING; SPIRITUALISM; UNIFICATION CHURCH; VIRGIN OF GUADALUPE.

BIBLIOGRAPHY

Flew, Antony. "Miracles." In *The Encyclopedia of Philosophy*, edited by Paul Edwards. 1967.

Gardner, Martin. *The Whys of a Philosophical Scrivener.* 1983.

Swinburne, Richard. *The Concept of Miracle.* 1970.

James A. Beverley

Missionary Movements

The designation "missionary movement" in the singular is something of a misnomer. Throughout the history of Christianity there have been many different missionary movements: Catholic, Orthodox, Protestant, British, American, Swiss, German, Scandinavian, and so on. Since the outbreak of the Protestant Reformation in the sixteenth century and the imperial expansion of various European political entities after that, there was an even greater proliferation in the number of such movements. There are in fact as many missionary movements today as there are churches working in many different parts of the world. The denominational plurality that characterizes the missionary enterprise is further complicated not only by the fact that different groups of missionaries identified themselves with the individual countries from which

A missionary visits an elderly Eskimo in Fort Yukon, Alaska, ca. 1970.   (Credit: CORBIS/Ed Eckstein.)

they came and shared the culture and political system of those countries but also by the variety of cultural contexts that were the objects of the Christianization they set out to accomplish. Because in their origins many missionary movements were country-specific, their methods of propagating the gospel and their perception of its meaning were largely shaped by their social and cultural backgrounds. This was natural enough. It has been an essential part of the spread of Christianity that wherever it went it was, at least partly, assimilated into the local culture and itself contributed to the transformation of that culture. Indeed, one of the unintended results of mission activity in many parts of the world today has been the rise of a large variety of local and, in some cases, independent forms of Christianity—so-called indigenous theologies.

But if these theologies bear enduring testimony to the principle of inculturation in the history of missions, we should not lose sight of the difficulties that this principle presents for any assessment of the mis-

sionary movement. Missionary theologies were themselves "indigenous"—they bore the many and varied social and cultural marks of their agents and thus were not culturally neutral. This is not to say that missionary activity was nothing but the expression of different cultural ideologies in the guise of religion, for whatever differences existed among missionaries, they all derived their motivation from the gospel of Matthew 28:19–20, the so-called great commission, according to which, before ascending to heaven for an interlude, Christ admonished his disciples to disseminate to the ends of the earth his message, the gospel or good news, of the impending reign of God to be inaugurated by the imminent return of Christ envisaged in Christian belief. Therefore the goal of missionary movements is to convert as many non-Christian peoples (indigenous peoples, Muslims, Jews, Hindus, Buddhists, and so on) to Christianity as is possible.

Historically, the desire to proselytize and to convert was founded on the belief that as a religion, Christianity is superior to all the others; that it is the only way to God, and therefore that all other religions are false or at least only partially true. However, when, in modern missionary movements, this contentious claim about the uniqueness of Christian faith was linked, as it often was, to colonial expansion, in which not only missionaries but also representatives of colonial adventurism believed in Christianity's potency as an agent of civilization, the line between the gospel and politics became blurred; the message of the gospel began to reflect national interests, thereby indicating the extent to which it, together with the methods and strategies used to propagate it, had been politically assimilated. The politics of this assimilation had devastating consequences for the evangelized, for it was on the basis of the manner in which these two separate projects were conjoined in missionary thought, even if not always deliberately, that whole cultures and societies were derided as ungodly and rejected as uncivilized, a move so typical of many missionary movements during the past few centuries of non-Western contact with Christianity.

This conjunction of religion and politics is clearly illustrated by missionary movements in North America. Although they were something of latecomers on the missionary scene and did not participate in the colonial projects of the expansionist imperial powers of the late nineteenth century, their representatives shared the outlook of most Europeans toward other inhabitants of the world—that they were lost and without true religion and thus needed to be brought under Christian influence. There was nothing unusual in the fact that American missionaries shared this view with their European counterparts because the rise of the modern missionary movement in the

United States was a result of the immigration of different religious groups from Europe to the United States. Some of these were made up of men and women who had participated in the Great Awakening of the eighteenth century that took place simultaneously on both sides of the Atlantic and that in certain respects inspired the missionary movement.

Although American missionaries were not part of the old expansionist imperial movement, they were not immune from thinking of the spread of the gospel through territorial expansion. At home their activities took place on an expanding frontier on which new cities had been established. Both the indigenous peoples and recently freed slaves were among those to be evangelized. The context in which this took place was one of spectacular economic growth. Between 1783 and 1914 America moved from being an essentially agricultural economy to achieving a high level of industrialization; its population became highly diversified; and Protestant churches, particularly in the late nineteenth century, increased considerably in number. The new wealth of rich families such as the Rockefellers, the Vanderbilts, and the Dukes was channeled into the cultivation of some of this growth through donations and philanthropic activity. The separation of church and state, which is such an important part of American democracy, also facilitated the freedom of religious groups, voluntary associations, and churches to propagate their beliefs.

A great historian of missions, Kenneth Latourette, noted how Christianity in this period adapted itself to this environment, becoming not just a religion of the frontier and expansion but also one of wealth and prosperity. This does not mean that missionaries set out to preach the virtues of colonialism and Mammon or that they were not specifically motivated by religious concerns. In fact, it is an interesting aspect of American missionary movements that although they developed in a context of increasing material prosperity, their religious message tended to be pietistic, otherworldly, and millennialistic as well as charismatic, tendencies that, with certain modifications, were to congeal into fundamentalism and prosperity theology as expressions of American Christianity in the twentieth century. In these perspectives, power and wealth are to be celebrated and not despised because they are results of God's blessing, fruits of Christian faith and commitment.

Again, all this shows some of the ways in which missionary movements in America inculturated their understanding of the gospel. It was this inculturated message that missionaries were to export beyond the American frontier to other parts of the world—the Pacific, Africa, Latin America, and Asia. The money missionaries took overseas was, of course, used to build hospitals, schools, and colleges—in short, to extend Western culture to non-Western peoples. The alliance between gospel and culture once again proved too strong to resist.

See also CHURCH AND STATE; CONVERSION; FREEDOM OF RELIGION; FUNDAMENTALIST CHRISTIANITY; GLOBALIZATION; PROSELYTIZING.

BIBLIOGRAPHY

Green, Vivian. *A New History of Christianity.* 1996.

Latourette, Kenneth Scott. *A History of the Expansion of Christianity: The Great Century A.D. 1800–1914.* 1941.

Tinker, George E. *Missionary Conquest: The Gospel and Native American Cultural Genocide.* 1993.

Walls, Andrew F. *The Missionary Movement in Christian History.* 1996.

Edward P. Antonio

Moon, Sun Myung.

See Divine Principle; Unification Church.

Moral Majority

In the aftermath of Watergate and the resignation of President Richard Nixon in 1974, millions of evangelical Christians voted for Jimmy Carter for president in 1976, contributing importantly to his narrow victory over Gerald Ford. In that same year, George Gallup reported that as many as fifty million Americans could be described as evangelicals, and *Newsweek* ran a cover story in which it dubbed 1976 "The Year of the Evangelical." Though disappointed by Carter's presidency, particularly his support of the Equal Rights Amendment, his grudging acceptance of abortion, and his belief that homosexuals should not be discriminated against because of their sexual orientation, conservative Protestants began looking for ways to use their newfound political muscle to push the country in a more rightward direction. At the same time, a tightly knit group of conservative political operatives, associated with such organizations as the Heritage Foundation and the Free Congress Foundation and calling themselves New Right or "movement conservatives," were actively seeking ways to enlist this evangelical army into their movement.

By the end of the 1970s, Jerry Falwell, pastor of the fundamentalist Thomas Road Baptist Church in Lynchburg, Virginia, was beginning to use his broadcast ministry—a half-hour daily radio program aired on approximately 250 stations, and a weekly television program that could be seen on more than 330 stations throughout the nation—to speak against gay rights, abortion, and other issues he traced to the influence of "secular humanism." In 1979, with the encouragement and assistance of New Right leaders, Falwell founded Moral Majority, declaring that it would be "prolife, profamily, promoral, and pro-American." Its stated aims included registering evangelical Christians to vote, informing members about what was going on in Washington and in state legislatures, lobbying to defeat leftist legislation, and pushing for legislation that would protect and advance a conservative social agenda.

Throughout the 1980 election campaign and for several years afterward, Falwell traveled extensively throughout the nation, telling pastors, mostly fundamentalist Independent Baptists, that their duty was "getting people saved, baptized, and registered to vote" and helping them organize chapters of Moral Majority. At the same time, an organization called Religious Roundtable worked to mobilize southern Baptists, and Christian Voice played a comparable role among charismatic and Pentecostal Christians. Because of Falwell's attention-getting message and style and his ubiquitous presence on television and in the press, Moral Majority became the best-known representative and symbol of the movement that came to be called the Christian New Right or, more simply, the Religious Right.

Moral Majority and its allied organizations helped elect Ronald Reagan and a Republican-majority Senate in 1980, but the Religious Right still lacked the political clout and organizational savvy to win significant White House or congressional support for its conservative social agenda. Falwell remained loyal to Reagan, but financial problems with his television ministry and a rapidly expanding Liberty University, of which he was founder and chancellor, demanded his increased attention. In 1986 he quietly disbanded Moral Majority, clearing the way for the appearance of more sophisticated and effective grassroots organizations.

See also CHRISTIAN COALITION; EVANGELICAL CHRISTIANITY; FALWELL, JERRY; FUNDAMENTALIST CHRISTIANITY; RELIGIOUS RIGHT; TELEVANGELISM.

BIBLIOGRAPHY

D'Souza, Dinesh. *Falwell, Before the Millennium.* 1984.
Falwell, Jerry. *Listen, America!* 1980.
Martin, William. *With God on Our Side: The Rise of the Religious Right in America.* 1996.

William Martin

Moral Rearmament

Moral Rearmament was the last and largest of several religious movements founded by Frank Buchman (1878–1961), an American Lutheran minister and evangelist. Buchman began his career working with young people in the United States, Asia, and England, believing that he could change the world most effectively through converting influential college students. He organized his followers into small groups where participants could confess their sins and share their religious experiences in an intimate setting; members would then seek to convert others through one-on-one evangelism. Buchman's followers listened for God's plans for their lives, and measured their behavior through a moral code centered on absolute honesty, purity, unselfishness, and love (the Four Absolutes). During the 1920s Buchman developed an international network of these small groups that became known as the Oxford Group Movement.

Starting in the 1930s, Buchman sought to apply this method to other relationships—within the family, between labor and management, and between countries. He believed that Western Christian democracies needed reinforcement in the face of materialism, communism, and unbelief. In 1938 he announced the campaign for Moral Rearmament (MRA), offering Christianity as an alternative to both communism and fascism. In the late 1930s MRA sought to prevent war by calling individuals on each side to confess their sins to the other and adhere to the Four Absolutes. During World War II it turned its energies to morale building, especially in industrial relations. MRA saw Christianity and communism as the world's two competing ideologies; during the Cold War it sought to defend the West, primarily by focusing on labor peace, strong families, and moral values. Through the 1950s the movement held international rallies and used the media skillfully; it achieved prominence by publicizing the involvement of world leaders, especially from the United States, the British Commonwealth, and Asia. Throughout its history MRA's critics accused it of being a cult or of ties to communist or fascist forces. Although they were groundless, these accusations limited MRA's world impact. The movement declined in the 1960s, partly because of a leadership vacuum after Buchman's death and partly because of the perceived irrelevance of its evangelical Christian worldview. The organization closed most of its offices in 1970, but the movement still has adherents.

Although little studied by scholars, the career of Moral Rearmament tells us a good deal about contemporary American religion. Buchman's small cell group, a departure from the large revival meetings characteristic of American evangelicalism, has become a model for evangelism, especially in the work of groups such as Campus Crusade for Christ. The model has also influenced modern popular psychology; Alcoholics Anonymous and other "twelve-step" recovery groups have their origin in this small-group work. MRA's involvement in world issues reflects the American Protestantism's tradition of looking to change the world. Unlike the social gospel movement of the early twentieth century, which focused on changing social and economic systems, however, MRA concentrated on changing the world through converting individuals. Its sophistication in using media and political contacts reveals the interconnections of religion and the social and political establishment.

See also CAMPUS CRUSADE FOR CHRIST; EVANGELICAL CHRISTIANITY; LUTHERANISM; TWELVE-STEP PROGRAM.

BIBLIOGRAPHY

Harris, Irving. *The Breeze of the Spirit: Sam Shoemaker and the Story of Faith-at-Work.* 1978.
Lean, Garth. *Frank Buchman: A Life.* 1985.
Sack, Daniel. "Disastrous Disturbances: Buchmanism and Student Religious Life at Princeton, 1919–1935." Ph.D. diss., 1995.

Daniel Sack

Mormon Church.

See Church of Jesus Christ of Latter-day Saints.

Mormon Temple

The Church of Jesus Christ of Latter-day Saints (LDS) encourages its members to participate in special ordinances that are performed only in LDS temples, in addition to regular weekly church services at local meetinghouses. Latter-day Saints, or Mormons, believe that temple worship was an important element of Israelite religion during Solomon's reign and that the Lord restored true temple worship to the earth when the LDS Church was organized in the 1830s. In 1836 Mormons built their first temple, in Kirtland, Ohio, and continued to build or plan a temple in every community as they moved west to escape persecution. Just four days after settling in Salt Lake City in 1847, President Brigham Young set aside a plot of land for the Salt Lake temple, which took nearly forty years to complete.

The Mormon Temple in Salt Lake City, Utah, ca. 1994. (Credit: © James Blank/Stock, Boston/PNI.)

Who May Enter the Temple

Admission to LDS temples is reserved for those members who can demonstrate their worthiness in annual interviews with their local bishop and regional stake president. Those who receive a "temple recommend" must obey church teachings on tithing (10 percent of income), dietary restrictions (no alcohol, tobacco, nonprescription drugs, or hot or caffeinated drinks), and chastity. Recommend holders must also declare their belief in Jesus Christ, support of the leaders of the LDS Church, and make their own commitments to live honestly and righteously.

The temple is primarily utilized by adult members, although worthy adolescents may perform proxy baptisms (see below) on a "limited recommend" until they are old enough to receive their endowments. Adults entering the temple must have been members for at least a year, and males must be ordained to the Melchizedek priesthood.

Sacred Ordinances

Several rituals are performed inside the temple, for both the living and the dead. Living members who are worthy to enter the temple will receive their "endowment" on their first visit. For orthodox Mormons, the endowment is a rite of passage from childhood into adulthood and must occur before a young adult goes forth on a mission (men at age nineteen, women at age twenty-one) or is sealed in a temple marriage. The endowment ritual, which lasts for several hours, begins with washings and anointings to cleanse believers in preparation for the knowledge they will receive. The endowment teaches Mormons about their sacred roles on earth and in the hereafter. Members make solemn covenants to God attesting to their faithfulness and obedience. They also receive a special garment, which they are expected to wear underneath their regular clothing for the rest of their lives, to remind them of the covenants they made in the temple.

Once they have received their endowments, adults may also participate in rituals that seal them to their nuclear families throughout eternity. For example, a man and a woman may take vows that they believe will seal their marriage not just "until death do us part," but forever. Any children born to parents who have been so sealed in the temple are said to be "born in the covenant" and will be automatically linked to their parents in the afterlife.

Other temple rituals are performed by living members on behalf of those who have died. Each temple contains a large baptismal font where such "proxy" baptisms are performed. (Mormons believe that individuals can still make spiritual choices after this life is completed; the dead, like the living, must receive the ordinances of baptism and their endowments before gaining access to the Celestial Kingdom, the highest tier of eternal paradise.) In addition to baptisms, living Mormons will also receive endowments by proxy for the dead and stand in for them as they are sealed to their families for eternity. While proxy baptisms may be performed by Latter-day Saints after age twelve, the endowments for the dead can be performed only by adult Mormons who have received their own temple endowments.

Recent Developments

In recent decades, several important developments have occurred regarding Mormon temple worship. As the LDS Church has expanded internationally, temples have been built to accommodate church members around the globe. There are currently LDS temples in every continent except Antarctica. As temple construction has expanded, the ceremony itself has been streamlined to make the rituals available to more Latter-day Saints. For example, key elements of the endowment ritual used to be performed by live actors, who would portray the creation, fall, and redemption of humankind. In the 1950s and 1960s, as the first temples outside North America were opened, these dramas were presented on film rather than through live drama. The medium of film enabled individual temples to hold endowment sessions in different languages, utilizing fewer ordinance workers. By 1990 this practice had become standard for all temples of the LDS Church, and temples today do not use live actors.

Changes in the temple ceremony, announced in 1990, eliminated the traditional pledge of a wife to obey her husband, while he promised to obey God. Today both partners covenant to obey God directly. Also, the endowment ceremony jettisoned some of the graphic "penalties" that templegoers had been warned might befall them if they ever revealed what had transpired during the temple ritual. Even so, Latter-day Saints regard temple worship as the most sacred core of their religious faith, and to preserve this hallowed nature, temple rituals are not discussed outside the temple.

The 1980s and 1990s were decades of vigorous temple-building for the LDS Church, with the 1980s seeing the dedication of twenty-six new temples, more than doubling their overall number worldwide. In April 1998 LDS president Gordon B. Hinckley announced that by the year 2000 there would be one hundred operating temples around the globe. Roughly a third of these would be new "minitemples," servicing a smaller geographical region and fewer members than traditional temples. All temples were to offer full services for baptisms, endowments, and sealings, but minitemples would forgo some additional amenities of larger temples, such as cafeterias.

See also ATTENDANCE; BOOK OF MORMON; CHURCH OF JESUS CHRIST OF LATTER-DAY SAINTS; LITURGY AND WORSHIP; MISSIONARY MOVEMENTS; PROSELYTIZING; RELIGIOUS COMMUNITIES.

BIBLIOGRAPHY

Andrew, Laurel B. *The Early Temples of the Mormons: The Architecture of the Millennial Kingdom in the American West.* 1978.
Packer, Boyd K. *Holy Temple.* 1980.

Jana Kathryn Riess

Mosque

The Arabic word *masjid* means "the place where one prostrates oneself in worship." All that God requires

Several Muslim men exit the Islamic Center in Washington, D.C., a mosque built in 1949, with a minaret that is 160 feet tall. (Credit: CORBIS/ Catherine Karnow.)

is that a place of worship should be set aside (Qur'an sura IX, 107–108), that it should be a sanctuary (sura IX, 17–18, and sura LXX, 11, 17), and that the direction of prayer should be indicated in some way: "And now verily We shall make thee turn (in prayer) toward a *qibla* (direction of prayer) that is dear to thee. So turn thy face toward the *masjid al-haram* (Mecca) and ye (O Muslims), wheresoever ye may be, turn your faces (when ye pray) toward it" (sura II, 144). No mention is made of a building, but every Muslim—both female and male—who has attained majority is bound to observe the five daily *salat* prayers of dawn, midday, afternoon, sunset, and late evening. In addition, Friday is the weekly day of communal worship (at midday) and incumbent on all adult male Muslims. Finally, salats are performed on the two Eids annually, one at the end of Ramadan, the other after the Hajj.

The first mosque was the house of the Prophet Muhammad in Medina. This was a simple rectangular enclosure containing rooms for the Prophet and his wives and a shaded area on the southern side of the courtyard that could be used for prayer in the direction of Mecca. This building became the model for subsequent mosques, which had the same basic courtyard layout with a prayer area against the qibla wall. An early development of this basic plan was the provision of shade on the other three sides of the courtyard. The roofs were supported by columns made of wood. Several features that were later to become standard features of mosques were introduced at an early stage. The first is the *minbar* (pulpit), which was used by Muhammad to give sermons; the second is a prayer niche called a *mihrab,* in the qibla wall. The minaret, a towerlike structure and the most conspicuous feature of mosques in many Muslim societies, has the least liturgical significance. Its purpose of calling the faithful to prayer is now redundant with the advent of electrical public address systems. Like the minaret, the domed mosque is also a later innovation. Thus the primary feature of a mosque is a qibla wall facing Mecca.

In the United States, unlike long-established Muslim societies, a majority of the mosques are housed in buildings originally constructed for other purposes. Thus we have abandoned churches, Masonic lodges, fire stations, funeral homes, theaters, private homes, and warehouses converted into mosques. A survey of 1997–1998 showed that of the nearly two thousand mosques, little more than a hundred were purpose-built. Initially, the poverty of both struggling immigrants and African-American Muslims prevented the believers from constructing mosques designed by architects. A number of crudely designed buildings emerged as mosques in Highland Park, Michigan (1919), Michigan City, Indiana (1924), Cedar Rapids, Iowa (1925), Ross, North Dakota (1926), Quincy, Massachusetts (1930), and Sacramento, California (1941). Many of these mosques were named "cultural centers" of the ethnonational population who built it, exemplified by the Albanian Cultural Center, the Arab Banner Society, the Indian/Pakistani Muslim Association, and the like. Many of these buildings had a hall for prayer but also served as ethnic clubs complete with a social hall for weddings, a ballroom dance floor, and even a basement for bingo!

Although historically the mosque experienced fourteen centuries of stylistic development, it is certainly an architectural novelty in the United States. The thematic and visual characteristics of mosque architecture in America must confront an alien environment, one that has its own deeply embedded historical and visual vocabulary. The response, then, of the architectural characteristics of the American mosque to its context is one of tension, resulting both from religious and cultural paradigms. While the building must respond to its own inner formal determinants (cultural and functional), it cannot ignore its regional setting. The stylistic features of mosques built since the late 1950s in America vary considerably. However, it is possible to identify three basic themes that prevail in the aesthetic content of the buildings. These are: traditional design transplanted from Islamic lands (e.g., the Islamic Cultural Center of Washington, D.C., designed by Abdur Rahman Rossi, an Italian convert to Islam and built in 1957); reinterpretation of historical prototypes (e.g., the Islamic Cultural Center of Manhattan, New York, designed by Michael McCarthy of Skidmore, Owings, & Merrill and built in 1991); and finally, innovative, unprecedented mosques (e.g., the Islamic Society of North America mosque in Plainfield, Indiana, designed by Syed Gulzar Haidar and Muhammad Mukhtar Khalil and built in 1981, and the Albuquerque, New Mexico, mosque designed by Bart Prince and built in 1986).

Functionally there are also some distinct characteristics—for example, most of the buildings do not operate strictly as places of worship alone but rather as places of public gathering; therefore many are called Islamic centers. They have facilities for a variety of uses: Islamic school on the weekend, library, conference center, bookshop, kitchen and social function hall, recreation facilities, residential apartments, and sometimes even a funeral home.

Since the American Muslim family is usually nuclear, the entire family turns out for worship, necessitating separate space for women, usually at a mezzanine level. Although women have never been barred from a mosque, lack of separate space prevented most women from going to mosques in traditional Islamic societies. However, in the American context, more and more women are taking their rightful place in the mosque along with their brothers, sons, and husbands.

See also ISLAM; MECCA; PRACTICE; PRAYER; QUR'AN.

BIBLIOGRAPHY
Holod, Renata, and Hassan-Uddin Khan. *The Contemporary Mosque: Clients, Architects, and Design Since the 1950s.* 1997.
Kahrea, Akel I., and Altif Abdul-Malik. "Designing the American Mosque." *Islamic Horizon* (October 1996):40–41.
Khalidi, Omar. "Approaches to Mosque Design in America." In *Muslims on the Americanization Path?*, edited by Yvonne Y. Haddad and John L. Esposito. 1998.

Omar Khalidi

Mother Teresa

(1910–1997), founder of the Missionaries of Charity.

Mother Teresa was born and named Agnes Gonxha Bojaxhiu in Skopje, northern Macedonia. At eighteen she joined the Sisters of Loretto, a group of Irish nuns who ran schools in India, and took the name Teresa in honor of the French saint Térèse of Lisieux. She spent seventeen years as a teacher and then a principal of a Calcutta high school for privileged Bengali girls. Then, in 1946, during a train ride to Darjeeling for a religious retreat, Teresa received a call in which she felt God directed her to leave her life as an enclosed sister to work on the streets with the poor. In 1950 the Vatican formally established her new order—the Missionaries of Charity. In addition to the usual vows of poverty, chastity, and obedience, the Missionaries of Charity vowed to give "wholehearted and free service to the poorest of the poor." Mother Teresa learned Hindi and Bengali, and she asked for and received Indian citizenship in 1948. In 1965 Pope Paul VI made her order a pontifical order, which opened the way to expansion outside India.

Mother Teresa went from relative obscurity in her work with the poor to a figure of international attention with the publication of Malcolm Muggeridge's *Something Beautiful for God* in 1971. Attention to Mother Teresa grew as she received honorary degrees and medals, including the Pope John XXIII Peace Prize in 1971 and the Presidential Medal of Freedom, awarded to her by President Ronald Reagan in 1985. In 1979 she was awarded the Nobel Peace Prize for her service to the poor. Mother Teresa became a well-recognized figure in the latter years of her life, meeting with American presidents and famous international personages. Widely regarded as a "living saint," Mother Teresa was an icon in the American media, which presented stark images of her caring for the dying and poor and spurning the trappings of wealth and power. In the 1980s and 1990s the term "Mother Teresa" became a catchphrase for anyone who was seen as extraordinarily charitable or holy, and she was seen as representing the Christian faith and the Catholic heritage at its best. Mother Teresa's appeal cut across ideological, religious, and national lines. For many Americans, disillusioned with religious institutionalism and conflict and with their own culture, which appeared increasingly materialistic as the century closed, Mother Teresa was a symbol of love, charity, and simplicity. Mother Teresa was voted American's Most Admired Woman in 1980, 1986, 1995, and 1996, growing more popular even as her health failed. After her death in 1997, calls were made to speed up the process for canonizing her as a saint.

Mother Teresa holds her hands together in prayer during a religious service on September 20, 1977.   (Credit: AP/Wide World Photos.)

At the time of her death Mother Teresa had created a network of nearly 600 homes spread across 130 countries that operated food centers, orphanages, leprosariums, AIDs hospices, and shelters for battered women, drug addicts, and the poor, unemployed, dying, insane, and aged. Mother Teresa spoke out against capital punishment and war. She was criticized for her adamant opposition to abortion and contraception.

See also MISSIONARY MOVEMENTS; ROMAN CATHOLICISM; SAINTHOOD.

BIBLIOGRAPHY

Doig, Desmond. *Mother Teresa, Her People, and Her Work.* 1976.
Egan, Eileen. *Such a Vision of the Street.* 1985.
Muggeridge, Malcolm. *Something Beautiful for God.* 1971.
Porter, David. *Mother Teresa: The Early Years.* 1986.
Sebba, Anne. *Mother Teresa: Beyond the Image.* 1997.

Marie Anne Pagliarini

Muhammad, Elijah Karriem

(1897–1975), religious and political leader.

Elijah Muhammad was the major leader from 1934 to 1975 of the Black Muslim movement, the Nation of Islam, which combined religious beliefs with black nationalism. Born Robert Elijah Poole on October 10, 1897, in Sandersville, Georgia, he was one of thirteen children of an itinerant Baptist preacher. In 1919 he married Clara Evans, and they joined the black migration to Detroit, where he worked in the auto plants. In 1931 he met Master Wallace Fard (or Wali Farrad or W. D. Fard), founder of the Nation of Islam, who eventually chose this devoted disciple as his chief aide. Fard named him "Minister of Islam," dropped his slave name "Robert Poole," and restored his true Muslim name, "Elijah Karriem Muhammad."

After Fard disappeared in 1934, Elijah Muhammad led a major faction to Chicago, where he established Temple of Islam No. 2 as the main headquarters for the Nation of Islam. He also instituted the worship of

Elijah Muhammad, African-American leader of the Nation of Islam, ca. 1955.   (Credit: © Archive Photos.)

Master Fard as Allah and himself as the Messenger of Allah and head of the Nation, always addressed with the honorific title "the Honorable." Muhammad built on the teachings of Fard and combined aspects of Islam and Christianity with the black nationalism of Marcus Garvey and Noble Drew Ali into a "proto-Islam," an unorthodox Islam with a strong racial slant. Whites were considered as devils.

The Honorable Elijah Muhammad's message of racial separation focused on the recognition of true black identity and stressed economic independence. "Knowledge of Self" and "Do for Self" were the rallying cries. His followers sold the Nation's newspaper, *Muhammad Speaks,* and established their own educational system of University of Islam schools and small businesses such as bakeries, grocery stores, and fish stores. They also followed his strict dietary rules outlined in his book *How to Eat to Live,* which enjoined one meal per day and complete abstention from pork, drugs, tobacco, and alcohol. In his major work, *Message to the Black Man,* Elijah Muhammad diagnosed the vulnerabilities of the black psyche as stemming from a confusion of identity and self-hatred caused by white racism; the cure he prescribed was radical surgery through the formation of a separate nation, either in the United States or elsewhere.

After spending four years in a federal prison for encouraging draft refusal during World War II, the Honorable Elijah Muhammad was assisted by his chief protégé, Minister Malcolm X, in building the movement and encouraging its rapid spread in the 1950s and 1960s. During its peak years the Nation of Islam had more than a half-million devoted followers, influencing millions more, and accumulated an economic empire worth an estimated eighty million dollars. With only a third-grade education, Elijah Muhammad was the leader of the most enduring black militant religious movement in the United States. Although he was not a charismatic speaker, he was a master manipulator, able to control powerful personalities such as Malcolm X and Louis Farrakhan. Elijah Muhammad died on February 25, 1975, in Chicago and was succeeded by one of his six sons, Warith Deen Muhammad. After Warith Deen Muhammad dismantled the Nation by moving the main body of followers to orthodox Sunni Islam, Minister Louis Farrakhan rebuilt it in 1977, using the teachings of Elijah Muhammad.

See also AFRICAN-AMERICAN RELIGIONS; BLACK MUSLIMS; FARD, W. D.; FARRAKHAN, LOUIS; MALCOLM X; NATION OF ISLAM; MUHAMMAD, WARITH DEEN; NOBLE DREW ALI.

BIBLIOGRAPHY

Clegg, Claude Andrew III. *An Original Man: The Life and Times of Elijah Muhammad.* 1997.

Essien-Udom, E. U. *Black Nationalism: A Search for an Identity in America.* 1962.

Gardell, Mattias. *In the Name of Elijah Muhammad: Louis Farrakhan and the Nation of Islam.* 1996.

Lincoln, C. Eric. *The Black Muslims in America.* 1960.

Malcolm X and Alex Haley. *The Autobiography of Malcolm X.* 1965.

Muhammad, Elijah. *How to Eat to Live.* 1972.

Muhammad, Elijah. *Message to the Black Man in America.* 1965.

Perry, Bruce. *Malcolm: The Life of a Man Who Changed Black America.* 1991.

Lawrence H. Mamiya

Muhammad, Warith Deen

(1933–), religious leader.

Born Wallace Mohammad to Elijah and Clara Muhammad in 1933, Warith Deen Muhammad ascended to the position of Supreme Minister of the Nation of

Imam Warith Deen Muhammad in a rare address by a Muslim leader during a Jewish Erev Shabbat service at Temple Israel of Greater Miami, on June 18, 1999. (Credit: AP/Wide World Photos.)

Islam immediately after his father's death in 1975. Wallace Muhammad as a young adult had always placed himself in contention with the philosophy of the Nation of Islam and his father. Studying Arabic and Islam under various tutors led him to "orthodox" Islam and away from the teachings of the Nation of Islam. His return as the Supreme Minister was both applauded and considered suspicious. His mounting denunciations of his father's teachings and the remolding of the Nation of Islam into an "orthodox" Muslim community were welcomed by some and detested by more than a few.

The name of the Nation of Islam was changed to the World Community of Al-Islam in the West in 1976, and temples were changed to mosques. The standard dress of men—bow ties and suits—gave way to adaptations of Muslim world dress. The dress regulations for women changed also. Supreme Minister Wallace Mohammad became Imam Wallace Muhammad, and an internal war began. As other ministers of the old Nation of Islam pulled away and formed other Nations of Islam with the original tenets and objectives, Imam Muhammad continued to steer the remaining community to Islam and open its doors to others. Each step in the process was heralded by a community and newspaper name change; *Muhammad Speaks* became *The Bilalian News.*

In 1980 the community was the American Muslim Mission and the newspaper was renamed *The Muslim World News.* Imam Muhammad totally dismantled the centralized governance of his community by giving his local imams autonomy. The early 1990s signaled another step in the process, and the community became the Muslim American Community, with a news organ called by its current name, *The Muslim Journal.* Today the Muslim American Community is loosely connected; its school system, dismantled in the 1980s, is being rebuilt. Throughout the process of redirecting the community formally known as the Nation of Islam, Imam Muhammad embarked on a number of initially unsuccessful but extremely important programs. AMMCOP (American Muslim Mission Committed to Purchase One Thousand Products Plus) was a well-structured cooperative buying program. This program was designed on the order of the large buying clubs around the country. CRAID (Committee to Remove All Images That Attempt to Portray the Divine) was designed to stimulate conversation and change in views on racial divinities in religion. Both of these programs are being revived.

In 1992 Imam Muhammad delivered the first address by a Muslim on the floor of the Georgia state legislature and was also the first Muslim to deliver an invocation on the floor of the U.S. Senate. Today Imam Warith Deen Muhammad is a respected leader of a large community of African-American Muslims engaging his community in a wide range of civic projects and interreligious dialogues. In 1999 he began a public reconciliation with Minister Louis Farrakhan concerning family disputes resulting in Elijah Muhammad's death in 1975.

See also FARRAKHAN, LOUIS; IMAM; ISLAM; MUHAMMAD, ELIJAH; NATION OF ISLAM.

BIBLIOGRAPHY

Marsh, Clifton. *The World Community of Islam in the West: From Black Muslim to Muslim, 1931–1977.* 1984.

McCloud, Aminah Beverly. *African American Islam.* 1995.

Turner, Richard Brent. *Islam in the African-American Experience.* 1997.

Aminah Beverly McCloud

Mullah

A mullah (from the Arabic word *mawlā,* meaning "master" or "lord") technically means a learned person with public functions of teaching and preaching in the community. As a title indicating religious education and the ability to communicate to the public, it applies to both men and women who undertake this function. In Iran it is also used for Jewish and Zoroastrian sages. Customarily it applies to men of religious learning who wear a turban, notwithstanding their religious affiliation. This connection with learning and teaching is connoted in a number of Persian compound verbs, such as *mullāh raftan,* meaning "to go to school" or "to learn a lesson," and *mullāh shudan,* "to become learned."

Although the title is commonly used by both the Persian-speaking Sunni and the Shī'ī communities for their religious functionaries, in the Shī'ite context, mullah denotes a kind of clergy whose functions include presiding at all those public acts that, according to the Sharī'a (Islamic law), require some kind of religious expertise and representational responsibilities—acts such as marriage ceremonies, funerals, and other social transactions involving two or more parties. Depending on the political-social status of the religious institution at different times in Iranian history, the term also sometimes carries a derogatory connotation when it refers to popular preachers, also known as *akhund,* whose religious knowledge is limited to basic teachings about certain devotional acts and whose main function is to recount the stories of the suffering (*ta'ziya*) of the Shī'ite imams. Both during the Constitutional Revolution in 1905 and the Islamic Revolution in 1978–1979 in Iran, the term "mullah" was applied to religious reactionaries who were seen as opposed to modernization through secularization of Muslim society. Shī'ite mullahs have continued to play a leading role in the social and political transformation of Shī'ite communities in Iran, Iraq, and Lebanon.

Historically, members of the religious class in Muslim communities were drawn from wealthy families, who could afford to educate their sons to become jurist-theologians (*'ulamā*). The classical works on the Qur'an exegesis, traditions, and jurisprudence were produced by these scholars, of whom some were given the title of mullah as a mark of respect for their learning. In modern times, mullahs are usually drawn from the lower and middle strata of society. After completing their early education in Qur'an schools (*maktab*) in their villages, these students, known as *tullāb,* between the ages of eleven and fifteen years, migrate to larger centers of religious learning (*madrasa*) in holy cities such as Mashhad or Qumm in Iran or Najaf in Iraq, where they pursue a set introductory curriculum in Arabic grammar, syntax, rhetoric, and logic on a personal, tutorial basis. The more advanced students are introduced to literary disciplines and dialectical theology (*kalām*). Students spend an average of three to five years at this introductory stage. The second stage of their education begins with the study of juridical terminology and texts. Depending on a student's intellectual and linguistic preparation, this stage requires from three to six years. It is only after successful completion of this second stage that a student begins to attend graduate lectures (*dars-i khārij*) given by prominent jurist-consults (*mujtahid*). The entire course of study takes some fifteen to twenty years. Very few among these *tullāb* finish the entire course to earn the title of *mujtahid* and thereby receive the permission (*ijāza*) to formulate independent opinions in matters of law. Whether one attains that high level of legal-theological education or not, once a person adopts the title of mullah it carries with it certain privileges in the community of the faithful. Under different Muslim dynasties some occupations were reserved for the mullah in civil and religious administration. In Iran mullahs were exempt from military service.

In the North American context, the Shī'ite mullah prefers to be called imam, the title usually adopted by the Sunni leaders of prayer. With his distinguished clothing (a cloak and a turban) and physical appearance in the otherwise unfriendly secular environment, a mullah/imam has become a symbol of Muslim religiosity for the majority of religious-minded Shī'ites, who follow him and through him emulate the grand ayatollah, the *marja' al-taqlīd* (the source of emulation), whom he represents in the community, collecting pious donations on behalf of the ayatollah and managing the community's religious affairs. He is also the source of stability in the fast-changing world of believers in a pluralistic environment.

See also IMAM; ISLAM; QU'RAN.

BIBLIOGRAPHY

Mallat, Chibli. *The Renewal of Islamic Law: Muhammad Baqer as-Sadr, Najaf and Shi'i International.* 1993.

Mottahedeh, Roy P. *The Mantle of the Prophet: Religion and Politics in Iran.* 1985.

Nafīsī, 'Alī Akbar. *Farhang-i Nafīsī.* 1343.

Sachedina, Abdulaziz A. *The Just Ruler in Shi'ite Islam: The Comprehensive Authority of the Jurist in Imamite Jurisprudence.* 1998.

Abdulaziz A. Sachedina

Music

American religious music has undergone an extraordinary transformation in the late twentieth century. Most of the major religious communities have made important changes in their music cultures since 1965. Virtually all of the mainline Protestant denominations have issued controversial new hymnals, while the Catholic church has endured the failure of an ambitious liturgical reform and then turned to traditional Protestant hymnody and new Pentecostal praise music to find effective songs for worship. American Jews have embraced the renewal of traditional synagogue music as well as a revival of Sephardic and klezmer musics. Native American nations have shared their music traditions with outsiders, while New Age movements have given music a central place in their beliefs and rituals. And while the number of religious works by major composers has continued a century-long decline, anthems for local choirs appear at unprecedented rates and concert hall performances of classical sacred works have never been more popular.

External forces have also shaped religious music, none more profoundly than its commodification and popularization through the mass-marketing of recordings and music videos. The multibillion-dollar gospel music industry offers the best illustration of how religious music has carved out its own commercial niche in American popular culture. This rapidly changing, market-driven quality is not new to American religious music. These processes of internal and external change are not new. A strong historical case can be made that American sacred music has constantly changed to meet the consumption patterns of the nation's unruly mass religious movements. These populist qualities have been especially prominent in the music culture of evangelicalism, America's largest Protestant movement since the eighteenth century.

While the development of American religious music since 1965 is precedented in important ways, it has also displayed important new patterns of growth and meaning, of which four are the most notable: denominational controversies over lyrical content and musical form in worship music, the renewal of music as a category of religious belief, the emergence of paraliturgical musics, and commodification with a concomittant blurring of sacred and secular musical styles. Taken together, these trends comprise a fair if not exhaustive picture of religious music in contemporary America.

Controversies About Worship Music

Most of the major liberal Protestant denominations have published new hymnals since the mid-1980s, including *The Hymnal, 1982* (Episcopal Church, 1985), *The United Methodist Hymnal* (1989), *The Presbyterian Hymnal* (Presbyterian Church U.S.A., 1990), *With One Voice* (Evangelical Lutheran Church in America, 1995), and *The New Century Hymnal* (United Church of Christ, 1995). Each of these hymnals has to some degree employed the principle of inclusive language in selecting and editing hymn texts. The inclusive language principle, a justice claim of liberation and feminist theology, mandates the removal of all expressions of gender, race, and class preference, as well as military metaphors, from the texts of scripture, liturgy, and sacred music.

Inclusive language has generated arguably the greatest explosion of new Protestant hymn and praise texts since World War I, some of it fine religious poetry indeed. While influential among theologians, poets, denominational leaders, and hymnal editors, however, inclusive language has proven controversial among the laity of even mainline denominations. Thousands successfully protested in 1986 when the editors of *The United Methodist Hymnal* proposed to exclude Sabine Baring-Gould's famous 1864 hymn "Onward, Christian Soldiers." *The New Century Hymnal*, which extended the inclusive language principle to the revision of the classic hymns of Anglo-American Protestantism, has provoked ongoing controversy in the United Church of Christ despite the denomination's pioneer endorsement of inclusivity in 1972. The other new hymnals have encountered similar resistance, suggesting that for liberal Protestants worship music may be the aspect of their religious culture most resistant to change. For at least a minority of this progressive theological and social vanguard, traditional hymns carry an irreducible element of historical identity and religious significance without which

The Mormon Tabernacle Choir and its conductor in Salt Lake City, Utah, ca. 1988. (Credit: CORBIS/ Phil Schermeister.)

they feel spiritually disoriented. On the other hand, denominational leaders, hymnal editors, and perhaps a majority of the laity see the new inclusive hymnody as the completion of a generation-long liberationist reform of the faith.

An analogous conflict between traditional and reforming ideas of worship music engulfed the American Catholic church in the aftermath of the Second Vatican Council (1962–1965). Vatican II produced the most comprehensive reform of Catholicism since the Council of Trent answered the Protestant Reformation in 1562–1563. Among its most important results was *Sancrosanctum Concilium,* the Constitution on the Sacred Liturgy (1963), an epic document that mandated vernacular translations of the mass and endorsed the inclusion of popular musical forms into worship. In the United States liturgical reform produced the folk mass, which featured unison hymns, responses, and guitar accompaniments composed in the style of the folk-music revival of the mid-1960s. Designed to attract youth to a renovated celebration of the Eucharist, the folk mass enjoyed initial success but quickly receded into anachronism as rock overwhelmed the folk revival in the popular musical taste of the 1970s. Many older Catholics, meanwhile, lamented the loss of the Latin Mass and resisted the folk mass and the imperatives of Vatican II's liturgical reform.

During the late 1970s and 1980s, the Charismatic Renewal, a massive resurgence of popular piety characterized by personal experience of the Holy Spirit, gripped the American Catholic church. The Charismatic Renewal inspired new praise songs, simple refrains musically related to the folk-mass style and popular folk-rock, and encouraged Catholic appropriation of evangelical Protestant and Pentecostal gospel hymns. Two popular hymn collections in the late 1980s marked the establishment of the new musical style. *Glory and Praise* (1987) brought the most widely used folksongs, praise songs, and Protestant hymns to urban and suburban parishes. The pilgrimage and praise songs of *Flor y Canto* (1989), the first major Spanish-language Catholic hymnal published in the United States, signaled the musical emergence of Hispanic-American Catholics among whose ranks the Charismatic Renewal had flourished with particular intensity. At the end of the twentieth century, Vatican II's imperative of liturgical music reform has been fulfilled in the American Catholic church, albeit in an unlikely way. Though hardly without conflict, the process of change has produced a distinctive, if not musically distinguished, body of singable and effective worship music written by and for American Catholics.

Music as a Category of Religious Belief and Practice

While music has always played an important role in the worship of the Christian West, its inherent power to move the human emotions and appetites has consistently been mistrusted by theologians. Other religious traditions understand sacred music quite differently. Several of these—including Greco-Roman, Hindu, Native American, and Wiccan—have enjoyed significant growth in late twentieth-century America. Elements from each of these traditions, moreover, have mingled together in the emergence of New Age spirituality, a wide and diffuse movement that has flourished on the east and west coasts during the 1980s and 1990s. The appearance of these non-Christian traditions has brought a wave of new speculation about the sacred powers of music and a new focus on the practice of chanting and toning.

Renewed beliefs about music's sacrality take many forms. Wiccans chant and howl to invoke the presence of the Earth Goddess; Native Americans sing and dance to unite with the ancestors and spirit beings. The most original contribution to American religious beliefs about music, however, has come from New Age spirituality in the form of three related assertions: that musical tone is an integral element of both the physical and spiritual worlds, that tone therefore can produce spiritual effects in the human body, and that when understood and used properly these effects can attune the human being to its most integrated, healthful, and spiritual state.

The first of these claims derives from the experiments of Greek philosopher Pythagoras (ca. 515–495 B.C.E.), who discovered that the tones of the musical scale can be produced from simple fractional proportions of a vibrating string. Pythagoras concluded that these mathematical ratios revealed the universe to be grounded in *harmonia,* the divine balance and proportion of being itself. Later Pythagoreans assigned specific emotional or spiritual qualities to different scales and chords. New Age thinkers reappropriated Pythagorean ideas and added new findings from acoustic, electromagnetic, light, and atomic theory to propose that the universe is constituted by mathematically ordered vibrations and that musical tone makes this cosmic order uniquely available to human beings.

New Age ideas about music's relation to the human soul and body come largely from a quite different source, the yogic traditions of Hinduism. The body is understood to contain seven spiritual centers associated with neural centers of the spinal chord and brain called *chakras.* These centers have specific powers which rise from the sexual at the base of the spine to the transcendental at the top of the skull. In yoga traditions like *kundalini,* meditation is combined with tone chanting to stimulate the *chakras* and release their spiritual potencies. At peak meditative moments, practitioners experience an integrating synthesis of these spiritual energies that produces enlightenment. These ancient Indic beliefs have provided New Age theorists with a model of body and soul that links music's cosmological and physical reality to the transformation of emotional and spiritual states.

From these appropriations of classical religions and contemporary science, New Age leaders prescribed the chanting of traditional sacred words or syllables and the toning of nontextual musical pitches as fundamental ritual practices for spiritual healing and enlightenment. Soon a rich variety of New Age listening, chant, and toning practices appeared, many of them theoretically grounded in a combination of Pythagorean and Hindu traditions. New Age artists including keyboardist Steve Halperin, pianist George Winston, saxophonist Paul Horn, and flutist Carlos Nakai gained great popularity during the 1980s with their recordings of New Age music characterized by slow melodic and harmonic movement and the employment of modal scales. By the late 1990s, New Age thinkers and artists had created an eclectic new theory of sacred sound, the basic premise of which is that by hearing or producing certain tones in a meditative state, the human body and soul can experience their proper balance and thereby gain physical health and spiritual integration into the cosmic harmony of being.

The Emergence of Paraliturgical Music

While there has been significant development of musical thought and practice in the major religious communities in the United States, the late twentieth century has been a time when sacred music has increasingly been composed and performed outside an explicitly liturgical context. One of the most prominent paraliturgical phenomena is the displacement of sacred music from the church to the concert hall, a process that began in Europe with the sacred oratorios of Handel and Haydn and the huge masses and choral seetings of Beethoven, Berlioz, Verdi, and Brahms. In the contemporary United States, Aaron Copland, Leonard Bernstein, John Adams, and others have composed successful large-scale settings of religious poetry, but their achievement pales before the immense recent popularity in the United States of the turn-of-the-century symphonies of the Austrian Gustav Mahler or the more recent 1976 *Symphony of Sorrowful Songs* by the Pole Henryk Górecki, massive late-Romantic or (Górecki) neo-Romantic works suffused with religious poetry and emotional spirituality. For many contemporary urban Americans, the concert hall has become the place where they hear their most meaningful religious music performed.

For even more Americans, the gospel concert has become the definitive paraliturgical setting. From its origins in the gospel hymns of the 1870s and gospel blues of the 1920s, gospel music has always been performed outside Sunday worship at revivals, song services, and choir and quartet competitions. But on the strength of a massive revival from 1974 through the 1980s, gospel music began to replace traditional hymnody as the sacred music of choice among millions of America's evangelicals and pentecostals. Some gospel music performers have become better known than television evangelists, and their concerts attract thousands to praise, pray, and testify to their faith. A good marker of gospel's recent growth is the annual Dove Awards ceremony sponsored since 1969 in Nashville by the Gospel Music Association. The first ceremony was a small local affair in which a dozen awards were presented. Thirty years later the Dove Awards take place at the immense new Grand Ole Opry auditorium, broadcasts live for three hours on the TNN cable television network, and presents accolades in more than fifty technical, production, and performance categories. Gospel music is the most popular form of religious music in contemporary America, and although it retains many evangelical beliefs and sentiments, it has become increasingly independent of traditional liturgical norms since the 1960s.

Further removed from formal liturgy is music written for secular contexts that holds religious meaning for hearers. Three examples illustrate this more peripheral form of paraliturgical music: jazz, Native American powwows, and the revival of klezmer and

Sephardic music among American Jews. Religious themes have played a persistent role in American jazz since its emergence around 1900. Duke Ellington's *Sacred Concert* (1934) and John Coltrane's *A Love Supreme* (1964) rank among the most noted jazz works with sacred themes, but countless jazz compositions have made musical or conceptual reference to religious beliefs and practices, especially to Christian, Islamic, and African traditions. Performed in the most secular of contexts, such jazz performances nonetheless convey powerful ideas of transcendence and sacred emotions to many listeners.

Powwows occupy an important paraliturgical locus for Native Americans. Distinguished from ceremonial rituals performed for the tribal community only, powwows are public social occasions for dancing, feasting, and games. Yet for powwow singers and dancers, their textually simple but melodically complex and rhythmically driving songs carry a powerful spiritual meaning best described by them as simply "being Indian." Since the early 1970s, powwows have taken on an important new dimension through the participation of many different nations at large—intertribal events including the Denver March Powwow, the Red Earth Powwow at Oklahoma City, and the Gathering of Nations Powwow at Albuquerque. On these occasions, singers and dancers compete and share their tribal cultures while a growing number of non-Indian Americans attend to engage in the spiritual and cultural traditions of Native America.

Since the Three Day War of 1967, American Jews have experienced a powerful renewal of paraliturgical musics from their historic diaspora, especially the communities dispersed by persecutions of the Sephardim in fifteenth-century Spain and of central European Ashkenazim in the Holocaust. During the 1970s, groups like Boston's Voice of the Turtle began performing folksongs and women's music collected from exiled Sephardic communities of the eastern Mediterranean, while other ensembles including Lev Liberman's band The Klezmorim and Hankus Netzsky's Kelzmer Conservatory Band created concerts from the traditional klezmer repertory of wedding, birthday, and Bar Mitzvah music from rural Ashkenazic villages of pre-Nazi and pre-Soviet Europe. Through their lyrics in Ladino and Yiddish and their Old World instrumentation, these musics powerfully evoke the everyday and celebrative worlds of medieval and early modern Judaism that have largely been lost to contemporary American Jews. At increasingly popular Sephardic and klezmer concerts, urban Jewish audiences during the 1980s and 1990s have experienced a potent identification with their Judaic heritage quite apart from the synagogue service.

Commodification and Stylistic Change

As religious music in contemporary America has moved beyond the confines of traditional liturgical form, it has encountered powerful external new influences from the secular music industry. Two of these influences, commodification and stylistic change, have had the greatest impact. Protestant hymnal and tune-book editors created a substantial music publishing enterprise during the nineteenth and early twentieth centuries, but the advent of radio, television, sound recordings, and music video has in recent decades transformed religious music into a multibillion-dollar performance and recording industry. The most fully developed sector of this industry is gospel music, whose production nexus at Nashville is indistinguishable from pop music centers in New York, Los Angeles, and Detroit. Gospel has in fact become a subset of the secular music business, with a Top Forty list and regular coverage presented alongside those for Pop, Rock, Hip-Hop, and Classical in *Billboard,* the industry's weekly journal. Commodification has also penetrated to the most basic level of religious music performance in America, rendering it as much a commercial activity as a sacred act. With the development of cheap techniques for producing audio compact discs, almost any sacred music ensemble or soloist, however humble, can provide recordings for their audiences, and a rapidly increasing number of them do.

The adoption of production and marketing methods from the secular music industry has perhaps inevitably led religious music to appropriate secular music styles. Gospel music again supplies the best illustration of this trend. For its first century, gospel music adhered to the stylistic limits of white gospel hymns and black gospel blues. During the 1950s and 1960s, African-American gospel artists led by Sam Cook and Aretha Franklin first successfully crossed over into the pop market, powerfully influencing the development of the rhythm and blues and soul styles. Since then the direction of musical influence has reversed, with virtually every new youth music style since the 1970s finding translation into gospel form. Gospel no longer connotes a single musical style; it simply means the use of lyrics which deliver some aspect of the evangelical message regardless of musical setting. Especially controversial has been the use of popular music styles associated with sex and violence, like heavy metal and rap, with gospel lyrics. Yet gospel performers in these styles, as well as rock, hip-hop, and world beat have enjoyed significant success. While the more traditional pop ballad style of Amy Grant and Steven Curtis Chapman continues to attract the largest audience, in the late twentieth century, gospel music and Christian music in general has become more stylistically diverse and more influenced by secular musical trends than at any time in American history.

See also CHAKRA; CHANTING; DANCE; ELVIS CULTS; IN-CLUSIVE LANGUAGE; LITURGY AND WORSHIP; NATIVE-AMERICAN RELIGIONS; NEW AGE SPIRITUALITY; REIKI; ROCK MASSES; SUN DANCE, VATICAN II; WICCA; YOGA.

BIBLIOGRAPHY

Dean, Talmadge. *A Survey of Twentieth Century Protestant Church Music in America.* 1988.

Gardner, Kay. *Sounding the Inner Landscape: Music as Medicine.* 1990.

Horse Pasture, George P. *Powwow.* 1989.

Joncas, Jan Michael. *From Sacred Song to Ritual Music: Twentieth-Century Understandings of Roman Catholic Worship Music.* 1997.

Marini, Stephen. *Sacred Song in America: Religion and Music at the Millennium.* 2000.

Slobin, Mark. *Subcultural Sounds: Micromusics of the West.* 1993.

Spencer, Jon Michael. *Protest and Praise: Sacred Music of Black Religion.* 1990.

Stephen Marini

Muslim Brotherhood

The Muslim Brotherhood, Al-Ikhwan al-Muslimum, was founded by Hasan al-Banna in 1928 in Egypt and quickly spread to surrounding Arab countries such as Syria, Sudan, Jordan, Kuwait, and countries in North Africa. It arose as one particular response to continued European imperialism and hegemony in Arab cultures. Al-Banna and his successors saw that influential Muslims adopted, then affirmed and promoted "Western" (i.e., secular) ideas over Islamic values as resources for confronting societal issues. The primary purpose was to return these Arab cultures to Islamic guidance. One could describe the Islamic Brotherhood as an Islamic cultural affirmation, a philosophical position, a social concept, and a political stance all rolled into one organization. Western societal foci on materialism, consumerism, and "individual autonomy without responsibility" were expeditiously labeled the core of Western values and what Muslim communities should avoid.

One early member and architect of the Muslim Brotherhood's philosophical stance was Sayyid Qutb (1906–1928). A portion of his text *Ma'alim fi al-tariq* (Signposts Along the Way) was circulated in the United States in the late 1960s as *Milestones.* This text alerted and engaged U.S. Muslims in a dialogue about the seductiveness of capitalism and consumerism/materialism. Muslims are to be discerning and moderate in their lifestyles, protecting themselves against *jahiliyyah* (the state of ignorance from the guidance of God).

Many Muslims interpreted the prescriptions of *Milestones* in their living to mean moderation in all things. Some Muslims interpreted the text literally and isolated themselves (as much as any American community could) from the larger society. The larger society is viewed as one with great potential, though lost in an ocean of arrogant ignorance. The general focus in many Muslim communities was and continues to be on perfecting their Islamic lives while in a jahili society. Communitywide adherence to the Islamic ideals, especially in a jahili society, has led Muslims to create their own financial institutions, for example. Muslim credit unions, investment corporations, leasing companies, and lending agencies follow Islamic injunctions against usury and are the preferred financial institutions among U.S. Muslims.

Negative American media on Islam and Muslims have served to further affirm, in the minds of individual Muslims and communities who follow the Muslim Brotherhood's precepts, that the West in general and America in particular are indeed in jahiliyyah. The Muslim Brotherhood's philosophical core has remained the same, though its manifestations in U.S. society have ebbed and flowed as America either focuses on or neglects its Muslims' existence. There is no distinct branch organization as such of the Muslim Brotherhood in the United States. The Muslim Brotherhood is alive in the minds and hearts of the majority of U.S. Muslims, though there is little interest among them in returning to the Muslim world, as it is seen to be steeped in a postcolonial maze.

See also BELONGING, RELIGIOUS; ISLAM; RELIGIOUS COMMUNITIES; SECULARIZATION; SPIRITUALITY.

BIBLIOGRAPHY

Mitchell, Richard P. *The Society of the Muslim Brothers.* 1969.

Aminah Beverly McCloud

Muslims.

See Black Muslims; Islam.

Muslim Students Association.

See Islamic Society of North America.

Mysticism

In an academic context, the term "mysticism" is generally understood as referring to a cluster of phenomena having to do with the unmediated contact with the divine or with the merging with an absolute understood in impersonal terms. In everyday usage, on the other hand, the term "mysticism" is associated with magic, with the occult, and in general with practices that seek to transcend the mundane realm—above all, the realm of ordinary, institutionalized religion. Even if the equation of the "mystical" and the "magical" may appear as inappropriate to some, including mystics, the history of religions provides enough examples of cases in which out-of-the-ordinary experiences are accompanied by supernatural, mysterious powers—indeed, it ought to be remembered that "mysticism" and "mystery" are etymologically related. In any event, neither in academic nor in nonacademic contexts is there an agreement as to the nature of the mystical. To begin with, one must consider the difficulties involved in trying to determine the meaning of terms such as "divine" or "absolute"—or, actually, one must confront the fact that such terms may be posited precisely because they defy definition. Furthermore, the claim that the mystics' experiences are not mediated by doctrine or ritual has been questioned by scholars since the early decades of this century. These scholars—besides pointing out that not many mystics have made such claims in the first place—have argued that, like everybody else, mystics function within a culture—that is, within a shared universe of meanings. This means that the religion within which mystics function or against which they react would necessarily mediate—that is, constrain or enable—the mystics' experiences. Against this position, some scholars of mysticism, referring to research in psychology and neurophysiology or to their own spiritual accomplishments, maintain that there are indeed experiences that transcend historical constraints. If research on mysticism is to go beyond sterile debates, scholars will have to take into account research in both the natural and social sciences—or, will have to stop assuming that the physical and the social sciences constitute self-contained domains.

A further problem with the concept of mysticism—one that will be especially relevant when discussing American developments—has to do with the difficulties one encounters when trying to differentiate mystical from other attempts to leave behind ordinary religiosity. In effect, it is not easy to distinguish attempts to transcend ordinary reality through mystical means from situations that involve messianic or millenarian ideologies. Even if one assumes that mysticism has to do mainly with achieving rarefied experiences, one can find examples of situations in which access to such experiences is achieved through the mediation of a spiritual guide—a guru or messiah. Similarly, mystical experiences can function as the catalyzers for millenarian movements—for cataclysmic events that are followed by a new era of peace and justice.

In the United States, interest in mystical approaches to religion can be traced back to Ralph Waldo Emerson (1803–1882), the New England Transcendentalist who was familiar with ancient Indian scriptures such as the Upanishads, as well as with Neoplatonism and with the teachings of the eighteenth-century Swedish visionary Emanuel Swedenborg. Then, at the beginning of the twentieth century, William James wrote one of the most influential accounts of mysticism, *Varieties of Religious Experience* (1902). Interest in mysticism and in Asian religions was reawakened during the Beat generation; one need only refer to Jack Kerouac's *On the Road* (1957) and *The Dharma Bums* (1958). During the 1960s, interest in mysticism has coincided with a distrust of institutional forms of religion, particularly when leaders of the main denominations have not assumed a critical attitude toward the government's activities. To these can be added occasional reports of visions or communications with Mary that repeat in an American context the European Catholic apparitions of Lourdes and Fatima.

One of the problems that students of mysticism share with scholars of the social sciences in general is the fact that a given social phenomenon can be said to have emerged as the result of diametrically opposed causes. Thus interest in noninstitutional forms of religion can be said to appear at times of relative peace and prosperity as a reaction against complacency and ossified religious practices, but also during periods of crisis when institutions have lost their prestige. An example of the first situation would be the post–World War II period when the Beat generation seemed to function as a reaction against the self-satisfaction of 1950s American culture. During the 1960s, on the other hand, the interest in Asian religions, in forms of noninstitutional religion, as well as in altered states of consciousness can be seen as a rejection of the technological and militaristic values of society, as well as of the passivity or outright complicity of religious leaders regarding the policies of the United States government in Southeast Asia. In both cases, some of those who rejected the socially accepted values engaged, like mystics in many traditions, in antinomian behavior, doing the reverse of what would be expected from ordinary people.

Among the groups that became popular during the 1960s and 1970s are the once ubiquitous Hare

Krishna, founded by Bhaktivedanta Swami Prabhupada. Although the psychological transformation induced by devotional yoga promoted by the International Society of Krishna Consciousness (ISKCON) can be traced back ultimately to the teachings of the sixteenth-century Indian mystic Caitanya, the movement was never popular in India, having been rather elicited by conditions in the United States. Indeed, the emphasis on transforming one's consciousness through mystical means, rather than by changing institutions through politics, was one of the avenues left to those who mistrusted American institutions. On the other hand, it would be worth exploring the parallels between the social conditions against which twentieth-century American devotees of Krishna Consciousness were reacting with those prevalent in northeastern India in the sixteenth century: on the one hand, youth alienation from a government engaged in aggression against Vietnam, and, on the other, Hindu protest against Muslim domination—in both cases, ecstatic devotion as a reaction against intolerable external conditions. Less ecstatic is the "gestalt consciousness" and the realization of Self sought by the adherents of the Human Potential Movement, popular during the 1960s and 1970s. In this movement, as in many others, one sees at work the still pervasive concern with therapeutic models and self-realization. Potentially deadly, on the other hand, are recent apocalyptic groups such as the Solar Temple, whose members committed suicide (or were murdered) seeking to transcend the human condition.

Interest in the mystical, intensified by the approach of the new millennium, may involve reading the many books found in the "metaphysical" section of most bookstores or harmless books such as James Redfield's *The Celestine Prophecy*, which takes place in a suitably mysterious Peru and is popular among college students. More pretentious, if equally harmless, are the many writings of "continental" authors, popular among academics of the postmodern persuasion—"continental" being for some academics at the turn of the millennium what "Oriental" used to be for 1960s dropouts. What deconstruction and postmodernism have in common with traditional forms of mysticism is the mistrust of reason as well as the concern with the relationship between identity and difference. However, traditional mystical teachings tend to emphasize identity and oneness, but postmodernism/deconstruction celebrates otherness and difference.

One should not conclude from the previous cases of mystical religion that mystical practices always take place outside the framework of mainstream religion. The ambiguity of mysticism becomes clear when one sees that intense experiences are sought and achieved in Protestant Pentecostal churches as much as in the Catholic Charismatic Renewal. In these cases, trance, possession, speaking in tongues, and the like, take place in a ritualized context—just as mystical experiences have tended to occur in all cultures. Similarly, academic celebrations of otherness and difference do take place within the safe confines of academia.

Despite the apparent clash between mystical goals and the values of a consumer society, in its current American form the mystical quest fits very well with the prevailing American ideology. In effect, the rejection of external constraints on one's behavior, the lack of interest in doctrinal issues, the abandonment of the unpleasant aspect of religion (for example, Americans' tendency to believe in heaven but not in hell), the concern with the self and with self-cultivation—in short, the desire for a religion designed by and for oneself, rather than one inherited by tradition—all go hand in hand with an individualist ideology in which the consumer, faced with an unlimited supply of inexpensive goods, is always right. It should be pointed out, however, that the fact that many contemporary Americans engage in mystical practices in order to improve their psychological and physical health, as well as their general well-being, should not be construed as the betrayal of a presumed essence of mysticism, for in many traditions mystical practices are intimately connected with the control of one's mind and of one's body—meditation has been an important component of most of the religions that have emerged in India, and in the Taoist tradition the goal is to attain immortality in one's own body.

Perhaps more telling than specific cases of interest in mystical teachings or membership in esoteric groups is Americans' desire for "experiencing," as opposed to just knowing about something in a detached way. This is shown by the frequency with which precisely the word "experience" is used in everyday American speech—for example in expressions as mundane as "dining experience" or "shopping experience." The fact that these expressions are promoted in the context of carefully orchestrated sales pitches does not prove that the thirst for experiencing is artificially induced—it shows rather that advertisers and purveyors of popular culture are quite aware of the pulse of American culture. We may conclude by noting that the peculiar tension between the search for experience and the concern with the self, on the one hand, and the prevalence of calculation and desire for economic advancement, on the other, is one of the central characteristics of modernity. In that sense, then, the current understanding of mysticism as that which transcends ordinary religion and ordinary experience appears as the perhaps necessary, modern counterpart of the rationalized world that emerged in the seventeenth century.

See also CATHOLIC CHARISMATIC RENEWAL; ENLIGHT-ENMENT; GURU; HUMAN POTENTIAL MOVEMENT; IN-TERNATIONAL SOCIETY FOR KRISHNA CONSCIOUSNESS; MAGIC; MEDITATION; NEW AGE SPIRITUALITY; OC-CULT; PENTECOSTAL AND CHARISMATIC CHRISTIAN-ITY; PSYCHOLOGY OF RELIGION; RELIGIOUS EXPERI-ENCE; RITUAL; SOLAR TEMPLE; SPIRIT GUIDE; SPIRIT POSSESSION; SPIRITUALITY; TRANCE; UPANISHADS; YOGA.

BIBLIOGRAPHY

Benavides, Gustavo. "Modernity." In *Critical Terms for Religious Studies*, edited by Mark C. Taylor. 1998.

Glock, Charles Y., and Robert N. Bellah, eds., *The New Religious Consciousness*. 1976.

Katz, Steven T., ed. *Mysticism and Philosophical Analysis*. 1978.

Robbins, Thomas, and Susan J. Palmer, eds. *Millennium, Messiahs, and Mayhem: Contemporary Apocalyptic Movements*. 1997.

Roof, Wade Clark. *Spiritual Marketplace: Baby Boomers and the Remaking of American Religion*. 1999.

Staal, Frits. *Exploring Mysticism: A Methodological Essay*. 1975.

Wuthnow, Robert. *After Heaven: Spirituality in America since the 1950s*. 1998.

Gustavo Benavides

Myth

Myths have attracted a great deal of interest among Americans since the 1960s. While many aspects of them may be fictive, myths often convey truths that stir people and compel their assent. Myths also command respect because of the close association they often have to religious rituals and other sacred events.

Myths vary from one culture to another and reflect the worldviews of particular peoples. But these worldviews and the myths representing them often contain overlapping and coinciding themes that reflect more universal dimensions of human experience. For this reason, the myths of any particular culture may have wide appeal and, as in the case of Greek myths, long outlast the society that produced them.

Three basic approaches to the interpretation of myths have developed in Western thought. Since the 1960s, each of these approaches has been pursued in creative and influential ways.

Rationalist Approaches to Myth

Many scholars have tried to explain how myths come into being and how they work in the human mind. The ancient Greek philosophers understood myths as stories that provided inexact pictures of reality. Heraclitus criticized the accounts of historical events written by Hesiod and Homer for relying too much on myth. Plato resorted to myth to avoid direct answers to controversial philosophical questions. Euhemereus argued that myths embellished and elevated stories about the exploits of human beings by depicting the humans as gods.

Beginning in the seventeenth century, Enlightenment scholars bent on discovering the rational nature of the world revitalized the ancient view that myth was an inexact form of expression inferior to pure philosophy or true history. This rationalist approach found its most famous expression in the *Comparative Mythology* (1865) authored by Friedrich Max Müller, a German linguist who lived and worked in Britain. On the basis of comparative analysis of Indo-European and Greco-Roman mythology, Müller argued that myths were allegories about nature. Myths sacralized natural phenomena, Müller believed, and typically focused on the sun and things related to the sun, such as sky and dawn.

Since the 1960s, when more appreciative approaches to the process of mythmaking became widely known and popular in the United States, the rational approach to myth exemplified by Müller has been harshly criticized. At the same time, there have been notable efforts to pursue the idea that myths represent things that actually happened. For example, in *The Short Swift Time of Gods on Earth* (1994), Donald Bahr argued that myths represent memories of important events in the distant past and, more specifically, that the origin myths of the Pima Indians of southwestern North America provide important clues about the more ancient Hohokam culture and its destruction.

Many Jews and Christians in the United States approach biblical narratives in much the same way, as important accounts of events actually occurring in the past, but accounts that are inexact as a result of embellishments that occurred in the telling or corruptions that crept in over time. After World War II, the German scholar Rudolph Bultmann prompted many Americans to "demythologize" the New Testament to separate out and lift up the essence of Jesus's teachings. In a recent variant of this approach, Elizabeth Schussler Fiorenza argued that the distinctive thrust of Jesus's life and message was his compassion for women and commitment to their equality. According to this analysis, later editors and interpreters of the gospel injected their patriarchal bias into the New Testament and corrupted its original, feminist message.

Of course, biblical literalists reject the whole enterprise of demythologization as well as use of the word "myth" to describe any part of the Bible. Nevertheless, their insistence on the historical and scientific exactitude of biblical narratives also reflects rationalist expectations of reality associated with an Enlightenment worldview.

Functionalist Approaches to Myth

A second, functionalist approach to myth is utilized by many social scientists, especially sociologists. This approach focuses on the role that myth plays in reinforcing social status, class and group difference, and other forms of social structure, convention, behavior. This approach can be traced to the work of the French founder of sociology, Émile Durkheim, whose *Elementary Forms of Religious Life* (1965; original French, 1912) viewed myths as explanations of rituals that maintained social cohesion in primitive societies. In Durkheim's view, the structure of religious rituals reflected and reinforced the structure of society. Moreover, people who gathered together for ritual events experienced an exhilarating awareness of the existence and power of their society. The myths that grew up around these rituals led people to conceptualize the existence and power of their society as God. As an idealization of society, God existed only in the minds of individuals. But as an entity much larger and stronger than anyone, God commanded religious devotion.

In American culture since the 1960s, social scientists have often utilized the general concept behind Durkheim's theory—namely, that myth is an idealized manifestation of social structure that explains, justifies, and reinforces that structure. Because this approach focuses on the socially conservative function of myth, liberal sociologists often emphasize the need to break through myths that perpetuate social inequality. At the same time, sociologists such as Robert Bellah and Peter Berger, who favor a return to the more cohesive kind of society that they believe was characteristic of the United States before the 1960s, regret the weakening of myths that once inculcated social cohesion and responsibility.

Transcendental Approaches to Myth

A third, transcendental approach sees myth as an expression of the very nature of human experience and essential to both personal and cultural development. This transcendental (or intersubjective) approach has become very popular in the United States since the 1960s, especially among people who conceptualize myth in terms of a larger interest in spirituality. The transcendental approach grows out of the work of the eighteenth-century German philosopher Immanuel Kant, and especially out of his emphasis on the constructive nature of the mind and the mind's inability to know anything outside or independent of itself. Transcendental approaches to myth are also indebted to the nineteenth-century German idealist Friedrich von Schelling, who went beyond Kant to define myth as an imaginative effort to describe the Absolute, the larger reality beyond the grasp of reason. This romantic, post-Kantian approach led to subsequent efforts to analyze myth as one of the essential phenomena (or nonempirical categories) characteristic of human experience of the sacred. It also invited psychological interpretations in which myth represented deep-seated human fears and desires. Especially through the phenomenological theories of Mircea Eliade and the psychological theories of Carl Gustav Jung and Joseph Campbell, this transcendental approach to myth has profoundly influenced American religious thought since the 1960s.

In the view of the Romanian scholar Mircea Eliade, who taught at the University of Chicago from 1956 until his death in 1986, myth and history were opposite and antagonistic ways of understanding reality. While history represented a chronological sequencing of more or less distinct events, myth represented the underlying dynamics of human experience that human events always recapitulated. In a mythic view of the world, nothing was ever really new. Moreover, the stories told about the persisting dynamics of life were deeply tied to experiences of the sacred. Inspired by Rudolph Otto's *The Idea of the Holy* (1923; original German, 1917), Eliade believed that the sacred was awesome, subjective apprehension of the larger reality beyond human reason. The sacred was also a collectively shared experience, he believed, involving a transconscious plane of awareness that was part of the universal human capacity for nonrational experience.

After developing his phenomenology of the sacred through studies of Yoga and shamanism, Eliade went on to compare the role of myth in primitive societies with what he regarded as the decadent but still persisting role of myth in modern society. While primitive people were intrinsically religious by virtue of being centered and saturated in mythic reality, Eliade believed, modern people found themselves adrift in the flux of time. But the terrible sense of meaninglessness that modern people suffered could be remedied by imaginative experiences that awoke the transconscious and stimulated the archaic capacity for sacred, mythic experience.

Eliade's concept of myth exerted a shaping influence on the field of religious studies in the United States during the 1960s and 1970s. As the field expanded rapidly during these years and established its independence from divinity school curricula and their predilection toward Christian thought, Eliade's theories offered a way to conceptualize religion as a universal phenomenon. Applying his phenomenology to a variety of different cultures, scholars not only produced new, interpretive accounts of various religions around the world but also argued for the existence of religious dimensions within various forms of popular American culture.

Eliade's theories were greeted with enthusiasm by many scholars in religious studies not only because they were applicable in many different contexts but also because they avoided bias toward Christianity, which the field was, in general, trying to overcome. Indeed, Eliade even blamed the Judeo-Christian tradition for originating the preoccupation with historical time that interfered with the immersion in myth that archaic people enjoyed. This anti–Judeo-Christian bias intrinsic to Eliade's work suited the countercultural sentiments prevalent among many academics during the 1960s and 1970s.

During the same decades, and for some of the same reasons, the psychological theories of the Swiss psychoanalyst Carl Gustav Jung and the American mythographer Joseph Campbell became popular among an even wider American audience. A student of Sigmund Freud's, Jung came to disagree with Freud's view of religion as a form of illusion. Utilizing a transcendental approach similar to that of Eliade's, Jung argued for the existence of a collective unconscious, a realm of the mind common to all humanity that provided the underlying dynamic structure for the ordinary consciousness of each individual. Jung understood the collective unconscious to be populated by archetypes that surfaced within individual consciousness, most clearly in dreams, but also in waking consciousness through the expectations that the individual bestowed on people encountered in daily life. Myths were of paramount importance to Jung because he believed that they represented the archetypes of the collective unconscious in vivid and compelling forms.

This Jungian approach to myth stimulated a great deal of personalized, spiritual interest. Because of the connection believed to exist between the individual psyche and the myths of all the world's religions, many Americans interested in exploring the depths of their own psyches were inspired by Jungian psychology to look to the myths of various cultures for inspiration.

This eclectic but highly personalized interest in myth contributed, in turn, to the strong interest in spirituality that began to sweep through many areas of American religious life in the 1970s. The Jungian approach to myth helped to fuel the tendency to distinguish spirituality, often perceived in terms of deep personal engagement, from religion, often perceived less positively in terms of institutional organizations and impersonal rules.

Similar to Jung's in many respects, Joseph Campbell's approach to myth played an even greater role in shaping American religious life after World War II. As a young man, Campbell renounced the Catholic Church for its repression of mythic play. A professor of literature at Sarah Lawrence College for thirty-eight years, and a national celebrity at the time of his death in 1989, Campbell had a lifelong fascination with Native American myths and Arthurian romance. Building on Jung's theory of the collective unconscious and its archetypes, and also on the German psychologist Eduard Spranger's emphasis on the importance for myth in adolescent development, Campbell argued for the supreme importance of the myth of the hero's journey in both individual and cultural life. Although the hero had many faces and the journey took many forms, Campbell believed that all these variants resonated with one another as particular expressions of a monomyth that was universal and fundamental to the human psyche. Campbell's theory of the hero's journey contributed not only to the burgeoning interest in spirituality among Americans after the 1960s but also to renewed interest in Christian mythology, especially among Catholics, more than a few of whom returned to the church with a new appreciation of Christ inspired by Campbell's concept of the hero's journey. Campbell's approach to myth also influenced George Lucas, the creator of the *Star Wars* film series, who based his ideas for *Star Wars* on Campbell's book *The Hero with a Thousand Faces* (1949).

See also ANTHROPOLOGY OF RELIGION; CAMPBELL, JOSEPH; ELIADE, MIRCEA; PSYCHOLOGY OF RELIGION; RELIGIOUS STUDIES; RITUAL; SOCIOLOGY OF RELIGION.

BIBLIOGRAPHY

Bellah, Robert. *The Broken Covenant: American Civil Religion in Time of Trial.* 1975.

Berger, Peter. *The Sacred Canopy: Elements of a Sociological Theory of Religion.* 1967.

Bultmann, Rudolph, et al. *Kerygma and Myth,* edited by Hans Werner Bartsch. 1953; orig. in German, 1948.

Dundes, Alan, ed. *Sacred Narrative: Readings in the Theory of Myth.* 1984.

Eliade, Mircea. *Myth and Reality,* translated by Willard R. Trask. 1963.

Fiorenza, Elizabeth Schussler. *In Memory of Her: A Feminist Theological Reconstruction of Christian Origins.* 1986.

Jung, Carl Gustav, and Clark Kerenyi. *Essays on a Science of Mythology,* rev. ed. 1963; orig. in German, 1949.

Moyers, Bill, with Joseph Campbell. *The Power of Myth.* 1988.

Amanda Porterfield

N

Names and Naming

In 1492, on the eve of the voyages to what would eventually be named the Americas, both the order of time (cosmogony) and that of the world were understood within European Christendom to have been spoken into being by God. As Europe's awareness of landmasses and peoples unaccounted for in either the Bible or classical sources slowly grew, the late medieval church was increasingly unable to claim absolute knowledge of the sacred origins of creation and the human race. The godlike task of renaming the world—or what Edmundo O'Gorman has called the "invention of America"—represented more than a transition from a Christian worldview to what would emerge as the Enlightenment. America was the first world whose order was understood to issue not from the mouth of God or the gods, but from human names and naming. The New World came to reflect a new understanding of time as created by human agency as "history" and of the material world as something to be shaped through the human imagination.

The emerging European worldview centered around a basic naming of itself as "civilization" and of other peoples as "savages." This discourse sought to give an account of the origins of and relationships among the peoples of the transatlantic world and to legitimate Europe's ideological and political subjugation of Africans and Amerindians. The non-European "other," precluded from defining the world, was expected to accept both European names and methods of naming. The historian of religion Charles H. Long has suggested it was not until the civil rights move-

ment of the 1960s that Euroamericans became fully aware of the ethnocentric dimensions of their historical narratives and the devastating sociopolitical implications of its significations for non-Euroamerican peoples.

The growth of ethnic studies programs in American academics since the 1960s has not only fostered reforms within the inherited structure and meaning of America, but has also served to bring its own significations of self and world into discussions of American identity. This development has been tantamount to a "reinvention of America," a return to the problematic question of how the New World should be understood, structured, and named. One response, epitomized in the title and content of Rudolph Acuña's *Occupied America* (1988), has been to emphasize the dynamics of colonization in the New World. This model—reflected in such American social developments as the Chicano movement (1965–1975), the Nation of Islam, and some Native American revitalization movements—advocates cultural and political resistance on the part of non-European cultures by renaming the New World in and through categories taken from non-European and/or precontact worldviews.

Another response, reflected in the works of such writers as Charles H. Long, the Chicana writer Gloria Anzaldua, and the Navajo novelist Leslie Marmon Silko, highlights the cultural exchanges in the New World context. While presupposing the dynamics of colonization, this model also seeks to emphasize the cultural "newness" of the Americas. Although intended primarily as a new name for Chicano/Chicana identity, Anzaldua's concept of "borderlands"—a variant of the Latin American idea *mestizaje,* or cultural "mixture"—contains profound implications of how the Americas, both North and South, might be re-imagined as a truly new world culture. A third conceptualization of American origins is to accept the central assumptions of Euroamerican identity and to work within them to effect greater inclusivity. This strategy was reflected by many of the pioneering leaders of the civil rights movement themselves, such as Martin Luther King, Jr., and Cesar Chávez, who struggled to extend the rights of life, liberty, and the pursuit of happiness to all Americans.

Other challenges to Eurocentric naming strategies are reflected in a current resurgence of conservative religious movements contesting Enlightenment explanations of human origins and purpose. These movements include the growth of the religious right beginning in the 1980s and the growth through the 1980s and 1990s of evangelical and pentecostal Protestantism, neotraditionalist trends in American Catholicism supported by Pope John Paul II, and the renewed emphasis on ritual in American Judaism. Especially since the nineteenth-century challenges to the divine authorship of the Bible, American religions not conforming substantially to Englightenment premises of historicity and human agency have suffered a fate similar to the naming practices of the "savage" peoples. Their resurgence at the end of the millennium clearly reflects the radical challenges to Enlightenment authority accelerated since the 1960s. It should be noted too that religions both within and outside of the Judeo-Christian tradition provided alternative naming strategies for those Americans at the social margins long before the discourses of ethnic studies, and continue to fulfill this function today—resignifying savages as persons created in a divine image.

While the Enlightenment worldview grew in influence, Europeans came also to rename the material world—signified in the Bible as God's creation—as nature. In America the seventeenth-century Puritan naming of the "wilderness" as a place of covenant between God and God's purportedly elect New England society gradually gave way by the eighteenth century to other Euroamerican conceptions of nature as a wilderness in need of taming. Euroamericans both continued and modified biblical sanctions of man's "dominion" of the Earth outlined in Genesis. Retaining the ideal of a hierarchical relationship between humans and the physical world, the American cosmology replaced the biblical ideal of dominion as stewardship or caretaking on God's behalf with the ideal of rational control of nature through mastery and application of scientific laws observable by human beings.

With the rise of industrial capitalism in America starting in the 1820s, this ideal came to be reflected in the notion of "progress," which brought together the ideals of civilizing and Christianizing "savages" and extending industrial capitalism across the continent in the name of Manifest Destiny.

Attempts since the 1960s to rename nature as something other than the "wilderness" thus parallel attempts to rename non-European culture as something other than savagery. From within the Euroamerican tradition, the New Age movement continues to advance what Martin Marty called a "harmonial" ethos advocating a reciprocal relationship between nature and American society. An integral part of American thought since the Transcendentalist writings of Ralph Waldo Emerson (1803–1882), harmonial thought ultimately originated in Puritan ideas of the wilderness as a place of divine revelation and human spiritual transformation. Other attempts to redress both individual and societal estrangement from the physical world have arisen in such Judeo-Christian movements as the Creation Theology of Matthew Fox, an excommunicated Catholic priest. Attempts to interpret the Bible from ecological perspectives interpret "dominion" in the context of other scriptural ideals of social and economic justice, and/or read Genesis independently of Greek spirit/matter dualism entering into the Christian canon through the letters of Paul. Finally, resignifications of Euroamerican cosmology emerge from within many conversations in ethnic and gender studies. While non-European traditions can obviously bypass Western cosmologies, ecofeminism engages in a renaming of the Western tradition itself. Writers like Rosemary Radford Ruether and Mary Daly, citing the origins of the human/nature dichotomy in the rise of early urban, patriarchal societies of the ancient Mediterranean and Near Eastern worlds, seek to salvage a "usable past" by which the West can rename itself.

As the world makes its transition into a new millennium, the task of renaming the Americas is made particularly urgent by a number of impending and daunting problems: environmental crises seemingly reflective of the West's estrangement from the physical world and continuing disparities and tensions between Euroamerican and non-Euroamerican peoples. The only explicit consensus among divergent attempts to resignify the Americas is that the old cosmologies and narratives are of questionable political or environmental use. Postmodern critiques of American identity tend to resuscitate premodern understandings of the potency of names and naming. An implicit understanding among critical American thinkers and leaders is that the future of their country, if not the world, depends very much on the way that people name and order it—either in light of pragmatic ends and objectives or in the name of a more-than-human authority.

See also CIVIL RIGHTS MOVEMENT; CREATION SPIRITUALITY; KING, MARTIN LUTHER, JR.; NATURE RELIGION; NEW AGE SPIRITUALITY.

BIBLIOGRAPHY

Foucault, Michel. *The Order of Things: An Archaeology of the Human Sciences.* 1970.

Gunn, Giles. *New World Metaphysics: Readings on the Religious Meaning of the American Experience.* 1981.

Long, Charles H. *Significations: Signs, Symbols, and Images in the Interpretation of Religions.* 1986.

McGrane, Bernard. *Beyond Anthropology: Society and the Other.* 1989.

Nash, Roderick. *Wilderness and the American Mind.* 1982.

O'Gorman, Edmundo. *The Invention of America: An Inquiry into the Historical Nature of the New World and the Meaning of Its History.* 1969.

Darryl V. Caterine

National Council of the Churches of Christ in the U.S.A.

Both the Evangelical Alliance (1867) and the Federal Council of Churches (1908) were forerunners of a new ecumenical entity, the National Council of the Churches of Christ in the U.S.A. (NCCCUSA), whose founding meeting was held in Cleveland in 1950. Initially composed of twenty-nine denominations and twelve interdenominational boards and agencies, NCCCUSA membership currently consists of thirty-four Protestant and Orthodox denominations, or communions. Some fifty-two million Christians are represented through these Trinitarian-based communions "in common mission, serving in all creation to the glory of God," as the preamble to its constitution states.

The NCCCUSA has metamorphosed throughout its almost fifty years of existence. At present it has two major units—one a gathering of many domestic programs in National Ministries; the other, Church World Service and Witness. There is also a General Secretariat, and an advocacy office, in Washington, D.C. Five commissions complete the structure: the Faith and Order Commission, the Interfaith Relations Commission, the Communication Commission, Ecumenical Networks, and an Inclusiveness and Justice Commission.

Among the many programs of National Ministries are Christian education, various justice and urban ministries, and church leadership support programs. The NCCCUSA is known globally for its Bible translation, the New Revised Standard Version, endorsed by Roman Catholics, Orthodox, and most Protestants. The Council's Friendship Press emphasizes mission studies and world issues. Currently NCCCUSA is the conduit and administrator of religious-based youth volunteer programs sponsored through U.S. AmeriCorps funding.

Church World Service and Witness has a long-standing history of aid programs that work not only with disaster relief and refugee resettlement but also with policy advocacy, community development projects, education, and leadership training. It is active among nongovernmental organizations at the United Nations regarding such matters as peace, banning land mines, and ending child prostitution in Asia. It also nurtures a global network of English-speaking congregations of citizens away from their home countries.

The NCCCUSA's General Assembly, composed of 270 delegates from the member communions, meets annually to set policy, adopt budgets, explore common issues, and model and celebrate Christian unity. Its officers and 60-member Executive Board meet three times a year and maintain oversight of the program activities of the council. Council membership includes eight Orthodox churches, five predominantly African-American Protestant communions, several "peace" churches, and "mainline" Protestant communions, among assorted others not readily categorized. The most recent addition is the Mar Thoma Syrian Church of India, received into membership in 1997. Although the Roman Catholic Church declines membership, it cooperates in many areas of the council's work. Numerous Protestant bodies considered fundamentalist or socially conservative evangelical do not participate in many council programs and are not members. Membership in both the NCCCUSA and the World Council of Churches is through member communions, not regional or national councils.

The headquarters of the NCCCUSA is at 475 Riverside Drive, New York, NY 10115.

See also WORLD COUNCIL OF CHURCHES.

BIBLIOGRAPHY

Cully, Iris V., and Kendig Brubaker Cully. *Harper's Encyclopedia of Religious Education*, pp. 445–447. 1990.

National Council of the Churches of Christ in the U.S.A. *One Body, One Spirit.* 1995.

Reid, Daniel G., ed. *Dictionary of Christianity in America,* pp. 798–799. 1990.

Peggy L. Shriver

Nation of Islam

According to accounts of the origins of the Nation of Islam (NOI), in the 1930s in "Paradise Valley" in Detroit, a silk peddler named W. D. Fard began to explain to small groups of Americans of African descent their history.

The Nation of Islam emerged on the American scene in 1931—the Depression years, at the time of the demise of the Garvey Movement and of the inaction of the black church. It arose in an era when the number of Ku Klux Klan members was increasing, immigrants were competing for jobs, and segregation was the social order. Even though it was known for political ideology and rhetoric against white racism, the NOI laid a firm religious foundation. Elijah Muhammad, the inheritor of the nascent movement of W. D. Fard, wanted to lift the "so-called Negro" out

of the deteriorating social circumstances that segregation and the absence of jobs were creating. Using both the Bible and the Qur'an as sources, he wove a cosmology that included themes such as the union of God and humanity—God in man (black); the notion that thought transcends both time and space; heaven and hell as being on Earth; and a final judgment. The original homeland was Mecca, Arabia, not Africa; and above all, God's name was Allah.

The goal of reconstruction was achieved, but the Nation of Islam was very much aware of "mainstream" Islam in the United States in the 1930s and 1940s, and of its emphasis on the Arab or Indian worlds, with the result that mainstream Islam demonstrated little interest in the problems of Americans of African descent. The central focus of the NOI was to reorient the spiritual vision of the black community away from peace in the hereafter to an understanding of God's favor and support for justice in the here and now, and to promote a united front of black men.

The "Ten-Point Program" underscored the difficulties of the black community in its emphasis on justice and equality for the "so-called Negro." Sustaining

Members of the Nation of Islam march in protest and affirmation in Washington, D.C., on Monday, October 16, 1995. In the background is the Washington Monument.   (Credit: AP/Wide World Photos.)

Followers of the Nation of Islam attending an annual Savior's Day Convention at the University of Illinois-Chicago Pavillion on Sunday, February 23, 1997.   (Credit: AP/Wide World Photos.)

this program is a belief system that has twelve "testimonies" in which mainstream Islamic beliefs are expanded to focus on the plight of Americans of African descent. These include belief that judgment will first take place in the United States; belief that Muslims should not participate in wars; belief that black women should be protected and respected as other women are; and belief that Allah (God) appeared in the person of W. D. Fard in July 1930.

The Nation of Islam, under the guidance of Elijah Muhammad, used this belief system to encourage its followers to abandon their slave surnames, pool their resources, make neighborhoods safe, build factories, purchase and run farms, and, in effect, build an economic system. Knowledge of self (black people's history), Arabic, math, science, and English formed the core of the NOI educational system. Without self-discipline, however, the economic and education systems would have no foundation.

Self-discipline plus abstinence from alcohol and drugs, a strict dietary regimen of one meal daily, and cooperative buying led the NOI into prosperity. Modest dress and behavior and sex segregation coupled with self-reliance and a sense of mutual responsibility formed the moral pillars of the community. The community kept itself from the mass consumerism and debt of Christmas by fasting from sunrise to sunset during the month of December. The apparent success of this regimen of self-help, austerity, and commitment was seen in the NOI's rapid expansion.

By the 1960s it was clear that the only written reference to a black theology on the American scene was the one articulated by the Nation of Islam. Also by the 1960s, the FBI's campaign to destroy the NOI surpassed the intensity of its surveillance of any other single group in the United States. The Nation of Islam won the hearts and total commitment of many, including Malcolm X, Muhammad Ali, and Louis Farrakhan. It also won the total commitment of J. Edgar Hoover and his FBI to its surveillance. The fiery rhetoric of Malcolm X and the apparent unwillingness of the government to cease police brutality against the nonviolent civil rights movement brought even more Americans of African descent into the NOI. The year 1963 saw the assassination of Malcolm X and internal strife, and the position of national spokesman for the NOI went to Louis X, later to be known as Louis Farrakhan.

Elijah Muhammad died on February 25, 1975, at the age of seventy-seven, leaving behind him a wealthy organization with national recognition. His son Wallace Muhammad became the elected leader of the NOI. Wallace Muhammad immediately began what was almost a complete dismantling of the philosophies and beliefs of the NOI that did not comport with mainstream Islam. Three years later the NOI had a new name, the World Community of Islam in the West. This symbol of a decisive new direction for the NOI caused the departure of its national spokesman, Louis Farrakhan, who launched what is now the largest of the splinter groups from the World Community of Islam in the West; he named it the Nation of Islam in 1979. Presenting a strong challenge to the black church, Farrakhan revived the theme of black unity by espousing the mainstream Muslim understandings of Islam, Christianity, and Judaism "as more or less expressions of the One True Faith." On June 13, 1993, a Christian pastor delivered the keynote address at Mosque Maryam for the first time. Despite his reputation in the Jewish community as an anti-Semite and his refusal to tame his rhetoric on the alleged misdeeds of that community, Farrakhan gave a musical performance for a Jewish audience in 1993. The Million Man March to Washington, in part sponsored by the NOI, was one outcome of the attempts of leaders of many black communities toward black unity.

The Nation of Islam at this time is working on several fronts. It has moved decisively into the political arena, not choosing sides but educating black voters and getting out the vote. It is also moving, cautiously, to engage mainstream Islam on its own terms. Women are now ministers, with some degree of support. The NOI is also involved in a number of interreligious dialogues and in rebuilding its economic bases.

See also AFRICAN-AMERICAN RELIGIONS; CIVIL RIGHTS MOVEMENT; FARD, W. D.; FARRAKHAN, LOUIS; MALCOLM X; MUHAMMAD, ELIJAH KARRIEM.

BIBLIOGRAPHY

Lincoln, C. Eric. *The Black Muslims of America,* 3rd ed. 1994.

McCloud, Aminah Beverly. *African American Islam.* 1995.

Muhammad, Elijah. *Message to the Blackman.* 1965.

Turner, Richard. *Islam in the African American Experience.* 1997.

Aminah Beverly McCloud

Native American Church

The Native American Church of North America (NAC) is a religious organization whose aim is to strengthen and protect the practice of peyote religion among Native Americans. Members seek health, guidance, wisdom, and good relations through a sacramental practice centered on peyote, a small, spineless cactus native to north-central Mexico and southernmost Texas. They pray to Grandfather Peyote, whom they also call "our Medicine" and "our sacrament," but many also pray to Jesus and consider their religion a form of Christianity. Many believe that peyote contains God's revelation in plant form, just as Jesus contained it in human form.

A peyote meeting can be called by individuals or families out of gratitude or need. Traditionally a tepee is erected for the meeting, at a secluded, pleasant site. As important as the meeting itself is the care with which the preparations are made, including the fashioning of fan, staff, water drum, and other implements used. Peyote meetings are led by a roadman, who is recognized for his knowledge and maturity but is not paid. Persons in several other roles assist. The meeting lasts from evening until morning. Essentially it consists of traditional songs accompanied with a water drum, alternating with individual prayers. Peyote music has a distinctive rhythm and style, with a fast drumbeat and a falling melody line. As the songs and prayers continue through the night, several times peyote buttons or peyote tea is passed around and consumed.

At dawn a woman known as Water Woman, who represents Peyote Woman, who originally brought peyote to the people, brings in a pail of water. Songs and prayers over this water mark the conclusion of the ceremony, after which the participants adjourn for a morning feast. This is a bare outline of the basic ceremony, several variations of which exist. They fall into three main classifications, known as the Big Moon, Half Moon, and Cross Fire versions. The extent to which and the manner in which Christian elements are incorporated in the ceremony are one distinguishing characteristic.

Controversy has plagued peyote religion because of the plant's mild psychoactive qualities. Peyote is sometimes sought as a hallucinogenic recreational drug, although obtaining and using it as such are illegal in the United States. Native American Church members describe their experience in far different terms. The primary benefits they report include general health and vitality; sobriety; healing of specific ailments; mental, emotional, and psychological clarity; and an abiding sense of kinship with fellow participants. Visions and hallucinations, if they occur at all, are said to be mere by-products of the healing process, often indicating areas of life where an individual needs to make changes.

Nonetheless, peyote religion, from its beginning, has had to fight for legal protection in the United States. From the 1880s through the late 1930s, and as late as 1963, members were forced to lobby Congress to halt proposed federal laws punishing the possession of peyote even for religious purposes. Quanah Parker (1850s–1911), a Comanche, was a vigorous and influential early advocate, as was Albert Hensley, a Ho-Chunk, a generation later. Their cause was supported by a long line of anthropologists, beginning with James Mooney (1861–1921). Despite success on the federal level, numerous state laws continued to prohibit the gathering, possession, transportation, and consumption of peyote for religious purposes.

In 1990 the U.S. Supreme Court was asked to decide on the constitutionality of these laws, in *Smith* v. *Employment Division of Oregon* (494 U.S. 872). It was argued that the laws threatened freedom of religion, and that there was no scientific evidence that peyote use by NAC members is harmful or addictive; but the Court affirmed the state prohibitions, ruling that freedom of religion in this case was a "luxury" society could not afford. This decision was widely protested by religious leaders of many faiths and by scholars. Definitive federal legislation was passed to grant full protection in 1994, as amendments to the Religious Freedom Restoration Act of 1993.

Today the peyote religion of the Native American Church is vigorous, despite opposition within some Native American communities, either from traditionalists representing older practices or from Christian congregations. Membership in 1990 was estimated at 250,000. Members often participate in other religious practices as well, but many younger members were raised without regular access to older local traditions. For many Native American people living in urban environments, or leading highly mobile lifestyles, and for many who do not speak the traditional languages of older ceremonial traditions, the Native American Church has been an invaluable source of sobriety, healing, community, and guidance.

See also BELONGING, RELIGIOUS; DRUGS; DRUMMING; NATIVE AMERICAN RELIGIONS; PEYOTE; RELIGIOUS EXPERIENCE; RELIGIOUS FREEDOM RESTORATION ACT; RELIGIOUS PERSECUTION; RITUAL; SOCIOLOGY OF RELIGION.

BIBLIOGRAPHY

Aberle, David F. *The Peyote Religion Among the Navaho.* 1966.

LaBarre, Weston. *The Peyote Cult.* 1938.

Slotkin, James S. *The Peyote Religion: A Study in Indian-White Relations.* 1956.

Smith, Huston, and Reuben Snake. *One Nation Under God: The Triumph of the Native American Church.* 1996.

Stewart, Omer C. *Peyote Religion: A History.* 1987.

Christopher Jocks

Native American Religions

Indigenous peoples across the United States developed distinct but complementary or even congruent religious beliefs and practices related to natural environments. There is no one "Native American religion," no homogeneous set of beliefs and practices; rather there are varieties of religious perspectives that share some commonalities. From the northeastern Haudenosaunee ("People of the Longhouse"/Six Nations/Iroquois) to the northwestern Wanapum ("River People"), from the southwestern Muskogee (Creek) to the southeastern Seminole, and ranging across the United States to include the Lakota (Sioux), Chippewa, Cherokee, and numerous others, native peoples developed a broad sense of spirituality rather than structured and stratified religions with unified and enforced beliefs. Native forms of spirituality tolerate alternative worldviews; they do not attempt to impose their understanding of the sacred on other peoples. This demonstrates not weak faith but an understanding that spiritual reality cannot be totally defined by any one culture. Such tolerance has enabled cultural integrity amid diffusion of beliefs and rituals. Only Hopi elders (or Arizona) of the snake society do a rain dance with live, venomous snakes clenched in their teeth, only the Diné (Navajos of Arizona and New Mexico) bury a newborn's umbilical cord next to their sheep corral, linking them to Mother Earth and to their community in life and death, and only the Wanapum (or Oregon and Washington) have Dreamers chosen by the Creator through spontaneous visions to use dreams and visions to guide communities and link them with the salmon cycle of the Columbia River; but the Hopi, Navajo, Wanapum, and all indigenous peoples regard their world as Mother Earth, a sacred and living nurturer, and care for her accordingly; and all recognize one

A Native American participant at the Sixth Annual Festival of Green Corn and Dance, Schemitzun '97, in Hartford, Connecticut, Thursday, September 4, 1997. (Credit: AP/Wide World Photos.)

for food, clothing, shelter, and tools, never for sport; and a prayer of gratitude is expressed to the individual animal or its species spirit (such as the deer people) for its gift of life to meet human needs. In the sun dance (Plains peoples), dancers hoping for a vision sacrifice a piece of flesh torn from their skin and chest muscle when dancing backward (blowing eagle bone whistles clenched in their teeth, while others drum the heartbeat of Mother Earth and sing sacred songs) from the center tree to which they are attached by ropes and skewers. The sweat lodge ceremony or "sweat" cleanses participants of physical, spiritual, and psychological ailments. In a dome-shaped structure made of bent willows draped with animal skins or heavy blankets, in total darkness representing the womb of Mother Earth, profuse perspiration occurs when an elder sprinkles water on hot rocks in a center pit. The purified participants emerge reborn. Indigenous peoples believe in guardian spirits, who might reveal themselves in animal form during a solitary vision quest. The animal guide imparts to its human relation particular powers or insights. Among the Oglala Lakota a bear brings healing power and courage, a wolf teaches cooperation in the hunt and family stability, a turtle guides women and shields warriors. In some cultures animals are clan totems: honored for their attributes or, more commonly, as guides and granters of special power who must not be hunted. Encounters with the spirit world usually occur in the natural world away from the community. New places of encounter become sacred; sometimes encounters are sought in places made sacred by others' experiences. Such sacred sites might be identifiable by symbolic markings or natural features, or might be known only to spiritual leaders, or might include an entire mountain or forest. Indigenous morality follows oral natural laws given to ancestors by the Creator. There is no "separation of church and state." Religious law is civil law. Morality is taught through stories and example and involves concern for the community as a whole, including future generations.

Great Holy One or Great Mystery or Grandfather and lesser spirits who guide, guard, and heal. Spirituality ordinarily focuses on present life—physical, social and psychological needs—rather than on an afterlife. Religious rites are communal or personal: An elder guides community worship, but individuals develop their own relationship with the sacred both individually—smoking the sacred pipe or singing a Spirit-given personal chant—and communally, passing a pipe around a sacred circle to be smoked by all, or focusing on the Spirit during a sun dance. The rising smoke of the sacred pipe offers to the Creator unified prayers from all creatures. Their unity is expressed also in a prayer often offered by elders before civic or religious gatherings: "Greetings, all my relations." The "relations" are not only one's ethnic group or all humans but also all living creatures. Life is sacred and taken only from necessity. Deer and buffalo are killed

Dreams, Visions, and Spiritual Leaders

Native peoples have a firm belief in the guiding power of dreams and visions. Visions are sought—through prayer, fasting, and heroic practices (such as a vision quest in which the supplicant spends four days fasting alone in a remote area seeking a connection with a guardian spirit, or during a sun dance when the supplicant dances over a four-day period in the hot sun, hoping for a message from the spirit world)—or a vision is spontaneous: a person at prayer receives an unexpected call from the Spirit through extraordinary images, words, and a powerful energy flow.

Prophets are men and women called to be messengers of the Spirit who sometimes foresee and interpret future events. Well-known prophecies come from the Hopi clans in the Southwest, and from the eighteenth-century Seneca leader Handsome Lake in the Northeast. Spiritual leaders (who might also be prophets) are extraordinary individuals gifted with spiritual powers, sometimes expressed through curative rituals; healers use their knowledge of herbs and mind-body connections. Nonnatives call native healers "medicine men" or "medicine women," but their abilities are spiritual as well as medicinal, and often more psychic than pharmacologic.

The term "shaman" is another misnomer, a term of Siberian origin but more widely applied by anthropologists, scholars of religion, and some "New Age" adherents. The spiritual leaders (by dreams, visions, and instruction) and healers (by intuition, instruction, and experience) seem to have extraordinary knowledge of the physical and psychological needs of

Ceremony participants leaving a kiwa after a meeting at the Fiesta de Santa Clara in Santa Clara Pueblo, New Mexico.   (Credit: CORBIS/Craig Aurness.)

their patients and of the remedies for those needs. Many have a secondary employment (carpenter, fisher, etc.) to financially supplement their primary calling as a healer. Healing powers are their gift from the Creator for the community; they do not charge for the use of sacred power (which is seen as residing in them or flowing through them), but they do accept posthealing gifts of gratitude. Noted twentieth-century spiritual leaders include Black Elk (Lakota); Phillip Deere (Muskogee); David Sohappy, Sr. (Wanapum); and Leon Shenandoah (Onondaga). In the nineteenth century, Wovoka (Paiute) had a vision and taught the ghost dance: His followers should dance, wear ghost shirts, and follow a way of nonviolence to see their ancestors return from the dead and bring a renewed world in which indigenous peoples would regain their lands and way of life.

Transcultural Diffusion

In the last half of the twentieth century, interest in native cultures generated by the publication of spiritual leaders' writings, American Indian Movement activism, and treaty negotiations has led to the diffusion of indigenous peoples' beliefs and practices among nonnatives. Indigenous spirituality-based ecological perspectives have become more appreciated and appropriated by other religious traditions and environmental organizations. Historians now recognize the contributions of Haudenoshaunee governance to the development of the U.S. Constitution. New Age groups have appropriated aspects of indigenous spirituality, sometimes with care, appreciation, and respect, but often superficially or for commercial purposes. Native elders hope that transcultural diffusion will stimulate respect for indigenous beliefs, culture, and sovereignty, and promote enhanced care for Mother Earth by the broader society.

See also BLACK ELK; ECOSPIRITUALITY; NATIVE AMERICAN CHURCH; NEW AGE SPIRITUALITY; PEYOTE; SHAMANISM; SPIRITUALITY; SUN DANCE; SWEAT LODGE; TOTEM; VISIONARY; VISION QUEST.

BIBLIOGRAPHY

Brown, Joseph Epes. *The Spiritual Legacy of the American Indian.* 1982.

Lame Deer, Archie Fire, and Richard Erdoes. *Gift of Power: The Life and Teachings of a Lakota Medicine Man.* 1992.

DeMallie, Raymond J., ed. *The Sixth Grandfather— Black Elk's Teachings Given to John G. Neihardt.* 1985.

Hart, John. *The Spirit of the Earth: A Theology of the Land.* 1984.

Hultkrantz, Åke. *The Religions of the American Indians,* translated by Monica Setterwall. 1980.

Lyons, Oren R., and John C. Mohawk, eds. *Exiled in the Land of the Free: Democracy, Indian Nations and the U.S. Constitution.* 1992.

Mails, Thomas E. *Fools Crow.* 1980.

Vecsey, Christopher. *Imagine Ourselves Richly: Mythic Narratives of North American Indians.* 1988.

Wall, Steve, and Harvey Arden. *Wisdomkeepers: Meetings with Native American Spiritual Elders.* 1990.

John Hart

Naturalism, Religious.

See Transcendence.

Nature Religion

Since the early 1970s the term *nature religion* has been used to denote religions that share a reverence for nature and consider it to be divine, sacred, or populated by spiritual beings. Practitioners of paganism and Wicca use the term as a descriptive umbrella for all earth- and nature-oriented spiritualities. Under nature religion they place spiritualities and customs they believe were prevalent before the expansion of the world's dominant religions. Nature religions thus include Norse, Celtic, and Germanic myths and folkways; polytheistic, pantheistic, animistic, fertility-oriented, and goddess-worshiping religions; shamanism and tribal (indigenous) religions; many New Age beliefs and practices; environmental spiritualities such as deep ecology; and the increasingly plural forms of contemporary paganism. Nature religions are often portrayed by contemporary pagans as having survived repression by the world's dominant religions, recently emerging from hiding or being revived through imaginative reconstruction based upon the surviving fragments of earlier repressed forms of nature-based spirituality.

This typical pagan understanding sees nature religions as resisting the centralized authority and global expansion of secularized, modern capitalism, as well as the world's dominant religions, which are said to desacralize nature, thereby removing constraints on its destruction. Pagans tend to view nature religions as pursuing decentralized social, economic, and religious communities as a path toward harmony with nature and intimate spiritual connections with a sacred world.

Some scholars express a similar understanding of nature religions. Others, however, through an anlysis of European and American history, understand nature religion to include a much wider range of phenomena. Indeed, they include under the "nature religion" rubric groups with whom most contemporary nature religionists would rather not associate.

In *Nature Religion in America,* Catherine Albanese argued that nature religionists, despite their rhetoric and their own perceptions, often seek not harmony with nature or other people but control and mastery over them. She analyzed the natural rights and republican philosophies of America's founders, for example, and found that their ideas were grounded in freemasonry and deism, both of which in turn claimed to ground religion, through reason, in nature. These two influential forms of nature religion in America perceived nature as sacred and certainly articulated the universalistic ideals of the Enlightenment. However, such nature religion, Albanese claimed, reflected republican nationalism and masked an impulse for the mastery of nature as well as nonelite humans. Moreover, such religion obscured and justified the worst features of the young, expansionist, agrarian nation.

Through an analysis of many additional examples of nature religion in American history, Albanese concluded that it is difficult for nature religions to escape the mastery impulse. She also noted the irony that in nature religion mastery is often pursued through magical or mystical means, through the attempted supernatural manipulation of the natural.

Scholarly attention to the ironies and "shadow side" of nature religion has increased. Ferry (1995), Kaplan (1997; 1999), and Olsen (1999), for example, recently documented the sometimes close connection between racist and far-right political movements, including Nazism and contemporary right-wing ecology movements in North America and Euope. Various nature religions—perhaps Ásatrú and certainly its racist counterpart, Odinism—fit this category as well. (Ásatrú and Odinism, forms of paganism that draw on pre-Christian Scandinavian and Germanic myths and folk cultures, are currently undergoing a revival in Northern Europe and America.)

Given their inventiveness and perhaps reflecting the penchant of participants to be influenced by scholarly analyses, some current forms of nature religion are developing science-based worldviews and cosmogonies that seek to eschew supernaturalism and resist the "mastery impulse." Deep ecology advocates usually view humans as only one species among others, for example, endowed with no special divine privilege. Meanwhile a number of newer organizations, such as the Epic of Evolution Society and the Society for Scientific Pantheism, as well as some practitioners of paganism and Wicca, are like-minded in this regard.

An interesting question for the future, therefore, is whether forms will evolve that overturn the "mastery impulse" and the supernaturalism that seem to be persistent, if ironic, characteristics of nature religion in contemporary America.

See also DEEP ECOLOGY; ECOFEMINISM; ECOSPIRITUALITY; NEOPAGANISM; NEW AGE SPIRITUALITY; PANTHEISM; SPIRITUALITY; WICCA.

BIBLIOGRAPHY

Albanese, C. L. *Nature Religion in America: From the Algonkian Indians to the New Age.* 1990.
Ferry, L. *The New Ecological Order.* 1992. Reprint, 1995.
Kaplan, J. *Radical Religion in America.* 1997.
———. "Savitri Devi and the National Socialist Religion of Nature." *Pomegranate* 7 (February 1999): 4–12.
Olsen, J. *Nature and Nationalism: Right Wing Ecology and the Politics of Identity in Contemporary Germany.* 1999.
Taylor, B. "Nature and Supernature—Harmony and Mastery: Irony and Evolution in Contemporary Nature Religion." *Pomegranate* 8 (1999): 21–27.

Bron Taylor

Navigators

The Navigators are an evangelical discipleship and evangelistic organization. Created in Southern California in 1933 by Dawson Trotman, a twenty-seven-year-old truck driver, the Navigators were begun as a program to evangelize the sailors of the Pacific Fleet stationed at naval bases in and around Long Beach. Influenced by several years' experience in Christian Endeavor work and with the Fishermen's Club of the Bible Institute of Los Angeles cofounder T. C. Horton, Trotman developed an intensive regimen of Bible memorization, prayer, and one-on-one mentoring, which he brought to the Navigators. Trotman was a tireless worker with a magnetic personality, and his insistence on daily evangelization and the "follow-up" of new converts created a core of eager workers intent on multiplying their group aboard ship.

The United States' entry into World War II sparked tremendous expansion of the Navigators. Prewar contacts with numerous evangelical leaders across the country proved very helpful, especially radio evangelist Charles E. Fuller's decision that all contacts made by military men and their families to his nationally broadcast *Old-Fashioned Revival Hour* be turned over to the Navigators. With the help of thousands of letters leading to potential contacts, the Navigators spread their work into the other branches of the armed forces. By 1944 the Navigators were represented on 350 naval vessels and within 450 army camps.

In the postwar period the Navigators branched out from their concentration on work among the military to target business and professional people and college students, as well as expanding their outreach to other countries. The organization moved its headquarters from Los Angeles to the Glen Eyrie estate in Colorado Springs in 1953 and soon opened a nearby youth camp, at Eagle Lake. Throughout this period Trotman and the Navigators played a key role in helping other evangelical organizations, such as Youth for Christ, Young Life, Campus Crusade for Christ, and Wycliffe Bible Translators, develop materials for Bible memorization and discipleship for workers and converts. Most prominent in this regard was the part Trotman and his assistant Lorne Sanny had in developing materials and overseeing follow-up efforts for Billy Graham's crusades.

In June 1956, while leading a Navigator conference at Schroon Lake, New York, Trotman drowned saving a young woman after a boating accident. Lorne Sanny took his place, serving as the Navigators' president until 1986. During his tenure the Navigators continued to expand, both in the United States and abroad. In 1975 the organization established a publishing arm, NavPress, and in 1981 it established a bimonthly periodical, *Discipleship Journal.*

By the late 1990s the Navigators were a thriving organization with a diverse set of ministries that continued an abiding commitment to the idea of personal evangelism and discipleship buttressed by in-depth Bible study and memorization of scripture. Newer efforts included NavYouth, created in 1995 as an organization for junior high and high school youth, which advocated a more personal, interactive relationship between youth and leaders. New ministries specifically targeting African Americans, Hispanics, and Asian Americans were also created. With an annual budget of about $100 million in 1998, the Navigators sponsored more than 1,800 workers in the United States and more than 1,900 others in 103 countries worldwide.

See also CAMPUS CRUSADE FOR CHRIST; EVANGELICAL CHRISTIANITY; GRAHAM, BILLY; JOURNALISM, RELIGIOUS; PUBLISHING, RELIGIOUS; TELEVANGELISM.

BIBLIOGRAPHY

Foster, Robert D. *The Navigator.* 1983.
Skinner, Betty Lee. *Daws: A Man Who Trusted God.* 1974.

Larry Eskridge

Near Death Experiences

In the 1970s interest in near death experiences (NDEs) reemerged, primarily associated with the popular appeal of Raymond Moody's *Life After Life* (1975). In this work, a respected physician used interviews of almost 150 persons to argue that commonalities in experiences of persons in near death conditions (who in fact did not die) are compelling evidence that death is a transition to another realm of existence. This is perhaps best symbolized by one fairly common NDE—that of traveling through a tunnel toward a bright light. Persons experiencing near death also often feel as though they have left their physical bodies, linking NDEs to the broad category of out-of-body experiences. Typically, people feel that it is revealed to them that it is not their time to die and thus they return to their earthly bodies. Other commonalties in NDEs include experiences of significant figures, typically friends or relatives, and perceptions of prominent religious persons. The vast majority of NDEs include positive emotional feelings such as joy and a profound peace. Still, one must be cautioned that the variety of experiences classified as near death are quite broad and that there is little unanimity in typical or ideal patterns of NDEs that have been scientifically verified. The most widely used measure of NDEs is an index developed by Ring (1980).

In contemporary surveys conducted in the Western world NDEs are common, likely to be reported by about 15 percent in random samples. Scientists report fewer NDEs than laypersons do and are also less likely to interpret their experiences as evidence for an afterlife. Both scientists interpreting their own NDEs and those studying NDEs of others tend to interpret these experiences as products of physiological changes occurring during extreme stress, or trauma characteristics associated with being near death— from accident, disease, or even attempted suicide. Most typically highlighted as possible physiological causal explanations for experiences reported in NDEs are oxygen deprivation, increased endorphin production, and changes in limbic system functioning. Figures typically reported in NDEs are likely to be identified as either simply hallucinatory or hypnogic imagery by scientists. No scientific evidence exists indicating that persons can have out-of-body experiences, including those in NDEs, that reveals to them factual knowledge unavailable to them as physically embodied persons. NDEs are heavily influenced by cultural and personal expectancies. Zaleski (1987) has provided the most critical account of NDEs across a broad historical spectrum, documenting the fact that NDEs have been reported in a variety of cultures since at least medieval times.

More common among laypersons reporting NDEs than scientists are interpretations granting evidential force to NDEs regarding an afterlife. Laypersons reporting general religious experiences are also more likely to report NDEs. Persons reporting NDEs are also are more likely than those who do not report NDEs to indicate belief in reincarnation and even believe that they have had contact with deceased persons in experiences other than NDEs. Not surprisingly, among those who give a meaningful interpretation to their NDE, positive changes in self-esteem, compassion, and increased internal control have been reported. Among the religiously oriented, decreased fear of death is associated with their interpretation that they have, however briefly, experienced the afterlife as legitimated within their faith.

In contemporary psychology, transpersonal psychologists have been most active in studying NDEs and providing a frame for interpreting them that avoids both physiological reductionism and an uncritical claim that NDEs are clear evidence of an afterlife. They also have been active in cross-cultural research on NDEs and the study of NDEs in children. An experience of a white light and of spiritual beings in NDEs in children most commonly parallel NDEs in adults.

Most typically NDEs are viewed by transpersonal psychologists either as adaptive processes triggered by near death or as transitional phenomena that are neither objective nor subjective, but simply human encounters with an acute awareness of death that NDEs necessarily trigger.

What seems most crucial is not simply the occurrence of NDEs but what frame one adopts to interpret them. For some, NDEs are religiously or spiritually meaningful in themselves. However, for most the meaningfulness of NDEs is probably their interpretation as supportive of an afterlife. While there is little scientific warrant for claiming that NDEs are indicative of an afterlife, it is also clear that many religions not only affirm an afterlife, but also provide a meaningful context that many use to interpret NDEs as a brief experience of that affirmation.

See also AFTERLIFE; DEATH AND DYING; PSYCHOTHERAPY; SUMMERLAND.

BIBLIOGRAPHY

Grof, Stanilav. *The Human Encounter with Death.* 1977.
Moody, Raymond. *Life After Life.* 1975.
Ring, Kenneth. *Life at Death: A Scientific Investigation of Near-Death Experience.* 1980.
Zaleski, Carol. *Otherworld Journeys: Accounts of Near-Death Experience in Medieval and Modern Times.* 1987.

Ralph W. Hood, Jr.

Neopaganism

Neopaganism is a new religious movement in the United States that had its beginnings in the 1950s but

A neopagan woman in Laytonville, California, wearing a winged costume with a rainbow-colored sash, ca. 1993.   (Credit: CORBIS/Phil Schermeister.)

saw its period of greatest growth during the 1970s and 1980s. Reports are mixed, but most observers agree that Neopaganism in the United States is well established and is growing steadily if not rapidly. It is impossible to say how many Americans practice Neopaganism, but most estimates (based on book sales, festival attendance, and the like) range from one hundred thousand to five hundred thousand.

Neopaganism in the United States was initially imported from Britain in the form of Witchcraft. Gerald Gardner, who popularized Witchcraft in England, described it as a pre-Christian, indigenously European religious tradition that had survived through secret teachings handed down along small group or family lines. Gardner himself claimed to have been initiated into Witchcraft in 1939 by an old woman who had received these traditions in an unbroken line dating back at least to the Middle Ages, when presumed witches were tried and executed in large numbers, especially in continental Europe. Goddess worship, group rituals on lunar and solar holidays, and the practice of magic were all key themes in Gardner's version of Witchcraft. From the start, Witchcraft was

a fractious religion, and new variants of it kept cropping up and vying for ascendancy. Several found their way in the 1950s and 1960s to the United States, where they were met by various complementary American occult traditions and a burgeoning religious counterculture that led to a dramatic flowering of Neopaganism. As it developed in the United States, Neopaganism gradually separated itself from its specifically European roots and began to adopt deities and religious practices from religions—especially tribal religions—worldwide.

There are several things that most Neopagans hold in common. First, Neopagans find the divine in the natural world, regarding the divine as radically immanent. For most American Neopagans, this extends to a commitment to environmentalist politics and often to vegetarianism. Second, ritual centers on natural events such as new and full moons, solstices, and equinoxes. Ritual typically involves the "casting of a circle" (an invocation of ritual space through blessings and ritual actions) and the "raising of energy" through drumming and chanting. Third, Neopagans practice magic, sometimes in the context of group ritual, but more often as a home-based religious practice. Most Neopagans have altars in their homes that contain objects from nature (feathers, flowers, stones, shells), images of gods or goddesses, divination tools such as runes or tarot cards, and items of personal importance such as photographs, all of which can be used to invoke magic or to cast spells. Fourth, Neopagans are officially polytheistic, worshiping a huge pantheon of gods and goddesses. However, this is often balanced by the view that all the deities are ultimately one and that this oneness is somehow feminine. Goddess worship and a concomitant use of female leadership in ritual have attracted large numbers of women to Neopaganism, some of whom have adapted it for specifically feminist use.

Neopagans in the United States are mostly antiauthoritarian and antidogmatic, downplaying doctrinal beliefs and formal initiations in favor of spontaneity and invention. This is especially apparent in the move from a Gardnerian-style hereditary Witchcraft—in which it was felt that an ancient body of secret knowledge had traveled relatively unscathed through centuries of official Christendom—to a happy admission that Neopagans are making it up as they go along. Despite the variety, even chaos, that this policy of spontaneous invention engenders, Neopagans are able to come together across their differences for shared ritual and worship. Several umbrella organizations exist, the largest of which is the Covenant of the Goddess. Regional and national festivals are held on an annual basis, and they draw solid and enthusiastic crowds. The ideal among Neopagans is the formation of a coven, a small group of practitioners (some say the optimum number is thirteen) who meet together on all the lunar and solar holidays and assist one another on an ongoing basis with their individual magical practices. However, such groups fall apart about as often as they form, with the result that Neopaganism at the local level is rarely very stable. Many Neopagans describe themselves as "solitaries" whose connection with other Neopagans is limited to reading the same newsletters and journals and attending the same festivals. To date, most Neopagans in America come to the religion as adults, but increasingly Neopagans are raising their children within the religion, creating a new and interesting phenomenon: second-generation Neopaganism.

See also ALTAR; CHANTING; CULT; DRUMMING; ECOFEMINISM; ECOSPIRITUALITY; GODDESS; MAGIC; NATURE RELIGION; OCCULT, THE; PANTHEON; RITUAL; TAROT; VEGETARIANISM; WICCA.

BIBLIOGRAPHY

Adler, Margot. *Drawing Down the Moon: Witches, Druids, Goddess-Worshippers, and Other Pagans in America Today.* 1989.

Eller, Cynthia. *Living in the Lap of the Goddess: The Feminist Spirituality Movement in America.* 1993.

Hutton, Ronald. *The Triumph of the Moon: A History of Modern Pagan Witchcraft.* Forthcoming.

Kelly, Aidan. "An Update on Neopagan Witchcraft in America." In *Perspectives on the New Age,* edited by James Lewis. 1993.

Cynthia Eller

New Age Spirituality

The New Age movement in America can be best understood as both a discourse community and a new social movement. As a discourse community, New Age denotes a group of people who embrace a shared core of social and religious values and speak about those values in a common language. As a new social movement, New Age denotes a loose grouping of individuals who have broken with the dominant capitalistic and Judeo-Christian ethos of late-twentieth-century America and who seek a new way of approaching personal spirituality, the natural order, gender, work, consumption, and the body.

Although the movement takes many different shapes and is continually changing, it is possible to delineate five features that distinguish it from other religious systems. The first of these is a generally optimistic view of humankind's future. Many New Agers believe that humanity is on the cusp of a planetary spiritual transformation, a kind of quantum leap in evolution that will occur at the level of human consciousness. This transformation will entail, among other things, a dawning awareness of the oneness of the human family, the intimate relationship between humanity and nature, and the innate divinity of all people.

A second characteristic of New Agers is their adoption of an ethic of self-empowerment that focuses on the realization of innate spiritual capacities as a prelude to both personal and planetary transformation. For many in this movement, it is necessary to go beyond established social codes and belief systems to realize a deeper wisdom and truth at the core of the self. This aspect of New Age religion embraces alternative healing therapies from across cultures and focuses on the holistic health of body, mind, and soul.

A third feature is the movement's attempt to reconcile the realms of religion and science in a higher synthesis that enhances the human condition both spiritually and materially. New Agers are not content to follow a purely materialistic science that is devoid of spiritual insight; at the same time, they are not willing to accept traditional religious doctrines that are clearly at odds with empirically verifiable scientific

A sunset ceremony for Earth, held by New Age nature worshipers at Big Sur, California, 1999. (Credit: © Joe Sohm/Chromosohm/Stock Connection/PNI.)

facts. The New Age movement looks forward to a society that reunites the deepest wisdom of both science and religion.

A fourth feature of New Agers is their eclectic embrace of a wide array of traditional and nontraditional spiritual beliefs and practices. New Agers are perennialists in the sense that they accept the existence of an ageless wisdom at the heart of the world's great religious traditions, and thus believe that all religions are a common treasury of spiritual practices that can be used as needed by contemporary seekers. Exclusivist claims to truth by traditional religions and national or ethnic elitism are soundly rejected by members of this universalizing movement.

A final characteristic of New Agers is their rejection of outer forms of authority, whether it be traditional religious hierarchies, political leaders, or academic experts. A cardinal tenet for New Agers is that truth lies within the individual and that it must be experienced personally if it is to remain uncontaminated by conventional ideologies and dogmas. Most New Age teachings encourage seekers to test any belief or practice against the standard of their own intuition. These teachings thus assume that within each person is a sacred reality that can know clearly the truth or falsity of any religious claim. Many New Age forms of spirituality promise to facilitate access to this "inner voice" or spiritual self.

Spirituality can be defined as beliefs and practices that attempt to bring a person into harmonious relationship with a sacred realm or being. The different forms that New Age spirituality takes can be confusing at first sight. *The Seeker's Guide: A New Age Resource Book*, for example, includes among its listing of practices goddess spirituality, biofeedback, meditation, Celtic Christianity, Kung Fu, acupuncture, sacred dance, rebirthing, past life regression, and sacred drumming. Although most of these practices existed long before the modern New Age movement began to emerge in the 1960s, what links them together is their challenge to the materialistic, patriarchal paradigm of modern Western industrialized culture. Each practice is regarded as a way of breaking through conventional social and psychological conditioning and of opening a person to the possibility of a deeper experience of relatedness to self, society, nature, and the sacred.

New Age spirituality generally accepts the existence of a universal energy that differs from more common forms of energy such as heat and light. This universal energy is believed to undergird and permeate all existence and has been called many names in different cultures, including *prana, mana,* odic force, orgone energy, and *ch'i.* For New Agers this energy is a natural energy that follows natural laws like electricity and is part of a subtle realm of vibration that sustains all life-forms.

New Agers use specific spiritual practices to bring themselves into dynamic relationship with this energy, thus allowing themselves to act as conductors and receptacles for it. Techniques for accessing "universal energy" for healing include Reiki, bioenergetics, acupuncture, acupressure massage, crystal healing, and exercises derived from Tantrism. In Reiki, for example, practitioners work with a "vital life energy" that flows through all living things and can be activated to heal conditions of physical disease or imbalance. Crystal healing involves using various kinds of crystals that are believed to transmit subtle energies. The crystals are worn around the neck or placed over sensitive points on the body that need healing.

Another characteristic form of spirituality in the New Age movement is channeling. This modern adaptation of traditional Spiritualist mediumship and shamanic trance aims to allow the channeler to become a vehicle through whom noncorporeal beings communicate with the human realm. To enter the special trance state, channelers disengage their minds from involvement with the sensory world of time and space. This state of disengaged attention is said to allow spirit entities to use the channel's physical faculties to counsel and heal those in need. The more well-known channelers, such as J. Z. Knight, organize weekend seminars during which they make themselves available to answer both personal and general metaphysical questions in a group setting.

Another important mode of New Age spirituality is related to the experience of death. New Agers believe that consciousness pervades the universe and that personal consciousness does not end with the death of the physical body. However, they are more interested in what the individual can learn from the death experience itself than in the learning that might take place in nonphysical realms. The works of Elisabeth Kübler-Ross on assisted death and dying, and texts such as the *Tibetan Book of the Dead,* have gained popularity in the New Age movement as guides for spiritually informed dying.

Another important facet of New Age spirituality involves neopagan rituals and beliefs. Those who participate in these rituals tend to draw on relatively localized traditions, such as Native American tribal religions, Celtic and Druidic paganism, and modern Witchcraft (although many Witchcraft practitioners reject the "New Age" designation). Some New Agers participate in Native American–inspired sweat lodges, vision quests, and drumming circles. Others are drawn to neoshamanic techniques such as chant, fasting, and ritual ingestion of mind-altering substances such as psilocybin mushrooms or peyote. By entering an altered state of awareness sometimes referred to as the "dreamtime," the participant hopes to experience contact with his or her deepest self and to unleash the forces of self-actualization.

In contemporary Witchcraft, participants celebrate seasonal festivals to experience a sense of connection with the gods and goddesses of nature. They also practice magic to gain personal empowerment. In a reversal of conventional Christian practice, the feminine aspects of selfhood and nature take precedence over the masculine, the physical and natural are accorded greater importance than the spiritual, and the human self is experienced as intrinsically good rather than fallen and corrupt.

New Age neopagans of all stripes often prioritize direct action as part of their spiritual path. For example, they may practice appropriate technologies; teach at New Age schools, institutes, and research centers; participate in protests against corporate environmental degradation; vote for ecologically friendly political candidates; or fight for animal rights.

New Agers often draw on the New Thought tradition in their practice of visualization and affirmation. In both of these practices there is a privileging of the faculties of imagination and creative thought and a belief in the inherent powers of the mind to manifest desired conditions. For many New Agers, daily meditation includes dynamic affirmations of health and prosperity and detailed imagining of a natural environment restored to its pristine state. The New Age movement has spawned a series of books and magazines that teach people to harness mental powers to create successful businesses, personal affluence, and fulfilling relationships. Researcher Paul Heelas has detailed the profusion of specialized training, businesses, and publications that have been inspired by New Age insights. Businesses ranging from IBM to General Electric and Pacific Bell have hired New Age consultants to conduct training for their workforce. Such training is designed to make employees more productive, managers more responsive and sensitive in their communications, and the workplace itself a more humane and nurturing setting.

New Age spirituality has not been without its critics, both from within and outside the movement. New Age theorist David Spangler, to cite one example, criticizes New Agers' tendency toward narcissism and a shallow, pastichelike spirituality. He also points out, however, that New Age spirituality is to be commended for its respectful attitude toward indigenous religious traditions and its attempts to resacralize humanity's view of nature. The former Dominican theologian Matthew Fox takes issue with the New Age movement's tendency to deny the shadow side of human nature—particularly the human capacity for evil and cruelty—and its upper-class elitism, which sometimes fails to take practical action to address the suffering of oppressed people. He is more positive about the movement's active search for a mystically informed cosmology and anthropology that transcends traditional Christianity's preoccupation with sin, guilt, and salvation.

While acknowledging its tendency toward becoming a kind of "designer spirituality," a form of spiritual practice based on personal whims and preferences, the New Age may constitute, in its more profound manifestations, a promising alternative spirituality for an emerging global culture. At its best, this spirituality points the way toward a rediscovery of personal responsibility, an affirmation of human potential, a realization of the importance of emotion in fully human relating, the establishment of a spiritually based ethic of ecology, an openness to innovative healing methods, and the first stirrings of an awakening to a universal human kinship that transcends long-standing ethnic, religious, and political animosities.

See also CELTIC PRACTICES; CHANNELING; DANCE; DREAMS; ECOSPIRITUALITY; FASTING; GODDESS; HEALING; LAZARIS; MACROBIOTICS; NATIVE AMERICAN RELIGIONS; NATURE RELIGION; NEOPAGANISM; NEW RELIGIOUS MOVEMENTS; QUANTUM HEALING; REIKI; SHAMANISM; SPIRITUALISM; SPIRITUALITY; THEOSOPHY; VISUALIZATION; WICCA.

BIBLIOGRAPHY

Heelas, Paul. *The New Age Movement.* 1996.

Hanegraaff, Wouter J. *New Age Religion and Western Culture: Esotericism in the Mirror of Secular Thought.* 1997.

Lewis, James R., and J. Gordon Melton, eds. *Perspectives on the New Age.* 1992.

Ferguson, Duncan S., ed. *New Age Spirituality: An Assessment.* 1993.

Phillip Charles Lucas

New Religious Movements

Throughout its history, the United States has provided a favorable cultural environment for religious innovation. The constitutional separation of church and state and the freedom of religion clause in the First Amendment have made it possible for independent-minded men and women to create new religious systems and communities that can exist largely free of governmental persecution or control.

During the late twentieth century, a number of trends have accelerated the pace of religious innovation in America. A nation that was once predominantly Christian is becoming the most religiously diverse country in the world. Not only are there hundreds of Christian churches; there are also now rapidly growing communities of Muslims (6 million), Buddhists (2 million), Hindus (1 million), and Sikhs (250,000). Within Christianity, denominational boundaries are becoming less important, with only about half of Americans now dying in the denomination of their birth. Religious switching—the transfer of membership from one denomination to another—is commonplace, especially when people relocate to a new city or marry someone from a different religion. Although many Americans believe in God, more than three-quarters claim a religious identity that has little to do with any organized religious community.

During the past thirty years, the country's fastest-growing religious communities have been churches that were once considered deviant by the mainstream; they include the Pentecostals, the Mormons, and the Jehovah's Witnesses. Meanwhile, mainstream Protestant congregations such as the Presbyterians, the Episcopalians, the Reformed Churches in America, and the United Methodists continue to lose members.

Sociologist Wade Clark Roof identifies the baby-boom generation as the "quest generation." His research indicates that members of this generation are more interested in experience than in theological doctrines and denominational identities. Many appear content to custom-design their own religion using elements from a wide variety of religious traditions. Baby boomers also appear to be much more open to participation in new religious movements (NRMs), groups that are characterized by their innovative solutions to the spiritual, psychological, and material needs of religious seekers in the contemporary United States.

The numbers of academic researchers studying NRMs has grown considerably between 1970 and 2000. Their research has greatly expanded our understanding of what kinds of people join NRMs, why members join and leave, the challenges of charismatic leadership in NRMs, the factors that are necessary for long-term movement success, and the ways in which new religions can serve as barometers of larger cultural trends.

The stereotypical picture of what kinds of people join NRMs and why has been well established by the anti-cult movement. Converts are either young, idealistic, gullible—and easy prey for persuasive recruiters—or they are maladjusted and marginal losers who are looking for a safe haven to escape personal responsibility. The results of careful research suggest that an accurate portrait of NRM converts is far more nuanced than the above picture would indicate. This research allows six generalizations about who joins NRMs and why:

1. Members of NRMs are recruited through preexisting social networks and through interpersonal bonds. In other words, friends recruit friends, family members recruit each other, and neighbors recruit neighbors. Contrary to the contentions of anti-cultists, not all people are equally susceptible to recruitment, nor are most converts recruited by strangers in public places. The evidence indicates that recruitment drives in public places are usually dismal failures. Rather, the majority of recruits come into contact with a movement because they personally know a member.
2. People drawn to NRMs are seeking emotional closeness—affective bonds of a deep quality—more than a new philosophy or ideology. As long as new recruits are fulfilled emotionally in the group, they are willing to remain as committed members.
3. People who join NRMs tend to have fewer and weaker social ties than nonjoiners and to be eighteen to twenty-six years of age. Part of the reason is that this age cohort is relatively free of social and economic obligations and commitments, compared to older adults. They have the time and the opportunity to search for spiritual fulfillment and to experiment with alternative lifestyles.
4. Persons who have not been reared in a religious family and who have no prior religious education tend to be more open to alternative spiritual paths.
5. People make rational decisions to join NRMs for direct rewards. These movements commonly offer positive inducements for joining: a loving community, heightened self-esteem, a sense of purpose, esoteric knowledge that promises self-empowerment, new career opportunities, powerful spiritual experiences, and new forms of social prestige. To the extent that people desire these things and cannot find them in conventional society, they are more likely to regard NRMs as attractive alternatives.
6. Psychological studies indicate that NRM members display no more signs of pathology than any youthful population. However, many recruits are distinguished by their inability to effect a successful transition from their families into

young adulthood. They wish to sever the parental bond and achieve independence but lack a sufficient sense of self to do so. The NRM provides a surrogate family—often complete with mother and father—and helps them separate from their birth family until they are ready for adult independence and responsibility. Once they have matured, members generally leave the NRM, typically within two years of joining.

NRMs often form around charismatic personalities who exercise a powerful influence over their followers. These leaders are perceived by their disciples to have special qualities that set them apart from ordinary people. Researchers such as Len Oakes and Anthony Storr have studied charismatic leaders and have helped to formulate a comprehensive psychological profile. To summarize their findings, NRM leaders often claim to have been given a special spiritual insight that has transformed their lives. Sometimes they believe the revelation has come directly from God, sometimes from an angel or a saint. Following their experience of new insight, the future leaders tend to become convinced that they have discovered the truth. This absolute certainty is part of their charismatic appeal. More than that, what is crucial is that their personal revelation is claimed to be universally applicable. In other words, charismatic leaders tend to generalize from their own experience and claim that their vision is true for all people.

Some research suggests that charismatic leaders are often isolated as children and remain that way into adulthood. They seldom have close friends and are more interested in their own inner life than in personal relationships. As teachers, they tend to attract disciples but not friends. They tend to be intolerant of criticism, believing that anything less than total agreement is equivalent to hostility.

Leaders of NRMs are often said to be unpredictable in their actions. They do not feel bound by traditions or rules, and because of their self-perceived elevated status they do not feel answerable to other human beings. This exalted vision of themselves puts these leaders at risk of becoming corrupted by power. Although many NRM leaders begin their missions in voluntary poverty, their success in attracting disciples can bring about a revision of values. It can be intoxicating to be adored and admired, and many charismatic leaders conclude that they are entitled to special privileges—including sexual and material favors not available to rank-and-file members.

Leaders of NRMs are said to demand huge sacrifices from their followers. They typically create closed environments in which members are expected to renounce everything that tied them to the world outside the group. Because they tend to place a high value on loyalty and devotion, NRM leaders often keep more independent and critically minded disciples at a distance and bring more loyal and devoted people into their inner circle. This can result in an organization run by loyal but not necessarily capable people.

Additionally, leaders in NRMs are said to be prone to paranoia, in the sense that they can become convinced, after negative publicity, that the world rejects them and that hidden enemies are seeking to destroy both them and their movement. In extreme cases—Jim Jones, for instance—this extreme sense of persecution can lead to psychic disintegration and a desire to take themselves and their followers out of this world to a better existence elsewhere.

Researchers have also considered the factors that are necessary to long-term success for NRMs. The first of these factors is cultural continuity. NRMs must build on the familiar—respect for the Bible, for example—or risk being labeled as too deviant. Such a label not only attracts hostile actions from normative institutions but also inhibits the recruitment of new members. The second factor necessary for success is the maintenance of a medium level of tension with the surrounding culture. The new movement must be familiar enough not to scare away potential converts but different enough to be sellable in the religious marketplace. In other words, it has to offer something other religions do not possess to appeal to religious seekers. A third condition for success is that an NRM must build an organization that maximizes the extent to which members are mobilized to help achieve the movement's goals. Typically, successful NRMs have a leadership hierarchy with clear lines of authority and well-defined roles for members. A fourth condition in success is the ability to attract and maintain a cross section of ages. The recruitment of young families is especially important, as this ensures future growth through fertility. Fulfilling this condition also makes the group attractive to people of diverse age groups. Several researchers have pointed out that NRMs typically recruit from one particular constituency and thereby limit their appeal to other sectors of society. This was certainly true of the NRMs of the 1960s and 1970s, which tended to recruit from the young counterculture population. This feature made these groups unattractive to middle-class, middle-aged, and senior populations. A final condition for success is the building of a dense but open social network. NRMs must create a strong sense of communal belonging, while at the same time maintaining a degree of openness to the outside world. To the extent that a group's internal social relations are weak, it will have difficulty mustering the collective effort required to keep itself vital, creative, and growing. On the other hand, if an internal social network is too all-encompassing, it will inhibit the formation of relationships with nonmembers that is necessary for successful recruitment of converts.

Research into NRMs has been an important addition to the study of American religion in general for three reasons. First, NRMs reveal a great deal about the tensions, problems, and general trends in contemporary culture. These movements are created by people who are looking for answers to problems that they and others are experiencing in their lives. In this sense, they reflect social and religious conditions in the larger culture. Second, NRMs also have been observed to be significant forces of innovation in American culture, typically creating small subcultures that act as testing grounds for new ways of living in a community, educating children, worshiping what is held to be sacred, earning a living, healing the sick, understanding gender, and establishing harmony with the natural world. To cite two examples, the Holy Order of MANS, an NRM established in 1968, founded America's first shelters for victims of domestic violence in the early 1970s. Today most American cities and towns have such shelters. The Shakers, a prominent NRM of the late eighteenth and nineteenth centuries, developed an architectural style and a style of furniture-making that has had a broad influence in subsequent American culture.

Finally, the study of NRMs is vital for a comprehensive understanding of American religious history. In a sense, the history of American religion is the history of one religious innovation after another. When the stories of alternative religious communities are omitted from American history, a very distorted picture of the rich diversity of the nation's religious culture is the result. During the past thirty years, prominent historians such as Catherine L. Albanese and Richard Wentz have begun to include substantive sections on NRMs in their works on American religious history.

NRMs will continue to play a significant role in American society, both as creative innovators of solutions to pressing social problems and as occasional expressions of collective fanaticism, extremism, and intolerance.

See also ANTI-CULT MOVEMENT; BELONGING, RELIGIOUS; CHURCH AND STATE; CULT; JONES, JIM; NEW AGE SPIRITUALITY; PSYCHOLOGY OF RELIGION; RELIGIOUS COMMUNITIES; RELIGIOUS EXPERIENCE; RELIGIOUS STUDIES; SOCIOLOGY OF RELIGION.

BIBLIOGRAPHY

Albanese, Catherine L. *America: Religions and Religion.* 1992.

Bednarowski, Mary Farrell. *New Religions and the Theological Imagination in America*. 1989.

Bromley, David, and Phillip Hammond, eds. *The Future of New Religious Movements*. 1987.

Ellwood, Robert, Jr., and Harry B. Partin. *Religious and Spiritual Groups in Modern America*. 1988.

Miller, Timothy. *America's Alternative Religions*. 1995.

Oakes, Len. *Prophetic Charisma: The Psychology of Revolutionary Religious Personalities*. 1997.

Roof, Wade Clark. *Spiritual Marketplace: Baby Boomers and the Remaking of American Religion*. 1999.

Storr, Anthony. *Feet of Clay: A Study of Gurus, Saints, Sinners, and Madmen*. 1996.

Phillip Charles Lucas

Newspapers, Religious.

See Journalism, Religious.

New Testament.

See Bible.

New Thought

The merger of the philosophical idealism popularized by Ralph Waldo Emerson converged with the interest in alternative healing methods in late-nineteenth-century America to give rise to Christian Science, a healing movement that emphasized the "Allness" of God and the unreality of sickness and evil. Its founder, Mary Baker Eddy, created a tight organization that left little room for disagreement or divergence, and soon after the founding of the Church of Christ Scientist, dissenting students began to form independent organizations. Among these organizations was the Christian Science Theological Seminary founded in 1886 by Emma Curtis Hopkins (1849–1925). Before retiring to private practice in 1895, Hopkins trained leaders from around the United States who would become the founders of the major organizations that would later constitute the New Thought movement (a name that came into common use during the 1890s).

While retaining Eddy's basic belief in God as the only reality and an emphasis upon spiritual healing, Hopkins's students felt free to diverge from Christian Science on numerous points. For example, Charles and Myrtle Fillmore, founders of the Unity School of Christianity, incorporated insights from Hinduism; and Melinda Cramer (1844–1906), founder of Divine

Science, de-emphasized the exclusively Christian presentation in her teaching. In the 1920s, Religious Science was founded by Ernest S. Holmes (1887–1960), one of Hopkins's last students.

By 1914, when the ecumenical International New Thought Alliance was formed, the movement had spread to Europe, and numerous new organizations had appeared across North America. It had also found popular expression in several best-selling books such as Ralph Waldo Trine's *In Tune with the Infinite* (1897). New Thought affirms the belief in God as universal, wisdom, truth, peace, power, beauty, and joy, and that human well-being results from a mystical alignment with the divine. The universe is seen as a body of God and human beings as spirits inhabiting a body.

Just as coming into conscious oneness with God, in whom there is no illness, produces health, so New Thought also teaches that oneness with God, in whom there is no poverty, also produces abundance. New Thought teachers affirmed that a conscious atunement with the divine and focus upon one's future could bring all of the rewards that the material world could offer. In its teachings on prosperity, New Thought most clearly demonstrates its absorption of the late nineteenth century's optimism and belief in the continued upward progress of the human race.

New Thought grew steadily through the first half of the twentieth century, and its perspective spread far beyond its representative organizations. In the 1950s, it found an unexpected ally in Norman Vincent Peale, a Reformed Church minister who had been inspired by New Thought ideas that he repackaged as "positive thinking," the subject of a series of best-selling books. Though giving little acknowledgment to his New Thought roots, Peale championed a positive approach to life and religion for several decades, and his work has been continued by another Reformed minister, televangelist Robert Schuller.

See also ALTERNATIVE MEDICINE; CHRISTIAN SCIENCE; HEALING; PEALE, NORMAN VINCENT; SCHULLER, ROBERT; UNITY.

BIBLIOGRAPHY

Braden, Charles S. *Spirits of Rebellion*. 1963.

Meyer, Donald. *The Positive Thinkers*. 1980.

J. Gordon Melton

Niebuhr, Reinhold

(1892–1971), theologian and social critic.

Reinhold Niebuhr, often considered America's greatest Protestant theologian and one of its most influential social critics, had a major impact on twentieth-century political life. Niebuhr helped shape the field of Christian social ethics; promote movements for Christian socialism and political realism; create organizations such as the Fellowship of Christian Socialists, the Fellowship of Reconciliation, and Americans for Democratic Action; and found New York's Liberal Party. He established the journal *Christianity and Crisis,* and in the 1940s served as an adviser to the U.S. State Department. His ideas provided the philosophical justification for the New Deal and offered a critique of idealistic foreign policies. For this reason he was admired by political figures on both the left and the right, including President Jimmy Carter and Ronald Reagan's ambassador to the United Nations, Jeane Kirkpatrick.

Born into an immigrant German community in Wright City, Missouri, Niebuhr attended Elmhurst College, Eden Theological Seminary, and Yale Divinity School. From 1915 to 1928 he served as a pastor at Bethel Evangelical Church in Detroit, where the oppressive labor conditions of parishioners in the automobile industry tempered the optimism of his liberal theological training. In 1928 he joined the faculty of Union Theological Seminary, New York, a position he held the rest of his life. Deeply influenced by the neo-orthodox theological ideas of Karl Barth, Niebuhr abandoned the romanticism of the Social Gospel and accepted the notion that the moral capacity of humans is limited by original sin. He found in the ideas of Augustine a basis for Christian ethics that took a "realistic" appraisal of human nature. In *Moral Man and Immoral Society* (1932) Niebuhr gave a theological basis for explaining the difference between personal and organizational ethics: Since collectivities are the extension of individual egoism, they are by definition incapable of sacrificial acts. This basic insight led to the conclusion that collectivities—especially businesses and governments—can only express self-interest.

Niebuhr scorned "moralism"—altruistic excuses given to justify self-interest. In his two-volume work *The Nature and Destiny of Man* he condemned the "sentimentalism" of optimistic views of human nature—including those of Mohandas Gandhi and Karl Marx. Niebuhr regarded history as characterized by irony rather than progress. He argued that love on a social plane can only be realized in justice. Although a pacifist in his youth, Niebuhr came to acknowledge the necessity of limited force in quelling violence and righting social wrongs. Social movements and "countervailing power" were necessary, he believed, in the face of oppressive organizations and unjust societies. He supported labor unions and government intervention, and he advocated movements for the civil rights

of African Americans as early as 1932. Though prosocialist, he condemned Stalin and communism. During the rise of the Vietnam War in the 1960s, he also criticized excessive U.S. presidential power. A persistent commentator on current events, Niebuhr was said to have held the Bible in one hand and the *New York Times* in the other. More than any other American public figure, he bridged the worlds of religion and public life.

See also CHURCH AND STATE; JOURNALISM, RELIGIOUS; PUBLISHING, RELIGIOUS; RELIGIOUS STUDIES.

BIBLIOGRAPHY

Brown, Robert McAfee, ed. *The Essential Reinhold Niebuhr.* 1986.

Fox, Richard. *Reinhold Niebuhr: A Biography.* 1985.

Kegley, Charles, ed. *Reinhold Niebuhr: His Religious, Social, and Political Thought.* 1984.

Lovin, Robin. *Reinhold Niebuhr and Christian Realism.* 1995.

Niebuhr, Reinhold. *The Children of Light and the Children of Darkness.* 1944.

Niebuhr, Reinhold. *Christian Realism and Political Problems.* 1953.

Niebuhr, Reinhold. *An Interpretation of Christian Ethics.* 1935.

Niebuhr, Reinhold. *Leaves from the Notebook of a Tamed Cynic.* 1929.

Niebuhr, Reinhold. *Man's Nature and His Communities.* 1965.

Niebuhr, Reinhold. *Moral Man and Immoral Society.* 1932.

Niebuhr, Reinhold. *The Nature and Destiny of Man.* 1941.

Niebuhr, Reinhold. *Why the Christian Church Is Not Pacifist.* 1940.

Mark Juergensmeyer

Nirvāṇa

The word *nirvāṇa* is commonly understood in contemporary America to be an Asian religious term meaning "enlightenment," or the highest possible spiritual experience. Actually, *nirvāṇa* is a Sanskrit word from South Asian Buddhism, literally translated as "blown out" or "extinguished." It derives from the Pāli Nikāyas (in which it is called *nibbāna*) and the Sanskrit Āgamas, collections of the earliest oral teachings of the Indian sage, the Awakened One or Buddha, who lived in the sixth and fifth centuries B.C.E. These teachings emphasized the fundamental four noble truths, beginning with the truth of suffering. The

Buddha spoke of the painful, disappointing qualities of human life, which he likened to the experience of being incessantly scorched by fire. The greatest pain of life was the burning quality of the mind, which resisted acknowledging this disappointment and dissatisfaction. In the remainder of the truths, he spoke of causes of suffering (the second truth), the promise of the extinction of suffering (the third truth), and the way suffering could be alleviated (the fourth truth) through discipline, meditation, and insight. The third truth, nirvāṇa, evoked the image of a raging fire being extinguished and calmed, and nirvāṇa is often understood to mean peace.

The Buddha refrained from philosophic or metaphysical speculation, insisting that this served only as an obstacle to the goal; instead, he taught that these truths must be directly experienced and realized and that words could not accurately express the true nature of that realization. On the topic of nirvāṇa, the Buddha refused to distinguish a separate, positive realm that contrasted to the painful qualities of human life; to do so would apparently make the actual realization more difficult. Instead, he emphasized the immediacy of recognizing patterns of suffering and renouncing them. Having cut the painful inertia, one could experience freedom in a practical way. This was nirvāṇa.

Given its inexpressibility, the Buddha's methods of teaching nirvāṇa were various, with four recognizable approaches: (1) nirvāṇa was described negatively, as the extinction of torturous emotions like passion, aversion, bewilderment, and especially the extinction of ego clinging; (2) it was depicted positively, as an actual experience of cessation described in lofty or allegorical terms, as immortal, cool, pure, a refuge, or a support; (3) the Buddha refused to say anything at all about it, remaining completely silent; and (4) it was described through paradox. Eventually, in the context of entire lifetimes of worthy ones, two general kinds of nirvāṇa were distinguished: the enlightenment attained during one's lifetime, in which painful habitual patterns were extinguished; and the complete nirvāṇa which occurred at death, in which all ties to the repetitive round of existence (saṃsāra) were cut forever, with no further rebirth. In the first kind of enlightenment, some remaining tendencies of karma remained, to be played out in the remainder of one's life; in the second kind, all karmic tendencies were exhausted, and the sage achieved a state of permanent cessation.

These ways of speaking about enlightenment dominated the early Buddhist tradition in South Asia, but as Mahāyāna Buddhism developed and more sophisticated understanding matured, new paradoxical interpretations of nirvāṇa emerged at the beginning of the first millennium. Early Mahāyāna texts such as the "Perfection of Wisdom" (Prajñāpāramitā-sūtras) proclaimed that there was no difference whatsoever between the repetitive cycle of suffering (saṃsāra) and extinction of suffering (nirvāṇa). Each notion depended on the other, and true liberation required transcending all such distinctions. Enlightenment, now called "insurpassable, true, complete awakening" (anuttara-samyak-sambodhi) was "awakening" (bodhi) from the dream of positive and negative, true and false, bound or freed. Certainly, words could not completely express the nature of realization, but skillful, well-chosen language could evoke the experience of awakening. In this context, nirvāṇa was no longer the extinction of suffering, but complete freedom from conceptuality, especially from belief in inherent existence. In general, however, in Mahāyāna Buddhist traditions, the word nirvāṇa was replaced by other terminology expressing this new sensibility about the highest goal.

American Usages

Today the word nirvāṇa, or rather its Pāli equivalent nibbāna, is used most frequently among meditation teachers of the Theravāda insight (vipassanā) tradition. The contemporary vipassanā movement originated in Burma early in the twentieth century, placing emphasis upon a direct, immediate path to nibbāna through the cultivation of insight. These innovators and their American students have widely taught vipassanā meditation since the 1960s; however, unlike their Asian mentors, the American vipassanā teachers rarely speak openly about nibbāna, perhaps downplaying the instant transformations so yearned for among American spiritual seekers. In vipassanā, the practitioner places bare attention, or mindfulness, on the experience of any phenomenon of life, noticing its impermanent, insubstantial, and painful dimensions, and abandoning assumptions and generalizations about it. When this is done in a sustained and concentrated way, there arises a desire to abandon attachment to that phenomenon, whether it is an object, an emotion, a thought, or an action. When this attachment is abandoned, the practitioner experiences successively cessation, peace, and a quality of contented joy that does not disrupt that peacefulness. At first this experience lasts only a few moments. Eventually, with the guidance of an experienced meditation virtuoso, the experience is extended to days at a time. This is knowledge of nibbāna. In order to progress further, even this knowledge must be abandoned and the experience of cessation must be more fully cultivated in order for full nibbāna to be attained.

American meditation teachers from other Buddhist traditions (such as Tibetan Buddhist, Zen, and Pure Land) generally speak little of *nirvāṇa*, because their Asian traditions drew from the Mahayāna approach, which emphasized awakening (*bodhi*) instead of cessation. However, these traditions have similarly expert descriptions of the path to enlightenment, with methods of meditation, guidelines for potential obstacles, and signposts of maturity which are to be followed.

See also BUDDHA; BUDDHISM; KARMA; MEDITATION; TIBETAN BUDDHISM; ZEN.

BIBLIOGRAPHY

Goldstein, Joseph, and Jack Kornfield. *Seeking the Heart of Wisdom: The Path of Insight Meditation.* 1987.

Hart, William. *Vipassana Meditation as Taught by S. N. Goenka.* 1987.

King, Winston L. *Theravāda Meditation: The Buddhist Transformation of Yoga.* 1980.

Welbon, Guy Richard. *The Buddhist Nirvāṇa and Its Western Interpreters.* 1968.

Judith Simmer-Brown

Noble Drew Ali

(1886–1929), religious leader.

Noble Drew Ali was the founder and prophet of the Moorish Science Temple of America, the first mass religious community in the history of American Islam and the black nationalist model for the Nation of Islam. He was born Timothy Drew on January 8, 1886, to parents who were ex-slaves in North Carolina. His earliest followers believed that he was an orphan for most of his childhood and was raised by the Cherokee Indians. After several years as a merchant seaman, he established the Canaanite Temple, the first Moorish-American community, in Newark, New Jersey, in 1913. In the 1920s, he renamed his community several times, as the Moorish Holy Temple of Science, the Moorish Science Temple of America, and the Moorish Divine and National Movement of North America, Inc., and founded new temples in several midwestern and southern cities. The Moorish-American community grew to approximately thirty thousand members and was the largest Islamic community in the United States before the ascendancy of the Nation of Islam in the 1950s.

Inspired by the political and cultural creativity of Marcus Garvey's Universal Negro Improvement As-sociation and the Great Migration of black southerners to the northern cities, Noble Drew Ali set up his headquarters in Chicago in 1923 and claimed to be the second prophet of Islam. His esoteric spiritual philosophy was constructed from Islamic, Christian, and Freemasonic sources. The Moorish Americans wore turbans and fezzes; they replaced their surnames from slavery with "El" or "Bey"; they created their own nationality cards and flag; and they called themselves "olive-skinned Asiatics," descendants of Morocco, instead of Negroes or colored people. In 1927, Ali wrote their sacred text, the *Holy Koran of the Moorish Science Temple,* also called the *Circle Seven Koran,* to teach his followers their pre-slavery religion, nationality, and genealogy. To support his case for a Moorish-American identity, he emphasized two important points: first, black Americans were really "Asiatics," the descendants of Jesus; and second, the destiny of western civilization was linked to the rise of the "Asiatic" nations—Asians, Africans, Native Americans, and African Americans.

In the *Holy Koran of the Moorish Science Temple,* Noble Drew Ali also argued that truth, peace, freedom, justice, and love were the Islamic ideals that his followers should emulate. However, in the late 1920s, corrupt businessmen joined the Moorish-American community. They embezzled a fortune from its small businesses and the Moorish Manufacturing Corporation and began to plot the prophet's death. His downfall began on March 15, 1929, when his business manager, Claude Greene, was murdered in Chicago. Noble Drew Ali was arrested and incarcerated for the murder and died mysteriously after he had been released on bond, several weeks later. The Moorish Science Temple of America survived in factions after Noble Drew Ali's death, and the Moorish Americans believed that their prophet would be reincarnated in his successor. Their community received official recognition for its Islamic linkages to Morocco from the Moroccan ambassador to the United States in 1986.

See also AFRICAN-AMERICAN RELIGIONS; ISLAM; NATION OF ISLAM.

BIBLIOGRAPHY

McCloud, Aminah Beverly. *African American Islam.* 1995.

Turner, Richard Brent. *Islam in the African-American Experience.* 1997.

Wilson, Peter Lamborn. *Sacred Drift: Essays on the Margins of Islam.* 1993.

Richard Brent Turner

O

Occult, The

"Occult" and "occultism" refer to spiritual concepts that are "hidden," not freely available to anyone without special understanding, training, or initiation. One finds awareness of the existence of occult or esoteric truths in most spiritual traditions. Often they have to do with knowledge of the inner dimensions or workings of the universe, with access to secret divine or human teachers, with such specialized skills as alchemy or astrology, or even with access to the true meaning of teachings given to the outer world in story or parable form, as when Jesus is quoted as having said to his inner disciples in the parable of the sower, "The knowledge of the secrets of the Kingdom of God has been given to you, but to the rest it comes by means of parables, so that they may look but not see, and listen but not understand." (Luke 8:10)

Teachings may be classified as occult for several reasons. They may be deliberately kept within a small group by an elite for the sake of that group's power and prestige. Or it may be held that they simply cannot be understood without preliminary training, just as calculus could not be grasped without training in basic mathematics, even though books on calculus might be readily available. Again, it may be considered that the occult wisdom cannot be received or employed without a special initiation that prepares one, perhaps emotionally and physically as well as intellectually, for its impact. Finally, it is sometimes honestly believed that the occult knowledge is so powerful that it would be dangerous for it to fall into the hands of anyone outside a small but responsible group, just as one would not give any low-ranking soldier in the army access to the atomic button.

This is because occult lore is generally thought to convey not only significant wisdom but also power. It may involve the secret names of gods and angels by which they can be invoked and enlisted as powerful allies. An important idea in Western occultism is the "great chain of being," the concept of hierarchies of gods or angels reaching from the human to the highest, and also down to demonic powers below. It may communicate the inner "correspondences" of sound, will, and substance that make the science of magic possible. The occultist may also learn to master such psychic phenomena as clairvoyance, telepathy, precognition, and astral projection. All this, in the wrong hands, could enable one to become a "black magician" of baleful force.

More positively, it must also be understood that occultism usually presents an intellectual worldview of some substance, offering a third option beside those of modern science and religion. In the occultist's picture of reality, everything is interconnected. Human thoughts and feelings are linked by very subtle lines of force with the remotest star, and influences can pass from one plane of the cosmos to another. To those who feel alienated not only by the mass society of modernity, but also by the impersonal, mechanistic universe of much of modern science, and no less by the remote, transcendent God of much conventional religion, occultism offers a universe in which matter and consciousness are deeply intertwined, so that thought and will can make a difference. One can contact helpers above who are more accessible than a transcendent divinity, and by knowing the right techniques make changes in one's situation. One may also find kindred spirits in occult orders, and human guidance from wise teachers of the wisdom.

Western occultism has roots in Hellenistic Neoplatonism, with its emphasis on the macrocosm-microcosm concept that everything below, especially in the human being, has a "correspondence" with entities on the universal plane. Each of the organs of the body, for example, has a particular correspondence with a certain sign of the zodiac, gemstone, and chant; these alignments could obviously be used for healing or magical purposes. Neoplatonic theurgy, or magical evocation, of gods—transmuted into angels in the monotheistic religions, Judaism, Christianity, and Islam—added awareness that this universe of interrelated energy is also alive, harboring interrelated consciousness and will.

This tradition manifested itself in antiquity in Christian gnosticism, and also in the Jewish secret sciences that came to be known as Kabbalism, in which correspondences were aligned with words and letters of the Hebrew alphabet, especially in the Torah. In both Jewish and Christian esoteric circles occultism maintained a quasi-underground life during the Middle Ages, perfecting such arts as alchemy and magical evocation, which grew out of the insights of the Hellenistic correspondences and theurgy. During the Renaissance the Neoplatonic/occult worldview emerged as a powerful intellectual force. Part of the classical and Platonic revival of the early modern era, occultism was abetted by input both from Kabbalism and from many newly discovered ancient texts such as the *Corpus Hermeticum*, containing much philosophical and magical lore and at first wrongly considered to be of very great antiquity.

The underlying worldview of Hellenistic and Renaissance occultism was essentially the same as that of pre-Copernican and pre-Newtonian science, including Ptolemaic astronomy and Galenic medicine. Thus occultism and early science were much less at odds in the Renaissance than they were after the emergence of modern science in the seventeenth and eighteenth centuries.

However, the older view, though subsequently perceived to be no longer viable as mainline science, maintained a continuing appeal as a way of seeing the inner meaning of the universe and of spiritual practices related to that view. An early movement in that direction was Rosicrucianism, appearing in Germany with the publication of anonymous pamphlets in 1614. Though it may never have had much sociological expression until recently, the term has long been used for those who, in the age of science, have preserved ancient lore associated with occultism and al-

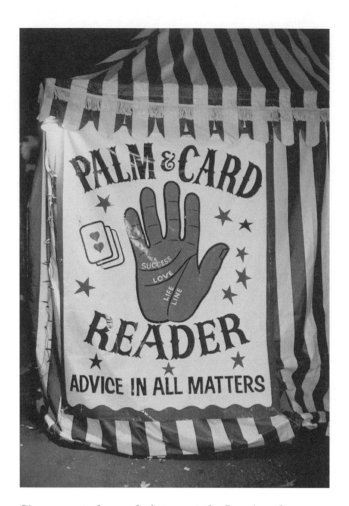

Sign on a palm reader's tent at the Los Angeles County Fair, ca. 1981. (Credit: CORBIS/Henry Diltz.)

chemy. The Freemasons, established in their modern form in 1714, incorporated some Rosicrucian and occult terms and concepts along with Enlightenment values into their rituals, including the idea of an ancient, half-forgotten wisdom attained through initiation. In America, a lodge calling itself Rosicrucian was established in Pennsylvania as early as 1694, and Freemasonry arrived in 1730.

In the nineteenth century, occultism continued to flourish, abetted by congenial themes in German idealism (the notion of a universe of consciousness and interconnectedness on all levels) and romanticism (the idea of the power of will and imagination; secret orders and the remote past as reservoirs of wisdom). In the United States these took the form of vogues for Swedenborgianism and mesmerism. Emanuel Swedenborg, undoubtedly influenced by Kabbalism and the occult tradition generally, in his own way saw vividly an inner spiritual meaning behind both the outer universe and the words of scripture, and communicated with angels. Anton Mesmer, the father of hyp-notism, held that in the trance state one could open one's mind to past, future, the farthest reaches of the universe, and the minds of angelic beings. Together these intellectual influences laid the foundation of spiritualism and its trance mediumship, which became widespread in 1848. Spiritualism could not be said to be highly occultist in itself, although some mediumistic communications were out of the same world of ideas as occultism, but it served to open popular consciousness to the concept of secret spiritual teachings newly unveiled today.

That was the message of the Theosophical Society, founded in 1875, and the first major book of its dominant figure, Helena Blavatsky, *Isis Unveiled* (1877). Together with Blavatsky's *The Secret Doctrine* (1888) and other writings, Theosophy held up the "Ancient Wisdom," known chiefly to occult fraternities past and present, as an alternative to the Victorian battle of worldviews, which Theosophists saw as shallow but dogmatic science versus no less narrow and dogmatic religion. The deeper wisdom known to the wise, they said, took into account the profound interaction of matter, mind, and will, and was transmitted by secret masters ensconced in such places as Egypt, India, and Tibet. Theosophy was a significant influence in the United States well into the twentieth century, affecting the spiritually based idealism of such progressives as sometime member of the Theosophical Society Henry Wallace, New Deal secretary of agriculture and vice president from 1941 to 1945.

In the 1890s, the famous Hermetic Order of the Golden Dawn, located principally in London, brought together a modern synthesis of occult theory and practice. Although it lasted little more than a decade in its original form, the Golden Dawn has been important in constructing twentieth-century images of occultism in the United States as elsewhere through its influence on such writers and sometime practitioners as W. B. Yeats, Evelyn Underhill, and Aleister Crowley. By then the standard modern social structures of occultism had appeared, characteristically represented not by church-type organizations but by a small, fairly intense and committed inner circle and a wide but diffuse outer circle of influence reached through books, tapes, lectures, and the like.

The 1960s witnessed an important upsurge of occultism as a major aspect of the "counterculture" of that tumultuous decade. The vogue for such occult arts as astrology, palmistry, the symbol-laden tarot cards, and in more esoteric circles ceremonial magic and out-of-the-body travel (sometimes with the aid of psychedelic substances) was of a piece with its rejection of rationalistic modernity and its desire to recover those aspects of spirituality, including the spir-

itual past, that modernity left out. The affirmation of occultism, in other words, became a symbol of opposition to modernism, to what was called the "establishment" or the "system," as well as its affirmation of a positive spirituality grounded in a magical, interlinked universe. Serious occultism in the twentieth century was often grounded intellectually in the analytic psychological systems of C. G. Jung, who himself affirmed the symbolic and psychological importance of much of traditional occultism and who contributed substantially to its revival. Occultists have interpreted such methods of divination as astrology or the tarot cards by means of Jung's concept of synchronicity, and have gone on to connect personality types suggested by astrological or tarot symbols with the "archetypes of the unconscious" made famous by Jungianism.

A residue of 1960s occultism has been perpetuated in what has been called, in the late twentieth century, the New Age movement. Its view of the importance of crystals, astrology, and spiritual healing certainly has ultimate roots in Neoplatonic correspondences, and its mediumistic "channeling" of transcendent teachers in the theurgy of the same tradition. Like an endless underground river, occultism, though usually disdained by the most respectable intellectual and religious leaders, continues to flow, changing, sometimes nearer the surface than at other times, but never quite dying out, always offering its alternative vision of cosmic and spiritual reality.

See also ASTRAL PLANES; ASTROLOGY; CHANNELING; CROWLEY, ALEISTER; GNOSTICISM; KABBALAH; MAGIC; NEW AGE SPIRITUALITY; PARANORMAL; PSYCHIC; ROSICRUCIANS; SPIRITUALISM; TAROT; THEOSOPHICAL SOCIETY; TORAH.

BIBLIOGRAPHY

Butler, E. M. *The Myth of the Magus*. 1948.
Butler, Jon. *Awash in a Sea of Faith*. 1990.
Kerr, Howard, and Charles L. Crow, eds. *The Occult in America*. 1983.
Melton, J. Gordon, Jerome Clark, and Aidan A. Kelly. *The New Age Almanac*. 1991.
Scott, Jennie Graham. *The Magicians*. 1983.
Yates, Frances A. *The Rosicrucian Enlightenment*. 1972.

Gracia Fay Ellwood
Robert Ellwood

Old Testament.

See Bible.

On Human Life.

See Humanae Vitae.

Opus Dei

The Prelature of the Holy Cross and Opus Dei—known best simply as Opus Dei ("The Work of God")—was founded by Josemaría Escrivá de Balaguer y Albas, a Spanish priest born on January 9, 1902, in Barbastaro, Spain. Escrivá was ordained to the priesthood in March 1925. During a retreat in Madrid in 1928, he allegedly "saw" God's expectation of him in the creation of Opus Dei. Originally a males-only organization, after 1930 it opened a section for women.

In 1943, the Priestly Society of the Holy Cross, the association for lay affiliates of Opus Dei who aspired to the Opus Dei priesthood, was founded. In 1946 Escrivá moved to Rome. Two years later he set up the Roman College of the Holy Cross for training members of the men's sections. In June of 1950, Opus Dei received its definitive status as the first secular institute approved directly by the Pope.

Throughout his life, Escrivá worked on behalf of Opus Dei. On June 26, 1975, he died suddenly in Rome. At the time of his death, Opus Dei was in all five continents and comprised some sixty thousand members of eighty nationalities.

In 1982 Opus Dei was made a personal prelature. This means that its clerical and lay members take spiritual direction from their own prelate in Rome and not—like other Catholics—from their local bishop. In May of 1992, "the Founder," as he is known by members, was beatified by Pope John Paul II.

The hallmark of Opus Dei spirituality, found in Escrivá's best-known work, *The Way* (1939), is the emphasis on laypeople seeking holiness in the context of their ordinary life, through the free and responsible exercise of their everyday work, and through an apostolate carried out within the ordinary structures of society. The broader objective of The Work, as members call it, is to seek a new Christendom through spiritual and apostolic ferment in the spheres of civil society and professional activities.

Opus Dei operates an international network of universities, schools, study and health care centers, student residences, and professional and vocational training institutes of various kinds. In addition to the membership ranks of Opus Dei (numeraries, associates, supernumeraries) and its priests, "cooperators" help the movement through prayer, work, and financial assistance.

Opus Dei has grown under the special favor shown the movement by Pope John Paul II. Like several other such phenomena in the postconciliar church (Cursillo; Neocatechumenal Way), Opus Dei is a highly ascetic revitalization movement that draws together idealistic people.

Although Opus Dei purportedly prefigured the reforms of Vatican II—notably the rehabilitation of the laity and the call for all Catholics to achieve holiness—critics of the organization have charged it with sectarianism and cultlike activity regarding some of its practices.

Controversy has centered on Opus Dei's hierarchical and secretive corporate structure, its subordination of women to secondary roles, its control of the minutiae of members' lives, and its alleged clandestine manner of recruitment. Objections have also been raised regarding the organization's rigid ultraconservatism and association with elites of wealth and power along with its members' excessive devotion to the founder.

Active concern over Opus Dei's "questionable practices" among American Catholics has come primarily from the Opus Dei Awareness Network, an organization of former members, concerned individuals, and families of some Opus Dei members.

Opus Dei came to the United States in 1949. There are currently over three thousand Opus Dei members with over sixty centers or residences for members in seventeen cities, typically located near large college campuses. The organization also operates a small number of high schools and sponsors retreat houses, programs for married Catholics, and outreach initiatives to the poor.

See also CURSILLO MOVEMENT; PAPACY; ROMAN CATHOLICISM; WORK.

BIBLIOGRAPHY

Le Tourneau, Dominique. *What Is Opus Dei?* 1984.

Martin, James. "Opus Dei in the United States." *America* (February 25, 1995): 8–27.

Tapia, Maria del Carmen. *Beyond the Threshold: A Life in Opus Dei.* 1997.

Walsh, Michael. *Opus Dei: An Investigation into the Secret Society Struggling for Power Within the Roman Catholic Church.* 1993.

Woodward, Kenneth. *Making Saints: How the Catholic Church Determines Who Becomes a Saint and Why.* 1996.

William D. Dinges

Ordination

Within human history religious communities often "set apart" or recognize special individuals for leadership. Sometimes there is a priestly clan, making religious leadership hereditary. In other situations anyone can be a religious leader, but he or she must be authorized or empowered through a special ritual or ceremony. In the Jewish and Christian traditions this is called "ordination."

Early Christianity remembered that Jesus called his disciples to service (*diakonia*), commissioning them to gather others who would also commit themselves to service. After his death and resurrection, the emerging church began to "set apart" certain persons for leadership responsibilities through "prayer and laying on of hands." This practice of ordination was defined by Jesus' relationship to the first disciples; by common practices within early Judaism; by secular customs borrowed from Greco-Roman, or Hellenistic, society; and by the theological ideas of the apostle Paul.

Jesus, as described in the first three gospels, was a reformer who provided an alternative approach to faithfulness within Judaism. He rejected the hereditary priesthood and many of the conventional patterns of Jewish religion. He invited his followers to move beyond the traditional leadership of the scribes and Pharisees. As the church developed, it also borrowed freely from the practices of first-century Judaism, where the elders "laid on hands" to bless each new generation of leaders. In like fashion, Christians began appointing elders (*presbyteroi*) to lead their congregations. The church was further influenced by Hellenistic society and patterned its leadership after local household mores. An overseer, or bishop (*episkopos*), became the head of each Christian community. Eventually there were specific qualifications required for such ecclesiastical household leadership, spelled out in the New Testament. Churches also designated still other persons as deacons (*diakonia*)— those who worked within and for the churches, embodying the caring mandate of the gospel. Deacons served as assistants to the elders and the bishops. All were ordained to service. Finally, the apostle Paul used the metaphor of the human body to insist that, just as the body needs all its parts to be healthy, various forms of ministry are needed by the church. Within the Jewish tradition, the ordination of rabbis accomplished the same purpose.

In addition to endorsing patterns of leadership, ordination has had at least five other purposes: (1) To preserve the link between the apostolic witnesses (those who knew Jesus firsthand) and the ongoing institutional church through "apostolic succession," where ordained leaders lay hands on the next generation of leaders and "pass on" (literally or symbolically, depending on the theology of the particular denomination) the power of Jesus' ministry. (2) To protect the Christian community from heresy by making sure that its leadership was trained in correct doctrine and was able to teach and preach correctly for the good of the faithful. (3) To exercise civic responsibility in times of political unrest and upheaval. (4) To maintain and protect the sacred mysteries of the eucharist and other sacramental acts. (5) To call some Christians to a more godly and holy life. This last purpose has had some unfortunate consequences, exacerbating artificial divisions between clergy and laity.

Ordination in the United States

Because so many different religious groups exist in the United States, it is impossible to make generalizations about the meaning of ordination. Some denominations, like the Quakers, reject ordination because everyone is considered a minister. In other denominations, like the Unitarians and many mainstream denominations, it is a recognition of functional responsibilities taken on by one on behalf of all—the moment of formal recognition for trained leaders. Among some Baptists or Pentecostals, ordination is not terribly important, because what is important is whether an individual leader is filled with the power of the Holy Spirit. At the same time, in more liturgical denominations, ordination remains a formal, sacred, and mystical rite whereby the power of Christ is channeled to the priesthood and the mysteries of the sacraments are protected.

In the last half of the twentieth century, three issues have generated great controversy related to ordination.

First, for almost two thousand years, only males were ordained. Women's ministries were valued by the early church and honored informally throughout the centuries, but only men could be ordained. In the modern era, arguments linking priesthood to the maleness of Jesus, or to the maleness of past leaders, have been challenged. Since the mid-nineteenth century, many women have actively sought ordination in Protestant denominations with increasing success. At the same time the insistence that ordination is only for males has become more vigorous, especially within the Roman Catholic church. Christian and Jewish groups continue to debate the question of women's ordination, even as the numbers of ordained women increase.

Second, in the development of Western European Christianity (Roman Catholicism) only celibate men were eligible for ordination. The fact that Jesus did not marry and the belief that the lifestyle required of priests should not involve active sexuality or family responsibilities suggested that only unmarried men were capable of being priests. By the sixteenth century, however, Protestant reformers challenged that assumption. They insisted that married clergy were more helpful to the Christian community and more in touch with ordinary life. Their argument was so persuasive that expectations went all the way to the other extreme, with many Protestant denominations coming to believe that clergy had to be married in order to model authentic discipleship within a Christian home.

Third, issues of sexuality, especially homosexuality, have forced many Jews and Christians to reexamine their understanding of ordination. As concerns about the sexual mores of clergy and public scandals have increased, denominations have tightened requirements for ordination and developed more intense patterns of support and discipline. Various texts and opinions about same-sex relationships and the long-standing silence or condemnation of gay men and lesbians among religious groups has made the question of the ordination of homosexuals one of the most divisive issues in the church. This question raises fundamental concerns about biblical authority, about distinctions between sexual orientation and practice, and about differences between clergy and laity. Theologians often have to remind faithful members of congregations and denominations that ordination is not an end in itself, but only a means to empower leadership for the ministries of the whole community.

See also CELIBACY; MINISTRY; ORDINATION OF WOMEN; PRIESTHOOD; RABBINATE.

BIBLIOGRAPHY

Ogden, Greg. *The New Reformation: Returning the Ministry to the People of God.* 1990.

Rademacher, William J. *Lay Ministry: A Theological, Spiritual and Pastoral Handbook.* 1991.

Schillebeeckx, Edward. *The Church with a Human Face: A New and Expanded Theology of Ministry.* 1985.

See also the apostolic letter *Ordinatio Sacerdotalis* by John Paul II (1994) and articles in *Origins* 30 (November 1995) and the *National Catholic Reporter* (December 1995).

Barbara Brown Zikmund

Ordination of Women

Ordination is the process by which persons are invested with the function or office of minister, priest, or rabbi. It varies according to religion but is the way each tradition designates those who will function on behalf of the community in its rituals and public life.

The long history of patriarchal sexism led to the discriminatory custom in most traditions of allowing only men to be considered for ordination. As U.S. society became increasingly aware of gender discrimination and as women entered many other professions, pressure mounted in the mid-twentieth century in virtually all religious groups to change their policies. Struggles that led to these changes have given a new, increasingly female face to the U.S. religious scene.

A pioneer in this effort was Jarena Lee in the African Methodist Episcopal (AME) Church. Although she was never ordained, her request for a preaching license in 1809, while denied, opened the question for public discussion. In 1894 Julia A. Foote was ordained deacon in the AME Zion Church in Poughkeepsie, New York; this was the first black denomination to so designate a woman.

The first white Christian woman to be ordained was Antoinette L. Brown, in 1853 by a Congregationalist church. Universalists ordained Olympia Brown and Augusta Chapin in 1863, and Unitarians followed with Celia Burleigh and Mary Graves in 1871. By the end of the nineteenth century the Northern Baptists, Disciples of Christ, and other Christian churches all ordained women. The various Methodist groups compromised on the question in 1939, gave full status to women in "traveling ministry" in 1956, and finally granted women full ecclesial standing in 1968 in the consolidated United Methodist Church. Holiness and Pentecostal churches ordained many women ministers, especially circuit riders.

Major steps forward for so-called mainline denominations came in the 1960s, when social forces, including the civil rights, women's, and antiwar movements, prompted large-scale cultural rethinking. Religious groups that once had seen themselves as exceptions to the rule found that egalitarian expectations were upon them. In 1964 Southern Baptists ordained Addie Davis. In that same year, the Presbyterian Church, U.S. (South), followed the Presbyterian Church (North), which had ordained women in 1955. By 1970 both the American Lutheran Church and the Lutheran Church in America had ordained their first women priests.

A dramatic development took place on July 29, 1974, when eleven women were ordained by three bishops in the Episcopal Church. This act of ecclesial disobedience was significant because it meant that women had broken through the "stained-glass ceiling" in a denomination that, like Roman Catholicism, had claimed that women's priesthood was theologically impossible and symbolically wrong. Other Protestant churches had coped with the social and psychological barriers to women's full acceptance, but this time it was the theological barrier that had been

*The Rev. Carolyn Tanner Irish acknowledges a
standing ovation at the conclusion of ceremonies
ordaining her as the first female bishop of the
Episcopal diocese in Salt Lake City, Utah, on May
31, 1996.* (Credit: AP/Wide World Photos.)

overcome. The ordination of the eleven was considered "irregular" but valid. After several years of debate the Episcopal Church agreed to the ordination of women in 1976, and the ordinations of those first priests were "regularized" on January 1, 1977.

The episcopacy was next, with the ordination of Methodist minister Marjorie Matthews as the first mainline Protestant bishop in 1980. Barbara C. Harris was ordained the first Anglican bishop in the world in 1989, when she became suffragan (assistant) bishop of the Episcopal Church, a scant dozen years after the first women in that denomination were ordained in the United States. (Chinese Anglican deacon Li Tim-Oi was ordained a priest in Hong Kong in 1944.)

Among Jewish women, the ordination question was equally problematic. Women were prohibited from becoming rabbis for similarly sexist reasons, most of which fell away over time. Women entered seminaries and engaged in pastoral practice while minds changed.

In all traditions feminist scholarship countered oppressive arguments and made theological sense.

The first woman rabbi ordained in the United States was Sally Priesand, by the Reform movement in 1972. The Reconstructionist movement ordained Sandy Eisenberg (Sasso) in 1974, and the Conservative movement ordained Amy Eilberg in 1985. Orthodox Jews still do not ordain women. A growing number of women are now serving in a wide variety of ministries in Jewish communities.

The Roman Catholic movement for women's ordination took hold in the United States in the 1970s, sparked by the Episcopalian women's success. The first meeting of the Women's Ordination Conference was held in Detroit in 1975. But the Vatican's 1976 *Declaration on the Question of the Admission of Women to the Ministerial Priesthood* left little doubt about the vehemence of the opposition. Church officials argued that the priesthood is not a right that can be given, but something that participates in "the economy of the mystery of Christ and the Church." The Vatican claimed the teaching unchangeable and the question closed.

Thousands of U.S. Catholic women engage in ministry, including, in some settings, sacramental ministry. In a 1994 papal pronouncement, *Ordinatio Sacerdotalis,* the argument was reiterated; this was followed in 1995 by a *Responsum* clarifying that the teaching against women priests, while not infallible, requires religious obedience. Despite these statements, it is widely assumed that the ordination of Catholic women will happen in the new century. The severe shortage of male celibate priests, the plethora of women ready and willing to be ordained, and the example of so many other religious groups make it likely.

Ordination of lesbian women is part of the larger struggle for the rights of gay, lesbian, bisexual, and transgendered people in their respective religions. This remains contentious in many circles, despite the fact that many homosexual persons are already ordained, albeit often hiding their sexuality.

Ordination is not necessary for women to function religiously. For example, the awarding of diplomas to women cantors, a role previously filled only by men, is revolutionary. The presence of hundreds of Catholic women in previously all-male seminaries is new. Some argue that ordination only co-opts women into the very structures that have previously oppressed them. The ordination of women, and the resistance to it, have proved to be important barometers both of how religious traditions treat their women and of how they interact with social forces beyond their gates.

See also CIVIL RIGHTS MOVEMENT; CLERGY; FEMINIST THEOLOGY; GENDER ROLES; LESBIAN AND GAY RIGHTS

MOVEMENT; MINISTRY; ORDINATION; PRIESTHOOD; RABBINATE; SEMINARIES.

BIBLIOGRAPHY

Braude, Ann. "Jewish Women." In *In Our Own Voices: Four Centuries of American Women's Religious Writing,* edited by Rosemary Radford Ruether and Rosemary Skinner Keller. 1995.

Chaves, Mark. *Ordaining Women: Culture and Conflict in Religious Organizations.* 1997.

Nadell, Pamela S. *Women Who Would Be Rabbis: A History of Women's Ordination, 1889–1985.* 1998.

Townes, Emilie M. "Black Women." In *In Our Own Voices: Four Centuries of American Women's Religious Writing,* edited by Rosemary Radford Ruether and Rosemary Skinner Keller. 1995.

Wessinger, Catherine, ed. *Religious Institutions and Women's Leadership: New Roles Inside the Mainstream.* 1996.

Zikmund, Barbara Brown. "Women and Ordination." In *In Our Own Voices: Four Centuries of American Women's Religious Writing,* edited by Rosemary Radford Ruether and Rosemary Skinner Keller. 1995.

Zola, Gary P. *Women Rabbis: Exploration and Celebration.* 1996.

Mary E. Hunt

Orthodox Judaism.

See Judaism.

P

Pacifism

The flowering of religious pacifism during the last half of the twentieth century in the United States comes from seeds scattered by earlier responses to war and social turmoil. The term "pacifism" emerged at the beginning of this century as a description of the diverse ways that people were working for peace. Thus those who based their pacifism in religion earlier in this century were the precursors of the many types of religious pacifism today.

There may be said to be three general species of religious pacifism that contribute to the diversity of contemporary religious pacifism. The first type is modeled by the Mennonites, who historically refused to participate in war of any sort and remained separate from attempts to influence politics. Such pacifists base their commitment on the view that Jesus and the early church were nonresisters to evil and kept apart from the world. The second type, exemplified by the Quakers, Brethren, and subgroups within many denominations, such as the Catholic Worker movement or the evangelical Sojourners community, also refuse to participate in war. However, such groups believe they are to promote peace and social justice in the world. These pacifists see Jesus as actively resisting injustice by nonviolence, and believe that Christ's spirit calls them to do so today. The third species includes those across all religious denominations who see war as sometimes justifiable, but believe their mission is to help prevent war. They do not see the early church speaking to social justice issues directly, but rather feel that Christians are obligated to protect innocent life

through involvement with the social order, as in Roman Catholic "just war" doctrine. Two developments from these roots show the diversity and influence of religious pacifism today: the spread of opposition to participation in war and the use of nonviolent action to challenge social injustice.

Representatives from the three historic peace churches—Mennonites, Brethren, and Quakers—advocated conscientious objection as the country reinstated the draft to prepare for World War II. The government did allow for conscientious objection, and those recognized as conscientious objectors (C.O.'s) worked in the Civilian Public Service (CPS) during the war. However, there were pacifists who refused to cooperate at all with the draft and went to prison, and some C.O.'s protested the government control of the CPS camps. Such actions generated ongoing efforts to expand the range of conscientious objection. During the Vietnam era, government recognition was enlarged so that today moral and ethical beliefs against participating in all war qualify for C.O. status. Groups such as the National Interreligious Service Board for Conscientious Objectors and the Friends Committee on National Legislation were formed during the war. They continue work today on behalf of pacifists and a range of social justice issues. Now, most Christian and Jewish denominations in the U.S. support conscientious objection and have created their own denominational groups that address issues of social concern. Further, some groups, such as the U.S. Catholic bishops, have advocated recognizing those who conscientiously oppose particular wars or nuclear war. The government, however, has yet to rec-

Indian pacifist leader Mahatma Gandhi, ca. 1930–1940. His writings and ideas have greatly influenced pacifist thinking in the United States. (Credit: CORBIS/Bettmann.)

ognize selective objection to war. Other religiously based groups, such as the Campaign for a Peace Tax Fund, have advocated conscientious objector status for taxpayers who want their taxes to go to nonmilitary spending.

The second aspect of the growth of religious pacifism in the second half of this century is the development of nonviolent action against social injustice. Dr. Martin Luther King, Jr., was presented the Nobel Peace Prize in 1964 for the combination of his Christian faith with the active nonviolence of Mohandas Gandhi. However, the nonviolent challenges to racial segregation that became standard in the civil rights movement after the Montgomery bus boycott of 1955 were connected to those who had been nonviolent activists as C.O.'s and draft resisters. These individuals were attracted to the Fellowship of Reconciliation (FOR), an ecumenical organization founded in 1914 to support religious pacifists. The FOR, chaired by former minister A. J. Muste, then offered leadership and training to early civil rights workers.

The success of nonviolent actions in the civil rights movement generated powerful links between pacifist opposition to war and efforts to correct social injustice. Religiously based nonviolent action spread to many social change groups. For example, in the 1970s the United Farm Workers used marches, strikes, boycotts, and fasting to highlight the plight of farm workers, sometimes breaking the law. During the 1980s, the Sanctuary Movement openly violated U.S. immigration law by providing help to Central American refugees. Also, campaigns against the proliferation of nuclear weapons that occurred in the 1970s and 1980s had initial leadership from religious pacifist groups like the American Friends Service Committee and the FOR. These efforts included work at the level of electoral politics that resulted in some governmental shift toward more control of nuclear weapons. Also, the campaign for the freeze on nuclear weapons development saw the spread of nonviolent actions aimed at symbolic destruction of those weapons by such groups as the Plowshares. Here radical pacifists, such as the Roman Catholic priests Daniel and Philip Berrigan, questioned the pacifist avoidance of the destruction of property used for war making.

In the 1990s many groups supported by religious pacifists have blossomed. Pastors for Peace sends medical supplies to Cuba in violation of the U.S. embargo. The Voices in the Wilderness campaign breaks the U.N. sanctions on Iraq by supplying food and medicine. Feminists for Life question war, the death penalty, and abortion. Many denominational groups are involved in a resurgence of activity against the death penalty. Members of the campaign to close the U.S. military training school for Latin Americans, the School of the Americas, have trespassed on property, prayed, and been arrested.

Thus, in the midst of many wars and much social injustice, religious pacifists have sought to remain true to their faith and responsive to the larger world at the close of the twentieth century. Because of this, religious pacifism is continuing to grow and diversify at the close of the twentieth century.

See also ABORTION; CAPITAL PUNISHMENT; CATHOLIC WORKER; CONSCIENTIOUS OBJECTION; KING, MARTIN LUTHER, JR.; MENNONITES; PEACE CHURCHES; QUAKERS; SANCTUARY MOVEMENT.

BIBLIOGRAPHY

Boyle, Beth Ellen, ed. *Words of Conscience: Religious Statements on Conscientious Objection.* 1983.

Chatfield, Charles. *The American Peace Movement: Ideals and Activism.* 1992.

Cooney, Robert, and Helen Michalowski, eds. *The Power of the People: Active Nonviolence in the United States.* 1977.

Kurtz, Lester R., ed. *Encyclopedia of Violence, Peace and Conflict.* 1999.

Lonnie Valentine

Paganism.

See Neopaganism.

Pantheism

Pantheism ("all God") is a family of views espousing total immanence—that is, the essential identity of the Divine and the world. It resembles but is distinguishable from panentheism ("all in God") in which the world is part of the Divine, the Divine also transcending the world. It stands in contrast to monotheism ("one God"), which tends to see God as separate from and transcending the world. It may contrast with polytheism ("many Gods"); but polytheism and pantheism may also be combined, with the many Gods seen as varied images of the Divine Oneness.

Modern forms of pantheism have major roots in Hindu Vedanta and the Neoplatonic tradition. The conception of God of Barukh Spinoza (1623–1677) was reached by reflective analysis; God is Substance, the changeless Unity underlying the fleeting many. God is not the external creator of Nature but is Nature as source: "Nature naturing," whereas the many things are "Nature natured." God does not possess intellect, will, or freedom, though "he" could be said to be the totality of thought.

Pantheistic themes appeared in about 1790 in German and English romantic thinkers, partly influenced by Spinoza and Indian thought. The romantics' starting point was not analysis but the human feeling-awareness of the Infinite Oneness that generates, permeates, and sustains the finite many. It is when we reflect on these experiences that we form specific images of God. The human imagination, its perception and creativity, are one with the Divine generative powers.

The New England Transcendentalists of the 1830s and 1840s drew upon these themes. Generally optimistic, they held a view that the world is one and one with God; the Divine Mind indwells the world in every part, and each part presents in microcosm the laws and meaning of the whole. This is especially true of the human soul, and thus the deepest human intuitions are divinely authoritative. Some of the Transcendentalists, such as Henry David Thoreau, translated these views into action against slavery.

Pantheistic elements also appear in the "metaphysical" movements of the mid-nineteenth century onward. They have roots in the visionary teachings of Emanuel Swedenborg that the world of Spirit is the ultimate reality, in Anton Mesmer's concepts of an invisible magnetic fluid permeating all things, and to some extent in Transcendentalism and Hindu ideas. Mary Baker Eddy, founder of Christian Science, taught that the only reality is infinite Mind and its infinite manifestations. Matter is unreal, disease is unreal; human beings are not material but spiritual. False ideas lead to disease, whereas knowledge of the Truth heals.

Among her followers was the influential Emma Curtis Hopkins, mother of the New Thought movement. Strongly feminist, Hopkins saw the present age as the period of the Spirit or Mother-Principle, the time for the rise of women. Her students formed such groups as the Unity School of Christianity and the Church of Religious Science. They affirm God as Universal Wisdom, Love, and Truth, and the universe as the Body of God. Matter is real, but secondary; a human being is an individualized expression of God. To move from sickness to health, from poverty to prosperity, is to manifest Divine Truth.

At the 1893 World's Parliament of Religions appeared the magnetic Hindu teacher Vivekananda, who founded the Vedanta Society. Its members taught the identity of Brahman, the impersonal Absolute, with Atman, the human self. By the disciplines of study and devotion, one may pierce the veil of Maya (enchantment) that makes the world appear to be separate things, and realize that all things and persons are essentially Divine.

Aldous Huxley, Ram Dass, and others informed by Hindu ideas influenced New Age thought, an amorphous movement of the 1960s and thereafter. Ranging from psychedelic religion and neoshamanism to near-death experience and UFO movements, it rejects dualistic and mechanistic worldviews and focuses on altered states of consciousness leading to both individual and planetary transformation: full realization that the cosmos is one and permeated by the Divine.

Pantheism is supported by intuitions and mystical experiences of the universe and all within it as one and Divine. It stands in tension, however, with intuitions of individual freedom and the reality of evil. If all is God, it would seem that human choice really cannot make a difference, nor can there be any basis for opposing evil and promoting good. Thus pantheistic movements tend toward quietism. However, despite the tension, individuals such as Vivekananda and Thoreau have been inspired by the perceived sacredness of all beings to take action on behalf of the oppressed.

See also CHRISTIAN SCIENCE; ECOSPIRITUALITY; HINDUISM; NEW AGE SPIRITUALITY; NEW THOUGHT; THEISM; VEDANTA SOCIETY.

BIBLIOGRAPHY

Eddy, Mary Baker. *Science and Health with Key to the Scriptures.* 1875.

Goddard, Harold Clarke. *New England Transcendentalists.* 1960.

Melton, J. Gordon. *The Encyclopedia of American Religions.* 1989.

Gracia Fay Ellwood
Robert Ellwood

Pantheon

Humans, in contemplating the ultimate questions of life, overwhelmingly posit the existence of a supernatural world. Confronted by the same problems of existence, various peoples have attempted to unravel mysteries and allay fears through encounters with this sacred realm. In polytheistic cultures, human contact with this world takes the form of interaction with sacred beings, or gods and goddesses. The culture of deities takes the form of a pantheon, a hierarchical structure wherein gods and goddesses live in a sacred community.

Although polytheistic systems most easily incorporate pantheons, monistic and monotheistic cultures may also possess similar images of the sacred. Monism allows for pantheons, viewing deities as emanations of the one divine reality. Although monotheism purports the existence of one, and only one, supreme deity, it has on occasion absorbed the pantheons of cultures it missionized, downgrading deities into helpers, such as angels or saints.

Whether a religion revolves around a polytheistic, monistic, or monotheistic view of the divine, pantheons possess a dynamic structure. Believers continually reexamine and reevaluate deities. New deities arise and take over the work of older deities and absorb their attributes. Deities merge, change gender and form, or fade away altogether.

Despite the diversity of cultures in existence, the functions and attributes of deities possess similarities the world over. Deities touch human existence at its most crucial junctures, dealing with issues of food, fertility, protection, birth, and death. The hierarchical structure of the pantheon often reflects the various functions of the deities, in turn, this sacred structure both reflects and creates the structure of human society and life itself.

The highest order of deities, generally associated with the sky, serve as the creators and guardians of cosmic and societal order. Deities associated with meteorological activities often take the roles of protectors or warriors. Earth deities fulfill tasks related to fertility and prosperity, both in the realm of food, such as gods and goddesses of the hunt or deities associated with agriculture, and in the realm of love and childbearing, dealing with romance, marriage, and procreation. Domestic and community deities also fall under this heading, protecting home and hearth. Underworld, or chthonic, deities rule the realm of sickness and death, often conversely associated with healing.

The realms of deities and humanity exist on different levels; however, certain deities, often tricksters, bring culture, art, technology, and esoteric knowledge and magic to humanity, helping people to bridge the gap between the mundane and the holy.

How a people understands its deities can range from viewing them as personifications or archetypes of abstract concepts to personal knowledge of them as mythological beings with their own histories, personalities, and distinct reality as persons. Often a belief system incorporates both understandings, with a divine ground of reality existing on a very remote, abstract plane, and the members of the religion's pantheon existing in a more immediate, immanent way, intimately concerned with the day-to-day aspects of an adherent's life.

In the United States today, three different groups possess readily recognizable pantheons. Native American religionists represent indigenous ideas of deity. Immigrants from India and Asia often bring their old religions with them, possessing a multitude of deities and supernatural entities. Africans hide their old ways in a syncretic fashion in religions such as Santería and Vodou. Finally, Neopaganism, a modern movement that seeks to revitalize the ancient religions of Europe, mainly adheres to a polytheistic view of the cosmos.

Various groups within Neopaganism vary widely in what pantheons they adopt and what practices they follow. Religions such as the Asatru follow one pantheon only and to re-create, or revitalize, an ancient European tradition in its entirety. The Asatru follow Norse or Germanic traditions, worshiping only members of the Norse pantheon, such as Odin, Freya, and Thor, and attempt to both conceptualize and worship them in the "old" ways. On the other side of the continuum, Wiccans often feel free to adopt deities from any pantheon in existence, often mixing and matching members from diverse pantheons. The main rituals of Wicca loosely follow the pre-Christian rituals of the British Isles; however, Wiccans view all pantheons as equally viable and real. Some witches limit themselves to an individual pantheon, with the gods and goddesses of ancient Egypt proving especially popular. Witches sometimes even adopt icons from popular culture, such as *Star Trek* or other fictional "universes." The central theme of Neopagan religions lies in the acceptance of both a goddess and a god, which may reveal themselves in a variety of forms.

See also GODDESS; NATIVE AMERICAN RELIGION; NEO-PAGANISM; SANTERÍA; THEISM; VODUN; WICCA.

BIBLIOGRAPHY

Farrar, Janet, and Stewart Farrar. *The Witches' God: Lord of the Dance*. 1989.

Farrar, Janet, and Stewart Farrar. *The Witches' Goddess: The Feminine Principle of Divinity*. 1987.

Jordan, Michael. *Encyclopedia of the Gods*. 1993.

Nancy Ramsey

Papacy

The papacy is the office of the bishop of Rome as successor of the Apostle Peter and visible head (under Christ) of the Roman Catholic Church. The origins of the Roman primacy are historically unclear, but from the earliest days of Christianity Roman bishops such as Clement assumed that they had the right and the duty to intervene or mediate in the disputes that rent other local churches, and their intervention was accepted. By the patristic age the church at Rome had acquired a reputation for orthodoxy, which gave special weight to its voice at ecumenical councils and in theological controversies. In the Middle Ages developments such as the temporal power and the growth and systematization of canon law added a political dimension to the authority of the bishop of Rome, and the cultural and ecclesial separation of the Eastern churches, which left Rome as the only apostolic see and the only patriarchate in the West, also contributed to the growing prestige and power of Rome among the Western peoples.

The Gregorian reform and the struggles between the church and the Holy Roman Empire during the Middle Ages led to an extremely high level of papal power, which culminated in the period from Innocent III (1198–1216) to Boniface VIII (1294–1303). The fourteenth century saw a reaction to this, as secular governments reaffirmed their rights, and the French domination of the papacy led to a seventy-year "Babylonian captivity" at Avignon. This was followed by the Great Western Schism, which divided Western Chris-

Pope John Paul II prays during an outdoor mass at Camden Yards in Baltimore on Sunday, October 8, 1995, at the conclusion of his 1995 visit to the United States. (Credit: CORBIS/Bettmann.)

tendom between two (later three) claimants to the papacy. This traumatic split was only solved by claiming that an ecumenical council could depose all three claimants, including the legitimate one, but this solution resulted in a century-long struggle by the popes to reaffirm their supremacy against the claims of the conciliarists. The conciliar movement had raised hopes of reform, which were frustrated by the success of the renaissance popes in evading the dangers of conciliarism—both to the papal primacy and to the more worldly convenience of the popes and their court. The failure of the popes to address reform was a major cause of the Protestant Reformation. Even after the Reformation, the popes continued to combine resistance to heresy with resistance to the reform of ingrained abuses, until the situation rendered the convoking of a reforming council at Trent unavoidable.

By the time the Council of Trent met, the emerging Protestant movement had come to believe that the development of papal authority over the previous fifteen centuries was both unwarranted and anti-evangelical; many of them identified the pope with Antichrist, and all were adamant that the papal office was unacceptable in a reformed Christianity. The council mandated sweeping reforms in Catholicism but also strengthened the Catholic position on those issues the Reformers had rejected. As a result of this sixteenth-century experience, Catholics came to feel that loyalty to the concept of the papacy was essential to the preservation of Catholicism; separation from Rome became inconceivable even for groups such as the eighteenth-century Gallicans, who disputed papal jurisdiction at the local level.

The French Revolution and the Napoleonic Wars ushered in an age of hardships for the papacy; revolutionary France tried to impose a schismatic constitution on the clergy and persecuted those priests who remained loyal to Rome, and with Napoleon's victories in Italy, two successive popes were dragged into captivity in France. While the Papal States were restored at the Congress of Vienna, Italian aspirations toward national unity led to the unpopularity of the papal government and to the gradual despoliation of the papacy's temporal power, which culminated in the fall of Rome to the Italian Army in 1870.

These developments, however, actually worked to the advantage of the papacy as a moral force. Catholics throughout the world came to see Pius VI and Pius VII as brave men who, with no weapons but their moral fortitude, stood up to the most powerful man in Europe, and later saw Pius IX as a holy old man abused and bullied by secularist power but never losing his dignity. At this time Catholics began to develop a dangerous tendency toward a personality cult of the reigning pope. Indeed, it was in 1870, as the last bastion of papal temporal power was about to crumble, that the First Vatican Council proclaimed the dogma of papal infallibility—the belief that when the Pope speaks *ex cathedra* on an issue of faith or morals, he is protected from error by the grace of the Holy Spirit. In spite of some opposition among bishops and intellectuals, this dogma was extremely popular among the rank and file of the church in all regions, and most of the bishops voted for it enthusiastically.

Attitudes toward the papacy in the newly independent United States were affected by all these developments. The Thirteen Colonies were, with one or two exceptions, heirs to the anti-Catholicism of British Protestantism, where the pope was burned in effigy every year on Guy Fawkes Day. The coming of independence brought religious freedom but also brought the feeling that papal power, even in purely religious matters, was incompatible with democracy, and that loyalty to the pope constituted "allegiance to a European prince"—which he was, at the time—and was in conflict with American patriotism. American Catholics had to walk a mental tightrope, insisting on their democratic spirit and on the compatibility of Catholicism with democracy while also remaining loyal to papal supremacy. Under pressure from the widespread Protestant version of medieval and Reformation history, they had to insist that they did not recognize any papal right to order Catholic Americans how to vote, or to interfere in their political life, while also insisting that there was no danger of such a thing occurring. At the same time, loyalty to the pope became all the more a sign of true Catholicism in that Catholics felt like a beleaguered minority that had to rally around the focal point of Catholic unity while insisting on their unimpeachable American patriotism. Mainstream Americans, however, remained deeply suspicious of the genuine Americanism of their Catholic fellow citizens, and these suspicions became especially odious in the 1928 presidential campaign, when Democratic candidate Alfred E. Smith's potential subordination to papal authority on political issues was hotly debated and contributed to his defeat by Herbert Hoover. The same fears were raised again in the campaign of 1960, but in the papacy of John XXIII they carried significantly less credibility and could not keep John F. Kennedy from the White House.

The Roman authorities in turn were ambivalent toward the American ethos. On the one hand, the new nation's religious freedom allowed the church to grow unimpeded, while the old Catholic nations of Europe often followed anticlerical policies and hindered papal governance of the local churches. Because of this, the beleaguered popes of the nineteenth century often expressed a sense of consolation at the sight of the American church when compared to the situation of the church in Europe. On the other hand, the democratic ideas prevalent in the United States could not but create discomfort in a Roman milieu that was still that of a princely court, and separation of church and state was a principle that Rome could tolerate in practice but could not—as more and more American Catholics were coming to do—accept as an ideal. A book that presented the American situation as a model to be imitated by Catholics under the French Republic caused such a scandal among conservative monarchists that Leo XIII felt the need to issue the apostolic letter *Testem Benevolentiae* (1899), which warned against a number of tendencies in American

Catholicism. The discomfort surfaced again in Rome during the 1940s when John Courtney Murray, S.J., published studies on church-and-state issues that presented the American experience as ideal rather than tolerable. Murray was silenced by the Holy Office in 1954 but was later brought by Francis Cardinal Spellman of New York as a *peritus* (expert) to the Second Vatican Council, where he wrote the draft for the Decree on Religious Freedom.

Mainstream American attitudes toward the papacy improved significantly after World War II, when the ascetic and imposing figure of Pius XII came to be seen as a bulwark against communism and thus a major moral force allied to the American effort to save the "free world" from atheistic Marxism. American Catholics, too, were enthusiastic about him, since he was conservative enough to be in tune with the spirit of the 1950s but had made a number of changes in liturgy and discipline that gave hope to the liberals and that in fact prepared the way for the Second Vatican Council.

The pontificate of John XXIII, however, was a watershed in the liberalizing of Catholicism. The new pope's personality charmed both Catholics and Protestants, and his encouragement of ecumenism, as well as his social encyclicals *Mater et Magistra* and *Pacem in Terris,* created a totally new climate in relations between Catholicism and other religions. The obvious freedom of debate that the non-Catholic observers discovered at the Second Vatican Council also eroded the centuries-old distrust of a monolithic papal church. Catholics, too, were excited by the heady new climate in which loyalty to the pope suddenly was equated with freedom to present bold new insights on belief and practice. If Pius XII had been in harmony with the spirit of the 1950s, John XXIII was one of the creators of the spirit of the 1960s. At his death in 1962 both Catholics and Protestants felt equally bereaved.

Initially Paul VI inherited the goodwill that John had elicited, since Paul was openly committed to continuing the process of the council and its reforms. But Paul's personality could not catch the imagination of the world as John's had, and events showed that Paul was of two minds about the brave new world that progressive Catholics had expected from the council. When, after convoking a blue-ribbon panel of experts to advise him, he ignored their almost unanimous counsel and reaffirmed the prohibition of artificial birth control in the encyclical *Humanae Vitae* (1968), he became extremely unpopular among American Catholics, who began to explore the legitimacy of dissent from the noninfallible *magisterium* (teaching authority of the church). The changes in the liturgy managed to displease both conservatives and progressives, vocations to the priesthood and religious life decreased drastically, and priests resigned from the ministry in unprecedented numbers. These developments cast a pall of gloom over the last years of Paul's pontificate.

After the brief pontificate of John Paul I, the cardinals broke precedent by electing a Polish cardinal, who took the name of John Paul II. He has combined great personal dynamism and charm with positions even more conservative than those of his Paul's last years, thus producing the anomaly of a pope who is personally extremely popular though his policies are widely questioned, opposed, or ignored. It is significant, however, that even in the circles that most oppose his theological and disciplinary positions, American Catholics still are not willing to consider any kind of separation from the papacy, only a redefinition of what constitutes due loyalty and permissible dissent.

See also CHURCH; CHURCH AND STATE; ENCYCLICAL; HUMANAE VITAE; ROMAN CATHOLICISM; ROME; VATICAN; VATICAN II.

BIBLIOGRAPHY

Fogarty, Gerald P. *The Vatican and the American Hierarchy from 1870 to 1965.* 1972.

Hennesey, James, S.J. *The First Council of the Vatican: The American Experience.* 1963.

Miller, J. Michael. *What Are They Saying About Papal Primacy?* 1983.

Reese, Thomas, S.J. *Inside the Vatican.* 1996.

Sullivan, Francis A., S. J. *Magisterium: Teaching Authority in the Catholic Church.*

Jaime R. Vidal

Paranormal

The concept of the supernatural event, which underlies the contemporary concept of the paranormal, has long had a part in religion. Colonists immigrating to North America brought with them traditions shaped by New Testament and medieval beliefs that the physical world is open to the influence of spiritual beings: God, angels, and demons. It was believed that God miraculously manifested his salvific power in the life of Jesus, and continued to intervene through occasional wonders wrought by saints. Furthermore, there was a widespread assumption that certain human beings could wield magical power either good, bad, or neutral. Magical systems are based on a view of the world as having correspondences, or "sympathy," between different things or different orders of being, making possible action at a distance in space or time—for example, the belief that the utterance of a curse or a blessing has an unmediated impact for ill or good on its object.

The Colonial and Antebellum Periods

By the fifteenth century, beliefs about the supernatural tended to become polarized, with both ordinary and extraordinary events often interpreted as being due to demonic activity. For three centuries paranoia supported by religious authorities manifested in waves of witch-hunts, including, in North America, the notorious New England trials and executions of 1692 and earlier. At the same time, however, there remained many people who considered various magical practices, such as astrology and the use of protective amulets, to be consistent with Christian beliefs.

Enlightenment rationalism and reaction to the witch-crazes caused beliefs in psychic phenomena and in the effectiveness of magical practices to wane in the eighteenth century, particularly among the educated and the powerful in society, though they continued much longer at the level of folk belief.

Nonetheless, there were significant religious movements stressing supernatural events and powers. The Shakers, immigrating to North America in 1774 under the leadership of Ann Lee, reported and highly valued various supernatural experiences such as clairvoyant visions and healing. From 1837 to the late 1850s, Shakers claimed visions of heaven and trance messages from Mother Ann and other first-generation pioneers as well as from angels and biblical prophets.

The successive waves of Protestant evangelical revivals also were accompanied by purportedly supernatural events (though many evangelicals did not welcome such phenomena or accounts of them). Among the evangelists, eighteenth-century Methodist itinerant clergy, for example, reported a number of precognitive dreams; a Calvinist clerical family claimed visions of Christ and Lazarus-like near-death experiences. Nineteenth-century revival converts experienced such phenomena as Christic visions, divine light flooding their surroundings, and nature glowing with celestial splendor. Many also believed that the life transformations (such as abrupt disappearance of addictions) in their ensuing lives were due to divine intervention.

The style of Christianity that developed among enslaved African Americans was influenced both by the revivals and by fragments of magical beliefs and practices retained from African religions. For example, praying to the Lord against the master was not altogether different from explicit practices of "conjure" and Witchcraft. That these beliefs and practices could embody genuine power is evident from Harriet Ross Tubman, conductor on the Underground Railway, whose autobiography tells of apparently successful praying-against as well as several instances of answered prayer in the form of telepathic warnings that enabled her to evade capture during her nineteen journeys of liberation.

Mormonism arose in the 1820s and 1830s in the upstate New York setting of competing evangelical groups. Its founder, Joseph Smith, Jr., reported that, guided by an angel, he found a cache of golden plates that he translated by means of a stone having supernatural powers. Some later Mormons practiced healing by laying on of hands, and reported near-death visions giving knowledge of the afterlife.

Mesmerism with its trances and healings, and Swedenborgianism with its beliefs in spirits and an afterlife were both influential in the early nineteenth-century United States, laying the groundwork for the Spiritualist movement, which began in 1848. One of the most important tenets of Spiritualism was the possibility of bringing messages to the bereaved from deceased loved ones, and it was here that paranormal knowledge—accounts by mediumistic communicators of specific events that the medium could not have known about normally—was highly valued when it was perceived to have happened. Spiritualists faced much opposition from mainstream religion.

The Years 1865 to 1961

Spiritualists tended to deprecate institutional religion as dogmatic, and recommended their own approach to the issue of life after death as comfirmable by scientific investigation. A few scientists and scholars rose to this challenge, but by the time the societies for physical research were established in the 1880s, the scientific study of mediumistic communication had largely separated from spiritualism as a religion. The societies continue to the present, and a number of prominent researchers (parapsychologists) have come to hold that there is in fact ample social-scientific evidence (if not proof) from the study of mediumship and other psychic phenomena that human personality does survive death.

It was parapsychologists who found the term "supernatural" too vague and freighted with religious overtones, and coined "paranormal" to refer to events that appear to violate taken-for-granted basic principles: the dependence of mind on brain, and the limitations on the ways one mind can interact with another mind and with matter. "Supernatural" and "paranormal" are not coterminous concepts; with the increase of knowledge, some healings or visions considered supernatural in previous centuries would not be considered paranormal today. In many cases there is insufficient information about a given historical case to settle the issue.

Another instance of the paranormal may be found in Pentecostalism. Pentecostalism is a renewal movement, whose members now number in the millions, that began at the turn of the twentieth century in Topeka and Los Angeles with glossolalia— "speaking in tongues"—by members of Holiness Movement churches. These incomprehensible utterances, though considered supernatural, are not definable as paranormal except when (as sometimes claimed) the speaker is using a recognized, unlearned language. Other characteristic activities were healings by laying on of hands; "prophecy" and "wisdom"—that is, spontaneous admonitions or homilies; and "discernment of spirits," seeing visions of spiritual beings. These manifestations sometimes involved apparent telepathy and clairvoyance.

Second Half of the Twentieth Century

In the 1960s and 1970s, Pentecostalism, under the name of charismatic renewal, appeared (and continues) in both Protestant and Catholic mainline churches, with the same basic phenomena. Unsurprisingly, much controversy resulted.

In Roman Catholic charismatic groups, these phenomena overlap with visions of the Virgin Mary and resulting pilgrimages to such places as Conyers, Georgia; Bayside, New York; and Santa Maria, California. In connection with Marian pilgrimages there have been reports of paranormal healings in response to prayer, of photographs showing inexplicable light, and of rosary beads of ordinary metal turning to gold—spontaneous modern alchemy. Church authorities are very slow to endorse these manifestations.

Metaphysical trance communications that have come to be known as "channeling" sometimes were accompanied by paranormal knowledge; an example is the well-documented work of Edgar Cayce, who diagnosed the ill health of hundreds of persons unknown to him. Beginning in about 1970, channeling was to become a major feature of the New Age movement, which envisions a radical transformation of the individual and of society. Different groups have used varying means toward these goals: meditation, exploring purported past lives, claimed contact with angels or spiritual guides. Many of these groups report and value paranormal phenomena as providing evidence for the truth of their beliefs; a few, however, consider such powers to be a temptation from the path to self-realization.

In sum, religious movements in North America, for the most part marginal, have manifested a range of beliefs, practices and happenings, that they consider supernatural; some of these in fact can be understood as paranormal. Traditional mainline churches tend to resist these developments.

See also AFTERLIFE; ANGELS; ASTRAL PLANES; ASTROLOGY; CHANNELING; DEVILS, DEMONS, AND SPIRITS; GLOSSOLALIA; MAGIC; MARIAN DEVOTIONS; NEAR DEATH EXPERIENCES; NEW AGE SPIRITUALITY; OCCULT, THE; PENTECOSTAL AND CHARISMATIC CHRISTIANITY; PSYCHIC; SPIRIT; SPIRITUALISM.

BIBLIOGRAPHY

Butler, Jon. *Awash in a Sea of Faith.* 1990.
Gudas, Fabian, ed. *Extra-Sensory Perception.* 1960.
James, William. *The Varieties of Religious Experience.* 1903.
Raboteau, Albert J. *Slave Religion: The "Invisible Institution" in the Antebellum South.* 1978.

Robert Ellwood
Gracia Fay Ellwood

Parish

Roman Catholic canon law stipulates that a parish is a defined community of the Christian faithful established on a stable basis within a particular church. The phrase "particular church" refers to a diocese or similar organizational structure. In the Roman Catholic tradition, parishes are established by, and are in communion with, their diocese and diocesan bishop, which are in turn established by and in communion with the Church universal and the Pope. Some Protestant churches, particularly those descended from European established churches, such as Episcopalians, Methodists, Lutherans, and others, borrow from this tradition and also use the term "parish." Protestant traditions that have congregationally oriented polities, such as the Baptist tradition, use the term "congregation" to emphasize local independence.

In the Roman Catholic tradition, parishes may be either "territorial" or "personal." Personal parishes are established for nonterritorial communities, such as those that are formed on the basis of ethnicity, nationality, language, participation in a specific college or university, and so forth. The functions common to parishes are: proclamation and formation, worship and sacramental celebration, charity and care, and outreach and social concerns.

In the United States, Roman Catholic parishes range in size from ten to ten thousand households; the average size of a parish is 843 registered families. In contrast, there are 36,170 Methodist parishes in the

United States, and their average size is 235 families. While the parishes of the United Methodist Church are more numerous than the parishes or congregations of any other church organization in the United States, the average size of each parish is typical.

Roman Catholic parishes are larger than Protestant congregations or parishes, in part because the Catholic tradition emphasizes a stronger sense of permanence and the Catholic sacramental tradition fits relatively congenially within a larger sized unit. Today, most Catholic parishes have a single priest assigned as pastor, who is responsible for the parish to the diocesan bishop. However, most parishes also have a number of others, including lay ministers, who serve either full or part time. The 30 percent of parishes with more than 1,000 families tend to have an average of five lay ministers, two deacons, and two vowed religious women ("nuns").

See also Congregation; Religious Communities; Roman Catholicism.

Bibliography

Coriden, James. *The Parish in Catholic Tradition.* 1996.
Dolan, Jay P. *The American Catholic Parish: A History from Colonial Times to the Present.* 1992.

Bryan Froehle

Passover

Passover or Pesach ("pass over"), one of the most significant Jewish holidays, begins the evening of 14 Nisan (late March to April). Traditionally, Jews outside Israel observe Passover for eight days; Jews in Israel and Reform Jews in North America observe for seven days. One of three biblical pilgrimage festivals (with Shavuot and Sukkot) when people brought agricultural offerings to the Temple in Jerusalem, Passover has its origins in ancient Near Eastern spring celebrations and is also called Chag Ha'Aviv ("the Spring Holiday"). However, the connection with history gives Passover its distinctive Jewish identity as a communal reminder and reenactment of the experiences of Egyptian slavery, the Exodus from bondage, divine revelation, and the formation of Judaism as a sacred community. Remembrance of these events is biblically mandated in Exodus 12:1–28. Many customs associated with Passover derive from earlier agricultural festivities, but all have been given Jewish meanings in terms of the Exodus. Most central is eating unleavened bread *(matzah)* throughout the festival. Once part of celebrations of the spring grain harvest, matzah came to symbolize the haste with which the Isra-

elites left Egypt, with no time to leaven their bread before baking it. Moreover, Passover observance requires that no leaven *(chametz)* of any kind may be eaten. Foods made from wheat, barley, spelt, rye, and oats, rice (for Ashkenazic Jews), and legumes, including beer and liquor, come under this category. The exception is the wheat flour used for baking matzah under rabbinic supervision in conditions that prevent any leavening; ground matzah may be used for baking. In traditional Jewish households, all regular dishes, cutlery, cooking utensils, and appliances are put away during Passover and replaced with items reserved for Passover use that have had no contact with *chametz;* directly before the holiday the house is thoroughly cleaned to remove all *chametz.* Many Jews also transfer ownership of any remaining *chametz* products to a non-Jew for the duration of the festival.

Although worship takes places in the synagogue on the first two and the last two days of the festival, which are considered full holidays, for most American Jews Passover's most central commemoration is the Seder (from the Hebrew word for "order"), a festive ritual meal, probably the most observed religious practice among North American Jewry. While Reform Jews may attend only one Seder, on the eve of the first day of the holiday, more traditionally oriented American Jews also participate in a second Seder, on the evening of the first day. Although components of the Seder have evolved over the centuries, the Seder framework remains flexible, allowing for adding new rituals and contemporary reinterpretations of Passover's fundamental themes. Central to the Seder is the Haggadah ("retelling"), the book that dictates the order of the ritual. The Haggadah, like the Seder itself, is a work in progress; while some of its contents date back two millennia, new material may always be added. In recent decades American Haggadot have been written focusing on issues such as civil rights, freedom for Soviet Jewry, and the role of women in Judaism. Since the Haggadah is a liturgical book for domestic use, regulations against adornment and illustration for scrolls and books used in the synagogue do not apply. Thus there is a long tradition of beautifully decorated and illustrated Haggadot; many examples of illuminated Haggadot manuscripts survive from the Middle Ages, while printed Haggadot past and present display a variety of artistic styles.

The primary functions of the Seder are educational and experiential. Since parents are biblically commanded to instruct their offspring on the centrality to Judaism of the redemption from slavery, the Exodus from Egypt, and the revelation of the Torah at Mount Sinai, many elements of the Seder are directed at engaging and entertaining children. Moreover, all who participate in the Seder should imagine

Jewish nursery school classmates at the Ramaz Hebrew Day School in New York on Thursday, March 25, 1999, cover their eyes during a blessing over the candles at the start of a Passover seder at their school.   (Credit: AP/ Wide World Photos.)

that they themselves are part of the Exodus generation reliving through this ritual the experiences of degradation, freedom, and commitment to religious service. Passover stresses that God alone brought the Israelite slaves out of bondage and led them to Mount Sinai, forming a mixed multitude into a people united by revealed laws and shared faith. The Haggadah's recounting of these events eliminates human agency as much as possible; Moses, so central in the biblical account, is barely mentioned.

The Seder appears to have been influenced by the Greek custom of holding sumptuous banquets accompanied by philosophical conversation, as in Plato's *Symposium.* Usual practices at such feasts—drinking wine and reclining at table—were adopted and imbued with Jewish symbolic meanings, while the philosophic discourse was turned into the Haggadah. In fact, the Seder is both a meal and a religious service; the five (sometimes six) foods on the Seder plate at the Seder table symbolically recall the Passover story. These include an egg *(betzah),* which evokes the Passover sacrifices that were offered in the Jerusalem Temple and the wholeness and continuity of life. A green vegetable *(karpas),* usually parsley or celery, represents the renewal of springtime; during the Seder, the

greens are dipped in salt water, reminiscent of the tears of the Hebrew slaves. A roasted shank bone *(zaro'a)* recalls the lamb sacrificed at the first Passover, while bitter herbs *(maror*—sometimes in two varieties) evoke the bitterness of slavery in Egypt. A mixture of chopped apples, nuts, and wine *(charoset)* is a reminder of the mortar the slaves were forced to mold into bricks; both maror and charoset are eaten, separately and together, during the Seder. The Seder table also holds a plate with three matzot, symbolizing the three divisions of ancient Israel: Kohen (priests), Levi (assistant priests), and Israel, the rest of the Jewish people. As the Seder begins, the middle matzah is broken in two; one half becomes the *afikomen,* a Greek term meaning "dessert," which must be eaten to end the ritual meal. This afikomen is hidden away and children search for it, demanding a gift in payment for its return. It is customary to drink four cups of wine during the Seder, based on four biblical promises of redemption (Exodus 6:6–7). An additional Cup of Elijah is placed on the Seder table as a reminder that Elijah will one day herald the advent of the messianic era, when all disputes will be resolved. Late in the Seder service, the door of the home is opened for Elijah. This symbolic reminder of ultimate redemption, like the afikomen, also sustains the interest and involvement of children.

The fifteen parts of the Seder service are recited and performed in a specific order. The central focus, the telling of the Passover story, *maggid* (narration), begins when the youngest child present asks four questions about what differentiates the Seder night from all other nights. The answers initiate the chronicle of slavery and redemption and explain the meaning of the three central Passover symbols: the paschal sacrifice, the matzah, and the *maror.* Following the eating of the Passover meal, the service concludes with selections from Psalms praising God for the many miracles of redemption, drinking of the final cups of wine, and songs and games. The Seder's final words, "next year in Jerusalem," refer literally to return to the biblical land of Israel and metaphorically to hopes for the time when all people will live in freedom and peace.

On the Sabbath, which occurs during Passover, the biblical book Song of Songs is read in the synagogue; it is appropriate both for its evocation of vitality and rebirth and as an allegory of the eternal relationship between God and the Jewish people that was forged through the Exodus experience.

See also Belonging, Religious; Food; Jewish Identity; Jewish Observance; Judaism; Religious Communities; Religious Persecution; Ritual; Synagogue; Temple; Torah.

Bibliography

Broner, Esther. *The Women's Haggadah.* 1994.

Dosick, Wayne. *Living Judaism: The Complete Guide to Jewish Belief, Tradition, and Practice.* 1995.

Raphael, Chaim. *A Feast of History: The Drama of Passover through the Ages.* 1972.

Steingroot, Ira. *Keeping Passover: Everything You Need to Know to Bring the Ancient Tradition to Life and Create Your Own Passover Celebration.* 1995.

Waskow, Arthur. *Seasons of Our Joy: A Celebration of Modern Jewish Renewal.* 1990.

Judith R. Baskin

Pastoral Counseling

Pastoral counseling is the practice of talking with individuals, couples, and families to increase their understanding of emotional and religious conflicts and to help resolve problems using religious and other resources. *Pastor* is a biblical word for shepherd, one who cares for the health and salvation of believers, as in the sentence, "The pastor is a shepherd of the congregation." Pastoral counselors are called and entrusted by religious communities to help people strengthen their faith in God. They are trained to listen, respond empathetically, make assessments, and provide resources for people who seek their help. "Christian modes of healing have always distinguished themselves by achieving a spiritual advance in connection with the healing process" (Hunter 1990, p. 497).

History of Pastoral Counseling

Pastoral counseling has been one of the tasks of religious leaders since the early Christian Church elected deacons and elders to organize visitation and distribution of food for widows and orphans (Acts 7). Pastors and other leaders have talked with people about their concerns, illnesses, and fears for many centuries, and guidelines for pastoral care and counseling have been available since Tertullian wrote about repentance and confession in the second century B.C.E.

Modern pastoral counseling in the United States began in about 1920, when Anton Boisen started the first clinical training program in a Boston hospital. He was influenced by the psychologies of Sigmund Freud and William James and followed the models of professional education of medicine and social work. The first book-length descriptions were published in 1936, and since that time the literature has focused on bringing the best insights of the new psychologies to ministry, especially the psychoanalytic traditions of Freud and Erik Erikson and the humanistic traditions of Carl Rogers. *Pastoral Psychology,* a journal edited by Seward Hiltner, was a primary forum for the new discipline beginning in 1950. Freud's insights into the human condition had dramatic impact on theology and pastoral counseling because they helped to explain pervasive forms of human sin and unhappiness and provided ways of helping people through changes in personality and faith. Carl Rogers put a more positive face on counseling by emphasizing empathy, acceptance, and positive regard. From dialogue with Freud and Rogers pastoral counseling developed coherent theories and practices and a movement that has had significant impact on religious communities and their ministries.

Contemporary Issues of Pastoral Counseling

Since 1965, pastoral counseling has experienced significant changes as religion and society have been challenged on many fronts. Several issues have dominated these debates:

1. What psychological theories should pastoral counselors utilize?

2. What makes pastoral counseling religious?
3. Should women be counseled differently than men?
4. What differences do culture and class make in pastoral counseling?
5. Who pays for pastoral counseling?

What Psychological Theories Should Pastoral Counselors Utilize?

Pastoral counseling in the early twentieth century adopted psychoanalytically oriented theories that focused on exploration of aggressive and sexual impulses in individuals for improved mental health. Most pastoral counselors met in one-on-one weekly sessions for many weeks to help individuals gain insight into their unconscious conflicts. Adapting this method for congregations has been challenging, since most people would not engage in such intensive, long-term counseling. In 1966 Howard Clinebell's *Basic Types of Pastoral Counseling* transformed the common understanding of pastoral counseling when he recommended new forms of pastoral counseling, including short-term family counseling. Dozens of schools of psychotherapy introduced new understandings of the best way to help people, and Clinebell argued that these new approaches had merit. During the last four decades of the twentieth century, many forms of pastoral counseling have became acceptable, including behavioral, cognitive, family systems, self-help, and other therapies. The result is a transformed landscape for practicing pastoral counseling and pluralistic understandings of the psychological foundations for pastoral counseling.

What Makes Pastoral Counseling Religious?

In 1966 Don Browning's *The Moral Context of Pastoral Care* reminded pastoral counselors that the religious and ethical dimensions of pastoral counseling were equally as important as the psychological. Browning argued that the various theories of psychology often functioned like religions—that is, they had ethical and philosophical assumptions that needed to be critically examined. For example, the assumption that the unconscious fears of individuals determine mental health may not be compatible with some theologies of prayer and inspiration by the Holy Spirit. This opened up whole new avenues of exploration often fueled by the question "What is pastoral about pastoral counseling?" Implied in this question is the concern that pastoral counselors often functioned as psychologists rather than religious leaders guided by Holy Scripture and religious traditions.

Exploration of the theological and ethical foundations of pastoral counseling opened up rich areas of creative thought. Within liberal Protestantism, spirited discussion of denominational traditions such as Lutheran, Reformed, Wesleyan, Baptist, Anglican, and Pentecostal became central concerns for pastoral counseling. Within Roman Catholicism, debates about the influence of Vatican II, historical spiritual direction, and pre–Vatican II theologies became important. Within evangelical Christian communities, authority of Scripture, spirit-filled worship and healing, and moral issues such as abortion and sexuality defined the shape of pastoral counseling. Jews of Reform, Conservative, and Orthodox views began to explore the different theological and ethical frames for pastoral counseling. Rediscovering the ethical and religious dimension of pastoral counseling at first fragmented pastoral counseling. But this diversity has developed into a source of creativity as pastoral counselors explore the contributions of their diverse religious traditions.

Should Women Be Counseled Differently Than Men?

Beginning in the 1970s feminist pastoral counselors began to raise questions about pastoral counseling of women. It quickly became obvious that the issues of women had been ignored or minimized during the early decades of male-dominated pastoral counseling. Issues such as childbirth, mothering, sexual abuse, violence against women, discrimination against women in work and income, menopause, aging, and other topics had not been addressed. In addition, some theories and practices of pastoral counseling were unfair to women—namely, blaming mothers for mental illnesses such as schizophrenia, and letting fathers off the hook for their responsibilities of parenting. Developments in the psychology of women and feminist therapies required significant revisions of pastoral counseling. As increasing numbers of women began practicing and writing about pastoral counseling, addressing gender equality and difference became mandatory for the field.

What Differences Do Culture and Class Make in Pastoral Counseling?

In 1968 James Cone's *Black Theology* suggested that the theologies and practices of religious communities needed to be reworked in the light of white race supremacy. Pastoral counseling during the early twentieth century, for example, did not acknowledge the impact of race and class on many African-American families nor the mental health implications of prejudice and economic vulnerability within white families. At the end of the twentieth century there are too few accredited African-American pastoral counselors. Also in the 1960s, Latin American Liberation theology raised similar questions about pastoral counseling with those who are poor. Roman Catholic priests who lived with the poor revised their practices of pastoral counseling. Many issues that pastoral counselors traditionally diagnosed as conflicts of sexuality and aggression were results of oppression and trauma from race and class violence. If pastoral counseling leads to adjustment to race and class oppression, then the values of justice and love are not served. Discovering how to diagnose the social situations of oppression requires revision of the theories and practices of pastoral counseling. For those who are oppressed by social and economic conditions, empowerment becomes the goal of pastoral counseling rather than insight and adjustment. As pastoral counseling became global, new forms of pastoral counseling informed by African, Asian, Australian, South American, and other cultures became available, disclosing the European and U.S. bias in many theories and practices. For example, honoring ancestors and trusting shamans became religious resources for many Christians who wanted to understand their lives more fully. Communitarian theologies made dramatic contributions to the ideas of relationship and families.

Who Pays for Pastoral Counseling?

Is pastoral counseling paid for by individuals, congregations, health insurance, or government? Because early pastoral counseling often followed a medical model of expensive individual sessions within health care centers, pastoral counseling was profoundly affected when insurance companies, government, and health maintenance organizations drastically changed the economics of health care in the 1980s. Third-party agencies refused to pay for many forms of mental health care, especially outpatient treatment and preventive counseling. Most individuals could not afford expensive pastoral counseling that was not subsidized. As a result, some U.S. pastoral counseling centers and training programs were forced to close. Some congregations provided funding for pastoral counseling centers, especially those organized under the franchise name Samaritan Centers, that provided high-quality, subsidized care in many communities. Other pastoral counselors focused on congregational care through support groups and short-term consultation. State licensing for counselors established secular criteria for care that often made pastoral counseling less available in many communities. Pastoral counseling as a ministry of congregations has historically been the central practice and is receiving added emphasis for the future.

In summary, pastoral counseling has been an important practice of religious communities for many centuries. During the twentieth century, pastoral counseling was dramatically changed by the introduction of modern psychologies. Since 1965 the theories and practices of pastoral counseling have been further transformed by new developments in psychology, theology, gender, culture, and economics. As religious communities revise their understandings of people in relation to God, pastoral counseling will continue to be an important resource in the twenty-first century.

See also PSYCHOLOGY OF RELIGION; PSYCHOTHERAPY.

BIBLIOGRAPHY

Browning, Don. *The Moral Context of Pastoral Care.* 1966.

Clinebell, Howard J., Jr. *Basic Types of Pastoral Counseling.* 1966.

Fitchett, George. *Assessing Spiritual Needs: A Guide for Caregivers.* 1993.

Gerkin, Charles V. *The Living Human Document: Revising Pastoral Counseling in a Hermeneutical Mode.* 1984.

Glaz, Maxine, and Jeanne Stevenson Moessner, eds. *Women in Travail and Transition: A New Pastoral Care.* 1991.

Graham, Elaine. *Making the Difference: Gender, Personhood and Theology.* 1996.

Graham, Larry Kent. *Care of Persons, Care of Worlds: A Psychosystems Approach to Pastoral Care and Counseling.* 1992.

Hiltner, Steward. *Preface to Pastoral Theology.* 1958.

Hunter, Rodney, ed. *Dictionary of Pastoral Care and Counseling.* 1990.

Lartey, Emmanuel. *In Living Colour: An Intercultural Approach to Pastoral Care and Counseling.* 1997.

Poling, James Newton. *The Abuse of Power: A Theological Problem.* 1991.

Pruyser, Paul W. *The Ministry as Diagnostician.* 1976.

Ramsay, Nancy. *Pastoral Diagnosis: A Resource for Ministries of Care and Counseling.* 1998.

Smith, Archie, Jr. *The Relational Self: Ethics and Therapy from a Black Church Perspective.* 1982.

Stone, Howard. *Using Behavioral Methods in Pastoral Counseling.* 1980.

Wimberly, Edward P. *Pastoral Counseling and Spiritual Values: A Black Point of View.* 1982.

James Newton Poling

Pastorate.

See Ministry.

Patriarchy

Although patriarchy has been the norm in most religions for most of recorded history, it has become a highly contentious term in contemporary American religion. Patriarchy (father rule) refers more generally to male authority within any social structure—family, country, religion—and has historically been associated with reduced power and freedom for women (e.g., dress codes, restriction of mobility outside the home, control of sexual activity, prohibition from voting or holding political office, exclusion from education and various occupations). While contemporary American society has—legally, at least—virtually abolished patriarchy, religion has long served to legitimate it and is the last remaining institution to claim that patriarchy should be maintained. Theoretical debates over patriarchy, therefore, have important practical implications.

First, scholars disagree over what exactly is meant by religious patriarchy and the impact it has on gender roles. Some traditions are patriarchal in their official structure but allow women considerable power within the home. Robert Orsi has described nineteenth-century Italian-American Catholicism as a public patriarchy, private matriarchy, and similar characterizations have been made of Judaism. Conservative Protestants officially promote male authority, but women have founded and led popular movements, particularly in early Pentecostalism and in healing ministries. In short, we need to distinguish between public (official) and private (domestic) elite and popular religion.

Second, there is considerable debate as to patriarchy's origins. One theory holds that religious patriarchy is tied to economics. Settled agricultural societies where women make an equal or greater contribution to the food supply than men often have female-centered creation myths and include women in public rituals, while the reverse is true in nomadic societies that depend primarily on hunting or herding of animals. Patriarchal religion became universal because the latter type of society developed weapons and techniques of warfare to overpower the former.

Another theory ties the rise of patriarchal religion to reproduction. Before man understood the reproductive process, woman's ability to give birth must have seemed magical. Patriarchal religion emerged either as a means to counter woman's power (e.g., menstruation taboos) or as a result of man's eventual recognition that reproduction requires his input and that to claim offspring as "his" he needed to control women's sexual activity.

Both these theories imply that patriarchy may have been preceded by a society in which men did not rule.

Some contemporary feminists have argued for the existence of a universal matriarchal religion that was suppressed by more patriarchal traditions (e.g., Judaism in the Middle East or the Vedic tradition in India), but the evidence is controversial. Much of the argument turns on whether archaeological findings of female figurines should be interpreted as goddesses, and whether societies who worship goddesses actually give women any authority.

Finally, and most important, there is the debate over religious patriarchy's future. Within American religious history, patriarchy was until recently accepted as normative, since it was clearly legitimated by Scripture. Until about the middle of the nineteenth century, God's curse that Eve must bear the pain of childbirth and that her husband "shall rule over you" was taken quite literally by most Jews and Christians to mean that women's primary role was raising children and that men should lead in church, at home, and in society at large. Patriarchal religion also dovetailed nicely with existing social and economic arrangements, as the newly independent nation and its emerging industrial economy benefited from keeping married women at home, raising children.

As the nineteenth century drew to a close, however, several factors combined to challenge the notion that patriarchy was God's will. One was a broader awareness of scientific theories, including evolution and biblical criticism, which led people to question the literal truth of the Bible. Another was the unintended consequence of the cult of domesticity (the notion that the home is a moral haven from the corrupt world of business and politics), which led women to become increasingly involved in church activities and later in moral reform movements such as temperance. Such involvement in turn motivated women to question their exclusion from religious and political leadership. Feminists began to challenge the notion that patriarchy is God-given and sought for new interpretations of Scripture that gave women greater equality.

Churches and synagogues were slow to respond. So-called mainline Protestant churches such as Congregationalists, Presbyterians, and Methodists were the first to officially abolish patriarchy by permitting the ordination of women in the late nineteenth and early twentieth centuries. Reform Jews followed suit in 1972 and Conservative Jews in 1985. Yet, as studies of women clergy have shown, such symbolic moves do not necessarily mean the actual structure of American religion is no longer patriarchal. Most churches and synagogues that permit women's ordination do not actually employ female pastors, and Roman Catholics, Orthodox Jews, and the majority of conservative Protestant churches still refuse to ordain women.

Because feminist criticism undermines the very foundations of conservative religion (scriptural inerrancy for Evangelicals, magisterial authority for Catholics, and halakah for Orthodox Jews), defending patriarchy has become a kind of identity badge or symbolic boundary that conservatives use to distinguish themselves from liberals. Yet unlike the nineteenth century, patriarchal religion is at odds with contemporary social and economic trends, inducing conservatives to claim that patriarchy isn't really sexist and actually empowers women.

A similar dilemma is faced by Hindus, Buddhists, and Muslims, whose numbers in the United States have significantly increased since immigration laws changed in 1965. These religions are historically every bit as patriarchal as traditional Christianity or Judaism, and many immigrants come from countries where feminism has yet to make a significant impact. In attempting to retain the younger generation and in seeking new converts, these religions have had to either modify their patriarchal structure (e.g., Zen) or develop an apologetic for it (e.g., Islam).

Feminists for their part are divided over how to respond to the persistence of patriarchal religion. While most continue to push for reform, more radical feminists assert that biblical imagery and language are inherently patriarchal and must therefore be rejected altogether. These women are often drawn to new religions, especially Neopaganism, that provide an alternative to patriarchy.

See also BIRTH; FEMINIST THEOLOGY; GENDER ROLES; GODDESS; INCLUSIVE LANGUAGE; MATRIARCHY; NEOPAGANISM; ORDINATION; ORDINATION OF WOMEN; TEMPERANCE.

BIBLIOGRAPHY

Baum, Charlotte, Paula Hyman, and Sonya Michel. *The Jewish Women in America.* 1976.

Barfoot, Charles, and Gerald Sheppard. "Prophetic vs. Priestly Religion: The Changing Role of Women in Classical Pentecostal Churches." *Review of Religious Research* 22 (1980):2–17.

Brasher, Brenda. *Godly Women: Fundamentalism and Female Power.* 1998.

Falk, Nancy, and Rita Gross. *Unspoken Worlds: Women's Religious Lives.* 1989.

Friedman, Lenore. *Meetings with Remarkable Women: Buddhist Teachers in America.* 1987.

Kaufman, Debra. *Rachel's Daughters: Newly Orthodox Jewish Women.* 1991.

Manning, Christel. *God Gave Us the Right: Conservative Catholic, Evangelical Protestant and Orthodox Jewish Women Grapple with Feminism.* 1999.

McCloud, Aminah Beverly. *African American Islam.* 1995.

Orsi, Robert. *The Madonna of 115th Street: Faith and Community in Italian Harlem, 1880–1950.* 1985.

Tannahill, Raey. *Sex in History.* 1992.

Christel Manning

Patron Saints and Patron-Saint Feasts

The invocation of patron saints is based on the concept that deceased Christians who were notable during their lives for virtue can aid living persons today by interceding with God for special graces and material favors. Jesus Christ and the apostolic church imitated the Jewish practice of citing the patriarchs as exemplars of particular virtues; Solomon for his wisdom (Matthew 6:29; Luke 12:27) and Abraham for his faith (Hebrews 11:57 ff). While invocation of Jesus as protector remains primary in Christianity, in the deaths of the deacon Stephen (Acts 7:55–56) and early martyrs such as Ignatius of Antioch (d. 107), the Roman persecutions multiplied the number of exemplars of Christian virtues. Because many of these martyrs were identified with the power of faith in a particular city or region, their bodily remains were buried in places of honor when the persecutions ended. Moralistic accounts of the virtues of the deceased saint were recorded, and on the anniversary of his or her death, rituals were celebrated reminding the public of the saint's virtue. Devotion to the virgin martyr Lucy (d. 304) in the Sicilian city of Syracuse follows this model.

Martyrs are "witnesses" (this is the meaning of the Greek word), and the testimony of their virtuous lives and holy deaths was considered to strengthen Christian practice. The hagiographies frequently present the martyrs as able to face death in a saintly manner because they led pious lives. The conclusion was that other Christians should do the same. By the end of the fourth century, not only martyrs, but also church leaders and persons of piety were afforded the status of saints. For instance, Martin (316–397), a former Roman soldier and bishop of Tours, was acclaimed as a saint even though he did not die as a martyr. Gradually, most Christian cities claimed some saintly person from within their population to have been a saint in life and to have become a protector after death.

The expansion of Christianity in Europe to include peoples who had never been under Roman rule allowed for each of these new nationalities to celebrate their own saints. Often the acceptance of Christ did not completely displace practices related to animistic religions, so that some saints appeared to appropriate powers of fertility or healing that were virtually identical with beliefs of the original religion. Christianity instituted practices meant to make the separation from the previous religion more definitive, such as requiring the adoption of the name of a Christian saint at baptism. Despite continual efforts from the church institution to control the proliferation of such cults, however, Christianity maintained many devotions to patron saints that mixed in elements of magic and belief in spells that were not consonant with the Gospel. Typical of popular excesses were the collection of relics—fragments of bone or pieces of cloth touched by the saint—to which were attributed miraculous healing or protection from evil. With the emergence of large medieval cities after the eleventh century, specific groups within a larger locality would choose a saint as exemplar of their collective effort at the Christian life. Thus, for instance, the Roman martyr Cecilia, who was believed to have been a musician, became the patron saint of musicians, while Joseph, foster father of Jesus, was patron saint of carpenters.

The Christian churches created by the Reformation tended to reject as saints all but persons described as holy in the Bible. Catholicism after the Council of Trent began a process of repressing suspect practices associated with patron saints without rejecting the concept itself. By emphasizing historical authenticity, the Bollandists created a new style of hagiography that relied more on documentation and legal testimony rather than legend or miracle. Simultaneously, a rigorous scrutiny was established by the Vatican for the canonization of saints. The Catholic Church and the Episcopal Church in the United States continue the practice of invoking patron saints. While the proclamation of sainthood is reserved to their hierarchy, popular religiosity continues to play a major role in fashioning devotions. Thus, for instance, the devotion to one of the apostles, St. Jude, as a patron of hopeless causes, is a twentieth-century development from a shrine in Chicago. The patron saints of particular countries, such as St. Patrick and St. Bridget for the Irish, St. Casimir for Poles, and St. John the Baptist for Puerto Ricans and French Canadians, are invoked in the United States by groups of those ethnicities. Some saints are patrons today because their names are frequently chosen for Christian children, as, for instance, Michael, Christopher, Matthew, Mark, John, and James for boys and forms of Mary and Ann, Barbara, Margaret, and Elizabeth for girls. Choice of such a name does not always imply devotion to the saint. Other patron saints are familiar because they are associated with a religious order that will name institutions after them; St. Ignatius of Loyola, for instance, is often declared as patron of Jesuit universities.

The sixty-ninth annual San Gennaro Festival is held on Mulberry Street in New York City's Little Italy neighborhood in September 1995. (Credit: AP/Wide World Photos.)

The most popular patron saints in the United States today include the following, with brief descriptions of their lives, some reasons for their popularity, and their feast day:

- *Ann, Mother of Mary:* Described in an early noncanonical text as wife of Joaquim and mother of Mary, she has always been considered a Christian saint. Her name is a variant of the Hebrew "Hannah" attributed to other pious women (I Samuel 1:1–2; Tobit 1:9; Luke 2:36–38). In the nineteenth century, St. Ann was often cited as an exemplar of feminine domesticity. Popular shrines to her are found in Québec, Canada, and Scranton, Pennsylvania. (July 26)
- *Anthony of Padua (1125–1231):* One of the early followers of the Franciscan Order, he was a university theologian at Bologna in Italy and died in

Padua. He is often pictured holding a book on which the child Jesus is seated, based on an account of a miracle during his life. Proclaimed a doctor of the church on account of his preaching, he is often invoked as a finder of lost things and as a supplier of bread to the poor. (June 13)

- *Bernadette Soubirous (1844–1879):* A French peasant girl who reported visions of Mary at Lourdes, which has become one of the most important shrines in Catholicism. She joined the convent of the Sisters of Notre Dame at Nevers. She was canonized in 1933. The 1940s motion picture of her life helped popularize devotion to her and the naming of Catholic girls born at that time. (April 16)
- *Bridget (ca. 450–525):* She was the founder of the first convent on Irish soil, at Kildare. A collection of apocalyptic prophesies is attributed to her, many of which suggest a special love for Ireland by God. (February 1)
- *Charles Lwanga (d. ca. 1885–1887):* He was leader of twenty-two martyrs, many of them pages in the court of the Ugandan ruler King Mwanga. They were sentenced to death for denouncing the corruption at court. He is popular among African Americans. (June 3)
- *Christopher (third century):* This is a name found among martyrs of the period, but possibly used only as a label for an anonymous Christian, much as one might label a "John Doe." Legends played on the meaning of the name, "bearer of Christ," and made Christopher into a ferryman who miraculously encountered Christ as a child. St. Christopher medals have been considered to offer protection for those taking a journey. (July 25)
- *Frances Xavier (Mother) Cabrini (1850–1917):* An Italian nun and founder in 1877 of the Missionary Sisters of the Sacred Heart, she became an American citizen at Seattle in 1909 while working for the welfare of immigrants. She was the first American citizen canonized, in 1946. (November 13)
- *Francis of Assisi (1181/82–1226):* Born into a merchant Italian family as Giovanni di Bernardone, during his youth the pursued frivolity and stylish French clothing (hence his nickname as "Francesco"). He founded the Order of Friars Minor (Franciscans) (1209) after his dramatic conversion to a life of poverty in service of the poor. He received the wounds of Christ, the stigmata, in 1224 and was acclaimed as a saint throughout Christianity even before his death. Accounts of his simplicity and acceptance of unspoiled nature made him a patron of ecologists and animal pets. (October 4)
- *John Vianney (the Curé of Ars) (1746–1859):* A parish priest in a small French village, he was noted for his austere and dedicated life. He is considered the patron of parish priests who do not belong to a religious order. (August 4)
- *Blessed Kateri Tekakwitha (Lily of the Mohawks) (1656–1680):* Born among the Mohawks of New York State, she was baptized by Jesuit missionaries. She spent many years aiding the needy in Montréal, Canada. She is considered a patron of Native American Catholics. (July 14)
- *Maria Goretti (1890–1902):* An Italian peasant girl, she was slain at age twelve while resisting rape. She was canonized in 1950 and proclaimed as a model for Catholic purity. (July 6)
- *Martin de Porres (1579–1639):* A Dominican lay brother of mixed African and Spanish parentage, he was born in Lima, Peru. Cited for many miracles during his life, he is considered a patron of African-American Catholics. (November 3)
- *Thérèse of Liseaux (The Little Flower) (1873–1897):* A cloistered Carmelite nun in France, she died young, of tuberculosis. Her diary (*Autobiography of a Soul*) was celebrated as an example of how sanctity could be attained without miracles during one's lifetime. The diary re-created in deft psychological detail how ordinary events could provide occasions for the practice of virtue. Her constant prayers for foreign missionaries made her their patron. She was proclaimed a doctor of the church in 1999. (October 1)
- *Thomas Aquinas (1226–1274):* A Dominican friar and professor at the University of Paris, he is considered the greatest exponent of the systematic explanations of Christianity, the *Summa Theologica*. Declared an angelic doctor, he is frequently invoked as patron of Catholic scholars. (January 28)
- *Thomas More (1478–1535):* An English writer and lawyer who became chancellor of England under Henry VIII, he was beheaded for refusing to recant the Catholic faith. Patron of Catholic lawyers. (June 22)
- *Vincent de Paul (1581?–1660):* He was a French peasant who, after his escape as a galley slave under the Turks, became a priest and founder of the Vincentians/Lazarists for men and the Daughters of Charity for women. He was notable for his service to the urban poor and is considered the patron saint of charitable works. (September 27)

See also Lived Religion; Ritual; Roman Catholicism; Sainthood; Shrine.

BIBLIOGRAPHY

Orsi, Robert. *Thank You, St. Jude: Women's Devotion to the Patron Saint of Hopeless Causes.* 1996.

For Catholic saints visit: www.saints.catholic.org and related sites.

For the Bollandist collection visit: www.kbr.be/~socboll.

Anthony M. Stevens-Arroyo

Peace Churches

"Peace churches" is the term commonly applied to the three oldest pacifist denominations in the United States—the Society of Friends or Quakers, the Church of the Brethren, and the Mennonites. None of these is a united body, embracing different and diverse organizational entities. Quakers, and Brethren and Mennonites to a lesser extent, run the gamut from fundamentalism to universalist liberalism.

Quakers

As the least ethnic and most acculturated of the peace churches, Quakers have been the most visible in peace activism in the United States over the past four decades. All persuasions of Friends remain formally committed, through doctrinal statements, to the support of conscientious objection, but their doctrinal differences otherwise manifest themselves in their attitudes toward war resistance and groups such as the American Friends Service Committee (AFSC). Liberal, unprogrammed Friends, largely affiliated with Friends General Conference or the small Conservative yearly meetings, have been most active in peace movements, draft resistance, and other forms of peace activism. Most American Friends, however, are in pastoral bodies. The most evangelical of these, Evangelical Friends International (EFI), makes conscientious objection a matter of individual conscience, and, while generally supportive of its members who embrace traditional Quaker pacifism, has had leaders who have been open in repudiating pacifism and supporting U.S. military actions. In the middle is Friends United Meeting (FUM), which embraces both pastoral and unprogrammed Friends. In its official statements it has remained committed to pacifism and has supported various programs to advance disarmament and a peace witness. But many individual members, including some leading Friends, and many affiliated congregations have openly broken with pacifism and peace activism.

These fractures, dating back to the Civil War, were clearly manifested during the Vietnam War. The AFSC was among the earliest religious groups to call for a halt to bombing and a negotiated peace settlement. A Baltimore Friend, Norman Morrison, attracted national attention in 1965 when he burned himself to death in front of the Pentagon as a protest. By 1967 the most radical Quaker peace activists had formed A Quaker Action Group for radical confrontation with U.S. policy. They chartered a ship, the *Phoenix,* and amid massive controversy took a shipment of artificial limbs to North Vietnam. For the rest of the war, the AFSC, the Friends Committee on National Legislation (FCNL), the Central Committee for Conscientious Objectors (CCCO), and numerous regional and local Quaker bodies and individuals were active in the antiwar movement. Some Friends actively resisted the draft, refusing induction and destroying draft cards. Others refused to pay certain taxes that they saw as supporting the war. The Quaker peace tradition also attracted antiwar activists who joined the society.

The activism of antiwar Friends, however, was not shared by all Quakers. President Richard Nixon remained a member in good standing in his California meeting group throughout his presidency. Most pastoral Friends of draft age were not conscientious objectors. And high-profile activism, like that of the *Phoenix* voyagers and draft resisters, drew fierce criticism from some Friends, who resented what they saw as unpatriotic actions.

These divisions have continued since the end of the Vietnam War. The AFSC and the FCNL have continued to back policies for disarmament, the end of the draft, and peaceful settlement of international conflicts. The Iranian crisis of 1979–1980, the Grenada invasion of 1983, the Gulf War of 1990–1991, and the conflicts in the former Yugoslavia have brought appeals from both groups, as well as from FUM and other Quaker bodies, against the use of force. And all of these conflicts saw support of the use of force by some Friends. The resumption of draft registration in 1980 again brought conflicts over draft resistance by some Friends.

The increasing commitment of the AFSC to support groups it perceived as oppressed, such as Nicaraguan and Salvadoran rebels and Palestinians in Israel, has brought charges that it was moving away from traditional Quaker pacifism. Well-known pacifist Kenneth Boulding engaged in a sit-in at AFSC headquarters in 1977 to protest what he saw as AFSC indifference to oppression by the Communist Vietnamese government.

Brethren

Like Quakers, the various groups with a German Baptist or Brethren heritage span the theological spectrum. The largest group is the Church of the Brethren; other Brethren groups include the Brethren Church, the Dunkard Brethren, the Old Order German Baptist Brethren, and the Grace Brethren. All trace their roots to Dunkard pacifists who emigrated from Germany in the eighteenth century. Their attitudes toward peace issues since 1960 have reflected their diversity.

The Church of the Brethren has remained officially committed to pacifism in a number of statements of its governing body, the Annual Conference. It has advised its membership against not only military service but also against noncombatant service. During the Vietnam War, many of its members were active in the antiwar movement. In 1970 the Annual Conference recorded its support for draft resisters as well as for registered conscientious objectors. The Annual Conference maintained the Peace Committee, which in 1978 was merged in the Social Concerns Committee, and has sponsored a series of peace seminars. Peace issues have been part of Brethren Sunday school curricula, and peace studies are part of the curricula of colleges affiliated with the church. Manchester College, for example, has maintained its Peace Studies Institute since 1948. On the other hand, acculturation has moved many Brethren away from pacifism. In this century a majority of members eligible for the draft have served in the armed forces in American wars, including Vietnam.

The position of the Brethren Church on peace issues has been similar to that of the larger Church of the Brethren. The Brethren Church remains officially committed to pacifism, and urges its members to register as conscientious objectors. Peace issues are promoted by its Social Concerns Committee and in its publications. Yet many members no longer support pacifism, and have served in the armed forces. Even some pastors have served as chaplains.

The positions of the most conservative Brethren groups, the Old Order German Baptist Brethren and the Dunkard Brethren, are similar. They enjoin pacifism on their members, most of whom registered as conscientious objectors during the Vietnam War. Yet these groups have resisted links with antiwar groups. In 1978, for example, the Old Order German Baptist Brethren officially condemned civil disobedience and antiwar demonstrations, enjoining instead subjection to civil powers.

The most fundamentalist of the Brethren groups, the Grace Brethren, have tended to follow the general course of other fundamentalist denominations on peace issues since 1960. A few older pastors still embraced pacifism, but such views were those of a small minority. Most Grace Brethren have more or less

openly supported U.S. use of armed force in Vietnam, the Gulf War, and other conflicts.

Mennonites

Mennonites have seen the greatest change over the past four decades. In 1960 all of the various Mennonite groups in the United States were still largely committed to the traditional Anabaptist theology of the Two Kingdoms. This theology separates the kingdom of the believer, where people live in strict obedience to New Testament command to "resist not evil," from the world that is subject to human authorities ordained by God. Thus while a Mennonite could not bear arms or engage in violence, neither could a Mennonite criticize governments that did so.

Change has been most apparent in the most acculturated of Mennonite bodies, the Mennonite Church, the Mennonite Brethren, and the General Conference Mennonite Church. Many of its members have moved away from Two Kingdoms theology toward a vision that sees all the world bound by the commandments of Christ. Thus violence is never in accord with the will of God. Mennonites also became more open to joining with people of other faiths in work to promote peace and in political action. Mennonites, for example, were active participants in the civil rights movement, in the antiwar movement of the Vietnam era, in the nuclear freeze movement of the early 1980s, and in various groups that opposed the draft. Peace studies became part of the curriculum of Mennonite colleges. The Mennonite Central Committee, which coordinates the social witness of the various Mennonite bodies, includes a Peace Section, which has been active in holding conferences and publishing peace literature.

Still, sociologists studying Mennonites have found considerable diversity. The most conservative Mennonites, especially in various Amish groups, still embrace the Two Kingdoms theology. They see involvement with "worldly" people as a threat to the separateness of believers, and civil disobedience and draft resistance as an irreligious violation of the commandment to accept human authority. Other Mennonites, more comfortable with political action, have seen the various peace movements as too linked to leftist and pro-Communist groups.

In 1976 Mennonites, most Quakers, and the Church of the Brethren joined together in a new organization, New Call to Peacemaking. The proposal to form the group came from evangelical Friends who feared a loss of the biblical basis of pacifism. The organization's first national conference was held in Green Lake, Wisconsin, in 1978. The New Call group sponsored conferences and publications to attempt to extend the peace witness within the constituent bodies and in the larger American society.

See also CONSCIENTIOUS OBJECTION; PACIFISM.

BIBLIOGRAPHY

Barbour, Hugh, and J. William Frost. *The Quakers.* 1988.

Brethren Encyclopedia. 1982.

Brock, Peter, and Nigel Young. *Pacifism in the Twentieth Century.* 1998.

Bush, Perry. *Two Kingdoms, Two Loyalties: Mennonite Pacifism in Modern America.* 1998.

Durnbaugh, Donald F. *Fruit of the Vine: A History of the Brethren, 1908–1995.* 1997.

Durnbaugh, Donald F., ed. *On Earth, Peace.* 1978.

Dyck, Cornelius J., and Dennis D. Martin. *The Mennonite Encyclopedia.* Vol. 5. 1990.

Thomas D. Hamm

Peak Experience

The term "peak-experience" was used by psychologist Abraham H. Maslow (1908–1970) to refer to states of unitive consciousness, or "moments of highest happiness and fulfillment," in people's lives. At such times, individuals feel detached from the mundane particulars of their individual lives and sense that they are at one with a fully integrated universe. They perceive things in a nonjudgmental or nonevaluative way, and they transcend their particular ego needs, becoming selfless or indeed "egoless." Moreover, their sense of time and location is often greatly distorted. Maslow further argues that during peak experiences people become more truly themselves. A common effect of the peak experience is to make life feel meaningful, or to reveal the "meaning of life." However, the peak experience itself has no further purpose. It is itself inherently valuable; it is not a means to any external end, but rather is important for its own sake.

In religious contexts peak experiences are often understood as mystical experiences. Maslow agreed with William James, John Dewey, and Erich Fromm that religion is not a single "social institution" or set of specific practices; rather, it is a "state of mind" that may be manifest in any aspect of everyday life. Indeed, Maslow explicitly divides religion into two types: the mystical, phenomenological "peakers," and the doctrinal, ritualized "non-peakers." For Maslow, the peak experience is the model of the religious revelation and the conversion experience, which in many religious narratives take place under the most ordinary, everyday conditions.

Complementary to the peak experience is the "plateau-experience," a notion Maslow developed at the end of his career. Whereas the peak experience is often an ecstatic overflow of the senses, the plateau experience is a calm, reflective moment of serenity during which the individual is able *both* to feel and to think about his or her situation. Unlike peak experiences, moreover, plateau experiences may be cultivated.

According to Maslow, the people most likely to have peak experiences, and to have them more often than others, are "self-actualizers." Self-actualizers are people who, for a variety of reasons, go farther than most toward fulfilling their individual potential, or as Maslow understood it, to finding their true selves. Maslow painted a strongly idealistic picture of self-actualizers: They are highly ethical, democratic, and selfless; they are not bound by culture or social ties; they are open to new ideas and appreciative of diversity; and they are capable of deeply meaningful interpersonal relationships.

Related to the notion of the peak experience is the notion of the "optimal experience," better known as "flow," developed by Mihaly and Isabella Csikszentmihalyi. An important difference between Maslow's theory and that of the Csikszentmihalyis is that whereas Maslow focuses on the peak experience itself, and the people who are most likely to have them, the Csikszentmihalyis are more interested in the activities that tend to generate flow experiences. Moreover, whereas peak experiences are understood as phenomenological—they are states of being and ends in and of themselves—flow experiences may occur during purposeful action, such as running, playing a musical instrument, or performing a religious ritual. Unlike Maslow, therefore—because the "paraphernalia" of religion are secondary, and possibly detrimental, to peak experiences—the Csikszentmihalyis show how religions actually can provide the "goals and rules for intense flow experiences."

See also CONVERSION; MEDITATION; MYSTICISM; PSYCHOLOGY OF RELIGION; RELIGIOUS EXPERIENCE; RELIGIOUS STUDIES; REVELATION; SPIRITUALITY; TRANSCENDENTAL MEDITATION.

BIBLIOGRAPHY

Csikszentmihalyi, Isabella Selega, and Mihaly Csikszentmihalyi, eds. *Optimal Experience: Psychological Studies of Flow in Consciousness.* 1988.

Csikszentmihalyi, Mihaly. *Flow: the Psychology of Happiness.* 1992.

Maslow, Abraham. *New Knowledge in Human Values.* 1959.

Maslow, Abraham Harold. *Religions, Values, and Peak Experiences,* 2nd ed. 1970.

Maslow, Abraham Harold. "Religious Aspects of Peak Experiences." In *Personality and Religion: The Role of Religion in Personal Development,* edited by William Alan Sadler. 1970.

Maslow, Abraham Harold. *Toward a Psychology of Being.* 1968.

Puttick, Elizabeth. "A New Typology of Religion Based on Needs and Values." *Journal of Beliefs and Values* 18 (1997): 133–146.

Wuthnow, Robert. "Peak Experiences: Some Empirical Tests." *Journal of Humanistic Psychology* 18, no. 3 (1978): 59–75.

J. Shawn Landres

Peale, Norman Vincent

(1898–1993), minister and author.

One of the most important currents in twentieth-century Christian thought has been the "gospel of prosperity," the idea that God wants his faithful peo-

A bespectacled Rev. Norman Vincent Peale holds the lapels of his cloak in this portrait from the 1950s at the height of his popularity as an author and speaker. (Credit: © Archive Photos.)

ple to prosper both spiritually and materially. The principal proponent of this gospel during the mid-twentieth century was Norman Vincent Peale, a Methodist minister whose "positive thinking" message struck a chord with millions of Americans struggling to work their way out of the Great Depression and to achieve personal success during the postwar era. The means to achieving success and prosperity, Peale argued, lay within the human mind and spirit. Drawing on the mental hygienics of nineteenth-century New Thought philosophy, Peale told his listeners that negative thinking led to failure and unhappiness. Positive thinking, in contrast, actually created the conditions for prosperity, health, and success in one's chosen profession. In crafting his gospel of this-worldly success, Peale tapped into a long-standing American interest in self-culture and self-empowerment, whose major nineteenth-century proponents included Ralph Waldo Emerson, Mary Baker Eddy, Ralph Waldo Trine, and Emma Curtis Hopkins.

Peale grew up in small-town Ohio, where his father, Charles Clifford Peale, rose from a Methodist circuit preacher to district superintendent and pastor of First Methodist Church of Columbus. The younger Peale attended Ohio Weslyan College and experienced a renewal of religious faith after overcoming a debilitating stutter. He worked as a journalist in Michigan before enrolling at Boston University's school of theology. Upon graduation, Peale successfully built churches in Brooklyn and Syracuse before receiving an appointment as senior minister at Marble Collegiate Church in midtown Manhattan. Peale's optimistic and ebullient preaching style soon drew thousands to the church's three Sunday services. His message of self-help, moral living, and hope appealed to Depression-era Americans struggling to keep their families afloat both morally and financially. Soon Peale was invited to start a new Saturday radio program, *The Art of Living,* which would run for forty years and turn Peale into a national celebrity. Peale also adapted his message to the new medium of television. His two programs, *What's Your Trouble?* and *Positive Thinking with Norman Vincent Peale,* were hugely popular during the "can do" Eisenhower era of the 1950s.

Peale's publishing successes outstripped even his broadcasting career. He began *Guideposts* during the mid-1940s as a newsletter and within ten years had built its circulation to more than one million readers. The still-popular periodical contains inspirational stories and quotations from ordinary people who have overcome adversity through belief in God and self. Peale's series of books on self-empowerment, the most popular of which was *The Power of Positive Thinking* (1952), helped define the postwar generation's ethos of faith in God, self-help, and material success.

Peale's personal star began to wane during the 1960s and 1970s, when his simple message of positive thinking seemed unable to speak to a nation traumatized by a loss of faith in conventional values and institutions. Television evangelists such as Robert Tilton, Frederick Price, and Robert Schuller, however, have embraced Peale's essential message and achieved considerable success by adapting the "gospel of prosperity" to their late-twentieth-century audiences.

See also JOURNALISM, RELIGIOUS; MATERIAL RELIGION; NEW THOUGHT; POPULAR RELIGION; PREACHING; PROSPERITY THEOLOGY; PUBLISHING, RELIGIOUS; TELEVANGELISM; SCHULLER, ROBERT.

BIBLIOGRAPHY

Detrich, Richard Lewis. *Norman Vincent Peale.* 1969.
Peale, Norman Vincent. *The Power of Positive Thinking.* 1952.

Phillip Charles Lucas

Pentagram

Every religion possesses a symbol that brings to mind the focal point of the belief system. For Christians, the cross or crucifix stands for the ultimate sacrifice and victory of Christ; Jews possess the Star of David; Taoist ideas revolve around the symbol of the Tao; and witches use the pentagram. The pentagram represents the order of the cosmos and appears as either a pentacle, or five-pointed star, or as a pentacle enclosed in a circle. Generally one point faces upward in Wiccan symbology; however, some British traditions use an upside-down pentagram to denote the higher degrees that a witch may obtain through training.

Typically, in the United States, the upside-down pentagram has been used by Satanists, representing the goat and often appearing as the head of the Goat of Mendes inside the five-pointed star. Anton LaVey, founder of the Church of Satan, claimed that the two upward points represented the horns of the goat and the three downward points the trinity turned on its head. In *The Secret Doctrine,* Madame Helena Blavatsky wrote that the reversed pentagram symbolized the Kali Yuga, the current dark age of materialism, sensuality, and violence. The pentagram is much older than contemporary Wicca and was known as a Qabalistic sign to the Freemasons and occult fraternities arising from the Rosicrucians. The pentagram's origins probably lie much earlier that this, with the earliest known examples appearing in Babylonian relics. Its earlier usage in Qabalistic magic shows through its

A black-and-white pentagram showing the basic pentagram design. Some pentagrams are multicolored and quite elaborate. (Credit: CORBIS/Christel Gerstenberg.)

meaning as a symbol of the four elements, elements that also play a major role in the tarot, astrology, and other occult forms of knowledge.

The pentagram functions as a magical symbol through its representation of cosmic order. Its five points represent the other elements of life, plus spirit, the source of magical power. Earth, air, fire, water, and spirit bound the life of a witch and are believed to enable witches to perform magic. Witches believe that meditation on the characteristics of each element allows them to visualize the order of the cosmos. For them, earth stands for stability, air controls the intellect, fire the passions, and water acts alternately as a purifying source and as the womb of all life. Spirit presides over these four elements and represents an immanent, sacred realm, the abode of the gods and goddesses.

Pentagrams used in magical rites are thought in some sense to control the elements they represent. Witches utilize the pentagram in invoking and banishing. In casting a circle, or in creating a sacred space in which to perform rituals, witches draw invoking pentagrams at each of the four quarters, inviting the element of that quarter to come and participate. After the ritual, a banishing pentagram at each quarter dissolves this link between the witch and the element represented. In most Wiccan cosmologies east is the direction of air, south of fire, west of water, and north represents earth. The element of spirit is said to dwell at the center of the circle. Through meditation on the pentagram and the order it represents, a witch aims to connect with all life and the power underlying the cosmos.

See also LaVey, Anton; Magic; Myth; Rosicrucians; Satanists; Wicca.

Bibliography

Farrar, Janet, and Stewart Farrar. *The Witches' Bible Compleat.* 1984; repr., 1991.
Valiente, Doreen. *An ABC of Witchcraft Past and Present.* 1973.

Nancy Ramsey

Pentecostal and Charismatic Christianity

American Pentecostalism traces its growth to a revival meeting on Azusa Street in Los Angeles in 1906. Although the Azusa Street revival galvanized the movement, the distinctive Pentecostal teaching on the baptism with the Holy Spirit had been formulated by Charles Parham, an itinerant independent evangelist, in Topeka, Kansas, late in 1900. For a few years, the notion that the uniform initial evidence of the baptism with the Holy Spirit was tongues speech elicited little popular response. Parham called this message the "apostolic faith" and claimed that an end-times awakening restoring New Testament Christian experience was under way. In the fall of 1903, Parham began revival and healing efforts that soon spread his message in Kansas, Oklahoma, and Texas. By 1906 one of Parham's African-American cohorts, William Seymour, began preaching the apostolic faith in Los Angeles. His efforts resulted in the revival that established the movement.

Pentecostal identity was molded by several assumptions: (1) the baptism with the Holy Spirit was for all believers, was an "enduement with power for service," and would always be manifested by speaking in tongues; (2) Christ was about to return, and Pentecostalism was a revival of New Testament Christian experience that would immediately precede his return; (3) speaking in tongues would facilitate the rapid evangelization of the world. The first Pentecostals were evangelicals who often felt marginalized by traditional Protestant churches. Their restless longing for "more of God" motivated them to network through camp meetings, Bible studies, voluntary associations, and subscriptions to religious publications. Some had already left established churches to participate in new denominations or movements. Adherents of the ho-liness movement found themselves especially challenged by early Pentecostals, whose beliefs mirrored their own except on the matter of evidence of the baptism with the Holy Spirit.

Within a decade Pentecostalism made a transition from religious movement to denominations. The movement had already fragmented over understandings of sanctification. Those who believed that sanctification was a "second work of grace" and that the baptism with the Holy Spirit was a third normative experience for every Christian comprised the holiness wing of the Pentecostal movement. The best known among this cluster of denominations are the Pentecostal Holiness Church, the Church of God (Cleveland, Tennessee), the Church of God in Christ, and two small apostolic faith movements, one with headquarters in Portland, Oregon, the other in Baxter Springs, Kansas.

Pentecostals who understood sanctification to be progressive organized the Assemblies of God, the International Church of the Foursquare Gospel, and the Pentecostal Church of God. By the 1920s disagreements over the Trinity led to the formation of denominations known collectively as "Oneness" or "Jesus Only" Pentecostals. Among these are various Apostolic churches, the Pentecostal Assemblies of the World, and the United Pentecostal Church.

Ostracized by most fundamentalists and ignored or ridiculed by most Protestants, Pentecostals kept to themselves until the 1940s. In 1947 leaders of several Pentecostal denominations created a forum in which to explore common concerns. They called it the Pentecostal Fellowship of North America. Its statement of faith excluded Oneness Pentecostals, and African-Americans were also conspicuously absent. After a program in 1994 focused on racial reconciliation, the Pentecostal Fellowship of North America was reorganized as the Pentecostal-Charismatic Churches of North America. Representatives of the Church of God in Christ joined the leadership of this association. Oneness Pentecostals remain excluded from all cooperative endeavors.

During the 1940s the larger white Pentecostal denominations began finding a degree of acceptance in the newly formed National Association of Evangelicals. In the 1970s and 1980s, Thomas F. Zimmerman, the general superintendent of the Assemblies of God, won the confidence of evangelicals like Billy Graham, Bill Bright, and Leighton Ford, as well as the friendship of Catholics, among them Cardinal Ratzinger. Zimmerman's influence brought white Pentecostals at leadership levels into cooperative endeavors with American evangelical associations concerned for national revival and world evangelization.

North American Pentecostal denominations experienced considerable growth during the 1970s and early 1980s, occasioned in part by a surge of Latino affiliation and the dramatic growth of the Church of God in Christ in urban America. Worldwide evangelization resulted in overseas constituencies in Brazil and South Korea that far exceeded North American membership. This overseas growth had been quietly proceeding for some time. It had gained popular notice as early as 1958 when *Life* magazine published "The Third Force in Christendom" by Union Theological Seminary President Henry Pitney van Dusen. In this important article Van Dusen noted the growing numbers in the United States and in Latin America of Pentecostals, Mormons, Adventists, and Jehovah's Witnesses, groups outside the range of the average Protestant's vision, and pondered the reasons for their successes. He also gave Pentecostals an alternative self-perception: Rather than being marginalized, they represented something distinctly different.

By the late 1950s other factors also brought Pentecostals greater visibility. Pentecostals, like healing evangelists Oral Roberts and A. A. Allen, had taken their message to radio and TV. Their citywide campaigns in tents and municipal auditoriums, while not attracting much middle-class notice, drew thousands of working-class and immigrant seekers.

Meanwhile, Assemblies of God pastor David du Plessis gained entrée to the leadership of the National Council of the Churches of Christ and the World Council of Churches. The goodwill of van Dusen and Princeton Seminary President John MacKay brought Du Plessis to the campuses of Princeton, Harvard, Yale, and other East Coast seminaries to explain Pentecostal experience. A gentle, humble man, Du Plessis achieved what no Pentecostal evangelism had yet accomplished: the opportunity to bring his Pentecostal testimony to the acknowledged church leaders of his day. They proved eager to learn about Pentecostal beliefs and practices. Du Plessis urged them to see the baptism with the Holy Spirit as an experience for all Christians regardless of denomination. He told them to stay in their churches and become a nucleus for renewal. This stance resulted in 1962 in the surrender of his Assemblies of God credentials.

On July 4, 1960, *Newsweek* carried an article about Dennis Bennett, an Episcopal rector in Seattle who spoke in tongues. Response to the article demonstrated that people scattered across the country and affiliated with several denominations shared Bennett's experience. This interest in Pentecostal spirituality was facilitated by the Full Gospel Businessmen's Fellowship International, an association created with the support of Oral Roberts by Demos Shakarian, a wealthy California dairy farmer. FGBMFI chapters

met in a neutral setting over breakfast or lunch to socialize, testify, pray, and speak in tongues. People who had never entered a Pentecostal church now heard the same message and had opportunity to respond. Youth movements, like the Jesus People, with their rejection of traditional institutions also promoted interest in the informal, experience-oriented worship of Pentecostals and charismatics.

These and other impulses forged the charismatic movement. Participants tended to be better educated, more affluent, and more professional than adherents of older Pentecostal churches. By the mid-1960s charismatic Christianity found expression in Roman Catholicism, too. This early charismatic movement tended to strengthen people in their commitments to their own churches. It had more to do with spirituality than with theology and practice. Whereas Pentecostal churches had long insisted on the verbal inspiration of scripture and the necessity of the "new birth," charismatics avoided the clichés to which Pentecostals were accustomed. Some spoke of "the filling" rather than "the baptism" with the Holy Spirit. Nor did they embrace the definition of *worldliness* that historically animated Pentecostalism. They smoked, drank, danced, and spoke in tongues. Pentecostals were bewildered. The Assemblies of God held officially aloof from charismatics until well into the 1980s, although some of its pastors enthusiastically embraced the movement.

A variety of new organizations and denominations emerged from traditional Pentecostal sources that offered ways for Pentecostals and charismatics to move beyond historical and theological differences. Several are youth-oriented: Youth with a Mission, a huge short-term missions program, established by the one-time Assemblies of God minister Loren Cunningham; and Calvary Chapel, established by the former Foursquare Church pastor Chuck Smith. In the 1980s televangelism also created new coalitions. Pat Robertson, a charismatic Southern Baptist, used his channel to build a political movement and a university. The Bakkers' PTL (Praise the Lord) ministry featured charismatics and Pentecostals on its programs and at its camp meetings. Assemblies of God minister Jimmy Swaggart built a television ministry that reached around the globe and raised millions of dollars for Assemblies of God missions. The public moral failures of these Assemblies of God televangelists have not discouraged a new generation of charismatic televangelists, like Rod Parsley and Rodney Howard-Brown. And Paul and Jan Crouch exert considerable influence through their cable channel, TBN. *Charisma* magazine, established by Stephen Strang, advertises and reports on this constituency in a glossy full-color monthly.

After an initial burst of fervor resulting in some theological assessments within traditional denominations, the charismatic movement in the denominations was domesticated by the creation of denominationally based renewal services to give oversight and coordination. Those who felt ostracized by their denominations or who despaired of renewing their churches gradually drifted to new affiliations. Some found homes in independent charismatic congregations. There they frequently met onetime Pentecostals who considered their congregations too staid or too conservative. Large congregations (sometimes built on foundations laid by older, smaller efforts) emerged, with pastors whose name recognition was secured by television ministries and publications in Christian bookstores. Several established nonaccredited Bible institutes that quickly enrolled thousands of students. Christ for the Nations (in Dallas) and Rhema (in Tulsa) are two of the most influential. In the course of such change, doctrinal discontinuities soon became evident. Whereas Pentecostals had a particular view of the baptism with the Holy Spirit and expected the baptized to speak in tongues, charismatics had sometimes argued that any spiritual gift might manifest Spirit baptism. Although they generally spoke in tongues, that experience did not hold the same place in their overall theology as it did for Pentecostals. After all, they were Methodists, Lutherans, Catholics, or Episcopalians with liturgy, history, and tradition molding their identity. And independent charismatics as well as large numbers of Pentecostals no longer emphasized tongues as they once had. Corporate worship featured prophecies, words of wisdom and knowledge, being "slain in the Spirit," or the gift of discernment more often than speaking in tongues. Some spoke of a "third wave." If Pentecostals represented the first wave and charismatics the second, movements like the Vineyard, Calvary Chapel, and independent charismatics represented a third phase of an overarching twentieth-century revival.

Once-despised Pentecostals found themselves contending with many voices on themes that had once been theirs. Stagnating growth gave the old notion of new revival tremendous appeal. When a revival broke out at Brownsville Assembly of God in Pensacola in 1994, Assemblies of God leaders wholeheartedly endorsed it as a harbinger of the awakening they craved.

The Pensacola Outpouring is related to several other contemporary movements, especially a revival in Toronto known as the Toronto Blessing, and the "laughing revival" promoted by Rodney Howard-Brown. Each of these has particular features, and Toronto and Pensacola have drawn revival-hungry Pentecostals from around the world. There they can expect to be "slain in the Spirit," to weep, dance, jerk uncontrollably, or sing the new revival music. Recent claims maintain that God turns participants' dental fillings to gold and that gold dust falls in Pentecostal services. Church-growth guru C. Peter Wagner suggests that the gold is a harbinger of God's glory. People travel to these places for particular spiritual "anointings" and then hope to carry the revival home. Prayer banners, music CDs, and how-to literature are available. These revivals have become profitable businesses. The World Wide Web brings their music and message around the world.

Pentecostal and charismatic Christianity focus on religious experience, divine immediacy, and expressive human response. Adherents of these movements manifest eager spiritual restlessness for "more of God" while also revealing shrewd entrepreneurial instincts that often build their ministries into profitable businesses. Over the century the focus has shifted from tongues speech to more dramatic physical "manifestations," spiritual warfare, and other spiritual gifts. Perhaps the most enduring theme throughout the century is evangelism.

See also BAPTISM IN THE HOLY SPIRIT; BROWNSVILLE REVIVAL; CATHOLIC CHARISMATIC RENEWAL; CHARISMATIC MOVEMENT; CHURCH GROWTH MOVEMENT; EVANGELICAL CHRISTIANITY; FUNDAMENTALIST CHRISTIANITY; GLOSSOLALIA; GRAHAM, BILLY; HOLINESS MOVEMENT; TELEVANGELISM.

BIBLIOGRAPHY
Arnott, John. *The Father's Blessing.* 1996.
Beverley, James A. *Holy Laughter and the Toronto Blessing.* 1995.
Blumhofer, Edith L. *Restoring the Faith.* 1993.
Du Plessis, David, and Bob Slosser. *A Man Called Mr. Pentecost.* 1980.
Hamilton, Michael, ed. *The Charismatic Movement.* 1975.
Poloma, Margaret. *The Assemblies of God at the Crossroads.* 1989.
Quebedeaux, Richard. *The New Charismatics II.* 1983.
Robey, Steve. *Revival in Brownsville.* 1999.

Edith L. Blumhofer

People's Temple

The People's Temple is best known for the mass suicides and/or murders of nearly all of its more than 900 members in Jonestown, Guyana, in November 1978. This followed the murder of Congressman Leo Ryan, plus four others, as Ryan's investigative mission

Members of the U.S. military place bodies of People's Temple members into coffins at the airport in Jonestown, Guyana, in November 1978. Some 900 members, including their leader, Rev. Jim Jones, committed mass suicide by poisoning themselves at their Jonestown compound there.   (Credit: AP/Wide World Photos.)

was ending, with some defectors planning to return with him to the United States.

Founded in 1956 in Indianapolis by Jim Jones, the People's Temple was a racially integrated congregation featuring enthusiastic, Pentecostal-style services with sometimes staged "faith healings" plus social service programs, including free meals for the poor. Jones became known in the community as a civil rights leader, but his integrationist policies aroused local hostility. In 1963 the People's Temple affiliated with the Christian Church (Disciples of Christ), a mainstream Protestant denomination whose polity emphasizes congregational autonomy. Jones's services were influenced more by Father Divine than by mainstream Protestantism, but his racial policies and social outreach were consistent with the social agenda of the Disciples (and other mainstream Protestant denominations) at the time. Jones developed a controlling leadership style, putting his own authority above the Bible and expecting followers to call him "Father." He borrowed Marxist-inspired socialist ideas plus the evangelical revivalist tradition. In 1965 he was ordained as a Disciples of Christ minister, but the congregation clearly did not fit traditional categories of religious organization.

In 1965 the People's Temple moved to Ukiah, California, reflecting Jones's fear of a nuclear holocaust, which he believed he could escape there. The con-

gregation gradually grew, attracting educated white professionals and alienated young people who admired the temple's racial policies, high cohesiveness, and social service goals. Its outreach expanded with campaigns to San Francisco and Los Angeles, recruiting many poor blacks. By 1972 the temple moved to San Francisco, where membership grew to perhaps three thousand. Jones again became active in local politics. But the congregation increasingly resembled a communal-type organization, with members surrendering all their resources to the group. Jones tightened his control, using strategies ranging from lengthy self-analysis meetings to manipulation of sexual relations to physical beatings. Control was through a circle of inner advisers and a planning commission. He initiated a fake suicide ritual with the planning commission in which members were asked to drink "poison" wine (alcohol was otherwise forbidden) before being told that it was only a test of their faith.

Controversies erupted outside as news of inside abuses became known, and Jones developed plans for moving again, this time to Guyana, South America, to establish his long-awaited utopian community isolated from the coming apocalypse and other threats. By 1977 most members had moved, taking guns acquired earlier for protection. But Jones and his followers could not escape their opponents back in the United States, as demonstrated by Congressman Ryan's visit.

Following Ryan's murder, Jones gave the suicide order to his followers. It will never be known how many suicide victims drank the cyanide-poisoned punch voluntarily to maintain their honor and escape possible retaliation for Congressman Ryan's murder, but armed guards ensured that Jones's last order before his death was followed.

See also ANTI-CULT MOVEMENT; BRAINWASHING; CHURCH AND STATE; COMMUNES; CULT; CULT AWARENESS NETWORK; FATHER DIVINE; JONES, JIM; PENTECOSTAL AND CHARISMATIC CHRISTIANITY; PSYCHOLOGY OF RELIGION; SOCIOLOGY OF RELIGION.

BIBLIOGRAPHY

Hall, John R. *Gone from the Promised Land: Jonestown in American Cultural History.* 1987.

Johnson, Doyle Paul. "Dilemmas of Charismatic Leadership: The Case of the People's Temple." *Sociological Analysis* 40 (1979):315–323.

Kilduff, Marshall, and Ron Javers. *The Suicide Cult: The Inside Story of the People's Temple Sect and the Massacre in Guyana.* 1978.

Doyle Paul Johnson

Persecution, Religious.

See Religious Persecution.

Peyote

Peyote is a small, spineless cactus (*Lophophora diffusa* or *Lophophora williamsii*) native to high desert regions from north-central Mexico to southernmost Texas. It has been used in religious healing ceremonies by many indigenous peoples in that area since pre-Columbian times, usually chewed into a paste and swallowed or taken as tea. Despite active persecution by colonial Spanish missionaries and the Spanish Inquisition, it survived and remains in use among some Huichol, Tarahumara, and Cora communities. Knowledge of the plant's properties and the associated ceremonies also spread northward until an organized religion with distinct Christian elements took shape in Oklahoma in the 1880s. There it was adopted by members of the many different Native American nations being relocated to what was then known as Indian Territory. This religion, with its several variations, is now institutionalized in the Native American Church (NAC).

Psychoactive effects of peyote ingestion are attributed to mescaline, one of the many alkaloids it con-

tains. Reported responses include euphoria, visions or mild hallucinations, vomiting, and mental clarity. It has never been shown to be addictive, or to cause genetic or other biological damage. In fact, members of the NAC report success in using it to treat alcoholism, in conjunction with membership in an NAC community. It is classified as a controlled substance by the U.S. Drug Enforcement Agency, and is illegal for recreational use. It was subject to punitive laws even for religious use in many states until full federal protection was granted in 1994.

See also DRUGS; DRUMMING; NATIVE AMERICAN CHURCH; NATIVE AMERICAN RELIGIONS; RELIGIOUS EXPERIENCE; RELIGIOUS FREEDOM RESTORATION ACT; RELIGIOUS PERSECUTION; RITUAL.

BIBLIOGRAPHY

Aberle, David F. *The Peyote Religion among the Navaho.* 1966.

Anderson, Edward F. *Peyote: The Divine Cactus.* 1996.

Brito, Sylvester J. *The Way of a Peyote Roadman.* 1989.

LaBarre, Weston. *The Peyote Cult.* 1938.

Slotkin, James S. *The Peyote Religion: A Study in Indian-White Relations.* 1956.

Stewart, Omer C. *Peyote Religion: A History.* 1987.

Christopher Jocks

Pilgrimage

A pilgrimage is a round-trip journey to a site the traveler considers sacred, usually a shrine. At their destination, and along the way, pilgrims engage in religious practices that might include ritualized speech, dress, and gesture. Pilgrimage sites sometimes stand far from the follower's home, and sometimes the length and arduousness of the journey are themselves spiritually significant. Whether or not the destination is distant and the journey difficult, most pilgrims, who are temporarily or permanently changed by the experience, carry something home with them. For contemporary pilgrims that can mean a range of artifacts—from holy cards and T-shirts to postcards and photographs. Upon their return, devotees recall and extend the sacred journey by wearing (or carrying) mementos, giving them to loved ones, or placing them in the home, thereby sacralizing domestic space and linking it with the pilgrimage site.

Approaches to the Study of Pilgrimage

There have been five main approaches to the study of pilgrimage. First, highlighting change over time, the historical approach has emphasized the distinctiveness of each pilgrimage and its embeddedness in the cultural context and the sponsoring religion. Second, a sociological view, inspired by the writings of Émile Durkheim, presupposes that pilgrimages reflect broader social processes; for example, they bolster social status and construct collective identity. Guided by the writings of Mircea Eliade and other religion scholars, a phenomenological approach has identified pilgrimage's common features by theorizing across religions and cultures. Claiming to be more sympathetic to the participants' interpretations, these scholars have seen pilgrimage as an encounter with the sacred. In opposition to functionalist sociological theories, they also have highlighted religion's *sui generis* character, criticizing those who reduce the phenomenon to social, cultural, or economic impulses. A fourth approach, anthropological, has had the most scholarly influence, and Victor Turner and Edith Turner have produced the most influential anthropological theory. For them, pilgrimage is a rite of passage: The pilgrim begins in the social structure, departs from it during the ritual, and then returns (transformed) to society. During the pilgrimage, the Turners argue, devotees stand in a liminal state, where the usual social hierarchies are suspended and an egalitarian spirit of "communitas" temporarily holds. In the 1991 book *Contesting the Sacred: The Anthropology of Christian Pilgrimage,* its editors, John Eade and Michael J. Sallnow, directly challenged the reigning Turnerian model. Eade and Sallnow saw contestation where the Turners found consensus. Pilgrimages, in this revisionist anthropological view, do not have a fixed meaning or produce a shared feeling of commonality. Rather, pilgrimage sites are social arenas where devotees negotiate meaning and power. A fifth approach to the study of pilgrimage comes from cultural geographers, who have drawn on the theories of Eliade, the Turners, and (more recently) Eade and Sallnow. S. M. Bhardwaj, C. Prorok, G. Rinschede, and other geographers have produced textured studies of contemporary pilgrimage sites, yet they have not offered a fully developed theory of religious travel. However, a greater sensitivity to the significance of space and place distinguishes the work of geographers, who have charted the flow of pilgrims and mapped the landscape of pilgrimage.

American Pilgrimage

Most scholars of pilgrimage have focused their attention on Europe, the Middle East, and Asia, although round-trip religious journeys also have been an important feature of religious life in the United States. The scholarly neglect is understandable, in part, since the relatively young nation has fewer ancient sacred

sites, and the predominant faith of the British colonies, Protestantism, eschewed pilgrimage, which seemed tainted by Catholic overtones. Nonetheless, U.S. Protestants have venerated some sites at home and abroad as spiritually significant, and their journeys—for example, Methodists' travel to the British birthplace of John and Charles Wesley or to American churches where the founders preached—take on some features traditionally associated with pilgrimage.

Pilgrimage has been even more central in other American faiths, and there are as many kinds of pilgrimage as there are types of shrines. The most basic distinction is between foreign and domestic pilgrimage.

Some American pilgrims—those with sufficient time and money—have traveled abroad to sites they considered sacred. A very small proportion of these journeys led to quasi-religious sites, those with civil religious importance such as American war memorials in Europe or other foreign sites with historical connections. For example, Alfred T. Story's 1908 guidebook *American Shrines in England* introduced American travelers to civil religious sites such as George Washington's and Benjamin Franklin's ancestral homes. Much more commonly, American travelers have visited the traditional pilgrimage sites in Europe, Asia, and the Middle East. Fast and relatively inexpensive air travel allows thousands of contemporary American Catholics annually to take guided tours of the great pilgrimage centers in Europe, Lourdes and Fatima, as well as newer apparitional sites such as Medjugorje and Mount Melleray. And each year many Christians—Protestant and Catholic—travel to the Holy Land. Some U.S. Jews imagine a trip to Israel, and the sacred sites there, as decisive for identity, even as a rite of passage to Jewish adulthood. During the turbulent late nineteenth century and again during and after the restless 1960s, small numbers of elite American Buddhist and Hindu converts homaged sacred sites in India and Japan, while Asian-American followers who entered the United States after the new immigration act of 1965 also have returned to holy places in their homeland. Pilgrimage to Mecca is a duty for all able Muslims, and by the 1990s approximately five thousand American followers were fulfilling that religious obligation each year.

If some American pilgrims have crossed national borders, others have traveled to destinations in the United States. Some of those destinations, such as battlefields and monuments, are quasi-religious, sharing some of the features of traditional pilgrimage sites. Journeys to the Stonewall Jackson Shrine in Virginia or to the Lincoln Memorial in Washington, D.C., can blur the lines between tourism and pilgrimage, since those sites have meaning for the celebration of America's civil religion. Visitors to some civil religious sites, such as the Vietnam Veterans Memorial in Washington, closely simulate ritual practice at traditionally religious shrines. By the end of the 1990s millions of visitors had left tens of thousands of artifacts and letters at that civic monument, just as Catholic pilgrims leave notes or crutches at healing shrines. As several scholars have noted, similar practices emerge at other U.S. tourist sites that claim secular status, including Graceland, Elvis Presley's Memphis home, where fans from across the country leave messages, flowers, and gifts during candlelight vigils.

But pilgrimage in the United States usually has been explicitly associated with religious traditions. American Indian peoples have long venerated certain natural and historical sites and returned regularly to perform prescribed rituals. As Vine Deloria notes in *God Is Red* (1992), however, the state's power sometimes constrains Indian peoples' ability to practice their faith because many have been displaced from their traditional homelands or forbidden access to holy places on federal lands. Nonetheless, Indian peoples still make round-trip religious journeys. So do many Roman Catholics, who established their first pilgrimage site on lands that would become the United States in 1620, when Spanish missionaries dedicated a small chapel to Our Lady of La Leche at St. Augustine, Florida. Since then, and especially in the twentieth century, many other shrines to Mary and the saints have appeared. And in the 1990s, Catholic pilgrims continued to visit hundreds of sacred places across the nation, including pilgrimage centers that develop around reports of miracles or apparitions. Some new religious movements also have consecrated sites as holy. For example, Christian Scientists visit the residences of founder Mary Baker Eddy and the monumental Mother Church in Boston, while Latter-Day Saints make journeys to regional Mormon temples as well as key sites of historical significance in Missouri and Utah.

Although they claim many fewer traditional sacred sites in the United States than in their homeland, post-1965 immigrants, who have transplanted a variety of faiths, have constructed (or renovated) thousands of places of worship. Some larger Hindu temples, Sikh gurdwaras, and Muslim mosques have functioned as local, regional, or national pilgrimage sites for Asian and Middle Eastern immigrants and their relatives. Although American Buddhist shrines have not appeared—there are no revered relics or sacred sites on U.S. soil—some temples draw pilgrims, often from a single ethnic group and Buddhist sect. For example, in 1996 more than 110,000 devotees, many of them Chinese immigrants, took the guided tour at southern California's Hsi Lai Temple, the largest Buddhist temple in the Western Hemisphere. The Jain Society of Metropolitan Chicago, which was the largest Jain center in North America when it opened in 1993, attracts both local Asian Indian immigrants and devotees who travel greater distances. Hindu immigrants from India and elsewhere first dedicated two major temples (in Pittsburgh and Flushing, New York) in 1977, and Hindu devotees have been especially successful in transplanting the ancient and vigorous Indian pilgrimage tradition since then. The first two temples, and the dozens consecrated since the 1970s, have attracted American pilgrims; and, as at many other religious and quasi-religious sites, new pilgrimage routes are constantly emerging in the United States.

See also Buddhism; Christian Science; Church of Jesus Christ of Latter-day Saints; Civil Religion; Eliade, Mircea; Elvis Cults; Hinduism; Holy Land; Islam; Jainism; Judaism; Mecca; Rome; Shrine.

Bibliography

Coleman, Simon, and John Elsner. *Pilgrimage: Past and Present in World Religions.* 1995.

Eade, John, and Michael J. Sallnow, eds. *Contesting the Sacred: The Anthropology of Christian Pilgrimage.* 1991.

Hanumadass, Marella L., ed. *A Pilgrimage to Hindu Temples in North America.* 1994.

Higgins, Paul Lambourne. *Pilgrimages USA: A Guide to Holy Places of the United States for Today's Traveler.* 1985.

Nolan, Mary Lee, and Sidney Nolan. *Christian Pilgrimage in Modern Western Europe.* 1989.

Park, Chris C. "Sacred Places and Pilgrimage." In *Sacred Worlds: An Introduction to Geography and Religion.* 1994.

"Pilgrimage." In *The HarperCollins Dictionary of Religion,* edited by Jonathan Z. Smith. 1995.

Reader, Ian, and Tony Walter, eds. *Pilgrimage in Popular Culture.* 1993.

Rinschede, G., and S. M. Bhardwaj, eds. *Pilgrimage in the United States.* 1990.

Turner, Victor, and Edith Turner. *Image and Pilgrimage in Christian Culture: Anthropological Perspectives.* 1978.

Thomas A. Tweed

Popular Religion

Popular religion may be defined as "the whole complex of underlying beliefs rooted in God, the basic attitudes that follow from these beliefs, and the expressions that manifest them. . . . [It is] the form of cultural life that religion takes on among a given people." This definition, taken from the Puebla Document issued by the Catholic bishops of Latin America in 1978, integrates social science and theological perspectives. The term "popular" in "popular religion" is derived from the Latin word meaning "from the people" and is not to be confused as the opposite of "unpopular." Popular religion became a unit of analysis as the early work of anthropologists noted differences between the official teachings of religion and the way it was practiced in local areas, especially poor and rural ones. In the early twentieth century, studies of comparative religion described the established institutions as "high" religion and the popular form as "low" or "folk" religion. Equally prejudicial are definitions that describe popular religion as "superstition" or "ignorance of the faith" or "survival of pagan elements." Such terminology carries unfortunate connotations of class prejudice.

Historical Considerations

The chief characteristic of popular religion is its salient difference from the religious practice controlled by clergy and institution. Because it contrasts with aspects of official religion, popular religion as a reality, if not as a term, has long been an internal concern of religious organizations. For example, scholars of the Judeo-Christian scriptures routinely discover traces of ancient Egyptian and Babylonian religions in biblical narratives. In Christian apostolic times, Gentiles and Jews clashed over observances of the faith. Popular religion played a role in later theological disputes that assumed the fault line of cultural divisions such as those between Antioch and Alexandria. Although often the transfer of popular culture into religious practice has been discouraged, it has proven impossible to practice religion without using some culturally derived forms.

Proselytizing religions with scriptures, including Buddhism and Islam, have all incorporated elements of local culture. Thus popular religion has its forms of popular Buddhism and of popular Islam as well as of popular Christianity. Judaism reflects the impact of culture by the distinction between Shephardic (Spanish) Jews and the Ashkenazi (German) Jews. The former developed prayers and rituals consistent with their location in a Mediterranean Christian world that was heavily influenced by Islam; the latter have other traditions, modified by life in northern and eastern Europe.

The influences from culture and from nonscripturally based religious beliefs are manifested typically in healing and divination. In fact, scholars of the Judeo-Christian scriptures routinely discover traces of this fascination with curing and telling the future in biblical narratives. The healing of body and soul has become an aspect of popular religion because although many scriptures relate miraculous cures worked by saintly figures in the past, they do not provide any directions for how to attain such miraculous cures in a contemporary setting. As early as the second century C.E., for instance, Christianity celebrated the curative powers attributed to certain saints in imitation of Jesus and the apostles, and the tombs of martyrs frequently became shrines where such favors were sought. Later, cures were connected to holy spots and powerful images such as statues and icons. Heavenly power was considered to work through these material artifacts. Such cults were popular—that is, "from the people"—but they were included in orthodox belief as efficacious manifestations of faith.

Islam has a vigorous popular religious expression. The Qu'ran affirms the existence of spirits (from which comes the English word "genie") who can affect human beings. Periodically, Islam has witnessed the emergence of popular religious movements that incorporated wonder working and spells as elements that brought legitimacy. Sufi mysticism depended on a communal dance and induced frenzy for much of its popular appeal. After the fifteenth century C.E., Muslim brotherhoods developed traditions of gifted wonder workers who could protect fellow members from harm, often outdoing competitors in producing potions, incantations, and spells. Islam encouraged pilgrimage. Frequently, local shrines such as the spot where a miracle had taken place or the tomb of a wonder worker were substituted for the trip to Mecca. These popular pilgrimages fostered popular Islamic religion, generating not only faith but also reports of favors received and a crop of material artifacts to memorialize the pilgrimage. Various of these elements are also found in medieval Christianity.

Rather than to urge their elimination, pre-Reformation Christian clerical focus generally sought to limit the exaggerations of popular cults. Often, petition for a cure included a request for protection against harm. By recourse to the sacramentals, material items such as medals, clothing items such as scapulars, as well as statues and candles were considered to provide protection from evil spells connected to the devil, spirits of the dead, or other religions. In a similar way, trances and dreams are interpreted as communications from God, suggesting that the reappearance among contemporary believers could be as legitimate as scripturally related revelations. Throughout the history of Christendom, mystics continually have related visions that carried messages of the future. In modern Catholicism, apparitions of Christ, Mary, and the saints have also been occasions for various forms of revelations. Despite the caution with which popular religion was treated, there was a long-standing tradition within Christianity to consider popular religion as a reservoir of legitimate public sentiment. The *sensus fidelium,* or the "sense of the faithful," was occasionally invoked as a factor in deciding the legitimacy of a doctrine.

The sixteenth-century Reformation introduced a sharp, biblically based critique of popular religion as it was practiced within European Christianity. By considering practices without a scriptural basis as questionable, Protestantism and the Reformation were able to reshape the practice of Christianity. Yet, particularly in Germany, Protestantism incorporated elements of popular religion. The nineteenth century brought an interest in culture as an expression of nationalism. Like folk art, folk religion was perceived as an unpolished version of more developed expressions but that nonetheless had importance as an uncorrupted expression of national particularity. Differences between folk religion and institutionalized practice were attributed to the lack of formal education among the poor. This view was challenged by a concept of popular religion as a vehicle for resistance to the imposition of a class-based religion by elite power. Karl Marx's colleague Friedrich Engels analyzed popular religion in his 1878 review of the Peasant War in sixteenth-century Germany, where he gave lower-class religious expression a utopian function as "cry of the oppressed." Influenced by Marxian theory, Antonio Gramsci in the early twentieth century considered popular religion as a "subaltern" protest against hegemonic religion. Ernst Bloch revisited these studies in a 1921 work that considered Thomas Münzer, the leader of the Peasant War in Germany, as a "theologian of revolution." Bloch's analysis considered popular religion as a form of class rebellion. The contemporary Latin American scholar Otto Maduro developed a Marxian concept of "religious production" to designate religious practice. The clergy or religious elites control the means of religious production, he said, while the popular masses are alienated from the results of their own experiences. Social and cultural historians today have come to view popular religion as a motivating force influencing peasant classes around the world.

Contemporary Analysis

The popularity among academics of a dichotomous separation of popular religion from institutionalized practice by reason of class has suffered an erosion. Popular religion is generally pictured today as essentially connected to its official expression. With nuances proper to the scholar and the subject studied, the different religious manifestations are depicted as parts of a continuum, with distinctions that are not as much contradictory as complementary. The ability of a religious institution to affect general society is dependent on, rather than antagonistic to, its popular expression. For example, it would be wrong to conceive of popular Catholicism as a religion different from institutional Catholicism; rather, each is an expression of a larger whole.

Contemporary scholarship on popular religion has assumed a multidisciplinary character wherein history, ethnography, and theology converge. Reflecting new sophistication in semiology and deconstructionist critiques, current studies often focus on the intent that motivates the use of religion and its rituals. Those most active at the popular end of the religious spectrum, the "folk," are given an active role in the creation of new religious meanings. In addition to class considerations, there are now issues of gender, social location, and race. For instance, holy water may be taken from a Catholic church and used in a Haitian Vodun ceremony. The meanings of holy water in both contexts are related, but the agency needs to be examined. Why do believers take material elements from one religious context and apply them in another?

The body of studies issuing from Spain and Latin America has tended to favor the term "popular religiosity." By examining the intentionality behind its use rather than the symbol itself, the analytical focus remains on the symbol-making rather than on the symbol. In the United States and northern Europe where study of popular religion has been shaped in a Protestant context, "material religion" has gained popularity as a term for a similar focus on agency. Thus, for instance, popular pictures of Christ that are hung on the walls of Protestant homes can be studied for changing perceptions of Jesus over generations among those who use these representations to express their faith.

Popular religion has long derived much of its symbolism from nature and the agricultural cycle of clearing, sowing, reaping, and storage. Some of the most visible symbols of seasonal change in U.S. society, for instance, derive from popular religion. The pumpkins of Halloween and Thanksgiving, the evergreen tree and the holly of Christmas, and the decorated eggs of Easter are among the most recognizable of these symbols, even if commercialization has obscured their origins in popular religion. The rites of passage from birth through maturity, marriage, and death also invoke a rich gamut of popular religious symbols and customs. Family gatherings, wedding receptions, wakes, and funerals vary not only from denomination to denomination but also from ethnic group to ethnic group even within the same religion and may be studied as popular religion.

When rejected by religious orthodoxy, popular religion may also generate new religions. In the contemporary United States, New Age beliefs mix symbols from various confessions to satisfy the believer. Afro-Caribbean religious forms such as *santería* have spread to non-Latino groups. Various forms of feminist religions, such as Wicca, have appeared. However, while these new religions may enjoy popularity, they are not necessarily manifestations of popular religion in the sense "of the people." Popular religion requires a social and communitarian character that is not identical with individualistic religious eclecticism. Until now, countercultural religious movements have been considered by definition as distinct from popular religion, which emerges from general society. But since the village setting of popular religion is rapidly disappearing in an age of global communications, analysis of popular religion may need to reexamine some of the premises of social location. Contemporary scholars suggest that popular or material religion in the United States has come to resemble a communitarian spirituality wherein interacting groups of believers are deeply touched by religious experiences that enrich traditional symbols and rituals.

See also ANTHROPOLOGY OF RELIGION; CHRISTMAS; HEALING; ISLAM; MAGIC; MATERIAL RELIGION; NEW AGE SPIRITUALITY; PATRON SAINTS AND PATRON-SAINT FEASTS; PROSELYTIZING; RIGHTS OF PASSAGE; RITUAL; ROMAN CATHOLICISM; SANTERÍA; SOCIOLOGY OF RELIGION; VODUN; WICCA.

BIBLIOGRAPHY

Bloch, Ernst. *Thomas Münzer als Theologe der Revolution.* 1921.
Díaz-Stevens, Ana María, and Anthony M. Stevens-Arroyo. *Recognizing the Latino Resurgence in U.S. Religion: The Emmaus Paradigm.* 1998.
Eliade, Mircea. *Patterns in Comparative Religion.* 1958.
Engels, Friedrich. *The Peasant War in Germany.* 1874; repr., 1926.
Espín, Orlando. "Tradition and Popular Religion: An Understanding of the *Sensus Fidelium.*" In *Frontiers of Hispanic Theology in the United States,* edited by Alan Figueroa Deck. 1992.
Flint, Valerie. *The Rise of Magic in Early Medieval Europe.* 1991.
Geertz, Clifford. *The Religion of Java.* 1960.
Gutiérrez, Ramón. *When Jesus Came, the Corn Flower Mothers Went Away.* 1991.
Maduro, Otto A. *Religion and Social Conflicts.* 1982.
McDannell, Colleen. *Material Christianity: Religion and Popular Culture in America.* 1995.
Ozment, Steven. *Protestants: The Birth of a Revolution.* 1992.
Rahman, Fazlur. *Islam.* 1966.
Sassoon, Anne Showstack. *Gramsci's Politics.* 1980.
Schmidt, Leigh Eric. *Consumer Rites: The Buying and Selling of American Holidays.* 1995.
Southern, R. W. *The Making of the Middle Ages.* 1953.
Stevens-Arroyo, Anthony M., and Ana María Díaz-Stevens, eds. *An Enduring Flame: Studies in Latino Popular Religiosity.* 1994.
Stevens-Arroyo, Anthony M., and Andrés I. Pérez y Mena, eds. *Enigmatic Powers: Syncretism with African and Indigenous Peoples' Religions Among Latinos.* 1995.
Taves, Ann. *The Household of Faith: Roman Catholic Devotions in Mid-Nineteenth-Century America.* 1986.
Tweed, Thomas A. *Our Lady of the Exile: Diasporic Religion at a Cuban Catholic Shrine in Miami.* 1997.
Wolf, Eric R. *Peasant Wars of the Twentieth Century.* 1969.

Ana María Díaz-Stevens
Anthony M. Stevens-Arroyo

Posada, La

Roughly translated as "the pilgrimage," La Posada commemorates the pilgrimage of Mary and Joseph to Bethlehem in fulfillment of Herod's command for a census. According to Christian tradition, the couple attempt to secure lodging at several inns before being allowed to bed down in a stable, where Mary gives birth to Jesus. It is this tradition that is played out annually at Christmastime in the solemn feast of La Posada.

While, according to Judy Blackwell, La Posada began in the sixteenth century as a communal liturgical event, in Mexico it has since evolved into a nine-day celebration involving the entire community. Though there are regional variations, including new expressions of the celebration in American Latino congregations, there are several key elements that constitute La Posada. Generally, the first Posada begins on the night of December 16, the feast day of La Vírgen de Guadalúpe, the patroness of Mexico. Often, in American Latino Catholic communities, La Posada is celebrated on this one evening and incorporated into a veneration of La Vírgen. Also, La Posada ritually reenacts the pilgrimage, with participants traveling in procession to a predesignated house and, after thrice being denied entry, are allowed in for the celebration. Another feature of nearly all Posadas is the musical accompaniment of the procession, generally provided by mariachis.

La Posada, then, is both a ritual reenactment of the pilgrimage of Mary and Joseph to Bethlehem, and a communal celebration in anticipation of the birth of Jesus at Christmastime.

See also BELONGING, RELIGIOUS; CHRISTMAS; LATINO TRADITIONS; LITURGY AND WORSHIP; MARIAN DEVOTIONS; MARY; MUSIC; PATRON SAINTS AND PATRON-SAINT FEASTS; ROMAN CATHOLICISM; SOCIOLOGY OF RELIGION; VIRGIN OF GUADALUPE.

BIBLIOGRAPHY

Díaz-Stevens, Ana María, and Anthony M. Stevens-Arroyo. *Recognizing the Latino Resurgence in U.S. Religion: The Emmaus Paradigm.* 1998.

Dennis Kelley

Positive Thinking.

See Peale, Norman Vincent.

Postdenominational Church

Substantial changes in worship style and organizational structure characterize many of America's fastest-growing churches. These congregations are not associated with one of the traditional denominations, but instead are founded as independent congregations or else are associated with networks and movements of churches that resist the organizational hierarchy that defines most denominations. These churches are often led by the founding pastor, who may not have received formal theological training, but instead reports having felt a strong "call" from the Holy Spirit to plant a church. Typically these churches began as a Bible study in this individual's home and then grew to a large enough scale that the group rented a public space for Sunday worship, such as a theater or school auditorium. Pastors of postdenominational churches are often relatively young; many have had dramatic conversion experiences; and they typically have demonstrated their leadership in a local church prior to deciding to plant a church of their own. During the early years of their ministry, these pastors are self-supporting and only when the church has reached a critical size of one hundred or more do they rely on the support of this fledgling congregation that has emerged under their leadership.

The postdenominational church is an amorphous entity with roots in the 1960s counter-cultural reaction to organized religion. Members of the so-called Jesus movement held worship in parks and on beaches, feeling that the spirit of Christianity was antithetical to the bricks and mortar, clerical vestments, ritual practice, and theological dogma that were associated with "institutional" religion. In recent years the focus of the post-denominational church has not been associated with countercultural reaction but instead is part of a restorationist movement to recapture the spirit of the early Christian church. Furthermore, there are pastors who identify with the postdenominational movement who are nevertheless part of denominational churches. Consequently, C. Peter Wagner, a professor of missions at Fuller Theological Seminary, who hosted the National Symposium on the Postdenominational Church in May of 1996, now refers to this movement as the "New Apostolic Reformation," since the goal is to model the contemporary church after the first-century gatherings of Christians. Another strain of this movement is connected to the Willow Creek Association, which offers consulting services and conferences for pastors who are searching for resources to build a "seeker-sensitive" church. In addition, popular speakers and workshop leaders such as Rick Warren (Saddleback Community Church) and Robert Schuller (Crystal Cathedral)—as well as consulting groups such as the Leadership Network—promote ideas that fit what has been called the "new paradigm" church.

Postdenominational churches typically share the following characteristics: They were started after the mid-1960s; the majority of congregational members were born after 1945; seminary training of clergy is optional; worship is contemporary; lay leadership is highly valued; the churches have extensive small-group ministries; clergy and congregants dress informally; tolerance of different personal styles is prized; pastors are understated, humble, and self-revealing; bodily, rather than merely cognitive, participation in worship is the norm; the gifts of the Holy Spirit are affirmed; and Bible-centered teaching predominates over topical sermonizing.

See also BELONGING, RELIGIOUS; CHURCH; CULT; DENOMINATION; JESUS MOVEMENT; NEW RELIGIOUS MOVEMENTS; RELIGIOUS COMMUNITIES; SEEKER CHURCHES.

BIBLIOGRAPHY

Miller, Donald E. "Postdenominational Christianity in the Twenty-First Century." *Annals.* 1998.
Wagner, C. Peter. *The New Apostolic Churches.* 1998.

Donald E. Miller

Prabhupada, Swami.

See International Society for Krishna Consciousness.

Practice

Participating in any religion entails not only holding specific beliefs but also engaging in characteristic ways of engaging in certain activities, such as singing, receiving strangers, sharing meals, and mourning the dead. Such activities are known as "practices."

Ordinary language points to some of the basic features of practices. Like playing a sport or a musical instrument, practices are learned from others over time, and those who do them have to practice them again and again. Accordingly, practices are social: They are learned and shared within social groups through explicit instruction or during the taken-for-granted course of everyday life, and they have duration beyond the life of an individual, sometimes extending across generations or centuries.

Another phrase evokes an interpretive problem regarding the importance and meaning of practices, however. "Practice what you preach" implies that it is possible to separate ideas from behavior, and indeed that ideas are more powerful than behavior, since they are presumed to guide it. This separation is also implicit when we speak of "putting an idea into practice." Thought or theory is one thing; action is something else.

During the 1970s and 1980s, theorists suspicious of neat divisions between thought and action offered more rigorous conceptions of practice that sought to explicate the close relationship between what people do and what and how people think. Thought and action, they noted, are intimately related. For example, various sorts of knowledge are available only within social spaces shaped by practices, including practices such as philosophy and science as well as cooking, carpentry, and prayer. One cannot separate the characteristic acts of practitioners from the thinking inherent in a practice. Moreover, practices are intrinsically full of meaning, not simply as the application of previously held thoughts but as activities that make sense within the life worlds of practitioners.

By the 1990s, the term "practices" appeared frequently in discourse about religion. In spite of significant overlap, however, specific uses of the term signal divergent emphases in how scholars and others understand religious life. Three basic uses are widely influential.

The oldest and most specific meaning of "practices" refers to disciplined activities deliberately undertaken to become attuned to the sacred, such as prayer, meditation, spiritual direction, and the study of sacred texts. In the West this understanding of practices is derived from ascetical and spiritual theology, which arose within monastic communities convinced that certain exercises would cultivate the human ca-

pacity to know and to love God. This tradition of practice, which also developed in distinctive ways among Protestants over the centuries, appears in numerous contemporary American works on Christian spirituality. By extension, the term also refers to devotional activities from Eastern religious traditions, and increasingly to exercises within New Age and other emergent spiritualities as well. Robert Wuthnow, in *After Heaven: Spirituality in America Since the 1950s* (1998), argues that "practices-oriented spirituality" is well adapted to the fluid, pluralistic context of contemporary America, since it draws individuals into serious, long-term spiritual commitments without requiring them to join stationary religious institutions.

A second sense of practices refers to a much wider range of activities—potentially, indeed, to anything people do. Arising from cultural anthropology, this approach interprets the meaning of the activities of everyday life, especially as they are done by ordinary people. By their nature down-to-earth, diverse, and open to change, practices embody religion as it is actually lived rather than religion as it is officially proclaimed (though sometimes these overlap). For example, the essays in *Lived Religion in America: Toward a History of Practice* (edited by David D. Hall, 1997) closely examine ten particular historical contexts, showing how ordinary people negotiated meaning amid social change by selectively sustaining and adapting such practices as gift exchange, hymn singing, and burial of the dead, mingling the heritage of their religious traditions with other material and cultural elements in creative yet ambiguous fashion. This overall approach to practices is influenced by the theoretical work of Pierre Bourdieu, Michel de Certeau, and Raymond Williams and is characteristically alert to how practices reinforce and/or resist structures of power.

A third understanding of practices flows from moral philosophy, and especially from Alasdair MacIntyre's concept of "social practices" (*After Virtue*, 2nd ed., 1984, pp. 187–188). Social practices are complex and coherent forms of cooperative activity; each pursues a good and involves practitioners in standards of excellence intrinsic to itself (e.g., chess, portrait painting, and inquiry in physics). Doing a social practice rightly requires specific virtues, posits a relationship with past practitioners, and extends the practice, fresh, into the future. Although MacIntyre did not develop the idea that a religion, or an activity within a religion, could be a social practice, his thought has attracted considerable attention from theologians intrigued by this idea. His normative sense of practices encourages reflection on the history, ends, and excellent performance of complex human activities; his insistence that practices are social challenges religious individualism, including the individualism that assigns ministry to ordained leaders rather than to the whole church; and his idea that practices both foster and require knowledge and skill situates theology within the common life of the church.

In all three of these approaches, contemporary interest in practices addresses concerns that are important to both scholars of religion and religious seekers. Practices resist individualism, since they are socially shared and have origins and horizons beyond the life span or comprehension of individuals, and yet they allow for individual agency because they are never completely subordinated to institutions. Practices are messy, changing shape boldly or subtly as circumstances change and as people negotiate, resist, or adapt to change. Practices belong to ordinary people and not simply to elites. Practices cut across the boundaries of the sacred and the profane. Practices bring thinking and doing, believing and living, together.

See also ANTHROPOLOGY OF RELIGION; BELONGING, RELIGIOUS; LIVED RELIGION; NAMES AND NAMING; PSYCHOLOGY OF RELIGION; RELIGIOUS COMMUNITIES; RELIGIOUS STUDIES; RITES OF PASSAGE; RITUAL; SOCIOLOGY OF RELIGION.

BIBLIOGRAPHY

Bass, Dorothy C., ed. *Practicing Our Faith: A Way of Life for a Searching People.* 1997.

Bourdieu, Pierre. *Outline of a Theory of Practice.* 1977.

Hall, David D., ed. *Lived Religion in America: Toward a History of Practice.* 1997.

MacIntyre, Alasdair. *After Virtue,* 2nd ed., 1984.

Murphy, Nancey, Brad J. Kallenberg, and Mark Thiessen Nation, eds. *Virtues and Practices in the Christian Tradition: Christian Ethics after MacIntyre.* 1997.

Ortner, Sherry B. "Theory in Anthropology since the Sixties." *Comparative Studies in Society and History* 26 (1984):126–166.

Wuthnow, Robert. *After Heaven: Spirituality in America Since the 1950s.* 1998.

Dorothy C. Bass

Prayer

The motto of the Benedictine monastic order is popularly cited (in Latin) as "*ora et labora*" (the force of the *et* in Latin provides an English rendering as "to pray is to work and to work is to pray," or "pray *and* work"). This terse couplet nicely provides the widest possible definition of "prayer" and at the same time provides a focus from which to analyze and understand this universal human phenomenon, which admits of no limitations by denomination, tradition, or circumstance, even though it is often formed by such factors. This motto does reflect, of course, the particular Benedictine commitment to a daily cycle of corporate, sung services of prayer and praise, as many as eight times each day, as the heart of its weekly, annual and vocational rhythms of life, all of which are known historically as the *opus Dei* (the work of God).

Thus prayer may be thought of as both a human activity and as touching on the divine. Further, it is, as the motto so succinctly says, an act of piety and also of the very essence of the never-ceasing "work" or "labor" or "effort" of life itself. The Benedictine monastic locus of such a definition reminds us that prayer is equally personal and corporate, just as it is both ritual and secular. One needs only to refer to the classic Jewish practice (also daily) of "davening," or the regular saying of one's private prayer and praise. It is customary in this tradition to speak the words just loud enough to hear the sound of one's own voice as a reminder that "all of Israel" is praying along. This bears a not surprising resemblance to the traditional Catholic practice of moving one's lips during the daily office of prayer (using a look known as the *Brievary*) even when entirely alone, or in a crowded public place.

Thus it is possible again to widen the definition/description of prayer by saying that this human-divine, personal-corporate, sacred-secular activity is an once a reaching "up" and a reaching "down," a reaching "out" as well as a reaching "in."

All of these characteristics are in that most loved and well-used corpus of prayer known to Christians and Jews as the Book of Psalms, the Psalter. The classically accepted genres of these 150 Hebrew poems express this universality very well: praise, hymns, thanksgiving, petition, and lament. For centuries these texts have formed the basis and heart of the daily *opus Dei* for both Jews and Christians. Also for centuries, these texts, together with certain New Testament "canticles" and liturgical formulas, have functioned as the sole body of corporate song in Christian public worship, whether in a sermonic or in a sacramental context.

The varied roles of prayer in contemporary American culture range from such highly structured practices as already mentioned to more spontaneous moments in public and private life. The 1980s and 1990s, which witnessed an extraordinary explosion of charismatic, spiritualistic, and ecumenically based patterns of liturgy, have also come to include more opportunities for spontaneous, spoken prayer, often associated with the sharing of "joys and concerns" by members of the worshiping assembly. There also has been considerable effort and experimentation to adapt the language of corporate prayer to the contemporary vernacular by Protestant churches, which for centuries used an archaic, Elizabethan form of English, and by Roman Catholic and Orthodox churches, which traditionally have used formal liturgical languages, not English. This has encouraged fuller participation by lay as well as clerical persons. Most notably and somewhat controversially, many churches have printed a new translation of the Lord's Prayer, produced by an international and ecumenical body known as the English Language Liturgical Consultation. This text cuts through the historic standoff between "debts" and "trespasses" in favor of a more literal rendering of the Greek as "sins." It also rids the verbs of ancient forms such as "art" and the formal "thee/thou" pronouns. Interestingly, Reform Judaism has found it important to move in a somewhat opposite direction just at the close of the century by adopting a "platform" that calls for a return of some use of the Hebrew language and Jewish customs in the context of its prayer and worship. But this simply underlines the fact that prayer and liturgy are always bridges between contemporary culture and concerns and traditional memories and identities.

More recently, independent, nondenominational local churches have developed in urban and suburban areas, often under the leadership of self-appointed charismatic persons. Many of these "megachurches" engage in highly informal styles of worship and prayer, often using the styles and media of public entertainment.

In spite of this sort of development, however, the incidence of spoken prayer in civic and public events has been subjected to growing criticism, if only under the impact of a pluralistic and secularistic consciousness. Prayers still grace the halls of Congress and other legislatures as well as sports events, but the focus of such praying is highly contextual, lacking much serious theological reflection or, as some would contend, integrity!

Debate continues in the United States with regard to prayer in the public school system. The assumptions involved in "the separation of church and state" vary from region to region but are increasingly subject to litigation and conflict. This is especially true at festival times, either religious or civic. Various strategies are often employed to circumvent some of these problems, such as silent prayer, interfaith celebrations, and the recovery of ethnic customs and festivals.

In short, the twentieth century has seen the stubborn continuance of prayer and religious observance, however much a highly secular mode of thought and behavior has come to characterize its latter decades. The sheer fact that the incidence of positive responses

A youth minister prays inside a chapel in Falls Church, Virginia, in September 1996. (Credit: CORBIS/Annie Griffiths Belt.)

to poll-taking regarding private prayer and participation in public worship regularly seems to be exaggerated and not in full accord with observable practice is perhaps evidence enough that the American people regard prayer as essential to the working out of their lives, however much the perceptible work and practice of prayer is obvious or not.

See also BIBLE; BOOK OF COMMON PRAYER; CHURCH; CHURCH AND STATE; DIVINITY; GOD; LITURGY AND WORSHIP; MEDITATION; MUSIC; PRACTICE; PRAYER BREAKFAST; PRAYER IN SCHOOL; RELIGIOUS EXPERIENCE.

BIBLIOGRAPHY

Hoffman, Lawrence, and Janet Walton, eds. *Sacred Sound and Social Change: Music in Jewish and Christian Experience.* 1992.

Irwin, Keith W. *Liturgy, Prayer and Spirituality.* 1984.

Martimort, A. G. *The Church at Prayer: The Liturgy and Time,* vol. 4. 1985.

Seybold, Klaus. *Introducing the Psalms.* 1990.

Taft, Robert, S. J. *The Liturgy of the Hours in East and West.* 1986.

Ware, Bishop Kallistos. *The Orthodox Way,* rev. ed. 1998.

White, James F. *A Brief History of Christian Worship.* 1993.

Horace T. Allen, Jr.

Prayer in School

At the time of America's founding as a nation, whatever schooling was available was largely in the hands of Protestant clergy. Not only were they among the better-educated, but also their role as teachers of the young reflected a widespread belief that a moral citizenry required spiritual training. It is safe to assume, then, that in addition to reading the Bible, students also participated in prayer. By 1962, in *Engel* v. *Vitale* (370 U.S. 421), the U.S. Supreme Court, in a near unanimous vote, declared that teacher-led prayer in public schools violated the Establishment Clause of the Constitution's First Amendment and was thus outlawed. Obviously much changed in the course of two hundred years.

What happened to prayer in public schools happened to many practices in American life as the United States realized its increasing diversity (including its religious diversity). Also at work was an expanding public bureaucracy that placed government in an administrative position that often unwittingly meant preferred treatment for one religion over another. Indeed, that situation is exactly what the Ohio Supreme Court realized in 1872 in its decision in *Board of Education* v. *Minor* (13 Am. R. 233). The circumstances were these: In Cincinnati, Catholics had gained such political strength that they were able to threaten to vote against public school bonds if the Protestant Bible readings (King James version) in the tax-supported schools were not stopped. The Cincinnati Board of Education called a halt to the long-standing practice, which led to a lawsuit to reverse the board's decision, which then went to the Ohio Supreme Court. In upholding the board's decision, the court noted that a civil government can have no religious opinion. It must, in other words, be religiously neutral. Between this Ohio action in 1872 and the 1962 *Engel* v. *Vitale* decision, a number of states outlawed mandatory prayer and Bible-reading (e.g., Wisconsin in 1890, Nebraska in 1902, Illinois in 1910).

The enormity of this change toward government neutrality in religious matters is underscored by noting earlier abuses when government was *not* neutral.

In 1854 the Maine Supreme Court upheld the expulsion of a Roman Catholic student for her refusal to participate in Protestant exercises. Something similar occurred in the Boston public schools, where Catholic students were beaten for not observing Protestant exercises. Just how "normative" many Americans, including judges, assumed Protestantism to be is also exemplified in a 1922 Georgia Supreme Court decision. Noting that the state-mandated Bible-reading in their public schools always employed the King James Version, some Catholic parents in Rome, Georgia, challenged the practice on the grounds that, by excluding the Catholic Douay Bible, the schools were violating the Georgia Constitution that denied tax money to "any sectarian institution." The Georgia court disagreed and offered three reasons why the exclusive use of the Protestant Bible was not "sectarian":

1. Differences between the two versions of the Bible are "not known to the ordinary lay reader."
2. Although tax-supported teachers lead the exercises, they teach the "creed of no sect."
3. The "real object" of the First Amendment's establishment clause is "to exclude all rivalry among Christian sects," and the King James Bible, while different from the Douay, is not anti–Roman Catholic.

Probably such blatant violations of the American religious libertarian spirits are now rare. The implications of religious pluralism filter down no doubt to all but the most isolated, homogeneous communities. First Catholics, then Jews, and now Buddhists, Hindus, and Muslims have moved into the American population in large numbers, along with Orthodox, Sikhs, Confucianists, Santeríans, and many others. Surveys show that three-quarters of American adults believe that people should be able to choose freely their own religion, so it is not surprising that pressures have declined to have public schools be surrogate religious educators. Moreover, the U.S. Supreme Court in the past five decades has ruled on many of the religious practices that were once commonplace in America's public schools, declaring many of them to be unconstitutional:

- In 1943, the practice whereby religious teachers came into public school classrooms and taught their particular religion to students whose parents gave permission was outlawed.
- In 1952, the Court approved the practice whereby students took similar instruction but only if it occurred off the school campus.
- We saw already that in 1962 the Court declared illegal teacher-led prayers in public schools; in

Three Annandale, Virginia, high school students join hands and pray in front of their school during National Student Prayer Day in 1998.   (Credit: Rob Crandall/Stock Connection/PNI.)

1963 so was the devotional reading of the Bible there made illegal.

- In 1980 a state-mandated practice of posting the Ten Commandments on the wall of every public classroom was declared unconstitutional.
- Five years later, a law calling for a minute of silence at the beginning of each school day was likewise outlawed.
- In 1992 the custom in which one or more clergy are asked to participate in public school graduation exercises was declared illegal.

Read one way, this series of U.S. Supreme Court decisions suggests that the Court is antireligious, and many Americans, believing that to be the case, object strenuously. But a more judicious reading suggests something else. What the Court is outlawing is not prayer, for example, but the state's *sponsorship* or *endorsement* of prayer, thereby losing its neutrality toward religion. Students, in other words, may pray in public schools if *they* choose to, subject only to restrictions of time, place, and manner. What is not permitted is for the teacher, school board, or state to lead such prayers or to dictate what prayers should be said. This constitutional demand for religious neutrality is illustrated in the 1990 case in which the Court ruled that if a public school makes its facilities available for after-school, voluntary club activities such as chess, stamp collecting, or swimming, it can *not* exclude a Bible study and prayer group. Again, the U.S. Supreme Court is not hostile to religion in public schools but merely insistent on what the Ohio Supreme Court found in 1872—that the state can have, sponsor, or endorse *no* religious opinions.

Violations occur, of course, especially in the southern states of the United States, where evangelical Protestantism has long dominated the culture (Dolbeare and Hammond, 1971). It is one thing for the U.S. Supreme Court to declare a practice to be unconstitutional and quite another for that declaration to be enforced. Enforcement requires the cooperation of such enforcers as teachers, principals, superintendents, school board members, and ultimately the attorneys general, governors, and legislatures. It also requires one or more aggrieved citizens who have the resources to challenge an unconstitutional practice in what can be a costly and protracted process. Obviously there are many communities where such enforcement is not desired and/or where such resources are unavailable. Prayer in public school continues in some places, in other words, even though it is illegal.

Why would this be the case? The answer is pretty clear: The First Amendment says, "Congress shall make no law respecting an establishment of religion, or prohibiting the free exercise thereof." While courts have outlawed school-sponsored prayer on the grounds that it violates the "establishment" clause of the First Amendment, many Americans *perceive* the court's actions as violations of the "free exercise" clause; government is improperly preventing them from exercising their religious freedom. Especially in small, rural communities, nearly everyone may identify as some kind of Protestant, with the result that nobody is offended by the continued use of prayer in their schools.

America is growing less rural, however, and its population not only gets larger but also vastly more diverse. Over time, therefore, even in those places where public school prayer is desired by many, the wisdom of governmental neutrality in matters of religion will be recognized.

See also CHURCH AND STATE; CIVIL RELIGION; FREEDOM OF RELIGION; PRAYER.

BIBLIOGRAPHY

Dolbeare, Kenneth, and Phillip E. Hammond. *The School Prayer Decisions: From Court Policy to Local Practice.* 1971.

Hammond, Phillip E. *With Liberty for All.* 1998.

Michaelsen, Robert. *Piety in the Public School.* 1970.

Nord, Warren A. *Religious and American Education: Rethinking the National Dilemma.* 1995.

Phillip E. Hammond

Preaching

Preaching is the oral declaration of the word of God, evident in the "forth-telling" of the Hebrew prophets and the proclamations of the Christian apostles. Matthew's Gospel says that Jesus "went about teaching in their synagogues and preaching the gospel of the Kingdom. . . ." (Matthew 4:23). The Apostle Peter preached one of the earliest recorded Christian sermons on the day of Pentecost (Acts 2:14–36). For Catholic and Protestant alike, preaching remains an intricate part of Christian worship. From the Reformation era of the sixteenth century, Protestants spoke of the "sacrament of the Word," with Martin Luther and others defining the church as that community "where the Word of God is preached, and the sacraments rightly observed." John Wesley helped foster a religious awakening in eighteenth-century England in part because of his practice of "field preaching," declaring the Christian message in "the highways and byways" for that segment of the populace who did not attend traditional services. The primary method of sermon preparation and delivery basically involves commentary on specific biblical texts, with application for personal and communal living.

In colonial America, preaching was the center of Puritan worship. Sermons were carefully organized and reasoned, uniting passages of scripture with doctrine and practice. These discourses were often one to two hours in length, many written out in manuscript form. It has been suggested that the average church member in colonial New England probably heard at least seven thousand sermons in a lifetime. The sermons of Puritan revivalists in New England and of camp meeting preachers on the western frontier reflected greater spontaneity and emotionalism in their homiletical style. George Whitefield, the "Great Awakener," was given to shouting and weeping in his efforts to bring sinners to repentance. Jonathan Edwards' classic "Sinners in the Hands of an Angry God," preached at Enfield, Connecticut, in 1741, created such powerful images that he was frequently interrupted by screams from the congregation. Nineteenth-century revival preachers such as Charles Grandison Finney and Dwight Lyman Moody called for conversion and Christian living in sermons aimed at the masses and preached in a simple, direct style. Mass evangelism characterized revivalistic preaching throughout the twentieth century. Billy Graham exemplified this style in his basic sermons, which presented the simple "plan of salvation" in a direct manner.

Female preachers were evident in many segments of American religious life before and after the Civil War. Sojourner Truth, an ex-slave who became an abolitionist leader, was a powerful preacher who addressed gatherings of both sexes throughout the North. She and another African-American women, Jarena Lee, were mystics who brought their piety and concern for human rights into the pulpit with boisterous, revivalistic presentations. Oberlin College in Ohio was a seedbed of revivalism and evangelical feminism and the first school to allow women to pursue degrees in theology. Lucy Stone and Antoinette Brown graduated from Oberlin in the 1850s. Brown served the Congregational Church in South Butler, New York. Stone served Unitarian congregations and chaired the American Women's Suffrage Association. Anna Howard Shaw held degrees in both medicine and theology. A graduate of Boston University School of Theology, she preached at the International Council of Women in 1888, noting that if women chose to obey God's call to preach, "what is man that he should attempt to abrogate her sacred and divine mission?" These women were among more than one hundred women in American Protestant churches who preached throughout the eighteenth and nineteenth centuries. In the twentieth century, the beginnings of the Pentecostal movement brought many women into pulpits, including Amy Semple McPherson, a Los Angeles preacher and founder of the Church of the Foursquare Gospel. Her sermons blended the feminine and the evangelical. Dressed in a long, flowing robe, she called persons to conversion and sanctification in a church where the baptismal waters were scented with rose petals. She testified to a divine calling, which, in spite of male opposition, instructed her to "preach the Word."

The late nineteenth and early twentieth centuries witnessed the rise of certain "princes of the pulpit," well known pastors of prominent churches. These included Phillips Brooks, at Trinity Church (Episcopal), Boston; Henry Ward Beecher, at Plymouth Congregational Church, New York; and Russell Conwell at First Baptist Church, Philadelphia. Their sermons were published widely, and they were popular speakers in churches and schools throughout the country. Much of their preaching reflected a progressive orientation of middle-class, upwardly mobile Protestantism.

During this period concerns among certain ministers for the social Gospel led to divisions over the nature and content of preaching. Some suggested that the preacher's task was the preaching of salvation, with the assurance that converted persons would work to change society. Others insisted that the social implications of the gospel required significant response from the pulpit. The preacher was a vehicle for helping bring in the Kingdom of God in its spiritual and social implications. The confrontation between fundamentalists and liberals in the early twentieth century brought further divisions over the nature of preaching in the church. Fundamentalists charged that liberals undermined dogma, choosing to promote psychology, sociology, and rationalism at the expense of the truth inherent in the "old, old story" of

Christianity. Princeton theologian J. Gresham Machen declared that modernism created a division between Christianity and liberalism, the latter incompatible with the former. Liberals such as Harry Emerson Fosdick, pastor of Riverside Church, New York, responded that the church could not ignore the changes in the modern world if the faith was to be preserved in a secular era. His famous sermon "Shall the Fundamentalists Win?," preached in May 1921, constituted a direct challenge to the ideals of fundamentalism. Sermons could be resources for fighting theological battles between various factions in the church. Fosdick was also known for his concern for "life situation" preaching that would address modern needs and concerns.

Preaching has also been utilized to challenge ethical and political issues in the church and the culture. Nowhere is this more evident than in African-American religious communions. Generally speaking, African-American preaching linked both evangelism and social concerns, proclaiming a gospel of liberation within the context of vibrant, enthusiastic worship. Martin Luther King, Jr., personified such a homiletical methodology, unashamedly declaring the Christian ideal while calling for freedom and civil rights for a segregated people. His "I Have a Dream" address at the Lincoln Memorial in August 1963 became one of the great expressions of the American dream couched in the rhetoric of the pulpit. King's "I Have Been to the Mountain" sermon, preached on the eve of his assassination in 1968, was a promise that freedom would ultimately prevail. The civil rights movement of the 1960s began in African-American pulpits throughout the nation.

During the latter quarter of the twentieth century, African-American preachers continued to address social and evangelical issues from churches large and small. Gardner Taylor, a longtime pastor in New York City, exercised a national influence and helped to found the Progressive National Baptist Convention in the 1960s. Los Angeles pastor E. V. Hill took a more conservative theological and social approach to preaching and was a popular preacher at Moral Majority gatherings. In 1988 James Forbes, an ordained Pentecostal minister and professor of preaching at Union Theological Seminary, New York, became pastor of Riverside Church, New York, the fifth senior minister and the first African-American in that position.

Radio and television have had significant influence on preaching in America. "Radio preachers," proclaiming their messages through local stations, were often caricatured for their boisterous sermons, their revivalistic style, and their hellfire content. Some scholars have explored the use of the "airwaves of Zion" as the medium of preaching for many pastors

and independent evangelists, from the hollows of Appalachia to urban storefront congregations. Even at century's end, these classic mountain preachers retained what is sometimes known as the "holy whine" or the "suck and blow" rhetorical cadences of their frontier forebears.

Television preachers also shaped public perception of preaching. Robert Schuller, founder and pastor of Garden Grove Community Church in Orange County, California, introduced popular psychology into the pulpit through his emphasis on "Possibility Thinking," asserting that sin was a poor self-image. Pentecostals such as Jimmy Swaggert, Oral Roberts (and his son Richard), Kenneth Copeland, and Benny Hinn linked preaching with faith healing and the promise of financial success. D. James Kennedy, pastor of Coral Ridge Presbyterian Church, Coral Gables, Florida; Adrian Rogers, pastor of Bellevue Baptist Church, Memphis, Tennessee; and Charles Stanley, pastor of First Baptist Church, Atlanta, were among those preachers whose conservative political and theological sermons were widely circulated through syndicated television broadcasts. Directly and indirectly, such programs defined the nature of preaching for many Americans inside and outside the church.

Contemporary approaches to preaching have been shaped by a variety of professors at universities, seminaries, and divinity schools whose lectures and books have been influential on preachers across the nation. Fred Craddock, professor at Emory University's Candler School of Theology; David Buttrick at Vanderbilt Divinity School; William Willimon, dean of the chapel at Duke University; Carolyn Knight, professor of homiletics at the Interdenominational Theological Center, Atlanta; and Episcopal preacher and professor Barbara Brown Taylor represent but a few of the influential teachers of preaching at the end of the twentieth century. During the last two decades of the twentieth century, ministers throughout the country utilized various approaches, some in multiple combinations. Some churches continue to use the lectionary, a three-year listing of Old Testament, Epistle, and Gospel texts that carries the congregation through major portions of the Bible in a systematic manner. Other preachers reject the use of prescribed texts, preferring a less ordered approach to the use of the Bible. Expository preaching, characteristic of many conservative ministers, placed great emphasis on the use of scripture and a verse-by-verse commentary on its meaning and application. Narrative preaching explored the nature of "story" in the biblical text and the participation of the particular individual or community in its timeless themes. Dialogue preaching invited conversation between or among two or more persons during or after the sermon presentation. Dialogue preaching was particularly popular in the 1960s and 1970s, as ministers sought to engage laity in discussion and interaction. Harry Emerson Fosdick's "life situation" preaching took many forms as used by conservative and liberal preachers in an effort to address the pressing needs and practical concerns of their flocks. Some preachers utilized various types of "incarnational preaching," by which they wove their own personal experiences into the biblical narratives. Others rejected that style as a far too personal, intimate, and even narcissistic approach to preaching. At century's end, "seeker-oriented" worship services, aimed at reaching the religiously nonaffiliated with the claims of the Christian faith, saw some ministers use drama, skits, overhead projectors, and videotapes to communicate their messages. "megachurches" (large congregations organized around marketing techniques) experimented with various forms of preaching styles to appeal to young people accustomed to more media-oriented presentations. Some even experimented with hologram images of their ministers, beamed simultaneously to separate locales. Certain preachers eschewed traditional pulpits, preferring to roam the platform or the aisles in an attempt to hold the attention of their audiences. Feminist or womanist (a method used by African-American females for reading and understanding the biblical text), as well as liberationist approaches to preaching were used by certain preachers intent on addressing oppressed and marginalized segments of the church. Feminists such as Old Testament scholar Phyllis Trible called preachers to read traditional texts in light of women's ways of understanding and participating in the biblical stories. Conservatives worried that these and other approaches would undermine orthodoxy in the pulpit and the pew. Questions regarding the nature and method of preaching divided Christians in both the pulpit and the pew, much as they had since the beginning of the church.

See also CHURCH; CIVIL RIGHTS MOVEMENT; GRAHAM, BILLY; KING, MARTIN LUTHER, JR.; MEGACHURCH; PEALE, NORMAN VINCENT; PRAYER; RELIGIOUS EXPERIENCE; RELIGIOUS COMMUNITIES; ROBERTS, ORAL; SCHULLER, ROBERT; TELEVANGELISM.

BIBLIOGRAPHY

Brekus, Catherine A. *Strangers and Pilgrims: Female Preaching in America, 1740–1845.* 1998.
Buttrick, David. *Preaching the New and the Now.* 1998.
Claypool, John. *The Preaching Event.* 1980.
Craddock, Fred. *Preaching.* 1985.
Handbook of Contemporary Preaching. 1992.
Hybels, Bill. *Mastering Contemporary Preaching.* 1990.
"Preaching in America." In *Dictionary of Christianity in America,* edited by Daniel Reid. 1990.
Proctor, Samuel. *"How Shall They Hear?" Effective Preaching for Vital Faith.* 1992.
Reuther, Rosemary Radford, and Rosemary Skinner Keller, eds. *Women and Religion in America,* 3 vols. 1981–1986.

Bill J. Leonard

Premillennialism

Premillennialism is the eschatological doctrine that Jesus will return for the true believers *before* the millennium, the thousand years of righteousness predicted in the Book of Revelation. Throughout church history believers have debated the precise meaning of the prophetic writings in the Bible—principally the Book of Daniel in the Hebrew Scriptures and Revelation at the end of the New Testament. Although many believed, for example, that Revelation was intended as a source of comfort to the persecuted early Christians, an assurance that God would eventually avenge their sufferings, others have chosen to interpret Revelation as a kind of "prehistory," a prediction of the sequence of events leading to the end of time. These literalists have generally divided between postmillennialists (those who believe that Jesus will return *after* the millennium) and premillennialists, who hold that the return of Jesus is imminent.

American evangelicals have vacillated to a remarkable degree between premillennialism and postmillennialism. Although some, notably the Millerites, held premillennial beliefs in the antebellum period, most were postmillennialists: They believed that Christ would return after the millennium, so they took it as their responsibility to bring on the millennium by working to reform society according to the norms of godliness. Postmillennialism, with its general optimism about the perfectibility of individuals and of society, animated most of the social-reform movements of the early nineteenth century—abolitionism, temperance, women's suffrage.

Premillennialism began to take hold after the Civil War, however, as evangelicals recognized that the teeming, squalid tenements of the cities, beset by labor unrest, would never resemble the precincts of Zion. Evangelicals also grew increasingly uneasy with the arrival of non-Protestant immigrants, most of whom did not share their scruples about temperance. In response to these social changes, which in turn were prompted by rapid urbanization and industrialization and unrestrained capitalism, evangelicals shifted their eschatology from postmillennialism to premillennialism, which insisted that the world was getting worse and worse and that the only hope was for Christ's return. Specifically, they adopted the variant of premillennialism called dispensationalism, or dispensational premillennialism, which divided all of human history into different ages, or dispensations, and insisted that human history was grinding imminently to a halt, that Jesus would return at any moment to rescue the true believers from the apocalyptic destruction awaiting the unrighteous. Dispensationalism, brought to North America from Great Britain by John Nelson Darby, became enormously popular among evangelicals during the decades surrounding the turn of the twentieth century, and its success was enhanced by the *Scofield Reference Bible,* published in 1909 by Oxford University Press, which provided a kind of template for reading a dispensational premillennialist interpretation into the Bible. In contrast to the social optimism implicit in postmillennialism, premillennialism was a theology of despair because it posited that this world was irredeemable and was careening toward apocalyptic judgment. "I look upon this world as a wrecked vessel," evangelist Dwight L. Moody declared toward the end of the nineteenth century. "God has given me a lifeboat and said, 'Moody, save all you can.' "

Evangelicals, especially fundamentalists, have for the most part held on to premillennialism throughout the twentieth century. They have invoked premillennialism as justification for their evangelistic appeals, as demonstrated by Billy Graham's crusades or *A Thief in the Night* by filmmaker Donald W. Thompson, and for their strong support for the State of Israel, which evangelicals believe will play a central role in the unfolding apocalyptic drama.

On the face of it, the rise of the Religious Right in the late 1970s represents a movement away from premillennialism and back toward postmillennialism because the leaders of the Religious Right seek, at least according to their own lights, to construct a godly society. While there is some justification for this interpretation—the Religious Right has been greatly influenced, for example, by the postmillennial interpretations of a movement called Reconstructionism—the majority of evangelicals remain premillennialist in their eschatology. They may act like postmillennialists, but they profess to be premillennialists.

See also DISPENSATIONALISM; ESCHATOLOGY; EVANGELICAL CHRISTIANITY; FUNDAMENTALIST CHRISTIAN; GRAHAM, BILLY; MILLENIALISM; RECONSTRUCTIONIST CHRISTIANITY; RELIGIOUS RIGHT; REVELATION, BOOK OF; TEMPERANCE.

BIBLIOGRAPHY

Balmer, Randall. *Mine Eyes Have Seen the Glory: A Journey into the Evangelical Subculture in America.* 1993.

Boyer, Paul. *When Time Shall Be No More: Prophecy Belief in Modern American Culture.* 1992.
Sandeen, Ernest R. *The Roots of Fundamentalism: British and American Millenarianism, 1800–1930.* 1970.
Weber, Timothy P. *Living in the Shadow of the Second Coming: American Premillennialism, 1875–1982.* 1983.

Randall Balmer

Presbyterianism

Presbyterian churches grew from the Western (Roman) Catholic tradition and underwent separation from Rome in the sixteenth century Protestant Reformation. Reformed Christianity, an international movement that sought to follow Scripture in all church life, gradually came to distinguish its Presbyterian from its Congregational sides. The Reformed have described themselves as "*ecclesia reformata, sed semper reformanda,*" "church reformed, always being reformed."

Presbyterians accentuate a Christian theology balanced between deference to tradition and openness to the new work of God's Spirit in every age. Balance characterizes their distinctive eucharistic doctrine, as the Lord's Supper becomes the "real presence" of Christ spiritually for believers. They affirm the classic Nicene and Apostolic symbols. They speak of the sovereignty (power) of God, of redemption through Jesus Christ by God's grace alone, and of the depravity (flawed nature) of human beings.

Most Presbyterians exercise government through representative local sessions, regional presbyteries and synods, and national general assemblies. They believe also in sharing power between ministers of the word (sometimes called "teaching elders") and ruling elders, and they ordain both clerical and lay leaders. Because Presbyterians affirm that "God alone is Lord of the conscience" and that believers are subject to Scripture as the chief authority for faith and morals, Presbyterians have not usually legislated detailed doctrinal codes.

Following the biblical interpretation of John Calvin, creedal statements from the Westminster Assembly of mid-seventeenth century Britain and other Reformed confessions, Presbyterians formed congregations in most American colonies but concentrated in the middle colonies. In 1706 a first presbytery was formed with Scottish, Welsh, Scotch-Irish (Protestants from Northern Ireland), and English Puritan leaders present. Dutch, Huguenot, German, Native-American,

African-American, and other ethnic groups were soon part of many colonial churches.

In the new United States of America, Presbyterians formed a General Assembly in 1789, with 419 congregations and fewer than 40,000 members (including baptized children not yet confirmed). Despite its small numbers, the Presbyterians had congregations in almost all the states, and its strength was considered second only to that of the Congregationalists, who were also Reformed.

Throughout the nineteenth century, Presbyterian churches grew, but their numbers increased more slowly than those of other, similar churches. Plagued by divisions concerning the nature of mission, the sin of slavery, the import of regional differences in culture, and the value of revivalism, Presbyterians spent considerable energy in debate and division.

In doctrine, Presbyterians together continued to emphasize the special work of the Holy Spirit in writing and interpreting of the Bible, a "spirituality of the Word." They also affirm especially the one church as the Body of Christ, the calling of all Christians to vocations that honor God, and serious attention to worship and stewardship in all of life. Family devotions, Sunday schools, and Sabbath observance (dedicating Sundays to worship, volunteer service, and nurture) were seen throughout the nineteenth century as indispensable for Presbyterian life. Presbyterians in 1900 owned more than two hundred colleges; more than a dozen theological seminaries; increasing numbers of orphanages, hospitals, camps, and conference grounds; and scores of boarding schools, especially for members of the racial and ethnic minorities within their membership. As a significant part of mainline, or mainstream, Protestantism, Presbyterian denominations have undergone many of the changes that have characterized American culture more broadly.

In the 1870s and 1880s, Presbyterian congregational and denominational life began to take on more formal tones. Denominational programs for funding and for mission became more numerous, and capital funds drives, weekly offerings, and special collections took the place of pew rents and annual tithes. Choirs grew more formal as well, and Sunday schools organized curricula, departments, and a hierarchy of superintendents. Ministers' studies soon became offices replete with typewriters, secretaries for those churches that could afford additional staff, and duplicating machinery as it became available. Associate and assistant pastors, directors of religious education, directors of music, youth directors, and custodians were common by the early decades of the twentieth century.

In 1960, though several Presbyterian denominations existed—including the Cumberland Presbyterian Church, which dates from 1810; the Orthodox

The Rev. Douglas Oldenburg of Decatur, Georgia, newly elected moderator of the Presbyterian Church U.S.A., stands ready to address the 210th General Assembly of the church in Charlotte, N.C., on Saturday, June 13, 1998. (Credit: AP/Wide World Photos.)

Presbyterian Church from 1937; and the Associate Reformed Presbyterian Church from 1822—only two denominations exceeded 250,000 in membership—the United Presbyterian Church in the U.S.A. (UPCUSA), with 9,383 congregations and 3,259,011 members; and the Presbyterian Church, U.S. (PCUS), with 3,995 congregations and 899,116 members. The UPCUSA had recently formed, in 1957, from a merger of the PCUS and the United Presbyterian Church in North America. Its headquarters were in New York City. The PCUS, or "Southern Presbyterians," had grown from denominational splits dating from the Civil War. Its offices in several cities were gathered in 1972 in Atlanta, Georgia.

Both denominations belonged to the National Council of Churches and to the World Council of Churches, and they helped form the World Alliance of Reformed Churches. Both afforded regional staff for mission, new church development, Christian education, and other specialized ministries. Although some congregations dissented, both denominations came in the 1960s to support the civil rights movement. First the UPCUSA ordained women, elders from the 1920s and ministers from 1956, and then the PCUS followed suit, ordaining women as both elders and ministers from 1964. First the UPCUSA in the late 1950s and then the PCUS a decade later began to lose members. A declining birth rate among Presbyterian women, diminished attention to evangelism and new church development as American demography made radical changes, discontent with the progressive stance of the denominations on matters of race and gender—all these and more reasons have been given for the membership losses. In 1974 dissenting congregations from the PCUS formed the Presbyterian Church in America, at first committed to racial segregation and consistently excluding women from ordination. Its membership grew from 67,345 in that year to 300,000 in 1996. Another small denomination, the Evangelical Presbyterian Church, grew from dissenting congregations in both denominations. Still other churches, such as the Korean Presbyterian Church in America, have grown from Asian immigrant roots.

In 1983, in part because some dissenters had departed from them, the two major Presbyterian denominations were able to merge and formed the Presbyterian Church (USA). In 1998 it reported 2,631,466 members, and 3,637,375 inclusive of children and associate members.

Issues that plague American society more generally also divide the UPCUSA and other Presbyterian bodies—whether the government should outlaw abortion; the ordination of self-avowed, practicing homosexual Christians; the nature of social witness and evangelical proclamation; the relationship of church and state; the place of women and men in marriage and family relationships as well as in the leadership of the church; and a host of others. At present, the UPCUSA and other Presbyterian denominations forbid the ordination of practicing homosexual Christians, alienating many of the churches and many members sympathetic to gay rights.

Many in the UPCUSA, including the holders of the highest offices in the church in 1999, Stated Clerk Clifton Kirkpatrick and Moderator Douglas Oldenburg, speak positively of its future. Indeed, refocused emphases on evangelism, new church development, partnership in mission, congregational initiatives, increasing support for theological education, and a friendlier atmosphere in many churches indicate vitality. Still, the obstacles are daunting—the intractability of positions concerning issues, the lack of stability in many congregations, the diminishing network of church-related institutions, and the dearth of sub-

stantial theological conversation among the leadership indicate challenges ahead for the Presbyterians.

See also ATTENDANCE; CIVIL RIGHTS MOVEMENT; LITURGY AND WORSHIP; LESBIAN AND GAY RIGHTS MOVEMENT; MAINLINE PROTESTANTISM; PRACTICE.

BIBLIOGRAPHY

Coalter, Milton J, John M. Mulder, and Louis B. Weeks, eds. *The Presbyterian Presence: The Twentieth-Century Experience,* 7 vols. 1990–1992.

Loetscher, Lefferts. *The Broadening Church: A Study of Theological Issues in the Presbyterian Church Since 1869.* 1954.

McNeill, John T. *The History and Character of Calvinism.* 1960.

Thompson, Ernest Trice. *Presbyterians in the South,* 3 vols. 1963–1973.

Thompson, Robert E. *A History of the Presbyterian Churches in the United States.* 1902.

Trinterud, Leonard. *The Forming of an American Tradition.* 1970.

Weeks, Louis B. *To Be a Presbyterian.* 1983.

Louis B. Weeks

Priestess

A priestess, under the broadest definition, is a female religious officiant corresponding to the male term "priest." However, usage of this term in the contemporary United States is more restricted than this. Female religious officiants in Protestant traditions are generally called ministers or worship leaders; in Asian religions they are typically given traditional Asian titles. In some priestly religions, such as Eastern Orthodoxy and Roman Catholicism, women are not ordained, but in those that do ordain women (such as Episcopalianism), women have become known as "priests" rather than "priestesses." It seems that women occupying traditional male religious roles take traditional titles along with these roles. It is only when women hold religious roles that are thought to be uniquely female that they are deemed priestesses. Thus the term is most commonly found among alternative religions in the United States that emphasize femaleness in the divine or regard certain religious states (such as possession) as being the special province of women. Neopaganism and Afro-Caribbean religions such as vodun (voodoo) and santería, for example, regularly make reference to priestesses.

Priestesses in these religions serve in a variety of roles: They are always ritual leaders; their counsel is sought in preparing magical spells or in establishing spiritual or meditative practices; they may be regarded as the "mother" of a religious community; and important decisions about the group may be referred to them. They are often thought to embody female divine power directly. A priestess, at least during ritual, may be the living representative of the Goddess; she may be the devoted servant of a particular goddess; or she may be possessed by various deities while in trance.

In neopaganism, ideas about who a priestess is and what functions she serves are related to the priestesses of classical antiquity. This era of pre-Christian paganism is often the model for neopaganism, and the fact that women officiated as priestesses in some of antiquity's most important rites is carried over in the neopagan assumption that some, if not all, ritual requires female leadership. Some neopagans believe that goddesses (or the Goddess) are more important than male deities (or male aspects of the Goddess) and that only women can represent her. Others stress balanced roles for the genders but insist that just as men must be present in ritual to represent the divine male, so must women represent the divine female. In some neopagan traditions, priestesshood must be earned through study, practice, and initiation by another priestess, but more often women become priestesses simply by taking on the role.

Afro-Caribbean religions draw on a different tradition in assigning priestesshood to women, namely that of West African religions. Spirit possession is more common in these religions, and priestesses are often connected to the worship of a specific deity. Admission to the priestesshood is generally more rigorous, and lines of spiritual authority are given greater emphasis. Priestesses may maintain a house where rituals are held and where people may come to consult with them or with the deities they represent.

See also AFRO-CUBAN RELIGIONS; FEMINIST THEOLOGY; GODDESS; NEOPAGANISM; SANTERÍA; VOUDOU.

BIBLIOGRAPHY

Budapest, Zsuzsanna. *The Holy Book of Women's Mysteries.* 1989.
Goodrich, Norma Lorre. *Priestesses.* 1989.
Tiesh, Luisah. *Jambalaya: The Natural Woman's Book of Personal Charms and Practical Rituals.* 1985.

Cynthia Eller

Priesthood

The historical roots of the priesthood in the Christian tradition are rooted in Jewish tradition, the New Testament, especially the letter to the Hebrews and the letter of Peter, and the Christian experience in the circum-Mediterranean world during the first few centuries of Christianity.

The Jewish priesthood tradition focuses on the Levites, the priestly role of Aaron and his successors, and Zadok, the High Priest appointed by King David. Although the Jewish priesthood had a variety of other elements, the focus on sacrifice and offering, in a context that mediates between God and humanity, became essential in the Christian notion of priesthood. The letter to the Hebrews reflects on Jesus as a kind of ultimate High Priest, whose personal sacrifice once and for all serves as a holy offering that mediates between God and humanity. On the other hand, the New Testament also contains reflections on the share every Christian has in the priesthood of Christ, the "common priesthood of all believers."

As early as the first church detailed in the Acts of the Apostles and the Pauline epistles, there was a certain pastoral division of labor. This division of labor developed and solidified in interaction with the Greco-Roman world of antiquity and the increasing complexity of Christianity as a social organization. Thus, as overseers (*episkopoi,* bishops) needed help, they worked first with ministers (*diakonoi,* deacons), who focused on the charitable, administrative, service, and pastoral needs of the community of believers. As the community grew, the need for presiders within a single community increased as well, leading to the institution of presiding elders (presbyters, priests). By the end of the first century of the Church, the local churches had the offices of bishops, priests, and deacons.

As Christianity grew under the Roman Empire, it borrowed more and more from the surrounding culture. By the time Christianity became the official religion of the Empire, it had adopted the Roman sensibility of "orders" or particular gradations of rank in thinking about ordained ministry; during the centuries that followed, these gradations became fixed as porter, lector, exorcist, and acolyte. There were also other orders and ministries in different times and places. The ministry and ordination of the priest came to reflect an increased emphasis on the experience of the Eucharist as a theophany or epiphany, an encounter with the divine, and less a community celebration. Consistent with this focus, the Latin word *sacerdos* and the Greek *hiereus* came to be seen as equivalent to the ministry of the presbyter. Thus the focus came to be more on the specialized, sacred role of the ministerial priesthood as someone set apart to help offer the bloodless sacrifice of the Mass.

Since 1972, the Catholic Church has ordained those who meet canonical requirements and are ap-

A large group of Roman Catholic priests from the Philadelphia Archdiocese participate in a Holy Thursday Mass at Philadelphia's Cathedral Basilica of Saints Peter and Paul on Thursday, April 9, 1998. (Credit: AP/Wide World Photos.)

proved for ordination to the three classic orders: diaconate, priest, and bishop, corresponding to the deacon, elder, and overseer of the early Church. The Catholic ministerial priesthood (as opposed to the common priesthood of all the faithful) is thus one of these three orders. The ordained, or ministerial priesthood, as distinct from the common priesthood of the faithful through baptism, has three key dimensions: ministry of the word, of sacraments, and of community leadership. In these ministries, the priest shares in the work of the bishop, which is the fullest expression of the Sacrament of Holy Orders in the Catholic Church. As an expression of the universality and shared communion of Church life, all priests serve for a particular diocese (or eparchy in the case of the Eastern Churches) or religious institute or province or other division of a religious institute under a bishop (or eparch) or religious superior. This is

referred to as "incardination." Diocesan (or eparchial) priests are ordained for a diocese (or eparchy). Religious priests are vowed members of religious institutes who are ordained for service to their religious community. Most diocesan priests serve parishes (some 18,962 parishes are in the U.S.); most religious priests do not.

Priests are formed in seminaries, an institution created at the time of the Council of Trent (*Cum Adolescentium Aetas,* 1563) that called for each diocesan bishop to establish a college to train poor youth for the priesthood in a way that would permit access to proper schooling and training. The Second Vatican Council (*Decree on Priestly Formation,* 1965) directed each national hierarchy to devise its national program of priestly formation. The most recent edition of the *U.S. Program of Priestly Formation* was published by the National Conference of Catholic Bishops in 1993.

Priesthood formation is now relatively more consistent across the country and around the world, with relatively high goals in the areas of academic, spiritual, pastoral, and personal formation. More than ever, too, standards are more similar in the formation of religious and diocesan priests. Consistent with long-standing tradition, a major seminary entails some six years of formation: two years of philosophy (in the United States, this is generally completed as the equivalent of undergraduate coursework considered as prerequisites to graduate study of theology in Catholic seminaries) and four of theology and pastoral preparation, completed in a M.Div. program at an approved seminary.

The spirituality of priests varies with their spiritual tradition in the case of religious priests, who draw on the rich traditions of their particular religious institutes and form of life, which emphasizes community and spirituality. In the case of diocesan priests, a key aspect of spirituality consists in the recitation of the liturgy of the hours, typically individually, and some spirituality that helps them relate to their ministry in the world, such as Ignatian apostolic spirituality. However, the nature of diocesan priesthood is unlike that of religious life; instead of a focus on a family or communal orientation, a diocesan priest may find a certain grace in a more "hermetical" form of spirituality. Hermits, after all, may be found both in remote, isolated places and in the middle of crowds—including parish crowds. To the degree that this expresses the reality priests experience, it informs their spirituality.

The number of Catholic priests in the United States peaked in about 1968 with some 37,500 diocesan priests (who primarily serve parishes) and 22,500 religious order priests (who primarily work outside of parishes). Ordinations in that year were 1,500, but steeply declined thereafter, particularly among religious order priests. At the same time, the number of resignations increased from fewer than 100 in 1964 to an average of about 300 per year, with a high point of 675 in 1970. Today, there are some 30,880 diocesan and 16,939 religious order priests. About one in four priests are over 70 years of age. Currently, about 450 priests are ordained each year in the United States, and about three in four of these are ordained to the diocesan priesthood. Assuming that the number of ordinations continues unchanged for the next 50 years, there will be no more than 16,875 diocesan priests and 5,625 religious priests under the age of 75 in the United States in 2050, perhaps many fewer if the trend of ordaining men later in life continues. In 1998, for example, almost 60 percent of those studying for the priesthood at graduate schools of theology were over 30. However, it should also be noted that significant increases in seminary enrollments have been noted over the past few years, and that any projection of the number of priests in the future depends on a variety of assumptions unlikely to hold that far into the future.

See also CHILD ABUSE BY CLERGY; MINISTRY; ORDINATION; ORDINATION OF WOMEN; PAPACY; PARISH; RABBINATE; ROMAN CATHOLICISM; SEMINARIES; VATICAN II.

BIBLIOGRAPHY

Ellis, John Tracy. *The Catholic Priest in the United States—Historical Investigations.* 1972.

Fichter, Joseph H., S.J. *America's Forgotten Priests—What They Are Saying.* 1968.

Fichter, Joseph H., S.J. *Religion as an Occupation.* 1961.

Greeley, Andrew M. *The Catholic Priest in the United States: Sociological Investigations.* 1972.

Hoge, Dean. *Future of Catholic Leadership: Responses to the Priest Shortage.* 1987.

Kennedy, Eugene, and Victor Heckler. *The Catholic Priest in the United States—Psychological Investigations.* 1972.

Walsh, James, John Mayer, James Castelli, Eugene Hemrick, Melvin Blanchette, and Paul Theroux, *Grace Under Pressure: What Gives Life to American Priests.* 1995.

Bryan Froehle

Prison and Religion

Historically, religion in the United States has played a significant role in the reform efforts to rehabilitate criminals, largely because the deeply embedded Judeo-Christian concepts of repentance and redemption suggest that people are capable of moral regeneration. The normative prescriptions for restoration of the human spirit are taught routinely in churches and synagogues. It is no wonder, then, that religious institutions have come to acquire a certain "ownership" of the problem of deviance and its moral remedy. Concerted rehabilitation efforts have been funneled into a wide variety of prison ministries. There are literally thousands of small, independent churches and religious organizations that operate prison ministries today. Services provided by prison ministries range from the distribution of Bibles and other religious materials to more comprehensive programs such as family counseling, legal aid, and victim-offender reconciliation/mediation.

In the past twenty years, one of the most promising developments in prison ministry is the emergence of the restorative justice model. Restorative justice is a process wherein stakeholder parties in an offense come together to resolve the problems and injustices imposed on victims. It is designed to repair harm, to achieve an agreement regarding compensation to the victim by the offender, and to involve the wider community in reducing crime outside the traditional criminal justice system. It recognizes the significance of community involvement in responding to crime rather than leaving the task to government alone. The restorative justice movement did not begin as an initiative of religious organizations, but it has been effectively harnessed and implemented by prison ministries that recognized consistencies with biblical principles of restitution. A leading advocate of restorative justice is Prison Fellowship International (PFI), founded by former Watergate figure Charles Colson. Colson founded Prison Fellowship (PF) in 1976 after his release from prison. Colson's own religious conversion and his firsthand observation of prison life led him to devote his energies and resources to working with prisoners to aid rehabilitation. In 1979 representatives from Prison Fellowship groups that had arisen in other countries formed the international organization PFI, which now is the largest and most extensive association of prison ministries in the world. PFI holds a nongovernmental organization (NGO) consultant status with the U.N. Economic and Social Council and is active in the U.N. Alliance of NGOs on Crime Prevention and Criminal Justice. Restorative justice is the principal thrust of PFI. The success of PFI's restorative justice programs has opened doors to correctional institutions around the country. Prison officials faced with overcrowding and lack of resources are often forced to warehouse inmates. Little rehabilitation is achieved under these conditions, and predictably, recidivism rates are high. Prison ministries that promote restorative justice programs such as PFI have independent financial resources and personnel, offer systematic and effective rehabilitation opportunities for prisoners who are willing to cooperate, and infuse compassion into inhospitable or sometimes hostile correctional environments.

Restorative justice programs include one or more of the following: (1) victim-offender reconciliation/mediation, (2) family group conferencing, (3) victim-offender panels, (4) victim assistance, and (5) prisoner assistance. Victim-offender reconciliation programs used trained mediators to bring victims and offenders together to discuss the crime and mutually work toward rectifying the harm suffered by the victims. This may involve restitution in the form of payment and monitoring schedules, in-kind services, or community service. PFI and other prison ministries train mediators to work with the courts and correctional institutions. Family group conferencing is similar to victim-

A group of inmates at Cook County Jail in Chicago pray with the Rev. Jesse Jackson in the jail's chapel on Sunday, February 23, 1997. (Credit: AP/Wide World Photos.)

offender reconciliation/mediation but incorporates participation of families, community support groups or religious organizations, social welfare officials, police, and attorneys in addition to the victim and the offender. Victim-offender panels are comprised of unrelated victims and offenders linked by a common type of crime, but not the particular crime directly involving the victim and the offender. In victim-offender or victim-impact panels, the offender must confront the pain of victims other than his or her own but who share the same victimization. Victim assistance programs provide services to victims as they recover from the crime and the arduous process of prosecution. Here prison ministries try to help victims from being revictimized, by the system. For example, prosecutors may decide to reduce charges and plea bargain a case even though the victim or the victim's family finds the decision unacceptable. Victims often find that they have no voice in the system. Neighbors Who Care (NWC) is one example of a national church-based organization that aids victims by linking them to support mechanisms and services provided by the church in the early days following victimization. Prisoner assistance programs provide ways for prisoners to make the transition from institutionalization to the external community. Incarceration can foster antisocial values and antisocial behavior, making reintegration into society difficult. The Detroit-based Transition of Prisoners (TOP) is a church-affiliated, nonresidential aftercare program providing accountability for former prisoners. TOP also enlists the aid of businesses, social service agencies, and community resources to facilitate reintegration for the ex-prisoner and his or her family.

Preliminary evaluation research on restorative justice programs has been encouraging. One study of juvenile corrections found that restitution agreements were reached in 95 percent of cases in family group conferencing and that completion of agreements was reached in 90 percent of cases without police follow-up. Offenders tended to show greater empathy with victims, demonstrated marked improvements in behavior toward families and police, and discovered stronger support networks. One study of victim-offender panels found that the recidivism rate was as much as five times greater for nonparticipants than for participants. Evaluation of the TOP program found that the recidivism rate for participants was only 9 percent, compared to the anticipated rate of approximately 50 percent based on risk-assessment scores. Courts and correctional institutions evidence an increasing willingness to work with religious organizations utilizing restorative justice programs at a time when incarceration rates have never been higher.

See also COLSON, CHARLES W.; HEALING; HUMAN RIGHTS; MINISTRY; PASTORAL COUNSELING; PRACTICE.

BIBLIOGRAPHY

Burnside, Jonathon, and Nicola Baker. *Relational Justice: Repairing the Breach.* 1994.
Galaway, Burt, and Joe Hudson. *Criminal Justice, Restitution and Reconciliation.* 1990.
Van Ness, Daniel, and Karen Heetderks Strong. *Restoring Justice.* 1997.

Stuart Wright

Process Theology

Process theology is based on the philosophy of Alfred North Whitehead (1861–1947), who, after a distinguished career as a mathematician in England, joined the Harvard faculty in 1924 and there developed a philosophy of becoming and relationship. His three most important books for what would become process theology are *Science and the Modern World* (1925), *Religion in the Making* (1926), and *Process and Reality* (1929). Early on, his philosophical system appealed to theologians as a way to make religion compatible with modern science, especially in regard to twentieth century physics and evolution. Beginning in 1934, Charles Hartshorne (1897–), then at the University of Chicago, systematically developed Whitehead's philosophy, with particular attention to its theological implications. Hartshorne's extensive writings on God include the important development of "neoclassical theism," with its revised understanding of divine perfection and the nature of God.

The defining features of process thought are its emphases on experience (to be is to be something for oneself), relationships (everything is partially constituted by its relationships), and change (reality is in process). Process theology embeds these principles in a theological framework in which creativity is the ultimate metaphysical principle and God is its ultimate embodiment.

In the process system, every unit of reality has some degree of freedom and is involved in the creative process, from the smallest particles to conscious minds to the most conscious mind of all, God. Because each moment of experience is to some degree self-determining, God cannot coerce life into a predetermined form. Process theologians speak of God's "persuasive power" in a world that is threaded through and through with freedom. One of the ways in which God works persuasively is to offer each subject an "ideal aim" toward the best possible decision that an entity can make in its own self-becoming. But every creature is free to choose how it responds to the influences of the world, including God's influence. Free creatures often decide against the divine aim, and hence evil arises.

The classical "problem of evil" (which begins with the assumption that God is all-powerful and could control everything if God chose to) is not a problem for process theology. God's creative, redemptive, and revelatory activities take place in a world where power is distributed among all living creatures. God neither violates the freedom of other creatures nor interrupts the natural order; rather, God acts noncoercively in the world through the power of love, goodness, beauty, and creativity. The process understanding of God's power in relationship to the power of others has been a significant contribution to the post-Holocaust discussion of evil.

Hartshorne offers a fully developed picture of a "neoclassical" view of God in which divine perfection is reinterpreted in light of the creative and social nature of reality. Above all, to be perfect means to be supremely related to all creatures; although all events are interrelated, God is the one being who is personally related to all. Likewise, in a world of change, divine perfection entails perfect responsiveness to all that happens. God is not the unmoved mover, but the "most moved," affected by the feelings and decisions of all creatures. Indeed, in the process system, "feeling" or experience is essential to existence; because God experiences the world in its fullness, God is the most sentient of beings, responding to every creature with immediate compassion and full awareness. It is especially this aspect of God's perfection that elicits the desire to worship God.

Though God is immanent in the world, as "fellow sufferer" and "companion," and incorporates the world in God's own becoming, God also surpasses the world and is not fully identifiable with it. This dialectic of divine immanence and transcendence is called panentheism—God is not all (pantheism), but rather is *in* all. Hartshorne speaks of the world as God's body, literally incorporate to God, but not the whole of God.

In a process metaphysics, God is not the exception to the rules that govern the universe, but the best exemplification of them. (In rejecting supernaturalism, process theology represents a form of religious naturalism.) What it means to be God is to maximize the qualities that are to some extent present in all creatures. For example, while all creatures have some knowledge, God knows all that can be known. (As the future is not yet, it is not knowable.) And while all creatures have some memory of the past (and are influenced to some extent by it), the world process and every event are preserved everlastingly in God. Particular events perish in the ongoing, creative flow of life, but all is remembered in the mind of God—and not simply as past fact, but present as an ingredient in the possibilities that God offers each becoming creature. Each entity has an affect on the world, both directly and through God, and each entity finds its immortality in its contributions to the divine life.

Neither Whitehead nor Hartshorne developed a specifically Christian form of process theology. That project has been given vigorous attention by Christian thinkers of the last quarter of the twentieth century, the most significant of whom are John B. Cobb, Jr., David Ray Griffin, Schubert M. Ogden, and Marjorie Suchocki. Weaving their understanding of Christian faith into a process metaphysics, they have developed a variety of forms of process theology. Several Jewish thinkers have been influenced by process thought, but a full-fledged Jewish process theology is yet to appear.

In advocating interrelatedness, freedom, and creativity as the hallmarks of life and in rejecting certain

aspects of classical theism, process theologians have been influenced by and contributors to many post-1960 liberatory movements, most prominently feminist and ecological movements. Moreover, because process theologians understand God as a natural part of all things, they have actively engaged in dialogue with science and other religious traditions. Indeed, in offering a holistic-relational view of the world, process theology has reinvigorated the dialogue between religion and many forms of human self-understanding. Rooted in a philosophy that is critical of many modernist assumptions (e.g., sense empiricism, substance ontology, etc.), process theology has become a source for constructive, postmodern theological inquiry at the close of the twentieth century.

See also EVIL; GOD; NEW RELIGIOUS MOVEMENTS; NATURE RELIGION; PANTHEISM; RELIGIOUS STUDIES; THEISM; THEOLOGY; WORSHIP.

BIBLIOGRAPHY

Brown, Delwin, Ralph E. James, Jr., and Gene Reeves. *Process Philosophy and Christian Thought.* 1971.
Griffin, David Ray, and John B. Cobb, Jr. *Process Theology: An Introductory Exposition.* 1976.
Hartshorne, Charles. *A Natural Theology for Our Time.* 1967.
Whitehead, Alfred North. *Process and Reality: An Essay in Cosmology.* 1929. Corrected edition edited by David Ray Griffin and Donald W. Sherburne. 1978.

Sandra B. Lubarsky

Promise Keepers

Started by former University of Colorado football coach Bill McCartney and his friend Dave Wardell in 1990, the Promise Keepers (PK) was a parachurch Christian men's ministry. Concentrated in the United States, the central goal of PK was to encourage men to become promise keepers who lived in accord with seven promises. The promises PK urged men to make included to "pursue vital relationships with other men," to practice "spiritual, moral, ethical, and sexual purity," to build "strong marriages and families through love," and to reach "beyond any racial and denominational barriers to demonstrate the power of biblical unity."

PK garnered significant public recognition for its ability to draw huge attendance to the all-male religious conventions it held in sports arenas across the United States. As a follow-up to convention attendance, PK encouraged men to form small accountability groups of four to ten men in their local communities that monitored the extent to which men

A crowd of several thousand Promise Keeper members raise their hands and sing during a men's conference on June 19, 1998, in Columbia, Missouri.   (Credit: AP/Wide World Photos.)

kept their PK promises. They subsequently established regional offices to oversee these accountability groups, and area task forces that worked to coalesce Christian men's interests and actions, especially in the area of race relations. Although the organization was characterized by explicitly evangelistic appeals, PK leaders insisted they did not wish PK to compete with local congregations or denominations for men's religious loyalty. The evangelistic goal of PK was not to get men to join the PK organization; instead, it was to get men to become promise keepers. Hence another of the promises PK asked men to make was to support their local pastor.

Arising during an era when women's rights were on the upswing, major controversies swirled around the PK movement with regard to its stances on women. The language of submission it used to depict a marital ideal was strongly attacked by the National Organization for Women, a leading U.S. feminist organization. PK's invitations to male pastors to attend workshops on men's ministries were criticized for ignoring the existence of female ministers and their interest in men's ministries. Finally, its exclusive targeting of men was questioned, even by some men within its own folds who wanted to involve their spouses in PK activities. In response to this barrage of criticism, PK altered some of its practices; most notably it began inviting female ministers to its men's ministry workshops.

The substantial material culture that developed around the PK organization contributed to its appeal. This primarily consisted of PK baseball caps, T-shirts, and sweatshirts, but was supplemented by a wide variety of other miscellaneous personal items. Marketed as an extension of this material culture was a huge array of books and magazines targeted at Christian men, which PK encouraged men to use as the focus of accountability group studies.

By the mid-1990s, only five years after its inception, PK was one of the best-known Christian ministries in the United States. Its substantial popular appeal was demonstrated on a national stage when it drew approximately one million men to its first national meeting, Stand In The Gap, held in Washington, D.C., on October 4, 1997. Yet this watershed event was quickly followed by considerable intraorganizational turbulence and decline. A policy change that curtailed the PK practice of charging entry fees to attend its stadium conferences plunged the organization into financial chaos and resulted in large swaths of staff layoffs. The poor publicity that ensued generated diminished popularity for the organization and placed its long-range continuance in serious doubt.

Among religious studies scholars, millennial experts deemed this popular religious movement an expression of late-twentieth-century millennial enthusiasm. In particular they noted the striking similarities between PK's support for male public displays of emotion—defining men as "weeping warriors"—and the weeping warriors associated with the Peace of God movement at the end of the first millennium.

See also BELONGING, RELIGIOUS; MASCULINE SPIRITUALITY; NEW RELIGIOUS MOVEMENTS; PRACTICE; RELIGIOUS COMMUNITIES.

BIBLIOGRAPHY

Abraham, Ken. *Who Are the Promise Keepers? Understanding the Christian Men's Movement.* 1995.

Brasher, Brenda E. "On Politics and Transcendence: The Promise Keepers at Washington, DC." *Nova Religio* 1, no. 2 (1998): 289–292.

Brenda E. Brasher

Proselytizing

Proselytizing, or proselytization, is associated with fervent evangelization and has played a prominent, if controversial, role in American religious life. Contemporary examples of proselytizing include Mormon missionaries who go from door-to-door to spread their good news and evangelists who hand out religious tracts on street corners. Anyone who has ever been asked by a friend to join a religious organization or who has been "witnessed to" (as it is referred to in some circles) by a devout believer has been the subject of proselytization.

In order to fully understanding the role of proselytizing in America, it is important to examine its origins in Christian thought. Since before the time of the writing of the New Testament, 'the term *proselyte* has referred to a religious convert to Judaism. With the advent of Jesus, however, the term's meaning began to encompass any man or woman who joined the nascent Christian religion. Evangelizers, motivated by a theology in which Christian truth claims applied to all peoples, have since carried the "gospel," or good news of Jesus' ministry, throughout the world to every continent including North America.

Successive generations of European Christians who settled in America sought inspiration from the Gospel of Matthew, in which Jesus is recorded to have said, "Go therefore and make disciples of all nations, baptizing them in the name of the Father and of the Son and of the Holy Spirit, and teaching them to obey everything that I have commanded you" (Mt. 28:19,

NRSV). This text, commonly referred to as the Great Commission, has been interpreted by many Christians as a mandate to proselytize not only to non-Christians but also to others within the Christian tradition who differ on points of doctrine or practice.

Intertradition Proselytization

In the early stages of European colonization of the Americas, much effort was expended on converting the indigenous populations to Christianity. Proselytization and missionary activities varied over time and place. However, we can loosely group them into Catholic and Protestant efforts.

Roman Catholic missionaries, like Father Junipero Serra, came to the Americas seeking to fulfill their obligation, as they understood it, to spread the domain of the Roman Catholic Church and to save the souls of American Indians. Serra, as other missionaries in the Spanish New World, worked closely with the political establishment. This intimate relationship between the Spanish government and missionaries was the result of the *Patronato Real de las Indas* of 1508. This agreement between the papacy and Spain ceded control of religious activities in the New World to the Spanish monarchy. Consequently, the government maintained de facto control over appointments to ecclesiastical hierarchy, the building of new churches and the expansion of missionary activities. Thus, it is not surprising that Serra, a Franciscan priest, was attached to a Spanish military expedition to the western American coast. When he arrived in Alta California in 1769, Serra proceeded to coordinate the construction of the now famous mission system along the Californian coast, as had been approved by the colonial government.

It is important to point out that, despite the best efforts of Serra and other missionaries, Native American Christian converts maintained many elements of their unique religious perspective. The result was a novel form of Christianity, containing elements of both orthodox Christianity presented by the proselytes and indigenous worldviews of the converts. For example, the Yaqui, who were converted by Jesuit missionaries, brought elements of their tradition to Catholicism. Christian rites were conducted by lay leaders, not priests. Though heavily Catholic in its orientation, Yaqui Christianity was not in communion with Rome.

For Protestant Americans, one of the most important early efforts at proselytization was the conversion of African slaves. While there was some initial opposition to the baptism of slaves because it was feared that baptized slaves would be set free, this opposition gradually gave way to organized evangelization efforts by the Anglican Church in the early eighteenth century. We have no accurate records on the rate of conversion of slaves and free blacks during this time period; however, historical accounts indicate that it was not until the Great Awakening of the mid–eighteenth century that large numbers of African-Americans were inspired to convert during the emotionally stirring revivals of the burgeoning Baptist and Methodist movements.

It is important to point out that, even though American Protestant colonizers did send missionaries to convert the American Indians, the Calvinist orientation of the colonists deterred extensive missionary efforts. The Calvinist doctrine of predestination promoted the idea that only a predetermined few were "elected" by God to be saved. Thus, proselytization efforts were seen as superfluous.

It was not until the nineteenth century that mainline American Protestants would reach the apex of their missionary efforts. Most denominations sent missionaries overseas, making foreign missions a prominent part of American religious life. There were also numerous ecumenical mission organizations, especially among liberal Protestants. Ironically, this ecumenism, which invited a fledgling sort of pluralism (i.e., pluralism within the Protestant tradition) would lead many Americans to question the imperialistic assumptions of foreign missions. Thus, the early twentieth century became a period of reevaluation of proselytization by Americans. For example, the Laymen's Foreign Mission Inquiry released *Re-Thinking Missions* in 1932. This report suggested that collaboration and not proselytization should be the goal of foreign missions.

Intratradition Proselytization

We have already examined several instances in which Christian missionaries tried to convert non-Christians. Yet of equal importance in American religious history is to understand how adherents of various Christian traditions have attempted to convert each other. Even in its colonial days, the United States offered immigrants a cafeteria-style choice of established churches. Over time, groups like the Puritans and the Anglicans became disestablished. In their stead rose denominations with which Americans were free to choose to affiliate themselves.

Even though there were differences in style and practice among denominations, the denominational system implied that denominations were essentially interchangeable. Thus, a system of competition among institutions for membership was created. In other words, while it may not have mattered to many Americans whether they attended a Baptist, Methodist, or Presbyterian church, it mattered very much to the denomination that it was able to attract and keep members. Winning converts became a sophisticated, market-driven process. The focus turned away from converting potential members to Christianity and more toward attracting Christians to a particular church. The result is that Americans found themselves in a religious marketplace in which they could seek their own spiritual path.

Pluralism and Evangelism

As previously noted, the term *proselytization* began to acquire a pejorative connotation for many Americans in the latter half of the twentieth century. It has often been identified with practices that are perceived as intrusive, invasive, and even culturally hegemonic.

As American culture has become more pluralistic, religious institutions have been forced to reevaluate their missionary efforts. One of the best examples of this evolutionary process is the "Declaration of Religious Freedom" (*Dignitatis Humanae*) released by the Second Vatican Council during the 1960s. Until 1908 the Catholic church in America was identified as a missionary church by Rome. Yet only half a century later, the Roman Catholic Church stated that "no one is to be forced to act in a manner contrary to [one's] religious beliefs." While not directly referring to proselytization, the "Declaration of Religious Freedom" opened the door to a more ecumenical outlook for American Catholics.

Yet proselytization is not seen as a negative activity by all Americans. Many traditions, such as the Church of Jesus Christ of Latter-day Saints, still consider proselytization central to their tradition. The Southern Baptist Convention as recently as the 1990s asked member congregations to witness to American Jews. Evangelical Christians can even purchase board games with titles such as "Missionary Conquest" whose goals include conquering and Christianizing the entire world.

See also CHURCH OF JESUS CHRIST OF LATTER-DAY SAINTS; DENOMINATIONS; ECUMENICAL MOVEMENT; MISSIONARY MOVEMENT; NATIVE AMERICAN RELIGIONS.

BIBLIOGRAPHY

Marty, Martin E., and Frederick Greenspan, eds. *Proselytism and Civility in a Pluralistic World.* 1988.

Josephine C. McMullen

Prosperity Theology

The Gospel of Prosperity, or prosperity theology, is a current in American popular culture with many institutional and literary manifestations that cross denominational boundaries; indeed, prosperity theology blurs the boundary between the religious, economic, and private institutional realms.

The theological underpinnings of the Gospel of Prosperity were present among the earliest colonists to the New World. The Puritan colonists, facing the hardships of life in newly founded settlements, believed that God would watch over His faithful, blessing their labors with prosperity. Personal and collective tragedy, conversely, was understood as providential judgment against those who had deviated from God's will. Although this theology has been revised and revitalized in response to the changing circumstances of American life, the basic equation of prosperity with moral virtue persists.

Max Weber's classic, *The Protestant Ethic and the Spirit of Capitalism,* documents well the emergence of prosperity theology. Industriousness and self-discipline became expressions of Protestant values in the secular realms of labor and domestic life. Financial success came to be understood as visible evidence of election to grace. Thus was formed an ideological link between capitalism, individualism, and religion in American culture.

As the basis of the American economy shifted from entrepreneurial capitalism to industrial capitalism, and Arminian thinking in American theology became widespread, so too was there a shift in prosperity theology. (Arminian thinking opposes the strict predestinarian doctrines of Calvin with the concept that salvation can be obtained by everyone.) The greater sense of individualism to which industrial society gave rise, combined with the Arminian notion of free will, lent themselves to a greater emphasis on self-determination. The myth of the self-made man, as expressed in popular Horatio Alger stories and Andrew Carnegie's classic, *Gospel of Wealth,* had a profound influence on all social classes. To those living in poverty, the new prosperity theology offered both an explanation for their present condition and, more importantly, a prescription for action to change their condition. Clean living, sobriety, hard work, and self-discipline would surely lead to prosperity. The rising middle classes were provided with an ethical basis for enjoying the conveniences that modern manufacturing techniques made readily available. Even "robber barons," such as Andrew Carnegie, could take comfort in knowing that by providing opportunities for gainful employment, they were contributing to the general welfare. Opportunities for economic success and the allure of the rewards of hard work gave the masses powerful incentives to live virtuous (hard-working, clean, and sober) lives. Persistent problems of poverty and the economic crisis of the 1930s, of course, cast a shadow over this optimistic viewpoint. The Social Gospel movement, which emerged in response to the economic struggles of the fourth and fifth decades of the twentieth century, may be understood, in part, as a critique of Prosperity Theology.

But the United States success in two World Wars and the economic recovery that accompanied military success revived the country's confidence in itself as a chosen nation. Unprecedented investment in institutions of higher education and economic expansion into the global marketplace, often subsidized directly or indirectly by the federal government, were seen as means of helping those Americans who would help themselves. It made sense again to think that anyone who really wanted to succeed in the United States could.

Implicit in this faith in free-market capitalism and democracy as the best of all possible worlds was a condemnation, sometimes stated explicitly, of those who did not experience success. If any one who was willing to work hard and live a virtuous life could succeed in America, it followed logically that those who experienced poverty had only themselves to blame. Along with a reaffirmation of faith in the Gospel of Prosperity, therefore, came a call for cutting back federal programs designed to ensure the general welfare. Ironically, the latest expressions of Prosperity Theology have argued that the very programs designed to alleviate poverty only serve to perpetuate it by making individuals dependent on government assistance and removing the incentives to improve one's own condition.

Today, Prosperity Theology may be readily observed in religio-economic corporations, think-tanks affiliated with the new Religious Right, and a growing abundance of self-help guides in print, video, and television media.

Religio-economic corporations such as Mary Kay Cosmetics and Amway, according to Bromley and Shupe, relate their products and services "to a higher cultural purpose . . . [that links] individual success to collective good" (1981, 234). Prosperity, according to such organizations, is the result of service to humanity.

Conservative think-tanks such as the Chalcedon Group in Vallecito, California, the Institute for Christian Economics in Texas, and the Contemporary Economics and Business Association, located at Liberty University in Lynchburg, Virginia, combine a literal reading of the Bible with neo-classical economic theories in their defense of free-market capitalism and their attack on government regulation of industry and public assistance programs. According to these thinkers, not only is free-market, competitive capitalism the best possible means of achieving distributive justice, but biblical law demands *laissez faire* capitalism and condemns government regulatory involvement.

Of course, most well known are popular expressions of prosperity theology in television and print media. Proponents such as Suze Orman, author of the bestselling book, *The Courage to Be Rich: Creating a Life of Material and Spiritual Abundance* (1999), are repackaging the ideas of Russell Conwell (*Acres of Diamonds*), Ralph Waldo Trine (*In Tune with the Infinite*), and Norman Vincent Peale (*The Power of Positive Thinking*) for a contemporary audience. Here the divine is portrayed as infinite abundance, and the way to prosperity is merely by attuning one's life to the divine will.

The central message of Prosperity Theology, that poverty is a sin because God wants you to be rich, is a powerful refrain that is certainly significant to understanding American religious culture. The refrain is persistent in American culture, though at some times it is heard more clearly than at others.

See also Free Will; Peale, Norman Vincent; Religious Right; Word of Faith Movement.

BIBLIOGRAPHY

Bromley, David G., and Anson Shupe. "Rebottling the Elixir: The Gospel of Prosperity in America's Religioeconomic Corporations." In *In Gods We Trust: New Patterns of Religious Pluralism,* edited by T. Robbins and D. Anthony. 1981, pp. 233–253.

Jordan, Bill. *The Common Good: Citizenship, Morality and Self-Interest.* 1989.

Terrie, Martha E. "Social Constructions and Cultural Contradictions: A Look at a Christian Perspective on Economics." *Journal of American Culture* 17, no. 3 (1994): 55–63.

Van Dahm, Thomas E. "The Christian Far Right and the Economic Role of the State." *Christian Scholar's Review* 12, no. 1 (1983): 17–36.

David W. Machacek

Protestantism, Mainline.

See Mainline Protestantism.

Psychedelics.

See Drugs.

Psychic

From the front pages of tabloids like the *National Enquirer* to the classified advertisements of more repu-

A female psychic reads tarot cards spread out on a table. (Credit: © John Coletti/Stock, Boston/PNI.)

table local weeklies and late-night television infomercials, psychics appear with their predictions or phone hot lines. They bend spoons, contact the dead, conduct miraculous healings, and make apocalyptic forecasts. Some psychics set up shop in small houses, where they dissect the past and predict the future for clients. The term "psychic" is derived from the Greek word *psyche* for "soul" or "spirit." Contemporary American psychics are so labeled because they say that they commune with the spiritual world, "channel" spirit entities, and demonstrate unusual skill at healing and extrasensory perception. Information about psychics flows through an informal network of workshops, books, magazines, tapes, videos, psychic fairs, and healing circles.

Some psychics claim to be clairvoyant (to see the future) or psychokinetic (to move material objects through acts of mental will—Uri Geller's spoon-bending is a famous example), while others say they hear and see spirits, sometimes bringing messages from the spirit world to humans (a practice called "channeling," with origins in nineteenth-century spirit mediumship). Diagnosis of illness and healing techniques such as psychic surgery are among the psychic's claimed skills. These techniques usually employ visualization or meditation and do not necessarily require the patient's physical presence. Psychic healers are eclectic, combining many methods, including flower remedies, herbs, colors, breathing techniques, fasting, dreamwork, t'ai chi, Yoga, herbs, and crystals.

Psychics' beliefs vary widely, but they usually attribute their abilities to a transcendent power outside themselves. Psychics cross the boundaries of religious traditions, aiming to draw on the powers of forces as varied as the Christian God, pagan Goddess, or impersonal energy. Many psychics are associated with the New Age movement, which has roots in New Thought, a metaphysical tradition that emphasized mental healing and developed from the teachings of Phineas P. Quimby (1802–1866).

Because psychics place themselves at the boundary between the spirit world and the world of humans, they may be ostracized or marginalized. Many psychics say they experienced a spiritual calling when they were children or adolescents, often during or after a period of illness. Edgar Cayce (1877–1945), a famous clairvoyant healer from Kentucky, lost his voice due to a serious illness and subsequently diagnosed and cured himself. Cayce's teachings continue to be spread through the Association for Research and Enlightenment (ARE). Like other psychics, Cayce's abilities seemed manifest when he was in an altered state of consciousness, such as meditation or a trance. Dubbed the "sleeping prophet," Cayce entered a sleeplike or trance state to practice his work. For psychics, trance is a dissociative state that allows the psychic to be displayed by another entity or to draw on knowledge or power otherwise unavailable.

Although psychic research has attempted to establish itself as a science, many skeptics (*The Skeptical Inquirer* journal is the most well known) continue to dispute all claims of psychic ability. Research into psychic phenomena was most significantly advanced by Duke University professor J. B. Rhine, whose Ph.D. was in botany. Rhine committed his life to adapting scientific methods to psychic research, renaming the field parapsychology and founding the Duke Parapsychology Laboratory in Durham, North Carolina, in 1940.

See also CHANNELING; HEALING; MEDITATION; NEW AGE SPIRITUALITY; NEW RELIGIOUS MOVEMENTS; NEW THOUGHT; OCCULT, THE; PARANORMAL; YOGA.

BIBLIOGRAPHY

Fuller, Robert C. *Alternative Medicine and American Religious Life.* 1989.

McClenon, James. *Wondrous Events: Foundations of Religious Belief.* 1994.

McGuire, Meredith. *Ritual Healing in Suburban America.* 1988.

Sarah M. Pike

Psychology of Religion

The psychology of religion consists of the systematic study and interpretation of religion using the methods and theories of contemporary Western psychology. "Religion" is most often understood to refer to individual experiences, attitudes, and conduct, but its referent is sometimes the diverse contents—images, doctrines, myths, rituals—of the historic religious traditions. Thus, broadly speaking, there are two variants of the psychology of religion: one of religious persons and another of religious content. Those who pursue a psychology of religious persons have tended historically to work within a single religious tradition, often with a personal commitment to the tradition and little interest in exploring it psychologically. Those who favor a psychology of religious content, on the other hand, commonly seek to reinterpret such content and trace out its origins, usually in terms of a particular psychological theory and sometimes in a comparative, cross-cultural framework.

Whatever their focus, the field's proponents have together pursued three related projects: (1) systematically describing religion, both as inner experience and outer expression, with the goal of clarifying religion's essential characteristics; (2) explaining the origins of religion, in history and in individual lives, and thereby illuminating its fundamental nature; and (3) tracing out the consequences of religious ideas, attitudes, experiences, and practices, both in individual lives and in the larger world. Whereas the second task typically challenges the self-understandings of religious persons and traditions, the first and third undertakings are consonant with traditional religious attitudes and even have roots in the historic religious traditions themselves.

The Inaugural Period

Although intimations of the contemporary psychology of religion can be found in eighteenth-century European theology and philosophy, it was in the United States, late in the nineteenth century, that the field finally took shape as a formal discipline. Two critical factors stand out. One was the growing enthusiasm, first in Europe and then in America, for extending the scientific attitude and methods into the human realm. Thus arose the new sciences of psychology and of the "history of religions," the latter promoted by the religious liberalism then in ascendance in the United States. The second factor was progressivism, the spirit of reform that swept across America at the turn of the century. Aimed at countering the destructive effects of industrialization, these reform efforts included the social gospel movement, which became widely influential in the liberal Protestant churches. Psychology and the other social sciences, likewise permeated by ethical concerns, lent support to these reform movements through the optimistic assumption that lives can be changed through systematic environmental interventions.

Most of the early advocates of the psychology of religion in America embraced both the new empirical psychology and the social gospel. Major contributors such as Stanley Hall, George Coe, and Edward Ames saw the psychology of religion as a way of reinterpreting or even reconstructing religion in more human-centered terms, to make it more effective in the modern world. Others, such as William James and James Pratt, were less set on reinterpreting religion than on establishing grounds for a new appreciation of it, especially as a means of individual and social transformation. Relying primarily on personal documents and questionnaire replies, these researchers set about to explore the dynamics of the religious sentiment and to propose new ways of engaging it in the more complex world of the twentieth century.

The climate that gave rise to the psychology of religion shifted rapidly, however, with the devastating blows of World War I and the subsequent economic and social crises. The great loss of confidence that spelled the end of progressivism and triggered the revival of religiously conservative views robbed the field of the interest and support it required for sustained development. At the same time, the dramatic rise of behaviorism and its ideal of an objective science undercut the study of subjective phenomena, including religious experience. Consequently, the psychology of religion went into a sharp decline in the 1930s and 1940s. It survived mainly in applied settings, notably in the work of pastoral counselors, and in the studies of a few dedicated scholars.

The Empirical Tradition

Beginning in the 1950s, the field underwent a gradual revival, paralleling the developments in the related areas of social and personality psychology that the slow retreat of behaviorism made possible. Two broad traditions emerged—the empirical and the interpretive—each with roots in the field's inaugural period. The empirical tradition, which can be traced back to Stanley Hall and his students at Clark University, embraces the model of the natural sciences, including their commitment to quantification and objective methods. Although the controlled experiment is considered the ideal, given its advantages for inferring cause and effect, empirical psychologists of religion largely agree that religion does not lend itself to laboratory study. Most use correlational techniques instead.

The majority of empirical psychologists of religion today pursue the first and third of the projects delineated above: describing religion in individual lives and tracing out its consequences. Description is undertaken only in a limited sense, however, for it is based on yes-no replies to standardized religiosity questionnaires and is reported in the form of numerical scores. The resulting data may then be subjected to factor analysis, a statistical procedure used to identify the underlying "factors" that account for the mathematical interrelationships of questionnaire items. Some assume that factor analysis reveals to us religion's essential dimensions or traits; others recognize that the number and character of the resulting dimensions are always contingent on both the types of questions asked and the nature of the participants who answer them.

Once religion has been satisfactorily operationalized—that is, identified and measured by some assessment device—the search for religion's consequences is undertaken by mathematically correlating participants' scores on the religiosity questionnaires with their scores on other measures, commonly of social attitudes or of various dimensions of mental health. Religiosity measures are sometimes also related to educational and socioeconomic variables as well as to physical-health status. The farther goal served by establishing religion's correlates is seldom explicitly stated, but from the work of James onward, it has often been the defense or the promotion of religion in the context of an increasingly secular society.

When promoting religion is the ultimate goal of the empirical psychologists, they are unlikely to be interested in the second project, explaining religion's origins. Furthermore, correlational procedures do not allow clear inferences about cause and effect. Yet some research of this type has been done, as in studies that have found significant relationships between images of God and such variables as mother and father images and level of self-esteem. It is debatable, however, if the latter variables play a causal role in the shaping of positive or negative God images, or if the God image—or some third variable—is the primary causal factor in the pattern of interrelationship.

Some of the earliest empirical speculation on causal factors in religion centered on physiological processes, including pathological conditions such as epilepsy, and the changes brought about by such voluntary practices as fasting, ecstatic dancing, and the taking of drugs. Recent advances in our knowledge of brain processes and the effects on them of various practices, including meditation and the ingestion of psychedelic drugs, have made possible more precise biological explanations. Basic research on the lateral specialization of the brain's hemispheres, for example, has prompted speculation as well as further investigations suggesting that striking religious or mystical experience is the result of exceptional electrical activity in the right temporal lobe. Whereas some conclude that establishing such physiological correlates reduces religious experience to electrical and chemical activity and hence invalidates it, researchers on meditation point to such correlates as evidence that meditation is genuinely and uniquely effective. We are faced here with highly complex philosophical issues.

The Interpretive Tradition

With its most conspicuous roots in the work of William James, the interpretive tradition follows the model of the human sciences. Rejecting the natural-scientific approach as essentially inapplicable to the study of human experience and expression, proponents of the human-scientific model employ a variety of methods chosen for their sensitivity to human subjectivity. Personal document analysis, historical and clinical case studies, interviews, and other such techniques provide entrée into the subtleties of individual religious experience, both ordinary and exceptional. If the object of study is the content of the religious traditions, attention is given to the various forms of objective human expression, such as the bodily movements of religious ritual or the images recorded in religious scriptures.

The project of describing religious phenomena lies at the heart of the interpretive approach. The phenomenological perspective is often explicitly embraced, signaling both a vigilance for unjustified assumptions or presuppositions and a commitment to the fullest and most faithful account possible of the phenomena under investigation. More an attitude than a set of prescribed methods, phenomenology requires either direct access to the object of study, in the form of one's own experience, or an exceptional capacity for empathic understanding of others' experience. For the descriptive study of mystical experience, for example, the German physician and psychotherapist Carl Albrecht was able to draw on his own intimate knowledge of meditation, whereas James, a professed outsider, undertook his classic work vicariously, with the aid of numerous personal documents written by "experts" in the religious realm.

Whether direct or vicarious, phenomenological description typically culminates in the identification of the phenomenon's essential features or traits. For some investigators, illumination of these traits marks the culmination of their work. Others go farther, seeking some interpretation of the descriptive material. Any of a variety of perspectives may come into play. One may undertake a "hermeneutical phenomenology," by means of which the phenomenon is situated in the broader context of human existence, itself understood phenomenologically. Alternatively, one may interpret the phenomenon in terms of one of the depth psychologies, whether it be Freudian psychoanalysis or one of its successors, Jung's analytical psychology, or yet another of the clinic-derived theories of personality.

Interpretation in terms of these psychologies marks a shift to the second of the field's projects: explaining the origins of religion in terms of psychological processes and suggesting thereby what the fundamental nature of religion is. Freud is well known for concluding that belief in a father-God is a product of the wishes and fears of early childhood, especially as they are shaped by the emotional complications of the Oedipus complex. Branding religion an "illusion," by which he meant a creation of wish fulfillment, Freud looked to the day when humankind would outgrow religion entirely.

Declaring this vision of the future to be itself an illusion, Freud's lifelong friend Oskar Pfister used psychoanalysis to explain the presence of neurotic trends in the Christian tradition and proposed that such insights might help to purify religious faith and practice. The views of certain object-relations theorists, who modified psychoanalysis by ascribing to human beings a fundamental need for relationship, are likewise more positive than Freud's. Religion, they concluded, is a system of therapy that compensates for bad object relations deep in the past and promotes wholeness through more satisfactory ones in the present. Jung, too, viewed religion as a vital resource; historically, he said, the individuation process of attaining psychic balance and wholeness has been promoted chiefly by the religious traditions.

Prospects for the Future

Other eminent psychologists, too, have weighed in on the question of religion, including Gordon Allport, Raymond Cattell, Erik Erikson, Viktor Frankl, Erich Fromm, Abraham Maslow, Eduard Spranger, and B. F. Skinner. Ironically, however, religion has throughout the twentieth century been a topic ignored by most psychologists. As a field of study, the psychology of religion has correspondingly long suffered neglect. Hopeful signs of change today include *The International Journal for the Psychology of Religion,* founded in 1990; the existence of three textbooks in revised editions; Division 36, Psychology of Religion, of the American Psychological Association; and European Psychologists of Religion, an informal group of scholars that has met every three years since 1979.

See also Body; Health; Meditation; Mysticism; Practice; Psychotherapy; Religious Experience; Religious Studies; Ritual; Sociology of Religion; Spirituality.

BIBLIOGRAPHY

Batson, C. Daniel, Patricia Schoenrade, and W. Larry Ventis. *Religion and the Individual: A Social-Psychological Perspective.* 1993.

Belzen, Jacob A., and Owe Wikström, eds. *Taking a Step Back: Assessments of the Psychology of Religion.* 1997.

Hill, Peter C., and Ralph W. Hood, Jr. *Measures of Religiosity.* 1999.

Hood, Ralph W., Jr., Bernard Spilka, Bruce Hunsberger, and Richard Gorsuch. *The Psychology of Religion: An Empirical Approach,* 2nd ed. 1996.

Paloutzian, Raymond F. *Invitation to the Psychology of Religion,* 2nd ed. 1996.

Pargament, Kenneth I. *The Psychology of Religion and Coping: Theory, Research, Practice.* 1997.

Wulff, David. M. *Psychology of Religion: Classic and Contemporary,* 2nd ed. 1997.

Wulff, David. M. "Rethinking the Rise and Fall of the Psychology of Religion." In *Religion in the Making: The Emergence of the Sciences of Religion,* edited by Arie L. Molendijk and Peter Pels. 1998.

David M. Wulff

Psychotherapy

Psychotherapy has been defined in a variety of ways. The most simplistic definitions is "soul-healing." This means that psychotherapy, no matter what particular form, is a process of restoring health to a person who is suffering mentally and emotionally. Understanding the soul to be the very core of the human being, the practice of psychotherapy tends to be reserved for the deepest concerns of life. Most often, psychotherapy addresses conflicts that reside within the personality.

Counseling is similar to psychotherapy, but the two tend to be differentiated. Counseling focuses on the minor stressors or irritations of life, offering immediate and practical problem-solving alternatives. Psychotherapy, on the other hand, attempts to explore the individual's life story with the hope of gaining insight into the circumstances that are causing personal problems.

Psychotherapy has two general expressions within American culture. One is psychotherapy *as* a contemporary American religion. The other is psychotherapy *within* contemporary American religion. In both instances, psychotherapy emphasizes a transformative relationship.

The "soul-searching" nature of psychotherapy is exactly what causes it to drift into functioning as a religion for some people. The focus is the human-human relationship. Developing its own language, rituals, sacred space, symbols, and revelation, one can easily place one's faith in the therapist as a divine presence and experience the process as worship or prayer. The psychotherapeutic process can imply spiritual satisfaction as one is healed from the pains of the past. A person confesses private pain and struggles to the benevolent therapist; and everyone knows that "confession is good for the soul." This can result in feelings of spiritual renewal.

Pastoral approaches to psychotherapy integrate theology and the behavioral sciences. The focus is the divine-human relationship. Whether the theology is Jewish, Christian, or Islamic, a pastoral approach engages human beings as spiritual beings with a divine origin. Rather than seeing humanity first and foremost through the eyes of psychological theory, pastoral approaches understand humanity to be in the image and likeness of God. From this perspective, psychotherapy becomes a tool for assisting one to overcome the deep pains of life. Within religion, psychotherapy is a means to an end instead of the end in and of itself.

Just as there is a distinction between counseling and psychotherapy, so there is a difference between spiritual direction and pastoral psychotherapy. Utilizing a medical model to illustrate the difference, pastoral psychotherapy is far more invasive than spiritual direction. The respect for the divine-human relationship is maintained, but there is a clear recognition that the depth of probing necessary to encourage healing is beyond the realm of spiritual direction inquiry. When the divine-human relationship is blocked by a problem deeply embedded in the personality, pastoral psychotherapy is required to facilitate healing the soul.

The ultimate goal of pastoral psychotherapy is to encourage a person to be fully human and fully alive. All parts of the human being are brought into harmonious relationship. The pains of the past are healed, and the broken relationships with God, self, and others are restored.

See also LITURGY AND WORSHIP; PASTORAL COUNSELING; PRAYER; PSYCHOLOGY OF RELIGION; RITUAL.

BIBLIOGRAPHY

Cushman, Philip. *Constructing the Self, Constructing America: A Cultural History of Psychotherapy.* 1995.

Rieff, Philip. *The Triumph of the Therapeutic: Uses of Freud After Freud.* 1966.

Lee Hayward Butler, Jr.

Publishing, Religious

The religions of the West propagate themselves through words, not the least of all printed words. This means that since the development of the printing press half a millennium ago in Germany, these religions have been engaged in publishing. Judaism, long given to lettering on scrolls, adapted easily to the world of print, and its leaders used publication to sustain community. The devotion of Jews and Judaism to "the Book" is well known. Catholicism has relied on book publishing of breviaries, devotions, and textbooks to nurture the faithful and then to reach out in apologetics or missionary activity to the non-Catholic world. Most forms of Protestantism, beginning with Martin Luther in the age of inventor and printer Johann Gutenberg, relied on publishing to make their way.

When these religions reached the colonies that became the United States, they found themselves internally divided, their denominations in competition. While steeples and domes beckoned believers to churches and synagogues, publishers and enterprisers had to appeal to individuals, often in isolation from each other. Some did this especially well in their efforts to convert others. Historian Frank Lambert in *"Pedlar in Divinity"* treated the colonies' most traveled evangelist, George Whitefield, as someone who understood the need to advertise and propagate—through print.

From colonial times into the present, religious publishing has prospered, making "Religion" one of the most productive categories in annual listings of book selling and purchasing in the United States. Most denominations have had their own publishing houses, such as the Methodist Book Concern, whose products were promoted by colporteurs (peddlers) and circuit riders across the frontier and in the new cities. Numbers of what today would be called "trade" houses, which were tied to no religious group in particular—one thinks of the old Harper & Brothers or Charles Scribner's Sons—either developed religious divisions or included religious titles in their general categories and reached millions.

Never has the venture of religious publishing, especially of books, burgeoned as it has in the final third of the twentieth century, a period that was, according to many, to be thought of as "secular" and thus lacking in religious interest. In those sectors of the culture where secularity or religious indifference has reigned, religious book publishing has appeared to be almost invisible. Religious titles—for example, books by evangelist Billy Graham—could outsell every book on the weekly best-seller lists but often go unmentioned. This situation began to change at the end of the century, when religious groups became ever more articulate, appealing, and even demanding. They and their authors and publishers had to be noticed.

One sign of this recognition has been in *Publishers Weekly,* the most notable book publishing trade magazine. For years it published semiannual "Religion" issues but was otherwise neglectful of the category. Now it offers regular roundups of the trade in religious and spiritual books and includes the impressive marketing situation of religious publishers in its appraisals of economic trends. Evangelicals speak up for themselves in the journal *Books and Culture,* and their books as well as those of moderate and liberal Protestants are advertised and get reviewed in journals such as *Christianity Today* and *The Christian Century.* Catholic publication thrives, and its productions get notice in journals such as *America* and *Commonweal.* The only complaint most authors and publishers carried into the turn of the millennium was that there was a general overlooking of religious books in major secular review organs such as *The New York Review of Books* and *The New York Times Book Review.*

Most religious books were sold through Jewish, Catholic, and Protestant stores, often on college and seminary campuses. But as evangelicals came to prominence, their large market, once reached through "ma and pa" or "Bible" bookstores, entered the mainstream in mall bookstores. Their books became available on the Internet.

Publishing today proceeds on several levels and through diverse channels. The market for serious religious scholarship, particularly of formal theology, remains very small. For that reason much serious work in religious history, archaeology, philosophy, and sometimes theology itself issues from university presses. As before, many denominations sponsor their own publishing firms to produce literature for church agencies such as Sunday schools, for developing personal piety, or for presenting arguments and calls to action on social issues. In Catholicism, religious orders and independents work through companies such as Paulist Press or Orbis Books, but some general trade publishers such as Doubleday have kept a Catholic line. There is also Doubleday's Anchor Bible series of translations with commentaries on books of the Bible, written by various Catholic, Protestant, and Jewish scholars. Nondenominational Protestant houses such as Eerdmans and Trinity cover the evangelical-to-mainstream scholarly front. And some privately owned companies such as Crossroad publish Catholic and Protestant books alike. However, many of the trade houses have phased out religion departments, though they may issue some religion titles in their general catalogs.

The two strongest trends in the end-of-century decades were the movement of evangelical publishing into the commercial mainstream and the trend toward "spiritual" lines that complemented or supplemented what had been "religious" only.

In the first of these trends, many of the expanding evangelical firms came to be owned by secular houses. Thus HarperCollins has made possible great outreach by Zondervan.

In the second trend, some publishers have catered to a sweeping national impulse to view most religion as institutional, corporate, traditional, and repressive. In its place, many authors and their readerships speak of "spirituality" as a separate domain, its books aimed more at individualists, seekers, and entrepreneurs. Whatever else that trend means, it suggests that in the world of publishing, purchasing, and reading of books, tens of millions of citizens demonstrate their dissatisfaction with the merely secular sphere. They demonstrate that the religious and spiritual searches are as intense as when Martin Luther propagandized through print and George Whitefield peddled divinity.

See also BIBLE; CONVERSION; JOURNALISM, RELIGIOUS; MISSIONARY MOVEMENTS; PROSELYTIZING; RELIGIOUS STUDIES; SPIRITUALITY; WISDOM LITERATURE.

BIBLIOGRAPHY

Edwards, Mark U., Jr. *Printing, Propaganda, and Martin Luther.* 1994.

Eisenstein, Elizabeth L. *The Printing Press as an Agent of Change: Communication and Cultural Transformations in Early Modern Europe.* 1979.

Lambert, Frank. *"Pedlar in Divinity": George Whitefield and the Transatlantic Revivals, 1737–1770.* 1994.

Martin E. Marty

Purification

Purification, and its attendant issues of purity and pollution, find expression in virtually all religions of the world. Purification rituals move a member from one pole of the continuum between purity and pollution to the other. Just as purity and pollution exist as a continuum, so religions vary along a line between those that express tantamount concern with purity issues and those that disregard the issue almost in its entirety. Nonetheless, more emphasis proves the rule, with purification serving as a major theme in religion. This theme touches on main issues of spirituality such as expiation, healing, renewal, and transcendence, as well as providing for the reintegration of the individual, society, and the cosmos. Despite cultural diversity, the playing out of these themes within religion reveals consistent patterns of ritual and belief.

Emphasis on the type or source of pollution varies greatly among different religiocultural contexts. Nonetheless, certain threads reveal a consistent categorization of purity issues. Concerns with bodily functions, social bonding, and boundary maintenance between the profane and the sacred comprise the three major focuses of religious attention to purity and pollution.

Issues surrounding bodily functions emphasize the provision of boundaries for purposes of control and purification. Of all bodily functions, menstruation and death universally receive attention as the most polluting. Feminist scholars consider issues of purity surrounding menstruation and pregnancy as means of control over and subjugation of women within society. Jewish laws of family purity, or the *taharat ha-mishpakha*, deal with issues of menstruation, reproduction, and sexual contact between husband and wife. Strict observers of *taharat ha-mishpakha* do not touch one another during forbidden days. Throughout a woman's period, and for an additional seven days after her cycle, she is *tahmay*, or impure. The *mikveh*, or ritual bath, takes place after this period of time. Upon completing the *mikveh* a woman may resume sexual congress with her husband. Since only married women can lawfully engage in sexual relations, only they go through the purification ritual of *mikveh*. This practice remains common only among Orthodox Jews.

Issues concerned with social bonding focus on rites of passage such as birth, adolescence, marriage, and death. Within many traditions, individuals undergoing status change prove most vulnerable to pollution. Rites of passage serve as means of protection and purification.

The final category, concerned with the maintenance of boundaries separating the profane from the divine, finds expression in often elaborate rites of purification enabling humans to approach divinity and serve to set individuals apart from the rest of society for the holy purpose of communing with the divine. In addition, setting apart, or consecrating, space and even time also serves this purpose. Thus rituals surrounding the consecration of buildings and natural areas, clergy, and laity all comprise part of this boundary maintenance.

Rites of purification likewise range greatly in scope and difficulty, from the Catholic ritual of crossing oneself with holy water prior to prayer and the ingestion of a sacrament to painful, prolonged, and dangerous acts of purgation. Five main tools of purification exist: fire, water, detergents, purgation, and scapegoats.

Fire rituals range from fire walking to the use of incense and fumigation. New Age fire walking workshops transport this ancient practice to the contemporary United States. Neopagans often make use of incense in purification preludes to ceremony. Rituals making use of water remain the most widespread. Christian baptism serves as the primary and best-known example of water purification; the Jewish *mikveh* remains less widespread and less well known. Detergents include the use of salt water, sand, herbal concoctions, ash, and other mixtures designed to cleanse the person on a variety of levels. Santería and Vodou use elaborate detergents in magical and initiation rites. The preparation and use of the detergents often prove quite arduous. All three forms of purification tools mentioned above involve the application of outside materials on the one seeking purification.

Purgation may either utilize physical or psychological means or even mix the two. These practices focus on interior cleansing. Fasting remains the most common means of purgation. Dietary laws serve as a means of maintaining purity. Among religions with dietary laws, Orthodox Judaism upholds the strictest codes, and for devout adherents eating serves an almost sacramental function. Emetics, such as the Native American sweat lodge, or *inipi*, ceremony also find widespread usage within religions. The sweat lodge ceremony, like the peace pipe ceremony, often serves as a prelude to other ceremonies. Among the Sioux, whose *inipi* ritual remains the best known of sweat lodge rituals, the sweat lodge is constructed of sixteen poles, bent to form an inverted bowl, which is then covered with hides, blankets, or tarps, and when in use the sweat lodge is closed off from outer air. A pit is dug in the center to hold heated rocks. Water poured over the hot rocks produces steam. A pipe ceremony usually precedes and follows the sweat lodge ceremony. Four separate sweats, representing the four directions, comprise the main ritual.

Psychological means of purification include penance, mortification, confession, sanctification, and the often more taxing and time-consuming practice of pilgrimage. Penance, mortification, confession, and pilgrimage remain primarily in the province of Catholic tradition. Protestant Christianity does include purification rituals above and beyond baptism. Doctrines of sanctification among holiness traditions reveal a rich psychological means of achieving ritual purity beyond that provided by baptism. According to Wesleyan theology surrounding the experience of sanctification, water baptism cleanses believers from sin, and the purely spiritual experience of sanctification then enables them to conduct a blameless life. Means of purification utilizing both physical and psychological elements revolve around human sexuality. Celibacy and strict rules surrounding marriage vows serve to maintain purity.

Finally, the use of substitutions, or scapegoats, as a means of satisfying severe purification rites remains widespread. On a symbolic level, the Christian view of the crucifixion of Jesus of Nazareth serves as a prime example of scapegoating. On a more physical level, the use of animal sacrifices in Santería and Vodou also serves at times as a purification tool.

See also Mikveh; Neopaganism; Quest; Rites of Passage; Ritual; Santería; Spirituality; Sweat Lodge; Vodun.

BIBLIOGRAPHY

Brown, John Epes, ed. *The Sacred Pipe: Black Elk's Account of the Seven Rites of the Oglala Sioux.* 1953.
Brown, Karen McCarthy. *Mama Lola: A Vodou Priestess in Brooklyn.* 1991.
Eliade, Mircea. *The Sacred and the Profane: The Nature of Religion*, trans. Willard R. Trask. 1957; repr., 1987.
Teluskin, Joseph. *Jewish Literacy.* 1991.

Nancy Ramsey

Q

Quakers

Members of the Religious Society of Friends, popularly known as Quakers, have never been dominant in number, but their influence on American culture has surpassed their size. With roots in radical Christian movements of seventeenth-century England, Quakers linked their religious experiences and convictions with their daily lives in ways that placed them at the center of controversy and cast them into leadership roles in movements advocating reform and social justice. While their worship practices have changed over four centuries, the Quaker commitments to pacifism and to social equality have remained constant, making their history particularly relevant in understanding Quakerism today.

Like Puritanism, Quakerism arose amid the social and religious upheaval of the Protestant Reformation in England. Initially Quakers shared the Puritan desire to reform the Church of England, but by the 1650s, when George Fox, credited with founding the Society of Friends, began preaching in northern England, differences between the Quakers and the Calvinistic Puritans were already evident. Most important among these differences, the Puritan doctrine of election ran counter to the more democratic and universalist Quaker belief in the Inner Light. Unlike the Puritans, who believed salvation to be limited to those predestined to be among God's elect, the Quakers believed that everyone had the capacity for salvation and that one had only to turn inward to be saved. The nickname "Quaker" reflected the physical shaking early Friends sometimes exhibited as they wrestled to find the Light within themselves.

The Inner Light is central to Quaker religious practices. Early Quaker worship was marked by silence, when Meetings sat quietly waiting for God to lead someone to speak. Early Friends wrote of the difficulty in finding a balance between inappropriate speech and the need to wisely use every opportunity to speak when God leads one to do so. The Inner Light also mandates that Quaker actions follow "testimonies" of honesty, simplicity, equality, and peace. Adherence to these ethical principles has placed Quakers in conflicted positions throughout American history.

From their earliest arrival in the American colonies, Quakers were seen as a "peculiar people." Their plain style of dress in adherence to their testimony of simplicity, their use of "thee" and "thou" to address all persons regardless of class or title, their refusal to remove their hats as a sign of deference that would violate their testimony of equality, and their refusal to take oaths in a court of law because it would imply that they were at other times less honest—these practices set them apart from the dominant culture. More importantly, however, their belief in the Inner Light threatened the foundations of Puritan culture, making the early Quakers seem like dangerous heretics who could not be allowed to spread their message in the colonies. When the first Quakers in America, Mary Austin and Anne Fisher, arrived in Boston in 1656, they were imprisoned as witches and their books burned. This harsh treatment notwithstanding, Quakers continued to arrive in increasing numbers, and

This simple but stately Quaker Meeting House in Easton, Maryland, was originally built in 1682 and still stands today.   (Credit: CORBIS/Lee Snider.)

anti-Quaker laws proliferated throughout the colonies. By 1658, punishment for Quakerism included imprisonment, deportation, whipping, ear-cropping, and death for repeat offenders. Among the most famous of these repeat offenders was Mary Dyer, who was hanged in Boston Common and symbolized Quaker martyrdom for later generations. At the end of the seventeenth century, almost every New England and mid-Atlantic colony had enacted anti-Quaker legislation, much of it reserving the harshest punishments for local converts to Quakerism.

The eighteenth-century Quaker population grew, and brutal persecutions of Quakers ceased. Owing to large land grants in Pennsylvania and in western New Jersey, Quakers were concentrated the mid-Atlantic colonies. Friends in these areas became successful, wealthy businessmen, and their names appeared in almost every list of political, legal, and civic leaders. One of the challenges facing eighteenth-century Quakers was how to reconcile their financial success with their testimony of simplicity. As the Revolution loomed large, Quakers also faced tests of their pacifist beliefs. Rather than violate Quaker practice that man-

dated strict neutrality and noninvolvement in war efforts, most Quakers relinquished their positions of political power. Even with diminished political power, the Quaker presence spread. Friends migrated westward into the frontiers of Pennsylvania and Virginia and also moved southwest, to the Carolina Piedmont. By the 1790s, Quaker communities dotted the Ohio Valley and were spreading into the Midwest, with many of the migrants fleeing from southern states to protest slavery.

As Quakerism spread geographically, the consensus that characterized eighteenth-century Meetings could no longer hold. Nineteenth-century debates resulted in a series of schisms among the Society of Friends. Most severe among them was the separation in the 1820s between Orthodox and Hicksite Quakers. Following Elias Hicks, a quietist who called for greater strictures against commercialism and wealthy lifestyles, the Hicksites opposed the so-called Orthodox Friends, who had begun to find pure forms of quietism less useful in facing the challenges of their daily lives. Hicksite Meetings, composed largely of recent immigrants and rural Friends, gained dominance in many rural areas, while Orthodox Meetings, including members of the socially cohesive business community, remained dominant in Philadelphia and other urban centers.

Central to the lives of nineteenth-century Quakers were reform efforts. Quaker women led campaigns for prison reform and women's rights, with four of the five women responsible for the 1848 Seneca Falls Convention being Quakers. From the 1830s onward, Quakers such as William Lloyd Garrison, Sarah and Angelina Grimké, and Lucretia Mott, heeding their testimony of equality, provided leadership in the abolitionist movement. When their peaceful efforts failed and the Civil War began, Friends faced traumatic decisions. Their testimony of peace in direct conflict with their testimony of equality, they were torn by their desire to support the Union cause, even though their faith prescribed complete neutrality. Many Quakers risked disownment and banishment from their Meeting by fighting in the war, and others found numerous ways to support them.

Beginning with these divisions and continuing through the twentieth century, the varieties of Quaker practices have become legion, with many contemporary Friends rejecting traditional quietism in favor of liberalism. What remain constant, however, are practices supporting the Quaker ethic. The American Friends Service Committee provides an institutionalized means of spreading the pacifist message and of renegotiating the meaning of the peace testimony in the face of global conflicts. Social justice and racial equality continue to be hallmarks of Quaker activism, with twentieth-century Quakers on the front lines of civil rights efforts, protests against the Vietnam War, and antinuclear activities.

Quakers are no longer a "peculiar people" marked by differences from the dominant culture, and contemporary Quaker Meetings are composed of members of that dominant culture, often attracting professional and working-class members dissatisfied with more mainstream denominations. If the image of Quakers has changed, their adherence to an ethics of peace and equality and their willingness to bring these beliefs into their daily lives link contemporary Friends to their seventeenth-century ancestors.

See also CHURCH; CHURCH AND STATE; CIVIL RIGHTS MOVEMENT; FREEDOM OF RELIGION; PACIFISM; PRACTICE; RELIGIOUS COMMUNITIES; RELIGIOUS PERSECUTION.

Quaker activists protesting the war in Vietnam (ca. 1970) by reading in public the names of American soldiers who have died there. (Credit: CORBIS/Hulton-Deutsch Co.)

BIBLIOGRAPHY

Bacon, Margaret Hope. *Mothers of Feminism: The Story of Quaker Women in America.* 1986.

Barbour, Hugh, and J. William Frost. *The Quakers.* 1988.

Brinton, Howard. *Friends for 300 Years: The History and Beliefs of the Society of Friends Since George Fox Started the Quaker Movement.* 1952.

Chu, Jonathan M. *Neighbors, Friends, or Madmen: The Puritan Adjustment to Quakerism in Seventeenth-Century Massachusetts Bay.* 1985.

Frost, J. William. *The Quaker Family in Colonial America: A Portrait of the Society of Friends.* 1973.

Jones, Rufus. *The Quakers in the American Colonies.* 1911.

Levy, Barry. *Quakers and the American Family: British Settlement in the Delaware Valley.* 1988.

Pushon, John. *Portrait in Grey: A Short History of the Quakers.* 1984.

Tolles, Frederick B. *Quakers and the Atlantic Culture.* 1960.

Worrall, Arthur J. *Quakers in the Colonial Northeast.* 1980.

Cristine Levenduski

Quantum Healing

Quantum healing is a controversial form of mind-body medicine wherein a fundamental change in consciousness is said to produce a profound healing of the body-mind. The term "quantum healing" was introduced by Deepak Chopra, M.D., in his book *Quantum Healing* (1989) to explain certain types of sudden and dramatic healing of the human body, such as spontaneous remissions, that are not understood by conventional medicine. Chopra postulates that these extraordinary forms of healing are related to understandings of quantum physics and of consciousness. Just as quantum physics aims to describe physical phenomena normally hidden at a subatomic level, so quantum healing is directed to healing the body-mind from a deep, unmanifest level of consciousness. The mind and body are expressions of this profound consciousness, which Chopra calls the "quantum mechanical body." Chopra identifies the quantum mechanical body with the quantum level of physical reality. He maintains that we can activate profound healing of the mind and body by consciously accessing this quantum level of our being.

Chopra developed quantum healing by combining principles of mind-body medicine with ideas from quantum physics; Transcendental Meditation (TM); and Āyurveda, the ancient Indian system of medicine that views health as a balance of mind, body, and spirit. After a number of years of traditional medical practice, Chopra became dissatisfied with the approach of Western medicine. In 1984 he was introduced to Maharishi Mahesh Yogi, the founder of the TM movement, who encouraged him to investigate Ayurveda. In 1985 Chopra became director of the Maharishi Ayurveda Health Center in Lancaster, Massachusetts, where his work with cancer patients combined modern Western medical treatments with TM and Ayurveda. Since 1993 he has devoted much of his time to writing and lecturing on mind-body healing, spirituality, and related topics. Chopra has become one of the most well-known and controversial advocates of mind-body medicine in the United States.

Deepak Chopra has been criticized for promoting and profiting from medical treatments not yet tested by scientific studies, nor consistent with established scientific concepts. For example, his fundamental premise postulating a deep connection between the ideas of quantum physics and the mind-body relationship is highly controversial. Even more speculative is his hypothesis that quantum physics provides a scientific explanation for the manner in which deep transformations in consciousness produce extraordinary forms of healing in the body. As a result, Chopra's integrity has been questioned because of his apparent attempt to legitimize and further promote his methods by implying that they are based on quantum physics.

Regardless of the ultimate accuracy of Chopra's theoretical explanations, however, mainstream scientific medical research has demonstrated that various mind-body interactions such as the "placebo effect" do exist and can have significant effects in healing. The effectiveness of Chopra's methods, therefore, should not be confused with the veracity of his theoretical explanation for them. At the same time, in mind-body medicine the effectiveness of a treatment method can depend on a subject's confidence in the treatment, which in turn can be influenced by the acceptance of the theoretical explanation provided for the treatment, regardless of its scientific validity.

See also QUANTUM PHYSICS; SPIRITUALITY; TRANSCENDENTAL MEDITATION.

BIBLIOGRAPHY

Chopra, Deepak. *Ageless Body, Timeless Mind: The Quantum Alternative to Growing Old.* 1993.

Chopra, Deepak. *Quantum Healing: Exploring the Frontiers of Mind/Body Medicine.* 1989.

Thomas J. McFarlane

Quantum Physics

Quantum physics, one of the main branches of modern physics, is the basis for our understanding of all fundamental particles and forces except gravity. Despite continuing controversy over its interpretation, quantum physics has been consistently confirmed by experiments and continues to provide the foundation for many modern technologies, such as atomic energy, lasers, and integrated circuits.

Quantum physics originated during the early twentieth century in response to emerging experimental evidence contradicting the classical laws of physics. According to classical physics, light consists of continuous waves of energy permeating space, while matter consists of particles localized in space. However, experiments showed light sometimes behaving as particles and matter sometimes behaving as waves. These violations of classical concepts forced physicists to search for new fundamental laws of physics. Quantum mechanics, the most elementary form of quantum physics, was discovered independently in 1925 by Werner Heisenberg and in 1926 by Erwin Schrödinger. Now, quantum physics also includes the more comprehensive theories of quantum electrodynamics and quantum field theory.

Although quantum physics is a widely accepted scientific theory, it is difficult to interpret in terms of commonsense notions of reality. The fundamental law of quantum mechanics, Schrödinger's wave equation, describes the state of a single particle by a single quantum wave. The intensity of this wave at any position represents the probability of observing the particle at that position. This quantum wave representing the particle's probable position can be mathematically transformed into a complementary wave representing the particle's probable momentum. Position and momentum are thus examples of complementary observable properties. Heisenberg's uncertainty principle states that a small uncertainty in one property necessarily results in a larger uncertainty in the complementary property. According to the standard Copenhagen interpretation of quantum mechanics developed by the Danish physicist Niels Bohr, this uncertainty represents not a mere lack of knowledge but rather a fundamental lack of definiteness in nature. Thus, to accurately describe quantum phenomena, we must use complementary descriptions. A particle, for example, can only be described as having an objectively existing position or an objectively existing momentum, not both.

In a famous paper published in 1935, Albert Einstein objected to the Copenhagen interpretation of quantum theory because of its inconsistency with certain natural assumptions about the nature of physical reality, namely that the properties of separated objects exist independently of each other (locality) and that objects have real properties independent of observation (realism). Einstein's argument was formalized in 1964 by John Bell, who proved that Einstein's assumptions do, indeed, contradict the predictions of quantum physics. Subsequent experiments have confirmed the validity of quantum mechanics and thus proved that realism and locality cannot both be true of our world. The implication is that one or both of the following is true: (1) Certain properties of physical objects do not exist independent of each other, or (2) certain properties of physical objects do not exist independent of observation.

Although observation appears to play an essential role in quantum theory, the fundamental nature of observation and measurement remains controversial. The problem of measurement derives from the fact that we observe only one of the possible values described by the quantum wave. Thus measurement is represented as a discontinuous "collapse" of the quantum wave of probability into a single actualized value. This sudden and spontaneous collapse, however, is not allowed by the laws of quantum physics. There is no explanation for how, when, or where measurement happens. Moreover, the laws of quantum physics do not predict which of the possible values will be selected in any single measurement.

This apparent break with classical determinism has been viewed by some as an opening within physical laws for the exercise of free will. Some researchers, for example, have speculated that consciousness can freely choose which possibility becomes actualized during a quantum measurement. It has also been suggested that certain parapsychological phenomena might be explained by this mechanism. To be compatible with physical laws, however, any such choices must conform to the probability distribution of the quantum wave. Therefore, if consciousness can exercise choice in selecting the result of particular quantum measurements, the result either violates the laws of quantum physics or has no observable effect.

In a fundamental analysis of the quantum measurement process, John von Neumann argued persuasively that consciousness is necessary for a measurement to occur. Because any physical system is described by a quantum wave of probability, the interaction of two physical objects will simply combine their two probability waves to produce yet another wave of probability. Thus the interaction of a physical system with a measurement apparatus will not result in an actual measured value. The observation of any physical system by any other physical system, therefore, will never result in a "collapse" of the probability wave into one actual value. For observation to occur at all, von Neumann concluded, a nonphysical consciousness is required. This activity of consciousness does not violate the laws of quantum physics, since it only serves to cause the collapse, and not to select or influence the value actualized. Because of this apparent role of consciousness in quantum mechanics, some physicists have suggested that the mind-body relationship can be explained using quantum theory. The codependence of observer and observed in quantum theory has also been compared with similar ideas in Buddhist philosophy.

The radical philosophical implications of quantum physics, although they are still controversial, suggest that (1) objects are intimately interconnected, (2) the observer and the observed are interdependent, and (3) consciousness plays an active role in observation. These new implications of quantum physics have prompted some physicists to interpret modern physics from the perspective of mystical worldviews. From such a perspective, some conceptual problems and paradoxes of quantum physics can be resolved. However, while these interpretations may be compatible with the evidence of quantum physics, they have not been established by scientific evidence and remain controversial.

See also BUDDHISM; FREE WILL; PARANORMAL; PSYCHOLOGY OF RELIGION; QUANTUM HEALING.

BIBLIOGRAPHY

Goswami, Amit. *The Self-Aware Universe: How Consciousness Creates the Material World.* 1993.

Herbert, Nick. *Quantum Reality.* 1985.

Stapp, Henry P. *Mind, Matter, and Quantum Mechanics.* 1993.

Wallace, B. Alan. *Choosing Reality: A Buddhist View of Physics and the Mind.* 1996.

Wilber, Ken, ed. *Quantum Questions: Mystical Writings of the World's Great Physicists.* 1984.

Thomas J. McFarlane

Quest

The term "quest," in many contemporary religious movements, designates a personal spiritual search. The implication of the term is usually that the seeker expects to find a particular kind of assistance in, or a resolution to, his or her search for greater meaning or for a deeper spiritual life.

There are a few prominent models for the notion of a spiritual "quest." The one most frequently cited is the traditional vision quest of North American Indians. Among Native American tribes of the Plains

cultural area, the typical adolescent boy's (and sometimes girl's) initiation involved going into the wilderness alone, and fasting and praying for a few days, until a specific kind of dream or (waking) vision occurred. In this vision, the seeker would ideally be visited by a figure, usually an animal but sometimes a human being or spirit, who would offer teachings and give a symbol that would serve as an amulet for assistance in the waking life. After the vision, the individual would return home and report the dream to a shaman or elder. Assuming that the quest was certified as successful, the figure who appeared in the dream would henceforth be regarded as the man's (or woman's) spiritual ally, similar to the idea of a guardian angel in Western religions. The symbol—such as a type of bird's feather or a musical instrument—would be worn or carried by the person on all significant occasions.

Other North American tribes also used the idea of a vision quest but did not necessarily require it as part of an adolescent rite of passage. The concept of receiving information about allies and important symbols in dreams or visions was quite widespread.

A second significant model for the idea of a "quest" comes from Eastern religions, particularly Buddhism, which classically portrays the "quest for enlightenment" as the most important practice a person can undertake. Enlightenment (nirvāṇa in classical Theravāda Buddhism, satori in Zen) is the ultimate goal of the religious life. The quest for enlightenment usually involves a commitment of many years, or an entire lifetime, under the guidance of a teacher who can instruct and monitor one's meditative practice and other aspects of one's daily life. In most Buddhist contexts, a person is expected to enter a monastery for this kind of intense instruction and discipline.

Several features are common to these two models:

1. A "quest" is very much an individual matter, even though it may take place in a communal context (such as a monastery).
2. The process involves some kind of altered state of consciousness, a vision or dream in the one case, enlightenment following on the practice of meditation in the other.
3. Both are a kind of initiation into a higher spiritual status, which in the model cases are acknowledged by a larger community.
4. In both these instances, the acknowledgment follows upon certification by a recognized religious authority.

The popular notion of a spiritual "quest" in contemporary Western culture borrows the first two of these: the lone individual seeking a spiritual goal, and the process involving some special insight or awareness. However, the seeker may or may not be officially certified by an authority or confirmed in any direct way by a community. The assumption is that if a person achieves satisfactory results from the quest, he or she will make the new insights central to life, and this normally will include finding a community that will accept these insights.

A third model focuses on community more directly: the "quest" for one's "roots." This direction for a quest has become popular, especially in ethnic communities, where one finds, particularly among people of Native American, African, Mexican, or Jewish descent, a search for spiritual values and practices within specific communal traditions. Traditions that are regarded as ancient are believed to be sources of deep wisdom, embodied in traditional beliefs or practices, so that in order to enrich the spiritual quality of life a person may take on a lifestyle that has not been practiced in the family for two or more generations. This kind of practice appears even in mainstream Christian traditions, where a return to the roots of Christian liturgy, for example, is regarded as a means of spiritual growth. In such examples a seeker is more likely to consider integration into an established religious community.

The notion of the spiritual quest was popularized from the 1960s through the 1980s by many religious writers, but perhaps none was more influential than the late Joseph Campbell. In his many books, notably *The Hero with a Thousand Faces,* he highlighted the personal spiritual quest—whether toward enlightenment or into the depths of one's ancestral past—as the primary model for modern religiosity. He emphasized the individual nature of the quest, the necessity for conquering obstacles, and the importance of receptivity to a higher awareness. Other writers of the same period illustrated the quest in different ways in their own lives, ranging from Alan Watts and Ram Dass, who appropriated Eastern traditions, to Carlos Castaneda, who represented the shamanic quest in Native American traditions. Many other writings followed, including secular versions such as the 1990s bestseller by Julia Cameron, *The Artist's Way,* which claimed to provide a step-by-step method of finding the true artist within oneself.

Gradually, the ideal of the quest permeated popular religious culture. So powerful did the concept become that a major publisher could use the word, all by itself, as the title of an advertising brochure for its 1999 offering of books on Jesus and early Christianity—another quest for roots. The academic referent of the word was unusual, however. For most of the millions of purchasers of spiritual books and tapes, "quest" continued to mean a highly individual search for insight that would bring both a greater happiness (or inner peace) and a greater insight or perspective on life itself.

See also BUDDHISM; CAMPBELL, JOSEPH; MYTH; NATIVE AMERICAN RELIGIONS; NIRVĀṆA; SHAMANISM; SPIRITUALITY; RITES OF PASSAGE; VISION QUEST.

BIBLIOGRAPHY

Campbell, Joseph. *The Hero with a Thousand Faces.* 1949; repr., 1972.

Dugan, Kathleen. *The Vision Quest of the Plains Indians: Its Spiritual Significance.* 1985.

Foster, Steven, and Meredith Little. *The Book of the Vision Quest: Personal Transformation in the Wilderness.* 1992.

Torrance, Robert M. *The Spiritual Quest: Transcendence in Myth, Religion, and Science.* 1992.

Tamar Frankiel

Quinceañera, La

The *quinceañera* celebration—a term derived from the Spanish word for fifteen (*quince*)—serves as both a "coming out" celebration for young women in Mexican and Mexican-American communities and a religious ceremony initiating the young woman into Catholic adulthood.

Tracing the roots of this complex rite can be somewhat difficult, as there is no real agreement on its particular origins, though it appears fairly obvious that the ceremony owes something to both Spanish court dances and native Mexican rituals of initiation. However, those who have studied this ritual have noted that since quinceañeras are virtually unknown in Spain, it seems logical to locate the genesis of the current celebration in the New World. In addition, the Spanish court dances were comparable to the American cotillion and similar "presentation" events, while quinceañeras take on a decidedly sacralized tone, as they are almost always accompanied by a Mass. It seems, then, that the quinceañera celebration represents a syncretic linkage between traditional Aztec, Maya, and Toltec puberty rites and the debutante-type balls of the Spanish from Mexico's colonial past.

As the term itself implies, the quinceañera takes place on or near the fifteenth birthday of the young honoree and includes two key elements: the Mass of thanksgiving and the dance. Though these two elements are necessarily separate in their official designation, in practice they are linked in a continuous flow of events such that the actual quinceañera can be thought of as one single event.

The Mass of thanksgiving, once celebrated as a regular Sunday Mass, is now most often a Saturday evening vigil, as that is more conducive to the celebration while still fulfilling the Sunday obligation. In addition, the honoree occasionally celebrates her confirmation during the quinceañera, to further emphasize her entrance into her adult life of faith. Whether accompanied by her confirmation or not, the quinceañera Mass is the first time the honoree receives the sacrament of Holy Eucharist as an adult.

The dance and celebration following the Mass should not be construed as merely a party, or *fiesta.* There are specific roles played by the honoree's fourteen *damas,* or attendants; their *chamberláns,* or escorts; the young woman's *padrinos,* or godparents; and her parents, their close friends, and even business associates. In addition, the honoree and her court perform dances and processions that are choreographed especially for the occasion.

For the young woman being honored with a quinceañera, the celebration ritually signals her entrance into adulthood in both realms accentuated during the celebration: the communal adulthood in the eyes of her friends and family, and her adult relationship with God in the eyes of the church.

See also BELONGING, RELIGIOUS; COMMUNION; LATINO TRADITIONS; LITURGY AND WORSHIP; RITES OF PASSAGE; RITUAL; ROMAN CATHOLICISM; SACRAMENTS; SOCIOLOGY OF RELIGION.

BIBLIOGRAPHY

Cantú, Norma E. *La Quinceañera: Towards an Ethnographic Analysis of a Life Cycle Ritual.* 1996.

Erivia, Sr. Angela, M.C.D.P. *Quince Años: Celebrating a Tradition.* 1985.

Dennis Kelley

Qur'an

The Qur'an is the scripture of Islam, consisting of revelations received by the Prophet Muhammad in Arabia during a period of about twenty-three years (610–632 C.E.). About the size of the New Testament and in Arabic, the Qur'an is the fundamental text of Islam. It is also regarded as the greatest masterpiece of the Arabic language.

Textual History

The word *qur'an* means both "reading" and "recitation"—it is both read from a written text and recited from memory. The name also stresses the importance of the contents of the Qur'an—it is scripture worth reading and reciting. Muhammad belonged to one of the clans of Quraysh, the ruling tribe of the coastal town of Mecca. Having rejected the idolatrous religion of Quraysh and other Arabs, he became accustomed to retiring for meditation to a cave outside Mecca. Here, at age forty, he received his first revelation, a short passage of a few verses, through the angel Gabriel. Thereafter the revelations came in small and large portions. The revelations were memorized by many of his followers. After the emigration of Muslims to Medina in 622 C.E., a systematic attempt was made, under Muhammad's supervision, to record the revelations in writing. The rudimentary writing materials available could not lead to the production of complete or finished copies—in the modern sense—of the Qur'an, and so a number of codices, prepared by different hands and differing in arrangement and sometimes in the amount of content recorded, came into existence. During the rule of the third caliph, 'Uthman, authoritative copies of the Qur'an were prepared and sent as "masters" to several major cities. It should be emphasized, though, that in Muslim understanding the primary method of transmission of the scripture is not written but oral. The extraordinary fact that millions of Muslims have memorized the Qur'an underscores another important point—that Muslims have consciously and methodically relied on memory to preserve the text of their scripture, which has been remarkably homogeneous through the centuries. The so-called "variant" readings, while important from historical and academic viewpoints, are not regarded as equivalent to the standard 'Uthmanic recension, which is in use throughout the Muslim world. Most modern Muslim authorities agree that Muhammad himself was responsible for the present arrangement of the Qur'an.

Structure and Themes

The Qur'an is made up of 114 chapters—called *suras*—which vary greatly in length. Shorter *suras* have one theme or specific themes and usually present no difficulty of understanding. Longer *suras* deal with multiple themes, sometimes with a large number of them, and it is often difficult to follow the train of thought. Part of the difficulty, however, arises from the nature of classical Arabic, the language of the Qur'an, which emphasizes brevity and conciseness. A number of modern Muslim scholars have concluded that there is a definite order to the verses in the individual *suras* and also to the *suras* taken as a whole, and that there are significant patterns of arrangement in many parts of the Qur'an. There is general agree-

Two young American Muslim girls (center and right) reading the Qu'ran with their teacher, Abdul-Munim S. Jitmoud, during Ramadan in Kansas City, Missouri.   (Credit: © Jeffrey C. Scott/Impact Visuals/PNI.)

ment that the Qur'an has a firm thematic focus. The major themes of the Qur'an include: (1) monotheism: there is only one God, the possessor of perfect attributes—"the most beautiful names"—and he alone deserves to be worshipped and obeyed; (2) prophecy and revelation: in order to guide humankind, God placed prophets among all nations and gave them revelation, Adam being the first prophet and Muhammad being the last; (3) the afterlife: on an appointed day God will resurrect the dead and pronounce judgment on them, rewarding the virtuous with heaven and punishing the evil in hell; (4) belief and action: right belief must be accompanied by right action, and both must be grounded in and imbued with *taqwa*—God-consciousness—the only true criterion of human excellence in the eyes of God, the distinctions of race, language, or color being meaningless; (5) social justice: a just society is one where gross social and economic disparities do not exist and whose affluent members take care of the less fortunate. In order to bring into existence a God-oriented, moral, and just society, the Qur'an institutes a comprehensive program of action that includes, on the one hand, ritual

(daily prayers, a monthlong annual fast, pilgrimage to Mecca) and virtuous practice (truthfulness in speech and conduct, kindness and generosity to strangers as well as to relatives, fulfillment of obligations toward others), and, on the other hand, a set of guidelines in several spheres—legal (marriage, divorce, inheritance), economic (approved and proscribed ways of earning and spending money, banning of usury or interest, *zakat* or mandatory charity), and political (electing qualified people to office and observing the principle of *shura* or consultation in important matters).

Interpretation

Classical sources lay down several principles of interpretation. The foremost is the principle of inner-Qur'an exegesis: the Qur'an often treats the same subjects in different places in different ways, one part of it thus throwing light on another. Muhammad is regarded as the most authoritative exponent of the Qur'an, and so his statements and observations (*Hadith*), which pertain explicitly or implicitly to the

Qur'an, constitute the definitive interpretation of scripture. The views and opinions of early authorities are also highly valued. Many classical commentaries deal with almost every aspect of the text—explaining the background of verses, discussing the meanings of words and grammatical constructions, and expounding the doctrinal and practical aspects of the Qur'anic message—though literary, theological, or juridical emphases are noticeable in individual works. Modern exegesis (critical interpretation), aiming to reach a broad audience, generally avoids discussion of grammatical and other technical matters, focusing on issues that have a direct theoretical or practical relevance in modern contexts. While all *tafsir,* or exegesis, seeks to remain faithful to the Qur'anic text, a broad distinction between exoteric and esoteric interpretation can be made. Exoteric interpretation, which is the dominant strain, is based on a more literal and more readily accessible—though not necessarily superficial—understanding of the text, whereas in esoteric interpretation an attempt is made to see, usually on subjective bases, meanings hidden behind the words. Sectarian *tafsir* also exists.

Translations

Owing probably to the view that the Arabic Qur'an is the only true Qur'an, Muslims for a very long time were opposed to translating the Qur'an into other languages. The imperative need to make the scripture accessible to the non-Arab believers in the United States and elsewhere eventually outweighed theological objections or reservations. Today translations of the Qur'an exist in many languages, including English, and new ones keep appearing. Typically, however, they are made by individuals rather than by sponsored committees, and little theoretical work exists to guide the translators or to evaluate their work in light of sound critical principles. Consequently, most translations fall short of the mark, and the beauty and grandeur of the original Arabic greatly suffers in them. Among the translations in common use are those by Muhammad Marmaduke Pickthall, Abdullah Yusuf Ali, A. J. Arberry, and Muhammad Asad.

Role in Muslim Life

The Qur'an has made a truly revolutionary impact on the lives of Muslims. From the very beginning it has served as the religious charter and constitution of Muslims, who have tried to engage with it on several levels and in different sets of circumstances. Besides being the basic text for liturgy and serving as a source of inspiration and solace, the Qur'an has provided a strong impetus to cultural and intellectual activity.

The rise of all the major Islamic disciplines of knowledge, for example, is directly or indirectly attributable to the Qur'an. Sound knowledge of the Qur'an is a basic qualification for all religious scholarship in Islam, and scholars of the Qur'an earn respect in society. The highly developed Islamic art of calligraphy revolves around the Qur'an: the arches, domes, and walls of mosques are often decorated with beautifully written Qur'anic verses. The equally refined art of Qur'an recitation is exhibited at the highly popular competitions where renowned reciters—both male and female—display skills mastered over the years. Muslims in the West try to maintain contact with the Qur'an. Children are encouraged to complete their first reading of the Qur'an at an early age, and such readings, when completed, are usually celebrated with fanfare. In several states in the United States where there are large Muslim populations—for example, New York, New Jersey, and California—there are boarding schools where, by arrangement with public schools, children memorize the Qur'an under expert guidance while continuing their other education.

Qur'an and Bible

The Qur'an is similar to the Bible in some respects and different in others. The essential theme of the right relationship between God and human beings is central to both, as are the attendant themes of prophecy, salvation, and the moral life. The Qur'an generally accepts the Biblical historical tradition. The Qur'an is different from the Bible in scope and structure: its focus is on the struggle of one man—the Prophet Muhammad—and his followers during a certain, much shorter period to establish Islam in the Arabian Peninsula. In addition, theme rather than chronology is its main organizing principle. Comparative study of the two scriptures—from an objective viewpoint—is a promising but still undeveloped area.

See also ALLAH; BIBLE; ISLAM; MECCA.

BIBLIOGRAPHY

Bell, Richard. *Introduction to the Qur'an.* Revised and expanded by W. Montgomery Watt. 1990.

Denny, Frederick M. "Qur'an and Hadith." In *The Holy Book in Comparative Perspective,* edited by Frederick M. Denny and Rodney L. Taylor. 1985.

Jeffery, Arthur. *The Qur'an as Scripture.* 1952.

Quasem, Muhammad Abul, trans. *The Recitation and Interpretation of the Qur'an: al-Ghazali's Theory.* 1982.

Rahman, Fazlur. *Major Themes of the Qur'an.* 1980.

Welch, A. T. "al-Kur'an." *Encyclopedia of Islam,* 2nd ed., 1954–, Vol. VI, pp. 400–429.

Mustansir Mir

R

Rabbinate

The term *rabbi* literally means "my master" and is derived from the Hebrew noun *rav,* meaning "great." Although the title does not appear in the Bible, its origins may be traced back to the rabbinic period in Jewish history arising, according to some scholars, after the destruction of the Second Temple. It was at this time that several generations of sages created a vast oral tradition that ultimately gave rise to a great literature in Judaism known as the Oral Law (which includes Mishnah, Gemara, Tosefta, Baraitha, and Midrash). The role of the rabbi then was completely different from what it has become. Originally, the title did not denote a full-time occupation but rather was used to distinguish those teachers who were properly authorized to function as interpreters and expounders of the Bible and the Oral Law. It was only during the Middle Ages that rabbis began to assume additional responsibilities, including preaching, teaching, and serving as the spiritual leader of the local congregation or community. As communal expectations and demands on rabbis increased, the custom of providing rabbis with emoluments developed, and in time the office of rabbi emerged.

The importance of local rabbis as communal leaders continued to evolve as communities increasingly relied on their rabbinate for guidance in a wide array of civil matters. Local rabbis assumed responsibility for the supervision of marriage and divorce proceedings, arbitrating moral dilemmas, and adjudicating legal contentions on the basis of their knowledge of Jewish law. In addition to these tasks, rabbis were expected to devote themselves to the study of the sacred texts in order to increase their wealth of knowledge.

Modern Period

In modern times the character and function of the rabbinate was again transformed primarily in response to the era of emancipation. As governments of various countries, particularly in Western Europe, granted Jewish residents the rights of citizenship during the nineteenth century, rabbinic authority in matters of civil jurisprudence waned. The more Jews acculturated within the general society, the more their rabbis were expected to possess a wider scope of knowledge. Although some rabbinical schools (called *yeshivot*) refused to modify their traditional curriculum, new rabbinical seminaries with a more comprehensive curriculum began to emerge. Relaxing the traditional emphasis on the study of Jewish law codes, these modern seminaries began to expose their students to the study of Jewish history, literature, philosophy, and homiletics. In time rabbis were expected to possess at least some familiarity with secular studies.

The role of the rabbi during modern times varies considerably from country to country in accordance with local conditions and needs. There are, however, a number of key responsibilities that the majority of modern rabbis have in common: teaching, preaching (in the vernacular), pastoral work (visiting the sick and officiating at life-cycle events), broad participation in the social life of the community, representing the Jewish community to the larger community, and serving as a spiritual leader and role model.

United States

From the onset rabbis in the United States have been expected to play a leadership role in a diverse array of cultural, social, and political activities that transcend the strictly religious and educational functions traditionally placed within the rabbi's purview. The modern American rabbi, like other religious leaders in the United States, is also called upon to serve as a personal counselor, a leader in the field of human relations, and an advocate for social justice within general society. American rabbis are expected to interpret Jewish tradition not only within the Jewish community itself but also to the community at large.

The rabbinate in the United States acquired a particularly distinct role, one that derives from the nation's unique cultural, political, and sociological characteristics. Separation between church and state, for example, has prevented one segment of the Jewish community from acquiring sanction or official recognition from the government. This situation contrasts with that of some European countries and the modern State of Israel, in which there developed a system of rabbinical hierarchy recognized by the state. This notion of a head, or chief, rabbi may be traced back to the fourteenth century, when the position of the *mara de-atra* ("the master of the locality") arose. In modern times this role has been formalized in various rabbinic offices such as that of the *Landrabbiner* (Germany), the Chief Rabbi (Great Britain and Israel), and the *Rosh Yeshivah* (Poland and Lithuania). In contrast to these practices, the vast majority of American rabbis do not submit themselves to the religious authority of another scholar.

The influence of congregationalism, the democratic spirit, and voluntarism—all so prominent in the religious life of the American nation—has also contributed to the rabbinate's distinctive features: U.S. Jewry embraced the notion that each congregation has, as a matter of principle, the right to exercise control over its own affairs. In the American synagogue members assume an equal right to direct their institution in accordance with their own convictions. Membership as well as participation in the synagogue is voluntary, not compulsory. In light of these characteristics, American rabbis must rely heavily upon the force of personal persuasion, as opposed to a licensed or imposed authority, in their efforts to exert spiritual leadership.

History

On the eve of the American Revolution, American Jewry—small in numbers—was already highly acculturated and entirely at home in the life patterns and general outlook of the fledgling nation. During the early national period there were no ordained rabbis in the New World. American Jewry relied largely upon knowledgeable laymen who served as religious officiants. Gershom Mendes Seixas (1745/6–1816), for example, served as the "minister" of Shearith Israel Congregation in New York from 1768 to 1776 and again from 1784 to 1816. Emanuel Nunes Carvalho (1771–1817) served as "minister" of Beth Elohim Congregation in Charleston from 1811 to 1815. In the 1830s Jewish immigration from central Europe increased, and a number of talented "ministers" (sometimes referred to by the title *hazzan,* which roughly meant "reader") left Europe in order to work in the United States. Among the most significant figures to come to the United States during this period were Isaac Leeser (1806–1868), who served as "minister" of Mikveh Israel Congregation in Philadelphia from 1829 to 1850, and Samuel Myer Isaacs (1804–1878), the *hazzan* of B'nai Jeshurun Congregation in New York from 1839 to 1847.

By the middle of the nineteenth century, American Jewry was large enough to attract ordained rabbis (rabbis with *semikhah,* a certificate of ordination) to its shores. The first ordained rabbi to settle in the United States was Abraham Rice (1800/2–1862) who arrived in 1840 and, shortly thereafter, was invited to became the rabbi of Congregation Nidche Israel, better known as Baltimore Hebrew Congregation. In 1845 Max Lilienthal (1815–1882) arrived and, after serving as the rabbi of a short-lived union of New York's German congregations and then as a schoolmaster, he became the rabbi of Cincinnati's Bene Israel Congregation in 1855. Undoubtedly the most significant rabbinic figure of the second half of the nineteenth century was Isaac Mayer Wise (1819–1900), who played a pivotal role in the creation of the Union of American Hebrew Congregations in 1873 (the oldest association of synagogues in the United States), the Hebrew Union College in 1875 (the oldest rabbinical school in the United States), and in 1889 the Central Conference of American Rabbis (the country's oldest rabbinical association).

After 1880 an unprecedented number of Jewish immigrants from eastern Europe began to arrive on these shores, and the number of American rabbis increased dramatically. Like the community they served, a significant percentage of these rabbis were themselves immigrants, and over time tensions developed between the rabbis who had trained in eastern Europe and those who had studied in the United States. Eventually, an ever-increasing number of American rabbis received their rabbinic education from an American institution of rabbinic learning such as the Hebrew Union College (which merged with the Jewish Institute of Religion in 1950), the Jewish Theological Seminary of America (1886), the Rabbi Isaac Elhanan Theological Seminary (1896/7), the Hebrew Theological College (1922), or the Reconstructionist Rabbinical College (1968).

Many rabbinical organizations have been established in the United States to support the professional needs of the American rabbinate, including the Central Conference of American Rabbis, the Rabbinical Assembly (originally the Alumni Association of the Jewish Theological Seminary of America; 1901), *Agudath Ha-Rabbonim* (the Union of Orthodox Rabbis of the United States, the oldest Orthodox rabbinical association in the United States; 1902), the Rabbinical Council of America (1935), and the Reconstructionist Rabbinical Association (1974).

In 1972 the Hebrew Union College ordained Sally J. Priesand, thereby making her the first woman in Jewish history to obtain rabbinic ordination from the faculty of a rabbinical seminary. The Reconstructionist Rabbinical College ordained its first woman rabbi, Sandy Eisenberg Sasso, in 1974, and in 1985 Amy Eilberg became the first woman ordinee of the Jewish Theological Seminary.

According to the Bureau of Labor Statistics, there are today approximately 4,500 rabbis currently employed in the United States; 1,850 associate themselves with the Reform Movement, 1,300 with the Conservative Movement, 1,000 with Orthodox Judaism, and 250 with the Reconstructionist Movement. A growing number of rabbis have acquired their titles by private ordination, and these individuals frequently serve synagogues or groups that choose not to associate themselves with one of the four primary movements in American Judaism. Of the 3,400 rabbis who align themselves with a movement that ordains women rabbis (Reform, Conservative, or Reconstructionist Judaism), approximately 500, or 15 percent, are women.

See also JUDAISM; MIDRASH; MINISTRY; ORDINATION; ORDINATION OF WOMEN; PRIESTHOOD; SYNAGOGUE.

BIBLIOGRAPHY

Gottschalk, Alfred. *To Learn and to Teach: Your Life as a Rabbi,* revised by Gary P. Zola. 1988.
Marcus, Jacob R., and Abraham J. Peck, eds. *The American Rabbinate: A Century of Continuity and Change, 1883–1983.* 1985.
Meyer, Michael A. *Hebrew Union College–Jewish Institute of Religion: A Centennial History, 1875–1975,* edited by Gary P. Zola. 1992.
Nadell, Pamela S. *Conservative Judaism in America: A Biographical Dictionary and Sourcebook.* 1988.
Nadell, Pamela S. *Women Who Would Be Rabbis: A History of Women's Ordination, 1889–1985.* 1998.
Olitzky, Kerry M., Lance J. Sussman, and Malcolm H. Stern. *Reform Judaism in America: A Biographical Dictionary and Sourcebook.* 1993.
Schwartzfuchs, Simon. *A Concise History of the Rabbinate.* 1993.
Sherman, Moshe. *Orthodox Judaism in America: A Biographical Dictionary and Sourcebook.* 1996.
Wertheimer, Jack, ed. *Tradition Renewed: A History of the Jewish Theological Seminary.* 1997.
Zola, Gary P. *The American Rabbinate, 1960–1986: A Bibliographic Essay.* 1988.
Zucker, David J. *American Rabbis: Facts and Fiction.* 1998.

Gary P. Zola

Rajneesh, Bhagwan

(1931–1990), religious leader.

Bhagwan Shree Rajneesh was leader of a high-profile religious group, popularly known as the "Rajneeshies," that drew considerable public attention in the late 1980s during a struggle between the group and local authorities over the operation of its commune, or "ashram," in the Pacific Northwest.

Rajneesh's idiosyncratic teachings melded components of Hinduism with those of the major world religions as well as classical Greek philosophy, the human potential movement, and Western psychotherapy. He was best known for his instruction on achieving enlightenment through sex with multiple partners. Because of this emphasis and his lavish lifestyle, including ownership of numerous Rolls-Royces, he became a media caricature of the guru as rake and supersalesman.

Born Rajneesh Chandra Mohan in the town of Kuchwara in central India, Rajneesh launched his career as a guru in 1966 after leaving his position as a philosophy professor at the University of Jabalpur. He set up an ashram in Bombay, later moving to Poona. From the outset Rajneesh's clientele consisted mainly of Americans, reported to number as many as fifty thousand.

In 1981 Rajneesh immigrated with some of his followers to a sixty-five-thousand-acre ranch near Antelope, Oregon, and named it Rajneeshpuram. Immediately his followers found themselves in serious conflict with their rural and small-town neighbors. Some ugly incidents, including the salmonella poisoning of local restaurant patrons and the firebombing of the office of city officials, were blamed, perhaps wrongly, on the Rajneesh organization. In 1995 two of Rajneesh's lieutenants were convicted of conspiracy

A portrait of Bhagwan Shree Rajneesh.   (Credit: © Archive Photos.)

to murder an attorney who had fought to close down Rajneeshpuram.

Rajneesh returned to India in 1986 and changed his name to Osho, an allusion to what William James had called the "oceanic experience," or mystical ecstasy. Rajneesh died in 1990 at Poona.

See also ASHRAM; COMMUNES; ECSTASY; GURU; HINDUISM.

BIBLIOGRAPHY
Gordon, James S. *The Golden Guru: The Strange Journey of Bhagwan Shree Rajneesh.* 1987.

Carl A. Raschke

Ramakrishna Movement

The Ramakrishna movement originated in India in the latter nineteenth century, based on the teachings of an Indian saint and mystic named Sri Ramakrishna (1836–1886). The movement was brought to the United States by the Bengali saint's disciple Swami Vivekananda (1863–1902), who represented Hinduism at the 1893 Chicago World Parliament of Religions. If Ramakrishna was the spiritual founder of the movement, Vivekananda stands out as the movement's chief organizer and publicist. Staying on after the Parliament, the swami lectured widely on Hinduism and founded the first Vedanta societies in America. As the first Asian religious movement to establish centers in the United States, the Ramakrishna movement may be said to have launched a new era in American religious history, pioneering the way for the numerous Hindu, Buddhist, and other Asian religious groups now active in the United States.

The Ramakrishna movement's message to Americans has been the Vedanta, a tradition that traces its inspiration back to the Upanishads, which originated as philosophical commentaries on the Vedas. As interpreted by Shankara, its most important early proponent, the Vedanta philosophy emphasizes a nondualistic view, arguing that all distinctions are unreal and that the only reality is Brahman. In addition to nondualism, the message presented by Ramakrishna swamis in the United States reveals a strong emphasis on Vedanta's universalism, compatibility with modern science, and ethical teachings. While presenting a broad, philosophical Hinduism to the American public, among close followers the movement has increasingly emphasized devotion to Ramakrishna and to Ramakrishna's wife, Sarada Devi, known to devotees as the "Holy Mother." Some have argued that the rising prominence of devotionalism threatens to undermine the movement's universalistic message.

While consistently denying any desire to propagate Hinduism or to convert Americans, the Ramakrishna movement has attracted a small American following numbering in the thousands. The membership has remained fairly steady since the 1890s, with a membership at present of approximately twenty-five hundred followers organized into twelve Vedanta societies. Historically, the typical follower has come from an educated middle- or upper-middle-class background; most have been female, many with earlier "spiritual seeker" roots; and a majority reveal prior Protestant upbringing. However, since the passage of the Immigration Act of 1965, which for the first time allowed significant immigration from India, Asian Indians have become increasingly prominent, a development that has brought important changes to the movement.

Organizationally, each of the Vedanta societies is headed by a senior swami, who looks to the Belur Math in Calcutta for direction. The worldwide movement consists of two guiding organizations, the Ramakrishna Math and the Ramakrishna Mission, with the Math representing the movement's monastic wing and the Mission directing the movement's extensive medical, relief, and educational programs in India. In practice, however, the two organizations operate as one, with the trustees of the Math serving as the Mission's governing board. In the early history of the American movement, individual Vedanta societies enjoyed a great deal of autonomy, with the local swami often playing a decisive role in each society's message and work. However, since World War II the Indian headquarters has steadily worked to establish greater control over the American centers, a manifestation of the Indian organization's increasing conservatism.

The significance of the Ramakrishna movement cannot be measured by its small numbers. Thanks to its long and continuous history in the United States and the intellectual stature of several of its U.S. swamis (Swamis Nikhilananda, Prabhavananda, Paramananda, and Akhilananda, among others), it has played a leading role in expanding American awareness of Hinduism and the Vedanta philosophy. Indeed, more than any other Hindu group, the Ramakrishna movement has served as the "official" voice of Hinduism in the United States, a role suggested by the movement's frequent invitations to represent Hinduism at interreligious congresses, as well as by the prominence of Ramakrishna movement translations and commentaries in contemporary bookstores and as texts in classes on world religions.

Today the Ramakrishna movement continues to work quietly, with major centers in such urban areas as Los Angeles; San Francisco; Chicago; Boston; New York City; Providence; St. Louis; Portland, Oregon; and Seattle. Also active in other Western countries, it maintains contemporary centers in Canada, Great Britain, France, Switzerland, and Argentina. Never concerned to reach a large audience, the movement promises to remain small. However, its early appearance on American shores, wide intellectual influence, and recognized position as the voice of Hinduism seem to guarantee that it will always be remembered as a pioneer in the introduction of Asian religion in America and the West.

See also Hinduism; International Society for Krishna Consciousness; Upanishads; Vedanta Society; Vedas.

BIBLIOGRAPHY

French, Harold W. *The Swan's Wide Waters: Ramakrishna and Western Culture.* 1974.

Jackson, Carl T. *Vedanta for the West: The Ramakrishna Movement in the United States.* 1994.

Yale, John, ed. *What Vedanta Means to Me: A Symposium.* 1960.

Carl T. Jackson

Ramtha's School of Enlightenment

Ramtha's School of Enlightenment, founded in 1987, emerged as one of the major organizational expressions of the New Age, a millennialist movement that swept through Western esotericism in the 1970s and 1980s. The school was founded by Judith Darlene "J. Z." Knight (b. 1946), a young housewife in Tacoma, Washington, who in 1977 had an encounter with a spiritual being who identified himself as Ramtha the Enlightened One. Shortly thereafter Knight began to channel Ramtha, and in the 1980s she became one of the most popular of New Age channelers.

Channeling messages from spiritual beings has been an integral part of modern esoteric movements since Emanuel Swedenborg (1688–1772) and continuing through Spiritualism and Theosophy. Through the twentieth century, more than a hundred groups built around channeled teachings have appeared.

Ramtha identified himself as a thirty-five-thousand-year-old warrior who had become a conqueror of nations. While recovering from an assassination attempt, he contemplated the nature of the universe, found enlightenment, and ascended from his mortal existence. In the present, speaking through Knight, he addresses his students as "masters" and reminds them of their ability to be creative, divine beings.

Knight presented Ramtha in weekend sessions held around the United States, but then in 1987 she ceased traveling and founded Ramtha's School of Enlightenment at her ranch near Yelm, Washington. The Ramtha school teaches a form of gnostic esotericism that views individuals as divine beings who have been trapped in this world by forgetfulness. It offers a set of spiritual practices designed to assist students to remember and again attain their divine status. Basic to the practice is "C&E" (consciousness and energy), a form of kundalini Yoga.

As the 1980s came to a close, the practice of channeling came under intense criticism, and the New Age movement as a whole distanced itself from the practice. Simultaneously, Knight became the focus of widespread criticism, some critics suggesting that the school had turned the Ramtha movement into a brainwashing cult that pushed members into weird and even dangerous practices. In 1996, as part of a larger study of the movement by an interdisciplinary set of scholars, Knight allowed herself to be monitored by a team of psychologists as she went into and came out of trance. The psychologists concluded that Knight was neither faking the process, nor was it a sign of pathology. Their work significantly contributed to the quelling of the controversy that had previously swelled around the school.

Since its founding, Ramtha's school has been especially attractive to people in their thirties, the average age of new members being thirty-five. The school thus stands in stark contrast to the many new religions that emerged in the West in the 1970s that drew recruits from young adults (eighteen to twenty-five). The school also has attracted a well-educated female majority, and well over half of the members are college graduates. As the 1990s come to a close, there are approximately three thousand students of the school, which has grown steadily during the years of its existence.

See also ANTI-CULT MOVEMENT; BRAINWASHING; CHANNELING; CULT; CULT AWARENESS NETWORK; MILLENNIALISM; NEW AGE SPIRITUALITY; NEW RELIGIOUS MOVEMENTS; YOGA.

BIBLIOGRAPHY

Knight, J. Z. *A Beginner's Guide to Creating Reality: An Introduction to Ramtha and His Teachings.* 1997.

Melton, J. Gordon. *Finding Enlightenment: Ramtha's School of Ancient Wisdom.* 1997.

Weinberg, Steven Lee, et al., eds. *Ramtha.* 1986.

J. Gordon Melton

Rapture

The word *rapture* comes from the Latin root *rapio*, meaning "caught up," and is taken primarily from 1 Thessalonians 4:17. The rapture refers to the belief held by some Christians that, near the end of the world, they will be lifted from the Earth to meet Christ in the air.

Not all Christians use the rapture concept. To understand which Christians use the concept, it is necessary to understand two other Christian concepts: the Great Tribulation and the millennium.

Based on biblical texts, the Great Tribulation is a seven-year period of great suffering taking place at the world's end. It is headed by an evil ruler called the Antichrist, who will have power over all the Earth's peoples. The millennium is the thousand years of peace and righteousness predicted in various biblical texts. Premillennialists are those who believe that the Great Tribulation will occur *before* the millennium. It is only these Christians—primarily conservative Chris-

tians in the United States and Britain of the past century and a half—who espouse the rapture.

Within Christian groups espousing the rapture, debate rages as to when it will happen. The most popular position is that it can happen at any time, but once it does happen, the tribulation will begin. Smaller numbers believe that the rapture will occur midway through the tribulation or at the end of the tribulation.

Though there were certainly earlier formulations, the concept of the rapture was not fully developed until the mid-1800s. In the United States, its acceptance is attributed to John Nelson Darby (1800–1882) of Great Britain. He placed ideas such as the rapture, the tribulation, and the millennium into a tight, cohesive system called dispensationalism, and he espoused this system with great fervor on his six trips to the United States from 1859 to 1874. His view of the rapture quickly gained popularity in the United States and became an important theme in conservative Protestant theology.

As detailed in Paul Boyer's *When Time Shall Be No More* (1992), the rapture concept has had a significant impact on modern American culture—especially since 1970—with an explosion of rapture/end times-related publications. The best-selling nonfiction book of the 1970s *The Late Great Planet Earth* was a modern translation of the rapture and the tribulation. It was first published in 1970, and by 1978, nine million copies were in print. More than thirty million copies are now in print. One of the best-selling fiction series of the 1990s—the *Left Behind* series—is about the rapture and the tribulation.

But the rapture is not just communicated through the thousands of books published about it. It is also the focus of numerous films, with titles such as *A Thief in the Night* and *The Road to Armageddon;* bumper stickers with messages such as "Beam Me Up, Lord" and "Warning: If the Rapture Occurs, This Car Will Be Driverless," as well as radio and television shows, magazine articles, seminary and Christian college classes, evangelistic tracts, Christian comic books, music, paintings, postcards, T-shirts, baseball caps, tattoos, and even rapture wristwatches.

The rapture concept has important implications. Conservative Protestants, believing that the rapture can occur at any time, are motivated to "keep right with God" and to evangelize others with fervor so others will not be left behind to face the horrible tribulation. Moreover, since their theology suggests that the world will get worse and worse as the rapture nears, motivation for social change is minimized. As some put it, to work for social change "is like polishing the brass fixtures on a sinking ocean liner" (Boyer 1992, p. 299).

See also DISPENSATIONALISM; JOURNALISM, RELIGIOUS; MILLENNIALISM; PREMILLENNIALISM; PROSELYTIZING; PUBLISHING, RELIGIOUS; RELIGIOUS EXPERIENCE; SECOND COMING.

BIBLIOGRAPHY

Boyer, Paul. *When Time Shall Be No More: Prophecy Belief in Modern American Culture.* 1992.

Gleason, L. Archer, Jr. *Three Views of the Rapture: Pre-, Mid-, or Post-Tribulation?* 1984.

Vander Lugt, Herbert. *Perhaps Today! The Rapture of the Church.* 1984.

Michael O. Emerson
Robyn Minahan

Rastafari

Rastafari began in Jamaica in the 1930s, but most scholarship recognizes its connection to earlier Jamaican folk religions, such as Revival. Rastafari started as a poor person's religion, drawing its membership from young unemployed men migrating from Jamaica's rural to urban areas. Because of their class origins and the persecution they faced, Rastafari developed a distrust for instituted authorities and the status quo (which it frequently refers to as "Babylon"). Though not necessarily an activist movement, Rastafari continues to have a strong concern for the oppressed and an acute awareness of racial and status inequality. At the same time, the movement is typically patriarchal and has been criticized for its treatment of women.

Rastafari emerged from at least four relatively separate strands associated with early founders Leonard Howell, Joseph Hibbert, Archibald Dunkley, and Robert Hinds. These leaders all shared an association with Marcus Garvey's Pan-Africanist movement and a concern with Ethiopia, a traditional symbol of African power and respectability that became even more important after the coronation of Emperor Haile Selassie in 1930. Experiences of marginalization, migration, and migratory labor further shaped the early worldviews of these founders, three of whom are known to have spent time outside of Jamaica.

In its early years, Rastafari's distinctive belief was in Haile Selassie as God ("Jah"). Through the 1960s, Rastafarianism developed other traits and practices for which it became well known and somewhat notorious. These include discussion ("reasoning") as a central ritual, ritual use of marijuana, wearing of matted hair ("dreadlocks"), bans on taking sharp objects to the body (e.g., no shaving or piercing), food proscriptions (e.g., no pork, alcohol, or things with blood in them), avoidance of the dead, development of an argot, and belief in repatriation to Africa. Several of these practices are rooted in Rastafari interpretations of Hebrew and Christian Scriptures, which continue to be authoritative but are subject to idiosyncratic interpretations in the "reasoning" process.

More recently, popular culture has been instrumental in the development and spread of Rastafari. Reggae music made Rastafari more acceptable to mainstream society; by the late 1960s Rastafari had moved beyond its lower-class origins and was attracting a new membership, especially on college campuses and in West Indian diaspora communities. Rastafari has spread to the United States primarily through migration and music.

Rastafari beliefs continue to evolve in new ways. The focus on Haile Selassie, still central in some groups, was weakened following the Ethiopian revolution of 1974 and Selassie's death in 1975. Now a primary concern is with recognition and liberation of the "I," a Rastafari notion of the self that is explicitly linked with a divine "I." The concern with repatriation to Ethiopia ("Zion") has also been mitigated and now is heard in general calls for a just world ("Zion"). Concern about race, though still present, is also less of a focus in contemporary Rastafari. Finally, the importance and visibility of women in Rastafari is increasing. This trend, combined with the increasing globalization of the movement, will decisively impact on how the movement develops in coming years.

Tamara I and Saloman Mu-sa-ya, leaders of the Rastafarian Nation in the U.S. Virgin Islands, ca. 1979. (Credit: CORBIS/Bettmann.)

See also AFRICAN-AMERICAN RELIGIONS; RITUAL.

BIBLIOGRAPHY

Barrett, Leonard E., Sr. *The Rastafarians.* Rev. ed. 1988.

Chevannes, Barry. *Rastafari: Roots and Ideology.* 1994.

Chevannes, Barry, ed. *Rastafari and Other African-Caribbean Worldviews.* 1998.

Hepner, Randal. "Movement of Jah People: Race, Class, and Religion Among the Rastafari of Jamaica and New York City." Ph.D. diss., New School for Social Research, New York. 1998.

Murrell, Spencer, and McFarlane, eds. *Chanting Down Babylon: The Rastafari Reader.* 1998.

Richard C. Salter

Rave

In 1988 the industrial "Acid House" music that pervaded underground clubs and warehouses in Chicago spread to England and gave birth to spontaneous all-night dance parties or "raves." Raves later migrated back to the United States, where thriving subcultures formed around the music-dance phenomenon in San Francisco, Los Angeles, and New York. More than just a "good time," rave culture has been characterized by a pervasive mysticism that fuses the technological and the spiritual.

For many ravers, the computer-driven, heavy, hypnotic technobeat of the music induces dance trance and mystical journeying. DJs, or "technoshamans," mix together an eclectic sampling of music and sounds, combining jungle noises, tribal rhythms, and chanting monks, with a fast industrial beat ranging from 140 to 160 beats per minute. Physically and spiritually merging with the music, many ravers cultivate a state of consciousness in which they "let go," allowing the music to lead them in a postmodern, neotribal, cathartic experience.

Other rave elements that help to cultivate the shamanic journey include the use of virtual reality technology, lasers, and psychedelic computer-generated images projected onto large screens. For some, the rave itself is a sufficiently mind-altering experience. Others use psychotropic drugs such as "Ecstasy" (touted as an important vehicle for enlightenment and spiritual evolution) or "smart drinks" (fruit juice and nutraceutical elixirs) to evoke and intensify the mystical experience.

Part of the allure of raves lies in the *quest* element involved in actually deciphering the rave's location. Information is passed on through word of mouth or a secretive system of mobile phones, toll-free numbers, and fax machines. Like a wild treasure hunt, the ravers search for clues to find their way to abandoned warehouses, open fields, beaches, and—in one case—a vacant airport runway. The mystery and intrigue of the quest tap into the archaic and mythic themes embraced by the closely related and overlapping subculture of cybernetic fantasy gaming. The nomadic quality of raves also speaks to the anarchic ethos among ravers, who tend to champion antistructure and spout "chaos theory."

Seeking to combine the spiritual power of the rave with efforts to revitalize Christian worship and make it more appealing to the twentysomething generation, former Catholic priest Matthew Fox and others organized a historic "Planetary Rave Mass" at Grace Cathedral in San Francisco in 1994. The multimedia rave featured large videoscreens flashing time-lapse nature footage evoking the cycles of life, death, and rebirth, all against a continuous background of hypnotic, ambient technomusic. A portion called "confessing our sins to God" that surrounded ravers with multiple screens showing graphic scenes of the Earth being polluted and desecrated in various ways was followed by group chants of "Lord, have mercy." Fox spoke with ravers of a medicine man who once said that "when a culture loses its spirituality, only the young can bring it back." Whether or not this is so, the neoshamanic, meditative, and mystical qualities of the rave constitute a particularly creative and vital youth-driven movement in contemporary spirituality.

See also CYBER RELIGION; DRUGS; MUSIC; MYSTICISM; NEW AGE SPIRITUALITY; QUEST; SHAMANISM.

BIBLIOGRAPHY

Lehmann-Haupt, R. "Sacred Raves." *Yoga Journal* (May-June 1995): 78–81.

Marshall, Jules. "Here Come the Zippies!" *Wired* (May 1994): 79–134.

Roof, Wade Clark, and Sarah McFarland Taylor, "The Force of Emotion: James's Reorientation of Religion and the Contemporary Rediscovery of the Body, Spirituality, and the Feeling Self." In *The Struggle For Life: A Companion to William James's The Varieties of Religious Experience,* edited by Donald Capps and Janet Jacobs. 1995.

Rushkoff, Douglas. *Cyberia: Life in the Trenches of Hyperspace.* 1994.

Sirius, R. U. *How to Mutate and Take Over the World.* 1996.

Sarah McFarland Taylor

Reconstructionist Christianity

While relatively unknown outside conservative Christian circles, the Christian Reconstructionists provided much of the intellectual underpinning for the rise of the New Christian Right in the latter half of the twentieth century. Reconstructionist thinkers grounded in strict Calvinism, including Rousas John Rushdoony, Gary North, Greg Bahnsen, and David Chilton, articulated a theological system called theonomy, which was based on the view that God's law, contained in the Bible, was applicable to all areas of life—not the least of which is civil government.

Reconstructionist Christianity can be understood as flowing from two theological distinctives: presuppositionalism and postmillennialism. Presuppositionalist epistemology holds that all reasoning begins with premises (presuppositions) for which there may be no proof. Reconstructionists derived this epistemology from Cornelius van Til, a professor at Westminster Seminary, where many of them studied. Reconstructionists teach that in the search for truth, one must begin either with God or with human reason (thus humanism) but that there can be no neutral starting point; that no aspect of life can be religiously neutral—not civil government, not science, not education. Thus they seek to bring all of life "under the lordship of Christ." From popularized versions of this system the New Christian Right has drawn its critique of "secular humanism" and called for "reestablishing America as a Christian nation."

As postmillennialists, Christian Reconstructionists stand apart from traditional American Fundamentalists, who are predominantly premillennial dispensationalists. Reconstructionists hold that Jesus' Second Coming will follow a "thousand-year" reign of the Kingdom of God (they are not literal concerning the thousand-year duration), which began at Christ's resurrection. They believe that the great tribulation promised in the Book of Revelation occurred with the destruction of the Temple at Jerusalem in 70 C.E. and that since the resurrection, it has been the responsibility of Christians to "usher in the Kingdom" by taking dominion over the Earth (as Adam and Eve were commanded to do at Creation). They expect the increasing "Christianization" of the world and a subsequent transformation of the world's nations into societies based on biblical law. These postmillennialist sensibilities have been imported into premillennialist conservative Protestant theological systems in piecemeal fashion as "Prosperity Theology" and as "Dominion Theology" (which, in turn, promoted involvement in business and politics).

While Christian Reconstructionist books and materials (including workbooks designed for use in Bible study sessions) were produced by a relatively small cadre of thinkers, the influence of the movement has been largely hidden for at least two reasons. First, the promotion of these views occurred in a diffused and informal manner. During the 1970s and 1980s Christian Reconstructionist materials were widely disseminated in the conservative Protestant subculture. New Christian Right leaders and pastors read Reconstructionist works, fundamentalist church bookstores sold the materials for individual and group Bible studies, and Christian schools and Christian home schoolers bought Reconstructionist curricular materials for use in their classrooms.

The second reason why the influence of this movement has been hidden is that Reconstructionists have been so unrelentingly consistent and have endorsed positions that the larger Christian Right found too extreme. Rushdoony has said in print, as well as in a PBS video with Bill Moyers (*God and Politics*), that democracy violated fundamental biblical principles and that the Book of Deuteronomy lists the death penalty as the punishment for homosexuality and "incorrigible" teens. Christian Right leaders have distanced themselves from Reconstructionist leaders while at the same time embracing many Reconstructionist views that seemed more politically palatable. For example, a 10 percent flat tax to replace the current graduated income tax was advocated by Reconstructionists as biblical (based on the biblical tithe) long before it was advocated by the Christian Right and then by more mainstream Republican politicians.

Important sources of Reconstructionist materials are Gary North's Institute for Christian Economics and Dominion Press, in Tyler, Texas, which publishes Reconstructionist books; North's newsletter *The Remnant Review;* and Rousas John Rushdoony's Chalcedon Foundation in Vallecito, California, from which *The Journal of Christian Reconstruction, The Chalcedon Report,* and other publications come. Key Reconstructionist works include Rushdoony's two-volume commentary on the Ten Commandments and their application for today, *The Institutes of Biblical Law* (1973); Bahnsen's exposition of presuppositionalism *Theonomy and Christian Ethics* (1974); Chilton's development of postmillennialism in *Paradise Restored* (Reconstruction Press, Fort Worth, Texas, 1985) and *Days of Vengeance* (Dominion Press, Fort Worth, Texas, 1990); and *The Biblical BluePrint Series,* edited by Gary North, which explores the application of Reconstructionist theology to every area of life (including government, education, and family, but also the welfare, banking, and taxation systems).

See also CIVIL RELIGION; FUNDAMENTALIST CHRISTIANITY; HOME SCHOOLING; MORAL MAJORITY; PREMILLENNIALISM; PROSPERITY THEOLOGY; RELIGIOUS RIGHT; SECOND COMING.

BIBLIOGRAPHY

Barron, Bruce. *Heaven on Earth?* 1992.

Juergensmeyer, Mark. *Terror in the Mind of God.* 1999.

Lienesch, Michael. *Redeeming America.* 1993.
Moyers, Bill. *God and Politics,* PBS video. 1987.
Shupe, Anson. "Christian Reconstruction and the Angry Rhetoric of Neo-Postmillennialism." In *Millennium, Messiahs, and Mayhem,* edited by Thomas Robbins and Susan Palmer. 1997.

Julie J. Ingersoll

Reconstructionist Movement, Jewish.

See Judaism.

Reform Judaism.

See Judaism.

Reiki

Reiki is a practice of spiritual healing in which practitioners use gentle touch and focusing of energy on appropriate parts of the body in order to heal. The term is a Japanese word translated, alternatively, as "universal energy" or "spiritually guided life-force energy." The philosophy of Reiki is that energy *(ki)* is universally available for healing and can be transmitted through the hands to heal. While we all theoretically have the power to heal in this way, Reiki offers a way to ensure a focused transmission of that energy, namely, a Reiki initiation by a teaching master. As part of that process, one learns to draw certain symbols with one's hand before beginning a healing, to focus the transmission of energy.

The Reiki practitioner, after drawing the appropriate symbol, places his or her hands on parts of the body that have been injured or that manifest illness. Frequently, practitioners and recipients of Reiki healing report intense warmth in the hands and areas of the body that are being treated. As a general rule, no specific thoughts or meditations are required in the practice, other than a general intent to use Reiki for healing. However, in recent years some American writers on Reiki have taught that it is helpful to focus one's thoughts and send positive mental energy as well.

According to Reiki's own traditions, this practice began in late nineteenth-century Japan as a result of the search of Dr. Mikao Usui (ca. 1865–1926), a Christian minister, for a healing method. He had learned from Buddhist traditions that the Buddha himself had been a healer but that the information on how to heal had been lost because Buddhism had emphasized

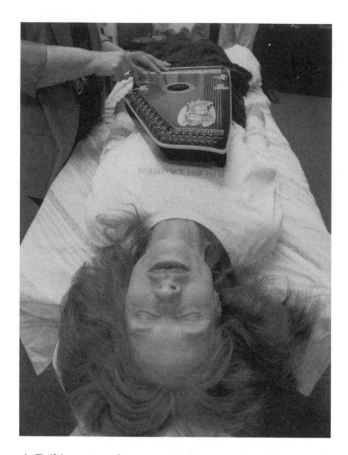

A Reiki master plays an autoharp on the abdomen of a participant in a Reiki healing session at the Reiki Institute in New York City on May 3, 1999. (Credit: AP/Wide World Photos.)

spirituality over physical healing. After studying in a Zen monastery for a time, Usui discovered formulas in Indian sutras that he believed would lead him to the keys to healing. After a twenty-one-day purification involving fasting and meditation, he had an experience in which he received the power to heal and symbols that would channel this power. The symbols, with instructions on how to draw them in the air with the hand, were passed down to his initiates along with his teachings.

Reiki was brought to the West by Mrs. Hawayo Takata (1900–1986) from Hawaii. She apparently claimed to be the only survivor of World War II who knew of the art of Reiki, although this claim later proved to be unfounded. In recent years, American practitioners of Reiki have made contact with Japanese counterparts who trace a different lineage from Dr. Usui's teachings. Disputes have developed over whether the symbols are supposed to be kept secret and what fees can be charged for teachings and healings. Questions about the historicity of Mrs. Takata's account of the movement have been raised. Moreover, some practitioners have claimed to receive additional symbols beyond the original ones traced to Dr. Usui.

There are several levels of initiation into the practice of Reiki healing. Different lineages of Reiki vary as to the number of levels, but most have three or four. Generally, a higher fee is charged for the higher levels of initiation. Moving through the levels, a healer gradually acquires the "keys" or symbols that enable him or her to perform different types of healing. For example, healing of emotional or mental problems uses a different symbol than physical healing alone; healing at a distance (when the practitioner cannot touch the patient) requires its own key. A person who has all the keys of healing is a master. In addition, one can become a teaching master, who can initiate others. In 1996, the movement claimed 5,000 teaching masters (teachers who can initiate others) and 500,000 practitioners (healers from first level to master) worldwide, mostly in the United States and Western Europe.

To date, no significant scientific studies of Reiki as a healing practice have appeared, and virtually all the information about Reiki comes from practitioners themselves.

See also ALTERNATIVE MEDICINE; BUDDHISM; HEALING; HEALTH; HOLISTIC HEALTH; QUANTUM HEALING.

BIBLIOGRAPHY

Rand, William Lee. *Reiki, The Healing Touch.* 1992.
Stein, Diane. *Essential Reiki.* 1995.

Tamar Frankiel

Reincarnation

The religious doctrine of reincarnation (literally, "back in the flesh," from *caro,* "flesh") was formulated by the ancient Indian sages. It is variously known as rebirth, transmigration, metempsychosis ("transfer of the soul from one body into another"), and palingenesis (literally, "again birth"). The term *transmigration,* moving from one state to another, is closer to the original Sanskrit word, *saṃsāra,* "what turns around forever." Reincarnation is the central doctrine for the Hindu, Buddhist, Jain, and Sikh religions, but the idea is prevalent in a myriad of other world religions and has even become popular in the modern West. Statistics claim that two-thirds of the world's population believes in some form of reincarnation.

Essentially, reincarnation is the belief that life does not begin with birth or end with death, rather, the individual self (or nonself, as in Buddhism) is eternal

and journeys from life to life taking on a series of births including human, animal, angelic, demonic, vegetative, divine, and astrological. The present existence is but a natural sequence of former life, and all physical, psychological, and social characteristics are determined by the moral law of cause and effect (Karma). Since what a person does automatically bears fruit in life—be it this one or the next—the idea of reincarnation practically motivates people to live ethically and morally, in accordance with their *dharma* (duty).

The concept of reincarnation evolved in the post-Vedic Aranyaka literature and was developed more fully in the Upanishads. The Bhagavad Gītā synthesizes the views of the Vedas, Upanishads, and several of the philosophical schools and presents the fundamental Hindu understanding. In this revered text, Lord Krishna explains that the individual is intrinsically immortal and that the body is only a garment worn externally by the self:

> As leaving aside worn-out garments
>   A man takes other, new ones,
> So leaving aside worn-out bodies
>   To other, new ones goes the embodied one.
> *Bhagavad Gītā, II:22*

Cremation at death is the norm, and the Upanishadic view of the eternal self taking on one of the two paths at the funeral pyre is reiterated in the Bhagavad Gītā. Through the path of *devayana* (that of the gods), the self or breath (Atman) goes through light and merges with the infinite light of lights (Brahman) and never returns. But through *pitriyana* (the path of the fathers), the self merges with the dark smoke and returns into the womb again:

> These are the two paths, light and dark,
>   Thought to be eternal for the world;
> By one, he goes to non-return;
>   By the other he returns again.
> *Bhagavad Gītā, VIII:26*

Although Buddhists reject the idea of an absolute self, reincarnation is equally vital to their ethical and ideological world. The twelve-link Chain of Causation explains the process by which life, birth, death, rebirth, and redeath continue. The root cause is ignorance, the basic illusion that individuality and permanence exist. Buddha's first Noble Truth states that there is nothing absolute, all is flux and motion, simply *dukha-dukha* (suffering). Hence without a substance, without any entity, the phenomenal individual migrates from one body to another—just as one lamp lights from another. Actions and psychic dispositions of a "me" keep echoing back. The wheel of saṃsāra can be broken by following Buddha's Noble Eightfold Path and attaining *nirvāṇa* (literally, "blowing out").

In Jainism, the living entity is called Jiva, and as long as it is enmeshed in Karma (meaning both action and the fruit of action), Jiva takes on birth and rebirth. Liberation can be attained by the Jina (conqueror), who stops the accretion of new Karma and sheds all that is of the past. Jain monks and nuns cover their mouths lest they breathe in and destroy any microscopic creatures. The whole universe, including stone and vegetation, pulsates with life and must not be harmed in any way.

In Sikhism, the body that we are in is a result of our past deeds, but love for and by the Divine can free us from the wheel of transmigration. According to Sikh scripture,

karmi avai kapra nadari mokha duar

Through actions we get our clothing
    But the divine gaze opens the door of liberation.

Redeath—not rebirth—disturbed these thinkers, and the goal of all the Indian religions is to break the cycle of transmigration and attain liberation (Moksha). Without a confining body, one aspires to the spaceless and timeless infinity. The Upanishadic prayer recited at funerals touchingly sums up the Indian ideal:

From untruth, lead me to truth
From darkness, lead me to light.
From death, lead me to immortality.

The West has also been familiar with the idea of reincarnation. Pythagoras is frequently cited for exclaiming, "Stop beating that dog—I recognize him by his voice as a friend of mine." Reincarnation is central to Plato's epistemology and is pervasive in his works, especially the *Phaedo,* the *Republic,* and the *Phaedrus.* Although Aristotle rejected the notion of reincarnation, Plotinus revived it in his Neoplatonism, which then influenced Western (i.e., Judaic, Christian, and Islamic) esotericism. For two thousand years Virgil's *Aeneid* was the standard text for Western education, and his account of reincarnation in book six kept the idea alive.

In North America many Native American tribes, like the Tlingits of Alaska, have believed in reincarnation as a glorious continuation of personal identity. The New Age movement and the immigration of Asians have further popularized reincarnation on the North American continent. The denial of the decisiveness of death is itself attractive to our society, which desperately clings to youth and life. Scholars in comparative philosophy, history of religions, and psy-

chology have brought the subject of reincarnation to the academic forefront. Diana Eck, a distinguished scholar of religious pluralism, compares reincarnation with resurrection. Although resurrection focuses on life itself and life now, both the Indian and the Christian phenomena "address the mystery of the ongoing irrepressible life that cannot be done in by death" (p. 115). Reincarnation is also being assimilated in various schools of psychotherapy and parapsychology. For example, past-life therapy (PLT) traces the cause of present physical and psychological problems to past life traumas and death experiences and has been claimed effective in treating phobias, fears, sexual dysfunctions, anger, insomnia, chronic headaches, and other disorders. Regarded at some point as foreign and absurd, reincarnation is becoming recognized as an important part of the American soil and psyche.

See also BHAGAVAD GĪTĀ; BUDDHISM; DHARMA; HINDUISM; JAINISM; KARMA; PSYCHOTHERAPY; SIKHISM; UPANISHADS; VEDAS.

BIBLIOGRAPHY

Deussen, Paul. *The Philosophy of the Upanishads.* 1966.

Ducasse, Curt John. *A Critical Examination of the Belief in the Life after Death.* 1961.

Eck, Diana. *Encountering God: A Spiritual Journey from Bozeman to Banaras.* 1993.

Edwards, Paul. *Reincarnation: A Critical Examination.* 1996.

Hess, David J. *Science in the New Age.* 1993.

Kaplan, Steven J. *Concepts of Transmigration: Perspectives on Reincarnation.* 1996.

Neufeldt, Ronald W. *Karma and Rebirth.* 1986.

O'Flaherty, Wendy Doniger. *Karma and Rebirth in Classical Indian Traditions.* 1980.

Olivelle, Patrick. *The Early Upanishads: Annotated Text and Translation.* 1998.

Sargent, Winthrop (translator). *The Bhagavad Gītā.* 1984.

Stevenson, Ian. *Twenty Cases Suggestive of Reincarnation.* 2nd ed. 1974.

Nikky-Guninder Kaur Singh

Relic

The veneration of relics is most usually associated with European popular Catholicism, although relics also have a place in Buddhism and Islam. Some Buddhists in Sri Lanka, for example, worship relics of the Buddha, believing that he is present in a relic of his tooth, notwithstanding Buddhist belief that the Buddha has

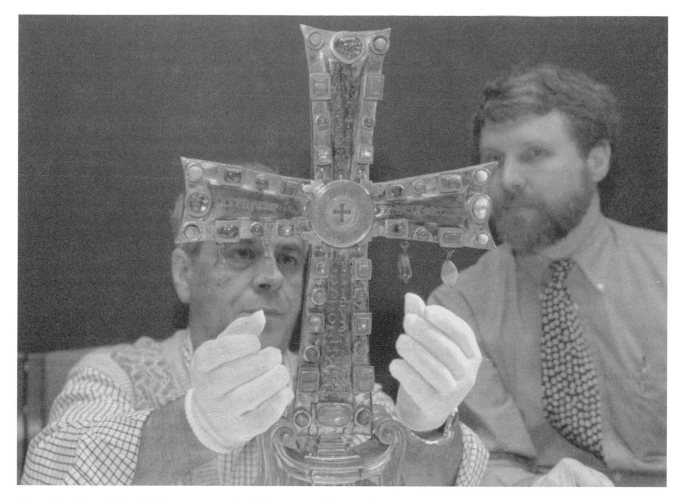

Arnaldo Mampieri, chief curator at the Vatican, and Bruce Christman, chief conservator at the Cleveland Museum of Art, examine a relic from the early Byzantine era: the "Cross of Justin II" (ca. 575 C.E.), believed by some to be a replica of the original crucifixion cross.   (Credit: AP/Wide World Photos.)

transcended this world. In Roman Catholicism, relics are objects that claim to contain actual physical remains (e.g., bones, teeth, blood) of Christ, Mary, the saints, and other holy people, or clothing and other objects worn or touched by the holy person. Relics are venerated because it is believed that the object itself is sacred and not solely a symbol of something sacred. The object's intimate association with the holy person is sufficient to make the actual relic worthy of veneration. Believers use the relic to invoke special favors—for example, touching a relic of a saint (e.g., a piece of clothing that is purported to have touched the saint in question) to heal an illness or as protection against danger. Perhaps the most famous relic today is the Shroud of Turin, which is alleged to be Christ's burial sheet.

In the early church, the tombs of the martyrs were used as altars for the celebration of the Eucharist, with the open tombs exposing the bones of the buried saints for viewing and touching by the people gathered. Belief in the sacredness of relics was encouraged by successive popes. They approved of the removal and transfer of the physical remains of various saints to Rome and other Catholic sites in Europe, and subsequently of relics to American churches, where, as in Europe, they were frequently used in the dedication of churches to Christ or to particular saints. The popularity of relics in Europe during the Middle Ages was advanced in part by returning Crusaders, who brought back relics they had pillaged as part of their conquests. The trade in relics, although historically encouraged by church officials, was also a source of concern. The Fourth Lateran Council (1215) prohibited both the transfer and the sale of relics. Abuses continued nonetheless, and during the Reformation the reformers included relics in their criticism of the use and sale of indulgences in the church. In response, the Council of Trent (1545–1563) enacted new and more restrictive rules for the veneration of relics but also reaffirmed their role in bestowing divine favors. The popularity of relics continued during the late sixteenth and seventeenth centuries (Carroll 1996, pp. 170–175), and their veneration is still an important part of the devotional life of many Catholics throughout the world, indicated, in part, by the numerous tourists who visit holy shrines and places of pilgrimage hoping for a cure from an illness or relief from some other burden. Although the Vatican approves of relics, church officials also caution that the veneration of relics should not be used to displace the centrality of the sacraments and a Christ-centered focus on the theology of redemption in Catholicism. The 1917 Code of Canon Law required that relics be authenticated by local bishops, and rules concerning the preservation and veneration of relics are enforced by the Vatican. The Second Vatican Council (1962–1965) noted that the use of relics should not eclipse worship of God in Catholic devotion. A subsequent revision of the calendar of the saints by Pope Paul VI resulted in a more critical approach to the study of relics and saints and in the removal of some popular saints, including St. Christopher, who was the patron of travelers. Notwithstanding Vatican concerns that relics not assume too great an importance in Catholic life, it is evident that their material presence, whether displayed in churches, cars, or living rooms, or more privately in scapulars or as attachments to medals, still provides many believers with a source of comfort and an immediate and visible reminder of the accessibility of sacred grace.

See also ALTAR; BUDDHISM; CHURCH; ICONS; ROMAN CATHOLICISM; SHRINE; VATICAN; VATICAN II.

BIBLIOGRAPHY

Carroll, Michael. *Veiled Threats: The Logic of Popular Catholicism in Italy.* 1996.

Moran, J. Anthony. *Catholic Shrines and Places of Pilgrimage in the United States.* 1994.

Nolan, Mary Lee, and Sidney Nolan. *Christian Pilgrimage in Modern Western Europe.* 1989.

Michele Dillon

Religious Communities

Religious communities are both gatherings of individuals who have common religious beliefs, habits, and practices and ideologies about the negotiated order of these gatherings. The term is multifaceted and, indeed, slippery. To employ "community" as a description of any group of people is to characterize the quality of their togetherness and not simply to provide a description of their gathering. Though frequently the term is used as a synonym for orders, residential religious groups, congregations, churches, synagogues, orders, or missions, religious communities are not simply spaces where religious ritual happens or organizational entities of religious life. The use of this term often implies an account of the type of religious culture that is valued and sometimes a kind of romanticism about the quality of relationships among members of the gathering.

The romanticism has both historical and contemporary faces. Historically, the concern about the effects of modern social structure, including the eclipsing of agrarian ways of life and the ascendancy of liberal states, animated many social theorists who wrote about religion. Ferdinand Tönnies, whose famous work *Community and Society* was published in 1887, was particularly concerned about the decline of community (*gemeinschaft*) and the expansion of society (*gesellschaft*). Tönnies believed that communities, including religious, familial, and neighborhood ones, were primary groups that socialized members not because of individual choice but rather because individuals were thrown together naturally. Societies—such as business associations, political parties, or other special interest groups—were secondary and socialized their members for rational, instrumental action for special purposes or goals. The values and habits that undergird communities were based on consensus and common moral norms firmly established in custom. However, modernity with its liberal state was undermining this sense of community, according to Tönnies. This transformation of the social structure from close-knit community to diverse society would result in individualism, fragmentation, and the relentless pursuit of material objectives overtaking communalism, convention, and common moral and religious norms. While Tönnies did not believe that a return to community was possible, he despaired about the heartless, self-serving character of modern society.

The contemporary resurgence of concern about community, and about the quality of religious communities in particular, also highlights deeply felt anxiety about the vitality of home, family, religious groups, and neighborhoods and a romanticist belief that a return to "traditional" values would reinvigorate community. The diagnosis of and solutions to the tensions about community have been the subject of considerable discussion within political philosophy, social theory, and sociology of religion in recent decades. Elizabeth M. Bounds's *Coming Together/Coming Apart* (1997) nicely chronicles the variety of current meanings of community, the role of religion in sustaining or establishing it, and judgments about sources of its

The village of Pleasant Hill, near Harrodsburg, Kentucky, was established in 1805 as a Shaker religious community. Today, the village, a part of which is shown here, has been restored and is operated as a historical museum. (Credit: CORBIS/Kevin R. Morris.)

decline in the United States. Bounds notes that discussions of community, especially within communitarian thought, are often typified by nostalgia and a tenor of despair. Since forms of religious life that were based primarily on the mutual reinforcement of home, family, and neighborhood ties no longer characterize U.S. religious life, religious communities are assumed to be weakened, perhaps so enfeebled as to be unable to support a tenable civil society. Questions are raised about how communities are created and maintained, given the corrosive effects of liberalism, capitalism, and individualism (see Bellah, et al., *Habits of the Heart*). Often this anxiety about the future of civil society is also related to recognition of the significant religious, cultural, class, racial, and ethnic diversity that characterizes the cultures of the United States.

The movements of alternative religions, intentional community, and women and minority group empowerment in the 1960s were often aimed at creating communal environments for raising families, pursuing self-fulfillment, or working for social change, in which an ethos of familiarity and trust could counter the alienating or oppressive forces of society at large. These movements sought to establish common purposes, core values, and a common lifestyle within local residential groups. Their internal order is established by strong leadership, consensus, and/or the exclusion of dissenters. However, these alternative religious communities emphasized expressive ideals even as they recombined them with moralities of authority, rules, and expedience—cf. Steven Tipton, *Getting Saved from the Sixties* (1982). Subcultural

norms, based on racial, ethnic, or gender commonality, and voluntarism promoted participatory movement communities and also created tensions about the degree to which homogeneity and the suppression of conflict have to be incorporated into this contemporary view of religious community. Thus the rhetoric of community was sometimes employed to construct consensus and to erect boundaries among religious groups within a milieu increasingly characterized by fluid (i.e., constantly changing) membership.

Thus to consider the meaning of religious communities, we must consider their history, the meaning of membership, and the means by which the communal life is negotiated. Therefore, three primary meanings of the term "religious communities" should be considered: religious communities as religious orders, intentional religious communities, and organizations as religious communities.

Religious Communities as Religious Orders

Religious communities can refer to religious orders or societies that are usually based on a long history of monastic life. These religious communities share a common life based on public vows, generally close physical proximity, an anticipated lifelong commitment by members, an accepted status order within the community, and the recognized power to exclude individuals from the group. Religious orders have been especially common within Roman Catholicism but are also represented within Episcopalianism and Anglicanism. Increasingly within the United States, Buddhist monasteries are also represented.

These religious communities order their lives according to tradition-based rules governing prayer, meditation, internal governance, and work in order to pursue a common religious goal, such as the care of the needy or the life of prayer. These rules also often specify the type of food, clothing, and possessions permissible for individuals in the religious community. For example, St. Benedict (ca. 480–547 C.E.), who is commonly accepted as the father of Western monasticism, wrote a guidebook, *The Rule of St. Benedict,* which indicated the times when monks prayed together throughout the day, provided guidelines for the responsibilities of superiors, and outlined precepts for doing the good work mandated of members of the community. *The Rule of St. Benedict* continues to provide a model for communal life for diverse religious communities, such as the Benedictine Sisters of Perpetual Adoration (a monastic community in St. Louis, Missouri) and the White Robed Monks of St. Benedict (a San Francisco–based, nonresidential, mixed-religious group of individuals who blend the Benedictine Rule with Zen Buddhism).

These two examples highlight both a traditional type of religious community based on traditional rules and established authority and a newer type of religious community, which though also based on rules—in this case *The Rule of St. Benedict*—also incorporates increased voluntarism and the explicit merger of religious traditions. This latter type of religious community has more in common with the movement of "intentional religious communities" particularly evident in the contemporary United States since the 1960s.

Intentional Religious Communities

Intentional religious communities, which are sometimes also called religious communes, homesteading groups, or religious cohousing, are groups of individuals of similar or like attitudes, goals, outlook, and worldview that are comprehensive in their functions, including residential or housing provision and work opportunities actually utilized by members for subsistence production of at least some of their necessities. Though they share much of the form of religious orders, their origins are in the 1960s. Early in that decade, Al Anderson founded and served as president of the Fellowship of Intentional Communities, a North American organization founded to promote shared living, which continues to exist today. This group highlighted a cooperative community movement emerging from the social experimentation of the 1960s and based in ideals of social change. Approximately 50 percent of the 540 intentional communities listed in the *Communities Directory* are religious in nature.

Unlike religious communities such as orders, intentional religious communities are often more voluntaristic, with members joining and departing with greater ease. The negotiated order of daily life is often also based more on the consensus of current members, rather than on the accepted orthodoxy of inherited tradition. Intentional religious communities attract and sustain members through their emphasis on ritual experience, affective communal ties, and often prophetic leadership.

The range of beliefs, rituals, and missions of these religious communities is extremely diverse. For example, the Ananda Communities, such as the one near Nevada City, California, are based on the teachings of Paramhansa Yogananda, the first well-known yoga teacher from India to teach in the West. Ananda Communities focus on Kriya Yoga, a technique of energy control through meditation that accelerates the individual's progress toward God. Community life is based on the discipline of thought and practice toward the goal of self-transformation and global enlightenment. Another intentional religious community is L'Arche, a Roman Catholic–based residential community movement founded in 1964 by Jean Vanier to create physical and spiritual fellowships that welcome people with mental disabilities. In general, intentional religious communities currently in existence tend to have their origins in the 1960s and to provide their members with common housing, religious expression, regimens for organizing daily life, and a countercultural social life.

Organizations as Religious Communities

Frequently denominations, congregations, churches, parishes, synagogues, or missions are identified as religious communities. This usage of "religious communities" is often an effort to speak or write about the diversity of religious organizations without privileging any one organizational form—for example, denomination or parish—or without naming all possible organizational types. For example, often in telephone directories or in newspaper listings of religious services, the term employed to designate the range of religious organizational types, from house churches to pilgrimages, is "religious communities." While perhaps a useful catchall term, this designation tells the reader nothing about the range of religious participation expected from groups' members, the norms of group and individual behavior, or common ritual lives. Rather it highlights the overwhelming acceptance within the United States that religious gatherings have as their primary characteristic the communal fellowship of like-minded people. Thus what they have in common is more important than their significant diversity.

Additionally, local and national interfaith or ecumenical groups have adopted the term "religious communities" to refer to their diverse constituencies. For instance, a National Council of Churches letter to President Bill Clinton in 1998, which urged humanitarian rather than military response to Iraqi defiance of United Nations mandates, began with the following introduction: "As religious leaders, we write respectfully to offer you counsel rooted in the experience and the deeply held commitments of numerous religious communities both within and beyond our membership." Religious communities, understood within this framework, are both specific organizations, whether denominations or congregations, and religious traditions, such as Orthodoxy, Judaism, or Pentecostalism. The term demonstrates the effort of such groups as the National Council of Churches or the Interfaith Alliance to take public stances based on shared moral norms even within a multidenominational, multireligious milieu.

The effort to speak with a communal voice for contemporary voluntaristic religious gatherings is always difficult. The rhetoric of community as often used by religious groups is an effort to model modern-day participation after forms of religious life that were based primarily on the mutual reinforcement of family, religious, and neighborhood ties that no longer characterizes most religious groups in the United States. It is, however, the case that these connections among familial, religious, and neighborhood ties may still characterize some groups, especially relatively newly arrived immigrants (cf. Warner and Wittner, *Gatherings in Diaspora*) or subcultural groups, such as gays and lesbians, racial, or ethnic congregations.

Even a quick search of local religious websites will yield a plethora of congregations that name themselves as authentic communities of caring where physical, emotional, and spiritual needs are met. That observation is not to call into question the many religious groups that do, indeed, meet those needs for their members. However, it is also to suggest that these congregations are composed of individuals whose choices to participate and to share their possessions, time, and spiritual energy are based on personal and/or familial autonomy, rather than on traditional rules, societal expectation, or intentionally formed group norms. Modern social order has resulted in an increased mobility that has strained the ties that bound generations to the places of their ancestors and has heightened personal autonomy. These and other factors have made religious belonging increasingly portable and optional. Membership means participation for the present time. The authority of religious groups is lodged more in their ability to create strong affective ties, to provide personal and public meaning-making, and offer ritual that promotes the experience of togetherness.

Thus religious communities are both the gatherings of like-minded faithful and the rhetorics that these groups and others employ to create and strengthen their common ties.

See also ATTENDANCE; CHURCH; COMMUNES; CONGREGATION; CULT; DENOMINATION; SECT.

BIBLIOGRAPHY

Bellah, Robert N., Richard Madsen, William Sullivan, Ann Swidler, Steven M. Tipton. *Habits of the Heart: Individualism and Commitment in American Life.* 1985.

Bounds, Elizabeth M. *Coming Together/Coming Apart: Religion, Community, and Modernity.* 1997.

Fellowship of Intentional Communities. *Communities Directory: A Guide to Cooperative Living.* 1996.

Hammonds, Phillip E. *Religion and Personal Autonomy: The Third Disestablishment.* 1992.

Homepage of the Benedictine Sisters of Perpetual Adoration (http://www.benedictinesisters.org/).

Homepage of the White Robed Monks (http://www.whiterobedmonks.org/welcome.html).

Tipton, Stephen. *Getting Saved From the Sixties.* 1982.

Tönnies, Ferdinand. *Community and Society,* edited and translated by Charles E. Loomis. 1957. (Original German edition published in 1887.)

Warner, R. Stephen, and Judith Wittner. *Gatherings in Diaspora: Religious Communities and the New Immigration.* 1998.

Yinger, J. Milton. *Religion, Society, and the Individual.* 1965.

Yinger, J. Milton. *The Scientific Study of Religion.* 1970.

Nancy L. Eiesland

Religious Experience

The idea of religious experience is relatively new. It gained scholarly prominence in the late eighteenth century, with Friedrich Schleiermacher's attempt (*On Religion,* 1799) to justify Christianity against Enlightenment rationalism. Thinkers from Descartes to Kant and Hume had dismantled the scientific and metaphysical justifications for religious belief. Historical studies of Scripture and of early Christendom had eroded faith in church authorities. Schleiermacher sought a base from which to defend religion against its "cultured despisers."

Roughly put, Schleiermacher argued that religion is best grounded in sentiments, not in ideas; he said that these sentiments are experienced directly, unstructured by thoughts and actions. Such experiences point beyond the natural realm. People experience, for example, a sense of utter dependence—something that cannot be comprehended within the bounds of the everyday world. As they reflect on this experience, they develop the idea of an all-powerful, benevolent God, the only possible source such an experience might have. This is an "overbelief," to use the term William James introduced in *The Varieties of Religious Experience* (1903). Its details are an intellectual elaboration of the experience itself. In this view, religious experience comes first, and religious ideas are crude attempts to explain experience in everyday terms.

For Schleiermacher, James, Rudolf Otto (*The Idea of the Holy,* 1917), and others who see experience as primary, religion cannot be destroyed by metaphysical or ecclesiastical criticism. Religious ideas, they say, make sense only to the extent that they express people's experiences in symbolic form. Though science and philosophy may attack such ideas, they cannot undercut the experiences themselves: experiences of dependence (Schleiermacher), of "the More" (James), or of "the Holy" (Otto). As long as people have such experiences, religion will endure. The idea of religious experience, then, is a weapon in the past two centuries' war between religion and rationalism—one with which religion has fought off the rationalist assault.

American Manifestations

The claim that religion is based in experience has had tremendous influence in late-twentieth-century America, feeding at least five different religious streams: Pentecostalism, Christian mysticism, Asian-based new religions, New Age religion, and American Evangelicalism.

Religious experience is central to Pentecostalism's appeal. Members of the theologically conservative Assemblies of God place great importance on "speaking in tongues," "being slain in the Spirit," and other events they regard as manifestations of divine favor. Charismatic Catholics—also often theological conservatives—embrace similar signs and wonders. Such Pentecostal groups have been among the fastest-growing religious bodies of the past thirty years—a testimony both to the allure of the extraordinary and to the popularity of its traditionalist clothing.

American mystics, too, seek the extraordinary, though often in a more liberal theological mode. The nineteenth-century Transcendentalists were among the first to embrace mystical ideas, along with a religious tolerance that set the tone for those to follow. Quakers followed in the early twentieth century, becoming until recently the most prominent American religion to host a strong mystical cohort. Their silent group meditation, in which each individual seeks guidance from the "inner light" common to all, sustains a religion that values experience more than doctrine. Yet Quakers are no longer alone. Many mainline churches now avidly explore the Christian mystical heritage, mining the medieval era in hopes of enriching modern life. The recent "Celtic Spirituality" movement among Catholics and Episcopalians, for example, offers Americans the contemplative techniques of Irish monks without the originals' cold and penury. Like Pentecostalism, its appeal lies in its combination of personal experience and traditionalism—though it reaches a far different audience.

Liberal mysticism has long shaped the American reception of Asian religions, especially Buddhism, transforming them in peculiarly American ways. The easing of immigration laws in the 1960s brought many Asian religious leaders to these shores, attracting disciples among the young. Several of the resulting groups followed the mystics in deemphasizing doctrine in favor of practice—and gave their members an almost experimental outlook. Techniques from silent *mudras* to "chaotic meditation" drew followers to new states of consciousness. As David Preston showed in *The Social Organization of Zen Practice* (1988), adepts regard these states as more important than creeds, though they do not necessarily see them as the highest religious goal. Survey research documents the allure of such experiences to followers of Asian-based religions generally.

The last two streams—New Age religion and American Evangelicalism—do not so much focus on actual religious experiences as they use the metaphor of experience to describe their religious insights. Both are individualist, though the New Age movement is much more eclectic. Eastern and Western, tribal and civilized, ancient and modern—there is scarcely a source that one or another New Age writer has not touted as helpful for "the spiritual quest." Indeed, the movement uses terms such as "spirituality" rather than "religion," and "quest" or "journey" rather than "doctrine," precisely because the former terms focus on individuals. New Agers see religion as an inward, not an outward, matter. They resist churches and external authorities, borrowing (or inventing) rites, hymns, and prayers only to the degree that they find them useful in their search for personal growth. To this way of thinking, individual experience is the touchstone of all religion. In contrast to Pentecostals and mystics, however, even reading the daily newspaper can be a religious experience—if it gives the individual a sense of spiritual progress.

American Evangelicals famously do not reject churches; they join them! Even those who avoid a doctrinaire or "fundamental" Christianity choose orthodoxy over eclecticism and respect church tradition, authorities, and especially the Bible. Yet they, too, speak the language of religious experience. Their call for individual conversion, their sense that God speaks to each person, their quest for a "personal relationship" with the resurrected Jesus all put the idea of individual experience at the center of religious life. Church, doctrine, and authority can guide one to the brink, one is told, but one must plunge in oneself—and this plunge alone brings salvation. In contrast to Puritan Calvinism, Evangelicalism promises its followers that they can directly experience their salvation. Neither the secular world nor rationalism can interfere with such leadings of the heart.

The idea that one can have a direct line to God resonates with American practical individualism— and also with late-twentieth-century America's distrust of institutions. Both lead one to value direct, unmediated experience. The five religious streams here listed are divided by their theologies, but all give such experiences the same weight and status in their worldviews.

Scholarly Approaches

Scholars have treated religious experiences in four main ways. The first follows Schleiermacher in treating religious experiences as raw data. It assumes that people first experience things, which they then interpret with overbeliefs. As some 30 percent of Americans claim to have had religious experiences, investigators do not lack for data. In *Where the Spirits Ride the Wind* (1990), Felicitas Goodman traced some of these to the ritualized body postures, dances, and rhythms present in many world religions.

Yet there is a problem. The Pentecostal experiences of "speaking in tongues" and "being slain in the Spirit" are not raw, but interpreted. To have them, one must know what each experience means, what having it looks like to outsiders, how and when it is appropriate, and so on. That is, one must be a religious insider: one must be able to interpret the experiences in order to have them. This is the reverse of Schleiermacher's claim.

In *Religious Experience* (1985), Wayne Proudfoot takes this as license to question the reality of religious experiences per se. Drawing on attribution theory, he argues that one cannot separate any experience from the ideas that grasp it. Any attempt to evaluate religious experience is thus inherently theological and closed to science.

Yet this is only true of everyday states of consciousness. Susan Blackmore's *Beyond the Body* (1992) presents a psychological model of altered states of consciousness—accidental, drug-induced, or created in meditation—that structure the relationship between ideas and experience differently. One can learn, for example, to generate meditation states in which ideas do not appear but that are still conscious. Blackmore advocates the investigation of such states while recognizing that any description of them made on returning to normal consciousness is subject to Proudfoot's strictures.

A final approach explores the experience of religious ritual, which it treats as shared experiences in time. Rituals focus people's attention. Like music, their sights and sounds channel participants' streams of consciousness in ways that cannot be reduced to mere ideas. But, *contra* Schleiermacher, these streams do not exclude ideas; indeed, ideas and experience here interpenetrate to produce a meaningful whole.

Despite their differences, all four of these approaches have provided fruitful glimpses at a much-cited but little-understood phenomenon.

See also Celtic Practices; Evangelical Christianity; Meditation; Mysticism; New Age Spirituality; Peak Experience; Pentecostal and Charismatic Christianity; Quakers; Quest; Ritual; Spirituality.

Bibliography

Balmer, Randall. *Mine Eyes Have Seen the Glory: A Journey into the Evangelical Subculture in America.* 1993.

Blackmore, Susan. *Beyond the Body.* 1992.

Czikszentmihalyi, Mihaly. *Flow: The Psychology of Optimal Experience.* 1991.

Heelas, Paul. *The New Age Movement: The Celebration of the Self and the Sacralization of Modernity.* 1996.

Hood, Ralph W., Jr., ed. *Handbook of Religious Experience.* 1995.

McGuire, Meredith B. *Pentecostal Catholics: Power, Charisma, and Order in a Religious Movement.* 1982.

Poloma, Margaret M. *The Assemblies of God at the Crossroads.* 1989.

Preston, David. *The Social Organization of Zen Practice.* 1988.

Spickard, James V. "Experiencing Religious Rituals: A Schutzian Analysis of Navajo Ceremonies." *Sociological Analysis* 52 (1991): 191–204.

Steere, Douglas V., ed. *Quaker Spirituality.* 1984.

James V. Spickard

Religious Freedom Restoration Act

Beginning in the 1960s, the U.S. Supreme Court interpreted the free-exercise clause of the First Amendment to provide significant protection for religiously motivated conduct. For example, the Court ruled that states could not deny unemployment compensation to Sabbatarians who refused Saturday employment, nor could they punish Amish parents who refused to send their children to high school. Although the Court's constitutional doctrine was complex and multifaceted, it generally required strict judicial scrutiny when a law had the effect of substantially burdening a religious practice. If the government could not demonstrate that the burden was justified by a "compelling" interest, an exemption from the law was constitutionally required.

In 1990, however, the Supreme Court adopted a dramatically different approach. In *Employment Division* v. *Smith,* the Court was asked to recognize an exemption for the sacramental use of an otherwise illegal drug, peyote, by members of the Native American Church. Not only did the Court refuse to do so, but it also declined to apply the strict judicial scrutiny that its precedents appeared to require. Marking a fundamental shift in doctrine, the Court declared that generally applicable laws that affect religious practices ordinarily do not require special constitutional scrutiny and therefore do not require religious exemptions. *Smith* essentially reduced the free-exercise clause to a prohibition on laws that discriminate against religion by targeting religious practices for special, disadvantageous treatment. Nondiscriminatory laws that burden religious practices, however substantially and for whatever reasons, would no longer be subject to serious constitutional scrutiny.

The Court's doctrinal shift was controversial, and it triggered widespread political criticism. Supported by a broad coalition of divergent interest groups, ranging from the ACLU to the Southern Baptist Convention, Congress concluded that the Court's new doctrine gave inadequate protection to religious freedom. Remarkably, Congress also concluded that it had the power to overturn the Court's interpretation of the free-exercise clause and to impose its own interpretation on the states. By nearly unanimous votes, Congress enacted the Religious Freedom Restoration Act of 1993 (RFRA), which was expressly designed to repudiate *Smith* and to "restore" the Supreme Court's preexisting doctrinal framework. Accordingly, RFRA stated that "Government shall not substantially burden a person's exercise of religion even if the burden results from a rule of general applicability," unless the burden "is in furtherance of a compelling governmental interest."

Not surprisingly, the constitutionality of RFRA itself was challenged, and in its 1997 decision in *City of Boerne* v. *Flores,* the Supreme Court invalidated RFRA, at least as it applied to state and local laws, thereby reinstating the restrictive approach of *Smith.* Whether RFRA remains valid as applied to federal laws is unsettled. At the state level, some legislatures have adopted or are considering state-law RFRAs to replace the invalidated federal statute. In addition, Congress is considering new legislation that would once again extend RFRA-like standards to many sorts of state and local laws. Whether this new legislation will be enacted is an open question, and, if it is, it is unclear whether the legislation will withstand constitutional scrutiny.

See also CHURCH AND STATE; FREEDOM OF RELIGION; NATIVE AMERICAN CHURCH; PRAYER IN SCHOOL; SECULARIZATION.

BIBLIOGRAPHY

Laycock, Douglas, and Oliver S. Thomas. "Interpreting the Religious Freedom Restoration Act." *Texas Law Review* 73 (1994): 209–245.
"Reflections on *City of Boerne* v. *Flores.*" *William and Mary Law Review* 39 (1998): 597–960.
"The Religious Freedom Restoration Act." *Montana Law Review* 56 (1995): 1–306.
"Requiem for Religious Freedom?" *University of Arkansas at Little Rock Law Journal* 20 (1998): 555–812.

Daniel O. Conkle

Religious Persecution

For those possessing even a cursory knowledge of Western civilization, the history of America, especially in the past four decades, hardly offers any example of religious persecution worthy of note. Certainly compared to the trials of the Spanish Inquisition; the systematic ghettoization, civil restriction, and oppressive church- and state-sponsored anti-Semitism of medieval Europe; the anti-Catholic laws of early modern England; or the violent purges of Anabaptists in Münster in 1534, or of Huguenots in Paris on St. Bartholemew's Day 1572, the United States seems almost to be the bastion of enlightened pluralism and freedom of religion envisioned by at least some of its founders.

And yet the United States has had its share of religious restriction, violence, and exclusivity, in many cases upheld by civil authorities. According to some scholars, the seeming contradiction between an ideological commitment to religious freedom and the impulse to establish a particular religious vision (and to persecute all rival visions) is knit into the very fabric of the nation. Particularly evident in the colonial period, the persecutory impulse can be seen easily among Massachusetts Bay Puritans, who harshly evicted Quakers from the colony and punished until death those stubborn enough in their convictions to return. As John T. Noonan, Jr., has most recently noted in *The Lustre of Our Country* (1998), this persecution was enacted despite a rhetorical attachment among the same Puritans to the rights of dissenters, based on their own experience of persecution. He and others have documented the numerous examples of religious feuding and persecution in early American life, despite the simultaneous development of the United States as a haven for Europe's most beleaguered religious minorities. In many cases the groups most victimized in

Europe held fastest to their own insistence on establishing a particular religious orthodoxy in their new homes.

Massachusetts thus served as a colonial refuge for Puritan Congregationalists while persecuting Quakers and Catholics. Maryland began its history as a refuge for Catholics then reverted to Anglican control by the end of the seventeenth century. Pennsylvania, established as a refuge for Quakers, refused Catholics visible houses of worship and maintained laws insisting that only believers in Jesus could hold public office. And even seemingly tolerant Providence Plantations (later Rhode Island), founded by the highly progressive Roger Williams after his own exile from Massachusetts, showed this same contradiction. Originally harboring Baptists, Quakers, and even a small Jewish community in Newport, the Providence Plantations restricted voting by the end of the seventeenth century to disfranchise Jews and Catholics. Nowhere in colonial America did full religious freedom exist.

And yet despite these contradictory impulses, free exercise of religion did prevail sufficiently to become a fundamental principle of American law. Writing in 1963, the historian Sidney Mead emphasized the de facto religious pluralism in place on American soil that necessitated the formation of an ideology favoring pluralism. In other words, the reality of free exercise, at least if one considered the colonies in toto, required that a rhetoric favoring free exercise be expounded and, ultimately, written into law. Those writing after Mead, including Noonan, have seen a more subtle process. Noonan has credited the triumph of free exercise in America (and the suppression if not eradication of its evil analogue religious persecution) to the rhetoric of theologians at Plymouth and Massachusetts Bay, to the reality that all four colonies mentioned above were approved in their religious expression by the officially Anglican kings of England (thus paving the way for the limited but still significant English Act of Toleration in 1688), and to the accumulated intellectual influence of three prominent critics of religious persecution of roughly that age: Roger Williams, Baruch Spinoza, and John Locke. Noonan has offered that all of these words, realities, and ideas were infused into American life and law by James Madison, as a conscious antidote to the hostilities and bloodshed for which Europe was already infamous in the premodern era.

Scholars have thus pictured the American experiment with religious freedom, and away from persecution, as largely if not wholly successful. And so, by and large, it has been. But what of the exceptions that linger, even into the second half of the twentieth century? While current American media interest in religious persecution often centers on U.S. censure of

Tibetan-American protestors sing the Dalai Lama's "A Prayer of Words of Truth" outside the Chinese embassy in Washington, D.C., on the night of October 28, 1997. The protest was against ongoing Chinese religious persecution in Tibet. (Credit: AP/Wide World Photos.)

discriminatory practices abroad, certainly there are numerous examples of persecutory impulses, at least, in American life to the current day.

For example, religious persecution often works in tandem (and is partially concealed as a result) with ethnic or political concerns. In the United States of the 1930s it was not unusual to find discrimination against Jews established in a variety of public and private spheres, including (but not limited to) restricted hotels, clubs, and resorts, residence restrictions, or quotas limiting admission of Jews to major universities. While such blatant discrimination atrophied, in part through widespread revulsion over the events of World War II and the Holocaust, as well as general considerations surrounding the civil rights movement of the 1960s, some scholars see subtle forms of the same impulse in anti-Israel rhetoric or the persistence of negative stereotypes of Jews. The scholar Gary A. Tobin, in *Jewish Perceptions of Antisemitism* (1988), confirms that institutional discrimination against Jews has declined markedly since World War II but that small extremist groups continue to persecute Jews in local communities. Sometimes, in rural communities particularly, this extremism manifests itself in the form of vandalism, grave desecration, and Holocaust revisionism, he states. And even beyond this, Tobin sees new anti-Jewish stereotypes emerging in the contemporary United States, often expressed by younger Americans in their attitudes toward Israel, and especially in their assumptions about American Jews' feelings or connections to the Jewish state. Other scholars, among them Harold E. Quinley and Charles Y. Glock in *Anti-Semitism in America* (1979), have similarly considered religious prejudice in its newer "political" form.

The same phenomenon can be seen with regard to other forms of entrenched religious discrimination that have resulted in persecution in America. Waves of anti-Irish sentiment that swept the country with the largest influx of Irish immigrants in the nineteenth century often masked, in only the most transparent of ways, the concomitant anti-Catholic animus that found its way into American political life. Prejudice against the Irish, and especially Irish Catholics, resulted in a variety of anti-Irish policies, formal and informal, including discrimination in employment and residence that were slowly erased over time. These impulses, though theoretically controlled by law, were still evident, if not as blatantly apparent, in opposition to the candidacy and presidency of John F. Kennedy, the first Roman Catholic to be elected to that office. Some might argue that ingrained prejudice, if not persecution per se, lies behind the fact that the United States has never elected a Jewish president nor, for that matter, a Muslim or an atheist.

Additionally some scholars see anti-Arab and anti-Muslim animus as not only a still vaguely permissible form of hate-mongering but also as a form of religious persecution. Recent examples might include early assumptions, especially by media commentators, that the bombing of a U.S. government building in Oklahoma City in 1995 was most probably the act of Arab Muslim terrorists.

Many other groups in the United States also claim to operate under severe handicaps, at the very least, imposed by the hostile mainline Christian majority. Among those who have recently claimed themselves subject to persecution are Wicca, practitioners of Scientology and New Age religions, atheists, and even some fundamentalist Christians who see constitutional protections against state-sponsored prayer in schools as limiting their free exercise of religion. Whether these claims represent true persecution or merely an appropriation of that term is a question that must be left largely to the subjective judgment of individuals and future scholars of American life.

See also Anti-Semitism; Atheism; Church and State; Civil Religion; Civil Rights Movement; Freedom of Religion; Holocaust; New Age Spirituality; Scientology, Church of; Wicca.

Bibliography

Brauer, Jerald C., ed. *The Lively Experiment Continued.* 1987.

Mead, Sidney. *The Lively Experiment.* 1963.

Noonan, John T., Jr. *The Lustre of Our Country: The American Experience of Religious Freedom.* 1998.

Quinley, Harold E., and Charles Y. Glock. *Anti-Semitism in America.* 1979.

Tobin, Gary A., with Sharon L. Sassler. *Jewish Perceptions of Antisemitism.* 1988.

Patricia Behre-Miskimin

Religious Right

Conservative Christians have been present in the United States since the beginning of the Republic. New England Puritans, for example, did not hesitate to address issues of politics and public morality. A Boston synod of 1679 detailed the sins of the age, including sexual promiscuity, the decline of religion, materialism, excessive litigation, insolent children who were given to lewd "company keeping," and a general corruption of the culture. Sermons addressed the moral and spiritual condition of the community, calling Christians to faithful service and good citizenship. Religious awakenings, which erupted in the eighteenth and nineteenth centuries, were understood by their supporters to provide spiritual renewal, civic order, and public morality.

In antebellum America the lines between liberal and conservative Christians were not clearly delineated. Protestantism in that period is generally referred to as Evangelical Christianity. Nineteenth-century evangelicals supported crusades against alcohol, prostitution, gambling, and other public sins. Racial controversies, however, led many southern Protestants to distance themselves from extensive involvement in public issues. By the end of that century large segments of American Christianity divided between "private" and "public" concerns. The former stressed the salvation of the individual as the primary method of redeeming the society, while the latter called the churches to "Christianize the social order" by working for justice and equality at all levels of community life. Those divisions became more pronounced in the twentieth century as liberals challenged traditional dogmas of biblical authority, salvation, and human nature. Fundamentalists warned that rationalism, evolutionist science, and theological liberalism were creating a social and ethical crisis in America. Funda-

Two activists of the Religious Right march in counter-protest during the Gay Pride Parade on New York City's Fifth Avenue, Sunday afternoon, June 27, 1997. The "Rosary of Reparation" sign on the left is said to be a "call for the repair of gay lifestyle." (Credit: AP/Wide World Photos.)

mentalism represents the foundation of the Religious Right in the United States. While many conservative Christians denounced modernism in pulpits and publications, they generally stayed out of the public arena. Their concerns increased with the racial unrest, anti-Vietnam protests, drug culture, and sexual permissiveness of the 1960s.

Political and religious agendas for these groups included opposition to government sanctions of abortion, pornography, film violence, the secularization of American life, homosexuality, and declining family structures. These conservative organizations supported some form of prayer in public schools, traditional "family values," and a renewal of "Judeo-Christian" influence in the nation. Many insisted that the United States faced a complete moral crisis, with liberal leaders of church and state promoting secularism and compromise on significant moral issues. Some questioned certain assumptions about the "separation of church and state," insisting that the founders of the Republic did not intend a radical differentiation between the two realms. Such an idea, they believed, had

led to the exaltation of "secular humanism" as the unofficial "religion" of the culture.

During the 1970s several conservative political leaders determined to bring conservative Christians into greater participation in the political process. Republican activists Paul Weyrich, Richard Viguerie, and Edward McAteer began a concerted effort to encourage evangelical conservatives to register to vote and enlist in a crusade to restore Christian values to the public square. They participated in the founding of religio-political coalitions that developed legislation, evaluated public officials and candidates, and attempted to reshape the moral context of the nation. They targeted churches, pastors, and laity, using religious radio and television as well as an extensive program of direct mail to reach their audience. They called these conservative Christians to enter the public arena to save the United States from spiritual and ethical collapse. Through their actions and the work of a growing number of pastors, the new Religious Right took shape. The rise of this movement paralleled, and many believe facilitated, the election of

Ronald Reagan as president in 1980, marking the beginning of what became known as the "Reagan revolution," a resurgence of conservative political emphases. With that, the Christian Right became closely connected with the Republican Party.

Functionally, the Religious Right is not one organization but a collection of political action agencies, lobbying groups, foundations, and church constituencies connected directly and indirectly through a variety of formal and informal networks. One of the earliest was the Religious Roundtable, a coalition of various religious groups formed in 1980. It brought together secular and religious conservatives in an effort to educate church members in political activism. The *Roundtable Report,* a publication primarily for pastors, provided basic information on such things as how to move a bill through Congress, lobby specific congressmen, and press for specific legislative actions. It issued one of the earliest documents instructing churches on ways to organize for political activity. The Roundtable's famous conference in Dallas, Texas, in 1980 was one of the earliest public forums for Religious Right causes. It brought together numerous political and religious leaders, including W. A. Criswell, longtime pastor of First Baptist Church, Dallas; Jerry Falwell; and fiery television evangelist James Robison, known for his denunciation of America's corrupt society. In a 1980 speech to that organization, Ronald Reagan declared: "You may not be able to endorse me, but I endorse you," linking his political agenda with those of the Religious Right. At that same meeting, evangelist and Southern Baptist Convention president Bailey Smith asserted that "God Almighty does not hear the prayer of a Jew," creating a national controversy over the attitude of the Religious Right toward other religions and their place in American life.

The Christian Voice was another small but influential segment of the Religious Right. It included a lobby, an educational foundation, and a political action agency. It began in 1978 in California as a lobbying effort on behalf of Proposition 6, an effort to limit the rights of state homosexuals (the measure failed). A Washington, D.C., office opened in 1979, listing an advisory board including Utah senator Orrin G. Hatch. In 1980 Christian Voice promoted a Christians for Reagan program, touting Reagan as the only candidate who could reclaim Judeo-Christian and biblical principles for the nation. It also instigated the practice of circulating "report cards" evaluating legislators as to their support for Religious Right causes. After the 1980 elections the Christian Voice and other Religious Right groups claimed to have been a major factor in the defeat of prominent Democratic liberals, including George McGovern of South Dakota, Birch Bayh of Indiana, and Frank Church of

Idaho. They claimed to have aided in the election of Senators Bob Dole of Kansas and Dan Quayle of Indiana in 1980. Quayle later served as vice president of the United States under George Bush, and Dole ran for president in 1996. Both ran as Republicans.

Perhaps the best known of the early Religious Right organizations was the Moral Majority, founded in 1979 by Jerry Falwell, pastor of the eighteen-thousand-member Thomas Road Baptist Church in Lynchburg, Virginia. Falwell became one of the most enduring ministerial spokespersons for Religious Right ideals. For more than two decades he was a frequent guest on television talk shows and news programs, providing commentary on the state of ethical and religious life in America. He frequently qualified his positions as those of "Bible-believing Christians" in contrast to other Christian groups, who did not accept his views. While the Moral Majority claimed to represent a broad conservative coalition including Mormons, Catholics, and others, its primary support came from independent Baptist churches and pastors. The independent Baptist movement represents one of the most fundamentalist segments of the diverse Baptist movement in the United States.

The Moral Majority opposed the Equal Rights Amendment (ERA), homosexuality, abortion, disarmament, pornography, drug use, and many welfare programs. Members gave strong support to the State of Israel, the death penalty, and a human life amendment. Falwell officially disbanded the Moral Majority in 1989, insisting that its work had run its course. His strong opposition to the presidency of Bill Clinton and his belief that the nation was again hurtling toward moral chaos led him to resurrect the organization a few years later. It waned toward the end of the century, particularly after the founding of another powerful group, known as the Christian Coalition. These groups took on many of the characteristics of political action agencies (PACs), funding issue-oriented media blitzes and other advertisements that benefited conservative candidates. Their actions had to be carried out with caution, lest they endorse candidates in ways that would undermine their tax-exempt status.

During the early 1990s, television evangelist Pat Robertson established the Christian Coalition, the largest organization representing the Religious Right. Its first director, Ralph Reed, soon became a major public spokesperson for rightward moral and political issues in American society. The group claimed significant influence in the election of a Republican majority in the House and Senate in the elections of 1994. Robertson, son of a U.S. senator and founder of the Christian Broadcasting Network, used his television program, the *700 Club,* to evangelize the public and address political and ethical concerns. He was a candidate for the Republican nomination for president in 1986. The Christian Coalition supported the moral agendas of earlier religious right groups while giving extensive attention to the election of candidates willing to promote those agendas in the political context. Opposition to abortion and homosexuality along with concern for traditional "family values" were major issues addressed by the Christian Coalition. They were particularly successful in encouraging conservatives to run for local and regional offices. Their record on the national level was somewhat mixed. Their impact on the Republican Party created divisions between conservatives and moderates in what was sometimes characterized as an internecine battle for the "soul of the party." Other Christian Coalition associates included Christian psychologist James Dobson, founder of the Focus on Family organization; D. James Kennedy, Florida Presbyterian pastor and television preacher; and California conservative Tim LaHaye. Reed left the organization in 1998 to become a political consultant to Republican candidates.

Also in the 1990s the movement known as Promise Keepers was founded, aimed at evangelizing men and energizing them in service to home and church. Their public rallies, often held at NASCAR racetracks, attracted huge numbers of men and elicited considerable media attention. The movement thrived among conservative evangelical congregations, leading some analysts to wonder if the organization was co-opted by the Religious Right. Its leaders denied any political motives save only the renewal of spiritual life among American males.

Other evangelical groups sought to distance themselves from the Religious Right, insisting that one could hold conservative theology apart from the right's political agendas. *Sojourners* magazine and Evangelicals for Social Action expressed agreement with certain conservative positions on abortion and family but rejected the idea of America as essentially a Christian nation. They also suggested that a genuine "pro-life" position required opposition to the death penalty and nuclear weaponry, positions eschewed by the Religious Right.

The election of William Jefferson (Bill) Clinton as president of the United States was a major concern for many individuals and groups associated with the Religious Right. During much of his term they presented significant opposition to his policies and his moral leadership. Jerry Falwell's organization circulated videotapes produced by Clinton's critics, accusing him of a variety of crimes. Many conservatives saw Clinton's affair with White House intern Monica Lewinsky and subsequent impeachment by the House of Representatives as vindication of their attacks against him. His acquittal by the Senate and continued high standing in popular polls were sources of great frustration to Religious Right proponents. It led Paul Weyrich, one of the movement's founders, to suggest that these efforts had essentially failed, that there was no moral majority in America. He urged the Christian minority to withdraw from the public sphere, working with the younger generation—through home and Christian schools—to prepare a new generation that would ultimately transform the country. Christian Coalition leaders disagree with Weyrich's assessment, encouraging the faithful to continue their course to effect political and spiritual change. Gary Bauer, longtime Religious Right leader, was a candidate for the Republican nomination for president during the election of 2000. Divisions in strategy did not mean that the organizations and activities of the Religious Right would vanish from the American religious and political scene.

See also BAPTIST TRADITION; CHRISTIAN COALITION; DOBSON, JAMES C., JR.; EVANGELICAL CHRISTIANITY; FALWELL, JERRY; FUNDAMENTALIST CHRISTIANITY; JUDEO-CHRISTIAN TRADITION; MORAL MAJORITY; PROMISE KEEPERS; ROBERTSON, PAT.

BIBLIOGRAPHY

Bromley, David G., and Anson Shupe, eds. *New Christian Politics.* 1984.

Fackre, Gabriel. *The Religious Right and Christian Faith.* 1982.

Falwell, Jerry. *Listen America!* 1980.

Hill, Samuel S., and Dennis S. Owen. *The New Religious Political Right in America.* 1982.

Zwier, R. "New Religious Right." In *Dictionary of Christianity in America.* 1990.

Bill J. Leonard

Religious Studies

"Religious studies" is now the descriptive term of greatest currency for the academic study of religion. In 1867, F. Max Müller first used the term *Religionswissenschaft,* the science of religion, to describe his comparative philological studies, which he hoped might uncover the essence of religion scientifically. This term and *Religionsgeschichte,* the history of religions, gained wide use among European scholars and in universities to describe the academic study of religion, which they saw as a human science on the model of Wilhelm Dilthey (1833–1911) in which the understanding of the actor or actors in social phenomena is integral. Science and history in its narrow sense would emancipate the study of religion from theology.

Here the heritage of the academic study of religion is clearly visible. Like earlier eighteenth-century European Enlightenment thinkers, such as Berkeley, Locke, Hume, and others, the new science or history of religions would seek to explore religion within the canon of reason rather than depending on the authority of revelation.

Today, more than a century after its origin, the modern study of religions involves substantially more elements than naively envisioned by the first students of religious studies. Indeed, one of the most important contributions of Ninian Smart to religious studies has been constantly to remind us that religious studies is a perspectival and comparative discipline that seeks to understand religion as a multidimensional phenomenon. By "multidimensional" he of course refers to the dimensions of the object of the discipline. Religion consists, among other things, of an authoritative narrative dimension (e.g., myth construed in its proper meanings), a doctrinal dimension, a ritual dimension, an experiential dimension, an institutional dimension, and an ethical dimension. Describing religious studies as a perspectival and comparative discipline immediately suggests that religious studies cannot be fully conducted within the frame of any one discipline and requires multidisciplinarity, drawing its methods and practices from the disciplines of the humanities and fine arts such as history, language study, literature, art and architecture, music, drama, and dance; from the disciplines of the social sciences, including anthropology, sociology, politics, and economics; and more recently from newer fields that often span the humanities, fine arts, and social sciences, such as global and international studies, gender studies, or ethnic studies. Religious studies in its broadest formulation then seeks to understand religion as a complex human phenomenon in history and in the contemporary world. However, by describing religious studies as a perspectival and comparative discipline, we are also able to understand the structure of the field and the classical theories and their reformulations that have advanced our understanding of religion.

We might describe one of the most important components of this structure broadly as the sociological or social-scientific study of religion. Already in the last decades of the nineteenth century there were a series of major contributions that arose from early fieldwork and folklore studies and that sought to put the origins of religion into an evolutionary context. These included E. B. Tylor's theory of animism (*Primitive Culture*, 1871), R. R. Marett's theory of pre-animism ("Pre-animistic Religion," 1900), and James Frazer's study of the relationship between magic and religion (his *The Golden Bough*, first published in two volumes in 1890, grew to twelve volumes by 1915). But the most powerful and theoretically enduring contributions came from Émile Durkheim (1858–1917), Max Weber (1864–1920), and Sigmund Freud (1856–1939), all of whom sought to provide a sense of the function and social processes of religion, even if those processes originated in the unconscious, as Freud argued. For example, Durkheim's *The Elementary Forms of Religious Life* (1912) sought to explain religion as the collective representation of society forged through an explosive discharge of social or individual energy that he called "effervescence." While Durkheim's work synthesized much nineteenth-century reflection on religion, he rejected the evolutionary thinking of his predecessors. His use of the word "elementary" does not mean the simplest in an evolutionary scheme. Instead, Durkheim understood "elementary" to mean the simplest in the sense of the most basic, that which would allow us to see precisely the religious nature of humans and would reveal to us an essential and permanent aspect of all human life. Equally essential to Durkheim's analysis of religion is the fundamental dichotomy between the sacred and profane. While most social theorists have utilized Durkheim's analytic works of the 1890s, his most important contributions to the study of religion come from a series of works begun with the *Elementary Forms* and continued in a series of monographs and lectures. These later works reveal a cultural program in which Durkheim came to understand that secular social processes have to be modeled upon the sacred world. This is why he called this project a "religious sociology." This later Durkheimian project would come to have immense influence on the semiotics of Ferdinand Saussure, the structuralism of Claude Lévi-Strauss, the comparative Indo-European mythological studies of Georges Dumézil, Roland Barthes's examination of the systems of symbolic classification that regulate a wide array of secular institutions and social processes, and postmodernist theorists such as Michel Foucault, who have carried the Durkheimian emphasis on the central social power of the sacred and profane even further into the social domain through the structuring power of symbolic patterns or discourses.

The Durkheimian tradition also gave rise to new studies of the relationship between traditional religions and the polity or state. Robert Bellah's classic essay on civil religion ("Civil Religion in America," *Daedalus*, Winter 1967, pp. 1–21) demonstrated how the modern nation-state could be invested with some of the same symbolisms as those traditionally associated with religion. This was followed by other studies that sought to explore civil religion in other nation-states (e.g., Charles S. Liebman and Eliezer Don-Yehiya, *Civil Religion in Israel*, 1983). The Durkheimian tradition's understanding of collective representations and the primacy of sacred and profane as both ontological (having to do with the fundamental nature of being or existence) and social categories resulted in new studies generated from field research. For example, Victor Turner's interpretation of ritual (*The Ritual Process*, 1969), while heavily indebted to Arnold van Gennep's *The Rites of Passage* (originally published in 1909) for the idea of ritual liminality and communitas, draws much from Durkheim. Likewise Clifford Geertz's densely detailed description and his efforts to study religion comprehensively as a cultural system (*The Interpretation of Cultures*, 1973) owe much to the Durkheimian paradigm.

A second major component of religious studies has been the phenomenology of religion, which traces its origin to Rudolf Otto's *The Idea of the Holy* (1917). Otto argued that the holy or the sacred was a *sui generis* category of experience, irreducible to the sum total of the empirical world. The manifestation of the sacred is characterized by two contradictory experiences—the sacred's *mysterium tremendum* and its *fascinans*. The *mysterium* suggests the total otherness of the holy, its radical unlikeness to the empirical world. The *tremendum* frightens us, fills us with awe, and repels us. But the manifestation of the holy is also accompanied by its *fascinans*—that which fascinates and draws us to it. The social structuring of the sacred as a system of power was comprehensively formulated in Gerardus van der Leeuw's *Religion in Essence and Manifestation* (originally published in 1933) and later revised in the work of Joachim Wach (1898–1955). However, the most theoretical powerful phenomenological analysis of religion has come from the work of Mircea Eliade (1907–1986). Among his major contributions are *Patterns in Comparative Religion* (originally published in 1949), *The Myth of the Eternal Return* (originally published in 1949), *Shamanism: Archaic Techniques of Ecstasy* (originally published in 1951), *Yoga: Immortality and Freedom* (originally published in 1954), and his three-volume *A History of Religious Ideas* (originally published in 1976 to 1983). Throughout these works Eliade attempted to explore what he called the morphology of the sacred or the forms that the sacred's manifestations took in history. These manifestations had a more primal and experiential form than the social structurations described by either van der Leeuw or Wach. A central category in his analysis was myth, which proved to be the key that could unlock the religious meanings of rituals. Eliade drew a sharp distinction between what he called *homo religiosus*, religious man, and the humans of archaic cultures and civilizations who ritually used myth to return the cosmos and human society to the time of the beginnings. Eliade was particularly sensitive to how archaic religious forms persisted in history and drew parallels between historiography and psychoanalysis and the traditional functions of myth and ritual.

Eliade's phenomenological study of religion achieved a prominence in religious studies as a result of the U.S. Supreme Court's 1963 decision in the *Schempp* case, which reinforced the separation of church and state while at the same time giving legitimacy to the academic study of religion in state-supported schools, colleges, and universities. Eliade's paradigm for the study of religion came with a new descriptive language that clearly marked it as different from theological studies as well as from older ways of studying religion. This new paradigm seemed most appropriate for the new context of the study of religion after this landmark court decision, which ushered in the century's most expansive period of growth in the United States of the academic discipline of religious studies. While Eliade described his contribution as belonging to the history of religions, subsequent critiques by Kurt Rudolph ("Mircea Eliade and the 'History' of Religions," *Religion* 19, no. 2 [April 1989]: 101–128) and Jonathan Z. Smith (*Imagining Religion: From Babylon to Jonestown* [1982] and *To Take Place: Toward Theory in Ritual* [1987]) have challenged his understanding of history as well as his interpretation of the central myths and rituals that lay at the heart of his phenomenology. Eliade believed that all religious meanings could be harmonized as modalities of the sacred. More recent studies have suggested that this consensus is a scholarly construction and that a central dynamic of religious traditions is conflictual meanings. For example, Bruce Lincoln has shown that classification systems expressed in myth and ritual often embody conflict, both legitimating the status quo or delegitimating it and opening the way to new possibilities of thought and action (*Discourse and the Construction of Society: Comparative Studies of Myth, Ritual, and Classification*, 1989).

See also ANTHROPOLOGY OF RELIGION; ARCHETYPE; ELIADE, MIRCEA; ETHICS; FREEDOM OF RELIGION; MYTH; PSYCHOLOGY OF RELIGION; RELIGIOUS EXPERIENCE; REVELATION; RITES OF PASSAGE; RITUAL; SOCIOLOGY OF RELIGION.

BIBLIOGRAPHY

Alexander, Jeffrey C. "Introduction: Durkheimian Sociology and Cultural Studies Today." In *Durkheimian Sociology: Cultural Studies*, edited by Jeffrey C. Alexander. 1988.

Capps, Walter H. *Religious Studies: The Making of a Discipline.* 1995.

Kitagawa, Joseph M. "The History of Religions in America." In *The History of Religions: Essays in Meth-*

odology, edited by Mircea Eliade and Joseph M. Kitagawa. 1959.

Oxtoby, Willard G. "*Religionswissenschaft* Revisited." In *Religions in Antiquity: Essays in Memory of Erwin Ramsdell Goodenough,* edited by Jacob Neusner. 1968.

Sharpe, Eric J. *Comparative Religion: A History.* 2nd ed. 1986.

Smart, Ninian. *Dimensions of the Sacred: An Anatomy of the World's Beliefs.* 1996.

Vries, Jan de. *The Study of Religion: A Historical Approach.* 1967.

Wach, Joachim. "Introduction: The Meaning and Task of the History of Religions (*Religionswissenschaft*)." Reprinted in *The History of Religions: Essays on the Problem of Understanding,* edited by Joseph M. Kitagawa, Mircea Eliade, and Charles H. Long. 1967.

Richard Hecht

Retreat

The retreat developed in the sixteenth-century Roman Catholic Church as a way of helping priests, other members of religious orders, and soon thereafter lay people to grow in their faith by way of an intense time spent in contemplation and meditation away from the day-to-day world. The classic retreat manual is the *Spiritual Exercises* (1544) of St. Ignatius of Loyola, founder of the Society of Jesus, or Jesuits, a Catholic religious order. The origins of retreats can be traced in part to practices designed to help members of religious communities that provide ministry in the world (the "apostolic" communities founded over the past five hundred years) to cultivate a kind of more intensive monastic or hermit-like spirituality, by way of rigorous silent retreats. Thus annual retreats were required by St. Ignatius for every Jesuit, with a longer, thirty-day retreat prior to final profession of vows or definitive commitment. Many other religious orders followed suit.

These newer apostolic communities emphasized work in the world rather than the begging and preaching of the classic itinerant or mendicant orders such as the Franciscans, Dominicans, Carmelites, and Augustinians, or the relatively more otherworldly, cloistered life of the properly monastic orders such as the Benedictines and Cistercians. Active in the "apostolate"—the work of the members in ministering to the needs of the world—members of these new communities ran schools, hospitals, and missionary and charitable enterprises with an energy and commit-

ment nourished by their spirituality, which in turn was informed or enhanced by these regular retreats.

It soon became clear, however, that a short, intensive spiritual experience devised to help the vowed Catholic religious to perform their work in the world could also be of use to other Catholic religious, diocesan priests, and particularly the laity. The retreat was thus adapted and typically shortened to serve the spiritual needs of the laity.

As new religious communities, such as the Passionists and Redemptorists, dedicated to parish preaching and cultivating religious devotion among the laity, grew in the eighteenth and nineteenth centuries, they took the retreat format to parishes in the form of "missions"—multi-day affairs that involved a structured process of preaching, prayer, and confession. Retreats are to be sure not individual prayer experiences: they involve a retreat director, preacher, spiritual director, or other person skilled in prayer, and they utilize a particular retreat manual or method.

Up to the mid-1960s in the United States, many Catholic retreat centers were built. They were often associated with a men's religious order known for retreats or with parish missions, such as the Passionists, Redemptorists, and Jesuits. There were also some diocesan-sponsored or privately organized retreat houses such as at Malvern in the Archdiocese of Philadelphia, organized by local businessmen and conducted largely by priests of that archdiocese. Many older traditions of religious life, such as the monastic and mendicant communities, maintained or developed traditions of welcoming outsiders for brief visits and spiritual sustenance.

Since the late 1960s many women religious and laity have increasingly become involved in sponsoring retreat houses and giving retreats, serving as retreat directors and spiritual directors. Many worked from within the traditional framework of the Ignatian *Spiritual Exercises* or some other traditional format, but many others combined traditional formats with a more explicitly psychological approach, including a focus on the relationship between spiritual self-actualization and personality types, specifically feminine spiritualities, religious insights, and creation spiritualities influenced by the great religions of Asia or the nature religions of pre-Christian Europe or the Americas. Over the past thirty years, interest in retreats in the United States has risen steadily, as evidenced by the growing number of retreat houses throughout the country.

See also CENTERING PRAYER; CREATION SPIRITUALITY; MEDITATION; PARISH; PRAYER; PRIESTHOOD; RELIGIOUS COMMUNITIES; ROMAN CATHOLICISM; SPIRITUALITY.

BIBLIOGRAPHY

Christian-Meyer, Patricia. *Catholic America: Self-Renewal Centers and Retreats.* 1989.

Cooper, David A. *Silence, Simplicity, and Solitude: A Complete Guide to Spiritual Retreat.* 1999.

Pennington, M. Basil. *On Retreat with Thomas Merton.* 1995.

Bryan Froehle

Reunions

A reunion is an assembly of people linked by common experience or by ancestry for the stated purpose of reaffirming their common ties. Types of gatherings include family reunion, church homecoming or church anniversary, cemetery association day, camp meeting, and denominational conference center. Each of these types features convergence of religious and family themes, hence the labels "kin-religious gatherings" and "folk liturgies." Civic versions of these assemblies include town festivals and homecomings, community reunions, and school class reunions. All of these gatherings serve the function of reuniting individuals who live in scattered households, often at great distances from one another, who have left home to pursue their personal careers; reunions are most often organized by those who have stayed at home.

The reunions combining religion and kinship are commonly held in summer or at holiday periods, at country churches, camp meeting grounds, cemeteries, or at the "old home place" of a family. These are organized around a reassembly of all the descendants of one common ancestor, descendants of persons buried in a cemetery, or descendants of persons who were founders of a particular church. In honor of the deceased ancestors, the living relatives come together on a regular basis, usually annually on a particular day, and share a common meal and often a church service or a program of some kind. The meal is the central activity. It is based on traditional foods prepared by the mothers of families—in the American South the foods include fried chicken, ham, casseroles, pies, and cakes. In some cases men barbecue or grill meats or fry chicken or fish outdoors. Families tell stories of their ancestors having settled new territories. In the South and East, stories focus on ancestors from Scotland, Ireland, England, or other European countries who entered this continent in colonial times. In Tennessee, the Midwest, and Texas, the focus is on ancestors who entered the territories from South Carolina or New England in later migrations westward. These stories form a body of foundation narratives that chronicle the settlement of the United States and connect kinship and religion in significant ways.

The gatherings have been analyzed as a pilgrimage system in the Protestant world, in which people who left home to seek their fortunes in response to the ethic of individual achievement now create rituals of return as a way of symbolizing the imagined lost past of home, church, community, and extended family (Neville 1987). This version of pilgrimage contrasts sharply to the Catholic pilgrimage studied by Turner and Turner (1978), in which individuals *leave* home to go outward to saints' shrines and faraway holy places. The Protestant, who sees his or her life as a personal journey or pilgrimage, *returns* to sacred places and sacred rituals of reunion.

As folk liturgies, the reunions can be seen as a form of symbolic inversion of indoor formal church liturgy, especially the Mass. They are celebrated outdoors by families, with women as officiants instead of priests, and with the commensal meal consisting of ordinary food instead of the sacralized elements of the Eucharist. In this way, reunions provide a cultural expression of a Protestant world that is an inversion of the Roman Catholic one. While reunions have been studied most extensively in the southern United States among Protestants, research on Catholic reunions is now also under way.

Historically, Protestant reunions are related to the Covenanting tradition of Scotland and to field preachings and outdoor services in England and early America. In today's mobile, heterogeneous society, families of all traditions have adopted the custom of holding reunions, and instruction books and articles on how to plan a reunion are popular in the secular media. Secular reunions, including town and school, could be said to be expressions of the American civil religion. All of these types of gatherings provide examples of ritual processes in contemporary America not defined by the classical understanding of ritual, confined to church services or formal celebrations. Ritual, seen in this model, is an expression of culture, stating themes that lie close to the meanings and values of a cultural system and providing a window through which to view some of the deeply rooted understandings that a people hold about themselves and about their world.

See also ATTENDANCE; BELONGING, RELIGIOUS; CIVIL RELIGION; FOOD; LITURGY AND WORSHIP; LIVED RELIGION; MAINLINE PROTESTANTISM; PRACTICE; RELIGIOUS EXPERIENCE; RITUAL; ROMAN CATHOLICISM; SHRINE; SOCIOLOGY OF RELIGION.

BIBLIOGRAPHY

Neville, Gwen Kennedy. *Kinship and Pilgrimage: Rituals of Reunion in American Protestant Culture.* 1987.

Neville, Gwen Kennedy. *The Mother Town: Civic Ritual, Symbol, and Experience in the Borders of Scotland.* 1995.

Turner, Victor, and Edith Turner. *Image and Pilgrimage in Christian Culture.* 1978.

Gwen Kennedy Neville

Revelation

A revelation is any event that is interpreted subjectively to be a message from the otherworld, understood variously as the realm of the ancestors, spirits, deities, or God. As such, revelations lie at the heart of every religion. Through revelations the faithful receive knowledge about ultimate reality, guidance for constructing meaningful lives, and the possibility of relationship with the divine.

In a pluralistic society such as the United States, any definition of revelation must apply equally to all faiths. Mircea Eliade, who taught the history of religions at the University of Chicago in the latter part of the twentieth century, also used the term "hierophany" to provide a more universal understanding of the phenomenon. Hierophany combines the Greek words for sacred and appearance and describes the human perception of a separate and sacred realm making itself felt. Thus both the reality of the sacred and its distinction from ordinary experience are part of the subjective experience. In some religions, the hierophany is believed to have occurred primarily in the past, as recorded in scripture. In contrast, other traditions are built around ongoing revelation, where it is felt that the entire creation serves as a window onto the divine. "The cosmos in its entirety can become a hierophany" (Eliade 1957, p. 12).

Apart from the source of the revelation and its content, there are many ways in which messages from the otherworld are conveyed. Joachim Wach, Eliade's predecessor at the University of Chicago, argued for a phenomenology of the types of revelation: "In my view, a theory of the types of revelation is a task for the history of religions, a task that must be undertaken independently from the philosophical question about the essential nature of revelation" (Carpenter 1995, p. 8, n. 8).

The most common type of revelation is that of visions and voices, encountered in dreams and in the light of day. Here the message from the otherworld is experienced by means of the senses and the imagination, which derives from sense experience. The Lakota Indians relate how White Buffalo Calf Woman visited their ancestors during a time of starvation, gave them the sacred pipe, and taught them how to treat one another. After instructing them in the Seven Sacred Rites, the basis of Lakota religion, she turned into a white buffalo calf and then left them. Sometimes voices are heard and interpreted as sacred messages. American Muslims are guided by the Qur'an, their sacred scripture comprising the words that God spoke to Muhammad. The Prophet recited what he heard, and this was written down. Further, revelation might take place during dreaming. Christine Downing began to study ancient goddess traditions after feminine images of the divine spontaneously appeared in her dreams: "For me the quest for the goddess began with a dream" (Downing 1988, p. 30). In one dream she is sent out in search of the goddess; then falling asleep in a cave, the dreamer dreams of yet another cave deep below the surface of the Earth. She enters and feels the presence of the goddess, although she cannot see her.

In visions and voices, the message is seen, heard, or felt, as in ordinary sense experience. In divination, the message is encoded in patterns that are found in the natural world, and a specialist "sees" and interprets the message for others. Traditions of divination popular in American culture include astrology, palm reading, reading tea leaves or coffee grounds, and the tradition of interpreting tarot cards.

A third type of revelation is spirit possession, during which a spirit from the otherworld enters a person or object to convey a message. Spirit possession can be partial or complete. In partial possession, the medium is conscious and senses a guiding presence; this is sometimes referred to as inspiration. The inspiration of the Holy Spirit is a central theme of Christian experience. Total possession occurs in vodun (voodoo), where the spirit medium serves as a vehicle for the ancestors and saints. When the spirit arrives, the medium's own ego consciousness ("big guardian angel") is forced to leave the body and wander, as it does during sleep. Once the spirit departs, the medium has no memory of what happened.

In the spirit journey, the soul—or spirit—of the person leaves the body in a coma or trancelike state and travels to and from the otherworld. Only a trained specialist, a shaman or holy person, is able to make the journey without dying or going crazy. The Lakota medicine man Nickolas Black Elk recounts how he lay in a coma for twelve days while his spirit ascended into the presence of the grandfathers. There he learned sacred teachings about the destiny of his people.

Incarnation, another form of revelation, takes place when a being whose home is primarily in the otherworld takes on a mortal life—is born, lives, dies—to help people in one way or another. Christians regard Jesus Christ as a divine incarnation, revealing the presence and nature of God. Tibetan Buddhists, many of whom have resettled in the United States after the occupation of their country by the Chinese, regard the Dalai Lama as the incarnation of the bodhisattva of compassion, Avalokiteśvara.

Finally, mysticism, too, is a form of revelation. In the mystical experience the boundary between the two worlds briefly dissolves so that the human comes into union with the divine. Mystics of all traditions insist that the initiative for union comes from the otherworld, although there is much that a person can do to prepare for such an encounter. J. Krishnamurti, who spent most of his life living and teaching in the United States, emphasizes the receptivity of the mystic: "[T]here must be total emptiness and only then that otherness, the timeless, comes" (Krishnamurti 1976, p. 168).

Approaching revelation as a historical event that involves subjective interpretation—the event is interpreted as a message from the otherworld—allows us to see the value that revelations hold in various religious traditions. Discerning the different types of revelation further elucidates the variety of religious expressions encountered in contemporary American religions.

See also ASTROLOGY; DIVINITY; DREAMS; MYSTICISM; NEAR DEATH EXPERIENCES; PARANORMAL; SPIRIT; SPIRIT POSSESSION; TRANCE.

BIBLIOGRAPHY

Carpenter, David. *Revelation, History, and the Dialogue of Religions: A Study of Bhartrhari and Bonaventure.* 1995.

Deninger, Johannes. "Revelation." In *The Encyclopedia of Religion,* edited by Mircea Eliade. 1987.

Downing, Christine. *The Goddess: Mythological Images of the Feminine.* 1988.

Eliade, Mircea. *The Sacred and the Profane: The Nature of Religion.* 1957.

Krishnamurti, J. *Krishnamurti's Notebook.* 1976.

Neihardt, John G. *Black Elk Speaks: Being the Life Story of a Holy Man of the Oglala Sioux.* 1932.

Wach, Joachim. *The Comparative Study of Religions.* 1958.

Beverly Moon

Right, Christian.

See Religious Right.

Rites of Passage

Contemporary American life pulsates at an enormously fast-paced tempo. Cars rush to work and rush home delivering overworked citizens to isolated dens where the television routinely takes over, anesthetizing viewers into a comfortable complacency until the next day's rush back to work begins the whole process over again. We hardly find time to catch our breath, let alone mark the passages of our lives with a ritualistic sense of the sacred. Ancient cultures and indigenous traditions around the world used to offer initiation rites into the various phases of human life, but modern Americans have largely lost this tradition. Our world was long ago demythologized leaving us bereft of powerful rites to provide the ongoing process of life with a sense of meaning.

Joseph Campbell (1907–1987), the American mythographer and folklorist, decries this loss of myth in a number of his works. He follows the Swiss psychologist Carl G. Jung (1875–1961) in championing the importance of myth and ritual, especially for uprooted moderns who so often suffer from alienation and a pervasive sense of meaninglessness—what Jung calls the disease of our age. Rituals provide avenues for "participation mystique," participation in mystery, the experience of the "numinous," or the profoundly awesome.

The journalist Gail Sheehy has also noted this glaring lack of ritual to shepherd us through life's transformations in her popular book of 1974, *Passages: Predictable Crises in Adult Life.* She remarks that although some attention is paid by psychologists to the difficult passages of childhood and adolescence, the successive stages of adult life rate hardly any notice. She cites Erik Erickson as one of the few psychologists to have offered any awareness of continuing passages after adolescence. The ruling concept appears to be that we fight our way through childhood and the confusions of adolescence only to plateau out into our twenties and cruise through to the finish line on a straight, unmarked path. This paucity of attention to passages through adult life, she says, leaves our potential for continued growth undeveloped. Her book seeks to contribute toward filling in these gaps. She lists these recognizable phases in life: birth, adolescence, and marriage, and also the passages into what she calls the "trying twenties," the drive to extend a root system in the thirties, the "mid-life crucible" of the forties, the sense of renewal in the fifties, then the culmination of life's work, the resting on one's laurels, and the "denouement into decline."

Certainly some rituals remain to mark the attainment of important stages in life. Many of us mark the reaching of a new year at our birthday with some sort of acknowledgment, though few among us may recognize it as an occasion to honor the commencement of a new cycle in our lives. We celebrate various holidays through the year, but what is missing is precisely a sense of the sacred. They are regarded largely as holidays—excuses to enjoy days off from work—but the metaphor has died. We no longer perceive them, by and large, as holy days.

Ritual still surrounds the culminating events of life such as weddings, graduations, and funerals, but what happens to us in between these momentous events? Sheehy notes that other cultures have done more to provide a lifelong nexus of ritual forms to recognize these passages, such as the Hindu system's Four Stages of Life. In this context the religious perspective offers a "sacred canopy" to use Peter Berger's language, providing a container for sacralizing the ongoing experience of life from the student phase, through householder stage, to *dharma* phase, the period entered in midlife when the natural tendency is to be occupied with a search for deeper meaning, culminating in the *moksha* stage in the sixties, and beyond, when all Hindus can aspire to take up some version of the life of the *sannyassi* (holy man) and his quest for salvation.

A similar ritual framework might be cited in the ancient Greek tradition of the archer-goddess Artemis, recognized as the goddess of perilous passages. Each of life's difficult transitions from birth to death was honored by prayers to Artemis to deliver the individual through the narrow passage, as if each such event were a new birth through a perilous birth canal, which could end in death: The perilous passage might kill us.

Today we lack such rituals and are left to flounder through the profound changes in life with a clumsy gait, a forlorn fear, and a nagging sense that there must be something wrong with us. If we had a ritual system to render sacred these predictable and perfectly normal passages in life, we might be able to combat this sense of meaninglessness and infuse our lives with a deeper experience of the sacred.

How different it used to be in the ancient past! Evidence from the Paleolithic cave paintings in France and Spain attest to a profound ritualistic sensibility. Many sites show evidence of adolescent initiation rites, based on the presence of footprints in the soft clay of the cave floors. These footprints, undisturbed for thousands of years, remain as a silent witness to the amazing power of ritual. Many of these ritual sites are miles deep in the caves, in areas very difficult to access. It is as if the ritual necessitated a journey deep into dangerous territory, to undergo an ordeal and a triumphant emergence for the transformed souls who are rebirthed out of the cave, the womb of the deep Earth Mother.

Jean Clottes tells of one spectacular archeological find. The eyes of late twentieth-century explorers were the first in tens of thousands of years to fall upon an incredible sight: At the back of a closed-in passage miles deep in the cave, they witnessed—still standing undisturbed—a bear skeleton. It stood upright on its hind legs with its skull on the ground between its feet and its skeleton covered with a much-maligned bear pelt. As researchers approached it, they discovered, still as fresh as the day they had been trampled in the earth, adolescent-sized footprints in the soft clay, going round and round the bear skeleton, its pelt showing signs of having been repeatedly stabbed by spearheads. Some ancient ritual of adolescent initiation to the mystery of the hunt was frozen here, to stand as a testament for all time, bathed in utter silence and the profound, absolute darkness of the cave's protective walls.

When we say that these adolescents were being initiated into the mystery of the hunt, we petition an important category that Joseph Campbell termed the "company of braves." Primal cultures typically feature such a community, a company of the tribe's brave men who are ritually inaugurated into a sacred duty to protect the tribe from danger and to provide for the tribe's needs by engaging in the hunt, a kind of ritualistic dance in which men and beasts are united in an unspoken pact to partake of each other's life energy. Providing sustenance and protection of the innocent are the archaic tasks, if not to say drives, of the males in the society. Are these drives "hard-wired," rooted at an instinctive level in the masculine consciousness? If so, these primal societies provided a built-in mechanism to honor and celebrate these vital energies, as adolescent boys were put through a ritualistic ordeal to achieve "bravery" and to earn the respect of the grown men who regularly participated in hunting magic. The well-known vision quest tradition among the plains Indians of North America is an example of such a profound initiation ritual: The youth who embarks on the quest returns a brave, as in the similar "walkabout" ritual of the aboriginal Australians and the circumcision and other cutting rituals adolescent boys endure in traditional African cultures.

This sort of initiation rite is almost completely lacking in our contemporary culture. The lack of a sacralizing ritual leaves adolescents to flounder through this stage on their own, bonding with peers who are experiencing the same passage, left to feel completely misunderstood and unappreciated by their parents, teachers, and guardians of the ruling social order into which they are tacitly expected to enter and assume their appropriate place.

Initiation rites are typically supposed to be provided by the religious traditions of a culture. And indeed, the dominant religions of our culture do retain some such rites. There are the Bar and Bat Mitzvah rituals in Judaism, and Confirmation in the church rituals in Catholicism and some forms of Protestantism. But these Western traditions long ago adopted intellectual and/or renunciative norms; their rites of passage into adulthood are characterized by a pronounced cerebral quality. The Jewish boy or girl memorizes Bible passages, leads the congregation in prayer and offers an address modeled on the form of a sermon. It is a ritual introduction into a legalistic framework that he or she now takes on as a personal responsibility. Similarly, the Christian youth undergoing Confirmation is ritually initiated into an all-encompassing system of dogma, with attendant rules and regulations to be followed with diligence. Certainly there is room within the ritual itself for the initiate to experience a profound, spiritual awakening, the presence of the divine filling his or her soul. But this kind of numinous experience probably happens all too infrequently in actuality.

Campbell and Jung claim that traditional Western religions have long ago ossified. The original core experience of the mysterious that rituals are designed to inculcate long ago faded to leave only the external forms of adherence to dogma and strict practice. Rituals like the Bar Mitzvah or Confirmation do not initiate the youth into the mystery of his or her own body. The surging energies experienced in adolescence are never engaged in the initiation rite. Unlike the powerful rituals of primal societies, the Bar Mitzvah boy is not newly initiated into a company of braves nor instilled with the sense of a new potency coursing through his veins. Leading the congregation in prayer may, indeed, be scary, but it is not primal. It is nothing like facing down a huge woolly rhinoceros charging at his face, armed only with a wooden spear.

As Joseph Campbell puts it, the ruling mythologies of our culture are at least two thousand years out of date for our contemporary experience. We do not inhabit the desert world of ancient Jerusalem anymore. Our world is a high-tech, fast-paced wonder of computers and the burgeoning information superhighway. To be initiated into the ancient law or the church is, in most cases, finally irrelevant to the immediate fascinations of the contemporary mindset. It does not provide a mechanism for participating in mystery, even if that is what it was originally designed to do.

This ossification of our traditional religions has left moderns craving for a genuine experience of the numinous. Currents in contemporary culture will always spontaneously invent new modes for such experience. These new ritual forms represent an authentic surging up of primal energies, authentic since they have been authored by participants in contemporary culture and stem directly from contemporary experience.

The contemporary practices of piercing and tattooing that were all the rage in the popular culture of the 1990s might be seen to represent precisely this. It is a new shamanism, as these are long-standing practices shamans have cultivated all over the world. The young person of the 1990s might have been through a Bar or Bat Mitzvah or Confirmation, but that was obligatory—imposed upon them by their parents' expectations and so, not authentic. But the night they went to get their first tattoo or piercing put them through a genuine ordeal. They chose to undergo pain that had to be endured over some period of time. They decided purposefully on the specific tattoo or area to be pierced. These acts of penetration into their flesh left them ritually scarred—marked for life with the proud sign of the ordeal. They forged a new identity during these rituals, as they emerged from out of the darkened tattoo parlor, a marked person, a changed person. The experience might have been entered into in solitude or shared with peers, but it was most emphatically not enjoined by, or typically approved of, by the parental units. It was the sheer intensity of raw, immediate, physical experience the youth was craving. The tattoo and piercing became sacred rituals, rites of passage into a new authentic self.

But what has become of the sacred company of braves? Where is the community of elders who welcomed the newly transformed youth into the mystery of the hunt? The youth today might sport a stylish new tattoo, but then he simply returns to regular life. There is no righteous fight to join to provide for dependents or protect them from harm, though this was not always the case in the modern world until very recent times.

The generations that fought both World Wars I and II had no lack of a righteous fight to engage their primal postadolescent energies. There was a strong company of braves to join as well as a sharply demarcated battle to protect the innocent and combat injustice. These generations experienced no emptiness, no longing for the intensity of experience. Boot camp forcefully—and ritualistically—inaugurated them into the mystery and power of their own bodies. These generations of young men had their primal need to join a respected company of braves well satisfied.

But in the postwar era, the battlegrounds of the righteous fight began to be profoundly obscured. Members of the generation that came into adolescence during the 1950s were rebels, but without a cause. This was the generation that invented rock and roll, the new, virtually exciting pathway for experiencing the numinous and for directly engaging the surging energies of the body. It was not precisely a company of braves, but it was an authentically created avenue for satisfying the desired intensity of experience.

This ritual form continued to engage the generation that came into adolescence in the 1960s. They also had a righteous fight to fight, as they inaugurated the "street-fighting" mode of powerful social protest. The war in Vietnam and the war against the war provided these youths with an avenue for the intensity of experience. But with the 1970s a kind of pervasive disillusionment set in, perhaps born of Watergate, and the young had no real righteous fight to join, no ritual introduction into a company of braves, the traditional model for this carried by the military brotherhood having been distinctly soured after the humiliations of Vietnam. Apathy and self-centered greed became the hallmarks of this age, culminating in the culture of greed of the 1980s.

The 1980s also brought in a conservative swing, a kind of backlash against the complexity that had marked the entire century. The harkening for a more simple, traditional set of "family values" and a swing toward fundamental—that is, basic, simple—forms of religion stamped the young of that era with a conservative quality. This almost seems unnatural for youth, a time in life when rebellion seems to be built in by nature. The youth culture of the 1990s was marked by this conservative legacy but seemed strangely schizophrenic—so often conservative in political values, yet wild in their quest for powerful experience in rave clubs and in the Gothic fascination with the macabre, the cult of death.

Still there was no righteous fight to join, no well-defined set of causes, as if the youth of the 1990s seemed to be resigned to worldwide destruction. It is as if they were "dancing in the wasteland," cultivating a purposeful sense of not caring while the world devolved into violence and chaos. This was apathy with an edge, and a real fascination for violence emerged. The primal company of braves has distorted into inner city street gangs and rural white supremacist and militia movements, filled with young men fascinated with guns and bombs and dedicated to an ugly violence. If there were an honorable avenue for channeling these energies, a way in which young men could earn the genuine respect of the peers and elders and be honored by society for their authentic bravery then perhaps we might avoid the drive-by shootings, gang violence, and school shooting rampages we experienced in the 1990s. In other words, if there were honored, recognized rites of passage for earning genuine power and respect, these distortions might be transformed.

But how do we reinfuse our culture with primal rituals? Not only are adolescents left without an initiation into a company of braves, but the subsequent natural passages of life remain without any ritual forms. The attempts of individuals like Robert Bly and

Sam Keen to reintroduce shamanic rituals in the emergent "men's movement" reflect an authentic move toward the resacralizing of our lives, as the conservative Christian Promise Keepers might also be said to represent. These are rituals for adult males that perhaps go some distance toward re-creating an authentic company of braves. All well and good, but they are largely fringe movements, whereas the majority in mainstream culture remain unengaged.

And these rituals are for men only. Where are the primal rituals to initiate the female into the profound mysteries of her own body and to honor her continued transformations through the various stages of life? Such rituals virtually do not exist in our culture, and women are left to experience their own mysteries in isolation. Joseph Campbell said, "woman is the mystery," a profound comment with far-reaching implications. The awesome changes that render the woman capable of creating new life are going to happen within her body in any case. Still, these profound transformations need some ritual avenue to be made consciously meaningful.

While such rituals do not exist for the majority of women, the pagan religions of Wicca, Goddess, and the Earth have perennially provided spiritual containers for the mysteries of the female experience. The contemporary resurgence of such primal forms of religion is a result of the same thirst for the experience of the numinous, for the sacralizing of the stages of our lives. The fact that our contemporary culture has witnessed a strong welling-up of such primal religious forms demonstrates the extreme importance of the need for meaningful rites of passage.

See also ARCHETYPE; BAR MITZVAH AND BAT MITZVAH; CAMPBELL, JOSEPH; DREAMS; GODDESS; MASCULINE SPIRITUALITY; PROMISE KEEPERS; RITUAL; SELF-MUTILATION; VISION QUEST; WICCA.

BIBLIOGRAPHY

Berger, Peter. *The Sacred Canopy, Elements of a Sociological Theory of Religion.* 1969.
Bly, Robert. *A Gathering of Men.* Video. 1990.
Bly, Robert. *Iron John: A Book About Men.* 1990.
Campbell, Joseph. *Myths to Live By.* 1972.
Campbell, Joseph. *The Power of Myth.* 1982.
Campbell, Joseph. *Transformations of Myth Through Time.* Video. 1990.
Clottes, Jean, and David Lewis-Williams. *The Shamans of Prehistory, Trance and Magic in the Painted Caves.* 1996.
Erikson, Erik H. *Childhood and Society.* 1950.
Jung, Carl G. *Aion. Collected Works.* Vol. 9, part II. 1959.
Jung, Carl G. *The Archetypes and the Collective Unconscious: Collected Works.* Vol. 9, part 1. 1959.

Jung, Carl G. *Memories, Dreams, Reflections*. 1961.

Keen, Sam. *Fire in the Belly: On Being a Man*. 1991.

Neugarten, Bernice L., ed. *Middle Age and Aging*. 1968.

Sheehy, Gail. *Passages: Predictable Crises of Adult Life*. 1974.

Sharon L. Coggan

Ritual

Since the 1960s, Americans have become more self-conscious about the importance of ritual in their lives. This increased awareness has led to new forms of ritual practice as well as to new appreciation of traditional forms.

Rituals are deliberately performed, repeatable acts that give structure to human life. They organize the flow and interactions of daily life. They also define important events, both for individual lives and for the communities and societies in which individuals live. Thus rituals define the growth of social institutions, changes in public leadership, and social responses to natural catastrophe as well as birth, adulthood, marriage, and death. To a significant extent, people express their humanity and define both their personal and their social identities through ritual.

Religious Ritual

Religious rituals engage people in the life of a religious community and its beliefs. Through religious rituals, people learn about the meaning of religious life and come to experience what is sacred for them, both as individuals and as members of a religious community. Religious rituals are deliberately performed, repeatable acts in which people enact and embody the beliefs of their religious communities. As a result of participating in these religious actions, people often find themselves uplifted, cleansed, and healed. Thus religious rituals lead to powerful experiences in which people find deeper meaning in life and find their ordinary lives enlarged and transformed.

Because of the powerful effects that religious rituals can have, some scholars have seen ritual as the foundational element of religion. In *The Elementary Forms of Religious Life* (1965; original French, 1912), the French founder of sociology, Émile Durkheim, argued that religion originated in group rituals that established social identity and social cohesion among primitive peoples. In Durkheim's view, priests and other religious leaders created myths about God to explain the exhilarating power that people experienced during these rituals. As Durkheim understood it, God was actually an idealization of society, and the power that people attributed to him was actually the power of the group. By virtue of this relationship between God and society, Durkheim believed, the rituals associated with God served as means of inculcating social identity and enforcing social structure.

While Durkheim's work has contributed to awareness of the power that rituals have to coerce social conformity, the writings of Arnold Van Gennep, Victor Turner, and Mircea Eliade have contributed to awareness of the importance of religious ritual for deepening and savoring the meaningfulness of life. These writings have contributed to greater appreciation of ritual in American popular culture since the 1960s, as well as to many scholarly efforts to understand the nature and effect of ritual in other cultures.

A contemporary and compatriot of Durkheim's, Van Gennep studied ceremonial rites practiced in a variety of different cultures. He argued that initiation, defined as a rite of passage from one social group, emotional state, and religious condition to another, was the most important element of religious ritual and that it was present in other types of ritual, including rites of birth, marriage, and death, as well as in more explicitly initiatory rites defining adulthood and religious responsibility. Since the 1960s, when his work first became available in English, Van Gennep's work has contributed to greater understanding of the universal importance of rites of passage, not only within the fields of sociology, anthropology, and religious studies but also in American culture more generally. In its discussion of the ritual dimensions of the life cycle that many Americans go through, Gail Sheehy's *Passages* (1976) is one example of the popularization of Van Gennep's work.

Building on Van Gennep's analysis of rites of passage, the British cultural anthropologist Victor Turner focused on the state of liminality, or unstructured in-betweenness, that participants in these rites experience as part of their passage to a new state of life. Turner developed his theories through fieldwork study of the Ndembu tribe in Zambia and, after moving to the United States in the 1960s, applied them to many different forms of ritual process, including those associated with American hippie culture. Turner argued that in the liminal state, initiates were lowly, without any real status, and dependent on guides and mentors for basic instruction. At the same time, they were also perceived as being directly in touch with sacred powers of transformation and thus imbued with a kind of holiness, as a result of a temporary existence outside the structures of society. Turner discovered that people in this state of liminality enjoyed an extraordinary kind of egalitarian fellowship with one another, which he called communitas.

Turner's theories of ritual process, liminality, and communitas have attracted considerable attention, not only among scholars of religion but also among organizational leaders interested in strategies of effective socialization. In the 1990s, for example, in at least one American Catholic university, first-year undergraduates were recruited for weekend retreats based on Turner's theories. During these retreats, students were led through a ritual process in which they bonded with one another, depended on spiritual leaders for guidance, and then returned to the normal routine of college life with greater discipline and an increased sense of both personal and social responsibility.

The Romanian scholar Mircea Eliade taught at the University of Chicago during the 1960s and 1970s and, during those years, exerted as much influence on the growing field of religious studies as anyone. Like Turner, Eliade drew from Van Gennep's work on initiation rites and their importance for religious life. But unlike Turner, Van Gennep, and Durkheim, all of whom focused on the relationship between ritual and social structure, Eliade was primarily interested in the patterns of subjective experience in which participants in initiation rites were immersed. In traditional religious cultures around the world, Eliade believed, initiates reenacted the creation myths of their cultures and found themselves, as he put it, "in illo tempore," at the beginning of time. Through initiation rites that recapitulated the process of world creation, Eliade believed, initiates were swallowed up in sacred time and in the cosmic events described in origin myths.

Eliade was harshly critical of modern life, which he regarded as a deliberate, destructive effort to desacralize the world. At the same time, he believed that opportunities for immersion in the sacred still existed in modern society and encouraged inventive efforts to rediscover it. Largely through his extraordinary influence on the field of religious studies, Eliade helped to inspire many practical efforts to refocus and even reinvent religious life. For example, his influence can be seen in Starhawk's *Dreaming the Dark* (1982), which offers guidelines that readers can use to create their own Neopagan rituals.

Sacramentalism in American Culture

During the same decades that Americans became interested in ideas about ritual based on the work of Van Gennep, Turner, and Eliade, Catholic attitudes toward ritual came to exert unprecedented influence on American culture. Deep investment in the rituals of the Catholic Church, and especially in the holy sacrament of the Eucharist, characterized most Ameri-

can Catholics who, in many other respects, were often quite different from one another. Unlike many Protestants who rejected the idea that the Eucharist was itself a means of grace, Catholics believed that Christ was present in the sacrament and united himself with participants through it. While American culture before the 1960s was strongly influenced by Protestant tendencies to regard many forms of religious ritual as superstitious practices or merely formalistic shows of faith, as Catholics joined the middle class in increasing numbers after World War II, Catholic tendencies to appreciate ritual as the centerpiece of religious life became an increasing part of mainstream American culture. Catholic reverence for ritual, along with a more general Catholic readiness to perceive God's presence in the world, has contributed to increased appreciation of ritual in the broader culture of the United States.

Catholic influence in American religious life has also increased as a result of the Second Vatican Council in the early 1960s, during which the Catholic Church officially opened its doors to the modern world. Since Vatican II, many American Catholics have expressed enthusiasm for liturgical vitality and innovation and also for better understanding of the ritual practices of other religious groups. Since the 1960s, Catholics have helped to inspire liturgical reform in several Protestant denominations in the United States. They have also led the way in establishing ecumenical dialogues with Hindus and Buddhists that have promoted respect for eastern meditation practices as potential aids to Christian worship. In combination with feminist interest in rituals that celebrate natural life, and feminist rejection of the patriarchal structures of the Catholic Church, innovative forms of Catholic sacramentalism may also have contributed to enthusiasm for alternative religious rituals associated with the Goddess and Mother Earth.

See also ANTHROPOLOGY OF RELIGION; ARCHETYPE; ELIADE, MIRCEA; MYTH; NEOPAGANISM; PSYCHOLOGY OF RELIGION; RELIGIOUS STUDIES; RETREAT; RITES OF PASSAGE; ROMAN CATHOLICISM; SOCIOLOGY OF RELIGION; STARHAWK.

BIBLIOGRAPHY

Eliade, Mircea. *Rites and Symbols of Initiation: The Mysteries of Birth and Rebirth.* 1958.

Giles, Paul. *American Catholic Arts and Fictions: Culture, Ideology, Aesthetics.* 1992.

Porterfield, Amanda. *The Power of Religion: An Introduction to Comparative Religion.* 1997.

Turner, Victor. *The Ritual Process: Structure and Anti-Structure.* 1969.

Van Gennep, Arnold. *The Rites of Passage,* translated by Monika B. Vizedom and Gabrielle L. Caffee. 1960; orig. French, 1908.

White, James F. *Christian Worship in North America, a Retrospective: 1955–1995.* 1997.

Amanda Porterfield

Roberts, Granville Oral

(1918–), evangelist, television minister, and college builder.

Oral Roberts has done much to define and spread pentecostal/charismatic religion in the twentieth century. He was born on January 24, 1918, in Pontotoc County, Oklahoma. Roberts's father, Ellis Roberts, was an itinerant evangelist in the small Pentecostal Holiness Church. While a teenager, Oral Roberts believed that he was divinely healed of tuberculosis, and shortly thereafter he became an ordained minister in the Pentecostal Holiness Church. In 1947 he made a bold decision to give up his position as pastor of a church in Enid, Oklahoma, to launch an independent healing ministry. In the second half of the twentieth century, Roberts was the most famous pentecostal evangelist in the world; he developed fresh methods of fund raising and collected hundreds of millions of dollars to support a diverse assortment of ministries. In addition to conducting revivals in many nations, he launched innovative radio and television ministries in the 1950s. In 1965 Roberts opened a university in Tulsa that was named Oral Roberts University. In 1980 Roberts set out to add a hospital and medical school to the university. While the university was a successful educational enterprise, the medical school survived for only seven years. By the end of the 1980s Roberts had turned over most of the responsibility for his ministry and the university to his son Richard Roberts.

Often ridiculed during his early years as a "fake healer" and charlatan, Roberts usually had an uneasy relationship with the press and with mainstream American religious leaders. However, in the late 1960s Roberts made a series of bold decisions that for a time improved his public image. In 1968 he stopped holding tent revivals and discontinued the television programs that had featured the tent healing lines. A few months later, in a risky and expensive venture, Roberts released a series of professionally produced television specials that were aired in prime time. At the same time, Roberts left the Pentecostal Holiness Church to become a member of the prestigious Boston Avenue Methodist Church in Tulsa. In the 1980s Roberts's public image once again plummeted. He

Oral Roberts addresses a crowd at Fort Mill, South Carolina, on March 7, 1987, during the National Church Growth Conference. (Credit: CORBIS/ Bettmann.)

was criticized by many Tulsa leaders who opposed the building of the huge City of Faith Hospital, and by the media because of the extravagant fund-raising tactics he used to fund his excursion into medical education. In addition, while no hint of scandal ever touched Roberts and his wife, Evelyn, his ministry suffered because of widespread criticism of televangelists following the exposés of Jim Bakker and Jimmy Swaggart in the late 1980s.

Oral Roberts was a pivotal figure in twentieth-century Protestantism. He pioneered many of the television techniques that made possible the rapid expansion of religious television in the 1970s and 1980s, and he also devised many of the fund-raising strategies used by later television ministers. His prime-time specials in the early 1970s, which were modeled on the popular variety shows of the decade, were critically acclaimed and encouraged a bevy of imitators to produce religious programming that could compete with commercial television.

Probably more important in the long run, more than any other person, in the 1960s Roberts anticipated the spread of the pentecostal emphasis on the gifts of the Holy Spirit and divine healing into mainstream Protestant churches and the Roman Catholic Church. As early as the 1950s, Roberts's tent campaigns included people from many different churches, and in the 1960s he consciously turned his attention to ministering to nonpentecostal Christians. Through his preaching and writing and in scores of conferences at Oral Roberts University, Roberts encouraged a revision of pentecostal theology that made it more palatable to mainstream Christians. By the end of the twentieth century Oral Roberts had become a patron saint to millions of charismatic Christians around the world.

See also EVANGELICAL CHRISTIANITY; HEALING; PENTECOSTAL AND CHARISMATIC CHRISTIANITY; SWAGGART, JIMMY; TELEVANGELISM.

BIBLIOGRAPHY

Harrell, David Edwin, Jr. *Oral Roberts: An American Life.* 1985.

Robinson, Wayne A. *Oral: The Warm, Intimate, Unauthorized Portrait of a Man of God.* 1976.

Roberts, Evelyn. *His Darling Wife, Evelyn.* 1976.

David Edwin Harrell, Jr.

Robertson, Marion Gordon "Pat"

(1930–), televangelist, media entrepreneur, politician.

One of the chief architects of modern religious television programming and of the conservative religious/political coalition that formed in the 1980s and 1990s, Pat Robertson was the son of A. Willis Robertson, a Virginia politician who served in the U.S. House of Representatives for fourteen years and in the U.S. Senate for twenty years. Pat Robertson graduated from Washington and Lee University in 1950 and, after serving as a Marine officer during the Korean War, received a law degree from Yale University in 1955. In 1956, after a series of personal and business disappointments, Robertson embarked, at the urging of his deeply religious mother, Gladys Churchill Robertson, on a religious journey that began with an evangelical "born again" experience and a subsequent pentecostal "baptism in the Holy Spirit."

While studying theology at an evangelical seminary in New York City, Robertson was attracted to pentecostalism, and in 1957 he had a tongues-speaking experience, thus becoming one of the first of millions of mainstream American Christians identified with the charismatic movement. He worked briefly with a slum mission in New York City and as minister of education at a Southern Baptist Church in Norfolk, but

in 1960 Robertson plunged into religious broadcasting, buying a defunct UHF television station in Norfolk. Incorporated as the Christian Broadcasting Network (CBN), Robertson's broadcasting empire grew slowly in the 1960s. Its survival was assured by a number of innovative decisions made by Robertson, including recruiting a nucleus of backers known as the "700 Club," instituting fund-raising telethons, and adding a popular talk show program to the station's schedule at the instigation of Jim Bakker, whom Robertson employed in the mid-1960s.

Beginning in the 1970s, CBN expanded very rapidly, aided by technological advances in cable and satellite broadcasting. The network adopted the name "The Family Channel" in 1985, and by the end of the decade it was one of the largest cable networks in the country. In 1987 the annual budget of CBN was more than $200 million, and the channel's programs were aired on nearly two hundred stations. By the 1990s CBN had become a privately held business with a symbiotic relationship to the other parts of Robertson's ministry. In the 1970s Robertson moved his organization to Virginia Beach, Virginia; in addition to CBN, the ministry supported a variety of activities, including

Televangelist Pat Robertson speaks at the National Press Club in Washington, D.C., on June 10, 1992. (Credit: REUTERS/Steve Jaffe/Archive Photos.)

a graduate university and professional school called Regents University.

Considering his background and education, Robertson's interest in politics was predictable. When the Religious Right began to coalesce in the late 1970s, Robertson wholeheartedly threw his support behind the movement. He was one of the organizers of the "Washington for Jesus" rally in 1980, which attracted an estimated two hundred thousand conservative Christians in a march on Washington. In 1988 Robertson ran for the Republican nomination for the presidency, having received petitions signed by more than three million voters supporting his candidacy. Though his campaign fizzled, Robertson remained a behind-the-scenes force in Republican politics. In 1990 he backed the founding of the Christian Coalition and supported a variety of other conservative legal and political causes.

Pat Robertson's contributions to the rise of the Religious Right were unique in a number of ways. Robertson was unashamedly charismatic in theology. He prayed for divine healing and used the language of the pentecostal/charismatic subculture on his program *The 700 Club,* and he won the confidence of millions of listeners belonging to a variety of American churches. As a leader in the loosely knit charismatic movement, he tapped into the fastest-growing religious movement in the twentieth century. Never a tent evangelist or even a conventional preacher, Robertson brought to the pentecostal/charismatic movement a sophistication and knowledge of politics and economics that were critically important. Robertson's television message mingled recognizable charismatic theology with doses of conservative political and economic advice.

The pentecostal/charismatic movement that Robertson symbolically led in the 1980s and 1990s was ideally suited for political marshaling. Compared to the fundamentalist coalition headed by Jerry Falwell, pentecostals and charismatics were more ecumenical and flexible. In addition, the movement demonstrated a genius for the creation of cell-type organizations within churches, a tactic that transferred easily to the establishment of grassroots political organizations. Pat Robertson combined the religious fervor, business acumen, cultural sophistication, and political savvy necessary to both the CBN empire and the Christian Coalition.

See also BAPTISM IN THE HOLY SPIRIT; EVANGELICAL CHRISTIANITY; FALWELL, JERRY; PENTECOSTAL AND CHARISMATIC CHRISTIANITY; RELIGIOUS RIGHT; TELEVANGELISM.

BIBLIOGRAPHY

Harrell, David Edwin, Jr. *Pat Robertson: A Personal, Religious, and Political Portrait.* 1987.

Morken, Hubbert. *Pat Robertson: Religion and Politics in Simple Terms.* 1987.

Hadden, Jeffrey K., and Anson Shupe. *Televangelism: Power & Politics on God's Frontier.* 1988.

David Edwin Harrell, Jr.

Rock Masses

Rock Masses are large-scale New Age celebrations performed since the early 1980s that combine elements of the Catholic Mass and Christian seasonal festivals with other sacred and secular texts, set to contemporary musical styles such as jazz, rock, pop, rap, and hip-hop. Rock Masses are products of several influences, including the Catholic folk Mass of the 1960s, rock gospel music of the 1970s, praise songs from the Charismatic Renewal movement, secular Top Forty music styles, and the music and creation spirituality of the New Age movement itself. Although rock Masses have been performed throughout the United States, they are primarily a bicoastal phenomenon, with the New Age movement most directly inspiring and supporting them.

The chief architect of the rock Mass is jazz saxophonist and ecology activist Paul Winter, whose 1981 work *Missa Gaia/Earth Mass* defined the genre. Commissioned by Dean James Morton of New York's Episcopal Cathedral of St. John the Divine, *Missa Gaia* was a sprawling work for jazz ensemble, vocal soloists and choir, percussion choir, and organ that celebrated Earth (*gaia* in Greek) as a single living entity. *Missa Gaia* included musical settings for the Ordinary of the Mass—Kyrie, Gloria, Sanctus, Benedictus, and Agnus Dei—along with hymns, solo songs, and organ fantasias. Winter's settings ranged across a broad musical spectrum, from Brazilian dance and African-American spirituals to traditional Anglo-American hymn tunes, pop ballads, and twentieth-century French writing for organ. The most original aspects of the music, however, were the recorded voices of wolves and whales played during the service and melodies Winter fashioned from them for several of his settings.

Missa Gaia premiered on Mother's Day 1981 and has been performed annually since then at the cathedral on the first Sunday in October, the Feast of St. Francis of Assisi. Winter has also conducted performances around the nation and overseas. *Missa Gaia's* success has fostered a series of similar presentations of Winter's "Earth music" at the cathedral, including annual winter and summer solstice celebrations as well as a carnival series during the 1990s. While Winter's musical expressions continue to evolve through these works, most recently including Celtic and Russian influences, they all follow the ritual form established by *Missa Gaia;* extended multicultural performances of sacred, secular, and original music; and texts celebrating the changing seasons and eternal synergy of Mother Earth.

Another style of rock Mass has recently appeared in the form of Matthew Fox's TechnoCosmic Masses and Techno Rituals at his University of Creation Spirituality in Oakland, California. Fox, a controversial ecotheologian who was dismissed from the Dominican Order in 1994 and later ordained an Anglican priest, celebrated the first TechnoCosmic Mass in April 1996 in New York City. Since then, more than twenty-five of these celebrations have been performed, most of them in the San Francisco Bay Area.

Fox's celebrations have much in common with Winter's, including an emphasis on the sacrality of nature and the employment of multicultural music, but there are important ritual and musical differences between them. Fox organizes his Masses around specific spiritual themes, such as the sacrality of the body, diversity and kinship, angels, the African diaspora, and the divine feminine, while Winter repeats the great calendric festivals and themes, filling them with gradually changing content. Although they take place in secular meeting halls and gymnasiums, Fox's TechnoCosmic Masses include official celebrations of the Eucharist, with himself as celebrant; Winter's *Missa Gaia* and solstice celebrations are designed for and performed in the world's largest Gothic-style cathedral but are not formal liturgies. Fox's rituals are "raves" in which participants dance and shout for hours, while Winter's are spectacles witnessed by a seated audience. Fox's events feature several different performing groups and recorded music of the most recent styles, including rap and hip-hop, while Winter carefully composes and orchestrates ensemble performances in an evolving and highly personal musical style.

These comparisons and contrasts between Paul Winter's celebrations in New York and Matthew Fox's in the Bay Area reveal the continuing growth and development of the rock Mass and of New Age spirituality in the 1990s. A highly diverse and eclectic religious movement, New Age spirituality has generated many new forms of ritual and sacred music, of which the rock Mass is the most complex, creative, and monumental. As such, the rock Mass is likely to be the New Age's most lasting ritual form and liturgical legacy.

See also CREATION SPIRITUALITY; ECOSPIRITUALITY; MUSIC; LITURGY AND WORSHIP; NATURE RELIGION; NEW AGE SPIRITUALITY; PRACTICE; RAVE; RELIGIOUS EXPERIENCE; RITUAL; ROMAN CATHOLICISM.

BIBLIOGRAPHY

Albanese, Catherine L. *Nature Religion in America: From the Algonkian Indians to the New Age.* 1990.

Winter, Paul. *Celtic Solstice.* 1999.

Winter, Paul. *Missa Gaia/Earth Mass.* 1982.

Winter, Paul. *Solstice Live.* 1993.

Stephen Marini

Roman Catholicism

Catholicism is the largest of the world's Christian denominations, with nearly a billion members entering the millennium. Derived from the Greek word for "universal," "catholic" has long been considered a defining characteristic of Christianity. The adjective "Roman" initially came into use during the Reformation as a deprecatory term for loyalty to the papacy. "Roman" is properly used to describe Catholics of the former Latin rite, as distinct from the various language traditions of other Catholic traditions. Thus, for instance, the Ukrainian Catholic Church, also called "Uniate," professes loyalty to the papacy but uses a liturgy that is not based on Latin. The common usage, which refers to Christianity linked to the papacy, is followed here.

Contemporary Catholicism is considered older than Protestantism because after the sixteenth-century Reformation, Catholicism preserved many of the institutions of medieval Christianity such as the mendicant orders, Marian devotions, and belief in Purgatory. Most of these owe their modern survival to approval by Church authorities. At the time of Francis of Assisi, for example, the mendicant orders emerged from among various movements urging return to evangelical poverty and popularizing lay preaching. But approval by the hierarchy allowed Franciscans, rather than Waldensians, to prosper. Although not found in Scripture, belief in Purgatory was derived from a theological premise that anyone not fully perfect in the faith would escape eternal punishment in Hell but still required purification to enter Heaven. As attested by Dante's epic poem, this was an important element in medieval Christian piety. Continuity with medieval Christendom is not absolute, however, because Catholicism allows for modification of institutions and beliefs to reflect social change. As a result, Purgatory is not as central to contemporary Catholic piety as it was when fear of punishment was generalized throughout society.

Catholicism in the United States

Roman Catholicism was the first Christianity brought to the Americas, in 1493. Puerto Rico, presently under

Cardinal John J. O'Connor, the Roman Catholic archbishop of New York, speaks in New York City on December 14, 1987. (Credit: AP/Wide World Photos.)

U.S. rule, had its diocese of San Juan established in 1511, and the first bishop to take possession of his diocese in what is now the United States was Alonso Manso in 1513. Catholicism was established in Florida in 1526, and the parish at St. Augustine (1565) is the oldest continuous Christian congregation in the fifty states. The Catholic faith entered New Mexico in 1598, radiating from there to other parts of the Southwest, Texas, and California.

English-speaking Catholics came to America under the leadership of Cecil Calvert, second lord of Baltimore, who founded the colony of Maryland in 1634. However, England's antagonism against Catholicism carried over to the American colonies, and prohibitions against the establishment of Catholic churches was a key facet of the prejudice against Catholics that characterized the colonial period. The 1776 War of Independence and the enactment of the U.S. Constitution in 1789 brought greater tolerance for Catholics. The vitality of this postrevolutionary American Catholicism counted among its members a convert, St. Elizabeth Ann Seton, and notable clerical immi-

grants, such as St. John Neumann and Blessed Felix Varela.

Expansion into Louisiana after 1803 and the settlement of territories beyond the Alleghenies brought the U.S. church jurisdiction over the preexisting Catholicism of parishes and mission churches that had been established by the Spanish and the French. The large number of incoming Protestant and English-speaking settlers reduced the original Catholic population of these conquered areas into minorities, who were inclined to conform to a subordinate role in a predominantly Protestant country.

A steady stream of Catholic immigrants pushed the church in the United States to develop new institutions of service, such as Catholic schools, and new attitudes toward religious practice in a pluralistic society that imparted a recognizable character as uniquely American. The mass immigration of Irish Catholics during the potato famines (1846–1848) and the expansion westward after the conquests of Texas (1838) and Mexico (1848) were events that ushered in a new era for the church that increased its membership and material resources. This influence became national, particularly after the Civil War.

Gains in social power came at a price for Catholics. The U.S. church faced a virulent anti-Catholicism during the nativist movement and the Know-Nothing riots (1844) that projected Protestantism as the only truly "American" religion. There were also doubts as to the loyalty of Catholic soldiers in U.S. armies who would have to fight Mexican Catholics in 1848, a fear expressed fifty years later in the 1898 war against Spain. Following the model previously used to incorporate Florida, Indiana, and Louisiana, the English-speaking Catholic bishops, most of whom were U.S. citizens, emphasized their commitment to the United States and its form of government. This embrace of the United States meant that Catholicism rejected a role as irridentist defender of the natives in the conquered Mexican Catholic areas of Texas, the Southwest, and California. Unlike Poland and Ireland, where Catholicism became a nationalist religion in resistance to foreign invasion, the U.S. Catholic Church fostered the assimilation of the resident peoples to the newcomers. Named "pious colonialism," this policy harmonized concern for ministry toward the conquered peoples with maintenance of their social and cultural subordination to the foreign invader, the United States. Although Catholicism did not totally ignore its preexistent Spanish heritage—as, for instance, in the adoption of a Spanish colonial architectural style for church buildings—Spanish-speaking Catholics were often treated as if they were newly arrived "immigrants" to come to the United States, rather than the inhabitants of a conquered land.

Catholicism and Americanization

Throughout its history, the U.S. Catholic Church has wrestled with its identification as an institution of immigrants. Outspoken nineteenth-century intellectuals such as Orestes Brownson and ecclesiastics such as John Ireland, archbishop of Minneapolis-St. Paul, considered the survival of cultural traits from the homeland as detriments to full assimilation of immigrants into American society. On the other hand, many bishops feared that the loss of immigrant culture would lead to the loss of the Catholic faith. Both sides came together, however, to repudiate the suggestion in 1891 of Peter Paul Cahensly, a German layman, that called for the creation of multiple ethnic parishes under ethnic bishops in the United States. On the premise that once English was learned, ethnic differences would disappear, bishops preferred to funnel immigrants into scattered national parishes that celebrated Mass and offered services in the native tongue of immigrants. The Vatican saw dangers in conforming Catholicism too closely to loyalty to the government and in 1899 issued *Testem Benevolentiae*, condemning an ill-defined tendency called "Americanism" as a distortion of Catholic faith in the United States.

Catholics prospered in early twentieth-century America and built an impressive network of churches, universities, schools, hospitals, and social services in major U.S. cities such as Boston, Philadelphia, New York, and Chicago. Immigrant leaders often spearheaded these efforts, such as St. Frances Cabrini, helping preserve traditional loyalty to Catholicism in a new land. The Depression added the ferment of a Catholic radicalism in the person of Dorothy Day of the Catholic Worker Movement, and the New Deal reflected many of the premises of Catholic social teaching as embodied in papal encyclicals. In the 1950s the television show *Life Is Worth Living*, with Bishop Fulton J. Sheen, brought the clarity of Catholic doctrine into the consciousness of mainstream U.S. society. As the fault lines of ethnic neighborhoods collapsed, frictions among groups such as the Irish, Italians, and Polish diminished, Catholics entered late into the civil rights movement, but they entered it nonetheless, although faced with the difficult task of educating their own members to oppose the de facto segregation of many northern cities.

Restructuring of American Catholicism

The Cuban Revolution and the election of John F. Kennedy, the first Catholic president, ushered in the 1960s, and the decade closed with U.S. society deeply divided about the Vietnam War, civil protest, the War on Poverty, race, and ethnicity. Catholicism worldwide undertook a critical restructuring of its organization, rituals, and doctrines in the Second Vatican Council (1962–1964). By redefining the church's relationship to the modern world, the council molded a new way of thinking about the mission of Catholicism. Ecclesiastical authority was challenged when it attempted to control debate about matters such as birth control and abortion. Vatican II also mandated the creation of national councils of Catholic bishops to mediate between the papacy and local needs, thus establishing a greater degree of local autonomy in every country. Today various activist groups, such as Pax Christi on the political left and Catholics United for the Faith on the right, address contemporary social issues by appealing to Catholic teaching. But although differing in the interpretation of Catholic teachings, each professes loyalty to the church.

In the United States, Vatican II had a profound impact on the number of men and women dedicating themselves to church service as priests and brothers, nuns and sisters. Between 1970 and 1990 the number of priests and sisters in the United States dropped precipitously. This loss of personnel produced a severe problem in Catholic agencies, particularly Catholic schools. Faced with rising tuition to accommodate the salaries of lay teachers replacing the free labor of sisters, many parochial schools were forced to close because they had become too expensive for the parish members.

These social factors produced a pragmatic need to reshape many of the institutions of U.S. Catholicism and to legitimate changes with theological arguments. There is organized support for the restoration of a married clergy in the Roman rite and for the ordination of women to the priesthood. The Theology of Liberation, which began in Latin America, introduced Marxist terminology into the analysis of church responsibility, thus reinforcing the responsibility of church leaders to frame policy by reference to global issues of injustice. The National Council of Catholic Bishops (NCCB) has advocated a government-run universal health care system and has produced several significant documents that articulate church teaching on issues of particular importance in the United States. Economic justice, racism, and homosexuality have been addressed as matters for pastoral concern. The Catholic Church has been an outspoken opponent of anti-immigrant legislation and government measures designed to rob the poor of needed assistance.

The reforms of Vatican II have radically altered the style of Catholic worship. When required to provide services in "the language of the people," the NCCB decided to develop one official liturgy in English and another in Spanish, each fitting the linguistic uses

The bell tower of the Basilica of the Sacred Heart at the University of Notre Dame in Indiana, December 1996. (Credit: CORBIS/Layne Kennedy.)

common in the United States. Because this decision virtually coincided with a radical change in immigration law, the introduction of bilingual education, and the creation of political power for the Spanish-speaking people of the United States through the War on Poverty, the way was cleared for a Latino religious resurgence. In fewer than two decades, Latino militancy within the church and rapid demographic growth have made U.S. Catholicism into a bilingual, bicultural church. Of the estimated 61 million Catholics in the country in 1998, an estimated 23 million (38 percent) were Latinos. In some cities such as New York, Los Angeles, and San Antonio, Latinos are the majority of Catholics. Demographic projections suggest that within twenty years a majority of U.S. Catholics will be Latinos, marking a change as significant as the Irish immigration of the nineteenth century.

The Catholic Church in the United States entered 1998 with 19,677 parishes and 3,051 missions. Cath-

olics run 590 hospitals, 17,165 elementary schools, 1,357 high schools, and 241 colleges and universities. Church-affiliated social service centers treat 24 million clients annually. Although prosperous, Catholicism has not ceased to be an immigrant church in the United States. Current trends include outreach to new and diverse ethnic groups and a return by second- and third-generation Catholics to elements of a lost, preconciliar piety. The church has undertaken the professional training of large numbers of lay Catholics to assume ministerial roles in Bible study, charismatic prayer, the pursuit of social justice, and a permanent diaconate for married men. The future holds the prospect for a U.S. Catholicism that is clergy-poor and lay ministry–rich, with strong attachment to material aspects of religion and a rootedness in social justice concerns, characteristics long exhibited by Latino Catholicism. The challenge will be to mesh the interests of different Catholic constituencies within the same national institution.

See also BELONGING, RELIGIOUS; CATHOLIC WORKER; CELIBACY; CHURCH AND STATE; ECUMENICAL MOVEMENT; ENCYCLICAL; FREEDOM OF RELIGION; MESTIZO WORSHIP; PAPACY; RELIGIOUS COMMUNITIES; RELIGIOUS PERSECUTION; ROME; SOCIOLOGY OF RELIGION; VATICAN; VATICAN II.

BIBLIOGRAPHY

Burns, Gene. "Studying the Political Culture of American Catholicism." *Sociology of Religion* 57, no. 1 (1996): 37–54.

De Antonio, William, James Davidson, Dean Hoge, and Ruth Wallace. *American Catholic Laity in a Changing Church.* 1989.

Díaz-Stevens, Ana María, and Anthony M. Stevens-Arroyo. *Recognizing the Latino Resurgence in U.S. Religion: The Emmaus Paradigm.* 1998.

Dolan, Jay P. *The American Catholic Experience.* 1992.

Elizondo, Virgil. *The Future Is Mestizo.* 1992.

Fernández Armesto, Felipe, and Derek Wilson. *Reformations: A Radical Interpretation of Christianity and the World (1500–2000).* 1996.

Gleason, Phillip. *Keeping the Faith: American Catholicism, Past and Present.* 1987.

Hennessey, James, S. J. *American Catholics: A History of the Roman Catholic Community in the United States.* 1981.

Hughes, Philip. *A Popular History of the Catholic Church.* 1949.

Johnson, Mary, S. N. D. de N. "The Reweaving of Catholic Spiritual and Institutional Life." *The Annals of the American Academy of Political and Social Science* 558 (July 1998): 135–143.

O'Brien, David J. *The Renewal of American Catholicism.* 1971.

Schoenherr, Richard, and Lawence A. Young. *Full Pews and Empty Altars: Demographics of Priest Shortage in U.S. Catholic Dioceses.* 1993.

Anthony M. Stevens-Arroyo

Rome

Rome is the headquarters of the Roman Catholic Church and the see city of the pope, who holds his supreme rank in the church by virtue of being bishop of Rome. By the time of Christ and the apostles, Rome had become the capital of a world-class empire centered on the Mediterranean, and that included Palestine as one of its many provinces. Thus both the life of Jesus and the early extension of Christianity took place in the context of Roman power, and a Christian community arose in Rome itself at a very early time, possibly founded by the "visitors from Rome, both Jews and proselytes" who were present at the event of Pentecost (Acts 2:10). Certainly the founding of the Roman community antedates the coming of either Peter or Paul to the city, as can be seen from Romans 1:8–15. Paul's presence at Rome is attested in Acts 28:14–31 and elsewhere in the New Testament; Peter's presence there at the end of his ministry, and the martyrdom of both under Nero (Peter crucified upside down at his own request at Vatican Hill, and Paul beheaded on the road to Ostia) is a most ancient tradition, unanimously held by early Christian sources.

Rome's position as head of the empire ensured that its community would suffer to an outstanding degree from the persecutions unleashed by emperors from Nero to Diocletian and his immediate successors, and that it would produce many outstanding martyrs, whose memory was spread throughout the empire by visiting Christians. Its secular importance meant that many Christians would have to visit the city on commercial or political business, and this fact contributed to making its bishop a personage of empirewide importance in the loose confederation of Christian communities, a person whose intervention or arbitration in disputes or controversies that divided other communities was very soon accepted as natural. It was probably not clear to any of the parties involved at the time whether this authority and prestige came from his being bishop of the imperial city, from being in some sense the successor of Peter (or of Peter and Paul) in the leadership of that community, or from the Roman community's high reputation for orthodoxy and for fraternal concern for the well-being of the other local churches, but there is no doubt that all of these factors contributed to the situation.

Even before the legalization of Christianity there is some evidence that Christian visitors to Rome would venerate the tombs of Peter and Paul, as well as the resting places of the principal local martyrs such as Agnes or Lawrence; this was given an even greater impulse by the building of basilicas on the sites, under Constantine. To this day Rome remains one of the major places of pilgrimage in the Christian world; in a period when relics had a major attraction for Christian devotion, the bishop of Rome's position as custodian of the bodies of the Princes of the Apostles was also an important element in his spiritual prestige.

With the founding of Constantinople as the New Rome and Eastern capital, the bishops of the "Elder Rome" began to be apprehensive of the Eastern bishops' tendency to attribute Rome's primacy to its position as Mother City of the empire and began therefore to insist on the Petrine foundation of their see. This new emphasis was not completely accepted in the East but was sufficiently accepted as to provoke the Byzantine legend of the apostle Andrew (Peter's brother, who had been called before Peter and introduced him to Jesus) as founder of the church of Byzantium-Constantinople. Eventually the Eastern attitude coalesced into an acceptance of the primacy of Rome as a primacy of honor based on the city's rank in the empire, while the West insisted that the bishop of Rome had a primacy of jurisdiction based on his being the successor of Peter not only in the bishopric of Rome but also in the privileges given to him by Jesus in Matthew 16:13–19, Luke 22:31–32, and John 21:15–19. This divergence was a principal cause of the division between the Eastern and Western churches and is still a humanly insurmountable obstacle to their reunion. However, the Orthodox churches still consider that the "Throne of the Elder Rome" has the first place among the episcopal sees of the world and consider Rome a venerable city, consecrated by the blood of the apostles and martyrs.

In the Middle Ages the city of Rome remained a place of pilgrimage even when the pope was, as often occurred, absent from it for long periods of time. However, the increasing business of the local churches at the papal court, as appeals to Rome became more and more frequent and as the papacy reserved more and more cases to its direct jurisdiction, meant that gradually the object of the journey to Rome came to be not only the veneration of the Roman shrines but also seeing the pope himself, whether to transact ecclesiastical business or merely to receive his blessing. Both the veneration of the shrines and the paying of one's respects to the pope received extra impetus from Boniface VIII's proclamation of the first

Jubilee Year, or Holy Year, in 1300. Such jubilees, which offered special indulgences and spiritual privileges to those who make a pilgrimage to Rome during that year, were originally supposed to occur every hundred years, but they became so popular that they soon came to be granted every fifty and then every twenty-five years. While indulgences have lost much of their importance in Catholic devotion after the Second Vatican Council, Holy Years still see a significant increase in pilgrims to the shrines of Rome.

With the coming of the Renaissance the city of Rome also became a mecca for artists and connoisseurs of art, and to the attractions of the great shrines was added the attraction of the ruins of antiquity and of the palaces and churches of the Renaissance and baroque styles, especially the new basilica of St. Peter's, whose rebuilding began under Julius II and culminated with Michelangelo's dome and Bernini's colonnade. As temporal sovereigns the popes became important collectors of antiquities and patrons of the principal Renaissance painters, sculptors, and architects, so that the Vatican Palace and museums became treasure-houses of art that no tourist, whatever his or her religious beliefs, can afford to miss. Similarly, the papal ceremonies at St. Peter's and the other major basilicas became memorable spectacles, enhanced by the Sistine Choir's performance of the music of Palestrina and other major composers who had written music on commission from the popes.

While papal temporal sovereignty over Rome ended with Italian unification in 1870, the events leading to this only increased the emotional attachment of Catholics throughout the world to the pope, who was perceived as a holy old man bullied and persecuted by a secularistic government. In fact, the loss of temporal power only enhanced the popes' stature as spiritual figures in the Catholic community. And so, in spite of the secular and artistic interests that are combined with religious devotion in a modern Catholic's attitude to Rome, it still remains primarily a holy city, and a visit to it is never mere tourism; it always shares in the character of a pilgrimage that puts one in touch with the early church and with the living representative of the princes of the apostles. For American Catholics, Rome is a symbol of religious authority even in an age of greater religious freedom and choice.

See also CHURCH; CHURCH AND STATE; PILGRIMAGE; RELIGIOUS STUDIES; ROMAN CATHOLICISM; VATICAN; VATICAN II.

BIBLIOGRAPHY

Dvornik, Francis. *The Idea of Apostolicity in Byzantium and the Legend of the Apostle Andrew.* 1958.

Guarducci, Margherita. *The Tomb of Saint Peter.* 1960.

Pinto, Pio V. *The Pilgrim's Guide to Rome.* 1975.

Vidal, Jaime R. "Pilgrimage in the Christian Tradition." *Concilium 4* (1996).

Jaime R. Vidal

Romero, Oscar Arnulfo

(1917–1980), clergyman and martyr.

Roman Catholic archbishop of El Salvador, liberation theologian, and martyr, Oscar Arnulfo Romero was born in the rural village of Ciudad Barrios on August 15, 1917. He attended a Claretian school and then later the Jesuit-sponsored National Seminary in San Salvador, El Salvador. In 1937 he traveled to Italy and spent the next six years attending the Gregorian Seminary in Rome. Ordained to the priesthood in 1942, he later served as general secretary of the Central

Archbishop of El Salvador, Oscar Romero, in early 1980, shortly before he was assassinated (on March 24, 1980) in the chapel of a hospital he had established for terminal cancer patients. (Credit: CORBIS/Bettmann.)

American Bishops' Conference. He became a bishop in 1967 and was appointed archbishop of El Salvador in 1977.

Quiet and reserved by nature, at first Romero did little to speak out against human rights violations. In fact, as bishop he was an outspoken critic of liberation theology, which he claimed was a "rationalistic, revolutionary, and hate-filled" theology. A major turning point took place in 1977 after a priest named Rutilio Grande and a young boy were gunned down by a right-wing death squad for speaking out against the oppressive regime. Romero called this his moment of truth, his "Saul on the road to Damascus" conversion. After reading the work of liberation theologians and critically reflecting on the sociopolitical situation in El Salvador, Romero began to speak out against the violence, corruption, and suffering of peasant workers. This brought him into direct conflict with the ruling elite and the government, who often sanctioned or turned a deaf ear to these problems. His commitment to the poor led him to stop the construction of the cathedral in San Salvador to use the church's resources for the poor and for pastoral work. He encouraged the spread of Christian Base Communities (CBCs) and defended the rights of peasants to organize unions and political organizations. This prompted many government officials and bishops to accuse him of practicing partisan politics. He responded by stating that although politics and faith are connected, they are not the same and should not be confused. Political programs could not take the place of genuine faith, Romero stated. As the mass killings of peasants continued between 1978 and 1980, however, Romero became more outspoken in his defense of the poor. He called on the government and the military to put an end to the death squads. In reaction to his growing popularity among the masses in El Salvador, his opponents had him assassinated while saying Mass on March 24, 1980. His martyrdom has made him a role model for liberation theologians, Latino activists, and social justice advocates in the United States and around the world. His immense popularity in the United States has led to the production of three biographies and one movie about his life and ministry.

See also LIBERATION THEOLOGY; PASTORAL COUNSELING; ROMAN CATHOLICISM.

BIBLIOGRAPHY

Keogh, Dermot. *Romero: El Salvador's Martyr.* 1981.

Romero, Oscar. *A Martyr's Message: Six Homilies by Archbishop Oscar Romero.* 1981.

Sobrino, Jon. *Archbishop Romero: Memories and Reflections,* translated by Robert R. Barr. 1990.

Gastón Espinosa

Rosicrucians

The term *Rosicrucian* refers to a set of related esoteric groups that originated from a story of the arrival of ancient wisdom teachings into the West now believed to have originated with the German Lutheran minister John Valentin Andrae (1586–1654). Andrae reportedly authored and anonymously published three documents, "The Fama Fraternitas of the Meritorious Order of the Rosy Cross" (1614), "The Confession of the Rosicrucian Fraternity" (1615), and "The Chymical Wedding of Christian Rosencreuz" (1616), that announced the existence of the Rosicrucian Order, revealed its basic teachings, and invited seekers to contact it. According to these documents, the order began with Christian Rosencreuz (1378–1484), who as a young man left his native Germany to study occultism with masters in Muslim lands. He returned in 1407 and began the order, which existed quietly until the public announcement in 1614.

When they were unable to contact the order, occultists across Europe began to create Rosicrucian groups using the three documents and other occult materials, and by the end of the seventeenth century, such orders could be found in England, France, and other European urban centers. Rosicrucian symbology was integrated into speculative Freemasonry, and French Rosicrucianism contributed to the antimonarchical ethos that led to the French Revolution. In the decades after the revolution, the movement suffered from the general attack upon supernaturalism from Enlightenment thinking and all but disappeared. Before its disappearance, however, one small German Rosicrucian group, the Chapter of Perfection, migrated to America in 1684 and settled in Germantown, Pennsylvania. The teachings of this short-lived group contributed greatly to the magical folklore of the region.

Occultism began its modern revival in the nineteenth century. The French magician Eliphas Levi and other thinkers constructed new occult systems that were quite compatible with the new science. Rosicrucianism emerged as one of those scientific occult systems in the 1850s when Pascal Beverly Randolph (1825–1875), an African-American spiritualist, developed a new set of occult teachings and practices (including sex magic) for the Rosicrucian Fraternity. Randolph was the first of several American practitioners to began a Rosicrucian group claiming authority from older Rosicrucian groups in Europe, groups not otherwise known to exist. By far the most successful of these was H. Spencer Lewis, who in 1915 launched the Ancient and Mystical Order Rosae Crucis, now headquartered in San Jose, California. Through its broad advertising program and its use of a correspondence course, AMORC has become the largest Rosicrucian group in the world, with lodges and study groups on every continent.

Rosicrucian ideas were revived in England in 1866, when Robert Wentworth Little (1840–1878) and several Masonic colleagues formed the Societas Rosicruciana in Anglica. Out of it would come the Societas Rosicruciana in Civitatibus Foederatis, formed by Charles E. Mayer and fellow Freemasons who received their authority from England. Like the parent body, the SRCF membership was limited to Masons. However, one of the SRCF members, Sylvester C. Gould, would form an open membership version of SRCF as the Societas Rosicruciana in America in 1907. This later order would thrive for a generation under the leadership of Gould's talented successor, George Winslow Plummer.

A second strain of Rosicrucian thought began in 1907 with Carl Louis Von Grasshoff, best known by his pen name, Max Heindel (1865–1919). In Europe at the beginning of the twentieth century, he was taught by an unnamed teacher, believed to be the German theosophist Rudolf Steiner. Steiner was articulating a more Christ-centered form of theosophy that would in 1914 cause him to leave the Theosophical Society. Heindel absorbed this Christocentric occultism and moved to America to found the Rosicrucian Fellowship, now headquartered in Oceanside, California. The fellowship would in turn lead to the founding of several additional Rosicrucian orders, the most successful being the Lectorium Rosicrucianum. From its base in Holland, the Lectorium Rosicrucianum has spread across Europe and North America, in spite of its having almost been destroyed by the Nazis.

Despite the lack of support for the account of Christian Rosencreuz, the idea of a Christian occult mystical order has continued to draw people, and Rosicrucianism has thrived as an established element in the twentieth-century occult revival. These new Rosicrucian groups share a name, story, and symbol, the rose cross being derived from the crest of the Protestant reformer Martin Luther. But while Rosicrucians share a few basic occult beliefs, each group teaches quite a distinct form of occult thought and emphasizes its own distinctive practices.

See also FREEMASONRY; OCCULT, THE; SPIRITUALISM; THEOSOPHICAL SOCIETY.

BIBLIOGRAPHY

Allen, Paul M., ed. *A Christian Rosenkreutz Anthology.* 1968.

MacIntosh, Christopher. *The Rosy Cross Unveiled.* 1980.

J. Gordon Melton

Rosseau, Leoncia Rosado

(1912–), evangelist, social activist.

Pioneer Puerto Rican Pentecostal woman evangelist, drug rehabilitation program founder, and cofounder of the Damascus Christian Church, "Mama Leo," as Rosado Rosseau is affectionately known, was born on April 11, 1912, in Toa Alta, Puerto Rico. The second of five children, she was converted during a revival sweeping the Disciples of Christ Church on the island in 1932. Shortly thereafter she became a Pentecostal and received her religious calling to go into the ministry. She preached all over Puerto Rico and had to battle sexism in the ministry. She claims that *"Nosotras las mujeres no trataban como soldado de 3ra clase"* (We women were treated as third-class soldiers). She claims to have received a vision from God to carry the Pentecostal message to the Spanish-speaking population in New York City. In September 1935 she left Puerto Rico for New York City, where she came under the healing ministry of Francisco Olazábal in Spanish Harlem. In 1937 she received her certificate of divinity. After Olazábal's death, she and her husband, Francisco, left the Latin American Council of Christian Churches and founded Damascus Christian Church (DCC) in Spanish Harlem in 1939. By 1987 the DCC numbered fifty-six churches in New York, New Jersey, Florida, Ecuador, Mexico, the Dominican Republic, Puerto Rico, and the Virgin Islands. Although targeted to the Spanish-speaking population, the DCC opened its first English-language ministry in 1981.

Rosado Rosseau is famous not only for her allegedly powerful preaching style, healing ministry, and mystical experiences but also for founding the Damascus Youth Crusade drug rehabilitation program in 1957. This was one of the first grassroots rehab programs founded within a church in New York City. It provided rehabilitation for drug addicts, alcoholics, ex-convicts, prostitutes, and gang members. An estimated 250 to 300 young people have gone through her rehab program into the Christian ministry. Her evangelistic social ministry has attracted the attention of New York City mayors and governors such as Nelson Rockefeller. At age eighty-five she was still pastoring her own church and ministering in her drug rehab programs.

Rosado Rosseau has served as a pioneer in urban ministry and as a role model for young women seeking to go into the ministry.

See also DRUGS; EVANGELICAL CHRISTIANITY; FEMINIST SPIRITUALITY; LATINO TRADITIONS; MINISTRY; ORDINATION OF WOMEN; PENTECOSTAL AND CHARISMATIC CHRISTIANITY.

BIBLIOGRAPHY

Korrol, Virginia Sánchez. "In Search of Unconventional Women: Histories of Puerto Rican Women in Religious Vocations Before Midcentury." In *Barrios and Borderlands,* edited by Denis Lynn Daly Heyck. 1994.

Villafañe, Eldin. *The Liberating Spirit: Toward an Hispanic American Pentecostal Social Ethic.* 1992.

Gastón Espinosa

S

Sabbat

Wicca, also known as Witchcraft or the Craft, seeks to reestablish the link to the earth and the cycle of seasons by following what Wiccans call the "Wheel of the Year." Celebrations, known as Sabbats, serve as the spokes of the Wheel, reminding practitioners of humanity's intimate connection to nature. The Lesser Sabbats, tied to the solstices and equinoxes, and the Greater Sabbats, purportedly tied to harvest and livestock cycles, occur approximately every six weeks. Through observance of the Sabbats and Esbats, rituals taking place every new and full moon, witches keep in touch with the progression of the year and nature's rhythms.

The names of the various Sabbats differ from tradition to tradition; this entry lists the most commonly accepted names. These names, the timing of the Sabbats, and most elements of these ritual celebrations draw from the meager evidence of ancient British and Celtic traditions, as well as the few survivals of these ancient practices. However, many contemporary Wiccan witches feel free to improvise, adding to what they know of old traditions. As Wicca ages, its own contemporary traditions gain authority, and Wiccans no longer feel a pressing need to legitimize their rituals by tying them to ancient practices. Even with innovations, the Wheel of the Year and the underlying meaning of each Sabbat generally remain the same. Nonetheless, Wiccans practicing in climates far different from that of the British Isles complain that harvests and seasons in their homeland do not follow the an-cient cycles. Wiccans in Australia especially find the ordinary Wheel of the Year difficult to follow. Many Wiccans in these areas seek to fit the Wheel of the Year to the seasons and cycles they actually experience.

The Wiccan year begins with Samhain, or Halloween, considered the holiest of the Sabbats. During Samhain the veil between the worlds is thinnest, allowing for communication between the living and the dead. During Samhain celebrations, witches remember those who died in the preceding year and welcome those due to be born in the coming year. Samhain also serves as a good time for magic involving the banishing of negative elements from one's life and for welcoming new, positive factors. Because of the enhanced communication between worlds, witches claim Samhain night as the most auspicious night of the year for divination.

Yule follows Samhain, taking place on the winter solstice; it celebrates the rebirth of the sun. With the rebirth of the sun, the God is reborn. Yule logs, wassailing, yule trees, mistletoe, and visits from the Holly King make up this festive Sabbat. Wiccans in the United States tend to retain the secular aspects of Christmas, viewing these as pagan holdovers from a pre-Christian Europe. Imbolc, also known as Candlemas or Brigid, a Greater Sabbat, falls on February 2 and celebrates the end of winter and the first signs of spring with a festival of lights. Wiccans teach that through the celebration of this Sabbat they aid the coming of spring and new life. Eostar, or the spring equinox, contains, like Yule, many familiar elements, with eggs and rabbits representing the fertility of the earth. As new life begins in spring, so Eostar marks an auspicious time for new beginnings.

Beltane, taking place on May Eve (April 30), stands at cross-quarters from Samhain, and witches consider this Greater Sabbat almost as important as Samhain. Far from being somber, Beltane celebrates fertility and the marriage of the Goddess and the God. Dancing the Maypole and jumping over the Bel-fire ensure human fecundity in the year that follows. The Maypole represents the phallus, or male fecundity. The festive nature of Beltane celebrations make this Sabbat a popular one.

Litha, or Midsummer, the summer solstice, not only celebrates the height of the sun's power but also remembers the impending death of the God, who is reborn at Yule. Like Beltane, Litha functions as a fertility festival. Lughnasadh, also known as Lammas, takes place on August 1 and celebrates the death of the God and the first fruits of harvest. The Sabbat derives its name from the Celtic god Lugh. Just as Imbolc celebrates the first signs of spring, so Lughnasadh commemorates the first signs of fall. Finally, Mabon, the fall equinox, marks the completion of the harvest and the close of the year.

Through observance of the Sabbat, Wiccans not only remember the cycles of seasons but also reenact the story of the Goddess and the God, a mythology central to their religion. The Wheel of the Year orders their religion and their day-to-day lives.

See also RITUAL; WICCA.

BIBLIOGRAPHY

Farrar, Janet, and Stewart Farrar. *The Witches' Bible Compleat.* 1984; repr., 1991.
Starhawk. *The Spiral Dance: A Rebirth of the Ancient Religion of the Great Goddess.* 1989.
Valiente, Doreen. *An ABC of Witchcraft Past and Present.* 1973.

Nancy Ramsey

Sabbath, Jewish

The seventh day of the week, in the Jewish calendar, is known as Shabbat or Shabbos. Extending from shortly before sunset on Friday evening until dark on Saturday night (because the Jewish day begins at sunset), its celebration has been a hallmark of Jewish practice for thousands of years. In the Hebrew Bible (Old Testament), observance of the Sabbath is one of the Ten Commandments and is mentioned numerous other times as well.

In particular, the biblical texts speak of "remembering" the Sabbath and of "guarding" it, mentioning restrictions on the work of building, gathering food, traveling, and making fires on that day. The oral tradition of Judaism over the centuries specified the details of the celebration as well as the restrictions. The mystical tradition honored Shabbat as a "Queen," the feminine aspect of divinity, manifest in the world through the Jewish people, especially on this day. Shabbat, the day of rest and peace, is honored above all other ritual observances and is among the first things taught to a prospective convert to Judaism.

In contemporary American culture the day is honored in different ways, depending on the Jewish subculture or denomination to which one belongs. However, there are some near-universals. For virtually all Jews who have some form of religious observance, Friday night is accompanied by the ceremonial lighting of candles and a special meal, initiated with a ceremonial blessing of wine and two loaves of bread. Synagogue services are also offered in most Jewish communities, usually on Friday night and Saturday morning, unless the community is too small to support weekly services. Beyond this, observance varies widely.

In the most observant segments of Judaism (Orthodox), the Sabbath is a day of complete abstinence from work as well as a joyous celebration. What constitutes work, aside from the obvious pursuit of one's occupation, is carefully defined in Jewish law. In modern culture, for example, the observant Jew will not drive or ride in a car, answer the telephone, write, or use a computer. All cooking must be done before Shabbat begins, but it is permitted to keep food warm in certain ways. One must walk to synagogue; thus the residences of Orthodox Jews tend to be clustered in proximity to their prayer communities.

In addition, observant Jews customarily have three long, relaxed meals—one on Friday night, one at midday on Saturday, and one at twilight. The meals often include traditional foods such as braided bread *(hallah)*, chicken soup, fish, meat, and favorite foods of the children. Having guests in one's home is common, as is singing and talking about religious topics at the table. Conversation about business or ordinary weekday activities is discouraged. Sexual relations between husband and wife are considered a special delight of Shabbat night. Prayer services are conducted in a slower, more relaxed manner than on weekdays, and gatherings for conversation or Torah study are common in these communities. Adults commonly take a nap in the afternoon. Shabbat ends, an hour or more after sunset, with a special ceremony known as Havdalah, honoring the distinction between the seventh day and the six working days. A party to "escort the Sabbath Queen" out is sometimes held as well.

Less observant communities include some but not all of these practices. For example, Conservative Judaism allows its members to drive to synagogue on Shabbat and to use electricity but does not permit business to be done on this day. Reform Judaism, which regards Jewish law as optional and originally eliminated most ritual observances, encourages Shabbat as a way of gathering family and community together. Business activities are discouraged but permitted in certain contexts—for example, a visiting lecturer might sell his books at the synagogue on Shabbat. In recent years the Reform movement has urged on its members more awareness and acceptance of the importance of Shabbat in Jewish life.

In some contemporary communities the spirit of Shabbat is more important than the letter of the law. While a general framework of abstaining from weekday activities is maintained, the emphasis is on a deep experience of the Sabbath. The theme is completeness and peace, as in the traditional greeting of the day, "Shabbat shalom" (Sabbath peace). (The Hebrew word for peace has the same root as the word "complete.") In alignment with traditional Judaism, practitioners try to make Shabbat "a taste of the world to come"—that is, the future messianic age of perfection. Conflict and arguments are to be avoided, worship should be intense and devotional, and singing and dancing are used to lift the mood of those present in the celebration. Since Shabbat is an aspect of divinity, the experience of it is understood to bring a person closer to God. The rediscovery of Shabbat by many Jews was a source of inspiration for liturgical renewal in the late twentieth century as composers, cantors, and designers of ritual found new ways of expressing the spiritual experience of the day.

Another practice that became common in a variety of settings is the "Shabbaton," an organized synagogue/community experience that brings people together outside their nuclear families. Whether in a regular synagogue or a retreat setting, a Shabbaton frequently features guest lecturers, community meals, and time for study and interaction. For example, a synagogue might organize a Shabbaton to attract newcomers and guests who are not part of the regular community, or an organization might host a Shabbaton for teenagers. By offering an intensified experience of learning and community interaction, people can experience Shabbat outside the limitations of their own homes.

Abraham Joshua Heschel called the Sabbath a "cathedral in time." This captures much of the spirit of contemporary Shabbat celebration: an elaborate architecture of communal energy, using the materials of common worship, common meals, and the natural cycle of the day through evening, night, morning, afternoon, and twilight. Each Shabbat is differentiated according to the customs and preferences of each community but is recognizable to everyone as a unique and distinctive religious structure. A Jew familiar with the basic structure of Shabbat can go to almost any Jewish community anywhere in the world—except perhaps the least observant—and find essentially the same rhythm and sense of purpose to the day.

Historically, a few non-Jewish groups have observed a Sabbath on Saturday, most notably the Seventh-Day Adventists. However, they did not incorporate Jewish law or mysticism into their observance. In very recent times a few non-Jews have proposed returning to a concept of a Sabbath that is inspired by contemporary Judaism: a spiritual day of rest designed to create a rhythm of life more in tune with a greater consciousness.

See also ATTENDANCE; BELONGING, RELIGIOUS; JEWISH IDENTITY; JEWISH OBSERVANCE; JUDAISM; LITURGY AND WORSHIP; PRACTICE; PRAYER; RELIGIOUS COMMUNITIES; RELIGIOUS EXPERIENCE; RITUAL; SYNAGOGUE; TEMPLE; TORAH.

BIBLIOGRAPHY

Heschel, Abraham Joseph. *The Sabbath.* 1996.

Kaplan, Aryeh. *Sabbath: Day of Eternity.* n.d.

Muller, Wayne. *Sabbath: Restoring the Sacred Rhythms of Rest.* 1994.

Zborowski, Mark, and Elizabeth Herzog. *Life Is with People: The Culture of the Shtetl.* Part 1. 1995.

Tamar Frankiel

Sacraments

The role of the sacraments in the Christian tradition has been a source of theological conflict since the Reformation, when the reformers declared that only two sacraments were instituted by Christ: Baptism and the Eucharist. In America, debate over the meanings of the sacraments, what they conferred, and who could legitimately receive them were sources of division among the early New England Puritans and subsequently caused a number of splits within Protestantism. Today most Protestants continue to acknowledge two sacraments (called Ordinances by Baptists), although the Society of Friends, for example, does not recognize any sacramental rituals. The second half of the twentieth century has seen a greater consensus among some Protestant denominations (e.g., Episco-

A Catholic priest wearing a white robe places a wafer on tongue of a girl wearing a white veil during her first communion.   (Credit: © Michael Weisbrot/ Stock, Boston/PNI.)

palians, Lutherans, Methodists, United Church of Christ) in their understanding of the sacraments that has facilitated greater liturgical cooperation among these churches. Sacraments are a core feature of Roman Catholicism and are seen as endowing everyday life with grace. In the Catholic Church there are seven sacraments, three of which (Baptism, Holy Eucharist, and Confirmation) initiate believers into the faith tradition, two of which are sacraments of healing (Penance/Reconciliation and Anointing of the Sick), and the remaining two (Matrimony and Holy Orders/Ordination) are seen, in part, as sacraments of service to others.

Sacraments involve the use of visible signs (e.g., words, actions, and material objects, including candles, bread, wine, chrism, and specific garments) to invoke what is invisible and transcendent. The celebration of the sacraments is communal and rich in symbolic evocation. As liturgical rituals, the sacraments serve to demarcate important stages in the individual life cycle and affirm individuals' integration with the larger community. For example, even when there is only a priest and one other person present, as is usually the case with the sacrament of Penance/ Reconciliation or the Anointing of the Sick, the in-

dividuals participating in the enactment of the sacrament are linked symbolically with Christ and with the universal Catholic community. The celebration of other sacraments, especially Baptism, Confirmation (which imprints the gifts of the Holy Spirit on the person being confirmed), and Matrimony, require the presence of "witnesses," and the respective liturgies specifically invoke the important obligatory role of these witnesses and of other friends and family present, to maintain a nurturing community for the persons receiving the sacrament in question. In Catholic teaching, therefore, although the sacrament of Matrimony clearly has a functional role in sanctifying and maintaining a major social institution, it also has important symbolic purposes, whereby, for example, the unity of the married couple signifies the mutuality of committed relationships in general, the unity of the church with Christ, and the unity of the whole Catholic community.

Catholics' most frequent and public encounter with their sacramental heritage is through attendance at Mass and participation in Holy Eucharist (Holy Communion). The Eucharist commemorates the Last Supper that Christ had with his twelve apostles, at which his exhortation to "Do this in remembrance of me" has been interpreted by the church down through the ages as Christ's command to continue his sacred ministry on earth. The Eucharist is the core sacrament in Catholicism, and all other sacraments are linked with it. Whereas Communion in most Protestant traditions is seen as a symbolic commemoration of the Last Supper, the Catholic Church teaches that the consecration of the bread and wine by the priest during Mass changes the whole substance of the bread and wine into the actual body and blood of Christ so that his presence is fully real in the Communion's species (doctrine of transubstantiation). Not all Catholics necessarily believe in the true corporal presence of Christ in communion, but see communion as the symbolic affirmation of communal solidarity. Nonetheless, they still value the consecration as the most sacred act in Catholicism, and receiving the Eucharist represents Catholics' demonstration of their belief in and commitment to the Catholic theological tradition. Since the Eucharist is the pinnacle of Catholic sacramentality and of Christ's presence in the world, the church encourages Catholics to partake of Communion as often as possible. In the past, most Catholics would refrain from receiving Communion if they perceived themselves to be in a state of sin, and Catholics who regularly received Communion were also frequent users of Penance (Confession). Since the 1970s, however, as part of the many changes experienced in the post–Vatican II church, there has been a significant shift in Catholics' disposition toward

Confession and the Eucharist. American Catholics in particular appear to be distinctive. They are significantly more likely than European Catholics (excluding Ireland) to attend Mass on a regular basis and to receive Communion (48 percent) but not to go to Confession (only 14 percent report regular Confession). At the same time, similar to their European counterparts, American Catholics' attitudes and behavior, especially in regard to sexual morality, deviate from official church teaching. Nine of ten American Catholics, for example, believe that one can use artificial contraception, and a majority believe that a person can have an abortion, or engage in same-sex sexual relations, and still be a good Catholic. Unlike in the past, Catholics' disagreement with official church doctrine on particular issues does not prevent them from attending Mass and receiving Communion. For many Catholics, it is loyalty to the Catholic sacramental and communal tradition rather than adherence to official church teaching on sexuality and other select issues that has become the hallmark of a "good" Catholic (Hout and Greeley 1987).

Catholics' commitment to participation in the sacramental life of the church also accounts, in part, for Catholics' disagreement with the Vatican on women's ordination. The sacrament of Holy Orders (Ordination) consecrates men for the priesthood, permitting them to exercise sacred power within the church (e.g., whereas anybody with a sincere sacramental intention can, in an emergency, baptize a person or administer the Anointing of the Sick, only an ordained priest can consecrate the bread and wine into the body and blood of Christ). According to official church teaching, women are excluded from the priesthood to maintain the church's constant tradition and the will and intention of Christ, who called only men to be his apostles. Women's exclusion from ordination has been challenged in recent decades by both lay Catholics and many Catholic theologians. They argue that the Vatican's reasoning contravenes both the historical role of women in the early church and scriptural narratives in which the exemplary actions of Jesus demonstrate the equality of all before God (Dillon 1999). In addition to the theological reasons favoring women priests, calls for the ordination of women have taken on greater practical urgency in recent years not only on account of the elimination of barriers against women's full participation in other institutional domains, but also due to the shortage of priests available in some areas to celebrate Mass and consecrate the Eucharist. Nonetheless, Pope John Paul II has insisted that the issue of women's ordination is theologically settled and not open to debate (unlike the celibacy requirement for priests, which is not divinely prescribed but a church law that can be rescinded at any time). In view of the symbolic importance of the Eucharist to Catholics, however, and its pivotal role in embodying Catholic sacramentality, theological and practical reasons may compel a shift in official church teaching toward a more inclusive understanding of who can be ordained.

See also BAPTISM; COMMUNION; MARRIAGE; ORDINATION; ORDINATION OF WOMEN; RITES OF PASSAGE; ROMAN CATHOLICISM.

BIBLIOGRAPHY

Dillon, Michele. *Catholic Identity: Balancing Reason, Faith, and Power.* 1999.

Greeley, Andrew. "Protestant and Catholic." *American Sociological Review* 54 (1989):485–502.

Hout, Michael, and Andrew Greeley. "The Center Doesn't Hold: Church Attendance in the United States, 1940–1980." *American Sociological Review* 52 (1987):325–345.

Schüssler Fiorenza, Francis and John P. Galvin, eds. *Systematic Theology: Roman Catholic Perspectives.* 1991.

Michele Dillon

Sacrilege

Sacrilege is generally defined as an offense against the sacred. Sacrilege derives from the Latin word *sacrilegium* (*sacer,* sacred and *legere,* to gather). In its Greek and Latin usage sacrilege is understood as the crime or sin of stealing any object consecrated to the worship of divinities. In its modern usage sacrilege refers to the physical or visual violation of the sacred. Sacrilege differs from blasphemy only in form: Sacrilege is physical and visual; blasphemy is spoken or written.

Sacrilege results from the violation of codes that designate the proper interpretation and use of sacred things, including sacred persons, places, objects, and symbols. Sacred things receive their meaning and power from religious groups who hold them in high esteem. Religious groups also establish norms, rules, and procedures that govern their meaning and use. The improper use of sacred things may elicit averse reactions from believers who attach strong sentiments to them. What is sacrilegious to one person may not be to another. Two criteria are used to determine whether sacrilege has occurred: the intention of the offender and the interpretation of the sacrilegious act or object. For example, artists may not intend to profane religious symbols, but religious persons may interpret their art as sacrilegious.

Physical violations of sacred things are usually referred to as desecration and include acts such as vandalism and the theft of church property. A more striking example is the excavation of Native American burial sites for universities and museums. Many Native Americans protest excavation because it violates their sacred beliefs regarding death and burial. In response, Congress created the Native American Graves Protection and Repatriation Act of 1990, which requires the return of Native American artifacts and the preservation of their sacred burial sites. Church arson and bombings are the most frequent type of sacrilege in its physical form. From 1980 to the present, thousands of church arsons have occurred in the United States, the majority against African-American Baptist churches. As a result of these crimes, Congress enacted the Church Arson Prevention Act of 1996, and President Clinton created the National Church Arson Task Force (1996).

Visually and symbolically, sacrilege assumes three general forms: syncretism, secularization, and profanation. Syncretism refers to the blending of religious traditions. Syncretistic religious art, for instance, combines sacred symbols from diverse religious traditions. Because it is not antagonistic toward religion, syncretistic art rarely incites accusations of sacrilege. Secularization involves the diminution or elimination of the traditional religious meanings of sacred things. Profanation occurs when sacred symbols are degraded by improper use or when they are mixed with profane symbols. In either instance, the meanings of sacred symbols have been altered or the codes regulating their use have been violated. Other factors increase the possibility for sacrilege. For the visual arts, the more significant the sacred symbol and the more realistic its representation, the greater the likelihood that it will offend. For example, many of the most controversial sacrilegious works of art contain easily recognizable representations of Jesus or the crucifixion.

The following examples of sacrilege from American visual culture aroused public controversy: Popular music singer Madonna's *Like a Prayer* (1989) is perhaps the most well-known sacrilegious music video. In the video Madonna is erotically kissed by an African-American saint while lying on a pew inside a church. One of the most controversial examples of sacrilegious art is Andres Serrano's *Piss Christ* (1987). Serrano's photographic art shows a plastic crucifix submerged in a jar of the artist's urine. Director Martin Scorsese's film *The Last Temptation of Christ* (1988), based on a novel by Nikos Kazantzakis, created tremendous dissension because it alters the biblical account of Christ's life. In fact, Christ's last temptation is to live a solely human life without fulfilling his obligation to die and be resurrected. The most recent example of sacrilege onstage is playwright Terrence

McNally's *Corpus Christi* (1998). In McNally's play the Jesus character, Joshua, has sexual relations with his disciples and is crucified as king of the queers.

Antagonism toward sacrilege may produce conflict among cultural and religious critics. These conflicts over the control of public expression have come to be known as the culture wars. On one hand, cultural critics view efforts by religious critics to censor artistic expression as a violation of their First Amendment right to free speech. On the other hand, religious critics view sacrilege as a form of religious bigotry and as a threat to the public image of religion. As illustrated by the recent McNally play, sacrilege continues to be a controversial issue in American culture.

See also Blasphemy; Freedom of Religion; Heresy; Secularization; Syncretism.

Bibliography

Dubin, Steven C. *Arresting Images.* 1992.

Meyer, Jerry D. "Profane and Sacred: Religious Imagery and Prophetic Expression in Postmodern Art." *Journal of the American Academy of Religion* 65 (1998):19–46.

Westin, Alan F. "The Miracle Case: The Supreme Court and the Movies." *Interuniversity Case Program* 64 (1961):1–38.

Jonathan F. Cordero

Sainthood

In the Catholic and Eastern Orthodox Churches (and to some extent among some of the older Protestant denominations) a saint is a person who has followed the Gospel to an eminent degree and is therefore presented to the faithful as an example of Christian life and an intercessor before God.

From earliest times this decision has involved both a spontaneous popular appreciation of the individual's extraordinary holiness *(fama sanctitatis)* and an official recognition of this popular feeling by ecclesiastical authority. In the early days of Christianity the normal indication of sanctity was martyrdom—giving witness to Christ unto the shedding of one's blood. Members of the local community who had shed their blood for the faith were remembered on the anniversary of their death, when the community gathered for Eucharist around their tombs, which were used as altars for the celebration, and since every Eucharist had to be celebrated by the local bishop or his delegate, such celebration implied episcopal approval of the martyr's status. At a very early date Christian communities began to send letters to the communities of

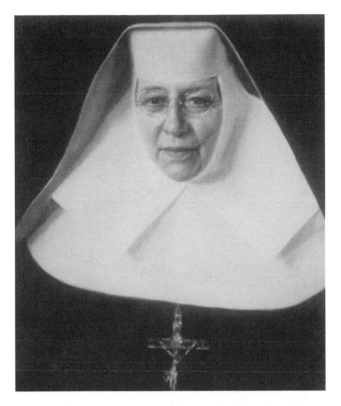

A nearly photo-realistic painting of Blessed Katherine Drexel, Foundress of the Sisters of the Blessed Sacrament, on display in Bensalem, Pennsylvania. She was beatified in 1998. (Credit: AP/Wide World Photos.)

other cities referring the martyrdom of its members, and this could result in the adoption of the martyr's feast by other communities, especially if the martyr in question had some connection to the community of the other city, or had suffered in circumstances that caught the imagination.

With the Peace of the Church, martyrdom became rare, but a result was recognition that there were other types of sanctity: asceticism, leadership in the community, defense of the faith against heresy, etc. In the Middle Ages a popular recognition of sanctity remained essential, but in the West the official approval came to take two different forms. For persons whose holiness was of merely local significance it was enough that the popular *cultus* be ratified by the local bishop by actions such as giving permission for the enshrining of the person's body or the celebration of his or her feast. It was still possible for such a cultus to spread to other localities with the approval of their own bishops, as long as this spread remained relatively limited. But for persons whose significance or extraordinary holiness transcended merely local interests, it became customary to request papal approval and in-

scription in the calendar, or *canon* of the Roman Catholic Church. Such canonization would imply approval of the cultus for the church.

By the thirteenth century the papacy began to demand serious inquiries about the genuineness of a candidate's holiness at the local level before it would proceed to further investigation at the Curia; it also refused to consider persons whose sanctity did not seem relevant enough by Roman standards—although normally such rejected candidates could still enjoy a local cultus. Well-attested miracles also came to be considered an essential requirement, providing supernatural sanction for the church's decision.

In 1642 Pope Urban VIII codified the practice that had been gradually developing by placing the process of canonization in the hands of the curial Congregation of Rites and giving it guidelines that had to be followed in the process. Persons who had died before 1642 and had a long-standing local cultus would be allowed to keep it and could eventually have the cultus officially confirmed by Rome—although such a confirmation was only permissive, and did not commit the church irrevocably. For persons who died after 1642, however, any kind of formal cultus would immediately disqualify their candidacy, thus effectively asserting absolute papal control over canonizations, although popular extraordinary holiness remains a prerequisite for the introduction of a candidate's cause. If the candidate survived detailed scrutiny of his or her life and writings, and if the requisite miracles were forthcoming, the pope would proceed to the ceremony of beatification. This meant that the person's name was now prefixed with the title "Blessed," his or her picture could be exhibited in churches with a glow of light (not quite a halo) around the head, and the person's feast could be celebrated in local calendars, usually those of the beatified person's country or religious order. Further examinations and miracles would result in canonization, after which the person would receive the title "Saint," be depicted with a full halo, and the anniversary of his or her death was often added to the calendar for the whole Western Church.

After Vatican II this process came to be seen as too slow and cumbersome, and as making it virtually impossible for anyone to be recognized as a saint until long after he or she had ceased to be relevant to the situation of the Christian community. The long and expensive process also had the unintended result of giving an advantage to candidates from religious orders, since their communities had the institutional resources to pursue a cause that could take more than a century to be successfully completed. This meant that the calendar was filled with priests, monks, and nuns, while there were very few married people or persons pursuing a Christian vocation in the secular world, aside from early martyrs or medieval kings and queens. As a result of this discontent Pope John Paul II in 1983 changed and simplified the procedures leading to beatification and canonization. One of the most important changes was the abolition of the promoter of the faith (commonly known as the "devil's advocate"), whose role had been to find objections to the supposed sanctity of the candidate. Since the cause could not proceed until his objections had been satisfactorily rebutted (which could take years of research), this official was one of the principal causes of delay and expense in canonizations. On the other hand, his role was to ensure that no unworthy person was raised to the altars as a result of misguided enthusiasm or political manipulations, and the knowledge that a candidate had to pass through all his objections with flying colors was reassuring in the case of potentially controversial beatifications. As a result of these simplified rules John Paul II has canonized and beatified more persons than any single pope in history, including relative contemporaries, such as victims of the Nazis in Central Europe and of leftist militias in the Spanish Civil War. However, liberal Catholic heroes such as John XXIII, Dorothy Day, and Archbishop Oscar Romero are still far from beatification.

One issue on which a paradigm shift may be occurring is the long-standing question as to whether a saint is primarily an extraordinary person to be admired, or a model to be imitated by ordinary people—a brother or a sister who simply did ordinary things in an extraordinarily selfless way. The "extraordinary" model of a person who is the moral equivalent of a genius, and who is to be admired and honored by those who cannot reach such heights, is losing favor in America; indeed, one obvious American candidate for sainthood, Dorothy Day, was known to despise talk of her sanctity not just out of humility, but because it would let others off doing the kinds of things she did. However, the Third World and the simpler people in the First World still cling to the image of a saint as someone intrinsically better than themselves, who can serve as an intercessor, protector, and "friend at court" precisely because he or she is *not* an ordinary Christian but a hero of the faith. And it is the simple people, rather than the intellectuals, who produce the extraordinary holiness that is essential for any saintly cult.

Another recent development is the great increase in American saints canonized or beatified in the second half of the twentieth century. Before 1960 the only saints of North America were French Jesuits martyred by Native Americans in Canada and New York State, and St. Frances Cabrini, an Italian nun who dedicated her life to work among immigrants. The 1960s saw the beatification and canonization of St. Elizabeth Ann Seton, a young New York widow in the early nineteenth century who converted to Catholicism and founded the U.S. branch of the Sisters of Charity. Since then other beatifications and canonizations have included St. John Neumann, a native of Bohemia and bishop of Philadelphia; St. Rose Philippine Duchesne, who brought the Religious of the Sacred Heart to Missouri; Blessed Katherine Drexel, a Philadelphia socialite who founded a religious community dedicated to Native Americans and African Americans; Blessed Teresa (Mother Theodore) Guerin, founder of the Sisters of Providence; Blessed Junípero Serra, founder of the California missions; and Blessed Kateri Tekakwitha, a Huron convert in the seventeenth century. The causes of Father Solanus Casey, a Capuchin friar who served for many years in Detroit; of Félix Varela, a Cuban priest who labored in New York in the nineteenth century; of Pierre Toussaint, a Haitian slave who helped found the Catholic community in New York; and of Henriette Delille, a free African American from New Orleans who founded a black community of sisters, are among the many American causes being considered in Rome.

The Orthodox Church in America has also recently canonized a number of North American figures: Sts. Herman and Juvenaly, monks and missionaries in Alaska; St. Innocent Veniaminov, first bishop of Alaska and later metropolitan of Moscow; St. Peter the Aleut, martyred for the Orthodox faith in California; St. Jacob Netsvetov, the first Native Alaskan Orthodox priest; and St. Alexis Toth, an Eastern Catholic priest who was driven out of the Roman Catholic church by Western Catholic prejudice and who became the champion of Orthodoxy in America. Other saints who died elsewhere but served in the United States for some time have been canonized by other Orthodox jurisdictions and recognized by the American church. The Russian Orthodox Church Outside Russia has canonized St. John Maximovich, metropolitan of San Francisco in the 1960s.

The Episcopal and Lutheran Churches have added commemorations of many Americans to their calendars in recent years, but prefer not to use the term "saint" (at least officially) for postbiblical persons so commemorated.

See also EASTERN ORTHODOXY; MIRACLES; ROMAN CATHOLICISM; ROMERO, OSCAR; VATICAN; VATICAN II.

BIBLIOGRAPHY

Brown, Peter. *The Cult of the Saints.* 1981.

Cunningham, Lawrence. *The Meaning of Saints.* 1980.

Delehaye, Hippolyte, S.J. *The Legends of the Saints.* 1962.

Vauchez, André. *Sainthood in the Later Middle Ages.* 1997.

Woodward, Kenneth L. *Making Saints.* 1990.

Jaime R. Vidal

Salvation

The idea of salvation is rooted in a conception that the world and the human condition are not as they once were or should be; salvation is the radical change or transformation that sets them right. It may mean a total or partial transformation of the individual, in this world or beyond death; it may mean a change of the social order, or a new cosmos.

The term "salvation" originally had only a Christian reference; it is now used to apply also to other religions, especially the so-called Great Religions that originated in the Axial Age (between approximately 600 B.C.E. and 600 C.E.). The cosmic religions that prevailed before this period, and that still do in some places, tend to be this-worldly in their concern. There is resort to Divine figures and/or rituals to meet needs for bodily well-being, for children, for help against impurity, chaos, enemies, death. Although there is interest in a spiritual world to be entered after death, it is not usually the standard by which the present life is judged.

But in the Great Religions, especially Buddhism, Hindu religion, Zoroastrianism, Christianity, and Islam, a profound otherworldly theme appears, sometimes coexisting with this-worldly concerns. It promises that by means of Divine help, spiritual discipline, or both, radically defective earthly life can be transcended, gradually or all at once. In the five Great Religions named above, such transcendence, whether in the flesh or in a purely spiritual state, is the primary meaning of the term "salvation," whereas resolution of this-worldly needs and distresses may be considered the term's secondary meaning. In Judaism, Confucianism, and Taoism this-worldly concerns tend to be primary.

The majority of immigrants to North America have been of Christian background, holding to a view of salvation that centered on atonement through Christ's death for sin against God, with forgiveness, renewal of life, and a promise of Heaven for the individual, and, to a varying extent, expectation of renewal for the community or the world. Like other Protestants, seventeenth-century Puritans held that the principal means of salvation lay in the Bible, a light to both the individual and the government. Puritans tended to see themselves as God's instruments to subdue the dark wilderness and build a Promised Land, a new Eden. In contrast, the Quakers who settled in Pennsylvania saw salvation more as an awakening from the spiritual death that manifested in materialism, inequality, violence, and religious intolerance; the principal means of salvation they found in a silent opening of the self to the Divine Spirit within every individual and the religious community. Quakers also held the ideal of building a new Eden in the wilderness.

In the eighteenth and nineteenth centuries occurred a series of major revivals called the Great Awakenings, originally influenced by the Methodist experience of the warmth of God's love in one's heart. By means of Bible-reading, preaching, and prayer, listeners were urged to repent from the sin that doomed them to hell, be born again, and receive Christ and the Holy Spirit. This focus on an emotional, life-transforming experience has come to inform the language of salvation in U.S. religion. Although this conception of salvation was primarily individual, it had a part in Christian efforts to transform society, notably in pressing for abolition of African slavery.

For many enslaved persons themselves, a rebirth experience of a powerful Divine Presence in their souls undermined society's message that they were mere chattels. The enslaved had an intense longing for Heaven, but in the Bible they also found subversive, this-worldly themes of salvation, especially the Exodus, in which God delivers his oppressed people from Egypt. This encouraged resistance and escape. In slave religion the longed-for Promised Land thus had dual meanings. The Exodus tradition was to be revived in the 1950s and 1960s in the birth of the civil rights movement in black churches.

Liberal Protestantism deemphasized transcendent religious experience along with ideas of atonement, Hell, and Heaven. It focused on the healing of souls from addiction, meaninglessness, and despair, and the healing of society from poverty, discrimination, and injustice through social and political action.

Jewish conceptions of salvation include a search for meaning in the wake of the Holocaust and centuries of exile and oppression. Salvation is particularly realized on a community level, and atonement with God must be manifest in reconciliation between and among individuals. Action to improve society is also important.

Although there were Roman Catholics on the North American continent from the early days, not until the nineteenth century did Roman Catholic Christianity became an important force there. Catholic views of salvation share with Protestant views the importance of forgiveness and transformation of life through Christ's atonement, but for Catholics good works are essential to this process. Furthermore, the means differ; it is principally through the sacraments, and the help of the saints, that the faithful are reconciled to God and prepared for the Beatific Vision of God in heaven. Certain religious and lay groups have traditions of charitable work among the underprivileged, but mainstream Catholic salvationism in the United States has stressed transcendence.

One significant exception to this pattern appeared from the 1960s onward in the Liberation Theology movement, which appropriated biblical themes of Exodus and the Kingdom of God to oppose poverty and oppression and attempt to build a new society on earth.

Hindu and Buddhist conceptions of salvation have had a substantial influence in the United States in the twentieth century. Tending toward transcendence, these religions teach that every deed creates a karmic reaction in future incarnations, so that we are bound to a perpetual round of suffering. Hindu Vedanta offers freedom by realization, through meditation, that Brahman, infinite Being-Consciousness-Bliss, is immanent in the universe, one with the soul. Buddhism offers freedom through Enlightenment—that is, the realization, by means of meditation and other altered states, that the individual self is illusory and that all we experience is mind-created.

These Eastern ideas, minor notes in North America until the 1960s, were widely diffused via the counterculture and influenced the amorphous New Age movement. Here what is wrong with the world is a mechanistic, dualistic outlook, which fosters isolation, exploitation, and militarism. The means to change are spiritual experience and spiritual discipline; the goal is transformation of consciousness for the individual and the healing of social and ecological ills.

The search for salvation arises out of need for the transcendent—for contact with the Divine, ultimate fulfillment—as well as for this-worldly transformation: meaningfulness, healing, and renewal for the person and the world.

See also Civil Rights Movement; Liberation Theology; New Age Spirituality; Quakers; Transcendence.

BIBLIOGRAPHY

Brandon, S. G. F. *Man and His Destiny in the Great Religions.* 1962.

Eliade, Mircea. *Cosmos and History.* 1959.

Ellwood, Robert S., and Barbara McGraw. *Many Peoples, Many Faiths.* 1999.

Rabateau, Albert. *Slave Religion.* 1978.

Werblowski, R. J. Zwi. *Types of Redemption.* 1970.

Gracia Fay Ellwood
Robert Ellwood

Salvation Army

In little more than a hundred years, the Salvation Army transformed itself from a despised and persecuted evangelical mission to the largest charitable fund-raiser in the United States. One of the few extant expressions of the ninetieth-century Holiness tradition that teaches sanctification, or a second baptism, and empowers believers for service, The Salvation Army remains true to founder William Booth's rallying cry "Soup, soap, and salvation!" In the last half of the twentieth century, however, Salvationists have been better known for soup and soap—that is, their vast array of social services—than for evangelism.

In 1861 William Booth resigned from a British Methodist denomination to start an itinerant ministry. Holding outdoor services in the London slums, he and his wife, Catherine, an early proponent of women's right to preach, sought the poor and destitute. But when Booth discovered that pressing material needs prevented many from hearing the gospel message, he began providing basic necessities, too. In 1879 Booth changed the name of his "Christian Mission" to the Salvation Army, and the military metaphor soon defined the structure, dress code, and identity of the organization. Instead of clergy, laity, and churches, the Salvation Army had officers, soldiers, and corps. Soldiers signed "articles of war" be-

Salvation Army street musician plays a baritone horn to get passing Christmas shoppers to give Christmas donations to the needy. (Credit: Bernard Gotfryd/ Archive Photos.)

fore enlisting in "active engagement" and donning their uniforms.

Booth's army arrived in the United States in the early 1880s, and its noisy bands and street-corner services elicited outrage from the pulpit and contempt from the press. When not marching through the streets, soldiers brought their campaign to the slums. Among their early efforts was a "Garret, Dive, and Tenement Brigade" of women officers serving in Manhattan's Lower East Side. By day the slum sisters cleaned, cooked, and tended children; at night they proselytized in brothels and saloons. Few were saved, but Salvationists, believing the work was itself a Christian witness, augmented their outreach and, by the turn of the twentieth century, ran shelters, soup kitchens, orphanages, and homes for unwed mothers. The organization was seen as a religious do-gooder group, but its status rose when, during World War I, members selflessly served American troops at the front lines. For almost a decade afterward, "Sallies," as Salvation Army women were called, were celebrated on stage and screen, and the Salvation Army was hailed as an exemplar of nonsectarian service.

The 1950 Broadway musical *Guys and Dolls* was the last time a starring role was written for a Sallie, but the Salvation Army still enjoys wide support. In 1997 donors contributed $1.1 billion to its $2.5 billion budget, which, in turn, subsidized programs including resident alcoholic rehabilitation centers, shelters for transients, halfway houses for ex-convicts and addicts, medical facilities, group homes, family programs, outreach to battered women and families with AIDS, thrift stores, employment bureaus, day-care centers, prison work, and emergency relief. Since religious witness is part of many Salvation Army programs, the organization accepts a limited amount of governmental funding. Relying on private support also allows the Salvation Army to follow its conscience, as in 1998, when it refused to comply with San Francisco's domestic partners law. While the Salvation Army provides social services for people with the HIV virus and AIDS, officials chose not to condone domestic partnerships between gays and lesbians in their workplace policy.

Salvationists describe their faith as a "practical religion" or a "religion of action," but they also subscribe to a conservative Christian theology (and concomitant social stands). Their eleven doctrines affirm traditional evangelical beliefs, such as the divine inspiration of Scripture and the atoning death of Jesus Christ. Since the organization's inception, Salvationists have done things differently than many of their coreligionists. Women have always had equal access to ministry; the sacraments of Baptism and the Lord's Supper are not practiced, and innovation has been the byword of evangelical outreach. Innovation has also changed the Salvation Army's structure. William Booth's army was an oligarchy, but today's organization is run democratically. Its global headquarters is in England, but national and territorial units worldwide have considerable autonomy and, as a result, distinctive regional profiles. The U.S. Salvation Army has four territorial divisions, and its policy is formulated by regional heads and the national commander. The Salvation Army in America is known for its abundant resources and diverse programs despite its modest size of 468,000 members. (There are about 3 million Salvationists worldwide.)

The Salvation Army's very success presents a singular challenge: how to keep its evangelical identity strong while appealing to a diverse public. Balancing its two foci—religious witness and social ministry—is the ultimate goal. Salvationists also face the same issues currently confronting American society: integrating increased racial and ethnic diversity within its ranks and providing women with equal access to top levels of leadership.

See also CONVERSION; FOOD; HEALTH; HOLINESS MOVEMENT; PREACHING; PROSELYTIZING; SALVATION.

BIBLIOGRAPHY

McKinley, Edward H. *Marching to Glory: The History of the Salvation Army in the United States, 1880–1992,* rev. ed. 1995.

Murdoch, Norman. *Origins of the Salvation Army.* 1994.

Winston, Diane. *Red-Hot and Righteous: The Urban Religion of the Salvation Army.* 1999.

Diane Winston

Sanctuary Movement

In the 1980s and early 1990s, the Sanctuary Movement was an interdenominational effort to give aid to Central American refugees to whom the U.S. government had denied asylum. President Ronald Reagan in 1981 was the most militant Cold Warrior in two decades. Fearful that Communists intended to create new "Cubas" in Central America, the Reagan administration reacted vigorously to any possible Communist threat. It supported the Contras (counterrevolutionaries) against the left-wing government of Nicaragua and backed right-wing governments in Guatemala and El Salvador against leftist revolutionaries. Rapidly escalated violence generated a stream of refugees fleeing war and terror from both the left and the right.

Influenced by liberation theology and appalled at rising violence in Central America, groups and individuals from liberal, pacifist, mainline Protestant, and Roman Catholic churches resisted Reagan's foreign policy. Religious groups had previously involved themselves in opposition to government Cold War policy—for example, during the Vietnam War—but the Sanctuary Movement was the first time that religious groups led the resistance to administration policy. A Latin American Catholic movement that gained strength in the 1970s, liberation theology was drawing increasing attention in U.S. churches. It taught that the best way to practice Christian faith in Latin America was through aiding the poor and oppressed by political action and changing unequal social and economic systems.

The Sanctuary Movement began in 1981 in Tucson, Arizona, not far from where many Salvadorean and Guatemalan refugees had been trying to cross the border into the United States. Quaker Jim Corbett attempted to assist the refugees through official immigration channels. Unfortunately, immigration officials awarded political asylum to refugees from governments the administration opposed, like Nicaragua, but deported refugees from those it supported, like El Salvador and Guatemala. As the homes of his Quaker friends filled with undocumented refugees, Corbett proposed creating religious-refugee sanctuaries on the model of the antebellum underground railroad for escaped slaves. Presbyterian minister John Fife and his Hispanic congregation agreed to offer sanctuary—that is, protection from arrest, prosecution, or deportation—and the movement began. Other Tucson religious leaders, like Father Ricardo Elford, supported him.

On March 24, 1982, Fife's congregation publicly announced its existence as a "sanctuary." Immediately some churches in the San Francisco Bay Area followed suit, led by Gus Schultz's University Lutheran Chapel in Berkeley, which had pioneered sanctuary for draft resisters in the 1960s. The Sanctuary Movement quickly spread across the Southwest and then north to Chicago, Seattle, New York, and Boston. At its height, 600 congregations and religious organizations nationwide were Sanctuary sponsors or cosponsors.

In 1982 the original sponsor of Sanctuary, the Tucson Ecumenical Council, approached the Chicago Religious Task Force on Central America about coordinating the national movement. The Chicago group then organized the National Sanctuary Alliance as well as communication and fund-raising organizations. Tension developed between the Tucson group, which was Protestant-led, decentralized, and inspired by civil disobedience, and the Chicago group, which was Catholic, centralized, and inspired by liberation theology. The Chicago leaders wanted Sanctuary to educate the nation and influence government policy.

They disagreed with Tucson activists by wanting to accept only victims of right-wing violence instead of refugees from all violence. The Tucson group's approach frustrated the Chicagoans, who saw Central American violence in terms of unequal political, economic, and social structures that they had a religious duty to challenge. Threat of a complete rift was overcome in 1984, but throughout the Sanctuary Movement activists drifted toward one group or the other.

At first wary and ambivalent about Sanctuary, the government finally took action, partly in irritated response to positive publicity in CBS and PBS reports. Government agents infiltrated the movement, and prosecution began in 1984. Of several scattered trials, the most publicized was a trial of sixteen Tucson Sanctuary leaders in 1985. Most were convicted, but the judge suspended the sentences. Widespread publicity from the trial led hundreds of churches, synagogues, and city councils to declare themselves as sanctuaries, and three somewhat separate sanctuary movements emerged by 1987–1988 in southern California, southern Arizona, and South Texas. However, Sanctuary's difficulties included ideological divisions, funding, and refugees' problems: psychological and physical scars; ethnic, religious, and political division; and worries about relatives kidnapped or left behind.

As Central American violence waned in the late 1980s and early 1990s, Sanctuary also wound down. Yet it represents a historical, explicitly religious challenge to American government policy. Sanctuary signifies such church-state issues as the role of conscience, spiritually-inspired civil disobedience, and faith-based antigovernment activism. Sanctuary by no means gives definitive answers to these issues, yet it brings them into uniquely stark relief.

See also LIBERATION THEOLOGY; ROMEO, OSCAR.

BIBLIOGRAPHY

Coutin, Susan Bibler. *The Culture of Protest: Religious Activism and the U.S. Sanctuary Movement.* 1993.

Cunningham, Hilary. *God and Caesar at the Rio Grande: Sanctuary and the Politics of Religion.* 1995.

Davidson, Miriam. *Convictions of the Heart: Jim Corbett and the Sanctuary Movement.* 1988.

Mark Stoll

Santa Claus.

See Christmas.

Santería

The Lucumí and Nago people from present day Nigeria, in Africa, were enslaved by the British, French, and Portugese and brought into the New World, where they were consigned in Cuba to Spanish plantations. By 1728 "Ulkumí" people, as they were then known, were found among the enslaved in Cuba. The plantation economy took form during the early nineteenth Century. It is estimated that the importation of Nagos and Lucumís from the Ojo Kingdom reached 275,000 to 350,000 people between 1820 and 1860. By the late 1800s these enslaved Lucumí and Nago people were known as Yorubas, their linguistic identification. These Yorubaland people brought a powerful religious cosmology that served to counter their enslavement and the Spanish form of Catholicism. In the 1840s, the Yoruba were a minority among the enslaved, representing 34 percent of the Africans in Havana, but their religious system, known as Ifá, spread among other enslaved nations. Due to the intensive exploitation of the enslaved on the Spanish plantations, their average life expectancy was seven years. This high mortality rate necessitated the legal as well as illegal importation of Africans to work the plantations, reintroducing Ifá religion and culture throughout the nineteenth century.

By the beginning of the twentieth century, Ifá represents the African religious form, while La Regla de Ocha (the Rites of Ocha) and Lucumí religious forms are Cuban. Lucumí became an ethnic identification for all Yorubas in Cuba. Forms of Ifá religion can be found throughout the Caribbean and South America, including Brazil where it is known as Cantomblé.

The word *santería* is translated as "the worship of saints." Santería focuses on earthly pursuits, divination, and providing the individual with a spiritual balance between good and evil. It is an animist religion that combines ancestor worship and mediumship. Europeans mistakenly viewed Ifá beliefs as similar to their Christian afterlife concerns, and the combined practice was allowed to buttress enslavement. This led to viewing Ocha as a syncretic religion that incorporated Catholicism into itself.

Since the 1930s, the syncretic paradigm has been used to explain the combining of two incompatible belief systems into one: Yorubaland's Ocha and Spanish Catholicism. This is the Eurocentric explanation for the use of saints at the altar of Ocha believers. Nevertheless, Ocha maintained an African religious orientation, which distinguishes it from Catholicism. This differentiation in cosmology led many believers to have both an afterlife orientation (Christianity) and a here-and-now belief (Ocha). Believers often add saints to their altars, a remnant of the Spanish

A statue of the Santería goddess Yemaya, on display and for sale in a store in Miami, Florida, on September 20, 1995. (Credit: AP/Wide World Photos.)

colonial era when Africans were forced to veil their worship, and this has contributed to a history of secrecy in the religion. Further, many believers sought legitimacy by using the iconography of Catholicism.

The *orisàs,* ancestor deities of the Yorubaland people, number more than three hundred in Cuba, although not more than sixty identified with saints. One example, Saint Lazarus the Leper, was identified with the Orisà Babalú Ayé, to whom supplicants who are sick and infirm provide votive offerings. These offerings (*ebbó*) are often given after divination and can include the blood-letting of animals. The tools for divination (interpretation of significance) are Ifá's Opele, where eight pieces of concave and convex coconut shells, affixed to a chain, are tossed on a tray; and the Diloggún, where sixteen unfastened corrie shells are similarly tossed. The third form of divination is the Obí, oftentimes done with four unfastened coconut shells, two of which are covered in white, and are tossed on the ground or on a tray. The Obí form is the most popular among Cubans. A *bàbálao*, an initiated priest, interprets and determines significance (*la letra*) by casting these shells.

Most believers are not initiated priests, but belong to a ritual kinship system where the *bàbálao* is godfather to a membership of godchildren who belong to a house of worship (Ilé Lucumí) or more popularly known as a Casa de Santería. It is a male-dominated religion, but women are making inroads into many roles. The Yorubaland language is used at ceremonies, but in the Americas it has lost much of its vocabulary, intonations, and accentuation, associated with the African variant. Worship is individualized, but generally festivals (*bembé*) occur for the *orisàs* in which an orchestra plays three *batá* drums and a chorus sings. In the absence of an orchestra, recorded music is played. Ilés de Lucumí have existed in Florida, especially Tampa, since before the Cuban Spanish American War (1898). In United States today, the belief system is mostly found in other areas where Cubans have settled and where there are concentrations of other Latinos/Hispanics, such as in California, Chicago, New Jersey, and New York.

See also AFRO-CUBAN RELIGION; ANIMAL SACRIFICE; DRUMMING; POPULAR RELIGION; SYNCRETISM; VODUN.

BIBLIOGRAPHY

Bascom, W. *Ifá Divination.* 1969.

Benavides, Gustavo. "Syncretism and Legitimacy in Latin American Religion." In *Enigmatic Powers: Syncretism with African and Indigenous Peoples' Religions Among Latinos.* Edited by Anthony Stevens Arroyo and Andrés I. Pérez y Mena. 1995, pp. 19–46.

Brandon, George. *Santería from Africa to the New World: The Dead Sell Memories.* 1997.

González-Wippler, Migene. *Santería: The Religion.* 1989.

Law, Robin. "Ethnicity and the Slave Trade: 'Lucumi' and 'Nago' as Ethnonyms in West Africa." *History in Africa* 24 (1997): 205–219.

Midlo Hall, Gwendolyn. Databases for the Study of Afro-Louisiana History and Genealogy, 1699–1860: Computerized Information from Original Manuscript Sources. Baton Rouge, LA: Louisiana State University Press. 1999.

Midlo Hall, Gwendolyn. *Social Control in Slave Plantation Societies: A Comparison of St. Dominque and Cuba.* 1972.

Murphy, Joseph M. *Santería: An African Religion in America.* 1988.

Ortiz, Fernando. *Cuban Counterpoint, Tobacco and Sugar.* Trans. Harriet De Onís. 1940. Repr. 1970.

Ortiz, Fernando. *Los Negros Brujos.* 1906. Repr. 1973.

Pérez y Mena, Andrés I. "Cuban Santería, Haitian Vodun, Puerto Rican Spiritualism: A Multicultural Inquiry into Syncretism." *Journal for the Scientific Study of Religion.* 37 (1998).

Pérez y Mena, Andrés I. "Religious Syncretism." In *The Latino Encyclopedia.* 1996.

Pérez y Mena, Andrés I. *Speaking with the Dead: Development of Afro-Latin Religion Among Puerto Ricans in the United States.* 1991.

Andrés I. Pérez y Mena

Santos

Santos is the Spanish name for sacred images of the Catholic saints, the Virgin Mary, the Magi, Christ, and other religious characters and episodes from the Bible and Catholic folklore. These images are usually carved in wood and then decorated with paint, metal, and precious stones. They are commonly found in Catholic churches and household altars throughout Spain, Latin America, and Latino communities in the United States. *Santos* were extremely popular in Puerto Rico, especially in rural areas with limited access to priests and churches. This entry will focus primarily on the folk art of carving saints (*santería*) on that island.

Hand-made images of saints played a key role in Catholic devotions in Puerto Rico until the middle of the twentieth century, when they were displaced by industrialization, urbanization, and migration. In addition, Protestant missionary efforts since the U.S. invasion of 1898 sought to eradicate the cult of the saints from Puerto Rico. Most traditional *santos* are now held in private collections, galleries, and museums, and have become objects of commercial consumption and speculation, especially by art collectors and tourists.

The earliest surviving examples of *santos* were probably brought from Spain and other European countries, such as Italy and France, during the sixteenth century. These painted sculptures followed closely the academic models of the time with regard to materials, techniques, scale, composition, and color. The first known Puerto Rican *santos* imitated the baroque style prevalent in Spain at the end of the eighteenth century. Like their Spanish prototypes, these images sought to reproduce as realistically as possible the human body, the landscape, and other aspects of the physical environment. The oldest Puerto Rican *santos* did not differ greatly from the folk religious sculpture of Spain, Mexico, Guatemala, and Santo Domingo during the Spanish colonial period.

Roughly between 1750 and 1898, Puerto Rican *santería* developed a distinctive style. The images gradually lost their natural appearance, while their posture adopted a frontal, rigid stance, either sitting or standing. Their anatomical proportions were deliberately deformed to stress their supernatural character. Traditional costumes were often abandoned; facial expressions were softened; and new characters and scenes were portrayed. Puerto Rican *santeros* increasingly represented local religious traditions such as the Miracle of the Virgin of Hormigueros, the Three Kings and the Three Maries, and the Lonely Soul. By far the most popular figure during the colonial period was the Virgin of Monserrate, transplanted from Catalonia but transformed into a black or mulatto woman. Other favorite subjects were the Three Kings, the various apparitions of the Virgin (especially at Candlemas and Bethlehem), Saint Anthony of Padua, the Nativity, and the Crucifixion.

The nineteenth century witnessed a veritable explosion of Puerto Rican santos to satisfy a growing demand for objects of worship, particularly in the most isolated peasant areas. The art of sculpting saints was especially popular in the inner highlands, along the central mountain range. There, a subsistence farming population of mixed Spanish, African, and indigenous origins developed a folk version of Catholicism centered on the cult of the saints in domestic shrines. Hence *santos* tended to be small—typically fewer than twelve inches high—because they had to fit within a humble niche.

Today most of the *santeros* remain anonymous, although several have become well-known artisans. The majority still learn their craft informally, usually by becoming apprentices to older family members, friends, or neighbors. Formerly, *santeros* used simple tools and indigenous woods (such as cedar and mahogany) to carve their images; they are now manufactured in a wide array of materials. Since the 1950s the Institute of Puerto Rican Culture has promoted the carving of saints through folk art festivals and museum exhibits. *Santos* represent a rich cultural patrimony, primarily of Hispanic Catholic origin, but mixed with African and indigenous traditions. As such, they have become symbols of Puerto Rico's national identity, as well as the most significant religious icons for Puerto Ricans and other Latino groups in the United States.

See also MARY; SAINTHOOD; SANTERÍA; ROMAN CATHOLICISM; VIRGIN OF GUADALUPE.

BIBLIOGRAPHY

Curbelo de Díaz, Irene. *El arte de los santeros puertorriqueños* (The art of the Puerto Rican santeros). 1986.

Lange, Yvonne. "The Household Wooden Saints of Puerto Rico." Ph.D. diss., University of Pennsylvania. 1975.

Quintero Rivera, Angel G., ed. *Vírgenes, magos y escapularios: imaginería, etnicidad y religiosidad popular en Puerto Rico (Virgins, Magis, and Scapulars: Imagery, Ethnicity, and Popular Religiousity in Puerto Rico).* 1998.

Tió, Teresa. *Esencia y presencia: artes de nuestra tradició* (Essence and Presence: Arts from Our Tradition). 1993.

Tsang, Jia-sun. "A Closer Look: *Santos* from Puerto Rico." Electronic document. http://www.si.edu/scmre/santos_e.html. July 1998.

Vidal, Teodoro. *Santeros puertorriqueños. (Puerto Rican Santeros).* 1979.

Jorge Duany

Satanic Bible

Continuously in print since its initial publication in 1969, *The Satanic Bible* by Anton Szandor LaVey (1930–1997) is the foundational text for the contemporary Satanic movement. Written in a compelling, aphoristic style, *The Satanic Bible* offers a hedonistic alternative to mainstream Christianity, emphasizing indulgence over abstinence, rational self-interest over altruistic sacrifice, and activity in this world over dreams of a future existence. In LaVey's formulation, Satan is not a supernatural being but a human principle, and Satanism a system of self-actualization based on positive thinking, goal-oriented action, and the elimination of sexual guilt and other impediments to personal gratification. Though contemptuous of conventional morality, Satanism is not wholly antinomian. LaVey instructs his readers to "do unto others as they do unto you," to respect the rights of others, and to protect children and animals. *The Satanic Bible* sets forth the precepts of Satanism and includes instructions for rituals and invocations. Other works by LaVey include *The Compleat Witch* (1971; reissued in 1989 as *The Satanic Witch*), a training manual in erotic manipulation; *The Satanic Rituals* (1972), a collection of rites designed "to elevate the self"; and two collections of essays and epigrams. There are several organizations devoted to Satanism, most notably the Church of Satan, which LaVey founded in 1966. But the relatively small memberships of these groups belies the much wider impact *The Satanic Bible* has had as inspiration for a number of youth subcultures.

See also DEVILS, DEMONS, AND SPIRITS; LAVEY, ANTON SZANDOR; NEOPAGANISM; SATANISTS.

BIBLIOGRAPHY

Barton, Blanche. *The Secret Life of a Satanist: The Authorized Biography of Anton LaVey.* 1990.

LaVey, Anton Szandor. *The Compleat Witch.* 1971. Reissued as *The Satanic Witch.* 1989.

LaVey, Anton Szandor. *The Devil's Notebook.* 1992.

LaVey, Anton Szandor. *Satan Speaks!* 1998.

LaVey, Anton Szandor. *The Satanic Bible.* 1969.

LaVey, Anton Szandor. *The Satanic Rituals.* 1972.

Bradford Verter

Satanists

There are three categories of Satanism—(1) theological depictions of Satan in Christianity; (2) countercultural satanic churches; and (3) a 1980s outbreak of satanic cult fear in North America and Europe. The focus here is on the second category, specifically the Church of Satan and the Temple of Set, the two most significant satanic churches that emerged out of the 1960s countercultural movements. Most of the other satanic churches (Universal Church of Man, Our Lady of Endor Coven, Satanic Orthodox Church of Nethilum Rite, Kerk du Satan–Magistralis Grotto and Walpurga Abbey, Church of Satanic Brotherhood, Order of the Black Ram and the Shrine of the Little Mother, and the Temple of Nepthys) were small, ephemeral groups that represented schismatic breakaways from or innovations on the Church of Satan. The various satanic churches flourished primarily during the 1970s; their combined membership never amounted to more than a few thousand, and most now count only a few hundred members. In addition, there is a long-standing Christian tradition of juxtaposing Satanism to Christian belief and practice. The history of identifying and searching out Satan-worshipers traces most directly to the sixteenth-century witch hunts. The *Malleus Maleficarum* (ca. 1486) and *Compendium Maleficarum* (ca. 1620) served as the Christian manuals for depicting and combating Satanism. Conservative Christianity has continued to postulate the active, contemporary presence of Satan and to use Satanism to bolster Christian solidarity. Finally, during the 1980s a wave of satanic subversion fear swept North America and Europe, centering around claims of the existence of a massive, international, underground, hierarchically organized satanic network. Satanists putatively were involved in a range of nefarious activity; the most horrific allegations involved the abduction of children, child abuse, commercial production of child pornography, sexual abuse and incest, and ritualistic sacrifices of young children. At the height of the subversion episode ritual abuse victims were estimated at fifty thousand annually, and there were numerous sensational ritual abuse prosecutions. The subversion episode dissipated rapidly as professional associations challenged the validity of repressed-memory evidence offered by claimants, no convincing physical evidence was produced to support allegations, court convictions were reversed, and American and European governmental investigations concluded that conspiracy claims were without foundation. There are no meaningful connections among the three types of Satanism.

Church of Satan

The Church of Satan was founded by Anton Szandor LaVey (1930–1997). The colorful accounts of LaVey's early life (working as a lion tamer, appearing in *Rosemary's Baby,* having an affair with Marilyn Monroe) are now disputed. After attending City College in San Francisco during the 1950s, his lifelong interest in the occult surfaced publicly during the 1960s. On April 30, 1966, LaVey pronounced himself the black pope. With filmmaker Kenneth Anger, LaVey organized both the Magic Circle, gatherings to discuss occult phenomena, and a topless nightclub act called the "Witches' Sabbath," which promoted his beliefs. LaVey became a media celebrity as a product of the eccentric persona he cultivated (e.g., driving a coroner's van, painting the walls of his home black, acquiring exotic pets, and using a nude woman as an altar in rituals) and the string of Hollywood stars who associated with his church. The church prospered during the 1960s, perhaps reaching a peak membership of a few thousand, but with the decline of the 1960s counterculture suffered a membership decline from which it never recovered. LaVey then went into seclusion until the early 1990s, when he resurfaced briefly before his death in 1997. Prior to his death, one of his daughters renounced him and joined the rival Temple of Set.

The Church of Satan is avowedly hedonistic, anti-establishment, elitist, and individualistic. Satan is conceived as a force of nature, a reservoir of power within each being that permits humans to be their own gods. In the *Satanic Bible* (1969) LaVey propounds indulgence and gratification over abstinence; vital existence, not spiritual pipe dreams; undefiled wisdom as opposed to hypocritical self-deceit; deserved rather than wasted love; and responsibility only to the responsible. The countercultural orientation is evident in the church's emphasis on free sexual expression and open contempt for Christianity; its elitism is reflected in members' self-designation as the ultimate underground alternative and the Alien Elite. The individualistic stance is reflected in the beliefs that human life is sacred and that individuals are their own redeemers. The church is organized into local units referred to as grottoes; in the mid-1970s grottoes could be found in major cities across the country. Sex magic, healing, and destruction are the major rituals, with the most important holiday being each Satanist's birthday. The church is currently administered by the Council of Nine.

Temple of Set

The Temple of Set was founded by Michael Aquino in 1975. Aquino, at the time an army lieutenant, attended a LaVey lecture in 1969, soon thereafter joined the church, was ordained as a priest in 1971, and quickly rose to a position of leadership just below LaVey. Within a few years the relationship between LaVey and Aquino deteriorated as Aquino charged LaVey with selling priesthoods. Aquino claims to have invoked Set in a ritual on June 21, 1975, during which Set ordained him as the successor to LaVey and the Church of Satan. The conversation is recorded in Aquino's *The Book of Coming Forth by Night* (1985).

Temple of Set philosophy proclaims that the universe is a nonconscious environment possessed of mechanical consistency. In contrast to the universe and occasionally violating its laws is Set (the Egyptian god of night), a metaphysical being formerly known under the Hebrew misnomer "Satan." Over the period of a millennium, Set has altered the genetic makeup of humans to create a species possessing an enhanced, nonnatural intelligence. The objective of the Temple of Set is to realize that potential through individual empowerment. This means rejecting cultural constraints and enhancing achievement of personally defined goals, developing the discipline requisite to attain those goals, and asserting individual will. The Temple of Set rejects traditional congregational organization in favor of structure involving local chapters called pylons. Pylons are equalitarian, cooperative networks of practicing initiates. The total membership of the pylons has never been more than a few hundred. The Temple of Set was briefly swept up in the 1980s satanic subversion episode when Aquino was accused of sexual abuse of children. Aquino denied the allegations, and no charges were filed following a police investigation.

See also LaVey, Anton Szandor; Satanic Bible.

Bibliography

Bromley, David, and Susan Ainsely. "Satanism and Satanic Churches: The Contemporary Incarnations." In *America's Alternative Religions,* edited by Timothy Miller. 1995.
Richardson, James, Joel Best, and David Bromley, eds. *The Satanism Scare.* 1991.

David G. Bromley

Schechter, Solomon

(1847–1915), Jewish scholar.

Solomon Schechter was born in Focsani, Romania, on December 7, 1847. His father was a Habad Hasid. Solomon left Romania for Lemberg, Austria, where he studied in a rabbinical school with Joseph Nathanson. Schechter was twenty-four when he decided to study for a degree at the rabbinical school in Vienna and earned his living as a private tutor.

He felt somewhat out of place as a pious Hasidic Jew in fashionable Vienna. While he changed his Hasidic garb for a tailcoat, a stiff shirt, and trousers, he still wore his beard. From 1875 to 1879 he devoted himself to rabbinical studies at the Jewish Seminary in Vienna and at the University of Vienna and from there he went to the Berlin, where he continued his studies with such scholars as Israel Lewy. At the University of Berlin he took courses in philosophy and history. He liked his studies but did not like the anti-Semitism of Germany.

In 1882 Claude Goldsmid Montefiore, invited him to be his tutor in rabbinics in London. Through Claude Montefiore he met Joseph Jacobs, an expert on Jewish folklore; and Israel Zangwill, editor of a Jewish weekly. Schechter, Jacobs, and Zangwill had a common interest in keeping Jewish culture and religion alive.

Schechter met Mathilde Roth, they fell in love, and in 1887 were married. He taught, and spent much time at the British Museum and at the Oxford library, where he found an obscure manuscript of *Pirkeh Aboth de Rabbi Nathan* (Teachings of the Fathers of Rabbi Nathan). After many months of work he published another edition of the *Pirkeh Aboth* and dedicated it to Claude Montefiore. Schechter's reputation was established, and two years later his essay on Leopold Zunz (a Jewish scholar in Germany) won Schechter the New York Jewish Ministers' Association prize.

In August 1888 Ruth, their first child, was born. Two years later Frank was born just as Schechter was appointed to teach rabbinics at the University of Cambridge. In 1890 he became a lecturer in Talmud, and in 1899 he became professor of Hebrew at University College, London.

Fragments of ancient Hebrew documents found in Cairo, Egypt, inspired Schechter to find the source of those documents. One was part of the Jerusalem Talmud, and the other turned out to be part of a book written by Ben Sira titled *Ecclesiasticus,* written in the second century B.C.E.

Two of his colleagues, Dr. Charles Taylor, master of St. John's College at Cambridge, and Donald MacAlister, a Scottish professor, encouraged Schechter to go to Cairo. Oxford sponsored his research trip.

The grand rabbi of Cairo showed him where the Genizah (repository for old books and manuscripts) of the ancient synagogue could be found. Schechter uncovered thousands of documents scattered amid dust and sand. He persuaded the rabbi that the documents should be taken to London, where they could be more thoroughly studied. Schechter had gathered more than a hundred thousand document fragments.

Before returning to London, Schechter traveled to the Holy Land to visit with his brother at Zichron Yaakov. Wherever Schechter walked in the land of Israel he felt that he was walking on holy ground.

Schechter brought back the Genizah manuscripts and the ancient Ark of Cairo's Old Synagogue. Schechter received an honorary degree from Cambridge University, the first ever awarded to a Jew by that university.

In 1899 Schechter and Taylor published *The Wisdom of Ben Sira.*

In 1901 Schechter accepted the presidency of the faculty of the fledgling Jewish Theological Seminary in New York City. He was to pioneer training rabbis in Conservative Judaism. While he loved his work at Cambridge and the Genizah discoveries, he found it difficult to raise his children there according to the Jewish tradition. In the spring of 1902 he arrived in New York and began to organize the Jewish Theological Seminary into an important center of Jewish learning. His impact on Jewish education in the United States was considerable. He brought such famous Jewish scholars as Louis Ginzberg, Talmudist; Alexander Marx, historian; Israel Friedlander, Bible scholar and historian; and Israel Davidson, a specialist in Jewish medieval literature, to the Jewish Theological Seminary.

He was a traditionalist, but was willing to accept change if it was introduced deliberately rather than arbitrarily. As a religious Zionist he believed that Zionism could restore "Jewish nationality in the Promised Land, accompanied by a renewal of Jewish life."

Schechter worked to improve the quality of teaching and the level of the teachers who would instruct a new generation of Jews to be proud rather than embarrassed that they were of the Jewish faith. He had seen how prosperous English Jews had lost interest in their religion and sought to counter this trend when he came to the United States. He believed that children could receive a good Jewish education only if their schools were well run. He instituted training courses for teachers and appointed Dr. Mordechai Kaplan, one of the seminary's lecturers, to head the Jewish Theological Seminary.

On the eve of the Sabbath, November 20, 1915, he died of a heart attack. He had chosen the burning bush as the seminary's symbol. For Schechter the Eternal Light of the Torah would forever keep Judaism and the Jewish people alive, in the United States and throughout the world. As a result of the thirteen years he served as president of the Jewish Theological Seminary, the foundation was laid for American Judaism as a vital area of scholarly concern.

See also ANTI-SEMITISM; HASIDIM; JEWISH IDENTITY; JEWISH OBSERVANCE; JUDAISM; RABBINATE; RELIGIOUS STUDIES; ZIONISM.

BIBLIOGRAPHY

Davis, Moshe. *The Emergence of Conservative Judaism* (1963).

De Mattos, Norman. *Solomon Schechter: A Biography* (1948).

Eisenberg, Azriel Louis. *Fill a Blank Page: A Biography of Solomon Schechter* (1965).

Schechter, Solomon. *Some Aspects of Rabbinic Theology.* 1909.

Schechter, Solomon. *Studies in Judaism.* 1896.

Herbert Druks

School Prayer.

See Prayer in School.

Schuller, Robert Harold

(1926–), minister, televangelist.

An ordained minister of the Reformed Church in America, Robert Schuller has been an influential megachurch pastor, a popular televangelist, and a prominent proponent of "possibility thinking."

Nurtured by a Dutch Calvinist family in northwestern Iowa, Schuller attended Hope College and Western Theological Seminary, denominational schools located in Holland, Michigan. During his seminary years he met and married Arvella DeHaan who, along with their five children, would play a significant role in the development of his ministry. Following a five-year pastorate near Chicago, in 1955 Schuller moved to Orange County, California, where he organized the Garden Grove Community Church (Reformed Church in America). Stymied in his attempts to find a traditional worship center in burgeoning post–World War II California, Schuller boldly initiated holding Sunday services in the open air from the top of a refreshment stand at the Orange Drive-in Theater. Demonstrating marketing savvy, he took out newspaper ads with a

Rev. Robert Schuller delivering a candlelight Christmas Eve service from the pulpit at this Crystal Cathedral in Garden Grove, California, on December 24, 1997. (Credit: AP/Wide World Photos.)

clever invitation: "Come as you are, in the family car." The congregation outgrew two buildings before the architect Philip Johnson was commissioned to design a twenty-million-dollar, three-thousand-seat, glass and steel sanctuary. Completed in 1980, this magnificent worship center, named the Crystal Cathedral of the Reformed Church in America, has become a popular tourist attraction.

A visionary leader, Schuller has always regarded his congregation as an experiment in church growth. With the establishment of the Robert H. Schuller Institute for Successful Church Leadership in 1969, he began to share the secrets of his success. During the last three decades of the twentieth century, thousands of church leaders, including many American mega-church pastors, have been influenced by this type of institute, which mixes how-to formulas and practical principles with a heavy dose of success stories. In an effort to help preachers hone their speaking styles, in 1992 Schuller opened the Fuqua International School of Christian Communications.

In 1970 Schuller introduced the *Hour of Power,* one of the most popular and long-standing television ministries produced in America. Featuring upbeat mainstream Protestant music, interviews with famous guests, and Schuller's dynamic messages, the *Hour of Power* has gradually gained millions of international viewers, with broadcasts carried to countries such as Korea, Japan, and Russia.

Schuller has authored more than thirty books, most of which promote "possibility thinking," the ideological drive wheel of his ministry. Closely related to the "positive thinking" of Norman Vincent Peale, a friend and mentor who served Marble Collegiate Church (Reformed Church in America) in New York City, Schuller's message is an amalgam of therapeutic psychology, mind conditioning, New Thought, and positive biblical texts. While "possibility thinking" provides practical prescriptions for health, wealth, and happiness, this popular message is undergirded by what Schuller has called the theology of self-esteem. In *Self-Esteem: The New Reformation* (1982), Schuller argues that, in an increasingly secularized culture, a theocentric message fails to gain a hearing from the unchurched. Schuller offers an anthropocentric approach that begins with the human condition and human needs. Suggesting that the essential human problem is not arrogance or pride but lack of self-esteem, Schuller proposes that the "new reformation" is one that restores human dignity and self-worth. While his attempt to reconstruct reformed theology generally has been rejected or neglected by established theologians from both ends of the theological spectrum, it has influenced Christian psychologists and missiologists.

Robert H. Schuller has had an enormous impact upon popular American religion since 1960. His *Hour of Power,* church leadership institutes, and popular motivational books have given him broad visibility. Moreover, his positive message of individual pluck, persistence, and positive thinking has struck a rich and abiding strain of popular American religion.

See also MEGACHURCH; NEW THOUGHT; PEALE, NORMAN VINCENT; TELEVANGELISM.

BIBLIOGRAPHY

Nason, Michael, and Donald Nason. *Robert Schuller: The Inside Story.* 1985.

Schuller, Robert H. *Move Ahead with Possibility Thinking.* 1967.

Schuller, Robert H. *Self-Esteem: The New Reformation.* 1982.

Schuller, Robert H. *Turning Hurts into Halos and Scars into Stars.* 1999.

Voskuil, Dennis N. *Mountains into Goldmines: Robert Schuller and the Gospel of Success.* 1983.

Dennis N. Voskuil

Science of Creative Intelligence.

See Transcendental Meditation.

Scientology, Church of

The Church of Scientology is a distinctly American religious movement that emerged in the second half of the twentieth century, and it is one of the few such movements that has sustained organizational stability and growth. By the 1990s the church had branches in more than seventy countries and claimed a membership of several million based on participation in various church-sponsored programs. The church is sometimes described as New Age, given its individualistic, human potential orientation, and as quasi-religious, given its blending of religion and therapy. In comparison to other such movements, Scientology is tightly, hierarchically organized and has self-consciously chosen a religious identity.

L. Ron Hubbard: Founder of Scientology

The Church of Scientology was founded by Lafayette Ronald Hubbard. There are conflicting accounts of Hubbard's life. These range from Scientology's photographic biography *L. Ron Hubbard Images of a Lifetime: A Photographic Biography* (1996), to highly critical accounts such as Russell Miller's *The Bare-Faced Messiah* (1988). Hubbard was born in Tilden, Nebraska, in

L. Ron Hubbard, the founder of Dianetics and the Church of Scientology. (Credit: Fotos International/ Archive Photos.)

1911. Many themes that became relevant to Scientology's development and Hubbard's leadership style— sailing and aviation; travel and exploration; workings of the human mind; fiction and nonfiction writing— can be traced to activities and interests he developed during his teenage and young adult years. Through the 1930s he devoted himself to writing and publishing different genres of fiction, most notably science fiction. During World War II he was commissioned as a naval lieutenant and saw combat in the Pacific. Toward the end of the war, while he was hospitalized, he began ruminating on the nature of the human mind, laying the groundwork for his subsequent development of Dianetics.

In 1950 *Dianetics: The Modern Science of Mental Health* was published, and Dianetics quickly became a popular alternative to traditional therapy. Shortly thereafter Hubbard formed the Hubbard Dianetic Research Foundation to offer classes and train practitioners. As Dianetics developed, practitioners reported puzzling findings, incidents, and details from their previous lives. These reports led Hubbard to postulate the existence of an immortal essence for each individual that existed across lifetimes. These immaterial, immortal spiritual entities possessing virtually infinite powers he called thetans. The discovery of thetans led to the emergence of Scientology, with a spiritual rather than simply a therapeutic orientation. Hubbard spent the next two decades developing successively higher levels of Scientology thought and practice.

Hubbard served as administrative and spiritual leader of Scientology until 1966, when he resigned his organizational positions to pursue further research. He formed the Sea Organization, a church unit staffed by advanced members, that was located on oceangoing ships until in 1975 when it was moved to a land base in Florida. Hubbard continued to relinquish organizational control over Scientology; by 1980 he withdrew from public life and remained secluded until his death in 1986. Church leaders announced that Hubbard's body had become an impediment to his work and that he was continuing research on another planet.

Dianetics and Scientology Technology

According to Hubbard, the basic human objective is survival, and the mind functions to solve survival-related problems. The structure of the mind is triadic, composed of the somatic, reactive, and analytical minds. The somatic mind regulates the basic mechanisms that sustain an organism's life. The reactive mind operates on a nonvolitional basis but exerts influence over individual thought and action. The analytical mind is the conscious, analytic, problem-solving component. During periods of trauma, the analytic mind shuts down and the reactive mind assumes control, forming detailed memory records of experiences. Hubbard named these records engrams. The engrams in the reactive mind cause emotional and irrational responses to anything that produces an association with the original experiences. Engrams undermine the capacity for individuals to engage in survival-promoting behavior, to achieve personal development, and to reflect humanity's essential goodness. Instead, individuals engage in behavior that is individually and socially destructive. The goal of Dianetics therapy involves a process termed auditing, which eliminates engrams by identifying, recalling, and extinguishing traumatic experiences. When this process is complete an individual is pronounced "Clear." Scientology continues the auditing process to eliminate engrams accumulated from past lives so that individuals can fully express their essential nature.

The drive to survive and express individual essence occurs across a number of what Hubbard terms "dynamics." The eight dynamics constitute an ascending hierarchy of needs for: (1) individual survival, (2) sexual reproduction and family survival, (3) group and nation survival, (4) species survival, (5) survival of all life forms, (6) survival by the physical universe, (7) survival by the individual as a spiritual entity, and (8) survival through infinity/oneness. The highest level of survival therefore involves a spiritual entity uniting with the universe. Individuals who succeed in eliminating all accumulated trauma and achieving full self-expression are defined as operating thetans.

Organization

The organization of Scientology is threefold. One set of groups organizes the practice of Scientology and the training of practitioners. Local units consist of hundreds of missions and churches, which operate as licensed franchises offering introductory levels of

The headquarters of the Church of Scientology in Los Angeles, California. (Credit: Fotos International/ Archive Photos.)

Scientological training on a fee-for-service basis. Above the church/mission level are a number of types of organizations: (1) Saint Hill Organizations, which function as colleges for auditors and ministers; (2) a variety of advanced training units, which provide the highest levels of Scientology technology; (3) the Sea Organization, which parallels traditional monastic orders and staffs advanced and management organizations; (4) the Religious Technology Center, which oversees the quality of Scientology training and licenses local churches; (5) the Church of Scientology Spiritual Technology Organization, which preserves Hubbard's writings; (6) Celebrity Centers, which assist artists in developing artistic and communication skills; (7) the International Association of Scientologists, which disseminates information on religious and civil rights to members; and (8) the Church of Scientology International, which functions as the umbrella unit for all Scientology churches and organizations.

Social betterment groups apply Hubbard's technologies in the larger society. These include (1) Narconon and Criminon, which provide drug education and rehabilitation services to drug users and criminals; (2) Applied Scholastics, which employs Hubbard's educational technology to teach students how to learn and eliminate barriers to effective study; (3) The Way to Happiness Foundation, which disseminates Scientology's moral code; and (4) the Association for Better Living and Education, which coordinates and publicizes the various betterment programs.

Social reform organizations include (1) the Citizens' Commission on Human Rights, which primarily targets abusive practices in psychiatry; (2) the National Commission on Law Enforcement and Social Justice, which combats abuses by national and international policing agencies; and (3) the World Institute of Scientology Enterprises, which offers training in a variety of business skills.

Controversy

Scientology has been embroiled in controversy since its inception. Both the American Psychiatric Association and the American Medical Association dismissed *Dianetics* soon after its publication. The U.S. Food and Drug Administration launched an investigation of possible violations of unlicensed medical practice. The transition from Dianetics to Scientology was followed by an Internal Revenue Service challenge to Scientology's status as a church. The tax-exempt status of the church was revoked and was not reinstated until 1993. For its part, Scientology has always adopted a militant posture toward critics; during its early history the church engaged in covert campaigns to intimi-

date, discredit, and neutralize opponents. Most notable was the infiltration of government agencies and the theft of documents, which resulted in the imprisonment of several high-level church leaders. The church has renounced its former tactics and dismissed leaders responsible for them, but it continues to acknowledge use of all possible legal means to combat opponents. The church remains the target of governmental control efforts, particularly in Europe.

See also HUMAN POTENTIAL MOVEMENT; NEW AGE SPIRITUALITY; NEW RELIGIOUS MOVEMENTS; PSYCHOTHERAPY.

BIBLIOGRAPHY

Bromley, David, and Mitchell Bracey. "Religion as Therapy, Therapy as Religion: The Church of Scientology as a Quasi-Religious Therapy." In *Sects, Cults, and Spiritual Communities: A Sociological Analysis,* edited by William Zellner and Marc Petrowsky. 1998.

Church of Scientology. *The Scientology Handbook.* 1994.

Church of Scientology. *Scientology: Theology and Practice of a Contemporary Religion.* 1992.

Wallis, Roy. *The Road to Total Freedom.* 1977.

David G. Bromley

Séance

The séance is the central ritual in Spiritualism, a religious movement that emerged in mid-nineteenth-century America. Spiritualism is based on the belief that the spirits of the dead can be contacted in séances through individuals called mediums, that spiritual enlightenment and harmony with the universe can be gained from this experience, and that séance phenomena constitute scientific proof of human immortality.

The early séance was typically held in a quiet and dimly lit room in the home of the medium. There, the medium entered a trance, fell under the control of spirits, and passed messages to the participants, usually a dozen or so in number. Messages in the earliest gatherings came by means of an alphabetic code, but mediumistic speaking and writing quickly became the norm. Messages ranged in purpose from personal consolation to spiritual and moral elevation, and created a religious experience both individual and communal. The religious function of the séance was underscored by the development of regularly meeting groups and orders of ritual, including prayer and the singing of hymns. These features continued to characterize the séance as it became part of the Sunday

A group of people stand in a circle around a table during a séance in Cassadaga, Florida, in September 1990. (Credit: © Dilip Mehta/Contact Press Images/PNI.)

services established by Spiritualists seeking to institutionalize the religion during the late nineteenth and twentieth centuries.

Attendance at séances cut across lines of race and class, but they were especially popular in the 1850s, in the Northeast and the Midwest, and among white middle-class theologically liberal Protestants. The appeal of the séance lay in its ability to address the profound spiritual unease many Americans experienced as a result of theological, social, and cultural change. It allowed believers dissatisfied with the abstract deity of liberal Protestantism to establish contact with a plane of being at once spiritual and human. It assuaged concerns that the increasing cultural authority of science would diminish the importance of things spiritual. Its tranquil domestic setting provided believers with a spatial and a spiritual counterpoint to the increasingly commercial, competitive, and urban society taking shape around them. It provided women with empowerment and authority in a culture that exalted their spiritual qualities while affording them few opportunities for religious leadership. The séance also, of course, eased the grief caused by the common occurrence of premature death in Victorian America, while the more sensational "spirit manifestations" entertained an American public continually hungry for novelty.

The séance aroused hostile as well as favorable attention, in part because orthodox theologians suspected occult activity and in part because mediums were suspected of fraud. Debunking appeared almost at the outset, culminated in a series of damaging exposures during the 1870s, and continues to the pres-

ent. It has often operated to undermine the religious appeal of the séance.

Yet the séance continues to provide thousands of Americans with religious fulfillment. Most obviously, it persists as the central and defining element of Spiritualist religious worship. It was also incorporated by Universal Hagar's Spiritual Church, a Spiritualist-influenced African-American organization that was established in Detroit in 1923 and that maintains a significant membership in several eastern and midwestern cities. The closely related practice of spirit "channeling" has become an important element of the contemporary New Age movement. The continuing place of the séance in American religious life suggests the enduring quest for spiritual illumination from a higher spiritual world.

See also AFTERLIFE; ASTRAL PLANES; CHANNELING; ENLIGHTENMENT; MUSIC; NEW AGE SPIRITUALITY; PRAYER; RELIGIOUS EXPERIENCE; RITUAL; SPIRIT; SPIRITUALISM.

BIBLIOGRAPHY

Baer, Hans. *The Black Spiritual Movement: A Religious Response to Racism.* 1984.

Braude, Ann. *Radical Spirits: Spiritualism and Women's Rights in Nineteenth-Century America.* 1989.

Carroll, Bret E. *Spiritualism in Antebellum America.* 1997.

Moore, R. Laurence. *In Search of White Crows: Spiritualism, Parapsychology, and American Culture.* 1977.

Bret E. Carroll

Second Coming

The belief that Jesus Christ will return to Earth at the end of time has long been a fundamental Christian doctrine. As the Apostles Creed, avowed by millions of Christians each Sunday, puts it: "He will come again to judge the living and the dead." For many believers, the Second Coming is associated with the Millennium, the thousand-year reign of justice and peace foretold in Revelation 20–21.

Specific interpretations of the Second Coming have varied widely, however, and remain a source of disagreement among Christians in contemporary America. In Catholic doctrine, the manner of Christ's return is generally viewed as a mystery, known only to God. In the Protestant tradition, one important strand of belief, generally designated as postmillennialism, holds that the Second Coming will follow a long cycle of gradual human betterment. Jonathan Edwards, amid the revival fervor of the 1740s, foresaw

Two Asian men hold placards on a New York City street in 1998, announcing the second coming of Jesus and the end of human history, to take place in 1999. (Credit: © Robert Brenner/Photo Edit/ PNI.)

an outpouring of divine grace through prayer circles, evangelism, missionary activity, and so forth. By the late nineteenth century, a somewhat secularized post-millennial vision focused on ameliorating the social problems associated with industrialization such as slums, child labor, and exploitive working conditions. Theologians such as Washington Gladden and Walter Rauschenbusch elaborated the theological underpinnings of such reform effort. President Woodrow Wilson during World War I incorporated this hopeful tradition of millennialist thought in his soaring portrayal of America's mission to spread peace and democracy worldwide.

While becoming less literalistic theologically, a postmillennialist vision suffused twentieth-century American life, especially in the liberal Protestant denominations, inspiring campaigns against child labor

and slum housing in the Progressive era; peace movements in the 1920s and 1930s; and civil rights activism in the 1950s and 1960s. Martin Luther King, Jr.'s, 1963 "I Have a Dream" speech at the Lincoln Memorial, saturated in biblical imagery, offered millennialist images of an America free of the stain of racism.

In contrast to postmillennialism, however, a very different view of the Second Coming, premillennialism, also exerts vast influence in contemporary America. According to this view, human history is not progressing inevitably toward righteousness and justice but rather is becoming increasingly wicked and conflict-ridden—a process that will soon culminate in a horrendous epoch when satanic forces will seem all-powerful. But just as conditions become most desperate, Christ will return and vanquish the forces of evil.

As long ago as the 1830s, William Miller of upstate New York became convinced through his study of Scripture that Christ would return in about 1843 or 1844. Some of his followers pinpointed the date even more precisely. Thousands were swept up in the Millerite movement. The subsequent "Great Disappointment" discredited date-setting, but not premillennial speculation. The most fully elaborated formulation of this scenario for the Second Coming is premillennial dispensationalism, first taught by the British dissenter John Nelson Darby (1800–1882), a founder of the Plymouth Brethren, and popularized in America by the Rev. Cyrus Scofield and others.

Premillennial dispensationalism envisions a precise sequence of end-time events drawn from apocalyptic texts in the books of Daniel, Ezekiel, Mark, II Thessalonians, and Revelation. This sequence begins with the "Last Days"—usually assumed to be the present age—when wickedness will increase and other evidences (including the restoration of the Jews to Israel) signal that the end is near. Next will come the Rapture, when all true believers will join Christ in the air, followed by a horrendous seven-year period, the Great Tribulation, when a demonic figure, the Antichrist, will rule the world, forcing everyone to bear the dread "Mark of the Beast," the number 666 (Revelation 13:16–18). As the seven years end, the armies of the earth gather at Megiddo in Israel (hence the Battle of Armageddon). At this cataclysmic moment, Christ returns with his saints, destroys Antichrist and his armies, and establishes his millennial kingdom in Jerusalem. After a final uprising by the Antichrist comes the Last Judgment, when every person who has ever lived will be consigned to heaven or to hell. With this final drama, human history draws to a close.

Premillennial dispensationalism remains profoundly influential in contemporary America, promulgated by evangelical and pentecostal churches, televangelists, paperbacks, videocassettes, and even Internet web sites. In a 1996 poll, 42 percent of Americans agreed with this statement: "The world will end in a battle in Armageddon between Jesus and the Antichrist." Post–World War II popularizers demonstrated great skill in weaving current events—from nuclear war and the Communist threat to the computer, abortion, pornography, the global economy, environmental hazards, and Islamic fundamentalism—into their scenario of Last Days events that herald the long-awaited Second Coming.

See also ADVENTISM; APOCALYPSE; DISPENSATIONALISM; ESCHATOLOGY; EVIL; HEAVEN; HELL; PREMILLENNIALISM.

BIBLIOGRAPHY

Boyer, Paul. *When Time Shall Be No More: Prophecy Belief in Modern American Culture.* 1992.

Rauschenbusch, Walter. *A Theology for the Social Gospel.* 1917.

Weber, Timothy P. *Living in the Shadow of the Second Coming: American Premillennialism, 1875–1925.* 1979.

Wojcik, Daniel. *The End of the World As We Know It: Faith, Fatalism, and Apocalypse in America.* 1997.

Paul Boyer

Second Vatican Council.

See Vatican II.

Secret Societies

Secret societies—associations whose existence, membership, purpose, or ritual is revealed only to their members—exist throughout the globe and among both traditional and industrialized peoples, ancient and modern. Most are open to men only, are at least partly religious in purpose, and involve more or less elaborate rituals of initiation. Most combine spiritual functions with social, cultural, psychological, political, or economic ones, suggesting the close interrelationship between religious and secular activities.

Indigenous American men commonly formed such societies, and they continue to exist in Indian cultures. Most have been devoted to the development and transmission of sacred knowledge, healing techniques, and religious rituals considered necessary for the well-being of the larger group. Initiates passed through a ritual ordeal and were required to maintain secrecy in the interest of preserving the efficacy of their practices.

White Europeans likewise founded secret societies devoted to spiritual wisdom—largely outside the Christian tradition—and were experiencing a proliferation of them when they colonized North America. Drawing on ancient gnosticism, Christianity, Renaissance mysticism, and Enlightenment rationalism, and stemming from medieval Catholic confraternities and guilds, secret societies were from the outset an important part of American religious and cultural life. The Rosicrucian order in particular was familiar to English intellectuals and German pietists of seventeenth-century America, but mysticism faded among literate colonists during the eighteenth century, and only in the twentieth was the Fraternitatis Rosae Crucis founded in Pennsylvania (1902) and the Ancient Mystical Order Rosae Crucis in California (1915). They continue to restrict their knowledge to members, but direct an active national advertising campaign to those seeking a spiritual alternative to mainline religions.

It was through Freemasonry, imported from England, that Rosicrucianism and other forms of religious mysticism found an institutional home in colonial and nineteenth-century America, though the rituals of Masons and most American secret societies that followed focused less on the sustained pursuit of higher wisdom than on the instillation of basic moral and ethical principles. First established in the colonies by 1730, Masonry blended ancient paganism, Christianity, Enlightenment deism, and political republicanism into an ideology that spread among the urban middle classes and greatly influenced the founders of the nation. The symbol of the all-seeing eye atop an Egyptian pyramid, incorporated into the national seal and appearing on the back of the one-dollar bill, is the most familiar of the order's substantial contributions to the iconography of revolutionary republicanism and of the "civil religion" that identifies the American political system with transcendent truth. A religiously infused patriotism continued to characterize American secret societies in the nineteenth and twentieth centuries. For example, the Improved Order of Red Men, established in 1834 as the first indigenous white American secret society and still operative, claims descent from such secret revolutionary era patriot societies as the Sons of Liberty and St. Tamina associations. Patriotic orders past and present couple republicanism with Judeo-Christian monotheism and blend biblical, pagan, mystical, and republican symbolism in their rituals.

Secret societies suffered declining membership during the 1820s and 1830s amid charges that they threatened republicanism, religious orthodoxy, and family devotion, but rebounded in the 1840s and entered a period of remarkable growth and proliferation sometimes called the "golden age of fraternity." Their new appeal lay in revised rituals that salved the religious, gender, and class anxieties of middle-class Protestant men of the Victorian period—particularly those of liberal denominations—by offering a spiritual alternative to what they considered "feminized" churches and sentimentalized liberal theology. The new rituals, often penned by liberal ministers, replaced the benign, deistic God of earlier fraternal ideology with an angry, patriarchal God reminiscent of the Puritans and older ceremonies, with elaborate initiation dramas emphasizing human sin, pain, death, and baptismal rebirth. The "masculinized" religion and male fellowship of the lodges counteracted the socially and spiritually alienating effects of an emerging modern urban and industrial society in which middle-class men were expected to be aggressively competitive and seek material success. By the end of the century, about 5.5 million of 19 million adult American males belonged to at least one of several hundred different secret fraternal orders. Continuing opposition from evangelicals and women led most orders to establish women's auxiliaries, which remain vital service organizations. As men of the early twentieth century increasingly found outlets for communal impulses in the corporate workplace and for tender emotion in family life, fraternal orders declined in popularity. The orders also truncated their rituals to allow for more of the social activity and benevolent work for which they are now best known. Their social status and membership remain greatly diminished, but contemporary challenges to male identity posed by technological change, economic shifts, corporate downsizing, and demographic shifts in the workplace have led some New Age masculinists to again promote the fraternal lodge a male spiritual space.

Secret societies also emerged to meet the religious needs of men other than white middle-class Protestants. Philadelphia tailors established the Knights of Labor in 1869, convinced that working-class resistance to the power of corporate capital required a secret labor organization and a Protestant theology of social justice. After 1879, however, the association jettisoned its secrecy and much of its mystical ritual. While such orders as the Masons and the Red Men welcomed ethnically defined chapters, men of many non-Protestant ethnic groups formed separate orders that both celebrated their religious and cultural distinctness and asserted their place in American life. The Knights of Columbus, an Irish-American society founded in 1882 by a Catholic priest, became the best known of these. It promotes knowledge of Catholicism in the interest of furthering interfaith understanding and has con-

tributed a distinctly Catholic element to American civil religion by successfully lobbying for the establishment of Columbus Day as a national holiday. African Americans have formed several societies, most notably the Prince Hall Masons, established in 1791 as a separate Masonic group. These middle-class organizations have derived their structures and rituals at least in part from West African sources, promoted a racially oriented Christian fellowship, and contributed to a spiritually infused campaign against racial oppression in the nineteenth and twentieth centuries.

Other Americans, meanwhile, formed secret societies to assert a white Protestant national identity against the increasing cultural and religious pluralism of American life. Rising Irish Catholic immigration in the late 1840s and 1850s stimulated the formation of several nativist and anti-Catholic societies. One of these, the Order of the Star-Spangled Banner, joined with many similar societies to spawn the clandestine American Party of the 1850s. Also known as the Know-Nothing Party because its members refused to answer questions about it, this powerful and briefly successful political organization was dedicated to preserving its vision of a native-born Anglo-Saxon Protestant society by curtailing Catholic political power. The slavery issue destroyed the party, but not its ideas and concerns. Larger and more diverse waves of immigration in the late nineteenth and early twentieth centuries led a former Methodist clergyman in 1915 to revive the Ku Klux Klan, a secret terrorist organization inspired by a religious and patriotic vision of Anglo-Saxon Protestant "Americanism." Particularly strong in the South, West, and Midwest, it targeted Catholics and Jews as well as blacks, adapted Protestant hymns and rituals to express its creed of white spiritual superiority, and attracted more than two million members in the 1920s. It declined again in the 1930s amid public criticism but has experienced periodic reinvigoration. Now reduced to a few thousand members, it seeks an improved public image, has dropped its opposition to Roman Catholicism, and continues to attract public attention.

Secret societies have also had a significant influence on alternative American religious movements. The rituals, symbols, and organization of Mormonism—itself suspected in its early years of being a secret society—derived at least in part from Masonic models, and theosophy, a movement devoted to spiritual illumination, has drawn heavily on the traditions of ancient, European, and American secret societies. As diverse as those who join them, secret societies have addressed Americans' many spiritual needs and anxieties and reflected the myriad currents of American religious life.

See also Belonging, Religious; Civil Religion; Freemasonry; Ku Klux Klan; Ritual; Rosicrucians.

Bibliography

Carnes, Mark C. *Secret Ritual and Manhood in Victorian America.* 1989.

Chalmers, David M. *Hooded Americanism: The History of the Ku Klux Klan,* 3rd ed. 1987.

Dumenil, Lynn. *Freemasonry and American Culture, 1880–1930.* 1984.

Kuyk, Betty M. "The African Derivation of Black Fraternal Orders in the United States." *Comparative Studies in Society and History* 25 (1983):559–592.

Muraskin, William. *Middle-Class Blacks in a White Society: Prince Hall Freemasonry in America.* 1975.

Bret E. Carroll

Sect

The term "sect" is identified with small religious groups that are generally seen in opposition to a more dominant religious belief system. This opposition may be visibly manifested in habits or forms of dress that signal a separation from mainstream society, physical isolation from society, or criticism of social norms. Because of these traits, sect members have sometimes been labeled as sociologically marginal, or deviant.

One of the most useful analytical definitions of the sect is found in the church-sect typology developed by Max Weber and Ernst Troeltsch. In this typology the "sect" is defined in opposition to the "church." Whereas the archetypal model of the church is the universal Catholic Church, the archetypal model for the sect is the band of apostles who followed Christ. In his church-sect typology, Weber identifies a number of characteristics by which the sect can be identified. One of the chief characteristics is voluntary membership. Members of the sect make a conscious decision (often prompted by an individual conversion experience) to accept the rules and beliefs of the faith community. Such communities tend to be democratic and self-governing, rather than hierarchical, and consequently tend to remain small in size.

Because of their opposition to the status quo, such sects are often perceived to be revolutionary or deviant, enacting their beliefs through their lifestyle and behavioral choices. These decisions often result in a withdrawal from the world and its institutions and values; exclusiveness in both attitude and social structure; an intense sense of fellowship among members; and an attitude of ethical austerity, often of an ascetic nature, in opposition to the worldliness of secular society.

A number of scholars have argued that the sect type of religious organization is difficult to sustain beyond the first generation of believers. H. Richard Niebuhr (1929) believed that the second generation rarely inherits the religious fervor of their parents. In addition, he believed in the lessons taught by Weber's *Protestant Ethic,* that the disciplined and ascetic lifestyle practiced by sect members would eventually lead to a worldly success that would cause sect members to form an accommodation with, rather than isolation from, secular society. Niebuhr felt that eventually sects would mature into denominations—that is, Christian assemblies divided by race, class, and caste but living in accommodation with the values of secular society. J. Milton Yinger (1946) argued that not all sects developed into denominations and coined the term "the established sect" to refer to second- and third-generation sects that retained their separation from secular society. Yinger included Quakers, Mennonites, and the Amish within this subtype.

Still another approach at classifying sects is attempted in the later work of Yinger (1957), and in Bryan Wilson (1959). This approach attempts to classify sects by their worldviews. Yinger distinguished among (1) acceptance sects, characterized by individualism; (2) aggressive sects, characterized by their rejection of society as evil; and (3) avoidance sects, characterized by pessimism and concentration on life in the hereafter. Wilson's work also distinguished among sects by their worldviews. Among those he identifies in his work are (1) conversionist sects that focus on evangelism; (2) adventist sects that focus on the imminent overthrow of the current social order; (3) pietist sects that tend to withdraw from the world and direct attention toward the life of the community, who are seen as the elect; and (4) gnostic sects that emphasize a special body of knowledge and offer a new teaching of the Christian doctrines. Of these four, he believes that conversionist sects are the most likely to develop into denominational types of organizations because their emphasis on evangelism brings them into direct confrontation with the secular world to accomplish their goals, and thus they are more likely to embrace secular values. Scholars suggest that since the 1970s, the influx of non-European immigrants, increasing exposure to non-Western world religions, and the approaching millennium have introduced new religious models that have stimulated the formation of new religious sects.

In contemporary usage, the terms "sect" and "cult" often denote overlapping concepts that may be used interchangeably by the mass media. Both terms are used to denote a religious group marginalized by society for its unusual religious beliefs or practices, and both terms are perceived by many to have negative connotations. Several scholars, including Rodney Stark and William S. Bainbridge (1987), distinguish between sects and cults by identifying sects as reform movements that have split from one of the mainstream churches or denominations, and cults as new religions formed around a charismatic leader and generally of a highly innovative character.

See also AMISH; ANTI-CULT MOVEMENT; BELONGING, RELIGIOUS; CHURCH; CHURCH GROWTH MOVEMENT; CULT; CULT AWARENESS NETWORK; DENOMINATION; MEGACHURCH; MENNONITES; NAMES AND NAMING; NEW RELIGIOUS MOVEMENTS; POSTDENOMINATIONAL CHURCH; QUAKERS; RELIGIOUS COMMUNITIES.

BIBLIOGRAPHY

Niebuhr, H. Richard. *The Social Sources of Denominationalism.* 1929.

Stark, Rodney, and William S. Bainbridge. *A Theory of Religion.* 1987.

Troeltsch, Ernst. *The Social Teaching of the Christian Churches,* vols. 1 and 2, translated by Olive Wyon. 1981.

Weber, Max. *Economy and Society: An Outline of Interpretive Sociology,* vols. 1 and 2, edited by Guenther Roth and Claus Wittich. 1956.

Weber, Max. *The Protestant Ethic and the Spirit of Capitalism.* 1920.

Wilson, Bryan. "An Analysis of Sect Development." *American Sociological Review* 24 (1959):3–15.

Yinger, J. Milton. *Religion in the Struggle for Power.* 1946.

Patricia Mei Yin Chang

Secularization

Secularization is commonly thought to be a process of religious decline, the eclipse of religious ideas and institutions by nonreligious ones. While this common-sense definition may seem obvious enough, both the concept and the evidence are among the most hotly debated topics among students of American religion. How should secularization be properly defined, and once defined, what will count as evidence for or against the hypothesis?

This debate is especially important because the idea of secularization has been closely tied to theories of modernization and thereby to the basic theoretical foundations of the social sciences. The German sociologist Max Weber, for instance, wrote of the "disenchantment" of the world, meaning that increasingly modern people do not perceive the world to be ruled by mysterious sacred forces, but by understandable processes that are subject to study. The French sociologist Émile Durkheim did not expect the sacred to disappear, but he did expect it to become highly generalized, amorphously resident in the ideals of our culture or in the idea of "sacred" human worth. Both were writing near the beginning of the twentieth century, in Europe, where "secularization" also meant the loss of property and power by the established churches.

These early ideas hint at the several ways in which secularization can be defined and the consequent variations in the evidence that might count toward a conclusion. The most basic definition has to do with the separation of religious authority from state authority, what is commonly known in the United States as "separation of church and state." In this sense, most modern nations are "secular." They are governed by political authorities that owe little, if any, allegiance to religious institutions. At least since the last of the colonial established churches gave up its privileges in the early nineteenth century, then, the United States has been secularized.

But that assertion seems to fly in the face of the immense institutional vitality of American religion and the fact that nearly all of the population regularly claims (in public opinion polls) to believe in God. The strength or weakness of religious institutions and religious ideas are additional dimensions to the secularization question that must be taken into account. While there is considerable debate about how many people can be found at religious services on any given weekend, estimates vary between 25 and 40 percent. In addition to the number who attend with some regularity, even if not every week, another 20 percent or more claim some affiliation with a religious body, while attending more sporadically. And still others are "mental affiliates," describing themselves as identified with a religious tradition even though not formally a member or a regular participant.

In this country, then, it is more normal to have a religious affiliation than not, a fact that contrasts dramatically with some European countries, where religious attendance is common among only a tiny fraction of the population. Overall levels of religious participation have remained relatively stable since the 1940s in the United States, despite a decline in membership and participation among the "mainline" Protestant bodies (Methodists, Presbyterians, Episcopalians, and the like) that dominated American culture in the nineteenth century and remained strong until the 1960s. While they have lost members and organizational strength, many other religious bodies— evangelical Protestants, Catholic churches swollen by immigration, new immigrant religious bodies from Hindus to Muslims—have grown.

Recently, scholars have argued that the voluntarism of the religion system in the United States helps to account for this organizational strength. Because religion was not supported by the state, every religious organization had to generate its own support. Those that did not meet the needs of enough people would cease to exist. And when there were new people and new needs, no legal obstacles stood in the way of religious entrepreneurs who wished to begin new religious groups. Ironically, because government was "secular," ample social space was left for religious organizations to flourish.

But what of the influence of these religious organizations? Another way to understand secularization is to look for the ways in which religion is privatized. That is, having lost its legal authority, has religion also lost its ability to influence the public world of work and politics? Here the evidence is much less clear. Some argue that American culture has trivialized religion, making it merely an individual preference to be indulged in one's leisure time. Others argue that religious ideas often play a key role in public policy debates (from abortion to war) and that religious figures, such as the Rev. Dr. Martin Luther King, Jr., or the Rev. Pat Robertson, have clearly exercised influence in the public arena. Beyond politics, others point to the growing presence of religious symbols, characters, and narratives in the mass media. Few would argue that the public airwaves and policy arenas are pervasively religious, but it is also clear that American culture is not utterly devoid of religious content.

A final aspect of secularization that has often been debated is the plausibility of religious beliefs in an age of reason and science. Throughout the twentieth century, people have debated evolution and creationism, cloning and space travel. Science clearly has enormous respect as a source of knowledge about the world, but most people have found it quite possible to simultaneously accept science and also believe in the reality of divine presence and power. In the pragmatics of everyday life, most people do not seem to need the elaborate theological and philosophical theories of accommodation worked out by scholars. Indeed, the very religious communities whose ideas seem to stand most at odds with modern scientific ideas about the world have thrived, at least in part because a pluralistic situation favors those groups best able to articulate a distinct identity.

The question of secularization in contemporary American culture is, then, a complicated one. Legally, secularization was long since effected. Culturally, many aspects of everyday life and mass media operate without apparent religious influence. And there has been significant decline in the organizational strength of the religious bodies that formerly held privileged positions in American society. However, other religious bodies have gained in strength, and the overall picture is still one of organizational health, fostered in large measure by the country's voluntaristic religious system. The extent to which those organizations can influence public life varies, and no definitive case can be made about long-term decline (or growth). Religious ideas are sometimes questioned by science, but just as often exist alongside science, offering an alternative or supplemental way of understanding the world. While secularization is a commonsense assumption about American society, it is far from a uniform fact that is universally accepted.

See also BELONGING, RELIGIOUS; CHURCH; CHURCH AND STATE; CHURCH GROWTH MOVEMENT; CIVIL RELIGION; FREEDOM OF RELIGION; FUTURE OF RELIGION; IMPLICIT RELIGION; MATERIAL RELIGION; POPULAR RELIGION; RELIGIOUS COMMUNITIES; RELIGIOUS STUDIES; SOCIOLOGY OF RELIGION.

BIBLIOGRAPHY

Berger, Peter L. *The Sacred Canopy.* 1969.
Casanova, José. *Public Religions in the Modern World.* 1994.
Demerath, N. J. III and Rhys H. Williams. *A Bridging of Faiths: Religion and Politics in a New England City.* 1992.
Finke, Roger, and Rodney Stark. *The Churching of America.* 1992.
Hadaway, C. Kirk, Penny Long Marler, and Mark Chaves. "What the Polls Don't Show: A Closer Look at U.S. Church Attendance." *American Sociological Review* 58(6) (1993):741–752.
Lechner, Frank. "The Case Against Secularization: A Rebuttal." *Social Forces* 69(4)(1991):1103–1119.
Smith, Christian. *American Evangelicalism: Embattled and Thriving.* 1998.
Warner, R. Stephen. "Work in Progress Toward a New Paradigm for the Sociological Study of Religion in the United States." *American Journal of Sociology* 98(5)(1993):1044–1093.

Nancy T. Ammerman

Seder, Christian

Since the 1970s, a growing number of Christians have begun celebrating the Seder, the traditional Jewish Passover night, often giving it a Christian meaning. Christians who celebrate the Seder relate to its meaning in a variety of manners. Liberal Protestants and Roman Catholics have been motivated by the spirit of interfaith dialogue that came about in the 1960s and

1970s, in the wake of the Second Vatican Council. They have organized Seder demonstrations, or have joined with Jewish congregations in celebrating the Seder. Many Unitarian congregations have adopted Passover in addition to other religious traditions' holidays as part of their pluralistic character. Conservative evangelical Christians have also shown interest in the Seder, but from a different perspective. Evangelical missionary organizations such as the Chosen People Ministries or Jews for Jesus have organized Seder demonstrations in conservative churches as a means of promoting interest in the Jewish people and their role in history, as well as gaining support for the missionaries' own work. Jews who believe in Jesus, both in separate messianic Jewish congregations and in evangelical churches, have been celebrating the Seder as well.

A number of Christian evangelical organizations and congregations, such as Jews for Jesus, have written their own Haggadot, the liturgical literature for Passover celebrations. Such evangelical Haggadot often omit the Midrashic passages that quote from the sayings of Mishnaic rabbis, instead incorporating the Christian faith in Jesus as the Messiah and the Son of God into the text. They view the three matzos on the Seder plate as representing the Trinity, with the disappearance of the broken middle matzo at the beginning of the Seder and its reappearance at the end as symbolizing Jesus' death and resurrection.

The Christian celebration of the Seder signifies a break with traditional Christian views of Judaism and a growing interest by Protestants and Catholics in the Jews and the Jewish religious heritage.

See also ECUMENICAL MOVEMENT; EVANGELICAL CHRISTIANITY; FOOD; JEWISH OBSERVANCE; JEWS FOR JESUS; JUDAISM; JUDEO-CHRISTIAN TRADITION; MAINLINE PROTESTANTISM; PRACTICE; RITUAL; ROMAN CATHOLICISM.

BIBLIOGRAPHY

Cohen Nussbaum, Debra. "Christianizing the Passover Seder." *Sh'ma* 29, no. 560 (1999): 1–2.

Feher, Shoshanah. *Passing Over Easter.* 1998.

Fisher, Eugene J. "Seders in Catholic Parishes." *Sh'ma* 29, no. 560 (1999): 4–5.

Lipson, Eric Peter. *Passover Haggadah: A Messianic Celebration.* 1986.

Sevener, Harold A., ed. *Passover Haggadah for Biblical Jews and Christians.* 1987.

Somerville, Robert S. "Christians Celebrating the Passover Seder." *Sh'ma* 29, no. 560 (1999): 2–3.

Yaakov S. Ariel

Seeker Churches

If you combine a rock concert, a shopping mall, and a self-help seminar with a young, nondenominational evangelical church that meets in a theater, school, or warehouse, you begin to get a picture of a seeker church. A seeker church designs its programs and services to attract its target audience of "Unchurched Harry," a midcareer, suburban professional male who does not attend church but probably was raised in either a mainline Protestant church or in the Roman Catholic Church. By developing an innovative model for reaching unchurched baby boomers, seeker churches are growing rapidly in the United States and even internationally as they seek to re-form the practices of evangelical churches.

The most prominent seeker church is the United States is Willow Creek Community Church, the self-proclaimed largest church in America, which attracts more than fifteen thousand people from suburban Chicago to its services every weekend. This modern American cathedral features a winding drive around a picturesque lake, a forty-five-hundred-seat theater offering a high-energy service with live band, professional lighting and sound, dramatic presentations, and topical messages on practical concerns. Willow Creek, however, does not look like a church. It has no crosses or religious symbols on display, even on its exterior. Willow Creek's extensive complex of dark brick and smoked glass buildings resembles a modern community college or corporate training center. Its facilities include a conference center, a cafeteria food court and atrium dining area, three basketball courts, a wing of offices, a chapel the size of many churches, a bookstore, and endless hallways of Sunday school rooms and nurseries that rival the most expensive private day-care centers.

Large, contemporary churches such as Willow Creek and Saddleback Valley Community Church, in Orange County, California, represent one of the most influential movements in American Protestantism because thousands of pastors from across the country are not only flocking to these churches to learn more about their new model of ministry but also establishing their own seeker churches. This broad movement, unlike previous movements within Protestantism that were associated with a particular theology (such as neo-orthodoxy or fundamentalism or the social Gospel), is not defined primarily by doctrine or denominational affiliation. Instead, the seeker church movement is distinguished by its emphasis on a particular methodology. Seeker church pastors retain traditional evangelical tenets, such as the authority of the Bible or the divinity of Christ, but reject more traditional forms of church services and organization.

What seeker churches have in common is that they are all committed to using new methods, frequently drawn from marketing principles, to reach those who currently do not attend church. These methods include using contemporary music and developing topical messages that apply biblical teaching to issues from daily life and the self-help movement's concern with fulfillment, as well as providing excellent child care, featuring a wide variety of choice in small groups and other ministries, creating an informal atmosphere, and deemphasizing denominational identity. Seeker churches stress the importance of authenticity—of making religion personally relevant not through inherited liturgies and creeds but through dynamic services; teachings that relate Christianity to everyday life; and intimate small groups. They also tend to train their own leaders, rather than to rely on seminaries or denominations. While there is not one single model that defines the seeker church (e.g., Willow Creek urges pastors to offer separate services for seekers and believers, while Saddleback offers just one type of service), many seeker churches are relatively large (with more than a thousand attendees), and their leaders look to the shopping mall, Disney, and other customer-sensitive companies to shape the practices of the twenty-first-century church.

The most dramatic evidence of the influence of the seeker church movement is the growth of the Willow Creek Association (WCA). From its founding in 1992 to 1998, the WCA's membership grew to more than twenty-two hundred churches, ranking it in the top 10 percent of American denominations based on the number of member churches. It is growing internationally as well, with chapters in Australia, England, Germany, and New Zealand and with more on the way. Nondenominational and Baptist churches are the two largest types of churches within the WCA. As significant as its size is the fact that the WCA represents a new kind of denomination—a postmodern denomination that stresses flexibility, specialization, flat authority structures, and the market as the primary source of accountability. Just as mainline Protestant denominations formed large bureaucracies in an age of corporate vertical integration (e.g., General Motors), so the WCA embodies the kind of flexibility that technology allows—and that low levels of denominational loyalty require.

The emergence of seeker churches stems from major cultural shifts since the 1960s that have influenced where and why people decide to participate in organized religion. Religious affiliations such as Baptist, Roman Catholic, and Presbyterian are less stable and enduring than they were previously. This declining significance of denominational loyalty has restructured American religion in profound ways. For example, two-thirds of the baby-boomer generation, what Wade Clark Roof (1993) has labeled the "generation of seekers," at some time in their adult lives left the church in which they were raised. Many remained religious dropouts, although one-quarter of all baby boomers who left the church at one point have since returned. What many of these seekers have in common is a do-it-yourself mentality toward religion in which they want to choose their own form of religion rather than rely on the authority of a tradition or a religious community. These seekers choose freely from an increasingly diverse array of spiritual options. This contemporary culture of choice encourages people to create new types of communities rooted primarily in an achieved identity (based on choice) rather than in an ascriptive identity (based on birth). By designing services and programs that emphasize authenticity, informality, and the practical benefits of belief, seeker churches are an innovative and effective response by evangelical churches to this cultural environment.

See also ATTENDANCE; BELONGING, RELIGIOUS; EVANGELICAL CHRISTIANITY; NEW RELIGIOUS MOVEMENTS; POSTDENOMINATIONAL CHURCH; RELIGIOUS COMMUNITIES.

BIBLIOGRAPHY

Miller, Donald. *Reinventing American Protestantism.* 1997.

Roof, Wade Clark. *A Generation of Seekers.* 1993.

Sargeant, Kimon H. *Re-forming the Church.* Forthcoming.

Wuthnow, Robert. *The Restructuring of American Religion.* 1988.

Kimon H. Sargeant

Self-Help Movement

The self-help movement is a historical development that, though widely presumed to have transpired, is very difficult to define. It is loosely analogous to a broad shift in American culture away from traditional Protestant emphases on sin and salvation toward therapeutic models of emotional and psychological healing or "recovery." As a social movement it is also predicated on the steady increase of small groups, though notions of what a "self-help group" actually constitutes vary widely, tend to be vague, and are frequently subject to debate. Robert Wuthnow, who has chronicled the movement in some detail, follows the demarcation of *The Self-Help Sourcebook* to characterize such groups as those that "generally provide mutual aid or mutual support to their members, are composed of peers who share common experiences or situations, are run by and for their members, and operate on a voluntary, nonprofit basis" (Wuthnow 1994). Self-help group directories today typically include organizations dealing with problems ranging from addiction, bereavement, disabilities, and health concerns to familial issues, abuse, debt, and sexuality.

With historical analogues in occupational guilds, trade unions, salons, and civic clubs (among numerous other groups), the modern self-help movement can be said to have originated with the founding of Alcoholics Anonymous (AA) in the mid-1930s and to have escalated dramatically during the latter half of the twentieth century. Mutual support or recovery groups emerged into being out of a shared need for encouragement (in cases of alcoholism, as well as of certain diseases) and the common goal of lobbying for government recognition and funding for particular disabilities. By the 1990s the self-help movement had become increasingly identified with such AA derivatives as Al-Anon, Adult Children of Alcoholics, Overeaters Anonymous, and myriad groups concentrating on such topics as gambling, drug abuse, and sexual addiction and using a twelve-step model of healing. Although it is virtually impossible to obtain precise statistics on self-help groups, researchers during the early 1990s estimated that eight million to fifteen million people were participating in such a group, with no perceptible ebb in sight. Women have typically outnumbered men, and participation has been overwhelmingly (though certainly not exclusively) white.

Observers such as Alfred Katz have located several common characteristics of self-help groups, characteristics that are generally applicable to both twelve-step groups and to non-twelve-step groups. Such groups tend, first, to engage in a process of cognitive restructuring, in which members' sense of despair about their problem is reduced, their belief in their own efficacy is enhanced, and new sources for self-esteem are developed. Participants are encouraged to learn adaptive skills such as methods of reducing stress, controlling pain, and changing behavior and are expected to give and receive positive reinforcement of desirable behavior and reassurance about the future. Groups are also characterized by a focus on personal disclosure of private feelings, ideas, or fears, with the group as a whole striving to help individuals overcome their sense of isolation. It is believed that by increasing individuals' sense of affiliation and empowerment while facilitating new coping skills, participants will both help others in need and achieve therapeutic goals for themselves. Leadership of such groups is most often fluid, though participants may become attached to particular facilitators as "charis-

matic leaders." Some groups, such as AA and similar twelve-step groups, have developed thoroughgoing sets of beliefs and rituals and require or expect full acceptance of these by participants; other groups, however, allow maximum flexibility among members, existing more as a source of general support than as a particular ideology about the healing process.

The relation between the self-help movement and American religion is a complicated and contentious one, the two appearing from some perspectives to be deeply at odds and from other perspectives to be merely two sides of the same coin. Religious conservatives, whether Christian, Jewish, or some other affiliation, tend to criticize the self-help movement for encouraging narcissism, exacerbating a sense of personal victimhood, glorifying the goodness of the individual at the expense of an awareness of evil, and, above all, teaching participants to deny divine and priestly authority in favor of the authority of the inner self. Yet it is not difficult to see how even traditional religious organizations have been influenced by the self-help movement and have incorporated its therapeutic rhetoric into their own belief systems. To take the example of evangelicalism: Evangelical organizations for the study of psychology began appearing during the early 1950s, and by the 1960s a surge of Christian counseling centers that provided mental health services from a biblical perspective came into view. By the 1970s, churches themselves were bulwarks of self-help groups, and terms such as "addiction," "intimacy," "self-esteem," and "codependency" have increasingly become common parlance even in such traditional forums as sermons (Witten 1993). Evangelical diet groups emerged locally and went national, modeled on the framework of self-help groups while adding a biblical emphasis thought to be missing in groups such as Overeaters Anonymous. In these and other ways, as David Watt has argued, evangelical Protestantism has shown itself to be "less a bulwark against than a variant of the therapeutic culture" (Watt 1991).

From another angle, many commentators have suggested that the self-help movement itself is a kind of new religion for thousands of Americans who, for whatever reason, no longer feel at home in more conventional religious settings. Participants themselves regularly complain about the ways in which a traditional Christian or Jewish background has bestowed on them a sense of sinfulness and inadequacy, and many participate in self-help groups with a frequency, consistency, and enthusiasm suggesting a strong religious attachment. Some secular commentators have criticized the movement for some of the same failings as their religious counterparts have noted, denouncing the movement for its "failure to acknowledge that there are hierarchies of human suffering," pointing to the alleged tendency to exaggerate personal pain as evidence of the "selfism" and "narcissism" of therapeutic discourse (Kaminer 1993). Whatever the case, it is quite clear that the movement has been a crucial component of religious life throughout the twentieth century and has, in a fundamental way, helped change the way religion is practiced in America.

See also NEW RELIGIOUS MOVEMENTS; PASTORAL COUNSELING; PSYCHOLOGY OF RELIGION; PSYCHOTHERAPY; RITUAL; TWELVE-STEP PROGRAMS.

BIBLIOGRAPHY

Kaminer, Wendy. *I'm Dysfunctional, You're Dysfunctional: The Recovery Movement and Other Self-Help Fashions.* 1993.

Katz, Alfred H. *Self-Help in America: A Social Movement Perspective.* 1993.

Powell, Thomas J., ed. *Understanding the Self-Help Organization: Frameworks and Findings.* 1994.

Watt, David Harrington. *A Transforming Faith: Explorations of Twentieth-Century American Evangelicalism.* 1991.

Witten, Marsha G. *All Is Forgiven: The Secular Message in American Protestantism.* 1993.

Wuthnow, Robert. *Sharing the Journey: Support Groups and America's New Quest for Community.* 1994.

R. Marie Griffith

Self-Mutilation

Self-mutilation encompasses a wide variety of acts performed on the human body, including scarification (cutting), flagellation, branding, tattooing, and piercing. Although the meaning of these and other body modifications varies greatly according to place and time, the practices themselves are widely found in religious rituals throughout the world, including in North America. The ritual act of marking the flesh may have a number of functions, including mapping relations between human bodies and cosmic forces, serving as visible signs of rites of passage or initiation into a particular status or association, and promoting healing. Until recently, scholarly literature has associated rituals of self-mutilation with preindustrial or even archaic societies. Such practices as body piercing, scarification (cutting), and tattooing existed in the modern West but were thought to be folk expressions of sailors, criminals, gang members, or outlaws, conveying no particular religious significance. North American mental health professionals continue to consider most forms of self-mutilation as a pathology requiring medical intervention, not as a ritual expression to be understood within its various social contexts. As a result, very little attention has been given in North America to the spiritual dimensions of self-mutilation.

Wherever acknowledgment of self-mutilation has surfaced, so have sensationalist accounts and even legal proscriptions. Two examples include the Lakota Sioux sun dance and the practices of the Penitential Brotherhoods of the American Southwest. Many Native American ceremonies involve self-mutilation. The various sun dances of the Lakota Sioux and other Great Plains tribes typically include the piercing of a devotee's chest, tethering the dancer to a central pole until he (or, in rare cases, she) tears the flesh and breaks loose into freedom. From 1883 to 1934, at the insistence of U. S. Army officers and Christian missionaries who labeled the dances as pagan, the federal government completely banned them, and piercing as a sun dance ritual remained outlawed until the 1950s. Since the 1960s, however, there has been a revival of interest in the sun dance as an expression of Native American identity and spirituality. Another well-known example of self-mutilation is in the rituals of New Mexico's *Los Hermanos Penitentes,* a Catholic confraternity. Some members practice self-flagellation with whips and shoulder heavy crosses, particularly during Holy Week observances. At various times these practices have been restricted or even condemned by Catholic authorities.

The association of self-mutilation with renegade, archaic, or "primitive" cultures may explain the surge of interest in body modifications in North America in recent decades. A loosely organized cultural movement known as modern primitivism arose in San Francisco and other American urban areas in the 1970s. Its proponents self-consciously embraced paganism, primitivism, and tribal identity as a challenge to biblical traditions and medical models of understanding the relationship between spirituality and human bodies. Modern primitives practiced elaborate tattooing, cutting, and the piercing of nipples, navels, and genitalia. In the performance of ritual practices adapted from ethnographic reports on Oceanic, African, and Native American cultures, many modern primitives claim to have discovered pain as a path to spiritual ecstasy. Driven in part by media visibility in the 1990s, the aesthetic if not the spiritual practice of self-mutilation had quickly spread outside the subcultural niches where it first flourished.

See also BODY; ECSTASY; NATIVE AMERICAN RELIGIONS; PRACTICE; RELIGIOUS EXPERIENCE; RITES OF PASSAGE; RITUAL; SPIRITUAL PATH; SUN DANCE.

BIBLIOGRAPHY

Holler, Clyde. *Black Elk's Religion: The Sun Dance and Lakota Catholicism.* 1995.

Rosenblatt, Daniel. "The Antisocial Skin: Structure, Resistance, and 'Modern Primitive Adornment' in the United States." *Cultural Anthropology* 12 (1997): 287–334.

Torgovnick, Marianna. *Primitive Passions.* 1997.

Weigle, Martha. *Brothers of Light, Brothers of Blood.* 1976.

Jesse T. Todd

Self-Realization Fellowship

The Self-Realization Fellowship (SRF) is a modern, Hindu-based tradition that has adapted to Western culture and attracted an international membership. It is closely linked to traditional Hinduism through its emphasis on certain practices, yet it transcends cultural boundaries through a philosophy that incorporates scientific vocabulary and pluralistic ideals. These emphases have made the Self-Realization Fellowship a foundational contributor to the Western appreciation of Indian religions while also providing a model for other transplanted traditions seeking an American audience.

The Self-Realization Fellowship was founded by an Indian swami named Paramahansa Yogananda (1893–1952). Yogananda's background and ideas are recorded in his most famous work, *Autobiography of a Yogi* (1946). As a youth he met his guru, Sri Yukteswar (1855–1936), who was part of a teaching lineage that strove to integrate Hindu spirituality with Western modernism. Yukteswar even wrote a book on the harmony of Hindu and Christian scriptures. These ideals formed a basis for Yogananda's own teachings, and in 1917 he formed the Yogoda Satsang Society, which continues to provide charitable services in India. In 1920 Yogananda was invited to participate in the International Congress of Religious Liberals in Boston. There he delivered a talk titled "The Science of Religion." He continued to find a receptive audience in the United States, especially among members of groups such as the Unitarians and the Theosophical Society.

Yogananda remained in the United States, first spending three years in the Boston area, where he established an ashram (spiritual center) as an extension of the Yogoda Satsang Society. When Yogananda went on a lecture tour beginning in 1924, halls were filled to capacity. In 1925 a center was established in Los Angeles to serve as Yogananda's headquarters, and in 1935 his organization was incorporated as the Self-Realization Fellowship. Subsequently, numerous centers have been constructed, not only in the United States but also throughout Latin America, continental Europe, and the United Kingdom.

Yogananda's success came from his ability to describe a path that incorporated spirituality into a modern lifestyle. His teachings combined classical Indian Yoga with a meditation technique called *kriya Yoga.* Classical Yoga is a system of physical and mental disciplines designed to lead the practitioner to a higher state of awareness. This aims to make it possible to understand the nature of the individual Self. In Indian Vedanta philosophy, the true nature of the Self is its identity with the all-pervasive Brahman, the Absolute (sometimes described as a personal God) that is the source and underlying essence of the entire cosmos. To attain this knowledge, Yogananda taught kriya Yoga, a style of meditation designed to withdraw the life energy from outer concerns and channel it inward.

Yogananda believed that Yoga philosophy and methods underlay all the world's religions; all traditions were trying to lead people to a direct understanding of the true nature of the Self and God. Therefore he advocated respect for the teachings of saints and scriptures from other religions. He also believed that Yoga was compatible with Western scientific methods. People should not accept a religion based on blind faith, he taught, but should subject its practices to their own empirical tests and choose a path based on personal experience.

The SRF emphasizes that Yoga is not only a means to achieve higher knowledge but also can have practical benefits for life in this world. Yogananda created a series of written lessons to offer, in his words, "inspiration and practical guidance for living every day in greater harmony with oneself and others, and for coping with the multitude of problems and pressures" in the modern world. These lessons, in the form of a correspondence course, include topics such as "How to Bring Spiritual Perspectives to Daily Life," "Finding Your True Vocation," "Creating Harmony in Marriage and Family Life," "Living Without Stress and Fear," and "Building World Unity."

The topic of world unity reflects the SRF's concern for improving life on global as well as personal levels. Yogananda told his followers "to serve mankind as one's larger Self," thereby extending the benefits of Yoga practices from the individual to the entire world. Classical Yoga practices begin with individual morality. In the Hindu system, actions (*karman*) produce results that affect the doer either in this lifetime or in a future rebirth. Thus behavior that harms another being will also have negative consequences for the evildoer, regardless of whether he or she is caught and punished. To avoid negative behavior, one practices appropriate actions and cultivates mental attitudes such as compassion. The SRF tries to promote good actions throughout the world by funding charitable organizations in the United States and India and has organized the Worldwide Prayer Circle to pray for those in need as well as for world peace.

The fellowship includes laity and a monastic order. The monks and nuns publish the writings of Yogananda and his direct disciples, provide spiritual counsel, conduct temple services, go on lecture tours, and serve as the fellowship's administration. Those who wish to take up the monastic life must be single, in good health, between eighteen and forty, free of family obligations, and students of the SRF lessons for at least one year. They take vows of simplicity, celibacy, obedience, and loyalty. The current head of the fellowship, Sri Daya Mata, is a nun ordained by Yogananda himself in the 1930s.

SRF membership is primarily middle-class, but it spans ethnic and age groups. The middle-class dominance reflects the literary nature of the tradition. Much of the popularization of SRF teachings comes through publications that are sold at cost. The actual impact of the group on American religion cannot, however, be measured by membership. SRF publications are widely read by nonmembers and have contributed to America's absorption of Hindu ideas. This is largely due to Yogananda's gift for expressing himself through scientific and even Christian vocabularies appropriate to his Western audience. It also reflects the timeliness of his teachings about incorporating spirituality into modern life and having respect for all religions as different versions of one human endeavor. These ideas have became themes in modern, pluralistic American society.

See also ASHRAM; HINDUISM; MEDITATION; YOGA.

BIBLIOGRAPHY

Wessinger, Catherine. "The Vedanta Movement and the Self-Realization Fellowship." In *America's Alternative Religions,* edited by Timothy Miller. 1995.

Yogananda, Paramahansa. *Autobiography of a Yogi.* 1946.

Cybelle Shattuck

Seminaries

Since the mid-twentieth century in American higher education, "seminary" has referred to a group of special-purpose institutions of higher education whose primary purpose is theological education: graduate professional education for ministers, priests, or religious professionals or graduate education in the various theological studies disciplines. These higher education institutions have other names, such as divinity school or school of theology, but most higher education institutions of this kind in the United States have the word "seminary" in their names. The Association of Theological Schools in the United States and Canada is the agency that accredits most seminaries, and it has approximately 240 member institutions. All these schools operate at the postbaccalaureate level (a bachelor's degree or its equivalent is required for admission), conduct programs of professional education (law schools, medical schools, and graduate business schools are examples of other kinds of professional education in American higher education), and consider themselves to be within the Christian tradition, and most of them provide some programs in the graduate, academic study of theological disciplines at the graduate level. There are also several Jewish seminaries in the United States, and those related to Reformed, Conservative, and Reconstructionist Judaism share educational and institutional similarities with the seminaries described in this entry. The schools for religious leaders in Buddhism, Islam, Hinduism, and other religious traditions present in America function differently, and tend to be identified with names other than "seminary."

History and Institutional Characteristics of Seminaries

The education of persons for the ministry was a motivating factor in the founding of many private colleges and universities in America. Gradually, the colleges and universities assumed broader educational purposes, and specific education for ministry moved to the theological schools, which were formed either as separate freestanding institutions or as college-related seminaries or university-related divinity schools. Currently, approximately 80 percent of the seminaries in North America are freestanding institutions and 20 percent are related to a college or university.

Most seminaries would identify themselves with one of three major families of Christianity in North America: Roman Catholic, Mainline Protestant, or Evangelical Protestant. Mainline and evangelical are arguable distinctions, but most Protestant seminaries would classify themselves as more closely related to one of these two major communities of Protestants or Protestant denominations than to the other.

Seminaries are primarily nineteenth- or twentieth-century institutions, although a few can trace their histories to the late 1700s. The oldest seminaries in North America were founded in the first half of the nineteenth century and tend to be related to denominations that would identify themselves as Mainline

The Burr and Burton Seminary in Manchester, Vermont, built in 1829, shown in this photo from ca. 1985. (Credit: CORBIS/Lee Snider.)

Protestant. During the second half of the nineteenth century, a number of seminaries were established in the South, following the Civil War–era separation of many American denominations (including Baptist, Methodist, and Presbyterian) into independent southern and northern denominations. A number of seminaries were founded around the turn of the twentieth century, as different immigrant groups arrived in America bringing immigrant churches with them. The Scandinavian Lutherans, western and southern European Roman Catholics, and eastern European Orthodox established seminaries not long after they became established in America. More than half of all the seminaries related to the Association of Theological Schools (ATS) were founded in the twentieth century.

Since the 1960s, seminaries have been affected by several shaping forces. Because seminaries grow out of the broader enterprise of religion, the most salient changes in seminaries reflect the changes more broadly experienced in American religion. Three of these changes are of particular importance. First, Mainline Protestantism has changed. Mainline Protestants, with whom almost half of all American seminaries could be identified, has experienced a substantial decline in membership—almost 30 percent in many mainline denominations—and that has had an impact on seminaries. Interestingly, the number of students has increased, but the students are, on average, older and are enrolled in a greater variety of degree programs. Second, membership of the Roman Catholic Church continues to grow, but the number of men presenting themselves as candidates for the ministerial priesthood has declined since the 1950s. While the enrollment of men studying for ordination has decreased, the total enrollment in Catholic seminaries has actually increased. This enrollment phenomenon is the result of the increase in students enrolled in programs such as the Master of Pastoral Studies, a degree program for persons preparing for nonordained professional ministry. Third, since World War II, one of the most interesting changes in American Protestantism has been the growth in numbers of persons who could be described, in one way or the other, as Evangelical Protestants. Most of the seminaries founded since World War II identify themselves as Evangelical Protestant. The growth in seminaries over the past forty years—both in the number of schools and the number of students enrolled in those schools—has been greatest among seminaries that identify with Evangelical denominations or the Evangelical wings of mainline denominations.

Some changes in seminaries since World War II have a less direct correlation with changes in religious denominations; they are the result of influences that have constituted significant shaping forces in the seminaries. The first of these is the increasing percentage of students, faculty, and administrators who are women. While women have been enrolled in some seminaries throughout those schools' histories, their numbers were traditionally small. Over the past twenty five years, the percentage of women students in seminaries related to ATS has grown from 10 percent to more than 40 percent of the total enrollment. While the enrollment of women reflects increasing openness in many denominations to the ordination of women, the increase in the enrollment of women is as evident among many seminaries related to church bodies that do not ordain women as it is among seminaries serving those church bodies that do ordain women. The presence of women, in substantial numbers, as students, administrators, and faculty has changed the ethos and culture of many theological schools.

A second major change in seminaries is the number and kind of degree programs they offer. In the 1950s the typical seminary offered a degree program for students preparing for ordained ministry, in which the vast majority of students were enrolled and, perhaps, one or two other degree programs, which generally had much smaller enrollments. Few seminaries offered academic master's programs, and few offered professional degree programs other than the one for persons preparing for ordained ministry. Presently, most seminaries offer many degree programs to a larger variety of students. These multiple-degree programs have resulted in a diversity of educational goals and aspirations of students. Like the increasing percentage of women, the growth in degree programs is a substantive change in the ethos of seminaries.

Finally, the students themselves appear to be far more diverse than they were forty years ago. The typical student in 1950 had received an undergraduate degree from a church-related college, majored in an area such as religion, philosophy, or history that was taken to be a good undergraduate area of study in preparation for seminary study, and enrolled in the seminary immediately after completing the baccalaureate degree. In the 1990s, only a small minority of students would fit this profile. The majority of contemporary students in seminaries has completed undergraduate degrees in public colleges or universities, typically do not have undergraduate majors in religion or cognate fields, and have not enrolled in seminary directly upon the completion of their undergraduate degree program. The present student body in American seminaries is very diverse; most of the older homogenizing factors are no longer present.

Students

In addition to their diversity, there are a variety of other characteristics of the student bodies in American seminaries that contribute to the understanding of these institutions. Approximately seventy thousand students are enrolled in degree programs in seminaries that are members of the Association of Theological Schools in the United States and Canada. While not all seminaries are members of ATS, the vast majority are. About 42 percent of these students are pursuing the Master of Divinity degree, which is a three-year, post-baccalaureate degree program that educates persons for general pastoral ministry and is a requirement for ordination in many American denominations. Another 15 per cent of the students are in various professional master's degree programs designed to educate persons for a variety of specialized religious professional areas of work, such as religious education, social ministries, church music, or mis-

sions. The remainder of students are pursuing academic master's degree programs such as the Master of Theological Studies or a Master of Arts with a specialization in one of the theological disciplines, or research doctoral programs like the Doctor of Philosophy.

Students are studying at seminary for a variety of reasons. The majority hope to serve in vocational ministry contexts upon completion of their seminary education. These positions include working in parishes and congregations in a variety of ordained and non-ordained roles, working in church- or denomination-related agencies or institutions, in independent ministry organizations, as chaplains, or in other religious service in hospitals, industry, or military or other government-service chaplaincy. Others are studying in order to pursue careers in teaching or research in the academic disciplines related to theological study. Still others are studying in seminaries because they want to pursue advanced learning related to their own religious faith that is more academically rigorous than the religious education provided by parishes, congregations, or denominational agencies. Throughout the 1990s, approximately one-third of the students have been women and two-thirds men.

Seminary Curriculum

While seminaries offer a variety of degrees, the majority of students are enrolled either in the Master of Divinity or another professional master's program and are preparing for some form of ministry. While these degree programs have substantive differences in requirements and curricula, they share several common features that constitute the salient features of the seminary curriculum. All these degrees involve the equivalent of two or three years of full-time study— although most students take more than the minimum two or three years to complete their degree programs. The courses for these various degree programs reflect three primary areas of study: (1) Scripture and other sacred texts; (2) history, theology, ethics, philosophy, and comparative religions; and (3) studies in pastoral care and counseling, church administration, religious education, preaching, and sociology of religion—to attain skills necessary for professional work. The educational goals of seminary degree programs include knowledge of the content of the theological disciplines, the capacity to understand the social and cultural contexts in which religion is situated, proficiency in the skills necessary for religious leadership and the practice of ministry, and the development of personal and spiritual maturity. The educational goals of seminary are unique, in contrast to other areas of American higher education, in terms of this final category:

students are expected to develop the kind of personal and spiritual maturity that will give them integrity as religious leaders, as well as the knowledge and competence that enable them to do their work well.

See also EVANGELICAL CHRISTIANITY; JUDAISM; MAINLINE PROTESTANTISM; ORDINATION; ORDINATION OF WOMEN; ROMAN CATHOLICISM.

BIBLIOGRAPHY

Aleshire, Daniel and Matthew Zyniewicz, eds. *The Fact Book on Theological Education.* Published annually.

Carroll, Jackson, Barbara Wheeler, Daniel Aleshire, and Penny Long Marler. *Being There: Culture and Formation in Two Theological Schools.* 1997.

Gilpin, Clark. *A Preface to Theology.* 1996.

Miller, Glenn. *Piety and Intellect: The Aims and Purposes of Ante-Bellum Theological Education.* 1990.

Schuth, Katarina. *Seminaries, Theologates, and the Future of the Ministry: An Analysis of the Trends and Transitions.* 1999.

White, Joseph. *The Diocesan Seminary in the United States: A History from the 1780s to the Present.* 1989.

Daniel Aleshire

Separation of Church and State.

See Church and State.

Serpent Handling.

See Snake Handling.

Seventh-Day Adventism

Seventh-Day Adventism emerged out of the Millerite apocalyptic excitement during the latter stages of the Second Great Awakening to become one of the nation's largest indigenous churches. By the end of the twentieth century there were close to nine hundred thousand Adventists in North America and more than ten million worldwide. In their mission of proclaiming the second advent of Christ and a new world to come, Adventists have made a significant impact on the present world through a vast array of health-care, educational, and publishing institutions. Though less well known than fellow nineteenth-century prophets Mary Baker Eddy and Joseph Smith, the church's cofounder, Ellen G. White, exerted an influence that not only inspired the entire Adventist achievement

but that also indirectly extends to all Americans who consume breakfast cereal or who believe in "scientific creationism."

William Miller, a New York farmer turned Baptist revivalist, came to prominence in the Northeast by the late 1830s, proclaiming the imminent, premillennial return of Jesus Christ. Rejecting the widespread millennialist gradualism about revival and reform transforming America, the Millerites envisioned total reform through one cataclysmic act of divine intervention—fiery destruction of the present order followed by re-creation at Christ's return. Moreover, Miller believed that apocalyptic prophecy revealed the time of the event—initially estimated at about 1843 and eventually more precisely predicted as October 22, 1844. While belief that the twenty-three-hundred-day prophecy of Daniel 8:14 would somehow be fulfilled in the 1840s was widespread, Miller was distinctive in associating the "cleansing of the sanctuary" referred to in that passage with the literal return of Christ.

After the prophecy failed, the disappointed Adventists split into numerous factions. One of the smaller of these gradually coalesced around the conviction that the prophecy of Daniel 8:14 had indeed been fulfilled in 1844 in a transcendent sense. The "cleansing of the sanctuary," they maintained, referred to a cosmic "Day of Atonement" marked by Christ's final work of mediation and judgment in the "heavenly" sanctuary referred to in the New Testament epistle to the Hebrews. These future Seventh-Day Adventists were led by Joseph Bates, a veteran social reformer and Millerite leader; James White, a young schoolteacher with a background in the Christian Connection; and Ellen Harmon, a teenage former Methodist from Portland, Maine, who received divine guidance and encouragement for the movement through dramatic visions experienced in a trancelike state. White and Harmon married in 1846.

This group found its mission and identity under the apocalyptic rubric of the "three angels' messages" of Revelation 14:6–12. The first two had already gone forth, they believed, but it was their duty to proclaim the third and final message before Christ's return, which called out a people who "keep the commandments of God and the faith of Jesus." The "commandments of God" included the Sabbath commandment, and they insisted that the Bible mandates observance of the Sabbath on the seventh day of the week—Saturday, not Sunday.

By the early 1850s these Sabbatarian Adventists saw it as their mission to gather a "remnant" in the last days, marked by fidelity to the law of God and Sabbath observance, and the "spirit of prophecy" manifested in the ministry of Ellen White. Other distinctive beliefs included the cleansing of the heavenly sanctuary begun in 1844, conditional immortality, and "annihilationism"—the destruction of sinners in the end, rather than their unending torment in an eternal hell. While focused on preparation for the Second Coming, the Sabbatarian Adventists were very much engaged with the national dilemma over slavery. Passionately antislavery for the most part, they viewed slavery as evidence that the American republic is the "second beast" of Revelation 13, which has a benign, lamblike aspect but "speaks like a dragon."

An era of organization- and institution-building began in the 1860s under James White's leadership. The Seventh-Day Adventist church was officially organized in 1863 with headquarters in Battle Creek, Michigan, and a membership of about thirty-five hundred. Prompted by Ellen White's visions, the church quickly turned its attention to health reform. Adventists came to view physical health as intrinsic to Christian sanctification and preparation for Christ's return, and health care as a leading dimension of their mission to the world. Though generally leery of politics, their interest in health in part motivated them to intensive involvement in the Prohibition movement. Educational institutions and overseas missions were both launched in the 1870s. In calling America's "Protestant empire" to what they regarded as true Protestantism, Adventists stressed not only a biblicism marked by seventh-day Sabbath observance but also individual freedom from coercion in religion. They began publishing the *American Sentinel* in 1886 (changed to the current title, *Liberty*, in 1906) and formed the National Religious Liberty Association to advocate religious freedom and separation of church and state.

The years between the late 1880s and World War I were among the most dynamic in the church's history but also saw major crises that did much to determine the direction of the twentieth-century church. A revival uplifting the theme of salvation through faith in Christ alone brought with it a severe controversy between the advocates of the new emphasis (primarily Alonzo T. Jones and Ellet J. Waggoner) and the older leadership worried that the Adventist emphasis on the necessity of observing the law of God was being undermined. Ellen White sided with the "righteousness by faith" advocates—a decisive moment in Adventism's complex relationship to evangelical Protestantism. Adventists, though not unambiguously or without subsequent controversy, would adhere to the Protestant principles of justification by faith and the final authority of Scripture.

Meanwhile, John Harvey Kellogg, director of the church's Battle Creek sanitarium, was earning a reputation as one of the nation's foremost authorities on health matters. Though it was his brother Will who eventually turned breakfast cereal into a financial empire, it was John Harvey who invented the concept with cornflakes and granola. Kellogg saw humanitarianism as the essence of Adventism. In addition to medical work, he promoted a comprehensive outreach to the poor of the nation's cities in the 1890s, particularly in Chicago. Disputes with the clerical leadership over control of the church's thriving "medical missionary" work and his unconventional theology led to Kellogg's removal from the church in 1907 and the church's loss of the Battle Creek sanitarium and program of humanitarian activism in the cities, though the emphasis on health and medicine would remain as a legacy of both Kellogg and Ellen White. In the decades surrounding her death in 1915, the authority of Ellen White's voluminous writings was another hotly debated issue. Though White explicitly denied claiming "infallibility," a large segment of the church held that her writings virtually were just that; at the very least they were regarded as unerring commentary on Scripture. A. G. Daniells, a close ally of White's and president of the church from 1901 to 1922, took a more moderate position, affirming the authenticity of White's spiritual gift but recognizing her fallibility. His ouster from the presidency, in part because of this "soft" view of Ellen White's authority, signaled the victory of the near-inerrantist view, which prevailed until a new round of controversies in the 1970s.

The Adventists of the 1920s identified themselves with fundamentalism and had something of an impact on the fundamentalist movement. Historian Ronald Numbers has shown that Adventist scholar George McCready Price was a major influence behind eventual widespread acceptance in fundamentalist circles of "flood geology"—a cornerstone of "scientific creationism." Price's views on creation and flood in turn were shaped by Ellen White's writings.

In the twentieth century, Adventism has exhibited dynamic growth in membership and expansion of institutions, particularly outside the United States. By 1995 the church was operating more than 5,000 schools and nearly 600 health-care institutions, with assets totaling about $5 billion. Through the Adventist Development and Relief Agency the church had established humanitarian work in 120 countries.

At the same time, the church faces tensions that have become increasingly apparent since the 1960s, all revolving around the question of how to remain unified as one world church amid rapidly increasing diversity—ethnic, national, and theological. By 1990, African Americans constituted 25 percent of the church's North American membership and Latinos 8 percent. Achieving racial justice and harmony in the church remains a challenge, as Adventists struggle to overcome a racism that became deeply entrenched during the early and middle decades of the twentieth century.

With the world church's membership becoming overwhelmingly non-American and nonwhite while North America retains disproportionate financial clout and representation in world leadership, deepening fissures between the United States and the rest of the world church have become increasingly apparent in recent decades. Debate over the role of women has been the most striking issue along this line of conflict. While sentiment in favor of the ordination of women is strong if not overwhelming in North America, opposition from overseas divisions was a major factor in blocking initiatives for women's equality in the ministry at the General Conference sessions of 1990 and 1995.

Increasing diversity in theological outlook also strained the unity of the church in the second half of the twentieth century. The church's decision in 1909 to, at Ellen White's direction, develop a fully accredited medical school in Loma Linda, California, led in turn to gradual accreditation for the church's undergraduate colleges. The church's system of higher education not only became an engine of Adventist upward mobility in society and professionalization of ministry but also required faculty with the requisite graduate degrees from public universities. The result was a liberal stream of Adventism more open to change and progressive development in doctrine and more interested in engaging the wider society. The Association of Adventist Forums and its publication, *Spectrum,* established in the late 1960s, have given voice to liberal Adventism.

Scholarly study of Ellen White has probably been the most controversial legacy of liberal Adventism. *Prophetess of Health* (1976) by Ronald Numbers challenged the widespread view of White's writings as virtually infallible divine revelation by showing her usage of the works of other health reformers and that she changed her views on some topics over time. The work of Numbers and others eventually prompted even the denominational leadership to acknowledge that White's writings were far more dependent on literary sources than previously recognized.

At the same time as the church was being shaken by controversy over Ellen White, an increasingly identifiable "evangelical" movement was taking shape within its ranks. The evangelical Adventists stressed justification by faith alone; affirmed the authority of Scripture over that of Ellen White's writings; and rejected a view deeply cherished in some Adventist circles that the church's mission was to develop a "final generation" of perfectly sanctified believers, which would lead to the Second Coming. Evangelical Adventism became particularly controversial when its foremost advocate, the Australian Desmond Ford, publicly challenged the church's teachings concerning 1844 as lacking a biblical basis and as contrary to justification by faith. Ford was defrocked and scores of ministers and teachers also left denominational employment, but the issues have not gone away.

The American Seventh-Day Adventism of 2000 is, overall, arguably more "evangelical" than it was in the 1960s. Teaching in its schools and congregations tends to be more Christ-centered and more focused on basic Protestant doctrine. Evangelical books and CDs accompany Adventist-produced material on the shelves of church-operated bookstores. It is also more "liberal" in that critical scholarship has become a lasting if embattled presence, relations with other denominations are more congenial, there is greater participation in public affairs, and behavioral standards on such matters as entertainment and wearing of jewelry are less rigid and uniform.

Yet the final quarter of the twentieth century has also seen a reinvigoration of traditional Adventism and its unique identity as a "remnant" of exclusive significance in the culmination of the "great controversy." Thus American Adventism enters the twenty-first century with unresolved questions: Will it be a sect, focusing on its singular importance as the agency for God's truth in the last days, a stance favored by the traditionalists? Or will it, under evangelical and liberal influences, be more like a denomination with, to be sure, distinctive emphases, but at home among the larger family of Christian denominations?

See also ADVENTISM; APOCALYPSE; CHURCH AND STATE; CREATIONISM; DOCTRINE; ESCHATOLOGY; EVANGELICAL CHRISTIANITY; FOOD; FREEDOM OF RELIGION; FUNDAMENTALIST CHRISTIANITY; HEALTH; PRACTICE; PREMILLENNIALISM; PUBLISHING, RELIGIOUS.

BIBLIOGRAPHY

Bull, Malcolm, and Keith Lockhart. *Seeking a Sanctuary: Seventh-Day Adventism and the American Dream.* 1989.

Knight, George R. *Millennial Fever and the End of the World.* 1993.

Land, Gary, ed. *Adventism in America.* 1986.

Numbers, Ronald, and Jonathan Butler, eds. *The Disappointed: Millerism and Millenarianism in the Nineteenth Century.* 1987.

Vance, Laura L. *Seventh-Day Adventism in Crisis: Gender and Sectarian Change in an Emerging Religion.* 1999.

Douglas Morgan

Sexuality

Sexuality includes more than genital behavior. It also encompasses the capacity and yearning for union with each other and the divine. The *Presbyterians and Human Sexuality* report (1991), for example, defines sexuality as "our way of being in the world as embodied selves, male and female [which] involves our whole being and is intrinsic to our dignity as persons.... Sexuality is also an indispensable element in the divine-human encounter."

As an important element of human self-understanding and a powerful force in human lives, sexuality has been significant in religious contexts, both as a symbol of the divine-human relationship and as a drive in need of moral guidance from religious traditions.

Sexual Imagery and the Divine

Sexual and gender images for the holy differ from one religious tradition to another. Hinduism is vividly descriptive of its many gods and goddesses. Buddhism varies from nontheistic interpretations of reality in Theravāda to the wealth of symbolic imagery in Tibetan Buddhist mythology. Confucian/Taoist understandings of ultimate reality are linked to the female yin and the male yang, which, while not deities, are regarded as central constituents of the universe. Native American religious traditions are richly diverse in their views of the sacred, depicting the holy sometimes in male and sometimes in female terms. Neopagan rituals are often addressed to the Goddess.

Traditionally Judaism, Christianity, and Islam have used the male pronoun for God and have desexualized the divine. Yet the women's movement has encouraged a broadening of the narrowly male terminology for God used in worship and prayer in both Judaism and Christianity. Feminists in many congregations and denominations have pointed to the tradition's own rich store of metaphors both female and male—as well as nonpersonal—for the divine. The Christian Science faith, founded by Mary Baker Eddy in 1866, envisions the divine as male *and* female, a Mother-Father God.

Sexual relations and yearning provide metaphors for the divine-human encounter. The Song of Solomon, in Jewish and Christian scripture, vividly describes a frankly erotic relationship between a man and a woman. Christian and Jewish commentators have explained that the human-human sexual encounters in this book are metaphors for the divine-human relationship. Mystics in the Jewish, Christian, and Islamic traditions have utilized sexual imagery to describe their powerful experiences of ecstatic union with God. Similarly, Hindu sacred literature includes graphic myths of the many female cowherds filled with sexual desire for Lord Krishna.

Ethical/Social Issues of Sexuality

In the United State over the past thirty years, many religious bodies have undergone major disputes over the proper approach toward sexual issues. Traditional and progressive views may be found in both religious groups on a number of these topics. These debates raise fundamental questions about the meaning of sexuality.

Sexual Activity, Celibacy, Marriage, and Divorce

Alone among Christian groups, the Roman Catholic tradition requires lifelong celibacy for its clergy, reserving the holiest state for those who do not indulge in sexual activity. While Protestants have shared the Christian legacy of ambivalence toward sex, Protestantism has never expected or encouraged celibacy for its clergy. Eastern Orthodox Christians view created humanity, including human sexuality, more positively in general than do Catholics and Protestants, and reject celibacy for their clergy. Jews have no heritage of regarding celibacy as holy; in fact, sexual intercourse in the context of heterosexual marriage is seen in Jewish tradition as a path to holiness. Muslims have no tradition of celibacy. However, Buddhist monastic traditions require celibacy, and some Hindu devotees practice it as well.

Traditional Jewish and Christian moral approaches insist that God's will for sexual expression is to be found solely in lifelong heterosexual monogamous marriage, and they encourage celibacy for everyone not in the state of matrimony. The Roman Catholic leadership sees divorce as a falling short of God's ideal plan and will not allow a church-sanctioned wedding for remarried Catholics who have not obtained an annulment. These remarried Catholics are also officially not permitted to receive the Eucharist. Divorce and remarriage trouble some conservative Protestants, but there is a growing presence of divorced and remarried couples in these conservative churches. Many Protestant and Jewish groups make no issue of divorce and remarriage, except as a pastoral concern requiring counseling where emotions of loss are involved. In some liberal Protestant contexts there have been attempts to establish a ritual of divorce to bring, if not reconciliation, at least healing, where a marital relationship has been broken.

Muslim faith allows for but does not encourage polygyny, but of course in the U.S. context this is illegal. Originally, teachings of the Church of Jesus Christ of

Latter-day Saints also permitted multiple wives to Mormon men, but just before Utah became a state, the church ceased allowing this practice.

A growing number of Protestant and Jewish thinkers are reenvisioning the place of sexual activity in people's lives outside the context of marriage. They cite contrasts between late-twentieth-century American life and earlier times: Puberty comes earlier; the age of marriage, due to increased pursuit of educational opportunities, comes later; life spans are longer; divorce is much more frequent; there is more recognition of the sexual needs of the elderly. Thus many persons of faith spend a large proportion of their post pubescent lives unmarried. Some progressive voices in Judaism and Christianity suggest that it is unrealistic and perhaps unnatural to expect celibacy from people in all these situations, and that the result of the church or synagogue forbidding sex in all these areas is simply to push people away from their religious communities, thus depriving them of support, solidarity, comfort, and moral guidance when they need it. Some African-American Christians are rethinking traditional sexual mores, noting that the black understanding of sexuality has been distorted by the legacy of slavery and white racism.

Procreation and Birth Control

Procreation has a high value in Jewish sexual ethics. Tracing back to biblical times, when increasing the small Hebrew community was a social/political/military necessity, the Jewish position has been that reproduction is a central factor in marriage. At the same time, a very important reason for sexual expression is its role in contributing to the holiness of the married couple; in fact, Jewish law demands that a husband satisfy his wife sexually but does not require the couple to have as many children as biologically possible.

Roman Catholic moral theology has emphasized that the unitive role of sexuality (contributing to the loving intimacy between husband and wife) should not be separated from its procreative role. Thus, even though the authoritative teachings of the Roman Catholic Church recognize the importance of sex for marital bonding, they insist that every sexual act should be in principle open to the possibility of procreation. By this principle artificial birth control methods, barrier or biochemical, are prohibited, since they overtly interfere with the possibility of reproduction. Yet natural family planning (the rhythm method) is permissible, since couples not desiring further children simply abstain from sexual encounters during the woman's fertile time, and any sexual activity they participate in at other times is still open to reproduction. Also, sexual relations are allowed between a married couple when one or more of the partners is infertile (if not as a result of chosen sterilization), since the acts are in principle open to conception.

Protestant teachings in general assume the use of birth control in family spacing of children (with less approval for the idea of voluntary childlessness). Conservative Protestants may be somewhat more likely to encourage larger families, but this view is not particularly prevalent.

Ethicists in all three groups have encouraged birth control for ecological reasons (though the Roman Catholic hierarchy does not approve). They cite limits to Earth's food and water resources for human survival, and concerns about human overpopulation of the planet and the resulting devastation of ecosystems and diminishing of biodiversity.

Homosexuality

The level of inclusion of gay, lesbian, bisexual, and transgendered persons in faith communities is a particularly fiery area of debate. Questions involved include the origin of sexual orientation as well as the purpose of sexuality. Most groups recognize sexual orientation as part of someone's identity, not easily changeable by an act of will. Exceptions include the Muslim teaching that persons can choose to follow Allah's will and not be homosexual, and the attempts of some conservative Protestant groups to convert persons from their homosexual desires and "reorient" them into the fully approved lifestyle of heterosexual, monogamous marriage. The official Roman Catholic teaching accepts the reality and solidity of gay/lesbian *orientation* but suggests that persons with this orientation should devote themselves to celibacy, since homosexual *behavior* is regarded as sinful.

In a traditionalist understanding that sees sexual behavior as permissible only when at least potentially procreative, homosexual sexual expression is prohibited. Yet progressive thinkers advocating full equality for gays and lesbians have noted a double standard among some moderates and conservatives, who allow, between heterosexuals, sexual activity not aimed at procreation, while retaining the prohibition for gay, lesbian, and bisexual persons.

Congregations and groups are springing up in many Jewish and Christian denominations insisting on the acceptance of gays and lesbians into religious communities. Some groups articulate a position committed to accepting gay and lesbian persons but not allowing them to be ordained. Some denominations, such as Reconstructionist Judaism, press for a recognition of homosexual sexual activity as a gift and blessing from God just like heterosexual sexual activity, and subject to the same moral guidelines (mutuality, respect, love, commitment). On the basis of this accepting attitude, they believe that ordination should be open to qualified persons of any sexual orientation, and they believe that religious blessings of same-sex unions should be undertaken in the same spirit of holiness and celebration that heterosexual marriages are.

Abortion

Religious groups and individuals can be found across the spectrum on the abortion question. The official Roman Catholic position, shared by many evangelical Protestants, is that full personhood begins at conception (or very shortly thereafter); some Catholic moral theologians, though their positions are not approved by the church hierarchy, articulate a more nuanced approach. Orthodox Jews are, in general, opposed to abortion, but believe that the woman's life always takes precedence over the fetus's life. The most liberal Protestants and Jews believe that each woman should make her own choice.

Sexuality and Spirituality

There is a growing movement in American religious faiths to see the vitally important human characteristics of sexuality and spirituality not as opposed to each other but as integrally connected in healthy persons in community, blessings of the human life that complement and fulfill one another.

See also ABORTION; BIRTH CONTROL; BODY; CELIBACY; CHASTITY; DIVORCE, CHRISTIAN; DIVORCE, JEWISH; GENDER ROLES; LESBIAN AND GAY RIGHTS MOVEMENT; MARRIAGE; MARRIAGE, JEWISH; SPIRITUALITY.

BIBLIOGRAPHY

Douglas, Kelly Brown. *Sexuality and the Black Church: A Womanist Perspective.* 1999.

Federation of Reconstructionist Congregations and Havurot; Reconstructionist Rabbinical Association. *Homosexuality and Judaism: The Reconstructionist Position.* 1993.

Genovesi, Vincent J., S.J. *In Pursuit of Love.* 1996.

Nelson, James B., and Sandra P. Longfellow, eds. *Sexuality and the Sacred: Sources for Theological Reflection.* 1994.

Office of the General Assembly, Presbyterian Church. *Presbyterians and Human Sexuality.* 1991.

Olyan, Saul M., and Martha C. Nussbaum, ed. *Sexual Orientation and Human Rights in American Religious Discourse.* 1998.

Parrinder, Geoffrey. *Sexual Morality in the World's Religions.* 1996.

Spong, John Shelby. *Living in Sin? A Bishop Rethinks Human Sexuality.* 1988.

Waskow, Arthur. *Down to Earth Judaism: Food, Money, Sex, and the Rest of Life.* 1995.

Barbara Darling-Smith

Shamanism

The term "shamanism" is of Russian-Tungusic origin. Most generally, a shaman is a man or a woman who acts as a mediator between the spirit and physical worlds. Shamanism as a religious concept and practice came under the focus of Western eyes in northern Asia and Siberia, where it had relatively precise meanings associated with "magic" and trancelike states of human ecstasy. Ecstatic states that enable mystical experience and insight are thought to be a special and definitive characteristic of shamanism.

Traditional shamans were leaders of religious groups and wielded powerful spiritual gifts, including effective utilization of sacred fire, and the practice of magical, mystical flights wherein the spirit (and sometimes the body, too) defies the known laws of physics and travels to destinations far and uncharted. In fact, the mark of a shaman vis-à-vis other spiritual mediators is that the shaman is believed to enjoy the capacity to separate his soul from his body at will, allowing the former to travel to destinations that are otherwise restricted to physically embodied visitors.

Perhaps the central distinguishing factor of shamanism is a shaman's deft relationship with the spiritual world. Counted among the types of spirits over which shamans hold dominion are spirits of the dead, demons, and spirits that are believed to be found in nature, such as those common to rivers and animals, for example. Shamans control their helping spirits, though at times they can be possessed by them. Shamans often have conflicts and bouts with their spirits. The shaman often deploys the aid of spirits in divination, clairvoyance, and prophecy (the accurate foretelling of future events, or the ability to know and articulate with accuracy past events in a person's life). Shamans rely on the aid of helping spirits to divine events—past and present—in the lives of people who seek their aid. Although not an exclusively expert province of shamanism, healing with the aid of helping spirits is also a practice that marks shamanic techniques. People seek the healing aid of shamans for ailments of all types, including physical disease, discomfort caused by curses and Witchcraft, and for familial, social, or psychological problems. Seekers also come to shamans for extra help when in need of special favors from the spirit world.

A Native American shaman, wearing a large silver nose ring sits next to a young girl wearing a headdress with claws, in Haines, Alaska, in 1991. (Credit: © Alan Hicks/Allstock/PNI.)

In their oracular efforts and functions as benevolent healers, shamans typically cultivate efficacious relationships with animals. In Native North American tribes of the Southwest, for example, an owl is often the embodiment of a shaman's helping spirit. In Native North American lore, an owl manifests powers of warning and protection that aid the shaman in his or her work. More generally, a shaman is marked early in his or her life by a close relationship with animals. Animals are drawn to the shaman, and even wild beasts behave as tame and nurturing friends when in the presence of a shaman. The extraordinary affection displayed by animals toward any one individual is often the sign that a person has been "called" to shamanism.

Such a calling, or the trajectory to archaic religious or sacred specialists, has been the subject of much study in the history of religions. Drawing from the work of Mircea Eliade, David Carrasco has delineated

a pattern of shamanic calling and initiation that begins with: (1) a sensitive and troubled individual who (2) receives sacred knowledge through fantastic dreams and visions plus formal instructions under the (3) guidance of a great shaman, during which the initiate (4) forms relationships with helping spirits, usually in the form of animals, which enable the seeker to (5) grasp a deep truth and techniques that enable him or her to renew contact with that wisdom and (6) obtain the powers to heal varieties of sickness and to attack and kill enemies.

This pattern of initiation usually involves a great ordeal, sometimes experienced during a sickness that takes the novice to the brink of death, and introduces him or her to the terrors of finitude and spiritual forces. During this ordeal, which often includes ecstatic dreams, the hero is tested. He or she is symbolically killed and reborn into the vocation of singer, healer, and poet. This ordeal involves face-to-face encounters with terrible monsters, scenarios of chaos that may include visualizing the dismemberment and destruction of one's own body, community, and cosmos. This total crisis emerges into a new integration of the self and the acquisition of sacred knowledge that is to be used to benefit the community. This is the meaning and purpose of such religious ecstasy. Thus shamans are typically distinguished by the way they go about obtaining shamanic powers—through personal calling and experience that enable them to manipulate spiritual powers for the aid of a community.

In Native North American Indian tribes shamanic functions are common to most if not all tribal members as each seeks to cultivate special relationships to helper spirits, and with the animals. What distinguishes shamans is the intensity of shamanic powers, especially shamanic ecstasy, and the degree of their knowledge of myth and ritual. This degree of knowledge is particularly relevant in regard to rites of passage, hunting, warfare, and healing. Often a medicine man of a particular tribe displays shamanic techniques.

Euroamericans, too, have displayed shamanic tendencies, beginning particularly in the nineteenth century, with the Fox sisters in upstate New York. In 1848 the Fox sisters convinced others that they could communicate with spirits of the deceased. They staged elaborate séances in which seekers came to receive messages from beyond the grave that were communicated by a simple system of knocks. This practice of mediumship spread rapidly and gave rise to American Spiritualism. Similarly, and also in the nineteenth century, a Frenchman known as Allen Kardec developed a system for communicating with spirits and deploying them in the service of divination and healing; he elaborated this process into the religion of Spiritism. Spiritism spread throughout Latin and North America.

More recently, in 1968, anthropologist Carlos Castaneda published what he claimed to be a documentary account of his apprenticeship into shamanic techniques under the tutelage of Don Juan, a Yaqui elder and medicine man. Castaneda's work implicitly opened up Yaqui shamanism for a generation of Americans who were disenchanted with traditional Christian religions and bent on experimenting with fresh religious myths and rituals.

Since the 1980s at least this American impulse for religious seeking and experimentation has unfolded into what has been called the "New Age." New Age devotees eschew traditional Euroamerican religions in favor of practices derived from Eastern religions and from Native North Americans. A preferred religious practice of the New Age is shamanism. This penchant for shamanism is evinced by the burgeoning literature on the topic, including and especially Michael Harner's *The Way of the Shaman: A Guide to Power and Healing* (1980). If Carlos Castaneda implied that just about any American could become a shaman if he or she followed the right path, Harner promises as much to his American New Age audience. Looking to Castaneda, Harner provides a handbook of sorts, with a step-by-step guide to shamanism and healing.

Though not recognized as such, today shamanic practices are part of the everyday fabric of American life. It is hardly possible to visit any American city or small town without spotting a palm or card reader. Spiritual healing, psychic phenomena, astrology, and tarot specialties are profitable cottage industries in today's religious economy. Additionally, spiritual healing and communication with the spirit world are becoming increasingly mainstream in forms of American Christian evangelicalism. Shamanism today permeates many aspects of the collective religious imagination of American society.

See also DEVILS, DEMONS, AND SPIRITS; DREAMS; ECSTASY; HEALING; JOURNEY AND JOURNEYING; MAGIC; MYSTICISM; MYTH; NATIVE AMERICAN RELIGIONS; NEW AGE SPIRITUALITY; RITES OF PASSAGE; RITUAL; SÉANCE; SPIRITUALISM; TRANCE; VISIONARY.

BIBLIOGRAPHY

Carrasco, David. "A Perspective for the Study of Religion in Chicano Experience: *Bless Me, Ultima* as a Religious Text." *Aztlán* 3 (1982):195–222.
Eliade, Mircea. *Shamanism: Archaic Techniques of Ecstasy,* translated by Willard R. Trask. 1964.
Harner, Michael. *The Way of the Shaman: A Guide to Power and Healing.* 1980.

Luis D. León

Shavuot

One of the three Judaic pilgrim festivals, along with Sukkot, Tabernacles, and Pessah, Passover, Shavuot, on the sixth of the lunar month of Sivan, is the festival that celebrates the revelation of the Torah by God to Moses at Mount Sinai, fifty days after the Exodus from Egypt. Called "the Feast of Weeks," or "Pentecost" (the fiftieth day, that is, counting the days of the lunar months, normally twenty-nine days, from Passover, the fifteenth day of the lunar month of Nisan, followed by the lunar month of Iyyar, and then concluding with the sixth of Sivan), the festival is observed in synagogue worship, cessation of secular activities, and especially Torah study.

The Torah speaks of the festival at Exodus 34:22 as "the Feast of Weeks," "the day of the first fruits" (Numbers 28:26), and "the harvest festival" (Exodus 23:16). In the Talmud the feast is called *aseret,* "solemn assembly." Shavuot comes, in the natural year of the Land of Israel, at the end of the barley harvest and the beginning of the wheat harvest. At that festival pilgrims would ascend to Jerusalem to celebrate the festival. Shavuot also marks the end of the daily counting of the sheaf of barley, called the *'omer.* For fifty days, from the first night of Passover to the Feast of Weeks, holy Israel counts seven full weeks (Leviticus 23:15–16), noting the passage of the days from Passover to Pentecost. Because of its association with the first fruits, Israeli celebrations may include harvest ceremonies.

In synagogue rites the Book of Ruth is read. The figure of Ruth symbolizes the sincere convert to Judaism, and since conversion means acceptance of God's rule as set forth in the Torah, that book is deemed especially suitable for the occasion on which Israel accepted God's rule in the Torah at Sinai. It is also common to decorate the synagogue with plants and flowers; at home it is traditional to eat dairy foods, diverse reasons being given for the practice. In America it is common for synagogues to organize all-night Torah study sessions, with large numbers of young people staying up for the occasion.

In keeping with the theme of the revelation of the Torah, Torah study is the key motif of the festival. That is why, in Reform and some Conservative synagogues, Shavuot also marks the occasion of confirmation— that is, the conclusion of formal religious education of teenagers celebrating the giving of the Torah at

Sinai. Confirmation rites therefore form the center of festival worship at Reform synagogues.

See also JEWISH OBSERVANCE; JUDAISM; PASSOVER; SYNAGOGUE; TORAH.

BIBLIOGRAPHY

Gaster, Theodor H. *Festivals of the Jewish Year: A Modern Interpretation and Guide.* 1971.

Goodman, Philip, ed. *The Shavuot Anthology.* 1975.

Greenberg, Irving. *The Jewish Way: Living the Holidays.* 1988.

Schauss, Hayyim. *The Jewish Festivals: From Their Beginnings to Our Own Day.* 1933; rev. ed., 1969.

Waskow, Arthur I. *Seasons of Our Joy: A Handbook of Jewish Festivals.* 1986.

Jacob Neusner

Shivah

In Judaism, Shivah (the word for "seven" in Hebrew; unrelated to the Hindu god Shiva) is the seven-day intensive period of mourning following a funeral; its observance is described in the Babylonian Talmud (sixth century C.E.), and it has changed little in modern times. During Shivah the bereaved remain at home, away from everyday activities and concerns. Shivah begins with mourners sharing a "meal of consolation" prepared by friends; this reminder of life's continuity initiates the healing process. Friends and relatives visit the house of mourning throughout Shivah, offering condolences and sharing remembrances; callers bring prepared food to relieve the bereaved of daily chores. Since mourners are required by Jewish law to recite the *kaddish* (sanctification) prayer, services with a required minimum of ten worshipers are held in the home. Although the Sabbath counts as a day of mourning, Shivah is suspended from sunset Friday to sunset Saturday, and mourners recite kaddish at synagogue services. Recognizing work and family pressures, many contemporary liberal American Jewish communities reduce Shivah to three days.

Traditional observances for mourners during Shivah include sitting on the floor or low furniture; rending garments; and abstention from bathing, cutting hair, shaving, wearing leather, use of cosmetics, or sexual activity. In some homes mirrors are covered. Shivah ends on the morning of the seventh day. The twenty-three days following Shivah complete the Shloshim or thirty-day mourning period; during this time many mourners curtail activities and avoid celebrations. Mourners continue reciting the kaddish in communal worship for the next ten months.

See also DEATH AND DYING; JEWISH OBSERVANCE; JUDAISM; PRAYER; RITUAL.

BIBLIOGRAPHY

Dosick, Wayne. *Living Judaism: The Complete Guide to Jewish Belief and Practice.* 1995.

Lamm, Maurice. *The Jewish Way in Death and Mourning.* 1972.

Judith R. Baskin

Shrine

The original meaning of "shrine" in Old English *(scrin)* and Latin *(scrinium)* suggests that it is a box or repository. In this original and more limited usage, shrines are repositories for a revered body or venerated relic, and devotees often have commemorated holy persons by constructing shrines over tombs or placing remains in them. In its broader meaning, however, "shrine" refers to a sacred site that houses holy artifacts, promotes ritual practice, and attracts religious travelers, who often mark the time and extend the space of the journey by returning home with mementos. These sacred sites function as mediating spaces or transitional zones by allowing a vertical movement toward the sacred, elevating devotees and bringing low the transcendent, as pilgrims petition and thank the gods and saints. Shrines also allow horizontal movement outward into the social terrain and built environment. In this sense they culturally situate devotees by creating interpersonal bonds, negotiating social status, and constructing collective identity. Shrines differ from other places of worship such as Protestant churches or Jewish synagogues, which attract visitors on a more regular basis and from a narrower geographical range. In other words, shrines usually attract *pilgrims,* religiously motivated travelers who undertake infrequent round-trip journeys.

If we consider the term in its widest sense, most religious traditions have shrines, but the meanings and functions of those sacred sites vary widely. We can classify the variety of contemporary shrines in several ways.

Shrines can be classified, first, by religious tradition. So using this apparently straightforward scheme, we could note that El Santuario de Chimayo in New Mexico, currently one of the most frequently visited Catholic pilgrimage sites in the United States, is a Christian shrine. However, sometimes classifying shrines by religious affiliation can be more difficult.

Some sites inscribe multiple religious influences, and self-consciously ecumenical sacred spaces claim to venerate multiple traditions, as with the 1986 Light of Truth Universal Shrine at Satchidananda Ashram in Virginia. By the 1960s the American Methodist Historical Association officially had designated twelve sites, including Epworth Chapel in Georgia, as "national Methodist shrines." However, some religious followers, especially many Protestants, seem less comfortable using the term "shrine" to describe places with religious significance, even though, as that Methodist organization acknowledged, those sites sometimes take on many of the meanings and functions usually associated with shrines. Finally, classifying shrines by religious affiliation is problematic because that method overlooks quasi-religious sites. Some places that claim secular status nonetheless share some of the standard features of shrines—for example, nationalistic spaces such as the Washington Monument and the Vietnam Veterans Memorial and tourist destinations such as Cooperstown's National Baseball Hall of Fame and Museum, and Elvis Presley's Memphis home, Graceland.

Shrines also can be classified geographically, since they vary in placement and scope. Although there are very few of these in the contemporary United States, some shrines, such as Lourdes in France and Muhammed's tomb in Saudi Arabia, become international sites, drawing pilgrims from many nations. Others are national, as saints—such as St. James in Spain and Our Lady of Guadalupe in Mexico—become intertwined with the nation's history and identity. Regional shrines attract devotees from a few counties or states, while local shrines draw visitors from a single town or city. Narrowing the scope still more, some shrines decorate pathways or mark the boundary between domestic and civic space, as with Afro-Cuban yard shrines in Miami. Homes become sacred, too, as devotees place images and artifacts associated with holy persons on bedroom walls or living-room altars. And recent technological innovations, especially the Internet, have made some shrines even less spatially fixed: Web pages allow cyberpilgrims to e-mail prayers, check schedules, and take virtual tours.

Finally, shrines also can be classified by their origin and function, even if most contemporary sites share features of several types. *Commemorative shrines* recall the site of key historical or mythological events (e.g., a founder's vision or the world's creation), and pilgrims recount historical narratives or sacred myths about the deeds done there as they perform rituals that memorialize holy persons or transport followers to religiously significant times or places. Some Native American sacred sites, for example, are commemorative: Several mountains in New Mexico and Arizona

The Dalai Lama says a prayer in an authentic Tibetan shrine room at the Tibet House Cultural Center in New York City, on May 4, 1998. (Credit: AP/Wide World Photos.)

mark places where the Pueblo, Hopi, and Navajo peoples first were told to settle or first established their spiritual relationships with bear, deer, and eagle. *Miraculous shrines,* a second type, mark the site of miraculous interventions or sacred encounters, such as apparitions and healings. Many shrines acquire a reputation for their healing powers. The holy dirt at El Santuario de Chimayo, for example, draws Latino pilgrims who believe it has the power to heal body and soul, and those who are transformed leave notes or crutches to signal their thanks. Sometimes shrines also originate because followers find or acquire relics, objects considered sacred because of their association with holy persons *(built or found object shrines),* or because devotees want to give thanks that an individual or group was saved from some crisis or catastrophe *(ex voto shrines).* Other shrines are self-consciously constructed on sites that do not recall historical events, mark miraculous interventions, house ancient relics, or thank a deity. Some of these, *imitative shrines,* replicate images and architecture from older sites elsewhere, as with the many American Catholic sites whose design mirrors European pilgrim centers such as Lourdes and as with American Hindu centers such as Pittsburgh's Sri Venkateswara Temple, which recalls one of the most sacred sites in South India, the hilltop shrine of Tirupati. Other self-consciously created pilgrimage sites, *identity shrines,* celebrate saints or deities that mark ethnic, religious, or national identity. These shrines have been especially important to first- and second-generation immigrants, as they make sense of themselves in the new American cultural context.

These multiple types of shrines—classified by religion, geography, and origin—appear throughout the world, but some patterns emerge as we consider what has been most distinctive about U.S. shrines. First, with the exception of some Native American shrines, U.S. pilgrimage sites are relatively recent when compared with those from Europe, the Middle East, or Asia. Second, perhaps because of its vigorous civil religion and its relative economic privilege, which allows its citizens to construct and visit more sites, the nation seems to have a greater number of quasi-religious nationalistic and tourist places. Third, shrines have been more central in some religious traditions (e.g., Roman Catholicism and Hinduism) than in others and, with some exceptions, those long-standing patterns have held in America. So Catholics, with as many as 360 religious sites, have built the most shrines on American soil. American Buddhists and Muslims, who have constructed shrines in Asia and the Middle East, have not yet transplanted that tradition because their numbers increased substantially only after the 1965 revision of U.S. immigration laws, and these religious communities traditionally have constructed shrines on the tombs of holy persons or at the sites of historical events. That also explains a fourth pattern in the United States. Only religious movements that originated on the continent, such as the Latter-Day Saints or Mormons, can claim the American landscape as the site of their founding, so there are fewer commemorative, miraculous, and found-object shrines in the United States. In turn, Americans have built more imitative and identity shrines, which bridge for immigrants the homeland and the United States, a nation originally formed and continually transformed by migration.

See also ELVIS CULTS; HOLY LAND; MECCA; MIRACLE; PILGRIMAGE; RITUAL; ROME; VIRGIN OF GUADALUPE.

BIBLIOGRAPHY

Courtright, Paul B. "Shrines." In *Encyclopedia of Religion.* 1987.

Hanumadass, Marella L., ed. *A Pilgrimage to Hindu Temples in North America.* 1994.

Higgins, Paul Lambourne. *Pilgrimages USA: A Guide to Holy Places of the United States for Today's Traveler.* 1985.

Jones, George H. *The Methodist Tourist Guidebook.* 1966.

Linenthal, Edward Tabor. *Sacred Ground: Americans and Their Battlefields.* 1993.

Moran, J. Anthony. *Pilgrims' Guide to America: U.S. Catholic Shrines and Centers of Devotion.* 1992.

Nolan, Mary Lee, and Sidney Nolan. *Christian Pilgrimage in Modern Western Europe.* 1989.

Sears, John. *Sacred Places: American Tourist Attractions in the Nineteenth Century.* 1989.

Tweed, Thomas A. *Our Lady of the Exile: Diasporic Religion at a Cuban Catholic Shrine in Miami.* 1997.

Thomas A. Tweed

Shunning

The *Meidung,* known in English as "shunning" or "the ban," is a potent tool used by the Amish to maintain their strict behavioral standards and their old-fashioned common faith. Its use was at the very center of the founding of the Amish in Europe in the 1690s; Jacob Ammann was a Mennonite who had strong ideas about certain religious policies and practices, none more important than the precept that the community should enforce discipline by separating from itself those who did not meet its high standards.

Ammann and his followers rooted the practice of shunning in their understanding of Matthew 18:17, in which Jesus says of an errant believer who fails to respond to private admonition, "If he refuses to listen to them, tell it to the church; and if he refuses to listen even to the church, let him be to you as a Gentile and a tax collector." Ammann argued that other Mennonite elders were not applying the ban in cases that clearly called for it, and that the exclusion involved must be a total severance of social relations, not merely debarment from the communion service, as some other leaders taught. The conflict came to a head in Ammann's confrontation with the more moderate Hans Reist in 1693, and despite several unsuccessful attempts at reconciliation that ensued over the next several years, the Amish became a movement distinct from the larger, more liberal body of Mennonites.

Shunning is a last resort, used only after lesser sanctions have failed. Most violations of the *Ordnung* (the detailed system of regulations governing daily life) are addressed through private admonition and repentance. In more serious cases the offender is asked to make a public confession at a church service. One who remains unrepentant will eventually be shunned for a limited period of time, typically six weeks. Only thereafter—or following an unusually flagrant violation, such as the purchase of an automobile—is the permanent ban imposed; even then it may be lifted upon public repentance and cessation of the offending behavior.

Shunning involves a near-total cutting off of social relations. Amish in good standing may not do business with an individual under the *Meidung*. Although Amish may ride in motor vehicles when necessary, no ride may be in a car driven by a banned former member. Husband and wife may continue to live together when one is banned, but they may not engage in sexual relations. Family ties are drastically ruptured; the shunned are in effect disowned by their parents and siblings. Church members who refuse to honor the ban will themselves be banned.

Theologically, shunning is regarded as salvific medicine that will help the wayward member, who has sinned against God, return to the fold. It also serves to purify the church, which is regarded as a body of saved believers, and reaffirm its role as a bulwark against sin. In effect it serves as perhaps the most important instrument for the maintenance of Amish life and of the *Ordnung*. To outsiders the ban seems harsh and cruel, but it has played a vital role in the maintenance of Amish distinctiveness.

See also AMISH; MENNONITES.

BIBLIOGRAPHY
Hostetler, John A. *Amish Society.* 1980.
Kraybill, Donald B. *The Riddle of Amish Culture.* 1989.

Timothy Miller

Sikhism

Most of the memorable events that are of major importance to Sikh religious tradition have taken place in the productive agricultural region called the Punjab, which is largely in north India but extends beyond India's current border into Pakistan. The region's name literally means "five rivers" (*panj-ab*), and historically its produce depended on water available from the five tributaries that flow into the Indus River and then into the Arabian Sea. Since the nineteenth century, modern irrigation canals have carried water down from the foothills of the Himalayas, and more recently hybrid seeds have made the Punjab plains one of the world's great sources of food grains. Today most of the world's Sikhs, who number around 15 mil-

An American Sikh wearing a turban with a badge, a typical Sikh emblem, near Espanola, New Mexico, ca. December 1979. (Credit: CORBIS/Buddy Mays.)

lion, are descended from Punjabi farmers and from people who supplied them with goods and services essential to their agricultural livelihood. Punjabi language, kinship patterns, and cultural habits in general are interwoven with the Sikh ideals and teachings that were first revealed though the life and work of Guru Nānak (1469–1539).

The lineage of the ten spiritual masters who have highest religious authority for Sikhs begins with Guru Nānak and ends with Guru Gobind Singh (d. 1708). These are ten different human beings, but because they reveal and reflect the unity of a single timeless divine reality, a Sikh is likely to refer to any or all of them together, and to whatever derives from them, in the singular as "the Guru." In fact the traditional Punjabi name for what English speakers call Sikhism is Gurmat, which means the doctrine or teachings of the guru(s). From the time of the death of Gobind Singh, who did not appoint any human successor, the function of spiritual teaching has been served mainly by the Sikh scripture called the Adi Granth (literally, "the first book"), which is more popularly and appropriately known as the Gurū Granth Sahib. Its standing among contemporary Sikhs is similar to that of the Torah among Jews, the Qur'an among Muslims, and the Bible among evangelical and other conservative Christians. As the repository of spiritual truth and power, it is accorded highest respect and deference.

The central act for establishing a gurdwara, the Sikh of worship, is to install a copy of the Guru Granth Sahib at a suitably prepared site. Its very presence is in a sense the presence of the Guru.

Guru Gobind Singh added another dimension to Sikh identity, which already had geographical and ethnic as well as spiritual sources, in 1699 when he founded the Khālsā Panth in the Himalayan foothills at Anandpur. The ethos of the *khālsā,* a voluntary order composed of adult men and women initiates within Sikhism, is that of the soldier, and its symbols are those of military preparedness. Five emblems of membership that are always to be kept on one's person are uncut hair and a comb, a steel bracelet, short (under)pants, and a dagger or sword. Vows taken at the time of initiation commit one to follow a shared set of prescribed rules (*rahit*). Khālsā identity provides a complement to the universalist teachings of Guru Nānak and the inclusivism of the Adi Granth, which was compiled on the Punjab plains at Amritsar largely by the Fifth Guru and incorporates the poems and prayers of several Hindu and Muslim saints whose spiritual perspectives are compatible with those of the Sikh masters. The Khālsā also generates a dynamic tension within Sikh tradition akin to the tension between priestly and prophetic strands within biblical tradition.

Khālsā members never have been the majority within Sikh tradition at large, but their ethos pervades and enriches Sikhism—which otherwise might not have attained widespread recognition in the twentieth century as a world religion with its own distinctive religious rites and practices, sites and homeland, and organizational structure. The dynamics infused into Sikh tradition by the Khālsā provided a rallying point during British colonial rule in South Asia—particularly in support of the establishment and legal recognition of separate Sikh life-cycle rituals early in the twentieth century and then in favor of legislative provision for Sikh control of historically significant religious centers, including the large and lucrative ones at Amritsar and Anandpur during the 1920s—and after the end of colonial rule in the movement for creation of a Punjab state with a Sikh majority in the Republic of India.

Sikh presence in the United States was almost completely excluded by restrictive and discriminatory immigration laws until the 1960s. Then within a few years several factors brought Sikhism into prominence. Some of the American counterculture youths who were attracted to Eastern spirituality joined one of the several movements created by Punjabi immigrant Harbhajan Singh (Yogi Bhajan) in the 1960s and 1970s, including the Healthy Happy Holy movement and later the Sikh Dharma of the Western Hemisphere. The apparent conversions generated debate about what should be required in order to be considered a Sikh, and the degree of acceptance of these *gora* or white Sikhs and their leader by religious authorities in the Punjab fluctuated in correlation with shifts in local politics. At the same time, new immigrants with advanced technical and professional training settled in North America, became highly successful, and found themselves increasingly nostalgic about their Punjabi Sikh heritage. A few of them lent support to a movement for a separate Sikh state to be called Khalistan, which they envisioned would be independent of both India and Pakistan. In the longer term the perennial issues that are likely to continue to influence the development of Sikh communities in North America are very likely to be the same as those that socially define other religious groups—how families are to be preserved, children educated, traditional values honored and enacted, religious centers controlled, and success within the world ensured.

BIBLIOGRAPHY

Embree, Ainslie T. *Utopias in Conflict: Religion and Nationalism in Modern India.* 1990.
Hinnells, John R., ed. *A New Handbook of Living Religions.* 1997.
Kapur, Rajiv A. *Sikh Separatism: The Politics of Faith.* 1986.
McLeod, Hew. *Sikhism.* 1997.
McLeod, W. H. *Historical Dictionary of Sikhism.* 1995.
Oberoi, Harjot. *The Construction of Religious Boundaries: Culture, Identity, and Diversity in the Sikh Tradition.* 1994.
Thursby, Gene R. *The Sikhs.* 1992.
Tweed, Thomas A., and Stephen Prothero, eds. *Asian Religions in America: A Documentary History.* 1999.
Williams, Raymond Brady. *Religions of Immigrants from India and Pakistan: New Threads in the American Tapestry.* 1988.

Gene R. Thursby

Silva Mind Control

Silva Mind Control is a self-help technique for enhancing mental performance that has its roots in New Thought philosophy, parapsychology, and brain-wave research. The technique's founder, José Silva, was born in 1914 in Laredo, Texas, and spent his early life building a successful electronics business. He also studied psychology, Yoga, and Rosicrucianism and experimented with hypnosis to improve his children's IQ. Based on exhaustive research into brain functioning, Silva began teaching a distinctive method of relaxation, visualization, and meditation to a group of thirty-one students—90 percent of whom were women—in Amarillo, Texas, in 1966. By the early 1970s Silva had created a teaching organization and standardized his training into a Basic Lecture Series (BLS) that has remained remarkably consistent over the past thirty-three years. The BLS is currently being taught in more than one hundred countries and in twenty-nine languages; Silva Mind Control International has recorded its fastest growth in Latin America.

Typically, the BLS is presented in four segments over two consecutive weekends. The first two segments teach a method of controlled relaxation designed to slow brain-wave frequency to ten cycles per second, which Silva claims is the most effective frequency for problem-solving, self-healing, and creative thought. In the third segment, students learn to contact inner guides and to visualize mental screens on which to work out problems. The final segment teaches students to heal others with innate psychic abilities. Graduate courses are available for those wishing to teach the BLS as private contractors and for those interested in learning advanced holistic healing techniques. Silva's belief that actualizing human potential will help inaugurate a golden age of spiritual understanding places his organization squarely within the broader New Age movement.

See also MEDITATION; NEW AGE SPIRITUALITY; NEW THOUGHT; PSYCHOLOGY OF RELIGION; RELIGIOUS EXPERIENCE; VISUALIZATION.

BIBLIOGRAPHY

Powers, Analine M. *Silva Mind Control: An Anthropological Inquiry.* 1992.
Silva, José, and Philip Miele. *The Silva Mind Control Method.* 1977.

Phillip Charles Lucas

Simos, Miriam.

See Starhawk.

Snake Handling

Throughout most of the twentieth century, snake-handling Appalachian Christians, who refer to their practice as "serpent handling," have been and continue to be part of the region's most sensationalized and least understood religious tradition. Serpent handling epitomizes the religions of Appalachia as the first and often only tradition that comes to mind in the popular national consciousness. Serpent handlers are a small independent Holiness group distinctive to

A "serpent" handler practices his faith by handling a poisonous rattlesnake as a fellow member looks on during services at the Church of the Lord Jesus in Kingston, Georgia, on February 25, 1995. Handling the serpent safely is regarded as a test of faith in God. (Credit: AP/Wide World Photos.)

the mountains, small valleys, and plateaus of Appalachia. The most informed estimates average two thousand participants scattered throughout the region, excluding out-migration.

David L. Kimbrough's *Taking Up Serpents: Snake Handlers of Eastern Kentucky* (1995) affirms that serpent handlers are not peculiar unto themselves but are clearly a part of Appalachia's much larger and older independent, nondenominational Holiness tradition, from which they are distinguished in worship practices and beliefs only by the inclusion of serpent handling, fire handling, and drinking poison. Clear distinctions prevail between different theological traditions of serpent handlers, from Oneness or Jesus Only groups to Trinitarian groups, a common division in the larger Holiness-Pentecostal movements within and outside of Appalachia. As part of Appalachia's larger Holiness tradition, Kimbrough affirms serpent handlers' strong, plain-folk, camp-meeting heritage in the region, stating that their "practices and beliefs represented an intensification and elaboration of traditional norms" (p. 77).

More thorough and persuasive than any other scholar to date, Kimbrough evaluates long-circulating accounts and only recently discovered information that decisively identify the practice's most probable origins long thought to be associated with George W. Hensley. At a revival in 1910 near Cleveland, Tennessee, Hensley took literally Mark 16:18, "They shall take up serpents," as a command Holiness people should keep. *Taking Up Serpents* also provides a solid social history of serpent handling. It follows the path of the Saylor family of eastern Kentucky, one of Appalachia's premier serpent-handling families, from their Presbyterian heritage, which they brought with them when they first settled in Kentucky at the beginning of the nineteenth century, through their shift to Primitive Baptist Calvinism, and finally to Holiness traditions at the end of the nineteenth century. The Saylor family embraced serpent handling by way of Hensley's work in eastern Kentucky in the early 1930s.

The Saylor family social history demonstrates the strong historical and theological commonalities that unite the varieties of Appalachia's religious traditions rather than their apparent yet misleading differences that are more distinguishing than divisive. Kimbrough also provides a persuasive contextual framework that rejects the cliché of fatalism for a sacramental interpretation of serpent handling that expresses a hope-infused, situational realism.

The crush of media fascination in the 1990s, from best-selling novels and I-was-there accounts to feature stories on *Oprah* and *Dateline NBC,* became white-hot following publication of *Salvation on Sand Mountain: Snake Handling and Redemption in Southern Appalachia* (1995) by Dennis Covington, a *New York Times* reporter on Appalachia. Covington's repetitive flair for the dramatic more often than not is at the expense of careful accuracy about the real-life people he names and portrays; nonetheless he provides a human face to Appalachia's serpent-handling Christians. As of this writing, popular media continue to highlight serpent handlers as though they stand separate and apart from an all but invisible multitude of interrelated groups that together make Appalachia the nation's largest and—second only to New England—oldest regional religious tradition.

See also Appalachia, Religions of; Southern Religion.

Bibliography

Burton, Thomas. *Serpent-Handling Believers.* 1993.

Covington, Dennis. *Salvation on Sand Mountain: Snake Handling and Redemption in Southern Appalachia.* 1985.

Daugherty, Mary Lee. "Serpent-Handling as Sacrament." *Theology Today* (October 1976): 232–243.

Smith, Lee. *Saving Grace.* 1995.

Deborah Vansau McCauley

Society for Humanistic Judaism.

See Humanism.

Society of Friends.

See Quakers.

Sociology of Religion

The sociology of religion seeks to understand humanly constructed aspects of religion in their social context. In contrast to other viable approaches to studying religion, the sociology of religion searches for patterns and processes underlying the interdependence of religion and society. To do so, it relies on models, theories, observation, and analysis.

As an outgrowth of historical developments in Western thought—such as the Enlightenment, the industrial revolution, rationalization, and positivism—the sociology of religion suspends judgment on the transcendent truthfulness of any religion, studying instead the social genesis, roles, and meanings of religion for the people involved and for the larger society.

The history of the sociology of religion is brief. Despite earlier, isolated applications, the first major systematic studies in the sociology of religion began at the end of the nineteenth century in Europe. Émile Durkheim, Ferdinand Tonnies, Georg Simmel, Ernst Troeltsch, and Max Weber all made the study of religion central in their theories of society and their historical, comparative, and empirical research. The most active time came in the first two decades of the twentieth century, with the publication of still-influential books such as Weber's *The Protestant Ethic and the Spirit of Capitalism* (1904–1905) and *Sociology of Religion* (1920–1921), Troeltsch's *Social Teachings of the Christian Church* (1912), and Durkheim's *The Elementary Forms of the Religious Life* (1912). These works examined the role of religion in social transformation, the role of structural characteristics in religion on faith and practice, and the social cohesive functions of religion for society. Pessimistic about the fate of religion in contemporary societies, many of these works viewed modernization as corroding religious needs and beliefs.

Because these seminal European works had not yet been translated into English, the sociology of religion was rather limited in the United States in the first third of the twentieth century. Much of the engaging sociological work in religion during this time was in the tradition of community studies. These works focused on all aspects of single communities, including religious life. Many of the early American sociologists who focused specifically on religion began their careers as clergy or seminarians, and focused on social problems as their primary subject matter. As such, the sociology of religion was isolated from the larger field of sociology. For example, the publication of theologian H. Richard Niebuhr's important sociological book *The Social Sources of Denominationalism* (1929) went largely unnoticed by sociological journals.

In the late 1930s and early 1940s the sociological study of religion was limited primarily to members of the Catholic Sociological Society. An important exception to this pattern was Talcott Parsons, probably the most influential American sociologist of the mid-twentieth century. He translated Weber's works—including his works on religion—into English (1930), making Weber's work more accessible to English-speakers. Further, combining work from Weber and Durkheim, Parsons also incorporated religion into his theory of society.

Easier access and greater knowledge of the seminal European sociological works on religion, an increase in church participation, and an increased interest in institutional research after World War II provided a fertile environment for sociologists to focus on religion (McGuire 1997). Until the 1960s, however, sociologists focused on institutionalized religion. Religion meant the church, typically a Christian church. Individual religiosity meant participation in a church. With the exception of Parsons' writings, this narrow focus continued to isolate the sociology of religion from the larger discipline of sociology. Perhaps the most influential American sociologists of religion after World War II, but prior to the 1960s, were J. Milton Yinger, with works such as *Religion in the Struggle for Power* (1946), and Joseph Fichter, with works such as *Dynamic of a City Church* (1951) and *Social Relations in the Urban Parish* (1954).

In the 1960s, the sociology of religion expanded its scope and influence. Several influential books and papers were published, including Will Herberg's *Protestant-Catholic-Jew* (1960), Gerhard Lenski's *The Religious Factor* and Evelyn Underhill's *Mysticism* (1961), Benton Johnson's "On Church and Sect" (1963), Clifford Geertz's "Religion as a Cultural System," and Charles Glock and Rodney Stark's *Christian Beliefs and Anti-Semitism* (1966). In particular, 1967 was a watershed year for the sociology of religion, with the publication of Robert Bellah's "Civil Religion in America," Peter Berger's *The Sacred Canopy*, Thomas Luckmann's *The Invisible Religion*, and Alasdair MacIntyre's *Secularization and Moral Change*. Several of these works expanded the secularization theme running through many of the seminal works that had come out of Europe a half century earlier. These contemporary works argued that, with the advancement of science and pluralism, religion in the modern world would survive only in a weakened, individualized form, or in a secularized form called civil religion.

Soon thereafter, alternative perspectives on the fate of religion in modern societies appeared. Books such as Andrew Greeley's *Unsecular Man* (1972) challenged the commonly accepted framework of secularization. The debate between secularization and the persistence of religion continued throughout the remainder of the twentieth century, generating a good deal of research and theorizing.

While this central debate motivated much research in the sociology of religion, the field diversified—especially after 1980—to study all types of institutionalized and noninstitutionalized forms of religion. And it increasingly asked, "What can we understand about the nature of social life by examining religion?" (McGuire 1997).

The sociology of religion focuses on areas such as conversion, cults/new religious movements, religious marketing, personal religiosity, religious conflict, religious movements, rituals, syncretism (the combining of beliefs and practices from different traditions), organizational structure, ethnic and national expressions of religion, and the provision of meaning and belonging. Much work in the sociology of religion is concerned with how religion influences and is influenced by other aspects of society. These include religion's influence on and by the economy, education, gender roles, globalization, health, the mass media, material culture, moral attitudes, politics, social order, social change, science, and stratification.

The expansion of the sociology of religion in the English-speaking countries of the West is reflected by the growth of sociology of religion journals and annuals. Of the ten primary sociology of religion journals and annuals, only one was founded before 1950. Half of the ten originated since 1980. The increasing concern for religion's influence on and by other aspects of society is reflected in the titles of post-1990 journals and annuals, such as *Religion and American Culture; Religion and the Social Order;* and *Religion, State, and Society.*

See also ANTHROPOLOGY OF RELIGION; BASE COMMUNITIES; BELONGING, RELIGIOUS; PSYCHOLOGY OF RELIGION; RELIGIOUS COMMUNITIES; RELIGIOUS STUDIES.

BIBLIOGRAPHY

Johnstone, Ronald L. *Religion in Society*, 5th ed. 1997.

McGuire, Merideth B. *Religion in the Social Context*, 4th ed. 1997.

Reed, Myer S., Jr. "After the Alliance: The Sociology of Religion in the United States from 1925 to 1949." *Sociological Analysis* 43 (1982):189–204.

Reed, Myer S., Jr. "An Alliance for Progress: The Early Years of the Sociology of Religion in the United States." *Sociological Analysis* 42 (1981):27–46.

Warner, Steve. "Work in Progress Toward a New Paradigm for the Sociological Study of Religion in the United States." *American Journal of Sociology* 98 (1993):1044–1093.

Michael Emerson

Soka Gakkai

Soka Gakkai is a Buddhist movement imported to the United States by Japanese immigrants. Originally practiced mainly by the Japanese wives of American military men, the movement began to grow rapidly following changes in U.S. immigration laws in 1965. The new immigration laws, combined with the expansion of the Japanese economy into U.S. markets, brought growing numbers of educated Japanese professionals and entrepreneurs to the United States. These new immigrants gave Soka Gakkai access to a much broader recruitment pool and positioned the movement advantageously with regard to those young Americans most likely to take an interest in Buddhism—that is, young, educated, middle-class, white-collar workers in urban environments.

History

The movement was founded in Japan in 1930 by an educator, Tsunesaburo Makiguchi (1871–1944), who organized the Soka Kyoiku Gakkai (Value Creation Education Society) in an attempt to inject a dose of humanism into the Japanese educational system. Shortly before the entry of Japan into World War II, Makiguchi and his protégé, Josei Toda (1900–1958), converted to Nichiren Shoshu Buddhism—a sect that claims to teach the "true Buddhism" as taught by Nichiren, a thirteenth-century monk who believed that all individuals contained within themselves the potential for enlightenment and that this potential could be unlocked by exclusive devotion to the Lotus Sutra. Thwarted in their attempt to reform the Japanese educational system, Makiguchi and Toda were imprisoned on charges of *lèse majesté* for their refusal to cooperate with the Religious Organizations Act (1940), which created a three-religion establishment, centered on State Shinto and designed to promote patriotism and loyalty to the increasingly militarist regime.

Following Makiguchi's death in prison and the end of World War II, Toda reorganized the movement as a lay association of Nichiren Shoshu. In the chaotic aftermath of the war, Soka Gakkai grew rapidly, mostly among the displaced residents of urban environments. Daisaku Ikeda (1928–), Soka Gakkai's charismatic third president, led the international growth of the movement. Today, Soka Gakkai International (SGI) claims millions of members in about a hundred countries, with significant representations in the United States, Brazil, Britain, and Italy.

Doctrine and Practice

The fundamental truth expounded by Nichiren and promoted by Soka Gakkai is that every individual has the potential for enlightenment, and the key to unlocking that potential is contained in the Lotus Sutra, which is understood to be the most perfect expression of the Buddha's wisdom. By chanting the title of the Lotus Sutra, *Nam myoho renge kyo*, one forms a connection with the ultimate reality that pervades the universe—the karmic law of cause and effect. Soka Gakkai members chant this phrase, along with portions of the Lotus Sutra and prayers for world peace (collectively called *Gongyo*) in front of a personal copy of the *Gohonzon*, a mandala originally inscribed by Nichiren, which features the title of the Lotus Sutra surrounded by characters representing the "ten realms" of consciousness and is understood as something like a road map to enlightenment. The ten realms describe ten basic life conditions that everyone possesses and experiences—Hell, Hunger, Animality, and Belligerence, through Tranquility, Rapture, Learning, and Realization, to Bodhisattva, and ultimately Buddhahood or enlightenment. These "life conditions" are not understood as external circumstances imposing upon the individual, but rather as modes of being. Thus one's external circumstances are but a reflection of one's inner life condition, and by changing one's way of being in the world, one can improve the external circumstances of one's life.

Soka Gakkai, furthermore, promotes the belief that individual enlightenment is the first step toward world peace. As individuals learn to take responsibility for their own life condition and for the impact of their lives on the external world, they can work together to raise awareness of issues of intercultural understanding and tolerance, issues of the environment, and the threat of military technology. As an organization, therefore, Soka Gakkai sponsors a variety of educational, cultural, and political projects, and participates in the United Nations as a recognized non-government organization.

Soka Gakkai in the United States

Soka Gakkai has experienced phenomenal growth in the United States, mostly through the conversion of non-Japanese, middle-class baby boomers. The organization claims to have about 300,000 members in the United States, although 45,000–50,000 is probably a more realistic estimate of the number of currently active members. Today, ethnically Japanese members are a minority, constituting less than a fourth of all members. White members are the majority, while black, Latino, and mixed-race members represent significant minorities.

As elsewhere in the world, SGI-USA is active in efforts to promote art, culture, and education in the United States. Soka University, located in Southern California, is modeled on the pedagogical theories of Makiguchi. The Boston Research Center for the Twenty-first Century, located in Cambridge, Massachusetts, is dedicated to research on issues related to nuclear power and world peace. The Florida Culture Center provides a venue for a variety of cultural and educational events. These foci of activity are complemented by a variety of more local efforts to clean up parks, educate through traveling art exhibits, and entertain with a variety of musical and theatrical performances.

The Schism of 1991

For more than fifty years, Soka Gakkai existed as a lay movement affiliated with the Nichiren Shoshu sect. Its aim, in part, was to raise money as well as to obtain a dedicated following to support the priesthood. But latent tensions between the Soka Gakkai and the Nichiren Shoshu leadership came to a head in 1990 when the high priest accused Daisaku Ikeda, who remains the movement's primary spiritual figurehead and president of the international organization, of slandering Buddhism by asserting that the priests and laity are equal before the *Gohonzon*. Although a formal apology was issued by the Soka Gakkai leadership, and apparently accepted by the priests, tensions between Soka Gakkai leaders and the priests continue to grow. When the priests raised obligatory fees for funerary and other ritual services, Soka Gakkai leaders objected that the priests had become greedy and authoritarian. In November 1991, the high priest of Nichren Shoshu ordered the Soka Gakkai to disband and issued a writ of excommunication for all members who remained affiliated with the Soka Gakkai.

Ironically, Soka Gakkai seems to have benefited greatly from that split. The schism served to enhance the autonomy of the various national organizations, making it easier for these organizations to adapt to the needs of members and circumstances in their immediate environments. To fill the gap left by the priests, Soka Gakkai developed roles for voluntary "ministers of ceremony," who now preside over weddings, funerals, and other ritual services.

In the United States, the changes in SGI since the split suggest movement toward the congregational form that dominates in American religious organiza-

tions. There is a growing emphasis on the autonomy of local organizations and participation by members in making important decisions. This new autonomy, coupled with the declining presence of Japanese immigrants in positions of leadership, suggests that the organization will lose much of its remaining Japanese patina and become more and more like an American denomination.

See also BUDDHISM; JAPANESE-AMERICAN RELIGIONS.

BIBLIOGRAPHY

Eppsteiner, Robert. *The Soka Gakkai International: Religious Roots, Early History, and Contemporary Development.* 1997.

Hammond, Phillip, and David Machacek. *Soka Gakkai in America: Accommodation and Conversion.* 1999.

Hurst, Jane. "A Buddhist Reformation in the Twentieth Century: Causes and Implications of the Conflict Between the Soka Gakkai and the Nichiren Shoshu Priesthood." In *Global Citizens: The Soka Gakkai Buddhist Movement in the World,* edited by D. Machecek and B. Wilson. Forthcoming.

Tamaru, Noriyoshi. "Soka Gakkai in historical perspective." In *Global Citizens: The Soka Gakkai Buddhist Movement in the World,* edited by D. Machacek and B. Wilson.

David W. Machacek

Solar Temple

The Order of the Solar Temple, a small and little-known modern gnostic occult group, was thrust into the spotlight following the death of fifty-three members on October 3–4, 1994, in a murder/suicide event in rural Switzerland. The Solar Temple was one of several occult initiatory groups that were representative of the Neo-Templar revival that began among Freemasons soon after the French Revolution. These groups claimed to continue the very successful Order of the Temple, which had been destroyed in France in 1307. In 1804, Bernard-Raymond Fabré-Palaprat (1773–1838) announced the existence of an unbroken line of Templar grand masters who had operated through the previous four centuries and the following year created a new Templar order with himself as grand master. The original order founded by Fabré-Palaprat generated a number of similar groups.

Influenced by the Neo-Templar tradition, French occultist Joseph Di Mambro (1924–1994) founded the Golden Way Foundation in Geneva, Switzerland, in 1978. The foundation was a closely knit initiatory group that looked both toward a transformation of the world and the return of its initiates to their cosmic origin. It operated several front groups through which it recruited members. In 1982, Luc Jouret (1947–1994), a physician, joined the Golden Way and became its main public spokesperson. He spoke to perspective members through gatherings of the Amenta clubs. Those showing promise were introduced to the more occult teachings of the order. A few were then accepted into the inner order.

The order spread through the French-speaking world, with the majority of its more than four hundred members coming from France, Switzerland, and Québec. Drawing authority from a set of secret masters residing in Zurich, Di Mambro led the order.

The message of the Temple was apocalyptic, survivalist, and neo-gnostic. In the face of predicted upheavals in the world, many moved to Québec, which they saw as a safer environment. At the same time, their neo-gnostic teachings led them to look forward to escape from the earthly situation into the higher spiritual realms.

As early as 1990, Di Mambro discussed the idea of transit as an act of voluntary departure on a mission to bring the germ of life to another planet. The nature of that transit, vague at first, was by 1993 being associated with suicide. To prepare themselves for transit, members cut ties with the outside world. At the same time, various investigations of the group by outside agencies accelerated.

The final events began on September 30 with the murder of five people in Québec. Then on October 3, twenty-seven people died at Chiery, Switzerland, and the next day twenty-one at Granges-sur-Salvan. All three locations were torched. The number who were murdered is unknown. In December 1995, sixteen additional members of the groups committed suicide at Vercors, France. In the wake of these actions, the order was disbanded.

Following these events, anticult organizations have become empowered in France and Belgium, and both governments have taken suppressive actions against new religious groups operating within their borders.

See also ANTI-CULT MOVEMENT; APOCALYPSE; BRAINWASHING; CULT; CULT AWARENESS NETWORK; GNOSTICISM; OCCULT, THE.

BIBLIOGRAPHY
Mayer, Jean-François. *Il Templio Solare.* 1997.

J. Gordon Melton

Sophia

"Sophia" is the Greek word of feminine grammatical gender for the English term "wisdom" (Hebrew, *chok-mah;* Latin, *sapientia*). Divine Sophia-Wisdom, seen variously as the feminine side of God, as the Holy Spirit, as the Goddess, or as God's spouse, reached her peak of power in the Hellenistic era; was limited in her divine status by Jewish monotheism; was replaced in Christianity by the Holy Spirit, Jesus, and Mary; and was erased from Christological tradition by the church fathers. Recent feminist research has recovered Sophia-Wisdom in the Hebrew scriptures and Apocrypha (*The Wisdom of Solomon* and *Ben Sira*), and rediscovered her great influence in Hellenistic-Jewish, early Christian, and Gnostic circles.

Jewish wisdom theology presents God as the divine woman Wisdom, who appears as God's own being in creative and saving involvement with the world. As Sophia-Wisdom (or Wisdom-Sophia) God is present to the chosen people Israel. The woman Wisdom is a hidden treasure known only to God and the only one who knows God (Job 28); she is a street preacher and prophet (Proverbs 1:8) who is with God during creation (Proverbs 8:22–31) and identifies her own words, actions, and gifts with those of God (Proverbs 1:23; 8:6–9). She is a giver of life (Proverbs 4:13), architect of her home, hostess and liturgist at her festive table (Proverbs 9:1–6), the glory of God (Wisdom 7:25–26), and the mediator of creation (Wisdom 8:5–6), and she shares the throne of God (Wisdom 9:3). She creates everything, makes all things new again, and permeates the universe (Wisdom 7:23, 27; 8:1, 5). She appears on earth, lives among creation (Baruch 3:37), and works in history to save her chosen people. She is called sister, spouse, mother, beloved, hostess, liberator, justice-maker, and teacher. In her, the wisdom of women and the image of the divine are united.

Scholarly opinion suggests that Hellenistic Jews in Egypt conceived of divine Wisdom as prefigured in the Canaanite, Mesopotamian, and Egyptian goddesses Astarte, Ishtar, Maat, and Isis. Egyptian Judaism incorporated the mythology and theology of Isis into the figure of Sophia to lend power to its own integrating forces through the use of a female divinity. Like Isis, Sophia is a religious symbol with an unusual capacity to create unity, a divine savior using the "I am" style to proclaim her message of universal salvation.

In early Christian writings Sophia seems to disappear, yet a deeper reading shows that a submerged theology of Wisdom-Sophia permeates the Christian scriptures. Early Christian communities had access to and used early Jewish discoveries of divine wisdom to elaborate on the significance of the Holy Spirit, Jesus, and Mary. The complete unity between Sophia and the Spirit is expressed in Wisdom 7:22–23, 27, where Sophia assumes the functions of the Spirit. Spirit-Sophia's universal presence is analogous to God's

Spirit (Wisdom 7:24). These texts strengthen the fittingness of speaking about the Spirit in female imagery.

Early Jesus traditions interpreted the mission of Jesus as that of divine Sophia: proclaiming Sophia-God as the God of the poor, the excluded, and all who suffer injustice. What Judaism said of Sophia, Christian writers came to say of Jesus. Just as Wisdom received everything from God, so Jesus received everything from God (Matthew 11:27a). Just as Wisdom-Sophia is known only by God and is the only one who knows God, so Jesus has all wisdom (Matthew 11:27b, c). Just as divine Sophia gives her wisdom as gift, so also Jesus reveals wisdom to his chosen (Matthew 11:27d). Like Sophia-Isis, Jesus speaks in the "I am" style, and with the symbolism of bread, wine, and water invites people to eat and drink. Like Sophia-Wisdom, Jesus proclaims his message in the public square, is light and life of the world, calls people, and makes them children and friends. Paul describes Jesus as "the Sophia of God" (1 Corinthians 1:23–25; 2:6–8). Though she/he is the child and messenger of Sophia-God, Jesus-Sophia's woman Wisdom presence is pushed aside partly by John's Logos-Son-male theology, by resistance to the Gnostic version of Christianity that embraced Sophia, by the rejection of female leadership in the churches, and by the growth of sexism and patriarchy in Christian communities. Female wisdom imagery passed to the figure of Mary of Nazareth, the mother of Jesus, who became known as the Throne of Wisdom.

Sophia has reemerged in contemporary American feminist theology and spirituality. As proposed by Elisabeth Schussler Fiorenza and adopted by many feminist theologians, Sophia as the divine woman Wisdom continues her call for the liberation of all women, children, and men from the patriarchal, kyriarchal (male-priesthood-dominated) power in society and in religious communities. She invites all to rearticulate the symbols, images, and names of divine Sophia so that masculine-oriented God and Christ language is radically changed and the Western cultural sex/gender system is radically reconstructed.

See also BIBLE; DIVINITY; EASTERN ORTHODOXY; FEMINIST SPIRITUALITY; FEMINIST THEOLOGY; GNOSTICISM; GOD; GODDESS; JUDAISM; MATRIARCHY; ROMAN CATHOLICISM; SPIRIT; WISDOM LITERATURE; WOMANIST THEOLOGY.

BIBLIOGRAPHY

Cady, Susan, Marian Ronan, and Hal Taussig. *Sophia: The Future of Feminist Spirituality.* 1986.

Camp, Claudia V. "Sophia/Wisdom." In *Dictionary of Feminist Theologies,* edited by Letty M. Russell and J. Shannon Clarkson. 1996.

Johnson, Elizabeth A. *She Who Is.* 1992.

Schussler Fiorenza, Elisabeth. *Jesus: Miriam's Child, Sophia's Prophet.* 1994.

Diann L. Neu

Southern Christian Leadership Conference

The Southern Christian Leadership Conference (SCLC) is one of the most important organizations to emerge out of the modern civil rights movement. An interdenominational alliance of activist clergymen, the SCLC drew upon and extended the institutional power base already present in the black church. The SCLC became the main organizational vehicle by which isolated instances of resistance against Jim Crow segregation were coordinated into a mass movement spanning the South. With the motto "To Save the Soul of America," the SCLC was committed to the philosophy of nonviolence in exercising the moral imperative to oppose unjust laws.

Founded in 1957 by a group of ministers, with Dr. Martin Luther King, Jr. (1929–1968) as its first president, the SCLC developed out of the successful Montgomery, Alabama, bus boycott of 1955–1956. The SCLC was also instrumental in establishing affiliated organizations, one of which was the Student Nonviolent Coordinating Committee (SNCC). Founded in 1960 through the direct efforts of then acting executive director Ella J. Baker (1905–) and based primarily in black colleges and universities rather than in churches, the SNCC became the main organizational vehicle mobilizing student protest efforts across the South.

Between 1960 and 1965 the SCLC and SNCC, in concert with other organizations, gave the movement some of its greatest successes. The sit-ins (1960) and freedom rides (1961) helped integrate public facilities and interstate transportation; the SCLC's Operation Breadbasket boycotted certain businesses "not" operating in black communities for better job opportunities; the 1963 Birmingham, Alabama, demonstration led to the March on Washington that same year, during which Dr. King delivered his famous "I Have a Dream" speech; and passage of the Civil Rights Act (1964) and the Voting Rights Act (1965) were particularly meaningful for the movement and for the SCLC as its leading organization.

After these major successes, the SCLC's attention began to shift to the plight of blacks in northern cities.

*(From left to right) Dr. Joseph E. Lowery, Rev. Ralph D. Abernathy, and Rev.
Andrew Young sit at a news conference in Atlanta, Georgia, on April 11, 1968, a
week after the assassination of the Rev. Dr. Martin Luther King, Jr. Abernathy led
the Southern Christian Leadership Conference from Dr. King's death until 1977,
when he was succeeded by Rev. Lowery. Lowery remained at the helm of SCLC for
twenty years, leaving office on July 31, 1997.* (Credit: AP/Wide World Photos.)

Rev. Jesse Jackson (1941–) came to prominence during this time as director of Chicago's Operation Breadbasket. It was also during this period of transition that the growing Black Power movement, rejecting the principle of nonviolence, began to challenge the authoritative position of the SCLC. With Dr. King's assassination on April 4, 1968, Rev. Ralph D. Abernathy (1926–1990) became president of the SCLC. In 1977, when he stepped down, Rev. Joseph Lowery (1924–) took over leadership and remained as president until his retirement in 1997. At that time Martin Luther King III became the fourth president of the historic organization. Dr. King's widow, Coretta Scott King, remains on the board of directors.

In the decades since the civil rights movement, the SCLC has concentrated on maintaining those gains made earlier, continuing the struggle for the rights of the poor and the homeless, and keeping alive the legacy of Dr. King. Recent actions have included lobbying for congressional extension of the Voting Rights Act (1982), a march in support of establishment of the King national holiday (1983), protests against apartheid in South Africa, gun buy-back campaigns to help curb inner-city violence, and AIDS awareness and mentoring programs. The SCLC remains a politically engaged organization, working hard to continue the struggle for human rights and to realize Dr. King's dream.

See also CIVIL RIGHTS MOVEMENT; JACKSON, JESSE; KING, MARTIN LUTHER, JR.

BIBLIOGRAPHY

Blumberg, Rhoda Lois. *Civil Rights: The 1960s Freedom Struggle,* rev. ed. 1991.

Chappell, Kevin. "A New King." *Ebony* 3, no. 3 (1998): 124, 126, 128, 138.

"Dayton the SCLC Hold Gun Buy Back Campaign." *Jet* 84 (7) (1993): 34–35. Author anonymous.

Giddings, Paula. *When and Where I Enter: The Impact of Black Women on Race and Sex in America.* 1984.

Lincoln, C. Eric, and Lawrence H. Mamiya. *The Black Church in the African American Experience.* 1990.

"Martin Luther King III Named to Lead the SCLC."
    Jet 93 (26) (1997): 4–5. Author anonymous.
Morris, Aldon. *The Origins of the Civil Rights Movement:
    Black Communities Organizing for Change.* 1984.
Peake, Thomas R. *Keeping the Dream Alive: A History of
    the Southern Christian Leadership Conference from King
    to the Nineteen-Eighties.* 1987.

Milmon F. Harrison

Southern Religion

Southern religion is a distinctive cultural religious system that emerged as a result of various historical, demographic, political, and religious developments in the southeastern region of the United States. Although a multitude of new religious communities found a home in this area in the last decades of the twentieth century, a specific religious ethos, linked primarily to evangelical Christianity, developed over the course of the nineteenth and early twentieth centuries and has continued to shape the cultural landscape into the twenty-first. Just as other regions have exhibited fairly homogeneous cultural forms—the Puritans in New England the Mormons in and around the Salt Lake Basin, and the Lutherans in the upper Midwest—the power of southern religion depends on a vast majority of like-minded people from the same region agreeing on certain key values, meanings, and practices.

More than any other region of the United States, however, matters of race and church intermingled in the production of a peculiar religious identity. Indeed, the dividing lines between black and white contributed to the texture and tenor of southern religion, and the difficult task of maintaining boundaries helped determine many crucial ritual patterns and theological positions. Despite the very urgent concern with race relations and communal standards of conduct, at its core southern religion relies on strong, personal pieties and commitments that keep the individual securely wedded to a southern identity.

Historically, the contours of this religious system are fairly easy to trace. Although forged during a period of rapid denominational change, the evolution of a southern religion was not solely dependent on church affiliation. In other words, southern religion is not simply confined by doctrine and denomination but, as an example of a cultural religion, is the product of religious sensibilities spilling over into the larger social ecology of the South. For this reason it is essential to briefly describe the history and distinctive flavor of the key religious tradition that came to dominate the region: evangelical Protestantism.

Before evangelicalism swept through the region in the early nineteenth century, Christian explorers and settlers, as well as African slaves, were in the process of transforming the religious landscape. In the sixteenth century Catholic missionaries from Spain and France encountered—and looked for ways to destroy—indigenous religious cultures. Accompanying soldiers and explorers, missionaries brought a Christian message to the Calusa, Timucuans, Apalachee, and a variety of other native groups. This message of civilization and salvation made an impression on the local populations—in its name entire communities were chased out of their homes or wiped out, and religious expression of indigenous views became a mortal danger. In the wake of these changes, a radically new structure appeared, permanently transforming the religious environment: the Church.

In the colonial era the established Church of England attempted to dominate the religious culture of settlers, slaves and freed Africans, and native peoples in the region. During this period Anglicanism primarily served the upper classes and never gained a foothold in other communities. The ascendency of Christianity, however, was not threatened by the failures of Anglican leaders. Indeed, Christian principles were expressed by deists in government, backcountry Presbyterian ministers, and converted African slaves. After the Revolution and a perceived period of religious decline, however, the soil was ripe for spreading a distinctive Christian message, especially to the margins of southern society: poor, often isolated white families, blacks suffering under the weight of slavery, Indians whose lives were being turned upside down, and others trying to makes sense of life in the New World.

An evangelical hegemony emerged in the South in the antebellum period, thanks in large part to the enormous successes of Baptists and Methodists. Sparked by a series of revival meetings in the early nineteenth century, evangelicals developed methods to reach out across class lines and the racial divide and bring the individual, emotional experience of salvation to the forefront of religious life. The dedication, mobility, and unpretentious backgrounds of many evangelical preachers looking to save individual souls won over the majority of southerners in towns and villages throughout the region; their emphasis on a personal, saving relationship with Jesus Christ, however, did not weaken the collective commitment to maintaining a cruel social order based on slavery. The persuasive—and pliable—power of the evangelical message also spread among slaves as well, who not only reshaped it to fit their own circumstances but also influenced its expression in white churches.

The Civil War marks an important turning point in the history of southern religion. On the one hand, the denominational makeup of the United States

The Rev. Paige Patterson, president of the Southern Baptist Convention, listens to proceedings during the final day of the group's annual meeting at the Georgia Dome in Atlanta. Among proposals discussed at this session was a rebuke to President Bill Clinton for proclaiming June 1999 as Gay and Lesbian Pride Month. (Credit: AP/Wide World Photos.)

changed dramatically, with southern and northern Protestant churches breaking apart over the slavery question. Reconciliation between churches occurred after the war, except for the Southern Baptists, whose enduring presence in the South remains a key component of southern religion. On the other hand, evangelicalism acted as an unofficial "state" religion for secession-minded southerners. Indeed, it permeated the cultural and political landscape of the Confederacy, overflowing the denominational boundaries that separated Methodist from Baptist or Presbyterian from Disciples of Christ; the class boundaries that separated poor white laborers from plantation-owning slaveholders; and gender boundaries separating men from women. Most important, it provided religious legitimacy to a peculiar southern identity that flourished in the aftermath of defeat. Southerners relied on evangelical language and rituals to make sense of their loss, transcend the morally destructive forces confronting them, and reaffirm their special place in the cosmos.

From the end of the nineteenth century to the 1960s, evangelicals, and particularly Southern Baptists, continued to dominate the social scene in the

southern states, even though internal changes and diversification emerged as a result of class divisions, theological debate, and the development of separate black churches. Throughout the region individual and public morality, the centrality of the family in social life, and commitment to orthodox Protestant principles all were stimulated by the culturally entrenched evangelical ethos. In addition, the ongoing process of remembering the war proved to be a critical ingredient in the cultural religion emerging in the South. For whites, Confederate ideals were commemorated in a variety of rituals and sacred myths that grounded personal and collective identity in a distinctly southern system of meaning. For blacks, on the other hand, the Confederate defeat signaled the promise of America fulfilling its enshrined ideals of liberty, democracy, and justice and placed a special burden on southern African Americans to help achieve this goal.

Despite vast differences in interpretation, the meanings established for the Civil War heightened regional identification and, combined with shared evangelical views, solidified the central position of southern religion in the South. The coherence and stability of southern religion can be attributed to the fairly uniform beliefs and practices that emerged as a result of these historical developments and established a popular religious system that undergirds the strong commitments southerners have to their regional identity. Some of the key components of this religious system are that literal truth is contained in the Bible, which is the foundation for living a good Christian life; that a personal relationship with God is available to every human; that individual morality in conformity with Christian values is the basis for ensuring social order, though black evangelicals tempered individualistic tendencies by foregrounding congregational life; that baptism is a crucial life experience, indicating a symbolic death and rebirth into the Christian community; that spreading the message and converting lost souls is a top priority; that the family and the church are two sacred institutions that mediate private faithfulness and public behavior; and that external forces that threaten social stability must be met with righteous, Christ-centered actions.

From the 1960s to the closing decades of the twentieth century, southern religion continued to dominate the region. The rise of the religious right, the growing influence of fundamentalism, the election of Jimmy Carter, the popularization of the term *born-again*, the notoriety of southern televangelists—all brought attention to the peculiarity of the religious South and the conservative flavor of southern religion. The fact that southerners go to church more often than nonsoutherners, are more solidly evangelical in their theology, and tend to believe that religion is the primary answer to the ills of American society reinforces the notion that a cultural religious system outside denominational lines is a great source of meaning in everyday life.

On the other hand, it is important to note that southern religion is no longer contained within the confines of the South. Many have argued that, with the increasing national prominence of evangelicalism and the movement of southerners out of the region in the 1970s and 1980s, a process identified as the "southernization" of American religion and culture was taking place. If indeed southern religion is spreading beyond the bounds of the southern United States and helping to mold a national cultural religion, the priority of identifying with the South and its history may be diminishing as an important characteristic of this religious system.

Additionally, just as southerners have exported a particular cultural religion to the rest of the nation, the last few decades of the century have witnessed the importation of a variety of religious traditions into the region. Although Jewish and Catholic communities have played an important role in the history of religious life in the South, a new religious diversity is radically changing the landscape. The reasons for this diversification are numerous but include increased attention to and experimentation with alternative religious systems outside of Christianity in some of the larger cities; substantial economic growth in certain regions of the South that have attracted job seekers from around the nation; and a surge in the number of immigrants from other countries who have made the South their new home. These recent religious communities are being shaped by and have to respond to the reigning southern religion they encounter in their neighborhoods and places of business. The real question that has not yet been answered is, how will the presence of these diverse religious communities affect southern religion?

See also BAPTIST TRADITION; BORN AGAIN CHRISTIANS; EVANGELICAL CHRISTIANITY; FUNDAMENTALIST CHRISTIANITY; METHODISM; RELIGIOUS RIGHT.

BIBLIOGRAPHY

Ammerman, Nancy Tatom. *Baptist Battles: Social Change and Religious Conflict in the Southern Baptist Convention.* 1990.

Harrell, David E., Jr. *Varieties of Southern Evangelicalism.* 1981.

Hill, Samuel S. *Religion and the Solid South.* 1972.

Hill, Samuel S. *Southern Churches in Crisis.* 1966.

Laderman, Gary. *Religions of Atlanta: Religious Diversity in the Centennial Olympic City.* 1996.

Reed, John Shelton. *The Enduring South: Subcultural Persistence in Mass Society.* 1986.

Shibley, Mark A. "The Southernization of American Religion: Testing a Hypothesis," *Sociological Analysis* 52, no. 2 (1991): 159–174.

White, O. Kendall, Jr., and Daryl White, eds. *Religion in the Contemporary South: Diversity, Community, and Identity.* 1995.

Wilson, Charles Reagan, ed. *Religion in the South.* 1985.

Gary Laderman

Space Flight

In the last third of the twentieth century, humanity took its first steps toward becoming an interstellar species, but its religions remained largely earth bound. However, from the Temple of Issus in *The Gods of Mars* by Edgar Rice Burroughs in 1913, to the Temple of the Jedi in the *Star Wars* prequel by George Lucas in 1999, science fiction has imagined the religions of other planets and sketched the creeds of the future. The Jedi knights of *Star Wars* are warrior-priests, like Templar Zen masters, and a few novel religions, such as Scientology and the Terran Order, appear ready to realize that dream today. J. Michael Straczynski's television series *Babylon 5* is a religious drama of the twenty-second century replete with alien creeds, an underlying mythos of warring gods, and interplanetary transmigration of souls. Realistically, earthlings on *Babylon 5* tend to belong to traditional faiths, such as Judaism and Roman Catholicism, but a substantial minority of the citizens of its fictional future belong to a bewildering range of innovative cults.

The Church of Scientology, a space-oriented religion of major importance, emerged directly from science fiction. Its founder, L. Ron Hubbard, was a leading writer of the genre and first published about Dianetics, the precursor of Scientology, in the magazine *Astounding Science Fiction* in 1950. Many Scientologists report that their church has restored their buried memories of having been on other planets in previous lives. The fundamental doctrines of Scientology seem to encourage human exploration of the galaxy, but the church has set a higher near-term priority on clearing this planet from mental barriers to spiritual development.

The idea that space could have religious significance is not new, and back in 1758, Emanuel Swedenborg published *The Earths in Our Solar System Which Are Called Planets*, claiming he had made spiritual contact with extraterrestrials. Beginning in about 1947, a substantial "flying saucer" cultural movement has promoted the idea that "unidentified flying objects"

(UFOs) are real extraterrestrial spacecraft. The previous decade neared its close with a 1938 Martian invasion panic in which many people imagined that a radio dramatization of H. G. Wells's *War of the Worlds* was an actual news broadcast, and the 1940s ended with test launches of captured German V-2 rockets establishing the feasibility of spaceflight. Science fiction continued to stimulate the saucerian movement, first in the person of Ray Palmer, who founded saucer-promoting *Fate* magazine when he lost the editorship of the first science-fiction magazine, *Amazing Stories,* and culminating in the popular 1977 film *Close Encounters of the Third Kind.* Military balloon and parachute experiments gave rise to the "Roswell incident" and the widespread belief that the government possessed the wreckage of a crashed alien spaceship, complete with the bodies of its crew.

In 1954 a team of social psychologists headed by Leon Festinger carried out the first comprehensive study of an extraterrestrial-oriented religion, focused on the mediumship of "Mrs. Keech," who said she was receiving spiritual messages from the planets Clarion and Cetus. A being named Sananda psychically warned her to prepare for a great disaster that would cause total destruction for miles around, but he promised that flying saucers would carry her faithful group to safety and transcendence. In the same year, George King founded The Aetherius Society, claiming to have achieve telepathic rapport with the Cosmic Masters and to possess technology capable of exchanging spiritual energy between the planets. The Raelian Movement, founded by "Rael" after an encounter with space aliens in 1973, employs erotic forms of meditation to prepare for the advent of extraterrestrial Elohim, and it has recently announced that it intends to clone human beings artificially.

Belief in extraterrestrial saviors is often associated with a high degree of social-psychological dependency, in which people are incapable of achieving their own transcendent goals but submit themselves to near-total psychic domination. The extreme in spiritual submission is ritual suicide, and the two striking examples of recent years both belong to the saucerian movement. In 1975 Herff Applewhite and Bonnie Nettles organized a group oriented toward "human individual metamorphosis" that would transform them into immortal, androgynous superbeings, much as a caterpillar becomes a butterfly through transformation in a cocoon. In 1997, after Nettles had died of cancer, Applewhite became convinced that he could rejoin her on a spaceship accompanying the comet Hale-Bopp, and with thirty-eight followers he staged the Heaven's Gate ritual suicide. Murder combined with suicide was the fate of sixty-nine members of the Solar Temple in Switzerland, Canada, and

France in 1994 and 1995. Messages left by the group's leaders, Luc Jouret and Joseph Di Mambro, indicated that they were leaving the doomed Earth for safety on a planet of Sirius, with the help of extraterrestrial ascended masters.

When human beings take active charge of their own destiny and infuse human exploration of the galaxy with religious meaning, spaceflight itself becomes potentially sacred. In the 1990s, "Omicron" and his associates founded the Terran Order, with the ambition of creating a community of spiritual adepts who would guide humanity to the stars. The order's website offers immortality software designed to archive a person's mind for later resurrection in a freshly cloned body on a distant planet. The religious doctrines are closely connected to scientific theories in areas such as quantum cosmology, biological evolution, and artificial intelligence. It remains to be seen whether religious doctrines connected to science will be more persuasive in the twenty-first century than those connected to ancient agricultural societies. In part, the answer to this question depends on the extent to which theories and discoveries at the forefront of scientific knowledge are communicated effectively to the general public.

The scientific advances of the twentieth century constantly erode the plausibility of traditional religions, even as the liberal churches find it possible to believe that they have achieved a mutually respectful truce in religion's war with science. Many scientists work in such limited research areas that they themselves see little religious relevance of their work, and this is certainly true for aerospace engineers and scientists. Ironically, however, at the same time that the general public considers God's role as creator to be the most important divine attribute, quantum cosmology is busy explaining how the universe could have come into being without a creator as a random fluctuation in the space-time continuum. Space-based telescopes cooperate with ground-based instruments to study the expansion of the universe from the quantum singularity of the "Big Bang" to the currently complex structures through a combination of mechanical processes and blind chance. A host of writers argue that "the anthropic principle" demolishes the old argument from design for God's existence, saying that the world seems designed for our welfare simply because only in such a propitious place could intelligent life evolve and ask why its environment was so benign. Yet humans need to feel that life has a higher meaning, and in every era people have developed new conceptions of spirituality.

The last human beings visited the Moon in 1972, and the world's space programs currently have no commitment whatsoever to human flight to the planets. In a sense, the "space age" has been a colossal illusion, and humanity may be centuries away from real interplanetary colonization. Thus we may have entered a long period in which dreamers who long for the stars experience great frustration, seeing the technical possibility of interstellar travel but finding society unwilling to develop it. The result may be the eruption of numerous religious movements oriented toward spiritual transformation of humanity into a cosmic species.

See also ANTI-CULT MOVEMENT; ASCENDED MASTER; ASTRAL PLANES; BRAINWASHING; CREATIONISM; CULT; CULT AWARENESS NETWORK; DEATH OF GOD; EXTRATERRESTRIAL GUIDES; GOD; HEAVEN'S GATE; JOURNEYS AND JOURNEYING; PSYCHOLOGY OF RELIGION; SCIENTOLOGY; SOLAR TEMPLE; STAR TREK; UNIDENTIFIED FLYING OBJECTS (UFOs).

BIBLIOGRAPHY

Bainbridge, William Sims. Goals in Space: American Values and the Future of Technology. 1991.

Bainbridge, William Sims. The Sociology of Religious Movements. 1997.

Barrow, John D., and Frank J. Tipler. The Anthropic Cosmological Principle. 1986.

Cantril, Hadley. The Invasion from Mars. 1940.

Festinger, Leon, Henry W. Riecken, and Stanley Schachter. When Prophecy Fails. 1956.

Lewis, James R., ed. The Gods Have Landed: New Religions from Other Worlds. 1995.

Saler, Benson, Charles A. Ziegler, and Charles B. Moore. UFO Crash at Roswell: The Genesis of a Modern Myth. 1997.

William Sims Bainbridge

Spirit

"Spirit" is a religious concept in American history and culture that cannot be reduced to any one definition—its meanings are too various. At the beginning of the twenty-first century these meanings proliferate across multiple boundaries: theological, psychological, and philosophical, as well as institutional, ethnic, and gender. In the broadest sense, definitions of spirit have at their core a focus on persistent, existential questions. What is the "really real"—that is, the nature of reality and of the universe? Is there someone or something, energy or presence, that brings the universe into being and sustains it? Does that something lie outside the boundaries of the cosmos in other realms of reality? Or does it dwell within nature as an inextricable part of the whole? Of what substances

and forces, energies and organizing principles is it made up? What substances and forces, energies and organizing principles make up the human being? How do we as human persons most fruitfully name the sources of our experiences of depth or transcendence, "the More," as William James put it?

Responses to questions such as these emerge from the plurality of religious and secular worldviews that are at home in America at the beginning of a new millennium. The very variety of worldviews testifies to the fact that temptingly terse definitions of spirit, such as "incorporeality," "consciousness," "energy," "animating principle," "life source," or "inner dimension" offer a starting place for understanding the complexities of what spirit means. But they do not convey the density of meanings or the metaphysical and cultural struggles that have accrued around "spirit" in a religiously plural society that is also secular and consumerist.

In spite of the religious pluralism of present-day America, in a society whose historically dominant religious tradition is Christianity, "spirit" has strong, persisting connections with the Holy Spirit, the third person of the Christian Trinity. Diverse and even competing interpretations of the Holy Spirit have acknowledged to greater and lesser degrees their foundations in the Hebrew concept of ruach, "breath of God," and the Greek pneuma, or soul (pneumatology is the branch of Christian theology devoted to doctrines of the Holy Spirit). It is the function of the Holy Spirit in Christian theology to pervade, sustain, and sanctify the universe, to be the bridge between God and the world. The most versatile in form of the divine persons (wind, fire, dove, etc.), the Spirit is known to break forth in unpredictable and innovative fashion. The revivals that are so much a part of American religious history—the First and Second Great Awakenings of the mid-eighteenth and early nineteenth centuries, the holiness and pentecostal movements of the mid-nineteenth and early twentieth centuries through the charismatic renewals in Catholicism and Lutheranism in the 1960s and the political prominence of the religious right in the 1980s and 1990s—all of these are attributed by followers to the workings of the Spirit. This emergence is often accompanied by theological and political conservatism—back to the basics, back to the time of apostolic origins.

Paradoxically, invoking the Spirit also continues to serve as a strategy to counteract institutional or social restrictions. Numberless women have asserted a call by the Spirit to preach when their religious traditions have forbidden them to do so. Many prophets and founders of new religious movements report visitations of the Spirit as the source of their new revelations and the basis for claiming religious authority. In fact, new religious movements often come into being at least in part based on dissatisfactions with prevailing understandings of spirit and its relationship to matter.

In the mid-nineteenth century, Ralph Waldo Emerson (1803–1882) and other Transcendentalists speculated about the extent to which nature reveals or conceals and distorts spirit. They looked to the human heart and within nature itself as sources of wisdom and truth on the assumption that spirit dwelt within each. In response to the growing primacy of science as the arbiter of truth and fears about human abandonment in a mechanistic and soulless universe, Emerson's contemporaries, the nineteenth-century Spiritualists, sought knowledge of life after death. Based on messages from the spirits of the dead, they claimed the reality of a spirit world whose laws ran parallel to those of the material world and that could be learned just as surely as the laws of chemistry and physics. Joseph Smith (1805–1844) and those who followed the Mormon religion he founded engaged in developing a commonsense theology undergirded by an understanding of spirit as eternally existing invisible matter. Mary Baker Eddy (1821–1910), the founder of Christian Science, broke the growing tension between spirit and matter by declaring her loyalty to Spirit as the only reality and matter as ultimately an illusion that was the cause of sin, suffering, and death.

A leap to the beginning of the twenty-first century reveals ever more diverse groups of Americans struggling to find understandings of spirit and access to it that:

1. are coherent with post-Newtonian, even post-Einsteinian, knowledge about how the universe operates;
2. take into account discoveries in psychology and the biological sciences about the human person, such as the fact that we share more than 99 percent or our DNA with chimpanzees;
3. can accommodate the multiple religious worldviews available, from Eastern religions to beliefs about spirit and spirits among Native North Americans to theories about healing energies abroad in the universe;
4. recognize the manifold manifestations of religious vitality and creativity that lie outside institutional and academic boundaries;
5. have as their goal not only individual fulfillment and healing but also the good of particular communities in the larger society and the well-being of the entire planet.

All of this ferment and creativity have fostered the contemporary emphasis on spirituality. Attention to this phenomenon suggests a pivotal question: To what does the "spirit" in "spirituality" refer? To press that question is to discover that it is nearly impossible, or at least not satisfying, to speak of spirit or spirituality in the abstract. One is compelled to turn immediately to particular kinds of spirituality and to pursue what "spirit" might or can mean in any of them: Jewish feminist spirituality; Tibetan Buddhist spirituality; Roman Catholic creation spirituality; Celtic spirituality; New Age spirituality; womanist spirituality; gay/lesbian/bisexual/transgender spirituality; Lakota spirituality.

The list, if not endless, is very, very long. If spirituality in general refers both to a way of seeing the world and a way of acting on what one sees, definitions of "spirit" point in more particular directions to the very heart of a tradition or worldview or practice and to the acknowledgment that distinctions are required. The "emptiness" of Buddhist spirituality is not the equivalent of the Spirit in Christian spiritualities, for example, nor are the multiply described energies of the New Age movement reducible to one source. In other words, if "spirit" is to be understood in contemporary America, its meanings must always be sought out in a particular context. Spirit is always embodied in the beliefs and practices of a particular community. If, as the old saying goes, spirit bloweth where it will, it nonetheless cannot be felt or defined until it becomes the stuff of human experience.

Then again, even after an insistence on the plural nature of "spirit," and its propensity to take many forms, it must be acknowledged that there are efforts in American culture to articulate understandings of spirit that stress its unifying power. Many philosophers and theologians who place themselves in the lineage of early-twentieth-century American pragmatism believe that there exists an underlying American spiritual culture that has contributions to make to public life and the flourishing of society in all its diversity. They tie the meaning of "spirit" to possibilities of transcendence in nature that are, finally, finite and do not presuppose absolute meaning or any kind of underlying, unifying reality that exists independent of natural forces or human experience and efforts at transformation.

What becomes apparent in a brief survey of the meanings of spirit is that the power of this concept to inspire creative efforts at definition has not been diminished—not by the desupernaturalizing of the cosmos, the rejections of metaphysical absolutes, the competing worldviews of religious pluralism, or challenges to the house of institutional authority. "Spirit" continues to conjure images of transcendence in human experience and to lend its intimations of "the More" to American culture.

See also DEVILS, DEMONS, AND SPIRITS; FEMINIST SPIRITUALITY; MASCULINE SPIRITUALITY; NEW AGE SPIRITUALITY; SPIRIT GUIDES; SPIRIT POSSESSION; SPIRITUAL PATH; SPIRITUALISM; SPIRITUALITY; TRANSCENDENCE; TRINITY.

BIBLIOGRAPHY

Albanese, Catherine L. *Nature Religion: From the Algonkian Indians to the New Age.* 1990.

Anderson, Victor. *Pragmatic Theology: Negotiating the Intersections of an American Philosophy of Religion and Public Theology.* 1998.

Bednarowski, Mary Farrell. *New Religions and the Theological Imagination in America.* 1989.

Brown, Warren S., Nancey Murphy, and H. Newton Malony. *Whatever Happened to the Human Soul? Scientific and Theological Portraits of Human Nature.* 1998.

Miller, Timothy, ed. *America's Alternative Religions.* 1995.

Van Ness, Peter H. *Spirituality and the Secular Quest.* 1996.

Mary Farrell Bednarowski

Spirit Guides

Spirit guides are nonhuman or human entities that reside in the spiritual realm and make their wisdom available to the living. They take a variety of forms, including guardian angels, animal or nature spirits, elves and fairies, saints or ascended masters, and ancestors or descendants who have crossed over to the spiritual realm. Spirit guides assist humans in their daily lives even though they are not aware of the guides' presence, according to believers. Those who are interested are encouraged to seek out their guides to gain practical and mystical information, healing abilities, and protection from harm.

Historical Background

The contemporary concept of spirit guides is derived from the nineteenth-century spiritualist movement, which emerged from Swedenborgianism, mesmerism, and theosophy. Suffice it to say that the leading figures in these groups—Emanuel Swedenborg, Andrew Jackson Davis, and Helena Petrovna Blavatsky—were very deeply involved in mediumistic activities. These leaders all believed they made contact with spirits of the dead (either angels or highly evolved beings that imparted great wisdom), and in so doing, they ac-

quired information that was useful to the world of the living. Their experiences and the religious movements they awakened contributed to a growing belief that spirits could speak to and assist humans. Spiritualism spread quickly in America during the mid-1800s, with mediums popping up everywhere, offering a variety of séances. Even with the discovery of fraudulent communication by some famous mediums, spiritualism retained its hold. But it kept a fairly low profile on the American scene until the 1970s, when spiritualism clearly resonated with the New Age movement. This movement contained a wide variety of groups that encouraged spiritual development, held a holistic view of the cosmos, and had a therapeutic orientation. In the early 1970s Jane Roberts began channeling a spirit entity called Seth and published several volumes of his teachings. In the 1980s J. Z. Knight further popularized channeling through her public dialogues with Ramtha, a thirty-five-thousand-year-old warrior deity. These figures—and others that followed in the 1990s—stimulated interest in spirit communication. New Agers were drawn to holistic health conferences, divination workshops, and classes on spiritual development, and the concept of spirit guide became part of the common parlance.

In the early 1980s Michael Harner introduced modern methods of shamanic journeying, based on his prior experience with the Brazilian Jivaro Indians. With the aid of a steady drumbeat and guided visualization, seekers are taught to travel to the spirit world to discover their "power animal" guardians. It must be noted that Harner has been criticized by academics for offering pop shamanism to the masses. Even so, his method has enjoyed a great deal of success, offering those who can afford a tape or a workshop the opportunity to seek a guardian spirit without hallucinogenic substances.

Spirit guides have always been a part of Native American spirituality. The Tenino Indians, for instance, sent their children into the wilderness at night to find their helper guardian spirits. Among the Oglala Sioux, lifelong personal spirit guides are sought through strenuous vision quests requiring lengthy periods of fasting and movement deprivation designed to put them in touch with the spirit world. Nature spirits, animal spirits, and revered ancestors, all endowed with powerful qualities, are called upon for assistance in daily life as well as in the sacred sweat lodge. The medicine people, or shamans, are thought to be especially powerful, as they attract many spirit guides that help them fulfill their charge of healing in their communities.

Modern-day pagan groups, such as druids and witches, also use shamanic techniques to reach ecstasy and inner wisdom and to become closer to goddesses or gods. And though some may talk to elves in the forest or comment on grandmother spirit while walking by a stream, they do not generally speak of spirit guides. A great many people are currently captivated with a particular spirit guide, the guardian angel. This spirit frequently appears in jewelry, figurines, cards, books, and the popular television show *Touched by an Angel*. Unlike nature spirits, fairies, or dead ancestors, guardian angels do not seem to pose a problem for those who adhere to certain mainstream religions, such as Christianity. Clearly, angel fascination does not imply a wholesale acceptance of spirit guides. However, as more people become involved in Native American and other nature spiritualities, there may be a corresponding attraction to spirit guides. Regardless, judging by the plethora of Internet web sites and the volumes of trade books on this subject, interest in spirit guides may be expected to increase in the third millennium.

See also ANGELS; ASCENDED MASTER; CHANNELING; HOLISTIC HEALTH; JOURNEYS AND JOURNEYING; NATIVE AMERICAN RELIGIONS; NEW AGE SPIRITUALITY; RAMTHA; SHAMANISM; SPIRITUALISM; THEOSOPHY; VISUALIZATION.

BIBLIOGRAPHY

Andrews, Ted. *How to Meet and Work with Spirit Guides.* 1997.

Harner, Michael. *The Way of the Shaman: A Guide to Power and Healing.* 1980.

Heelas, Paul. *The New Age Movement.* 1996.

McGaa, Ed. *Rainbow Tribe: Ordinary People Journeying on the Red Road.* 1992.

Murdock, George Peter. "The Tenino Indians." *Ethnology* 19, no. 2 (April 1980): 129–149.

Tanice G. Foltz

Spirit Possession

The term *possession* covers a wide variety of human behaviors in which spirits are believed to enter and inhabit human bodies. These behaviors include spirit mediumship, automatic writing, shamanic soul travel, ecstatic prophecy, and other phenomena that take place in an altered state of consciousness and that often bring dramatic changes in a person's gestures, voice, and other expressions of personality. The interpretation and evaluation of these phenomena vary greatly according to particular contexts. In some places, possessing spirits are friendly beings to be welcomed, and possession is a condition to be actively pursued through means such as drumming, dancing, incantations, and breathing exercises. Often, however, possession is seen as an affliction to be avoided. Jewish and Christian traditions have generally associated possession with malevolent forces. Jewish lore speaks of a hungry ghost known as the dybbuk, whose possession of an individual results in madness and who can be exorcized by pronouncing the name of God. Many Christian traditions associate possession with Satan or his agents and prescribe special exorcism rituals to rebuke evil spirits by the use of liturgical implements or by simply invoking the name of Jesus.

While visionaries, prophets, and shamans have always inhabited the American landscape, spirit possession has drawn relatively little scholarly attention in North America, perhaps because of its association with marginalized religious movements. One form of possession, spirit mediumship, has been particularly popular in North America. It was commonly practiced among Shakers, especially during the period of ecstatic revival in the 1830s and 1840s known as Mother's Work; in spiritualism, a new religious movement that reached its apogee by the mid–nineteenth century; in theosophy; and in some forms of contemporary New Age spiritual practices such as trance channeling. In all these instances, spirits were believed to inhabit the bodies of adepts, dispensing spiritual guidance from worlds other than our own.

Spirit possession is a central ritual practice in Afro-Caribbean Christian traditions such as Santería and vodun, which represent a fusion of West and Central African spiritualities with European Catholicism. In *Mama Lola* (1991) Karen McCarthy Brown describes the possession rituals of vodun communities in New York City as elaborate healing rites that foster relations among spirit beings, the living, and the dead. At these events the spirits, who are related to both African deities and Catholic saints, mount and ride the bodies of their servers, dispensing practical advice, humor, and spiritual guidance. Possession is also a central ritual event in a number of other traditions of the African diaspora in America, including the spiritual churches of New Orleans.

The problem of scope in defining spirit possession comes sharply into focus in the case of Pentecostal and charismatic Christianity. Within these traditions, which are among the fastest-growing religious groups in contemporary North America, possession is associated with demonic forces who inhabit human bodies and cause physical, emotional, and spiritual distress. However, these Christians experience a phenomenon they call "baptism in the Holy Spirit," which may lead to trance states and ecstatic behaviors such as glossolalia, that is, speaking in unknown tongues. Among scholars there is no agreement about whether to include Christian spirit baptism as an example of possession. Yet as Felicitas Goodman has persuasively argued, the inclusion of Pentecostal spirit baptism in the range of human behaviors studied as possession would greatly enhance cross-cultural and comparative studies.

See also AFRO-CUBAN RELIGION; BAPTISM IN THE HOLY SPIRIT; CHANNELING; DEVILS, DEMONS, AND SPIRITS; ECSTASY; EXORCISM; NEW AGE SPIRITUALITY; PENTECOSTAL AND CHARISMATIC CHRISTIANITY; SANTERÍA; SHAMANISM; SPIRIT GUIDES; SPIRITUALISM; TRENCE; VODUN (VOODOO).

BIBLIOGRAPHY

Boddy, Janice. "Spirit Possession Revisited: Beyond Instrumentality." *Annual Review of Anthropology* 23 (1994): 407–434.

Bourginon, Erika. *Possession*. 1991.

Brown, Karen McCarthy. *Mama Lola: A Vodou Priestess in Brooklyn*. 1991.

Garrett, Clarke. *Spirit Possession and Popular Religion*. 1987.

Goodman, Felicitas. *What about Demons? Possession and Exorcism in the Modern World*. 1988.

Jacobs, Claude F., and Andrew J. Kaslow. *The Spiritual Churches of New Orleans*. 1991.

Jesse T. Todd

Spiritualism

The basic distinguishing feature of religious Spiritualism is belief in the reality of communication with the deceased, especially through mediumship, and the practice of this communication as a religious activity. Like the somewhat later Pentecostalism, modern Spiritualism originated within the free-spirited religious life of the United States, and then spread beyond its borders to become a significant presence worldwide. The Spiritualist movement is important historically not only for its own sake, but also because of its early connections with feminism, abolition of slavery, and other reformist movements; its provocative interaction with science and the mass media; and its role as a catalyst of popular religious liberalism.

The origin of the modern Spiritualist movement is conventionally attributed to the "Rochester rappings" experienced by the Fox sisters Kate (1841–1892) and Margaretta (1838–1893) in their upstate New York farmhouse in 1848. These young girls claimed they heard unusual tappings that seemed to have no natural origin or explanation. Perhaps inspired by the recently invented Morse code, they took them to be messages from the other world, later claimed to have been sent by the spirit of a murdered peddler. The news created a media sensation, and soon similar tappings were heard across the land. Indeed, rappings quickly proved to be cumbersome, and were superseded for the most part by trance mediumship. Spiritualist circles, formed to explore the new adventure, soon spoke of such other mysterious phenomena as table-tilting, spirit trumpets, apports (physical objects brought to a location by spiritual means), levitation, and the visible manifestation of the spirits in bodies composed of a fine substance called ectoplasm.

The intellectual background of early Spiritualism was twofold. First, mesmerism, experiments with hypnotism and trance induction in the tradition of the celebrated Viennese physician Anton Mesmer, were popular as stage and parlor performances in the 1840s. Together with Mesmer's own spiritualistic and parapsychological theories they afforded an easy transition to the mediumistic trance and séance states of religious Spiritualism. At the same time, the philosophy and example of Emanuel Swedenborg, a Swedish scientist who reported visits to Heaven and Hell, provided a plausible metaphysical framework for nascent Spiritualism.

Swedenborgianism was as popular as mesmerism in the cultural environment out of which Spiritualism emerged; the 1830s were called the "Swedenborgian decade" in America, and John Chapman, "Johnny Appleseed," had spread Swedenborgian tracts as well as appleseeds through the northern frontier areas where Spiritualism was to take especially firm hold. The two trends had already come together in 1847 in a massive book by Andrew Jackson Davis, *The Principles of Nature, Her Divine Revelations, and a Voice to Mankind,* a work delivered in trance (Davis had been a mesmerist) that combined Swedenborg's cosmology with the socialism of Charles Fourier. Davis was soon adopted as Spiritualism's chief theoretician, his highly optimistic view of personal and social progress in this world and the worlds to come shaping its open and liberal temper. In the 1830s the Shakers also reported experiencing a series of impressive spiritualistic manifestations, called "Mother Ann's work."

Spiritualism became an American vogue in the 1850s. Apologists for the new faith confidently proclaimed it to be the religion of the future, the faith most compatible with democracy, progress, and the new scientific world. All this was contrasted with the alleged oppressiveness and blind dogmatism of religions brought over from the past. Significantly, though, Spiritualism was also referred to as "the oldest religion in the world," its advocates being aware of its similarity to the shamanism of Native American and

A contemporary spiritualist displays some crystals in her hand, near Mount Shasta, California, ca. 1993. (Credit: CORBIS/Phil Schermeister.)

other primal societies, as though the vanguard of progress had now reached a point where it could reconcile itself with human beginnings. At the same time, Jesus was spoken of as a Spiritualist, and the early Christian church was said to have been Spiritualistic.

All these features relate much about early Spiritualism and its times. As a religion suited to the young republic's proud democracy, it affirmed the spiritual equality of all, since gifted mediums could be found in any sector of society, not only among the properly educated and ordained. In particular, in the 1850s Spiritualism was one of very few venues in which women could exercise religious leadership on a par with men. If women could rarely preach directly, they could give voice to wise spirits speaking through them. Those messages often endorsed feminism, and attracted the attention of women leaders such as Susan B. Anthony, Elizabeth Cady Stanton, and Victoria Woodhull. Many spirits were no less eager to advocate other major reform projects of the 1850s, including abolition of slavery, humane childbearing, prison reform, and the ending of capital punishment.

The science connection had several facets. At times contemporaries might have had some uncertainty as to whether the movement represented a new religion or popular science. While the subject matter, life after death, is traditionally associated with religion, the Spiritualist investigation of it sometimes involved careful scientific methods and precautions rarely before associated with matters of faith. Spiritualism boldly called for religious doctrine to be tested against modern science and the rationalistic assumptions of the Enlightenment. Spiritualists held that now, in the present enlightened age, as basic an aspect of religion as the soul's survival of physical death could be as much a matter of certainty as the composition of water. To be sure, the results of the scientific testing of mediumship were often ambiguous and controversial; but in the end, that only confirmed believers in their sense that theirs was a new kind of religion, with new standards of truth and generating new forms of opposition.

Hardly less important was the way Spiritualism was a new kind of religion in its manner of dissemination. As the first major religious movement of the age of widespread literacy, mass-market newspapers, and even the telegraph (significantly, one of the early Spiritualist magazines was called *The Spiritual Telegraph*), Spiritualism—ever a media sensation—was the first new religion to benefit from popular print reports as well as word of mouth and itinerant preachers. Not only that, but the new movement, which depended heavily on traveling star mediums and lecturers, could now send them around the world with the relative speed and comfort of hurtling trains and steamships, and did.

Despite these advantages, by the end of the 1850s Spiritualism was in some disarray. Not only had the impending Civil War crisis attracted nearly all the nation's attention, but also scandals involving fraudulent mediums had tarnished the image of the faith of the future. After the war it revived somewhat, as Spiritualism generally has after wars, when many of those who lost loved ones to the demons of battle turn to it in hope of contact and reassurance. By now, however, disparities among three aspects of the maturing movement could no longer be ignored and called out for resolution or separation. These might be called the religious, the philosophical, and the scientific aspects of Spiritualism, and in the latter third of the nineteenth century they more and more went their separate ways.

The religious aspect was focused on the original premise of communication with departed kin and with ancient spiritual teachers. Even in the early days there had been no lack of the latter, including mighty figures from the Bible or classical philosophers now returned to speak again. In Spiritualism's second, post–Civil War phase, those for whom this kind of mediumship was of special importance and who wished to experience it in an atmosphere of faith and belief moved toward making Spiritualism essentially an organized church. Problems obtained; in the late nineteenth century and even after, religious Spiritualism was divided over the teachings of the French Spiritualist H. L. D. Rivail, who wrote as Allan Kardec, and who, unlike Andrew Jackson Davis and most other early Anglo-American Spiritualists, espoused reincarnation. (Kardecist Spiritualism remains popular in Latin America, especially in Brazil.) In North America scattered Spiritualist churches appeared toward the end of the nineteenth century, offering regular Sunday services in a Protestant style but including spirit messages and mediumship in the service program. In 1893 a number of such churches formed the National Spiritualist Association, the most successful of numerous Spiritualist denominations.

Others wanted the Spiritualist worldview but did not care for the churchlike atmosphere or "trivial" mediumship associated with the conventional movement. Some, however, were willing to accept more intellectually sophisticated teachings from lips and pens reported to be inspired by great masters of wisdom, Eastern or Western. Many of these found their way to groups such as the Theosophical Society, founded in 1875, chiefly by two former ardent Spiritualists, Helena Blavatsky and Henry Steel Olcott. Others turned to "New Thought," Mormonism, or imported Eastern religions.

Still others were always really most interested in the scientific investigation of psychic phenomena promised by the Spiritualist upsurge, and were put off by religious or occultist overtones. Some of these were among the founders of the 1882 Society for Psychical Research in England and its U.S. ally the American Society for Psychical Research.

In each case, though, it is clear that Spiritualism first had the effect of liberating persons from dogmatic slumbers, or even from the great nineteenth-century revivals; significantly, the Fox sisters' original rappings had occurred in the "burnt-over country" of upstate New York. Whether or not converts stayed with the spirit faith, and wherever they went after it, they could not go back to exactly what they were before.

The 1920s might be called the "Silver Age" of Spiritualism. Then, in the aftermath of World War I, the faith enjoyed a revival of interest, and attendance at Spiritualist churches grew. That decade's best-known Spiritualist advocate was Sir Arthur Conan Doyle, the celebrated creator of Sherlock Holmes. Doyle's writings and tireless world-ranging lecture tours, including visits to the United States in 1922 and 1923, and above all his dramatic presentations of psychic photographs alleged to show spirits, attracted great attention and controversy. Another feature of this period was the development of African-American Spiritualism. A prominent example was the Universal Hagar's Spiritual Church, organized in Detroit in 1923 by George W. Hurley and numbering some thirty-seven churches by the time of Hurley's death in 1943.

However, no comparable upsurge of conventional religious Spiritualism obtained after World War II, despite growth of interest in psychical research, much publicity given celebrated independent mediums and psychics such as Arthur Ford or Edgar Cayce, and the 1960s fascination with alternative spirituality. Perhaps by now Spiritualist churches had become too conventional and fusty for what was essentially a countercultural concern.

Church-based Spiritualism continued to the end of the century in a number of loosely organized denominations. The movement has rarely submitted to tight institutional structures, for sociologically it has been largely a matter of the followers and clients of individual charismatic mediums/ministers, who usually prefer to operate independently, under their own inspiration. Its most characteristic institution apart from the local Spiritualist church is the "camp," representing a tradition going back to the nineteenth century. There is Cassadaga in Florida, originally a winter haven for northern Spiritualists who could there enjoy intensive study and experience in a balmy climate, and now an exemplary Spiritualist community. Lily Dale in upstate New York boasts the modest Fox home where the original rappings took place, now moved to this location, and Camp Chesterfield in Indiana has long drawn midwestern Spiritualists for summer activities. In general, though, contemporary Spiritualism in its church form seems to have little of its earlier vibrancy.

However, it could be argued that Spiritualism, fundamentally a fluid concept that has taken different forms in different ages, from primal shamanism to the nineteenth-century movement, emerged in the second half of the twentieth century in new forms. The UFO "contactees" of the 1950s and thereafter often continued the relation they claimed to an extraterrestrial mentor by allowing that entity to deliver trance discourses through the earthling's voice. The contact phenomenon thus showed similarities to the Spiritualist medium, believed to be giving expression to a high, godlike teacher; in fact, some contactees had a background in Spiritualism. Where once spirit entities were understood to be ancient masters of wisdom, now for UFO aficionados they were "space brothers," superior entities from other worlds come to give earthlings warning and encouragement.

Then, as the "New Age" movement took shape later in the century, one of its most striking aspects was "channeling," the communication in trance of messages thought to come from high teachers. The similarity to Spiritualism, especially to what J. Gordon Melton has called "teaching spiritualism," in contrast to the mediumship of "ordinary" departed relatives and others, is obvious. However, channeling has no evident direct link to classic Spiritualism, and its reported entities are often Eastern, or teach Eastern-type doctrines such as karma and reincarnation, in contrast to the largely Western bias of the older faith in North America. Thus has Spiritualism and its fundamental ideas survived.

See also AFTERLIFE; CHANNELING; DEATH AND DYING; EXTRATERRESTRIAL GUIDES; NEW AGE SPIRITUALITY; NEW THOUGHT; OCCULT; PSYCHIC; SEANCE; SHAMANISM; THEOSOPHICAL SOCIETY; TRANCE; UNIDENTIFIED FLYING OBJECTS.

BIBLIOGRAPHY

Braude, Ann. *Radical Spirits: Spiritualism and Women's Rights in Nineteenth-Century America.* 1989.
Moore, R. Laurence. *In Search of White Crows: Spiritualism, Parapsychology, and American Culture.* 1977.
Nelson, Geoffrey K. *Spiritualism and Society.* 1969.

Robert S. Ellwood
Gracia Fay Ellwood

Spirituality

Although the word "spirituality" was originally a Christian one, derived from the Pauline definition of whatever was under the influence of the spirit of God, its roots were planted firmly in the Jewish tradition of God's abiding presence. Until the twentieth century, religiousness and spirituality had similar meanings. In fact, many non-Western languages have no separate word for spirituality. Modernity, the growing distrust of authority, and the rise of secularism have contributed to shaping our present understanding of these words as different though related concepts.

The uncertainties of modernity have created problems that, for many, are no longer solved by traditional religious institutions. These concerns involve issues of identity, meaning, and a general loss of faith in authority and moral order. Authority's response to the attempts of 1960s activism to bring about peace, justice, and equality shocked many adolescents and young adults out of comfortable conformity. This period of disillusionment occurred at a time in the lives of baby boomers when people typically seek meaning and direction and contributed to a growing distrust of institutional authority and traditional leaders and solutions. But though many of these children of modernity were disillusioned and distrustful of tradition, they did not stop searching. A search for direction in a time of crisis is part of what makes us human.

In *A Generation of Seekers,* Roof (1993) argues that baby boomers are a generation of educated and active seekers who have rejected traditional religion and forms of worship. Having experienced estrangement from cultural institutions, this generation consists of middle-aged spiritual nomads on a search for personal meaning. Joined by the Generation Xers, they have developed a highly individualistic spirituality. Heelas (1996) points out that this personalized rather than institutionalized spirituality is to be expected in modernity, where a key aspect is a shift from an external locus of control to an internal one. When meaning and stability are no longer to be found in the world around us, the individual is forced to search within. Thus, for many, the self rather than the church or temple becomes the major spiritual resource. This gives spiritual meaning to some of the widely held concepts of modernity, such as the importance of autonomy, the search for authenticity, self-responsibility, and immediacy, and makes them accessible to all. The new, democratized spirituality can be seen as a cultural resource.

But if authority cannot be trusted, how does the self recognize truth? How does it strip away the layers of meaning embedded in our social institutions and in the ways we have been taught to think, behave, and be? For many, reason is not enough. No longer trusting what they have been taught to be true, these seekers turn to the spiritual truth that comes from their own subjective experience, and they privilege experience over belief and reason. Spirituality thus becomes both democratized and experiential.

The contemporary search for identity and meaning in experiential spirituality is holistic, grounded in lived experience and praxis rather than existing outside of it. Humans experience with their hearts as well as their heads, and with all their senses. This is where contemporary spirituality differs from the traditional otherworldly, ascetic practices of the past. If spirituality has reached a crossroads, as some theologians declare, this is where the road divides. One path, though individualistic and experiential, continues to be otherworldly, as can be seen in the popularity of "rapture" films of the 1980s, where Christians awaited the destruction of the world and their removal to a transcendent paradise. A further example is the world-denying spirituality of Heaven's Gate, where believers, some of them castrated, committed mass suicide in the belief that they would be transported to a spaceship above the earth's surface and take on "heavenly bodies."

Rather than otherworldly, the second path in the road is in and of this earth. Here, matter is imbued with spirit. The dualisms inherent in Cartesian philosophy are rejected. Spirituality is radically embodied. These dualisms are not limited to those of spirit and matter, mind and body. King (1993) points out that until fairly recently, a spiritual person was usually one whose spiritual practice included upholding and even reifying gender roles. The spiritual quest was traditionally a male journey, while for women spirituality often revolved around issues of obedience. Religion, as the guardian of this profoundly dualistic, otherworldly spirituality, saw the world, pleasure, and the human body as impediments ranging from distasteful to dangerous. However, beginning with the second wave of the U.S. women's movement in the 1960s, the cry "the personal is political" was quickly joined by "the spiritual is political." Feminist writers, artists, and theologians began to point out how the act of demeaning the body is profoundly linked to the societal demeaning and oppression of women. Male-dominated religions typically associate men, the mind, and culture, and place these in opposition to women, the body, and nature. When they also emphasize transcending the body and nature, the subjugation of women is given religious mandate.

While gender dualism is still much in evidence in many but not all groups' spiritual worldviews and practices today, the dichotomizing of spirit and matter is increasingly challenged. Pentecostalists, for example, affirm the body as a feeling, sensing self and privilege an experiential stance that is both communal and empowering. Creation spirituality places primacy on a nondualistic interconnectivity that is body-based and earth-based. New Age spirituality focuses on a radical holism that is an experiential, individualistic search, not for salvation but for self-actualization. Practitioners of Goddess or Gaian spirituality believe that both the body and nature are sacred and sources of spiritual revelation. Because of this, the divine is understood as immanent, and the erotic is celebrated as the interlinking life force in everything. It is creative energy empowered. From Native American spirituality these practitioners borrow the concept of the interdependent web of life in which humans are a very small part.

These groups are among the many that experience the divine in this manner. Different from religion though not entirely unrelated, contemporary spirituality is individualistic, experiential, embodied, nondualistic, and celebratory.

See also CREATION SPIRITUALITY; ECOSPIRITUALITY; FEMINIST SPIRITUALITY; MASCULINE SPIRITUALITY; NEW AGE SPIRITUALITY; SPIRITUAL PATH; SPIRITUALISM.

BIBLIOGRAPHY

Griffin, Wendy, ed. *Daughters of the Goddess: Identity, Healing, and Empowerment.* 1999.
Heelas, Paul. *The New Age Movement.* 1996.
King, Ursula. *Women and Spirituality: Voices of Protest and Promise.* 1989, 1993.
Roof, Wade Clark. *A Generation of Seekers: The Spiritual Journeys of the Baby Boom Generation.* 1993.

Wendy Griffin

Spirituals

Spirituals, despite the transliterated state in which they have come down to us, are one of the earliest bodies of material we have of African-American slave culture. With no authors, composers, dates, established texts, or even fixed melodies, they are impossible to situate accurately in time or in space, but they were probably created later than we might think, perhaps in the early years of the nineteenth century. They are the products of an interwoven blending of African tradition, the slave experience, and the evangelical Protestantism of the American South and its frontiers.

Spirituals are, first, religious songs. Their name probably comes from "spiritual songs," the term for the more informal hymns that were popular features of white camp meetings. As hymns, spirituals reflect the revivalistic, largely early Methodist, theology of the day. Even so, there are differences so marked as to make spirituals unique. The original music was African in nature, and the sympathetic whites who first tried to write it down during the Civil War were able

Members of the choir at the Trinity United Church of Christ in Chicago sing spirituals from the revised New Century Hymnal. The texts of some of these songs have been updated to be more gender-inclusive and to eliminate language considered offensive by minorities and people with disabilities. (Credit: AP/Wide World Photos.)

only to record a Westernized approximation of the original sounds. These are forever lost.

The spirituals' improvisational poetic lyrics are striking for their imaginative word usage and vernacular imagery: "I sweep my house with the gospel broom," "I'm going to sit at the welcome table," and "Fix me, Jesus," for example. Often spirituals recount biblical stories, a not uncommon literary device of nonliterate people. Some biblical narratives resonated more strongly than others, and there are numerous references to Daniel, Jonah, Noah, and other figures who remained faithful to God despite trials and testing. There is also identification with Israel in bondage, and the idealization of Moses as the divine agent of liberation.

Perhaps the most striking things about spirituals are their secret language and double meanings. There are covert calls to clandestine meetings. Many spirituals list family members, recalling those who had been sold away. These outwardly simple hymns are also freedom songs in which heaven, Canaan, Promised Land, and campground stand for Africa or Canada or the free states; shoes, wheels, and chariots are all devices for movement—that is, escape; the Jordan River represents the Ohio River, with freedom on the other side. The slaves articulated a broad and inclusive view of freedom and a radical vision of liberation: "Didn't my Lord deliver Daniel/And why not every man?"

With the end of slavery, virtually no whites had ever heard spirituals, and blacks wanted to forget them as part of a degrading slave past better forgotten. The touring Jubilee Singers of Fisk University, a freedpeople's school, introduced them in the 1870s to northern whites, who were captivated by the haunting melodies and vivid lyrics. As a result, words and music were preserved. Spirituals continue to exert power, particularly, as theologian James Cone points out, in their expression that faith is trust in God's work of liberation in the world and that Jesus is "God's black slave who has come to put an end to human bondage."

See also AFRICAN-AMERICAN RELIGIONS; CHANTING; DRUMMING; METHODISM; MUSIC; RELIGIOUS EXPERIENCE.

BIBLIOGRAPHY

Cone, James. *The Spirituals and the Blues: An Interpretation.* 1972.
Newman, Richard. *Go Down, Moses: Celebrating the African-American Spiritual.* 1998.

Richard Newman

Starhawk

(1951–), writer, religious leader.

Starhawk (born Miriam Simos), is a founder, philosopher, and leader of the contemporary Wiccan movement. Raised as a Jew, she became interested in Witchcraft while in her late teens. At first self-taught, she soon found teachers among a variety of Pagan, Wiccan, and other earth-based traditions. In 1979 she published her pioneering book *The Spiral Dance,* which introduced native, pre-Christian European traditions to an American audience generally unaware of the survival and authenticity of Witchcraft. This work was continued in *Dreaming the Dark* and *Truth or Dare.* Each of these books combines thealogy (Goddess philosophy), history, and a practical guide to ritual and community process, and each draws on a combination of traditional teachings and contemporary innovations. Wicca is presented as one of numerous religions, native to all regions of the earth, based on the cycles and teachings of the natural world.

Starhawk's writings outline a worldview rooted in the underlying value of relationship: the immanent relationship between divinity and creation; the interdependent relationship among all living beings; and the powerful relationship of community. She describes the Goddess as an inclusive, universal naming of the divine, experienced by human beings in both female and male, feminine and masculine aspects. In contrast to male-dominated traditions, Goddess religion emphasizes the presence of the sacred among and within material beings rather than its apartness or separateness. Starhawk argues that such an honoring of the connection between physical and spiritual is of particular significance to women in cultures in which they are taught to devalue and distance themselves from their bodies and power. Extending this care and respect to the earth itself as another living embodiment of the Goddess, Starhawk links Wicca to ecofeminist theory and activism. Political activism in a wide variety of areas is presented as essential to the expression of Wiccan ethics, based in understanding and expressing connection to all life. Starhawk's more recent works on death and raising children reflect the growth of the Wiccan movement in the United States. They also express the efforts on the part of Starhawk and Wiccan communities to create and re-create Goddess traditions inclusive of a fuller range of human life experience, especially that of people of color and their distinct Goddess traditions, as well as that of gay, lesbian, bisexual, and transgendered people.

In addition to her nonfiction writing, Starhawk has authored two novels, *The Fifth Sacred Thing* (1993) and *Walking to Mercury* (1997). Set in both the twentieth and twenty-first centuries, these fictional works combine historical and utopian settings and give narrative expression to the themes of spirituality, personal relationships, community, ecofeminism, transformation, and earth-based traditions that inform her other writings.

While best known as an author, Starhawk is also active in the ecofeminist movement. She teaches in a wide variety of settings, ranging from formal academic institutions to public lectures and trainings for Wiccan practitioners.

See also ECOFEMINISM; FEMINIST THEOLOGY; NATURE RELIGION; NEOPAGANISM; WICCA.

BIBLIOGRAPHY

Starhawk. *Dreaming the Dark: Magic, Sex and Politics.* 1982, 1997.
———. *The Fifth Sacred Thing.* 1993.
———. *The Spiral Dance: A Rebirth of the Ancient Religion of the Great Goddess.* 1989.
———. *Truth or Dare: Encounters with Power, Authority, and Mystery.* 1987.
———. *Walking to Mercury.* 1997.
Starhawk, Diane Baker, and Anne Hill, eds. *Circle Round: Raising Children in Goddess Traditions.* 1998.
Starhawk, M. Macha NightMare, and the Reclaiming Collective, eds. *The Pagan Book of Living and Dying: Practical Rituals, Prayers, Blessings, and Meditations on Crossing Over.* 1997.

Drorah O'Donnell Setel

Star Trek

A short-lived television series fueled by the creative genius of Gene Roddenberry, *Star Trek* aired for three seasons, from 1966 through 1968. Set in the twenty-second century, the central theme of the science fiction series was the exploration of outer space. Its story lines revolved around the space travels of the ship U.S.S. *Enterprise,* under the command of Captain James T. Kirk. The ship's mission, as announced in the opening moments of each episode, was "to explore strange new worlds, to seek out new life and new civilizations, to boldly go where no man has gone before."

The decisions and actions of Captain Kirk, a Ulysses-like character portrayed with casual offhandedness by William Shatner, were the series main focus; however, several supporting characters who comprised the heart of the *Enterprise* crew became hugely popular as well. The most prominent of these ancillary characters was Commander Spock (Leonard Nimoy). A

pointed-eared being from the planet Vulcan whose native populace embraced a behavioral standard of stoic, emotionless rationality, Mr. Spock was known for being able to achieve a Vulcan mind meld with any living creature merely by touching the base and side of its head. Other characters included Montgomery "Scottie" Scott (James Doohan), the ship's chief engineer; Lieutenant Uhura (Nichelle Nichols), the ship's communications officer (one of the first African-American woman to land a featured role in a television series); and Dr. Leonard "Bones" McCoy (DeForest Kelley), the ship's chief medical officer who was the emotional opposite of Spock, with a personality as impassioned as Spock's was passionless.

Though *Star Trek* produced an original corpus of only seventy-nine episodes, the fictional world it sketched attracted what are generally acknowledged to be television's most fervent and loyal fans. First known as Trekkies and later Trekkers, these fans stubbornly supported the series long after its demise. They organized *Star Trek* conferences and became famous for investing considerable money and effort to create their own *Star Trek* costumes. This intrepid and indefatigable fan support eventually attracted new monies and energies to the *Star Trek* phenomenon, which spawned an animated television series, numerous books, six full-length feature films starring much of the original cast, and eventually three spin-off television series, including *Star Trek: The Next Generation, Star Trek: Deep Space Nine,* and *Star Trek: Voyager.*

By their intense commitment to the series and its characters, Trekkers revealed the extent to which mass-mediated entertainment could take on a religious function for at least part of its audience base at the end of the twentieth century.

See also SPACE FLIGHT.

BIBLIOGRAPHY

Brasher, Brenda F. "Thoughts on the Status of the Cyborg: On Technological Socialization and Its Link to the Religious Function of Popular Culture." *Journal of the American Academy of Religion* 64, no. 4 (1996): 809–830.
Jindra, Michael. "Star Trek Fandom as a Religious Phenomenon." *Sociology of Religion* 55, no. 1 (Spring 1994): 27–51.

Brenda E. Brasher

Stations of the Cross

Stations of the Cross, also known as the Way of the Cross or Via Crucis, is a Roman Catholic devotion

A group from St. Catharine of Alexandria Roman Catholic Church in the Sunset Park section of Brooklyn, N.Y., reenact the story of the Crucifixion in the Via Crucis (Stations of the Cross) street procession on Good Friday, April 2, 1999. (Credit: AP/Wide World Photos.)

(also found in some Episcopal churches) commemorating certain incidents in the Passion of Christ in the form of a symbolic pilgrimage. The fourteen "stations," or stopping places, are represented by crosses, carvings, or pictures placed around the inner walls of a church, or outdoors along a road or path in a garden or woods. Since the basic form of the devotion (whether practiced individually or congregationally) is a symbolic pilgrimage, moving from station to station is essential to its practice; when the concourse of people makes this impractical, the person reading the prayers or preaching about the incidents of the Passion usually moves from one site to the other while the congregation follows with their eyes, and turn their bodies in the direction of each station. The devotion is sometimes practiced collectively on the streets, making a station at each corner, or at stated sites in a neighborhood.

The fourteen symbolic stopping places have been prescribed by authority since the seventeenth century, but there is no necessary form of prayers prescribed; a great number of prayers or meditations for this exercise circulate with ecclesiastical approval, and it is perfectly acceptable to pray or meditate at each station in one's own words while following them privately, or to preach on them extemporaneously when leading a congregation. However, it is customary to

precede the prayers or meditations at each station with the prayer "We adore you, O Christ, and we bless you," to which the congregation responds "For by your holy cross you have redeemed the world." Appropriate hymns are frequently sung between the stations, especially if the devotion is practiced outdoors and the stations are at some distance from each other. For obvious reasons the exercise is particularly popular as a Lenten devotion, especially on Fridays, and most especially on Good Friday.

The origin of this devotion seems to be in the tradition of pilgrims to Jerusalem of following the Via Dolorosa from the traditional site of Pilate's Praetorium to the sites of Golgotha and the Holy Sepulcher, meditating on the various traditional sites of evangelical or legendary incidents in the story of the Passion—for example, the place where Simon of Cyrene was forced to help Jesus carry the cross, the place where Veronica wiped Jesus' face, or the place where he spoke to the women of Jerusalem, as well as the places where he fell under the weight of the cross. The pilgrimage culminated in the basilica of the Holy Sepulcher, where the traditional sites of the Crucifixion, the anointing of Christ's body, and the empty tomb are shown. During certain periods the local Muslim authorities would not permit pilgrims to stop at these places or to kiss the ground or perform other acts of visible devotion, but eventually such acts became possible, and the pilgrimage along the Via Dolorosa, with stops for prayer and meditation, is now a feature of life in Jerusalem, especially on Fridays.

By the fifteenth century, returning pilgrims in various lands spontaneously began to set up reproductions—pictorial or symbolic—of the various stopping places on the Via Dolorosa, and these gradually became popular enough for Rome to approve the devotion and codify the fourteen stations, as well as to enrich the exercise with abundant privileges and indulgences. A modern development that has become widespread in the United States is to add a fifteenth station, to commemorate the Resurrection, to add a more Paschal dimension to the exercise, which used to end with the burial of Christ. However, since the "stations" do not actually represent incidents but places, the final station is the Holy Sepulcher, which is the place of both the burial and the Resurrection. It would therefore be more correct to not add a fifteenth station but instead to emphasize both the burial and the Resurrection in the fourteenth.

See also CHURCH; EPISCOPAL CHURCHES; JOURNEYS AND JOURNEYING; LENT; LITURGY AND WORSHIP; PILGRIMAGE; PRAYER; RITUAL; ROMAN CATHOLICISM.

BIBLIOGRAPHY

Pillai, C. A. I. Pillai. "The Way of the Cross: Resurrection." *Worship* 37, no. 4 (March 1963): 250–253.

Thurston, Herbert. *The Stations of the Cross*. 1906.

Jaime R. Vidal

Subud Movement

Subud is an international spiritual movement that began in Indonesia in the 1940s and came to the United States in 1959. Its core practice is the *latihan kejiwaan*, or "spiritual exercise/practice," which is considered to be an awakening of the inner self, a receiving of guidance from God, an acquired awareness of the variety of forces and motivations at work in our actions, and a gradual purification of the negative tendencies of the self.

History

The association consists of about five thousand members in seventy countries, with groups active in such diverse cultural and linguistic locales as Asia, Africa, western and eastern Europe, North and South America, and the Middle East. Members are not asked to give up their religion, nor must they have one. Its founder, an Indonesian civil servant, Bapak Muham-

mad Subuh Sumohadiwidjojo, described the latihan (which he began to receive spontaneously during the 1930s) as the history of the "inner content" of what the sages and prophets of God had transmitted to human beings in previous eras. Bapak saw his role as a continuation of that transmission in the contemporary era. "Subud" is an acronym for "*Susila Budhi Dharma*," terms that signify the qualities engendered in the latihan: character and conduct that is "truly human" and surrendered to the will of God. Bapak was acquainted with but not initiated in sufi (mystical Islamic) groups in Indonesia. He distanced himself from the title of shaykh, or teacher; his writings speak of the present need of human beings to experience for themselves the "inner reality of things" (self, religion, relationships, sacred scripture). Subud came to the West particularly through the efforts of John Bennett, the major transmitter of Gurdjieff's and Ouspensky's teachings, whose *Concerning Subud* describes his brief but influential involvement in the early days of Subud in England and America.

The Practice

Local groups across the globe meet once or twice a week, "latihaning" for thirty minutes, men and women in separate spaces. The practice is a nonstructured "ritual of surrender." Members are asked to sit quietly for a few minutes to clear their mind and heart from the influence of their self-willed thoughts and desires. Members then stand and are asked to simply receive the power of God with patience, submission, and sincerity. Individuals receive and interpret their own particular spontaneous movements, sounds, and feelings, which Bapak described as arising from their deepest self, which is "open" to the contact with the "great life force."

Structure and Activities

While the core activity of Subud is the latihan, the Subud organization defines itself as responsible for bringing the fruits of the practice into everyday life and for raising the quality of life for all beings on the planet. To this end, the organization has a social welfare "wing," Susila Dharma International (with nongovernmental-organization consultative status to the UN), which, with its explicitly noninterventionist, nonmissionary, and noncolonialist approach to development, has numerous projects across the globe, including Congo, Cuba, Columbia, India, and Indonesia.

See also SUFISM.

BIBLIOGRAPHY

http://www. subud.org.

http://www. SusilaDharma.org.

Lyle, Robert. *Subud.* 1995.

Sumohadiwidjojo, Muhammad Subuh. *Bapak's Talks: The Complete Recorded Talks of Bapak Muhammad Subuh Sumohadiwidjojo in English Translation.* Vol. 1 (Bapak's talks of June 1957 to June 1958). 1996.

Sumohadiwidjojo, Muhammad Subuh. *Susila Budhi Dharma.* 1991.

Webb, Gisela. "Subud." In *America's Alternative Religions,* edited by Timothy Miller, pp. 267–273. 1994.

Gisella Webb

Suffering

From the Latin *sufferre,* "to undergo," suffering is a situation of pain, sorrow, and/or anguish that is experienced physically, emotionally, or spiritually. Suffering can be personal and intimate as well as experienced by a group of people. This makes it difficult to distance ourselves from the emotional impact of suffering completely or consistently. Suffering can be the result of natural evil (e.g., earthquakes, diseases) or human evil (e.g., war, injustice).

For centuries, people have raised the question of why suffering occurs. This is referred to as the question of evil or the issue of theodicy (If God is all good and powerful, why do people suffer?). In Judaism, Christianity, and Islam, one school of thought believes that if a person or group suffers, it is punishment for sinful behavior and actions and a manifestation of divine justice. In Islam, suffering is not a theoretical problem, but a very concrete and practical reality. For Muslims, suffering is part of what it means to live and is not seen as a problem. This is due, in large measure, to the fact that the Qur'an (the sacred text of Islam) emphasizes God's omnipotence, love, and compassion. Allah (God) controls all suffering, and faithful Muslims must endure it.

The Jewish and Christian traditions do not emphasize suffering as a result of natural disaster. Both traditions ask why humans suffer. There is considerable debate as to whether suffering is the result of human disobedience that results in punishment from God. The story of Job in the Hebrew Bible and the words of Jesus in the Christian New Testament Gospel of Luke contest this view of suffering as punishment. Both traditions recognize that some sins, especially those that are the result of human excesses that are sinful (e.g., substance abuse), may bring about suffering (e.g., poor health). This is not seen as a form of divine judgment but as a correlation between sinful behavior and suffering.

From the first Jewish narratives of creation in the Book of Genesis in the Hebrew Bible, suffering has been seen as going against the goodness of creation. All forms of domination (e.g., classism, sexism, racism), hostility between peoples, and hostility between people and nature bring forms of suffering that signal a rejection of our connectedness to each other and from God.

For many Jews, Christians, and Muslims, suffering is believed to help contribute to one's moral character. For Christians, suffering is seen in the context of God's redemptive and sustaining love and of God's will. Some suffering is attributable to evil, but undeserved suffering must be endured by faith. Within Judaism and Christianity, contemporary liberation theologies challenge the idea that suffering may be good or redemptive. These theologies point to the suffering of those victimized by oppression and abuse. It is important to differentiate among suffering that is natural to life; suffering inflicted on others; and suffering that experienced as the result of injustice, oppression, or abuse. None of these are good or redemptive in themselves. Liberation theologies point to the suffering that result from choices made by a person who is trying to change or right a situation of abuse or oppression that contain the possibility of being good and redemptive.

See also EVIL; ISLAM; JUDAISM; JUDEO-CHRISTIAN TRADITION; THEODICY.

BIBLIOGRAPHY

Bowker, John. *Problems of Suffering in Religions of the World.* 1970.

Jonas, Hans. *Mortality and Morality: A Search for Good After Auschwitz.* 1996.

Kushner, Harold. *When Bad Things Happen to Good People.* 1983.

Soelle, Dorothee. *Suffering.* 1975.

Townes, Emilie M., ed. *A Troubling in My Soul: Womanist Perspectives on Evil and Suffering.* 1993.

Emilie M. Townes

Sufism

Sufism (Arabic: *tasawwuf*) is the term used in English for Islamic mysticism, initially a movement of pious individuals and later of institutionalized mystical orders widely dispersed throughout the Muslim world.

The first teacher in the Sufi tradition came to the United States in 1912. This was Hazrat Inayat Khan of

India, a Sufi in the Chishti lineage who married an American, although he eventually settled in Europe. His son, Pir Vilayat Khan, revived the movement in the 1960s under the name "Sufi Order in the West" or "Message in our Time." This Sufi movement, like a number of others to emerge in the United States, emphasized the spiritual element of the Islamic tradition and an essential truth at the core of all human religious experience. The formal requirements of the Islamic law and adherence to mainstream Islam were not required of followers. Some consider the early impact of such movements in the West to have arisen as part of an attraction to "Oriental wisdom" while their reflowering in the 1960s was due to the appeal of New Age spiritual eclecticism.

The United States has also been fertile ground for the Perennialist movement, a number of whose followers have strong links to Sufism. Academics such as Huston Smith and Seyyed Hossein Nasr have advocated the pursuit of a perennial truth and sympathetically presented Islamic teachings in the light of inner or mystical understandings. Frithjof Schuon (1998), a Swiss who ultimately settled in Bloomington, Indiana, was influential in disseminating a strand of this "Perennialist" or "traditionalist" understanding. At the same time he functioned as the head of a Sufi order known as the Miriamiyya, a branch of the Shadhili Order.

Another movement functioning in the United States that claims inspiration from the Naqshbandi Sufi Order is that of the followers of the late British writer Idries Shah (1997) and his brother Omar Ali Shah. Idries Shah was a prolific writer on esoteric themes and a popularizer of the Sufi teaching story epitomized by the wise fool character of Mulla Nasruddin. Idries Shah became a well-known and successful author and was influential in literary and psychological circles in both the United States and Europe. His successor in the United States is Stanford University psychologist Robert Ornstein. In the 1960s Ornstein, along with others such as Charles Tart, brought the ideas of attaining self-realization based on Eastern religious or Western esotericist approaches to consciousness into the foreground of third wave transpersonal psychology embraced by the counterculture movement of that time.

During the 1970s, changes in American immigration policy facilitated increased immigration from Asia and the Middle East. This brought Sufi groups more strongly affiliated with the practice of the Islamic religion and its law to America. Some of these groups, mainly based in large urban centers and serving a primarily immigrant constituency, continue to function much as they did in the original cultural context.

Other Sufi groups, which I have termed "hybrid" movements due to their appeal and adaptation to a broader American community, teach the practice of Islam as part of the spiritual training of Sufism. The most notable of these movements are the Naqshbandi Haqqani Order, the Helveti Jerrahi Order, and the Guru Baba Muwaihideen Fellowship.

The constituencies and the membership of these various American Sufi movements vary, since they represent diverse religious and social orientations. The Sufi Order in the West and the Idries Shah Movement have had a broader impact on mainstream American culture due to their publishing activities and outreach to other communities through transpersonal psychology, holistic health, and Sufi dancing. Members do not have to make radical lifestyle or social adjustments and tend to be white, middle-class spiritual seekers. Interest in these movements probably peaked in the mid-1970s. While the Sufi Order claims that ten thousand persons have taken an initiation with Pir Vilayat Khan, many more Americans have attended Sufi seminars or camps or have read their publications.

Perennialist or "traditionalist" Sufism along the lines of the writings of Schuon, Nasr, and Houston Smith has also reached a broad American cultural audience through media such as television interviews with Bill Moyers and publishing activities in both scholarly and popular contexts. The impact of these movements is primarily through ideas rather than due to participation in organized movements.

In the case of the hybrid or Islamic Sufi orders, impact on mainstream American culture is less significant, since the ideas propounded are more specific to Muslim concerns. The Naqshbandi Haqqani Order has twenty-two branches nationwide and a membership estimated at twelve thousand. It has become increasingly prominent in the immigrant Muslim community and has sponsored two "Islamic Unity Conferences," in Los Angeles (1996) and in Washington, D.C. (1998), each attended by several thousand U.S.-based and international delegates. Since Sufi interpretations of Islam—for example, the idea of charismatic leadership and the intercession of pious saints (auliya)—are not accepted by all Muslims, it should not be thought that such movements are supported by the entire American Muslim community. At the same time, many non-Sufi Muslims appreciate their success in drawing Americans to Islam.

Sufi practices involving prayer and meditation have required little adaptation to the American context. At the same time, the gender segregation in public and religious contexts practiced in many Muslim societies has been moderated among American participants. The traditional Sufi practice of pilgrimage to the tombs or shrines of departed Sufis has been transplanted to the American context, as the first generation of leadership, including Murshid Samuel Lewis (New Mexico), Guru Bawa (Pennsylvania), and Shah Magsoud (California), has been memorialized in American soil.

Sufism is practiced in both the Shi'i and Sunni branches of Islam, and a number of Shi'i Orders, including the Ni'matullahi and the Oveyssi-Shahmaghsoudi, have followings in both the Iranian émigré and the American communities. Sufism has had a proportionately smaller impact among African-American Muslims, although some interest has been sparked by activities of the Tijaniyya, an Africa-based order, and by the Naqshbandi Haqqani Order, which probably has the most diverse following among the Sufi orders in the United States.

See also BABA MUWAIHIDEEN; ISLAM; MYSTICISM; NEW AGE SPIRITUALITY.

BIBLIOGRAPHY

Hermansen, Marcia K. "In the Garden of American Sufi Movements: Hybrids and Perennials." In *New Trends and Developments in the World of Islam,* edited by Peter B. Clarke. 1997.

Jervis, James. "The Sufi Order in the West and Pir Vilayat Inayat Khan." In *New Trends and Developments in the World of Islam,* edited by Peter B. Clarke. 1997.

Webb, Gisela. "Sufism in America." In *America's Alternative Religions,* edited by Timothy Miller and Harold Coward. 1995.

Webb, Gisela. "Tradition and Innovation in Contemporary American Islamic Spirituality: The Bawa Muhaiyadeen Fellowship." In *Muslim Communities in North America,* edited by Yvonne Y. Haddad and Jane I. Smith. 1994.

Marcia K. Hermansen

Suicide, Assisted.

See Euthanasia and Assisted Suicide.

Summerland

Summerland is a Spiritualist term referring to a paradisal after-death state. It first appeared in 1845 in the published automatic writings of the youthful Andrew Jackson Davis, the "Poughkeepsie Seer." One of several concentric spherical planes surrounding the earth, the Summerland is the habitation of spirits of good will. Descriptions by mediumistic communica-

tors present the deceased as living a harmonious, quasi-physical life amid supernally beautiful houses, lecture halls, music, gardens, meadows, trees, lakes, streams, and animals. Like other spheres, the Summerland is a product of the minds of its inhabitants. A basic principle of Spiritualism is that "like attracts like"; thus deceased persons who are attuned to beauty, love, and learning are drawn together, and singly or in concert they create these delights, which appear to be altogether concrete. A spirit residing in this sphere may communicate with the living for their benefit; likewise, living persons while out-of-body may upon occasion visit the Summerland.

It is clear that the conceptions of Eden, Paradise, and Heaven from the Christian tradition have informed the Summerland. However, the latter has distinctive features, among them the ideas of halls of learning, of reunited families having their own homes, and of the spirits of infants being raised to maturity by nurturant adult spirits. Some of these ideas appear in the earlier writings of Emanuel Swedenborg, and in fact Davis reported that while he was entranced, Swedenborg dictated the material to him. Interestingly, William James reported that entranced persons unexposed to Spiritualist tradition will in many cases speak like Spiritualist communicators in the name of the deceased, describing the Summerland. Similar narratives are found among twentieth-century Near-Death experiencers.

See also NEAR-DEATH EXPERIENCE; SPIRITUALISM.

BIBLIOGRAPHY

Davis, Andrew Jackson. *The Principles of Nature.* 1845.
James, William. *The Principles of Psychology,* vol. I. 1955.

Gracia Fay Ellwood
Robert Ellwood

Sun Dance

The Sun Dance is one of the seven sacred rites given to the Lakota people by White Buffalo Calf Woman, a legendary figure said to have lived some "nineteen generations ago." These rites represent the basic structure of Lakota ceremonies. The first two rituals usually involve the sweat ceremony, which prepares people for purification, both spiritually and physically. During the sweat ceremony, one can also prepare for the Vision Quest, which is undertaken for the purpose of acquiring power and seeking a vision that will inform or facilitate benevolent privileges to the seeker. The seeker of a vision will try to find a person to guide them in a spiritual sense through the visionary experience. For societies that practice the Sun Dance, it is often the most important ceremony within their set of regularly practiced rituals. Offerings or vows made by the people during the year are, through prayers, supplications, and rituals, fulfilled during the annual celebration. There might be variations in details from tribe to tribe and even within a tribe, yet the principle structure of the ceremony remains similar in terms of its function and rationale.

In the past, there are references that attest to the fact that the Sun Dancers maintained their spiritual relationships to the sun by praying, scarifying their bodies, and fasting alone on a mountain away from the people. They would seek signs from the Great Mystery, *Wakantanka,* through dreams or visionary experience. An experienced Sun Dancer would care for them periodically by bringing them water and checking on their well-being. Usually a pit was dug, and the dancer entered the pit unclothed and covered himself with a buffalo hide for protection against the weather. Members of different tribes would come together to participate in the ritual. As people arrived from different Native Nations, they were instructed as to where the ceremony would be held. Guests then set up tipis in an outer circle around the ceremonial area. In Ella Cara Deloria's description of the Dakota Sun Dance, a crier would tell the people to prepare. Then they would dismantle their tipis and move to the ceremonial area, with the people making four ritual pauses along the way for the purpose of honoring the four sacred directions, the Four Winds. Once all the tipis were together in a large circle, the people's consciousness was directed to the ceremonial process.

Today the Sun Dance requires selecting a sacred ceremonial place that is considered clean and in its natural state. The Sun Dance usually is held during the summer months. Prior to the ceremony, religious authorities known as *wakasa wakan,* or "sacred persons," are responsible for the performance of the ceremony, which lasts for four days. After the camp circle of tipis is in place on the first day of the ceremony, a person is elected to dig a hole in the earth for the sacred Sun Dance pole, which was selected earlier and will be erected as the central pivot of the ceremony. Soil taken from this hole is used to form a square mound of earth on the west side of the Sun Dance pole. A lodge or arbor is then constructed, which surrounds the sacred hole in the center of the camp circle. The person who digs the hole is then instructed by the Sun Dance leader, who walks from the hole in the center toward the east for the purpose of placing wood stakes in the earth at every four paces. After sixteen wood stakes have been placed in position, the last one designates the placement of the sacred tipi. A special sweat lodge is created on the north side of the sacred tipi in the center of the dance grounds. Here the Sun Dancers and their ritual accoutrement are then purified and prayed over.

Sage is used to cover the ground inside the tipi, where an altar is created on the west side and a buffalo skull is adorned with sage, facing to the west. Tobacco offerings are placed on the sixteen stakes by the dancers. The people know that they must not pass through the marked stakes, which mark the path that the sun makes as it moves across the sky. During the ceremony, prayers are made to the spirit of the buffalo for the sustenance of the people and to ensure that there will be no shortage of food in the year after the Sun Dance.

The next day, preparation begins for the selection of the sacred tree, and rituals involved in the cutting of the tree are begun. The ceremonial leader blesses the tree with the pipe and sacred tobacco. A ritually pure girl is prompted to "count coupe," or strike, the tree four times with a ceremonial hatchet. Then, while songs are sung in praise of it, the tree is felled onto a bed of boughs and carried to the center of the Sun Dance grounds, all the while never once being allowed to touch the ground.

The next morning the sacred pole is decorated and people place offerings on it. Then the pole is raised and the end is slid into the hole and firmed up by placing soil around it to hold it in place. During these first three days, the dancers, who have promised to sacrifice by piercing their bodies, are instructed and they pledge to make the sacrifice to the sun. They pledge to dance in one of four ways: gazing at the sun, pierced, suspended, or dragging buffalo skulls.

On the last day, the dancers leave the sacred tipi and prepare for their ritual sacrifice. They are again led by the ceremonial leader as they all leave the tipi circling sun-wise four times. As the first Sun Dance song is heard, they dance in place and blow eaglebone whistles as the drums begin to play and they turn to the four directions of the winds, symbolically emulating the movement of the sun. During the ceremony, the dancers do not drink water and they fast. Periodically they are allowed to rest. The dancing continues for four segments and they, the singers, pray as they ritually smoke the pipe. As the singers finish the pipe ceremony, the dance begins again. As the time approaches for their ritual sacrifice, the dancers take turns lying on the buffalo robe as the Sun Dance leader prepares the dancers and pierces their skin. Others from the community may also ask to be pierced in symbolic support of the dancers.

As the dancers complete their sacrifice, the Sun Dance comes to its conclusion. The dancers have now gained the sacred power of the ceremony, and people step forward to be blessed by them. Some of them receive ritual objects that were used during the ceremony because they also contain power. The pole is left in place, as is the ceremonial arbor, until they erode or decay and return back to the earth.

See also NATIVE AMERICAN RELIGIONS; SWEAT LODGE; VISION QUEST.

BIBLIOGRAPHY

Brown, Joseph Epes. *The Gift of the Sacred Pipe: Based on Black Elk's Account of the Seven Rites of the Oglala Sioux.* 1982.

Deloria, Ella Cara. *Waterlily.* With a biographical sketch of the author by Agnes Picotte and an afterword by Raymond J. DeMallie. 1988.

Ines M. Talamantez

Survivalism

Survivalism is a loosely constructed system of belief and action centered around preparation for the destruction of the existing social order through a series of catastrophic events. While survivalism has roots in Christian premillennialism, it appears in the context of a wide variety of belief systems, reflecting the potency of millennialist belief in American culture more than the demands of any particular theological system.

Most survivalists are white males of a conservative religious and political bent. Survivalist practices enjoy their greatest popularity among members of the American paramilitary subculture, who seldom link survivalism with religious doctrine, and among militant racist and antigovernment groups such as Dan Gayman's Church of Israel and James Ellison's Covenant, The Sword and the Arm of the Lord, both Christian Identity organizations. Survivalism is not restricted to these subcultures, however, appearing at times among groups whose beliefs lie at the opposite end of the ideological spectrum. Elizabeth Clare Prophet's Church Universal and Triumphant, an heir to the Western metaphysical tradition passed down through Theosophical organizations and their kin, and environmentalist survival groups such as Ontario's Ark Two Survival Community are two recent examples.

Survivalists envision a variety of apocalyptic scenarios, including nuclear war, environmental holocaust, race wars, widespread disease, economic collapse, and divinely ordained Armageddon. Their means of preparing for these situations can include stockpiling food and weapons, developing combat skills, amassing knowledge of medical techniques, herbal remedies, and other "survival skills," and building retreats in wilderness areas.

It is difficult to assess the prevalence of survivalism in contemporary society, given that the phenomenon appeals to diverse groups of individuals and is transmitted through informal networks rather than stable institutions. Estimates are further complicated by the fact that most survivalists believe that a certain amount of secrecy is essential to the success of their endeavor. Stephen N. Linder, in *Survivalists* (1982), estimated that as many as three million individuals are involved in the movement. The movement enjoyed a brief but well-documented renaissance in the early 1990s. This fact, coupled with an assessment based on the wide array of survivalist publications available on the open market and on the number of Internet sites as well as at conventions and survivalist stores currently in operation, would seem to indicate growth in the movement over the past decade.

Survivalism, in something close to its current form, first surfaced in about the 1920s, though the term itself was not coined until the mid-1970s. The earliest survivalists—early Christian Identity figure William Kullgren is an example—were premillennialist Christians, specifically post- or mid-Tribulationists, believing that Christians would have to survive some or all of the Tribulation before being raptured off the earth.

Survivalism began to break away from its religious underpinnings in the first years of the nuclear age, as members of the American mainstream culture began to take seriously the prospect of a world-destroying nuclear holocaust. Survivalism took on its most modern form in the post-Vietnam era, gathering in much from the paramilitary subculture it spawned. While coexisting with religiously influenced forms, proponents of survivalism's most recent incarnation often take pains to distance themselves from explicitly religious motivations.

See also CHURCH UNIVERSAL AND TRIUMPHANT; DEATH AND DYING; IDENTITY CHRISTIANITY; MILLENNIALISM; PREMILLENNIALISM; THEOSOPHICAL SOCIETY.

BIBLIOGRAPHY

Barkun, Michael. *Religion and the Racist Right: The Origins of the Christian Identity Movement.* 1994.

Wojcik, Daniel. *The End of the World As We Know It: Faith, Fatalism and Apocalypse in America.* 1997.

Matthew R. Miller

Swaggart, Jimmy Lee

(1935–), radio and television evangelist.

Jimmy Swaggart was perhaps the most celebrated evangelist in the world in the 1980s, both because of huge revival campaigns he conducted in auditoriums and stadiums in the United States and overseas and also because of his popular radio and television programs. Born in Ferriday, Louisiana, Swaggart often attended church with two cousins who had highly successful musical careers, Jerry Lee Lewis, a rock'n'roll legend, and Mickey Gilley, a famous country music star. In later years Swaggart often used his relationship with Lewis to impress audiences. Reared in a pentecostal home, at an early age he had a conversion experience and received the baptism of the Holy Spirit, and at age twenty-three he became an itinerant evangelist. Ordained to the ministry by the Assemblies of God in 1964, Swaggart quickly became one of that denomination's most successful revivalists.

Swaggart was an exuberant and talented preacher, but he was even more gifted as a piano player and singer. In the 1960s he recorded a number of gospel record albums that were highly successful. In 1969 he launched a radio program, *The Camp Meeting Hour,* that was soon aired on hundreds of religious radio stations. In 1973 Swaggart's booming ministry began producing a television program that featured his musical talents and his dynamic preaching; by the 1980s he was seen on more than two hundred stations. By the early 1980s the Jimmy Swaggart Ministerial Association, headquartered in Baton Rouge, Louisiana, sponsored an active crusade schedule that crammed auditoriums in the United States and stadiums overseas; a monthly magazine, *The Evangelist,* which reached a circulation of nearly a million; the Family Worship Center in Baton Rouge that would seat seven thousand people; a small training school known as Jimmy Swaggart Bible College; and a direct mail department that distributed millions of records and books. Hundreds of millions of dollars poured into the Swaggart ministry in the 1970s and 1980s, and in addition to funding his own wide range of programs, he supported pentecostal missions abroad. Swaggart was particularly influential in Latin American countries, where he staged a series of huge crusades and regularly aired his television program in Spanish and Portuguese translation.

Swaggart was a part of a booming pentecostal/charismatic revival that was sweeping the world by the 1970s. Journalists often linked him with other television preachers such as Jim Bakker and Oral Roberts, and to some extent they were all part of the same worldwide revival. However, while most independent charismatic ministers were theologically tolerant and ecumenical, Swaggart remained strongly tied to his denomination, the Assemblies of God, and he preached an "old-time Holy Ghost" message. He was harshly critical of Roman Catholicism and of Protestant liberals, and he preached a strict code of personal

The Rev. Jimmy Swaggart waves a Bible in the air as he speaks to a crowd of 14,000 faithful at the Los Angeles Sports Arena on Sunday, March 30, 1987. (Credit: AP/Wide World Photos.)

morality. When Jim Bakker was accused of sexual misconduct in the spring of 1987, Swaggart strongly condemned his fellow evangelist's sexual indiscretions. Swaggart was not a central figure in the formation of the politically conservative religious coalition that first emerged under the leadership of Jerry Falwell in the late 1970s. Like many other pentecostal preachers, Swaggart was more or less apolitical, although he did back Pat Robertson's bid for the Republican nomination for president in 1988.

Only a few months after his attack on Bakker, Swaggart was himself accused of having liaisons with a prostitute in a seamy New Orleans motel. Swaggart's tearful confession of his sexual indiscretions, which received international press attention, effectively ended his career as a prominent evangelist. His ordination was withdrawn by the Assemblies of God in 1988, but he continued to preach in camp meetings held in Baton Rouge, and the ministry supported a limited television schedule. The post-1988 decline of the Swaggart ministry should not obscure the fact that for nearly two decades he exerted a massive influence on the musical and preaching techniques used by pentecostal evangelists around the world.

See also EVANGELICAL CHRISTIANITY; PENTECOSTAL AND CHARISMATIC CHRISTIANITY; REVIVALISM; ROBERTSON, PAT; TELEVANGELISM.

BIBLIOGRAPHY

Swaggart, Jimmy, and R. P. Lamb. *To Cross a River.* 1977.

Harrell, David Edwin, Jr. *All Things Are Possible: The Healing and Charismatic Revivals in Modern America.* 1975.

Razelle, Frank. *Religious Television: Controversies and Conclusions.* 1990.

David Edwin Harrell, Jr.

Sweat Lodge

Today the Lakota Sioux tradition of group sweating is common throughout Native America. The basic structures of the sweat ceremony described here are typical across much of Native America today. Each community and each leader, however, has a particular style, and various elements are modified by each according to taste and needs. The principles behind the sweat lodge ceremony are purification of the spirit through prayer and sacrifice, and cleansing of the body through intense sweating, which eliminates toxins through the skin. Praying during the ritual is either silent or verbalized. It is understood that this is an act of reciprocity for the gifts one receives from the earth, or it could be taken as a form of supplication or prayer for one's needs, either spiritual or physical. Visionary experience is also an important aspect of the sweat ceremony. One learns to pray and seek visions, often through the guidance of the ceremonial leader, an experienced person honored in the community. In some Native American cultures, men and women sweat separately and in others they sweat together. Today the sweat ceremony has become very popular as a way of bringing Native American peoples back into the traditional ceremonies that have survived in spite of missionization by the churches and acculturation by the government.

The number of people participating is determined by the size of the sweat lodge itself. Usually anywhere from five to ten people may participate. The structure is usually eight to ten feet in diameter and is created by bending (usually) sixteen willow branches to form a five-foot dome with the ends of the branches buried in the ground. At the center of the lodge is a pit of three to four feet in diameter dug into the ground (usually with bare hands) in which heated rocks are placed. This framework is covered to contain the steam that will be created in the lodge. Once buffalo robes were used for this covering, though canvas, blankets, and rugs are more typical today. The opening faces the east where the sun rises. The earth that was dug from the center pit is used to create a path to the east and to build a small earthen altar. Farther over is the fire used for heating the rocks, often referred to as "Stone People," to a glowing red. The fire is tended by the fire keeper, who will also ladle the heated rocks into the lodge.

One enters the lodge in a sun-wise direction after having been given permission to enter by the leader of the sweat group. From the door in the east, one crawls around to the south, back toward the west, and as far toward the north and east as there is room left. Once everyone has entered the lodge, the leader offers tobacco at the pit in which the rocks will be placed. The leader fills the pipe, prays with it, and then it is passed around the circle for each to pray with. Sage is also lit and used to smudge, or cleanse, everything and everyone present. The tobacco and sage incense prepares the body and mind for a spiritual experience and purification. The leader then calls to the fire keeper to bring in the first rocks, or "Stone People." The first four stones are placed in the four directions, identified with the Four Winds, and then topped by two more stones representing the sky above and the earth below. A seventh stone is then placed on top, often representing an eagle or the Great Mystery, *Wakantanka*. Each stone is prayed over as it is placed at the proper spot in the pit. After this foundation is established, the remaining rocks—as many as the leader calls for—are placed in the pit. The leader then calls for a bucket of water and directs the fire keeper to close the entrance to the lodge.

Once the lodge is closed, the leader begins praying and ladling water onto the hot rocks. Led in song and prayer by the leader, the people pray and sing together in the darkness amidst the often intense heat. Prayers are said each time that water is poured on the rocks. There are four rounds, each one usually climaxing with a blast of steam, intense heat, and prayer, and finally the entrance of the lodge is opened to let some fresh air in and to provide relief. At this point the refrain *"Mitakuye Oyasin!"* ("All my relations") is often called out. After the fourth round, everyone leaves the lodge in a sun-wise direction and walks around the lodge, in a sun-wise direction as well. The participants depart to dress and prepare for a communal meal together. The experience of the sweat and the sharing of food and conversation afterward create a powerful sense of community.

See also BELONGING, RELIGIOUS; NATIVE AMERICAN RELIGIONS; PURIFICATION; SUN DANCE; VISIONARY.

BIBLIOGRAPHY

Brown, Joseph Epes. *The Gift of the Sacred Pipe: Based on Black Elk's Account of the Seven Rites of the Oglala Sioux.* 1982.

DeMallie, Raymond J. *The Sixth Grandfather: Black Elk's Teachings Given to John G. Neihardt.* 1984.

DeMallie, Raymond J., and Douglas R. Parks. *Sioux Indian Religion: Tradition and Innovation.* 1987.

Powers, William K. *Oglala Religion.* 1977.

Walker, J. R. (b. 1849). *Lakota Belief and Ritual.* Edited by Raymond J. DeMallie and Elaine A. Jahner. 1980.

Inez M. Talamantez

The Rose Window of Temple Emanu-el, a synagogue in New York City, November 9, 1995. (Credit: CORBIS/Gail Mooney.)

Synagogue

A syngagogue is a building devoted to the practice of Judaism through prayer, study of the Torah, and practice of the religious obligations set forth by God through Moses to Israel at Mount Sinai; a community of Jews formed for the purpose of practicing Judaism. The synagogue, along with the associated cemetery, was the first institution Jews created in the United States, beginning in colonial times in New York, Philadelphia, Charleston, Savannah, and Newport, and it remains the principal institution for the practice of Judaism, including religious education, in the United States. Public worship ordinarily takes place in buildings constructed for that purpose, which set aside as the focal point of public worship an ark in which the Torah scrolls of the community are kept.

In Reform, Reconstructionist, and Conservative synagogues, men and women sit together; in Orthodox synagogues they are seated separately, and a *mehisah,* or partition, separates them; or the women are seated in balconies. Synagogue worship may be led, and the Torah may be read, by any qualified person (male in Orthodoxy). But in the United States it is common for synagogues to employ full-time clergy, called rabbis, who are qualified for service by knowledge of the Torah, and many synagogues also call on cantors, *hazzanim,* to recite the service. In addition to large public halls for community occasions, synagogues always encompass schoolrooms for regular class sessions for all age groups and often provide for smaller prayer spaces for occasions on which the congregation is few in number. In the United States, where large numbers of persons attend services on a few occasions during the year, such as the New Year (Rosh Hashanah) and the Day of Atonement (Yom Kippur), a synagogue will provide for expansion through folding doors and walls to open up the main sanctuary. But synagogue worship also takes place in private homes, and a congregation may number from ten upward.

The synagogue, a place of organized communal worship of God and study of the Torah, is well attested from the first century C.E. and certainly antedates that time, though its origins are still unclear. Many think that the synagogue originated after the destruction of the first Temple in 586, finding in Ezekiel 8:6, 14:1, 209:1 references to such an institution (e.g., "the little sanctuary" of Ezekiel 11:16). For Jews outside the Land of Israel, in any event, the synagogue was the center of the religious life. Synagogues small and large were built by Jewish communities wherever Judaism was practiced, and the synagogue has been the principal institution of that religion for nearly the whole of its existence. Prayer took the place of sacrifice, and the word for Temple service, *abodah,* "labor," was taken over as the word for prayer, "the labor of the heart." The liturgy of the synagogue morning and evening corresponds to the liturgy of the Temple when it stood. And from ancient times forward, the synagogue served not only as a center for prayer and Torah study but also as a meeting place for the Jewish community.

In the United States the conception of the synagogue as a community center, set forth originally by Mordecai M. Kaplan, founder of Reconstructionist Judaism, greatly broadened the scope of synagogue activity. The synagogue center includes not only a place for prayer and study but also space for a library, clubrooms, activities in music, drama, photography, dance, and sports, social and cultural programs, and even sports and swimming facilities, so that the synagogue-center serves as a center for all leisure-time activities. The center model redefined in broad terms the character of the synagogue and the Jewish community that it served, extending the definition of Judaism as a religion to include the Jews as an ethnic group.

Synagogues in the United States fall into six main groups: Reconstructionist, Reform, Conservative, integrationist ("modern") Orthodox, segregationist Orthodox, and Hasidic. Reconstructionist synagogues look for rabbis to the Reconstructionist Rabbinical College and follow the teachings of Mordecai Kaplan. Reform synagogues turn to Hebrew Union College–Jewish Institute of Religion and originate in the synagogue reforms first of liturgy, then of law and theology of nineteenth-century Germany, whence immigrants brought Reform Judaism to the United States. Conservative synagogues look to the Jewish Theological Seminary of America for rabbis; they differ from Reform synagogues in using more Hebrew in public worship and adhering more closely to the received liturgy and forms of prayer. Integrationist Orthodoxy, the Orthodox Judaism that affirms the possibility of observing the Torah and also participating in modern life, finds its rabbis at Yeshiva University. Segregationist Orthodoxy, which holds that the life of the Torah requires separation in all possible ways from all aspects of the Gentile world, takes shape around yeshivas, or intensive seminaries for Torah study. There are no important liturgical differences between integrationist and segregationist Orthodoxy, though there are important distinctions in the everyday life patterns of adherents to the one and the other. Hasidic groups conform to the norms of Orthodox Judaism in most respects, but they have some customs and convictions that distinguish them as well. Chief among these is the importance they assign to their rabbis, *rebbes*, who are not only teachers of the Torah, as in the normative synagogues, but also holy men and intermediaries between man and God. They dispense blessings and advice and are at the very center of Hasidic Judaism. Some Hasidic groups take shape around a small number of congregations, but others form worldwide organizations. The leading Hasidic Judaism is Habad, a.k.a. Lubovitch, which maintains representatives in every country in which Jews, however few, are located, and which further sends rabbis into prisons and other locations not commonly ministered to by mainstream synagogues and national organizations.

Synagogues in the several classifications form national synagogue organizations as well. These are as follows: Reform: Union of American Hebrew Congregations; Conservative: United Synagogue; integrationist-Orthodox: Union of Orthodox Jewish Congregations. Reform and Conservative synagogues also relate to overseas counterparts through the World Union of Progressive Judaism and the World Council of Synagogues, respectively. All American synagogue organizations maintain relationships, in addition, with Israeli counterparts.

In architecture, contemporary American synagogues have aimed at simplicity of design and decoration, using painting, sculpture, textiles, mosaics, and stained glass to create a sacred space. While for a long time the congregation was seated in long rows facing the *bimah*, or platform, from which the service was presented, a different pattern has taken shape in the recent past. The congregation is seated around the center point, or on three sides of it, with the ark at the back wall; a greater sense of community at worship is attained, in place of the experience of an audience at a play on a stage that the former pattern afforded. The auditorium plan of organization of the synagogue had the lectern in front of the ark, but the new pattern makes the ark the visual focus and sets the lectern to the side.

See also Congregation; Jewish Identity; Jewish Observance; Judaism; Kaplan, Mordechai; Rabbinate; Religious Belonging; Religious Communities; Torah.

Bibliography

Chiat, Marilyn. *Handbook of Synagogue Architecture.* 1982.

Heilman, Samuel C. *Synagogue Life: A Study in Symbolic Interaction.* 1976.

Liebman, Charles S. *Orthodoxy in American Jewish Life.* 1966.

Neusner, Jacob, ed. *Understanding American Judaism: Toward the Description of Modern Religion,* 2 vols. 1975.

Raphael, Marc Lee. *Profiles in American Judaism: The Reform, Conservative, Orthodox and Reconstructionist Traditions in Historical Perspective.* 1984.

Rudavsky, David. *Modern Jewish Religious Movements,* 3rd ed. 1979.

Sklare, Marshall. *Conservative Judaism: An American Religious Movement.* 1977.

Jacob Neusner

Synanon

The Synanon Foundation, founded in 1958 as a therapeutic group for alcohol and drug addicts, slowly evolved into a communal religious group that formally recognized its new status in 1975 with a change in its charter and five years later with the adoption of a new name, the Synanon Church. In its early stage, Synanon drew on the model of Alcoholics Anonymous in its efforts to assist drug addicts to drop their use of a range of illegal narcotics and controlled substances. Through the 1960s, under the leadership of founder Charles Dederich (1914–1997), its work expanded rapidly, and Synanon facilities opened along the American West Coast. In 1968, headquarters moved to rural Marin County, California, near the town of Marshal.

Like alcoholism, Synanon defined addiction as a permanent problem for former addicts, and many participants in the program moved into Synanon facilities for ongoing help. Facility residents organized themselves as a communal society and developed businesses that provided an economic base for their life together.

As with Alcoholics Anonymous, a spiritual/religious theme was integral to Synanon's approach, but only in the 1970s did a self-conscious theological perspective emerge. Synanon adopted a vague mystical worldview that drew elements from both Eastern (Buddhist/ Hindu) and Western (metaphysical) sources. The basic desire for cosmic, social, and individual unity was ideally expressed in the communal life and made operational in the Synanon Game, the group's primary ritual activity. The game had begun as an encounter group but became increasingly intense as a religious practice. People participated in the game on a regular basis. They were expected to be completely open and honest and receive the group's critique as a catalyst for confession, repentance, and ablution.

Synanon quickly became controversial for its aggressive approach to individuals, but found many supporters for its undeniable success with ridding people of their drug dependence and destructive habits. However, the group ran into significant trouble in 1978, when an attorney who had won a judgment against, the group was bitten by a rattlesnake that had been placed in his mailbox. Dederich and two others charged in the case pleaded no contest. Dederich avoided a jail sentence but was forced to resign as the group's leader. Soon afterward he admitted to a recurrence of the alcoholism that had been a major reason for starting Synanon.

Dederich's trial occurred in the hostile atmosphere generated by the deaths at Jonestown. It was followed by a series of hostile press articles; a book-length exposé; a sct of new lawsuits, some by former members who had rejected what they saw as an increasingly harsh, dictatorial life within the group; and a period of intense government scrutiny of the group's expanding business interests. The combined attack eventually resulted in the Internal Revenue Service's denying Synanon tax-exempt status in 1991. The resulting damage to their economic base forced the church to disband soon afterward, though remnants of the community survived through the 1990s.

See also BELONGING, RELIGIOUS; DRUGS; HEALTH; NEW RELIGIOUS MOVEMENTS.

BIBLIOGRAPHY

Garfield, Howard M. *The Synanon Religion.* 1978.

Mitchell, Dave, Cathy Mitchell, and Richard Ofshe. *The Light on Synanon.* 1980.

J. Gordon Melton

Syncretism

Syncretism refers to the mixture of religious ideas or practices from diverse sources. The earliest use of the term is in the *Moralia* of Plutarch, who spoke of the alliances that brought fractious Cretans together (*syn-Kretoi*) against a common enemy. This togetherness among things that have not been, and perhaps should not be, together gives the term its energy and openness to controversy. Syncretism in religion implies crossed doctrinal, liturgical, and institutional borders.

Writers committed to religious institutions have generally been hostile to unauthorized blending of religious symbols and have seen syncretism as a challenge to the integrity of religious traditions. The word became fixed as a term of disparagement in seventeenth-century Europe, when those opposed to movements of theological reconciliation among Protestant denominations and Roman Catholicism referred to unacceptable compromises as "syncretism." Today writers seeking respectful interreligious dialogue still may see the blurring of religious borders as "the threat of syncretism." (Wiggins 1996:64).

Theologians and missionaries have long used the term to deprecate new religious movements and folk religious initiatives as inauthentic or impure. Here the label of syncretism acts as a normative judgment that rests on notions of the superiority of an essential religious tradition and the need to protect it from dilution and adulteration. Contemporary practitioners of new alternative, or minority religions often resent the condescension connoted by the label of syncretism with its implications of confusion and inferiority.

The controversy surrounding the label of syncretism reveals a number of psychological, social, and cultural dynamics that illuminate how religions develop. By focusing on the arrangement of disparate elements in religious symbolism, the observer may see how social and personal religious experience is organized in a concrete historical situation. In particular the idea of syncretism illuminates the location and importance of borders in the construction of identity in religious communities and individuals.

The social dynamics behind the idea of syncretism reveal contestation about boundaries and power. Syncretism may be seen to originate "from above" or "from below," particularly in situations of religious mission, where issues of translation are paramount (Sanneh 1989). Elites seeking to "inculturate" Christianity among Native Americans or Buddhism among white Coloradans may self-consciously adapt ideas and practices in order to make them more readily understood and acceptable to the indigenous populations. Often this missionary quest to build local theologies still seeks to restrict access and religious expression within institutional boundaries. On the other hand syncretism may also arise "from below," in the ways that the missionized construct new meanings from the symbols that arise from different social contexts. Thus the Catholic saints take on new significance among practitioners of *santería* and the Christian cross speaks at several levels to members of the Native American Church. This phenomenon of reinterpretation was highlighted by American anthropologist Melville Herskovits as a two-way process of cultural interaction, in which familiar symbols take on new meanings and new symbols can be reinterpreted in the light of familiar associations. (Herskovits 1948: 553; also Apter 1991). In this way syncretism is the way that people can live in different semiotic worlds, allowing both their blending as well as their juxtaposition.

Syncretism can thus be seen as an adaptive strategy on the part of many different individuals and social groups to both cross and maintain boundaries. Syncretism may be the self-conscious attempt to integrate experience as seen in the rise of such traditions as Sikhism or Baha'i. Or it may be an accommodation to power as well as a critique of it, a kind of "cultural judo" in the words of Jamaican-American historian of religion Leonard Barrett. Here the folk on the margins of power accept the symbols of the elite only to subvert them with additional, unauthorized, and often ironic meanings.

It may be that the term "syncretism" is indelibly tainted with the politics of claims to and resistance against cultural hegemony. Several contemporary scholars have suggested abandoning the term, either because of its pejorative connotation, or because it is a universal process in the history of all religions, or because the precise boundaries of traditions simply cannot be determined. (Baird 1971; Ringgen 1966). Scholars have put forth alternative terms using words or phrases such as "combinatory" "mixing and matching," or even "religion à la carte"—all intended to highlight the processes of religious formation and boundary definitions.

Whether or not the term itself proves to be viable, the type of religious creativity that syncretism attempts to describe is real, important, and relevant to American religious life at the beginning of the new millennium. With the growth of global communications and travel, Americans are experiencing unprecedented cross-cultural contact and exchange. Identities are being simultaneously globalized and localized as individuals and groups struggle to connect to, and separate themselves from, a new world order. Parents of interfaith marriages are raising children simultaneously in two or more traditions. Individuals and groups are organizing their religious lives by freely blending and juxtaposing religious symbols from African, Asian, European, Native American, and even extraterrestrial sources. Individuals are claiming to be Buddhist Jews and Hindu Africans are forming voodoo ashrams. The rise of American Neopaganism, the growth of traditions such as Wicca, and the cluster of beliefs and practices associated with New Age spirituality attest to the fluency with which Americans are constructing new symbolic worlds. In the analysis of these traditions, the issues addressed by the term "syncretism" yield significant insights into the integration of experience by individuals and the construction of boundaries by groups.

See also ANTHROPOLOGY OF RELIGION; BAHA'IS; CRYPTO-JUDAISM; GLOBALIZATION; NATIVE AMERICAN CHURCH; NEOPAGANISM; NEW AGE SPIRITUALITY; RELIGIOUS EXPERIENCE; SANTERÍA; SIKHISM; WICCA.

BIBLIOGRAPHY

Apter, Andrew. "Herskovits's Heritage: Rethinking Syncretism in the African Diaspora," *Diaspora,* vol. 1, no. 3, 1991.

Baird, Robert D. *Category Formation in the History of Religions,* 1971.

Barrett, Leonard E. *Soul Force: African Heritage in Afro-American Religion,* 1974.

Droogers André. "Syncretism: the Problem of Definition, the Definition of the Problem," In *Dialogue and Syncretism, An Interdisciplinary Approach,* edited by Jerald Gort, et al., 1989.

Herskovits, Melville J. *Man and His Works,* 1948.

Ringgen, Helmer. "The Problems of Syncretism." In *Syncretism,* edited by Sven S. Hartman, 1966.

Sanneh, Lamin. *Translating the Message: The Missionary Impact on Culture,* 1989.

Schreiter, Robert J. *Constructing Local Theologies,* 1985.

Stewart, Charles, and Rosalind Shaw, editors. *Syncretism/Anti-Syncretism: The Politics of Religious Synthesis,* 1994.

Wiggins, James. *In Praise of Religious Diversity,* 1996.

Joseph M. Murphy

T

Talmud

The Talmud is a rabbinic work consisting of the Mishnah, the earliest formulation of rabbinic instruction (ca. 200 c.e.); and the Gemara, an extended commentary and elaboration of the Mishnah composed in the mid-sixth century. The Gemara is built on rabbinic teachings, from Palestine and Babylonia, of the third through the fifth centuries. But its received form, combining approximately equal amounts of attributed teachings and unattributed analysis and argumentation, is the work of Babylonian rabbis. A related work, also called a Talmud, was written by Palestinian rabbis. Still, *the* Talmud has always been the Babylonian (the Bavli).

A Hasidic man instructs his son in the Talmud and Bible, in Brooklyn, New York, ca. 1990. (Credit: CORBIS/Richard T. Nowitz.)

Since the early Middle Ages, the Talmud has served rabbis as the authoritative source for halakhic decision-making (*halakha* = Jewish law). To this day in the traditional Jewish community, no question in Jewish law can be answered without reference to talmudic precedents. For this reason the Talmud is the primary focus of study in traditional *yeshivot*.

Jewish reformers in the nineteenth century turned their back on the Talmud, and Talmud study continues to demand relatively little time in liberal Jewish schools. Consequently, the majority of contemporary Jews are ignorant of the Talmud. However, in recent years, as many Jews have sought to rediscover the roots of their tradition, the Talmud has regained a measure of popularity. The most outstanding product of this phenomenon is the English talmudic translation and commentary by Rabbi Adin Steinsaltz. The growing popularity of the Talmud is also a product of its nature: Rather than offering single definitive opinions, the Talmud more often analyzes and supports multiple opinions, hesitating to declare only one correct. The Talmud thus serves as a model of respectful pluralistic dialogue both for communities of Jewish laypeople and for academics who seek historical and theoretical precedents for "postmodern" discourse.

See also JEWISH IDENTITY; JUDAISM.

BIBLIOGRAPHY

Kraemer, David. *The Mind of the Talmud.* 1990.

Steinsaltz, Adin. *The Essential Talmud.* 1976.

David Kraemer

715

Tantra

Tantra refers to a family of esoteric religious cults originating in South Asia at an uncertain time, probably between 600 B.C.E. and 300 C.E. Because these were secret traditions, they had no formal institutions, scriptures, or visible exemplars at their inception. These cults probably revived aspects of pre-Vedic civilization, with an emphasis on the mother-goddess, yogic practice, and spiritual transformation with shamanic overtones. Eventually, tantra became mainstreamed (600–1000 C.E.), first in Buddhism and then in Hinduism, as powerful religious movements that revitalized their entire traditions. But because of esoteric elements, including unconventional methods, sexual symbolism and iconography, and a requisite bond of vow between guru and disciple, tantra has often been misunderstood by the more conservative elements of their root traditions and by other religions, especially outside of India.

Tantra is a Sanskrit word that means "continuity," and it refers most formally to a group of ritual scriptures, attributed to the Buddha or to Hindu masters. These texts appeared in manuscript form between 600 and 900 C.E. and were indecipherable, for they were written in "twilight language" (*sandhābhāsa*), a highly symbolic esoteric dialect that could not be interpreted without initiation and the personal guidance of an authorized *guru*. These texts, whether Buddhist or Hindu, spoke of the continuity of inherent sacredness of all aspects of the world, no matter how defiled they might appear. The tantras outlined the path to liberation through inner transformation, which included spiritual, psychological, and physical dimensions.

Although tantric traditions probably had common roots in Indian culture, the Buddhist and Hindu assimilations of tantra quickly developed quite distinct qualities, reflecting the basic views, sensibilities, and paradigms of liberation specific to each. Even when these traditions have a common iconography and symbolic language, the actual meanings and practices differ greatly from tradition to tradition. For example, though many Hindu tantric traditions focused on a powerful goddess, Śaivite traditions emphasized the male deity with a powerful but ultimately subordinate consort. Vaiṣṇava tantric traditions see the *śakti* goddess as the creative aspect of the male godhead; Śakti cults elevated the goddess to supreme status as Mahādevī, the "great goddess." Buddhist tantra spread throughout Asia but met reluctance in East Asia. Only Shingon survives in Japan, in a highly truncated form. The premier tantric Buddhist tradition developed as the "diamond vehicle" Vajrayāna in Tibet, where it was preserved in unbroken lineage until the Chinese invasion and Tibetan diaspora in 1959.

Tantra in America

With the rise in popularity of Asian meditation traditions in the late 1960s and 1970s, Buddhist and Hindu tantric gurus introduced their respective traditions to American students. Among the variety of tantric teachings, two will be discussed: Siddha-yoga, taught by Swami Muktananda; and Tibetan Vajrayāna, taught first by Ven. Chögyam Trungpa, Rinpoche. Each teacher was a traditionally trained, highly respected representative of his Asian tantric tradition; each was a pioneer in introducing tantra to American students; and each paved the way for further tantric teachings to be disseminated. At the same time, these charismatic, riveting gurus attracted controversy as they experimented with how to introduce tantric teachings in an American environment.

Swami Muktananda, the spiritual successor of Nityananda of Ganeshpuri, first toured the United States in 1970 with two American students, Ram Dass (also known as Richard Alpert) and Rudi (Albert Rudolph). Then and on successive tours, he boldly adapted a hallmark teaching from tantra's secrecy, the *śaktipāt,* a direct transmission that awakened the spiritual energy (*śakti*) dormant at the base of the spine in the subtle yogic body. When it is awakened, it becomes the *kundalinī,* which dramatically moves snake-like up the spine, awakening all the spiritual centers and opening the student to spiritual fulfillment. Muktananda's programs provided a context for this experience, and eventually Siddha Yoga centers were created to teach meditation and support spiritual development based on *śaktipāt.* Muktananda energetically continued his U.S. tours until his death in 1982 at the age of seventy-four. His American spiritual successor is a young woman who served as his translator, the former Malti Shetty (b. 1955), now empowered as Gurumayi Chidvilasananda, known for her spiritual depth, charisma, and continuation of her guru's *śaktipāt* transmissions.

When the twenty-year old Chögyam Trungpa, Rinpoche, fled Tibet in 1959, he had been under rigorous monastic training in Vajrayāna Buddhism since the age of seven. In 1970 Trungpa came to the United States, already fluent in English and Western ways from his years of study at Oxford. Almost immediately he began publicly teaching tantra but in American idiom, without the transmissions and practices that usually characterize the tradition. Instead, he called it an "open secret" that was the naked truth, a "spiritual atomic bomb," accessed through formless sitting meditation. He also spoke of the Tibetan tradition of "crazy wisdom" (*yeshe chölwa*), fearless wisdom that appears crazy only in the eyes of a confused, enslaved world. Eventually, with his students, he became more traditional, introducing vows and commitments, ritual practices, and textual study, laying the foundations for a thoroughly American Buddhist tantra. At his death in 1987, Trungpa left behind an international network of Vajradhatu (now Shambhala) Meditation Centers and a fully accredited university, Nāropa Institute, in Boulder, Colorado. His spiritual successor is his Tibetan son, Ven. Sakyong Mipham, Rinpoche, who blends his Asian and American heritages in a style more traditional than his famous father's.

Like their Asian forebearers, these tantric gurus sometimes attracted controversy because of their unconventional teaching methods, requirements for unquestioning devotion, or secular lifestyles, which were considered "unspiritual" in an American religious context. Critics suggested that tantra was not appropriate for an American context and should be shunned in favor of more gradual, scholastic, or conservative methods from the Asian heritage. Both teachers remained undaunted by these criticisms, confident that the American context was perfect for tantra because of the intelligence, spiritual aptitude, and ambition of American students. Still, their tantric successors have faced a variety of obstacles in the American setting, including sexual harrassment lawsuits, attrition or schism among members, and an aura of scandal which often surrounded their Asian predecessors.

See also BUDDHISM; HINDUISM; NEW AGE SPIRITUALITY.

BIBLIOGRAPHY

Bharati, Agehananda. *The Tantric Tradition.* 1970.

Hayes, Peter. *The Supreme Adventure: The Experience of Siddha Yoga.* 1988.

Snellgrove, David. *Indo-Tibetan Buddhism: Indian Buddhists and Their Tibetan Successors.* 1987.

Trungpa, Chögyam. *Crazy Wisdom.* 1991.

Judith Simmer Brown

Taoism

The word "Taoism," or rather "Tauism," first appeared in the English language in about 1839. The term is, in Nathan Sivin's words, a "source of perplexity," partly due to problems shared with other "-ism" words and partly due to the Western categorization of Chinese religion. Like "Zen," the word "Taoism" and the term "Tao" have taken on a life of their own in the West,

divorced from their contexts in China. This article briefly overviews the Chinese contexts of Taoism, the major shifts in Western understandings of Taoism, the pervasive appropriation of certain elements of Taoism by non-Chinese-American culture, and finally the Taoist religious life of Chinese immigrants.

As Sivin remarks, in contemporary usage, Taoist can refer to a certain frame of mind (carefree, spontaneous, "going with the flow"), but also to a religion, a political philosophy, a bibliographical classification, or a means of gaining immortality. Indeed, there is no precise Chinese term for Taoism. The nearest one comes is the two terms *tao-chia* and *tao-chiao*. These are sometimes translated as "philosophical Taoism" and "religious Taoism," respectively, but one can accept these translations only very loosely. Generally, tao-chia refers to expertise in an elite literary/philosophical tradition focused on a small number of classical texts from the late Zhou and early Han dynasties (ca. third century B.C.E. to first century C.E.), principally the Tao Te Ching by the rather shadowy figure Lao Tzu, the Chuang Tzu by an author of the same name, and subsequent traditions of commentary. In the early Han dynasty, the term tao-chia also implied a miscellaneous bibliographical classification that included many topics apparently unrelated to "Taoism"—treatises on agriculture and hydrology, for example. The term tao-chiao refers to a series of religious movements and traditions beginning in the late Han dynasty (second century C.E.) with divine revelations of the cosmic body of Lao Tzu to a certain Chang Tao-ling. We need not go into the details of the various religious movements over the centuries—T'ai-p'ing, T'ien-shih, Shang-ch'ing, etc. These religious traditions included such features as scripture, liturgy, ecclesiastical hierarchy, meditation, worship, and even monasticism. More important for now is to note the history of Western attitudes toward these two meanings of Taoism. In Hastings's *Encyclopedia of Religion and Ethics* (1916), for example, most of the article on Taoism concerns the ideas of the Tao Te Ching, and only as an afterthought is there a mention of "popular Taoism," "which is not unfairly described as a mass of superstitious magic . . . [which has] yielded to the love of the marvelous" (p. 201). In this view, the Taoism of the majority of Chinese resulted from an "inrush of superstition," a "deterioration." It has taken many years for Western scholars to decisively repudiate this judgmental stereotype, and it may take many more for popular books on Taoism to go beyond the Tao Te Ching. The dominance of that one text in the American image of Taoism is almost without precedent. It is said that the Tao Te Ching has been translated into English more than any other text except the Bible. "Translations" have been made by people who do not actually know Chinese. For example, Stephen Mitchell's best-selling translation begins with this admission.

One reason for this Rorschach-picture quality of the ongoing rephrasing of the Tao Te Ching is that the traditional text is itself highly ambiguous and probably corrupt. Even a very responsible translation steeped in Chinese commentarial tradition, such as that of D. C. Lau, must include many arbitrary resolutions of irresolvably ambiguous prose. Among the many ideas articulated in this rather rambling collection of poetic aphorisms is a polarity (though not a dualism) of yin and yang motifs, such as male/female, powerful/powerless, famous/unknown, and mountain/valley. The epistemology here is relativist, with a sense that no value is absolute; every value changes according to the context. Given the danger of taking rigid positions or going to extremes, the practical advice for survival in the violent late Zhou period is to yield, take the lower position, and be obscure. Some of the appeal for American readers, especially those in "countercultures," lies in the rejection of egotistical self-promotion or the aggressive domination of others.

This philosophical/literary Taoism is also appealing to Western environmentalists. Many of the metaphors in classical texts are from natural cycles: People are basically like plants—they start out as seed; they germinate inside the feminine (Earth); they are vulnerable when young but survive by being supple and yielding; they grow stronger but also stiffer; when they get too brittle they snap easily; they have a core of sap that must be guarded even at the expense of losing leaves, twigs, and branches; their death contributes directly to an ongoing fertility; and so on.

Elements of Taoism—symbols, practices, textual fragments—have been appropriated by non-Chinese Americans and have entered into popular commercial culture. The "yin-yang" symbol (more correctly the t'ai chi symbol) may be seen on surfboards, T-shirts, and product packaging. The rhetoric and practices of various martial arts such as t'ai chi and aikido include Taoist motifs: an alternation of yin and yang, an emphasis on gaining power through yielding or absorbing the opponent's blows, and an avoidance of postural extremes.

Perhaps the best-known example of appropriation of Taoism is the best-selling book *The Tao of Pooh* by Benjamin Hoff. He explains the ideas of the Tao Te Ching through A. A. Milne's character Winnie-the-Pooh. While this is charming in its way, Hoff makes Taoism and Chinese culture as a whole into an enchanted fantasy, a child's world. Taoism is paraphrased as a story of "a dumpy little bear that wanders around asking silly questions, making up songs, and going through all kinds of adventures, without ever

accumulating any amount of intellectual knowledge or losing his simpleminded sort of happiness" (p. xii). Such playful figures are certainly in evidence in Taoist texts, in the Chuang Tzu, and throughout Chinese literature, but again Taoism is reduced to only a happy attitude. Certainly this description has little to do with the Taoism (tao-chiao) of most Chinese.

We turn now to "religious Taoism." Chinese immigrants came to America especially during the mid-nineteenth century prior to the Chinese Exclusion Act of 1882 and again since the 1950s. They brought religious practices and built temples that can in many cases be identified as Taoist. However, in popular religious practice the strict sectarian classification becomes untenable due to the tendency to worship Taoist, Buddhist, and Confucian deities at the same site. Every major settlement of Chinese immigrants in North America supports at least one Taoist temple. The earliest Taoist temples in America are in San Francisco. The Kong Chow Temple, for example, was founded in 1857 and relocated in the 1960s to Stockton Street. The principle deity there is Kuan Ti, who embodies both martial and literati virtues. Founded in 1852, the Tin How Temple, on Waverly Place, commemorates T'ien Hou (a female "Celestial Consort" or "Empress of Heaven"). In addition to temple-based Taoism, there is frequent worship of tutelary deities (t'u-ti-kung) and Taoist ritual at funerals. There are also many T'ai chi clubs and traditional medical practices that may be considered more or less explicitly Taoist.

See also CHINESE-AMERICAN RELIGIONS; CONFUCIANISM; LITURGY AND WORSHIP; RELIGIOUS STUDIES; RITUAL; TAO TE CHING.

BIBLIOGRAPHY

Kohn, Livia. *The Taoist Experience: An Anthology*. 1993.

Pas, Julian. *A Select Bibliography on Taoism*. 1997.

Schipper, Kristofer. *The Taoist Body*. 1993.

Sivin, Nathan. "On the Word 'Taoist' as a Source of Perplexity, with Special Reference to the Relations of Science and Religion in Traditional China." *History of Religions* 17 (February–May 1978): 303–330.

Eric Reinders

Tao Te Ching

The Tao Te Ching (also Daodejing, Tao Te King) is a Chinese text dating from the fourth or third century B.C.E. and attributed to the obscure figure Lao Tzu ("The Old Master" or "The Old Boy"). It is foundational for all forms of Taoism, though interpretations of the text vary widely. Tao is literally "way" or "the way," as in "the way things are." Te is the "power" or "virtue" that comes through attunement with the Tao. Ching means a book or "classic." The text is divided into two halves, the Tao section and the Te section. However, a version of the text, dating from before 168 B.C.E. and found in 1973 at Ma-wang-tui, has instead the Te Tao Ching.

Among the many ideas articulated in this rather rambling collection of poetic aphorisms are a polarity (though not a dualism) of yin and yang motifs such as male/female, powerful/powerless, famous/unknown, and mountain/valley. The epistemology here is relativist, and no absolute positions are tenable. Meaning is produced in terms of contrasts (high/low, good/bad, etc.) that divide our experience. Extremes of any kind are only temporary, just as one reaching the mountain peak can only go downward. Extremes are thus momentary and lead inexorably to their opposites. The Tao Te Ching posits a fruitful, chaotic union of opposites, embracing all potential differences. This is one way to conceive of the Tao. The practical advice for survival in violent times is to yield, take the lower position, and be obscure. Some of the appeal for American readers, especially those in "countercultures," lies in the rejection of egotistical self-promotion or the aggressive domination of others. The monopoly of this one text in the American image of Taoism is almost without precedent, to the point that for many Americans, this text equals Taoism. It is often said that the Tao Te Ching has been translated into English more than any other text. "Translations" have been made by people who do not actually know Chinese. The ambiguity of the original text, together with its relative brevity and the cumulative tradition of repeated translation, lends it a mirroring or Rorschach-test quality: Translators diverge wildly from the letter of the text in pursuit of its spirit, which (as it turns out) usually corresponds closely to their own notions and ideals. Partly this is true of all translations, but in this case the traditional text is also corrupt and highly ambiguous. Even a very responsible translation steeped in Chinese commentarial tradition, such as that of D. C. Lau, must include many arbitrary resolutions of irresolvably ambiguous prose. A selection of translations of the first verse of the first chapter indicates this hermeneutic plenitude. Laus's fairly literal translation runs: "The way that can be spoken of is not the constant way; the name that can be named is not the constant name." This verse introduces the theme of the limits of language, a theme that develops into a polarity of the nameless, womblike chaos (the Tao) contrasted to the phenomenal world of names, distinctions, and order.

Anachronistically interjecting the notion of eternality, Paul Carus's translation runs: "The Reason that can be reasoned is not the eternal Reason. The name that can be named is not the eternal name." In his introduction, Carus compared Lao Tzu to Jesus, and the concept of Tao to the New Testament logos. The Christian analogy is repeated in E. H. Parker's 1904 translation: "The Providence which could be indicated by words would not be an all-embracing Providence, nor would any name by which we could name it be an ever-applicable name." He also translates the term Te as "grace." His candid willingness to read freely into the text without concern for philological rigor is clear: "I totally ignore all that both Chinese and foreigners have hitherto said as to Lao Tzu's meaning" (pp. 3–4).

Dwight Goddard's 1919 translation does not translate the word Tao. "The Tao that can be understood cannot be the primal, or cosmic, Tao, just as an idea that can be expressed in words cannot be the infinite idea." In his introduction Goddard remarks: "Laotzu saw in a glass darkly what Jesus saw face to face in all his glory, the Divine Tao, God as creative and redemptive Love" (p. 6). Although the Tao Te Ching has been used as a foil to critique the aggression of twentieth-century Western culture, the essentializing impulse to reduce difference to sameness informs the recent work of Stephen Mitchell, who claims that his lack of training in the Chinese language is overcome by fourteen years of Zen meditation, "which brought me face to face with Lao-tzu" (p. 14). He claims to have translated the "mind" of Lao Tzu. (The interchangeability of Taoism and Zen Buddhism is a common anachronistic assumption in popular writing.) Another modern interpreter, Brian Walker, considers the text "less a book than a living, breathing angel" (foreword). He considers Lao Tzu "less as a man who once lived and more as a song that plays, eternal and abiding." Mitchell and Walker among others claim that the Tao Te Ching is a feminine text, since "of all the great world religions the teaching of Lao-tzu is by far the most female" (Mitchell, p. ix). However, the possible feminism of the Tao Te Ching is somewhat ironic; the position of the female or the "spirit of the valley" is praised because it is lower, hidden, and yielding. The text thus leaves intact the patriarchy and gender construction of its milieu. The Tao Te Ching is now a fixture of mainstream American culture, having been quoted by Ronald Reagan ("governing a state is like frying a small fish") and appearing on greeting cards and calendars, in films and science-fiction novels.

See also CHINESE-AMERICAN RELIGIONS; CONFUCIANISM; RELIGIOUS STUDIES; TAOISM.

BIBLIOGRAPHY

Browne, Brian Walker, trans. *The Tao Te Ching of Lao Tzu.* 1995.

Carus, Paul, trans. *The Canon of Reason and Virtue.* 1909.

Goddard, Dwight, trans. *Laotzu's Tao and Wu Wei.* 1919.

Kohn, Livia, and Michael LaFargue, eds., *Lao-tzu and the Tao-te-ching.* 1998.

Lau, D. C., trans. *Lao Tzu's Tao Te Ching.* 1963.

Mitchell, Stephen, trans. *Tao Te Ching.* 1988.

Parker, E. H., trans. *The Tao-teh King, or "Providential Grace" Classic.* 1904.

Pas, Julian. *A Select Bibliography on Taoism.* 1997.

Eric Reinders

Tarot

The French term *tarot* refers to a variety of playing cards commonly used for divination. The typical deck has seventy-eight cards—twenty-two symbolic trump cards and four suits—swords, cups, coins, and batons (or wands)—of fourteen cards each. Each suit has ten numbered cards and four court cards. While there are a few games that utilize tarot cards, as a whole they are primarily used for fortune-telling. A tarot card reader will lay selected cards from a deck in a pattern before a client, and from the position of a particular card, when overturned, will determine its meaning. As is true of many areas of occultism, the tarot has re-

Tarot cards and related accessories. (Credit: CORBIS/Nik Wheeler.)

ceived but scant attention from the scholarly community.

The tarot's origin is lost to history, though tarot decks appear to have emerged as a variety of playing cards and to have become established in the occult community in France and Italy in the eighteenth century. There is little evidence to support speculation concerning their Egyptian origin, first proposed by Protestant minister and occultist Antoine Count de Gébelin (1719–1784) in his 1781 book *Le monde primitif.* In a subsequent publication he called the deck the "Book of Thoth," a label that has continued.

An anonymous friend of de Gébelin's suggested the culture of the Gypsies as an alternative origin for the tarot, an idea championed in several books by J. F. Vaillant, a researcher who had lived among Gypsies and become knowledgeable about their occult practices. Gypsies had adopted the tarot, and Vaillant saw the mobile communities as perfect instruments for distributing the cards. Vaillant's ideas were championed by popular occult writer Gérald Encasse (known by his pen name "Papus") in his 1899 book *Le Tarot des bohemians: Le plus ancien livre du monde.* The possible Gypsy origin of the tarot was hotly debated in the twentieth century, with inconclusive results.

Adam McLean, a highly respected occult historian, has suggested a Hermetic (i.e., Gnostic) origin for the tarot based upon his examination of the Tarocchia of Mantegna, a card deck that appeared in the mid-fifteenth century in Italy. McLean, drawing on the work of art historian Kenneth Clark, has argued that this deck can be traced to the city of Ferrara during the period that Marsilio Ficino and other scholars began to make their translations of the Corpus Hermeticum.

Whatever the ultimate origin of the tarot, it is generally agreed that the modern understanding of it can be traced to 1853 and the publication of *Dogma de la haute magie* by magician Eliphas Levi, the most important voice in the nineteenth-century occult revival in France. Levi, working with an older Marseilles deck, tied the cards to the Kabbalah, the Hebrew mystical-magical system. The twenty-two trump cards were identified with the twenty-two letters of the Hebrew alphabet. The four suits were related to the four letters in the Hebrew name of God, the tetragrammaton, and the several court cards to the stages of human life. The ten numbered cards in each suit were identified with the ten sephiroth, images pictured on the kabbalistic Tree of Life, a diagram representing the various levels in the kabbalistic universe.

Levi's hope of producing a new tarot specifically designed for magical purposes was not fulfilled until the tarot became part of the more comprehensive system for practicing magic devised by the Hermetic Order of the Golden Dawn (OGD), a magical order formed in England in the 1880s. OGD leader S. L. MacGregor Mathers and his wife, Moïna, collaborated on the new tarot for initiates, though they produced only one oversized deck. That deck was then given to all members as they progressed through the OGD system. They mastered the tarot in the process of making their own private duplicates. This deck was not published until the 1970s, many decades after the dissolution of the order.

Two members of the OGD produced new tarot decks. Arthur Edward Waite teamed with artist Pamela Coleman-Smith to create a deck originally released in 1910. It has surpassed all others in popularity through the twentieth century. Shortly thereafter, Aleister Crowley, who had had an angry break with the OGD and had become the British leader of a rival organization, the Ordo Templi Orientis (OTO), worked with artist Freda Harris to create an OTO deck, which he called the Book of Thoth. A complete set of masters was completed, but the deck was not published until 1969, when the OTO was experiencing a revival after having almost died out. The Book of Thoth is the second most popular tarot deck.

The OGD, the Waite, and the Crowley decks were used for divination but had a more important function. The individual cards, especially the trump cards, were seen as containing archetypal images that the initiate could meditate on and utilize to assist in an occult awakening. During the 1970s, as the New Age movement was emerging, the tarot would take on a third use, as a New Age tool for transformation. The New Age focused on individual transformation as a step toward broad social change. That transformation could be assisted by a number of practices, including older divinatory practices such as astrology and tarot. The New Age suggested that tarot readings, rather than predicting the future, could provide important information that an individual could use to make decisions about life questions.

The New Age tended to locate religious authority in the individual and encouraged adherents to find the tools that seemed to resonate with their present state. The search for a broader range of tools from which to choose led to the creation of many new decks, employing different kinds of art, from the abstract to the representational, and utilizing a variety of themes (Wicca, surrealism, feminism, Jungian psychology, tantra). During the last quarter of the twentieth century, several hundred new decks appeared, accompanied by a plethora of books to explain the different decks and to facilitate their use.

See also ASTROLOGY; GNOSTICISM; KABBALAH; MAGIC; MYSTICISM; NEW AGE SPIRITUALITY; OCCULT, THE.

BIBLIOGRAPHY

Douglas, Alfred. *The Tarot: The Origins, Meaning and Use of the Cards.* 1974.

J. Gordon Melton

Televangelism

"Televangelism" refers to the specific style of religious broadcasting identified with conservative Protestantism and the Religious Right. Its roots are in the fundamentalist radio ministries of the 1930s through the 1950s, but televangelists took advantage of changing Federal Communications Commission (FCC) regulations, the increasing availability of cable television, and a changing cultural climate to build vast media empires, most significantly in the 1980s.

History

Evangelism, revivalist preaching, and simple Bible-based Christianity have long dominated the American religious landscape. While claiming to be "old-time religion," evangelical and fundamentalist Christianity, perhaps paradoxically, have often been on the cutting edge of technological development and the utilization of that technology to further their antimodernist ends. Such is the case with televangelism. Though televangelists are much criticized for their huckster, "Elmer Gantry"-type characteristics, their obsession with fund-raising appeals is a result of both pressure created by mainline religion in the early history of broadcasting and the techniques that enabled televangelism to grow at the pace at which it did.

Scholars trace the roots of televangelism to the revivalist preachers of the nineteenth century, especially Charles Finney, Dwight Moody, and Billy Sunday, who developed and perfected evangelical religious programming. By 1960 the fight for broadcast time had expanded to include television time as well as radio. It was in this year that the National Religious Broadcasters (NRB) convinced the FCC to change its policy regarding public service broadcasting; from this point forward, the FCC determined that programming considered "in the public interest" was in the public interest whether or not the network was paid for airing it. Mainline religious broadcasters found it hard to compete with the fundamentalists, who were, by this time, skilled at raising money for paid airtime. Furthermore, the income-generating fundamentalists had

Evangelist Jim Bakker and his wife Tammy interview a guest on their television program on April 28, 1986, in Fort Mills, South Carolina. (Credit: CORBIS/ Bettmann.)

funds to spend on the purchase and development of the latest technologies.

Major Ministries

From Baptist Jerry Falwell and Presbyterian D. James Kennedy to nondenominational African American Fred Price, important television ministries have included representatives of the entire spectrum of Protestant traditions that make up evangelicalism and fundamentalism. But the most colorful, controversial, and prevalent are (or have been) the pentecostal ministries of Jimmy Swaggart, Jim and Tammy Bakker, Oral Roberts, and Pat Robertson.

While the television ministries of Falwell, Kennedy, Price, Swaggart, and Roberts have kept fairly traditional formats—broadcasting the church services of their respective congregations with their own sermons as the central focus of the program—it has been the pentecostal ministries of Jim and Tammy Bakker (Praise The Lord [PTL] Club) and Pat Robertson (700 Club) that have emphasized revivalist methods designed to evoke specific responses by their audiences. Rhetorical styles, the use of music, and even the orchestration of the physical environment were all carefully examined, planned, and controlled to bring about the desired response: fear, repentance, conversion, and dedication to the ongoing support of the ministry so that others might experience the

same. When broadcast technology became available, the religious traditions grounded in revivalism had skills that readily lent themselves to the new media.

Early regulation of radio by the FCC required stations to provide free public service programming. The most popular forms were religious in nature, produced by mainline denominations, provided free to networks, and aired by the networks at no charge to the religious institutions. Finke and Stark (1992) argue that the Federal Council of Churches (through which the mainline churches had access to the media) worked to freeze out the fundamentalists by requiring radio networks that wished to use the council's programming to air only council programming during free time and not to sell airtime to other religious programming. Networks typically prohibited the solicitation of funds during free "public service" airtime. The exception to this "cartel" (as Finke and Stark call it) was the Mutual Broadcasting System, which sold commercial airtime to fundamentalist broadcasters who were willing to pay and who used part of their airtime to solicit funds to pay for it.

In 1944 the NRB was formed, in part to work toward securing access to broadcast media for innovation and responding to market demands. The Bakkers' and Robertson's ministries have used state-of-the-art technology, a strong emphasis on sophisticated production values, and a news or talk show format to develop unique niches in the religious broadcasting market. They have also diversified well beyond their interests in television evangelism. Robertson has founded the Christian Broadcasting Network (CBN) and a university (formerly CBN University, now Regent University). The Bakkers, at the height of their influence, built a Christian theme park: Heritage USA.

It was also the Pentecostal ministries—Swaggart, the Bakkers, and Roberts—that were racked with sex and financial scandals in the 1980s. The Bakkers were criticized for their lavish lifestyle, paid for by their viewers, and then it was made public that Jim had had an extramarital affair that had been covered up with hush money from PTL funds. Swaggart's ministry faced similar controversy when it was made public that he had been a frequent visitor to prostitutes. Roberts's financial scandal reached its peak when he announced that if supporters did not contribute a specified amount of money within a specified time to his ministry, "the Lord will take me home" (i.e., he would die). These scandals ultimately brought down the Bakkers' ministry, as Jim landed in jail, Jim and Tammy divorced, and Tammy remarried. Swaggart was defrocked by the Assemblies of God. He made a televised emotional plea to God, his followers, and his family for forgiveness and refused to give up his ministry—although it has not recovered from the debacle and subsequent accusations of continued wrongdoing. Likewise, Roberts's ministry continued, but it never fully recovered from the scandal. The scandals affected all of televangelism for a time during the 1980s, but the ministry that came through the storm intact was Pat Robertson's 700 Club and CBN.

Cable access has also made regional and local ministries an important force. With few exceptions, the major televangelist ministries have been Anglo-Protestant, but local and regional evangelists who use broadcast media are much more representative of the racial and ethnic diversity in evangelicalism and fundamentalism.

Televangelism and American Culture

The first of the televangelists to attract widespread attention from the national media, scholars, and the nonevangelical public was Jerry Falwell. In 1979 Falwell founded the Moral Majority. Having previously preached that religious leaders should not become involved in politics, Falwell did a quick turnabout in which he became the national spokesman for the early New Christian Right (NCR), and the name of his organization became synonymous with that movement. In the initial flurry of activity surrounding the NCR and the 1980 elections, the size of the Moral Majority was significantly overestimated. It did, however, carry significant weight through the early 1980s.

By mid-decade, however, it had developed insurmountable negatives in public opinion polls, and Falwell disbanded it.

Although Falwell replaced the Moral Majority with a new organization (Liberty Federation), it was Pat Robertson's Christian Coalition that grew rapidly and took the place of the Moral Majority as the flagship organization of the Christian Right. In part it was able to do so because of its role in Robertson's failed bid for the Republican nomination for president in 1988; the Christian Coalition was built as a grassroots movement, precinct by precinct. When Robertson's presidential bid failed, the organization remained in place and became involved in elections and legislative politics at every level, from local to national.

There has been much scholarly debate as to the actual size of the audience for televangelism as well as over the impact of such programming on religious viewers and on potential converts. There is scholarly consensus that the number of televangelism viewers is not as high as the religious broadcasters claim. According to Hoover (1988), reasonable audience figures range from ten million to twenty million, although there is still significant debate on this point, largely due to vastly different forms of audience measurement. There is also a scholarly consensus that the televangelists do little in terms of their goals of evangelization, as viewers tend to be already connected with the evangelical/fundamentalist subculture.

While the impact of televangelism outside the evangelical/fundamentalist subculture may be minimal, its impact within the subculture itself has been much more significant. As Wuthnow (1988) has argued, religious broadcasting has served to foster the development of intradenominational, parachurch ministries, which have, in turn, contributed to the decreasing influence and "restructuring" of American denominationalism. As a nationwide phenomenon, televangelism has also undermined the regional distinctiveness of the various forms of conservative American Protestantism and has been a force for national uniformity and identity.

Finally, televangelism has undermined scholarly theoretical assumptions about religion. Widespread popularity of religious broadcasting has been part of the critique of secularization theory, and the televangelist's emphasis on the use and development of cutting-edge technology has belied the argument that fundamentalism is essentially an antimodern phenomenon.

See also BELONGING, RELIGIOUS; CHRISTIAN COALITION; EVANGELICAL CHRISTIANITY; FALWELL, JERRY; FUNDAMENTALIST CHRISTIANITY; MAINLINE PROTESTANTISM; MORAL MAJORITY; PENTECOSTAL AND

CHARISMATIC CHRISTIANITY; RELIGIOUS RIGHT; ROBERTS, ORAL; ROBERTSON, PAT; SWAGGART, JIMMY.

BIBLIOGRAPHY

Finke, Roger, and Rodney Stark. *The Churching of America*. 1992.
Hadden, Jeff, and Anson Shupe. *Televangelism*. 1988.
Hoover, Stewart. *Mass Media Religion*. 1988.
Wuthnow, Robert. *The Restructuring of American Religion*. 1988.

Julie J. Ingersoll

Temperance

Although alcohol use and abuse had been a part of American society since the arrival of European colonists, it was not until the nineteenth century that campaigns against alcohol took on the character of a mass movement. With the foundation of the American Temperance Society in 1826, evangelical concern for the moral regeneration of individual alcohol abusers started to be transformed into a broader campaign to purify society of the corrupting influence of alcohol. In these campaigns, reformers moved back and forth between moral suasion (attempts to discourage alcohol use through argument and example) and more coercive measures (such as governmental regulation and prohibition).

Beyond their attempts to curtail the use of alcohol, reformers found themselves drawn into larger political and social issues. For instance, after the formation of the Women's Christian Temperance Union in 1874, many women took their crusade for the moral improvement of America to such issues as women's suffrage and the labor movement. Some conservative temperance advocates were uncomfortable with such broader reforms, and in 1896 the Anti-Saloon League was founded, with a narrower focus on governmental prohibition of alcohol and a closer alliance with the conservative evangelical churches. In 1919 these narrower efforts bore fruit: The Eighteenth Amendment to the Constitution was ratified, and national prohibition went into effect shortly afterward. But while most Americans saw the danger of alcohol abuse, governmental prohibition brought on many problems. Corruption and crime went hand in hand with a burgeoning black-market liquor industry, and in 1933 the Eighteenth Amendment was repealed, ending the Prohibition era.

Since 1933 America has not come close to national prohibition of alcohol. Instead, efforts have moved back toward moral suasion as the primary method of combating alcohol abuse. The evangelical character of such efforts can be seen in Alcoholics Anonymous (founded in 1935), which asserted the notion that certain individuals, called "alcoholics," needed to appeal to a higher power to help them. This organization, with its "Twelve-Step" program, was the prototype for a variety of contemporary self-help groups that encourage a kind of temperance in relation to food, sex, anger, work, and many other aspects of life.

If there has been a contemporary resurgence of a more coercive national temperance movement, it has bypassed alcohol and has taken shape as the "war on drugs." Much of the earlier rhetoric decrying the corrupting influence of alcohol has been applied in the more recent crusades against marijuana, cocaine, heroin, and a variety of other substances. Once again, larger social and political issues have been brought into these debates, including questions about the role of government in regulating the lives of private citizens; questions about the links among drug prohibition, crime, corruption, and a black-market economy; and accusations of racism in the enforcement of antidrug laws. Perhaps in an effort to avoid such problematic issues, antidrug efforts to enforce and maintain certain ideals of purity have been framed in the language of public health. However, while both proponents and critics have appealed to notions of justice and freedom, to the degree that these notions differ, controversy is likely to continue.

See also DRUGS; HEALTH; TWELVE-STEP PROGRAMS.

BIBLIOGRAPHY

Blocker, Jack S. *American Temperance Movements: Cycles of Reform*. 1989.
Blocker, Jack S. "Temperance Movements." In *Encyclopedia of Politics and Religion*, edited by Robert Wuthnow. 1998.
Clark, Norman H. *Deliver Us from Evil: An Interpretation of American Prohibition*. 1976.
Gusfield, Joseph R. *Symbolic Crusade: Status Politics and the American Temperance Movement*. 1963.
Wagner, David. *The New Temperance: The American Obsession with Sin and Vice*. 1997.

Kerry Mitchell

Temple

Our word *temple* comes from the Latin *templum,* meaning any space demarcated as sacred—even a part of the sky. A temple is the place for housing a divine image or idea; it is a place where the devotee has access to the divine through worship and ritual. Indian temples serve as an intersection of a central vertical

Byodo-In, a Buddhist temple in the Koolau Mountains on the Hawaiian Island of Oahu.   (Credit: CORBIS/ David Muench.)

axis to the Divine and a horizontal axis for contemplation and circumambulation of that transcendent center. A temple can be grand and palatial, constructed in marble and inlaid with gold and precious stones; it can be a hut, a simple enclosure for a tree or a pillar or a stone. Temples are found in cities and villages, caves and mountains, deserts and islands.

In America temples are not only the sacred buildings of Jews and Mormons; they are also the sacred structures of Hindus, Buddhists, Jains, and Sikhs. The first encounter with Asian traditions on this continent was the meeting of the World's Parliament of Religions in Chicago in 1893. Indian metaphysical and aesthetic ideals did not begin to infiltrate meaningfully, however, until 1965, when the Asian Exclusion Act of 1917 was repealed. With noticeable immigration over the last three decades of the twentieth century, the architectural pattern of America is becoming a beautiful mosaic, with Hindu and Jain mandirs, Buddhist monasteries, and Sikh gurdwaras. These physical structures embody the spiritual *Weltanschauung* of their respective traditions. Fusing traditional and modern styles, many temples are built anew; many

others are converted from former churches and schools.

The archetype for the Hindu temple is the human body, with the two sides of the temple representing the hands, and the top of the temple, the head. The architecture closely follows the ancient temple manuals. One of the earliest and grandest Hindu temples in North America is the Sri Venkateshwara Temple in Pittsburgh, established in 1976. Modeled on the seventh-century Tirupathi shrine in South India, it has a fifty-foot towered gateway. The temple is dedicated to Sri Venkatesvara, an incarnation of Vishnu, the preserver god. He is flanked on either side by the goddesses Padmavati and Āṇḍāl. To Hindus the single formless reality (Brahman) reveals itself in millions of incarnations, male and female. Hindus visit their temples to see (darshan) and worship (pūjā) their manifested deity. They perform the ritual of Āratī, in which a fivefold lamp and incense are lit and encircled around the deity—accompanied by chanting of hymns, ringing of bells, and beating of drums. Hindu worship is a mode of remembering the cosmogonic process, and Āratī represents the union of the elements of fire, water, sound, smell, and ether. While in India each temple has a sanctum sanctorum (*garbhagriya,* literally, "womb chamber") for a particular deity, the temples in the West tend to be more inclusive to accommodate the diverse Hindu communities. (For instance, the Sri Shiva Vishnu Temple in Maryland is dedicated to both Shiva and Vishnu.)

The general structure of the Jain temple is similar to the Hindu temple. The distinctive feature is the imagery of the Tīrthaṃkaras, "those who have made the crossing" from the life of birth and death to ultimate freedom. The temples venerate the twenty-four Tīrthaṃkaras and also display auspicious and symbolic diagrams, like the wheel of the Jain law. In India the magnificent Jain temples are far from urban centers—out in the country or at high tops of mountains such as Abu (one of the Seven Wonders of India), Taranga, Palitana, and Girnar—but in the West they are established in the heart of cities. Outside of India, Jain temples also unite the different sects by combining images of the "white-clad" Svetāmbaras and the "sky-clad" Digambaras.

Buddhist temples in America are an outgrowth of the international spread of Indian, Sri Lankan, Chinese, Korean, Japanese, Thai, Cambodian, Vietnamese and other schools of both Theravāda and Mahāyāna Buddhism. The patterns reveal the influence of their ethnic cultures, but the enlightened Buddha, sitting serenely in the lotus posture, is the paradigmatic image shared by all of them. While statues and paintings show him directly, the Buddha is also presented abstractly in mandalas and symbolically by the stupa. The Indian ideal of the temple as the center of the universe has given birth to some of the most magnificent architectural displays. With the main shrine at the center, the temple complex is oriented to the cardinal directions, and sumptuous gateways, bridges, and balustrades express the link between the sacred and the secular world.

A Sikh temple is called a gurdwara, literally, a door (*dwara*) to ultimate enlightenment (*guru*). There are no images or sculptures incarnating a deity in any way, and the Gurū Granth, the Sikh scripture, is set at the very center of the gurdwara. The metaphysical poetry

Sri Venkateswara Swami Temple at Calabasis, near Malibu, California, ca. 1988.   (Credit: CORBIS/Dave G. Houser.)

in sensuous imagery is the sole visual and aural icon for the Sikhs. Just as the recitation of the intangible verses launches the worshiper to intuit the Unintuitable One, the Indo-Persian domes, minarets, and the black and white marble squares on the floor lead the eye toward infinity. Most traditional gurdwaras are associated with the lives of the ten Sikh gurus (from Guru Nānak to Guru Gobind Singh; 1469–1708). They are usually white in color and have large square halls and courtyards that provide an immediate feeling of expansiveness. A gurdwara is identified by the saffron triangular flag that flies over it. The flag is emblazoned with the khālsā emblem—a double-edged sword set in a circle, surrounded by two semicircular swords. A gurdwara has four doors, indicating welcome to people of all four castes. Harimandir, the Golden Temple at Amritsar in India, is the most sacred, but the biggest Sikh shrine is in Yuba City, California. There are more than 115 gurdwaras in America, 35 in California alone (the first was built in Stockton in 1909).

Shoes are removed in all Indian temples. No meat or alcohol is partaken in any of the sacred premises. As a sign of humility, the congregations seat themselves on the floor. In Sikh gurdwaras men and women have their hair covered out of respect for their holy book. Along with worship and religious discourses, all Indian temples in the West serve as a hub for social and cultural events. Language classes are taught, youth activities are held, and camps for young children are organized. Marriages are performed in the respective temples, and their rites are closely followed: a Hindu couple takes seven steps around Agni, the sacred fire; a Sikh couple takes four circles around the Guru Granth, the sacred book. During important celebrations, elaborate processions issuing forth from and culminating in the various temples are becoming a familiar sight in American metropolitan centers. While Hindus carry images of the goddess through the streets of American cities during Durgā Pūjā, the Sikhs carry the Guru Granth during Baisakhi. Such festivities enable the followers to share in their heritage, keep the foundations of the community strong, and create a multicultural and vibrant America. All the religions of India open their temples to *others,* and by entering into *that* sacred space we experience *our own* essential humanity.

See also BUDDHISM; CHURCH OF JESUS CHRIST OF LATTER-DAY SAINTS; HINDUISM; MORMON TEMPLE; MOSQUE; SHRINE; SIKKHISM.

BIBLIOGRAPHY

Brown, Kerry, ed. *Sikh Art and Literature.* 1999.
Coomaraswamy, Ananda. *Elements of Buddhist Iconography.* 1979.
Kramrisch, Stella. *The Hindu Temple.* 1946.
Laidlaw, James. *Riches and Renunciation: Religion, Economy, and Society Among the Jains.* 1995.
Meister, Michael W., ed. *Encyclopaedia of Indian Temple Architecture.* 1983.
Sarkar, H. *Studies in Early Buddhist Architecture of India.* 1966.
Singh, Nikky-Guninder Kaur. "The Sikh Religion." In *Arts of the Sikh Kingdoms,* edited by Sue Stronge. 1999.
Singh, Patwant. *The Golden Temple.* 1989.
Tweed, Thomas, and Prothero, Stephen, eds. *Asian Religions in America: A Documentary History.* 1999.

Nikky-Guninder Kaur Singh

Temple of Set.

See Satanists.

Temptation

Temptation is a Christian theological term meaning "enticement to sin." In classical theology, a person may be tempted by the world, the flesh, or the Devil (also known as the "Tempter") to commit acts contrary to Christian morality.

Throughout American history, changing conceptions of sin and salvation have redefined specific temptations. One might be tempted to excessive wealth or power, spiritual ennui, sensual pleasure, doctrinal deviation, or a violation of ethical mores. In a general sense, these things always provide occasion to sin. However, the specifics vary depending upon the religious tradition and the particular era. Such variations have often been the source of religious tension in the United States.

In nineteenth-century America, for example, most Protestants believed alcohol use to be inherently sinful. A Christian could be tempted by "demon rum" to a life of drunkenness and debauchery. Alcohol was seen as the source of poverty and moral corruption leading to the destruction of the Christian family and, ultimately, the nation. Liquor possessed such a powerful inducement to sin that Protestants sought to limit its use through both voluntary and legislative means. Roman Catholics, however, did not share Protestant views on alcohol, believing instead that spirits could be celebratory and pleasurable. Most Catholics refused to participate in Protestant prohibition campaigns. Protestants understood this to prove the moral and political deficiencies of Roman Catholicism. "Rum" thus served as a point of conflict between the Protestant majority and the growing Catholic minority in both theology and politics.

Even within traditions, however, temptation is not static. In the early twentieth century, evangelical Protestants identified smoking, drinking, dancing, make-up, movies, and secular music as sinful. By the 1980s, this list had been substantially modified. Some things might or might not be sinful under certain circumstances. "G" and "PG" films were generally acceptable; "R" and "NC-17" films were generally not. Many evangelical colleges dropped dress rules and prohibitions against dancing on campus. Drinking and smoking became health concerns rather than sins. For one generation of evangelicals, these moral taboos were absolutes. For their grandchildren, temptation depended upon a person's intentions. Older evangelicals often depict this as a loss of fervor or decline of faith on the part of the younger generation. Younger evangelicals think previous generations narrow-minded or irrelevant. Such patterns of generational tension repeat in other traditions.

No matter how much variation, however, temptation usually connotes sexuality. In contemporary America, the world (power, money, prestige) and the devil (as a personal being) have lost some currency as sources of temptation. Thus Microsoft billionaire Bill Gates is a cultural hero for some, and even Christians question whether Satan exists. But the flesh, from pre-martial intercourse to Internet pornography, is still a powerful draw to sin. Both religious and secular scandals are energized by sexual temptation. In the 1980s, televangelists Jimmy Swaggart and Jim Bakker were brought down by sexual misadventures. In 1999, Harvard Divinity School Dean Frank Thielmann was demoted when Internet pornography was found on his computer. Even President Bill Clinton admitted to the American public that he had given in to temptation in his affair with a White House intern.

See also SEXUALITY; TELEVANGELISM; TEMPERANCE.

BIBLIOGRAPHY

Hunter, James Davidson. *Evangelicalism: The Coming Generation.* 1987.

Menninger, Karl. *Whatever Became of Sin?* 1973.

Niebuhr, Reinhold. *Moral Man and Immoral Society.* 1932.

Shur, Edwin M. *Our Criminal Society.* 1969.

"Temptation." In *HarperCollins Encyclopedia of Catholicism,* edited by Richard P. McBrien. 1995.

Diana Hochstedt Butler Bass

Teresa, Mother.

See Mother Teresa.

Testimony

Primarily associated with evangelical Protestant Christianity and African-American churches, in particular the "born-again" piety customary to the ritual life of each, a testimony is an individual's personal faith story that is told to others. Testimonies tend to address one of two topics: Either they explain how and why people converted to their current expression of faith, or they describe extraordinary occurrences in people's lives that strengthened or restored their faith commitment.

Within the social worlds of the Christian congregations for whom testifying is a normal communal practice, a person's testimony functions as her or his narrative home within the religious group. It publicly divulges the details of the religious experiences whereby people discovered the divine pattern that now organizes their life. Intrinsically motivational, a good testimony reinforces the religious commitment of the person telling the story while moving those who hear it toward analogous behavior. Autobiographical in form and presenting rich descriptions of events in the life of the narrator, testimonies are told to achieve these twin rhetorical objectives. Hence, to the extent that the details of a person's life enhance either of these rhetorical objectives, they are included. Those that do not are scrupulously pruned.

While the details of a testimony are immensely personal, the story itself is inherently public. To withhold a testimony is to deny the story's truth. Because of a testimony's essentially public nature, the expectations of the religious community to whom a testimony is conveyed strongly shape its contents. Yet a striking characteristic of testimonies is their consistent individuality. Testimonies are invariably presented as personal narratives. Structural factors that may have influenced their composition, such as audience expectations, are never mentioned.

A testimony typically occurs in three parts. In a testimony's opening phase, the person testifying describes a time when she or he was existing in a state of loss or confusion, and had limited knowledge or vision to address this condition. Thus the opening phase of a testimony is a tale of suffering and woe. In the second phase of a testimony, the testifier describes the salvation event that relieved the confusion or suffering portrayed in the opening phase. Providing a stark contrast to the mournful tone of the testimony's opening phase, the second phase of a testimony is joyous and gleeful. Among Pentecostals it can be accompanied by shouting, glossolalia, or other manifestations of intense religious excitement. In the third and final phase of a testimony, the significance of the conversion or salvation event for the person and the audience today is detailed. Typically, testimonies end with an appeal for the conversion of those hearing them.

See also AFRICAN-AMERICAN RELIGIONS; CONVERSION; EVANGELICAL CHRISTIANITY; GLOSSOLALIA; PENTECOSTAL AND CHARISMATIC CHRISTIANITY; RITUAL; SOCIOLOGY OF RELIGION.

BIBLIOGRAPHY

Ammerman, Nancy T. *Bible Believers: Fundamentalists in the Modern World.* 1987.

Brereton, Virginia L. *From Sin to Salvation: Stories of Women's Conversions, 1800 to the Present.* 1991.

Brenda E. Brasher

Theism

Theism refers to belief in the divine. It is a personal choice that forms part of the social fabric as "believers" come together to form religious groups based on such beliefs. The opposite of theism is atheism, the denial that there is anything beyond human reason.

Theism is closely related to polytheism, the belief in many divinities, as well as to pantheism, the belief that everything is divine, and also to panentheism, the idea that everything is *in* the divine. Theism is a characteristic that many diverse religious traditions share, whether they call their divinity or divinities God, Goddess, the Buddha, Allah, Supreme Being, or the like.

As a belief system, theism has played a central role in the development of U.S. culture during the twentieth century. As a country founded on the principle of freedom to worship as well as on the separation of church and state (or of religion and government), the United States is a unique laboratory allowing competing forms of theism to coexist, if not always peaceably. In study after study, an overwhelming majority of the population call themselves "believers," though virtually no study has sorted out what the American people believe.

At the beginning of the twentieth century the United States was largely a three-religion culture. Protestants were in the majority, Catholics a growing second, and Jews a distant third. Native Americans, Hindus, Buddhists, and other small groups were all but ignored. The "God" of that society resembled most closely the liberal Protestant deity—a strong father figure who put emphasis on hard work and whose very presence was seen as ensuring progress.

Two world wars dampened this view. The magnitude of evil embodied in the Holocaust, the sheer numbers of war dead, and the inability of those who believed in God to stop the slaughter left a chastened neo orthodoxy in its wake. What kind of God would have permitted such cosmic destruction? In reaction, revelation came back into vogue as the source of knowledge about the divine. The Swiss theologian Karl Barth described "the God of the Gospels" as the real thing.

However, other intellectual and social factors came into play as well. Karl Marx's economic and political teachings regarded religion as "the opiate of the people." Sigmund Freud's increasingly influential writing took all theistic propositions to be mere projections of the psyche, naive at best and neurotic at worst. Darwin's theory of evolution cast aspersions on biblical creation stories and left little scientific room for a creator God. But the urge to believe persisted for most Americans despite these moves toward postmodernity.

Political theology was one such response in the 1960s. Far from being a way to placate the poor, a figment of a fertile imagination, or a sop for biblicists, the divine in this framework is a full-fledged player in social justice efforts. Humans cooperate with the divine in building a just society. Political theology laid the groundwork for the many liberation theologies to follow.

Meanwhile, a small but influential movement held sway in the 1960s and early 1970s. Radical theology, better known as the "Death of God" movement, proclaimed the end of belief in a personal God, the brand of theism that had predominated since the founding of the republic. As described in a cover story in *Time* magazine, the personal God of Christian and Jewish theism was pronounced dead on arrival in a culture that was increasingly secular, increasingly pluralistic religiously, and increasingly skeptical that any divine force could be at play. Whether the word "God" had lost its usefulness, or whether all theistic affirmations were considered intellectually bankrupt, the impact of this short-lived movement was undeniable. One could be a socially acceptable atheist in the United States.

From the 1970s on, in the wake of the Vietnam War, the civil rights and women's movements, and in the face of the sexual revolution, most claims to theism in the form of a personal God who ruled the universe, a reference point for universal laws and a moral compass, prompted questions and doubts. As a result, perhaps as a kind of backlash, two competing constructive theistic tracks emerged: progressive or liberation theologies, and conservative or evangelical approaches.

The progressive or liberation schools were built on the political theology model. Beginning in Latin America, where economic and political oppression was rampant, and proceeding north, where the gap between rich and poor was growing, the idea that "Yahweh, who does what is right, is always on the side of the oppressed" (Psalm 103:6) gave rise to a range of related but unique theistic strands in Christianity.

In the Latin American line, the God of liberation theology is a source of justice and mercy, a friend to people who are poor. Black theology takes a similar approach. In its lexicon, God is black, at one with those who suffer racial injustice. Likewise, feminist theology developed a radical critique of the patriarchal nature of even the most progressive approaches. Feminists connected patriarchal language and imagery for the divine with male power in society. Words such as "Father," "Lord," "Ruler," and "King" were replaced by inclusive, nonhierarchical imagery such as "Source," "Companion," "Friend," and "Spirit." Female images were rediscovered and/or introduced: "Shekinah," "Sophia-Wisdom," "God the Mother." Goddess worship returned to favor among some theistic people.

By the 1990s, lesbian, gay, bisexual, and transgendered people were initiating their theological arguments. One result was the claim that God is "queer." Ecological, and especially ecofeminist, models of the divine put special emphasis on natural images of the divine, including wind, breath, and cosmic spirit.

Given this diversity, theists could and did choose from among a wide variety of options in the linkage between their faiths and their worldviews. What all of these articulations have in common is an explicit appeal to the divine as an expression of and support for a particular social concern. Such forms of theism assume that images of the divine and names used to describe the divine are human constructs that have real economic and political consequences.

The same assumption is true of the other movement that grew from the aftermath of the 1970s and is often in conflict with the progressive approach. The conservative or evangelical movement, sometimes referred to as the "religious right," has a particular theism at its heart. By contrast with the progressive movement, its God is the God of the Christian scriptures understood in very literal terms such as Lord and Father. This God—and in this view there is only one—is in charge of the universe. Biblical authority is absolute. Conformity to the will of God is the human goal.

Late-twentieth-century culture in the United States has been shaped in large measure by these competing views of the divine. Such issues as abortion and the death penalty, for instance, are debated and voted on largely on the basis of conflicting theistic assumptions. Progressives generally tend to favor reproductive choice and oppose the death penalty; this position is based on their view of a divinity who encourages human freedom and gives life to all. Conservatives generally tend to oppose abortion and favor capital punishment; this is based on their view of a God who judges wrong deeds and exacts retribution.

These are complicated and difficult social conflicts in a society in which the normative position is theistic, albeit in a range of interpretations of the word. The U.S. religious landscape comprises all manner of belief systems now, including Hindus, Muslims, and Buddhists, not to mention sects and cults of various stripes, all of which place their faith in something more than human reason can grasp, thus qualifying as theistic. Such variety broadens the definition and expands the percentages of those who affirm the divine.

By contrast, in many European countries, and in Australia and New Zealand, the percentage of theists is much smaller. One reason for this is that in the United States there are a wide variety of options for theism—including New Age and other unaffiliated groups—that are readily available and socially acceptable. To be a believer is sometimes taken to be more important than what one believes.

Theism is so prevalent in the United States that a certain generic Protestant brand of it was dubbed "civil religion." It is expressed by the phrase "In God we trust" found on money and in prayers as part of the presidential inaugural ceremonies. Strong legal challenges to the "right" of communities to display a crèche at Christmastime or the "right" of military services to prohibit the wearing of religious gear are slowly eroding some of the liberal Protestant assumptions of God the Father that were so pervasive at the beginning of the twentieth century.

Capitalism places supreme value on money and the accumulation of resources, leading some to say that in the United States "money is God." The new rapprochement between science and religion is perhaps the most challenging dimension of contemporary theism. Whether the "big bang" was caused, allowed, or ignored by the divine, it is sure to influence the way Americans think about God. Thus far, theism reigns. Surely not all of the definitions of the divine correspond to what the country's founders had in mind when they conceived of "one nation under God." But the liberty to be theistic or not, as one chooses, and the justice required to respect people's various choices remain cherished American values. In the twenty-first century, the United States will still be, it seems, a theistic if differently theistic country. While most people still believe in what they call God, it takes a great deal of imagination and religious tolerance to discern just what they mean by it and how to live fruitfully with the diversity.

See also AGNOSTICISM; ALLAH; ATHEISM; CIVIL RELI-
GION; DEATH OF GOD; DIVINITY; GOD; GODDESS; LIB-
ERATION THEOLOGY; PANTHEISM; THEODICY.

BIBLIOGRAPHY

Armstrong, Karen. *A History of God: The 4000-Year Quest of Judaism, Christianity and Islam.* 1993.

Eck, Dianna L. *On Common Ground: World Religions in America.* 1997.

McFague, Sallie. *Models of God: Theology for an Ecological, Nuclear Age.* 1987.

Mary E. Hunt

Theodicy

The philosopher Gottfried Leibniz (1646–1716) coined the term "theodicy" from the Greek *theos* (God) and *dike* (justice, right). Theodicy literally means "the justification of God." It is the justification of a deity's justice and goodness in light of evil and suffering. There are many different understandings of suffering: It is brought on by sinful human actions, it is redemptive, it is from oppressive systems, it is abusive. The reality of suffering and evil is juxtaposed against a view of God as omnipotent (all-powerful) and loving. This presents a problem that inevitably ends with the question "Why do bad things happen to good people?" Implicit in the question is another one: "If God is all-powerful and all-good, why does God permit suffering and evil to thrive in the world?" These questions form the framework for theodicy.

In Judaism, the Torah and various reflections and commentaries on it (Mishnah, Talmud, Gemorrah, Midrashim, and rabbinic writings) suggest two reasons for the origin of sin. One is that it is the rebellion of humanity, and the other is that it is the presence of evil. People are created with the impulse for doing good and doing evil. Judaism is reluctant to attribute evil to the work of God. When there appears to be no other option, the response is "God created the Evil Impulse, but He also created its antidote, the Torah" (Kiddushin 3ob). The orthodox explanation of suffering is that it is punishment for sin. However, this explanation is not without some problems. One can find a number of protests to God where suffering is thought to be unwarranted (e.g., the Book of Job in the Hebrew Bible). Nevertheless, the traditional response to suffering is prayer and penance, because the assumption is that suffering results from sin. The good person must live a righteous life that is expressed in one's words as well as in one's actions. The ultimate question in Judaism is not the fact of suffering, but its distribution:

Why do the wicked prosper so often, while those who try to keep faith with God suffer?

In Christianity, the question of theodicy involves reconciling three traditionally affirmed propositions: God, the Creator, is omnipotent; God is benevolent (all good); and evil exists. The traditional Christian response is to attempt to preserve full divine omnipotence and benevolence. In reality, the focus is on divine omnipotence. This focus features a concern with power, specifically God's power—be it limited or unlimited—viewed as domination (neo-orthodox) or as persuasive (process theology). Therefore some traditionalists reject omnipotence and state that God's power is limited by other beings. Others argue that divine omnipotence is self-limited in that God decides to restrict God's power to allow humans to have free will. Still others contend that human free will does not inhibit or limit God's omnipotence. There is also a third alternative view of power in these traditional understandings of theodicy: power as enabling, empowering, and compassionate. This view comes from various liberation theologies (e.g., feminist, black, womanist).

More radical responses barely seem to justify God. The radical response to the theodicy issue actually questions the goodness of God. These theodicies of protest refuse to argue for God's justification because to do so would dishonor the memories of those who endured radical suffering (e.g., the Middle Passage in slavery, the annihilation of Native Americans, the Holocaust, domestic or sexual violence). Less radical responses to the theodicy question protect God's goodness by claiming that it is compatible with God's allowing evil and suffering to exist because evil and suffering are punishments for sin or a trial necessary for growth. Others in the less radical camp argue that God suffers with us. Whatever responsibility God might have for human suffering, God's goodness is established by God's willingness to share in that suffering.

Also within the Christian tradition there are those who do not address the theodicy question from the perspective of God's omnipotence; instead, they focus on arguing against the existence of evil. Some argue that if we look from an ultimate perspective, evil contributes to a more extensive and harmonious whole. Others appeal to a heavenly reward as compensation for any necessary sufferings on earth, which that will be unremarkable in light of the coming glory.

In Islam, the question of theodicy manifests itself in the problem of the apparent absence of God's control and power when it comes to suffering. This problem is solved in the Qur'an (the sacred text of Islam) with its repeated calls to the faithful to take God's omnipotence seriously. Suffering occurs only within

God's creation; therefore, suffering is not out of God's control. This means that suffering may raise questions about the nature of God, but it cannot occur as a problem because God's omnipotence is firmly established. This, however, calls into question whether the underlying assumption is that the universe is not in God's control. Suffering could be a problem because its existence questions the basic assertion that God has power over everything. Because of the complexity of the preceding discussion, there is much thought in the Qur'an devoted to substantiating and exemplifying that God is omnipotent and that suffering must be a part of God's purpose.

Muslims must expect to be tested. Suffering helps create a faithful disposition and also helps to distinguish those who are sincere in their faith from those who are not. Suffering not only forms character for the Muslim, it also reveals one's true nature. Simply put, the faithful must endure suffering or choose suffering as a way to achieve martyrdom, which leads to riches in the next life. This means that the fundamental attitude of Islam to the reality of evil and the presence of an omnipotent God (Allah) is that one must submit to the right relationship with God. Suffering is viewed as punishment for sin and/or a trial or test. Hence suffering is part of God's justice, and it only appears that the wicked prosper, for in reality they ultimately suffer unending agony after death.

See also EVIL; FREE WILL; LIBERATION THEOLOGY; MIDRASH; QUR'AN; SUFFERING; TALMUD; TORAH; WOMANIST THEOLOGY.

BIBLIOGRAPHY

Bowker, John. *Problems of Suffering in Religions of the World.* 1970.

Gutiérrez, Gustavo. *On Job: God-Talk and the Suffering of the Innocent.* 1987.

Jonas, Hans. *Mortality and Morality: A Search for Good After Auschwitz.* 1996.

Kushner, Harold. *When Bad Things Happen to Good People.* 1983.

Soelle, Dorothee. *Suffering.* 1975.

Townes, Emilie M., ed. *A Troubling in My Soul: Womanist Perspectives on Evil and Suffering.* 1993.

Emilie M. Townes

Theosophical Society

The organization known as the Theosophical Society is generally equated with the largest and most widespread of a number of groups that teach and disseminate those theosophical teachings based on the writings of Helena Petrovna Blavatsky (1831–1891). The Theosophical Society has its headquarters in Adyar, Madras, India. Other theosophical organizations include the Theosophical Society (Pasadena, California), the United Lodge of Theosophy (founded in Los Angeles), and Point Loma Publications (San Diego). Organizations that arose out of the teachings of Blavatsky but emphasize teachings originating from sources other than her include the Temple of the People (Halcyon, California), and the Word Foundation (Dallas, Texas).

The original Theosophical Society was founded on November 17, 1875, in New York City by sixteen individuals, only three of whom have retained their credentials as theosophical leaders and teachers: Helena Blavatsky; Henry Steel Olcott (1832–1907), the first president of the Theosophical Society; and William Quan Judge (1851–1896).

The basic teachings of the Theosophical Society have varied somewhat from its original stated goals to what it professes today. Originally, the society was established, in the words of its bylaws, "to collect and diffuse a knowledge of the laws which govern the universe." There is also evidence that the laws were to be applied; in other words, the practice of "magic"—defined as spiritual wisdom—was an unstated goal. The society also taught that spiritual wisdom was passed down through the ages by the great teachers of antiquity, among whom were Jesus, Buddha, Pythagoras, and Krishna. Furthermore, the great religious traditions such as Christianity, Buddhism, the Greek mystery schools, and Hinduism still retained much of this ancient wisdom, although it is encrusted with degraded later beliefs and practices that have nothing to do with it. By the 1880s the ancient wisdom described by Blavatsky became more associated with Hindu and Buddhist teachings because of her perception that it was retained to a greater degree there than in other religions.

Among the teachings adopted from Hinduism and Buddhism, as they were perceived by Theosophists, is rebirth (or reincarnation), the teaching that the essence of the individual (the "ego") takes on a physical body many times. Its complement, karma—"the Law of Cause and Effect"—states that for every intended action there is an effect. Karma therefore fuels future rebirths. These teachings are closely bound to the notion of the evolution and progress of the individual—on physical, mental, and spiritual levels.

Most Theosophists explain theosophy through the objectives of the Theosophical Society and through the three propositions presented in the introduction to Blavatsky's magnum opus, *The Secret Doctrine.* The three objectives are as follows:

1. To form a nucleus of the universal brotherhood of humanity, without distinction of race, creed, sex, caste, or color
2. To encourage the study of comparative religion, philosophy, and science
3. To investigate unexplained laws of nature and the powers latent in man

A synopsis of the three propositions is as follows: (1) the existence of an infinite and unknowable Absolute; (2) the cyclic nature (i.e., manifestation and dissolution, life and death) of the universe and all it comprises; and (3) the identity of the soul with the Universal Soul (of the Absolute) and the need for all souls to progress through the cycle of reincarnation to realize this identity.

In conclusion, members of the Theosophical Society perceive themselves as students persuing the truth as reflected in the objectives and propositions. The main activity of the society is the publication of basic theosophical classics and various outreach programs.

See also BUDDHISM; HINDUISM; KARMA; MAGIC; NEW THOUGHT; REINCARNATION; SPIRITUALISM.

BIBLIOGRAPHY

Besant, Annie. *The Ancient Wisdom.* 1939; repr., 1897.
Blavatsky, Helena Petrovna. *The Key to Theosophy.* 1889; repr., 1973.
Blavatsky, Helena Petrovna. *The Secret Doctrine,* 2 vols. 1888; repr., 1974.
Deveney, John Patrick. *Astral Projection or Liberation of the Double and the Work of the Early Theosophical Society.* 1997.
Gomes, Michael. *The Dawning of the Theosophical Movement.* 1987.
Gomes, Michael. *Theosophy in the Nineteenth Century: An Annotated Bibliography.* 1994.
Judge, William Quan. *The Ocean of Theosophy.* 1893; repr., 1987.
Santucci, James A. "Theosophical Movement" and "Theosophical Society." In *The Encyclopedia of Cults, Sects, and New Religions,* edited by James R. Lewis. 1998.

James Santucci

Thurman, Howard

(1899–1981), clergyman, educator, philosopher, poet, theologian.

Howard Thurman was one of the most significant figures of twentieth-century American religious and cultural life. The author of numerous books of sermons,

Rev. Howard Thurman addressing attendees at a dinner. (Credit: Arnold DeMille/Fotos International/Archive Photos.)

meditations, and essays, he was born in the segregated town of Daytona, Florida, ordained in the Baptist Church, and educated at Morehouse College (B.A., 1923) and Rochester Theological Seminary (B.D., 1926). Thurman began his career as a youth movement leader in the 1920s as a regular on the YMCA speakers' circuit. He studied with Quaker mystic and philosopher Rufus Jones at Haverford College (spring 1929) and returned to teach philosophy and religion at Morehouse and at its sister school Spelman College (1929–1932).

As professor of Christian theology and dean of Rankin Chapel at Howard University (1932–1944), he began systematic experimentation of his belief in interracial and intercultural relations through religious experience. During this period Thurman also led a "Negro Delegation of Friendship" to South Asia; this was the first African-American group to meet Mohandas Gandhi. In 1944 Thurman left his position at Howard University to cofound the first racially integrated, interreligious, and intercultural church in the United States, the Church for the Fellowship of All Peoples, in San Francisco. From 1953 to 1965 he served as professor of spiritual resources and dean of Marsh Chapel at Boston University—the first African American to do so. He continued his ministry as director of the Howard Thurman Educational Trust from its founding in 1965 until his death. Thurman's vision of a "friendly world underneath friendly skies" continues his rich legacy.

See also CIVIL RIGHTS MOVEMENT; MINISTRY; RELIGIOUS STUDIES.

BIBLIOGRAPHY

Fluker, Walter E. *They Looked for a City: A Comparative Analysis of the Ideal of Community.* 1988.

Stewart, Carlyle Field. *God, Being, and Liberation: A Comparative Analysis of the Theologies and Ethics of James H. Cone and Howard Thurman.* 1989.

Thurman, Howard. *A Strange Freedom: The Best of Howard Thurman on Religious Experience and Public Life,* edited by Walter Earl Fluker and Catherine Tumber, 1999.

Thurman, Howard. *With Head and Heart: The Autobiography of Howard Thurman.* 1979.

Walter Earl Fluker

Tibetan Buddhism

To understand Tibetan Buddhism and its significance to the contemporary United States, we must first understand Buddhism, then Tibet, then the combination. What is Buddhism? It is usually considered a religion. But the operative definitions of religion today fit only a third of the phenomena that make up the many forms of Buddhism—those in the categories of beliefs, rituals, and pattern maintenance in general. Most of Buddhism is, rather, concerned with pattern transcendence, through education, ethical discipline, literature, art, science, and philosophy. The Buddha's enlightenment was not a religious discovery, not a mystical meeting with "God," nor a mission to spread divine "Truth." It was, rather, presented as one human being's exact and comprehensive experiential understanding of the nature and structure of reality, the attainment of the final goal of all philosophical exploration and scientific investigation. "Buddha" is a title, meaning "awakened," "enlightened," and "evolved." A buddha's mind is just what most theists have thought the mind of God should be like, fully knowing everything in an infinite universe, totally Aware— thus by definition inconceivable, incomprehensible to finite, ignorant, egocentric consciousness.

Though it seems preposterous to those acculturated as we are in the United States, we must acknowledge the Buddha's claim of omniscience. Though definitional for every form of Buddhism, it is rarely emphasized, since this claim is sacrilege for theists and an impossibility for materialists. However, to be a Buddhist, one must believe that a buddha has evolved from an ignorant human to a state of knowing everything, and is thus able to give all beings a realistic refuge from suffering. Thus the purpose of a Buddhist's life, seen as a part of an infinite evolution, is to awaken such omniscience within oneself, to transcend the egocentric human condition, and to become a buddha. When one awakens as a buddha, suffering ends and happiness is complete. The infinite number of beings who have already become buddhas are naturally moved to share their happiness with all other beings, which they do all the time.

But even buddhas cannot force ignorant beings to become wise, and thus free and happy. Since beings are liberated from suffering only by their own free understanding, buddhas are forced to become teachers. Thus, Buddhism was always more an educational movement than a religious mission. The Buddha emphatically disclaimed any power as a creator. He critiqued the plausibility of any being having total power over all beings and things. He did not reject the existence of gods—he was not an "atheist." He is reported to have met gods, angels, and even devils, finding them just as real as any other beings and just as caught in ultimate ignorance. He found that gods also need the teachings of enlightened buddhas. Among a buddha's most important names are "God beyond gods" (Devatideva) and "Teacher of Gods and Humans" (Devamanushyashasta). Buddhism developed in India from the Buddha's time in the sixth and fifth centuries B.C.E., in what can be described as three main phases: the monastic (Shravakayāna), the messianic (Mahāyāna), and the apocalyptic (Vajrayāna), each dominant for around five hundred years, with the earlier phases flourishing in parallel.

The monastic phase emphasized monasticism, as necessary for individual liberation. It was socially revolutionary, stressing ethical dualism and creating a new institution consisting of schools for human freedom, beyond the control of religious or secular authorities. The ideal of this phase was the enlightened monk or nun, the saint or arhat. The lay community was pushed to live according to a tenfold path of good and bad evolutionary action, not killing, stealing, or committing sexual misconduct; not lying, slandering, abusing, or speaking frivolously; and not harboring malice, greed, or unreasonable convictions. The critical education and warrior-like training of the monastics produced tamed persons, free of the wildness of egocentric drives. The social result of this phase was the pacification of a previously warlike society, and the spread of values supporting urbanization and the merchant classes. During this phase, Buddhism as a monastic educational movement spread outside of India, to Sri Lanka, Central Asia, Iran, and west Asia.

The messianic phase, dominant from 0 to 500 C.E., stemmed from core monasticism to reach out into lay society to transform the social ethic through the nondualistic ethic of love and compassion. It was socially evolutionary, as the monasteries developed into universities. The ideal of this phase was the bodhisattva, the hero or heroine who vows to free all beings from suffering and transform all universes into the buddhaverse, embarking on a process of conscious evolution through millions of future individual lives to complete buddhahood. This phase elaborated the doctrine of the three bodies of a buddha, the bodies of truth, beatitude, and beneficial emanation.

Metaphysically, the notion of nirvāṇa as a safe place beyond the world is critiqued, and the ultimate nonduality of nirvāṇa and saṃsāra undergirds the nonduality of wisdom and compassion, of the monastic and lay communities, and of the Buddhist and non-Buddhist societies. The social result of this phase was to move Indian society, by now more civilized, toward a universalistic orientation, freeing the popular imagination of the colorful cosmos of the infinite buddhaverse. This phase spread wherever the monastic phase had spread, also moving beyond into China and further west in Asia.

The apocalyptic phase, dominant ca. 500–1000 C.E., was socially culminatory, with the monastic universities reaching out beyond the literate state into culturally marginal areas. It elaborated the furthest implications of the messianic phase by aiming at immediate transformation of the universe to buddhaverse. Its ideal figure is the female or male great adept (mahasiddha), an already actual perfect buddha maintaining an ordinary human form in history, exemplifying the kingship of each individual, contemplatively, ritually, and artistically. Messianic nondualism is here extended to everything, including sexuality and death; buddhahood is reconceived as bliss-void-indivisible orgasmic reality. There is an apocalyptic insistence on accelerating history and evolution, a realization of individual buddhahood and universal buddhaverse here and now, in this lifetime preferably, through magical, high-tech means. The social result was the elevation of women, the expansion of culture to marginal low castes, tribal members, and foreigners, and the permeation of high culture with aesthetic values. This phase spread everywhere that the previous phases had spread, reaching further to Indonesia, Korea, Japan, and Tibet. It was preserved in its original integration with the two previous phases only in the Shingon school in Japan and in Tibet.

Until recently, Tibet was a huge country of over one million square miles, unmistakably recognizable on a relief map of Asia as the highest plateau in the world, with an average altitude of 14,000 feet. It was as large as all of Europe. Its diverse regions were unified by intertribal wars from 500 B.C.E. to 500 C.E., with a royal dynasty emerging in the Yarlung valley near the Tsangpo River. This dynasty conquered an empire beyond the huge plateau that lasted from around 600 to 850 C.E. Its emperors began to import Buddhism as a cultural treasure from their Indian, Nepalese,

Central Asian, and Chinese neighbors, whom they often conquered and pillaged. Inspired by the great adept from India, Padma Sambhava, these emperors created a written language, commissioned huge numbers of translations, built temples and monasteries, ordained monks, and spread the Buddhist ethic, in spite of the fact that their conquest empire depended on violence and martial discipline rather than Buddhist gentleness and spiritual discipline. Around 850 C.E., internal dissension shattered the dynasty, and Buddhism was suppressed as the state cult, though it gradually took hold as a grassroots movement.

By 1042, the Bengali master Atisha came to a regionalized Tibet gripped by a popular fervor for the Buddhist lifestyle and began to teach the full panoply of concepts developed in India during the three phases sketched above. From his time through the seventeenth century, a medieval Tibet became more and more monasticized and less and less militaristic, experiencing a brief period of state unification as part of the Mongol empire during the late thirteenth and early fourteenth century.

Around 1400, a spiritual renaissance was ushered in by the lifework of the gifted lama Jey Tsong Khapa, who shared with Padma Sambhava and Atisha a special recognition by Tibetans. He attained full enlightenment in 1398, after an arduous six-year retreat. For the last twenty-one years of his life, his popular impact increased exponentially and set the tone for the next five hundred years. It was based on a new level of national dedication to Buddhism, making it the main aim of Tibetan life. Tsong Khapa founded the Great Prayer Festival in Lhasa in 1409, bringing the whole nation together for two weeks of prayer every lunar new year to celebrate an apocalyptic fortnight of miracles in Shakyamuni Buddha's biography. This became a core event for all of Tibet from 1409 until 1960, with the Chinese occupation of Tibet.

The centuries following the era of Tsong Khapa saw the rippling outward of this spiritual synthesis in a gradual process of transformation of the social, political, and physical landscape of Tibet. Monasteries were built on an unprecedented scale, with the Lhasa area alone constructing three major monasteries that came to house over twenty thousand monks (Lhasa's own lay population was no more than thirty-five thousand). The social climate became more peaceful, as fewer individuals were available for the armies of the aristocratic warlords.

One of Tsong Khapa's disciples, Gendun Drubpa (1391–1474), attained great awakenings and performed great deeds, founding the huge Tashi Lhunpo Monastic University in southern Tibet and teaching hosts of disciples. After his death, he turned up reincarnated as the son of a yogin couple. Eventually reunited with his disciples at Tashi Lhunpo, he was named Gendun Gyatso (1475–1542). He spent long years in retreat, gave great teachings, built important monasteries, and made daring inner voyages as an adept. His next reincarnation was Sonam Gyatso (1543–1588), who continued the universal spiritual education program, the building of monasteries, the taming of individuals, and his inner voyages as an adept. Invited to the court of the Mongol king Altan Khan, he tamed this formidable warlord and taught him that it was better not to sacrifice war captives to the ancestors and war gods, but rather to take refuge in the Three Jewels of Buddha, Dharma, and Sangha, and to practice renunciation, compassion, and wisdom, even becoming a buddha. Altan Khan was so impressed by his encounter with a person he obviously perceived to be a superior being that he gave him the name "Dalai Lama," "dalai" being the Mongol word for "ocean." Counting his two retrospectively renamed predecessors, Sonam Gyatso became known as His Holiness the Third Dalai Lama.

By the end of the sixteenth century, the secular rulers of Tibet felt overwhelmed by the popular dedication to enlightenment education, monastic vocations, and monastery building. As in both shogunate Japan and Protestant Europe, a period of violent persecution of monasteries ensued, with the fate of the country in the balance. The secular forces of the militaristic, aristocratic warlords tried to eclipse the rise of the monastery-centered, spiritual lifestyle, but the monastic leaders resisted. The Dalai Lama, by now the beloved spiritual leader of a huge population, called for help from the Mongolian ruler Gushri Khan, who had become his disciple. The Khan swept into Tibet and crushed the coalition of Tibetan warlords, disarmed them, and brokered a peace that elevated the main monastic leader to head the nation.

In 1642, almost exactly a thousand years after the first Buddhist temple was built in Lhasa, His Holiness the Fifth Dalai Lama (1617–1682) was crowned king of Tibet. He founded the Ganden Palace Victory Government, which Tibetans still consider their legitimate government, a unique form of government eminently suited to Tibet's Buddhist society. It was almost completely demilitarized, acknowledging the centrality of the monastic institutions in the national life and the priority given to nonviolence. He built the Potala Palace on the Red Mountain at Lhasa. His palace was three buildings in one: a monastery for the abbot, a fortress for the king, and a buddha realm or mandala for the adept.

The nobility was virtually expropriated, retaining the use of and income from parts of its hereditary estates only as salary for service to the Ganden government. Nobles were deprived of their private ar-

mies, losing their feudal power of life and death over their peasants. With thanks to the Mongolian supporter, the Great Fifth asked him and his army to go back to Mongolia, and Tibet became the first modern nation to be unilaterally disarmed. As the Protestant princes of northern Europe and the shoguns of Japan had seen, a nation could not afford a universal military and a universal monastery at the same time; this caused them to terminate their monasteries. In Tibet alone at this time, the monastery terminated the military instead and created a bureaucratic government to maintain a principled peace. International security was maintained by diplomacy and moral force, not by military prowess. During the 317 years of the Dalai Lamas' rule over Tibet, a remarkable society developed, the earliest postmodern society in the world. Completely demilitarized, it was utterly "educationalized," in that the monastic vocation thrived at the highest rate ever achieved in any society. It was not Shangri-la; Tibetans believe that Shambhala (their own mythic paradise on earth) exists in the northern polar region. They were highly aware of the all-too-human faults of their "Land of Snows." But they still felt specially blessed by the presidency of Lokeshvara, their archangelic messiah figure incarnate in the Dalai Lamas. It was the land of his sacred mantra, OM MANI PADME HUM, "Come! Jewel and Lotus Holder! Be with me!" It was a land of maximum opportunity for the individual intent on enlightenment. There was maximum low-cost, lifelong educational opportunity. There were minimum taxes, almost no military service, no mortgages, and no factories for material products. There was no lack of teachers.

Tibetan Buddhist practice can be summarized briefly as consisting of: (1) living in a multilife continuum of evolutionary lives, under the refuge of the Buddha, the dharma reality and teaching, and the community of enlightenment-oriented people; (2) finding that refuge represented by living, enlightened, incarnate teachers (lamas) who could administer the teachings to individuals in an optimal manner; (3) recognizing within the special preciousness of the human life-form and so making the most of this life opportunity; (4) acknowledging impermanence and the immediacy of death, making each moment precious; (5) accepting the evolutionary impact of every thought, word, or deed, hence taking responsibility for one's own fate; (6) recognizing the universality of suffering attendant upon the unenlightened, egocentric mind-set, hence resolving to develop wisdom free of delusion; (7) recognizing the common condition of all beings as suffering and interrelated, and hence developing love and compassion as the key to all evolutionary progress and ultimate happiness; (8) aspiring to attain perfect understanding of the nature of reality as the only way to find freedom from suffering; (9) cultivating a positive imagination and vision of the universe and the empirical self as the method of achieving relative happiness; and (10) rehearsing and perfecting control over the processes of death, between-state (the after-death, dreamlike transformation experience) travel, and the evolutionary life with a view to ensuring complete enlightenment for the sake of oneself and others. Though there is an infinite variety of theories and practices suited to a great variety of individuals, these ten developmental processes are common to all forms of Tibetan Buddhism.

Everything about post–seventeenth century Tibetan life was rationalized to facilitate the production of enlightenment; their unique psychological and social form of life is a kind of inner modernity. Most recently, this mentality has adapted quite well to the rest of the world's industrial modernity, in the United States and throughout the world, except when the encounter was violently forced, as it decidedly was when the Chinese Communists attempted to impose Marxist materialism, communistic egalitarianism, and an industrial focus on Tibetans, via an all-out assault on Tibetan Buddhism. They destroyed monastic institutions, monks and nuns, scriptures, outdoor monuments, mani stones, prayer flags, personal rosaries and prayer wheels, icons, paintings, photographs of the Dalai Lama, even knowledge of the Tibetan language. They instituted intensive communist thought reform and struggle sessions for decades. They killed members of the upper classes, forced redistribution of all forms of wealth, and imposed Chinese-language education and Maoist indoctrination. They enlisted all able-bodied persons in labor brigades, work gangs, and other production units.

These brutal measures caused the death of approximately 1.2 million people, destroyed all the architectural and artistic treasures of the Tibetan nation, and eradicated the intelligentsia entirely, except for a few people who survived the prison camps or who escaped into exile in the United States and elsewhere. Nonetheless, the attempts to eradicate Tibetan culture were a dismal failure. The minute the Chinese administration was distracted by the post-Mao disturbances in the early 1980s, the Tibetans rose up and began to rebuild their monasteries, to become monks and nuns, and to restore their previous social order based on occupation and talent. They traveled to India for pilgrimage and to receive initiations and teachings from the Dalai Lama and other teachers. The Chinese were astounded that such "primitive" thinking could have survived their thirty-year onslaught; but they uneasily acquiesced in the Tibetan choices, hoping to make Tibet, with its colorful monasteries, quaint monks, and ceremonies, an attractive tourist destina-tion. But by the late 1980s, monks and especially nuns began to make peaceful protests against the Chinese occupation, and the government again suppressed the monasteries with a heavy hand.

In exile in India, Nepal, and Bhutan, as well as in North America, Europe, and Australia, the Dalai Lama and about 150,000 Tibetan refugees have succeeded in keeping their unique civilization alive. They have their own school system, so young Tibetans can learn the Tibetan language, history, and some basic religious teachings. They have maintained a high rate of monasticism, with over 25,000 monks and nuns, making up about one sixth of the Tibetan population in exile. The curricula of the monasteries and nunneries continue to emphasize spiritual studies and practices, though a modicum of modern, secular learning is added to orient the religious in the contemporary world. Tibetan spiritual teachers have attracted large followings in Europe, the Americas, Australia, Japan, Taiwan, and Southeast Asia, and some have written best-sellers. The Dalai Lama has received the Nobel Peace Prize, and has met and is respected by most of the world's religious and secular leaders. The Communist Chinese regime still refuses to recognize him or his people's right of self-determination, and still succeeds in making other governments ignore the reality of Tibet as the price of trade relations.

Tibetans in the United States and elsewhere are a success story as refugee communities go, with little history of violence, crime, or persisting poverty, and they easily take to the professions of the modern economy. The last chapter of the amazing social experiment of Tibetan Buddhist civilization cannot yet be written, as it involves the coming experience of the political freedom Tibet will inevitably gain, as the restructuring of the big-power, twentieth-century colonialism that Russia only recently relinquished becomes global. Then we will see if a society touched by living buddhas, with a different popular sense of the purpose and value of human life, with a determined spiritual orientation, will adopt some elements of materialistic modernity. Which elements will it adopt, and which will it reject? Will Tibetans use computers to aid them in their quest for evolutionary perfection in Buddhahood? Will they militarize, never again to taste the bitterness of conquest and occupation by an outside power? Will they exploit and ruin their own environment? Will they industrialize in an external manner? The world will get a chance to see if a culture oriented to the possibility of becoming a perfect buddha can persist in a materially modern setting.

See also BUDDHA; BUDDHISM; DALAI LAMA; DHARMA; ENLIGHTENMENT.

BIBLIOGRAPHY

Dalai Lama, H. H. *Freedom in Exile.* 1988.
Dalai Lama, H. H. *World of Tibetan Buddhism.*
Lopez, D., ed. *Religions of Tibet in Practice.* 1997.
Rhie, M. H., and R. A. F. Thurman. *Wisdom and Compassion: The Sacred Art of Tibet.* 1991.
Thurman, R. A. F. *Essential Tibetan Buddhism.* 1996.
Thurman, R. A. F. *The Tibetan Book of the Dead.* 1994.

Robert A. F. Thurman

Tillich, Paul

(1883–1965), theologian, philosopher.

Regarded as one of the most influential modern Christian thinkers of the twentieth century, Paul Tillich was born in Germany but emigrated to the United States. Tillich, the son of a Lutheran pastor, received his Ph.D. from Breslau in 1910 and his licen-

Paul Tillich in his office at Harvard University.
(Credit: © Archive Photos.)

tiate in theology from Halle in 1912. His experiences as a chaplain with the German forces in World War I transformed his youthful nationalistic fervor and religious beliefs and set him on the road to his mature reflections on the human condition. In 1933 Tillich was dismissed from his prominent Frankfurt professorship for opposing Nazism, and for the next 22 years he taught theology at Union Theological Seminary in New York. Upon his retirement from Union, he accepted prestigious positions at Harvard (1955–1962) and Chicago (1962–1965).

Tillich emphasized that it is the "duty" of every theology to address the challenges of contemporary culture through an explication of the meaning, relevance, and truth of Christian beliefs and practices. Tillich described this process as a "method of correlation" between the fundamental "existential questions" arising from human existence and the "answers" to those questions found in the Christian message. Traditional Christian symbols are critically reinterpreted in light of prevailing modes of thought, and contemporary experience is in turn explicated in light of religious tradition. Tillich's correlational method informed all of his writings—his sermons collected in influential volumes, such as *The Shaking of the Foundations* (1948); popular classroom texts, such as *The Courage to Be* (1952) and *Dynamics of Faith* (1955); and his philosophically and theologically rigorous magnum opus, the three-volume *Systematic Theology* (1951, 1957, 1963). Deftly drawing from existentialist philosophy and psychoanalysis (among other modes of critical inquiry), Tillich argued that the questions arising from the anxiety and estrangement of the finite human condition are fundamentally religious; hence, they are properly addressed in terms of the religious experience whereby one is grasped by "being-itself" or the "power of being," which transcends "finitude." This power of being, as expressed through religious symbols such as "God as Creator" or "Jesus as the Christ," is both the source of our "courage" to resist the despair of finite existence and the integrating ground of our experience as artisans of culture. The religious dimension is, in other words, the underlying substance of culture, and cultural symbols are the form through which the religious dimension of our experience comes to expression.

Tillich has had an extraordinary impact on American intellectual and religious life since the 1950s. He wrote from a perspective that straddled the conventional boundaries between German and American cultural sensibilities, philosophy and theology, the modern scientific consciousness and traditional Christian faith, and the trust in the possibilities of reason that embued modern intellectual and political life before the world wars and the self-doubt of the postwar period. Tillich's creative insight on life between cultural worlds struck a chord with many liberal Christians and young Americans searching for religious and cultural renewal. Despite strenuous scholarly challenges, for example, to Tillich's theory of religion and view of God, his vision of the task of theology remains an influential classic model for many theologians.

See also GOD; RELIGIOUS STUDIES.

BIBLIOGRAPHY

Adams, James L., Wilhelm Pauck, and Roger L. Shinn, eds. *The Thought of Paul Tillich.* 1985.

Clayton, John P. *The Concept of Correlation.* 1980.

Kelsey, David H. *The Fabric of Paul Tillich's Theology.* 1967.

Pauck, Wilhelm, and Marion Pauck. *Paul Tillich: His Life and Thought.* Vol. 1. 1976.

Tillich, Paul. *Main Works/Hauptwerke.* Vols. 1–6. Edited by Carl Heinz Ratschow. 1987.

Stone, Ronald P. *Paul Tillich's Radical Social Thought.* 1980.

David G. Kamitsuka

Torah

"Torah," from the Hebrew root *YRH* ("teach"), has had a variety of meanings in the history of Judaism. In biblical contexts, "torah" meant simply "the teaching/law of so-and-so" (e.g., see Joshua 24:26) or "the law of such-and-such" (as at Leviticus 14:2). Later Torah came to refer in particular to the Torah of Moses (Genesis through Deuteronomy). But "Torah" had far broader meanings for certain Jewish groups, and for the rabbis, the term came to refer to any teaching accepted within the canonical rabbinic tradition. In fact, the rabbis claimed that two Torahs were revealed at Sinai—one written (the entire Hebrew Bible) and one "oral" (rabbinic teachings). When the rabbis spoke of the obligation to study Torah, they meant study of either.

In our age, "Torah" is used primarily to refer to the Five Books of Moses (the Pentateuch). Because this Torah is the first part of the Bible, Christian or Jewish, it is read and taught as scripture throughout the United States and beyond. However, in Christian tradition the Torah is part of the "Old Testament," yielding privilege of place to the New Testament. Furthermore, Paul's insistence on reading the commandments of the Torah allegorically, preferring their spiritual to their literal meanings, meant that, in Christianity, the extensive legal portions of the Torah are distinctly less significant. Hence, in Christianity the Torah has a secondary status. By contrast, in Judaism it is primary, and for many contemporary Jews, the Torah is the only part of the Hebrew Bible they have ever read.

In the late twentieth century, study of Torah among Jewish adults is an increasingly common phenome-

A Jewish scribe repairs the writings on a Torah scroll on Manhattan's Lower East Side, ca. 1989. (Credit: CORBIS/Richard T. Nowitz.)

non—an expression of renewed concern for Jewish continuity. For many Jews, though, the Torah scroll remains more a symbol than a source of instruction—an emblem of Jewish history, identity, and contributions to world culture.

See also BIBLE; JUDAISM; JUDEO-CHRISTIAN TRADITION.

BIBLIOGRAPHY

Holtz, Barry, ed. *Back to the Sources.* 1984.

Neusner, Jacob. *Torah: From Scroll to Symbol in Formative Judaism.* 1985.

David Kraemer

Toronto Blessing

The Toronto Blessing, also known as "the Father's Blessing" or "the renewal," began in the storefront facility of the Toronto Airport Vineyard Fellowship in January 1994, when participants in revival services manifested intense physical responses to prayer—crying, twitching, shaking, uncontrollable laughter, and falling to the floor in a trancelike state that lasted for hours. Word spread quickly through the Vineyard Fellowship, and the meeting place soon teemed with visitors. By mid-1994, people flocked in from across North America and Britain. Soon the crowds became more diverse as Australians, Europeans, Malaysians, Africans, and others found their way to the congregation's new, commodious quarters in a converted warehouse close to the Toronto airport. The revival's characteristic physical manifestations, folksy music, and dance spread beyond the Vineyard into congregations of many denominations whose pastors hoped for increased fervor in their ministries, especially in Great Britain, Australia, and New Zealand. Dancing, shouting, running, falling, and other raucous behavior led Vineyard Fellowship founder John Wimber in 1995 to expel the Toronto Vineyard Fellowship and its pastor, John Arnott. Some thirty Vineyard congregations withdrew from the Vineyard Fellowship in an expression of solidarity with Arnott and the revival. The Toronto congregation changed its name to Toronto Airport Christian Fellowship. After five years, revival services continued six nights each week, and Arnott has estimated that 2.5 million people have attended.

Criticism of the Toronto Blessing has come from both religious and secular media. Theologian critics challenge the emphasis on "manifestations," which they charge move beyond Scripture. Instances of barking, or a video of a devotee being led about on a dog leash, have been publicized to validate claims of fanaticism. The idea of going to a particular place to experience a particular phenomenon seems to some critics to be out of Protestant character. Claims by John Arnott of hundreds of people having their dental fillings turned to gold, of gold dust descending on worshipers, or of oil appearing on hands (gold and oil have been explained as symbols of God's spirit and glory) echo those of the more radical of the barnstorming healing revivalists of the 1950s.

While the Toronto Blessing has thrived outside the organized Canadian and British Pentecostal movements, its expressive character has deeply influenced numerous Pentecostal congregations, as well as many others in Canada and elsewhere. Pentecostalism never prospered in Canada. Through the Toronto Blessing, however, Pentecostal forms of spirituality have been widely publicized. International crowds drawn by the renewal movement have kept the services in the public eye. While the Toronto Blessing has directly influenced the practices of hundreds of international congregations, it has also affected the course of several other North American renewal movements that have spawned their own networks. Especially prominent are those associated with Rodney Howard-Brown and the "laughing revival" and with the Pensacola Outpouring, a long-running event at the Brownsville Assemblies of God in Pensacola, Florida.

The Toronto Blessing is one indicator of a turn that charismatic Christianity has taken. It leads away from traditional church forms that emphasize Christian education and nurture as concomitants of worship; its energies are devoted, rather, to indefinitely prolonged, emotionally exhausting, intense experiences, in which participants abandon themselves to what they regard as the presence of God. Thus, the Toronto Airport Christian Fellowship is not a typical church. Its approach to Christianity blends easily with the ubiquitous interest in spirituality in a postmodern culture.

See also BROWNSVILLE REVIVAL; NEW AGE SPIRITUALITY; PENTECOSTAL AND CHARISMATIC CHRISTIANITY; TRANCE; VINEYARD CHRISTIAN FELLOWSHIP.

BIBLIOGRAPHY

Arnott, John. *The Father's Blessing.* 1996.

Kuglin, Robert J. *The Toronto Blessing: What Would the Holy Spirit Say?* 1998.

Poloma, Margaret. "The Spirit and the Bride: The 'Toronto Blessing' and Church Structure." *Evangelical Studies Bulletin* 13, no. 4 (winter 1999): 1, 2, 5.

Poloma, Margaret. "Toronto Pastor Says God Is Filling Teeth with Gold." *Charisma* 14, no. 11 (June 1999): 39–40.

Edith L. Blumhofer

Totem

The word "totem" and other terms such as "taboo," "fetish," and "mana" were first noted by European travelers among tribal peoples in the seventeenth, eighteenth, and nineteenth centuries and were subsequently used to describe general religious phenomena. "Totem" is a North American Ojibwa term that was first reported as "totam" in 1791. Its first description is that of a tutelary (guardian) deity who watches over a hunter throughout his life, takes the form of an animal, and may never be hunted, killed, or eaten by the individual. By the early decades of the nineteenth century, some commentators noted that individuals or groups among tribal peoples stood in specific relationship to animals, birds, and plants, but little attention was given to placing this phenomenon into a general theory of the evolution of religion. Parallels were first drawn between the native peoples of North America and Australian tribal groups, where similar identifications were observed.

The earliest to regard "totem" as a universal stage in the development or evolution of religion was James Ferguson M'Lennan (1827–1881), whose first work was on the history of marriage. In trying to explain endogamous and exogamous marriage patterns, he noted relationships between marriage groups having similar or dissimilar totems, and from this he reasoned that religious traditions pass through a totem stage. He theorized that animal, plant, and bird gods precede anthropomorphic deities in time and in civilizational development. More sophisticated evolutionary theories advanced by William Robertson Smith (1846–1894), Andrew Lang (1844–1912), E. B. Tylor (1832–1917), James Frazer (1854–1941), and Wilhelm Schmidt (1868–1954) all employed "totemism" to describe a stage in the evolution of religion.

For example, Robertson Smith enlarged the ethnographic data on totemic deities through his fieldwork in Egypt and the Middle East and argued that "totemism" explained even biblical injunctions concerning foods and the origins of the Israelite deity. Frazer argued that "totemism" is an essential element in magical practices that precede other advanced forms of religion. Lang and Schmidt linked totemism to the presence of supreme deities and sky gods, but in diametrically opposite ways. Lang saw the totemic deity as one of the forms of the supreme deity. Schmidt argued that "totemism" is one of the degenerated forms of his primal monotheism.

Totemic deities and "totemism" played a central role in Émile Durkheim's *The Elementary Forms of Religious Life* (1912). He rejected the evolutionary thinking of both his contemporaries and earlier theorists. Drawing on Australian aboriginal traditions, Durkheim argued that "totemism" was one of the elementary forms that express the central idea of collective representation and that religion is eminently social. The term "elementary" as used by Durkheim does not refer to an early stage in the development of civilization and individual or collective consciousness, but rather means that which is the simplest, most exemplary instance of a form. The totemic relationship between tribal or clan groups demonstrated how a deity represents the social group and thus produces social cohesion and unity. "Totemism" also plays a central role in Sigmund Freud's extended cultural and historical studies, in which he attempted to move from individual psychopathology to collective or social psychopathology. In *Totem and Taboo* (1915) he drew parallels between the mental life of children and the religious life of "primitive" peoples. Totemic relations are an expression of guilt intended, he argues, to assuage the feelings of a violated father by a complete obedience to the father's command.

Other theorists, like Durkheim, rejected the evolutionary argument and instead sought to define the nature of totemic deities and their relationship to tribes and clans. For example, Arnold van Gennep defined "totemism" as (1) a relationship between a kinship group and a species of animals or plants that is expressed in (2) rituals that ensure the relationship to the totemic group, in (3) marriage regulations, and in (4) the totemic group's taking the name of its totem. Still others expanded the conception of totemic deities to include the *dema* deities of the Indonesian archipelago. Like totemic deities, the *dema* stand in specific relationship to social groups, but they do not necessarily take on the form of an animal, bird, or plant. In creation myths, *dema* initially appear as the first ancestors, who are transformed into deities, animals, and spirits through an act of violence. Claude Lévi-Strauss's structuralist anthropological study of totems, totemic deities, and totemic social relations is the recent comprehensive critique of the last century's evolutionary reflection on "totemism." He demonstrated that totemic deities and totemic relationships are located throughout the history of religious traditions. They are not confined to tribal traditions and are more importantly related to the fundamental binary oppositions of the deep structure of human reflection. Totemic ideas and concepts, then, are directly related to the structuring and communication of meaning.

"Totemism" as a distinct early stage in religious development or evolution does not exist. That was an erroneous idea of the last century and perhaps even of our own. Nevertheless there are totemic deities and totemic social relations that can help to elucidate the nature of kinship patterns and religious legitimation of authority in some religious traditions.

See also ANTHROPOLOGY OF RELIGION; ARCHETYPE; MYTH; PSYCHOLOGY OF RELIGION; RITUAL; SOCIOLOGY OF RELIGION.

BIBLIOGRAPHY

Durkheim, Émile. *The Elementary Forms of Religious Life,* trans. by Karen E. Fields. 1995.

Jensen, Adolf E. *Myth and Cult Among Primitive Peoples,* trans. by Marianna Tax Choldin and Wolfgang Weissleder. 1963.

Lévi-Strauss, Claude. *Totemism,* trans. by Rodney Needham. 1963.

Sharpe, Eric J. *Comparative Religion: A History.* 2nd ed. 1986, esp. pp. 72–96.

van Baal, Jan. *Dema: Description and Analysis of Marind-anim Culture.* 1966.

van Gennep, Arnold. *Mythes et légendes d'Australie.* 1906.

Richard Hecht

Trance

Trance is a perceptual state measurably different from wakefulness that is a common feature of ritual behavior throughout the world, including North America, where it figures prominently in a wide variety of religious traditions from Spiritualism to Santería. Trance states can be induced by drumming, chanting, clapping, and dancing as well as by breathing techniques, meditation, scrying (staring into a translucent object), and a variety of other methods. The function of trance states varies greatly according to tradition, time, and place, yet like other altered states of consciousness, trance is usually intended to facilitate communication between humans and spirits or deities.

Owing largely to the association of trance with mediumship, spirit possession, and the occult in North America, skeptics and orthodox religionists have often relegated trance to the margins of acceptable religious behavior, yet that has never dampened public curiosity. The nineteenth century produced a number of popular religious movements such as Spiritualism that featured trance as a central ritual. Spiritualist mediums, most of whom were women, would enter a trance state during public performances, claiming to speak with the dead, who often conveyed radical political messages as well as words of comfort. Spiritualism waned after 1860, yet it found enduring institutional expression in groups such as the National Spiritualist Association of Churches. Trance was also ritualized in meetings of the Theosophical Society, founded in 1876.

Interest in transpersonal psychology and in attempts to alter consciousness through meditation and other spiritual exercises led to a second eruption of interest in trance during the 1960s and after. Although the renowned psychic Edgar Cayce (1877–1945) had previously claimed to transmit messages from celestial beings and other spirit entities while in a trance state, it was Jane Roberts (1929–1984) who was first among a wave of New Age trance channelers. Roberts used trance states to connect with a spiritual entity she called Seth. In books such as *The Seth Material* (1970), Roberts published Seth's counsel on self-love and the divinity of humanity; these works circulated widely among readers interested in New Age spirituality. By the 1980s trance channeling proliferated, producing its own celebrities such as J. Z. Knight and Kevin Ryerson. During private readings and public performances at New Age gatherings, channelers like Knight and Ryerson would enter trance, then deliver messages from various spiritual entites ranging from ancient inhabitants of Atlantis to beings from other galaxies. Quite predictably, skeptics accused these channelers of defrauding their public.

Although trance channeling waned as a cultural phenomenon in the 1990s, interest in trance as a means of enlightenment continued unabated. The neoprimitive aesthetic and practice fostered by global youth culture included a style of popular dance music known as trance dance. At events of very long duration in urban nightclubs throughout North America and the world, young dancers met in loosely organized communities to induce trance states by rhythmically moving to heavily percussive, neopsychedelic music. Organizations such as the Texas-based Natale Institute have tried to connect this youth subculture with New Age neoshamanism, which promotes trance as a path to individual and collective healing.

See also CHANNELING; CHANTING; DANCE; DRUMMING; HEALING; NEW AGE SPIRITUALITY; PSYCHIC; SANTERÍA; SHAMANISM; SPIRITUALISM; THEOSOPHICAL SOCIETY.

BIBLIOGRAPHY

Brown, Michael. *The Channeling Zone: American Spirituality in an Anxious Age.* 1997.

Carroll, Bret. *Spiritualism in Antbellum America.* 1997.

Goodman, Felicitas. *Where the Spirits Ride the Wind: Trance Journeys and Other Ecstatic Experiences.* 1990.

Hughes, Dureen. "Blending with an Other: An Analysis of Trance Channeling in the United States." *Ethos* 19 (1991): 161–184.

Taves, Ann. *Fits, Trances, and Visions: Experiencing Religion and Explaining Experience from Wesley to James.* 1999.

Winkelman, Michael. "Trance States: A Theoretical Model and Cross-Cultural Analysis." *Ethos* 14 (1986): 174–203.

Jesse T. Todd

Transcendence

The term "transcendence" is used in philosophical and theological discussions about the relationship of God to the world. Its opposite is "immanence." Recently transcendence has been used as a technical umbrella term to designate the divine dimension as sensed by all religions, a generic term to include not only the God of monotheism, but also such "things" as the Hindu Brahman, the Taoist Tao, possibly the nirvāṇa of Buddhists, and any other ultimate or sacred dimension in religion, philosophy, or spiritual practice. In fact, a reference to some transcendent dimension in faith, ritual, obedience, prayer, or other acts might even be a way to define religion.

In the earlier discussions it was often said that Deists conceived of a transcendent God who created the world and then "withdrew" to let the world run its course. The opposite view was that of pantheists, who identified God with the world or with part of the world. Theists occupied a middle position, God creating the world and then having either a constant sustaining relation to the world or else occasional relationships to the world in acts of revelation, miracles, and, for Christians, the incarnation of Christ. God could also be conceived as having both a constant sustaining relationship and occasional special relations. "Transcendence" and "immanence" are, of course, metaphors, spatial terms for the superiority or identity of God's metaphysical or moral character with the world, especially humanity. Recently process philosophers think of all existents, including God, as both transcendent and immanent to each other.

Simplifying the complexities of historical traditions, transcendence of the divine can be seen in most of the world's religions. This transcendence often has a dual aspect of gift and demand, which can be seen in Judaism, Christianity, and Islam, three major monotheistic faiths. Thus for the early Hebrews God's election of and continuing faithfulness to his people "transcended" or exceeded their worth or merit to earn this election and faithfulness. At the same time, the demand that Israel be faithful "transcended" Israel's ability to maintain complete faithfulness. In the later Jewish rabbinical tradition the Torah is a sign of God's favor, again transcending Israel's merit, combined with the demand that the laws of God be obeyed, a demand exceeding Israel's capacity to completely fulfill. In the teachings of Jesus there is the Kingdom of God, which transcends human power to bring it about, plus the transcendent call for perfection. In Paul and the later Christian tradition both the law and the gospel, good works and grace, are beyond human power. At the heart of Islam is the cry that Allah is greater than any creature, that his mercy and judgment are far beyond any human mercy or judgment.

Transcendence may also be a useful term in understanding other religions. For example, Brahman seems to be a nonpersonal superior reality for some Hindus. Likewise, the transcendent Buddha body goes beyond this phenomenal world, and perhaps nirvana itself is transcendent. Also the Tao, which is unknowable and cannot be named, seems to transcend the myriad things of this world for Taoism.

Scholars disagree on the usefulness of transcendence as a term for understanding the religions of many indigenous peoples or contemporary Neopaganism. Is there a transcendent dimension in these religions, or does their apparent polytheism prevent a full disclosure of transcendence? There is evidence that these religions have as strong a sense of both the transcendence and immanence of the divine as any other. There is also controversy on whether the Confucian tradition has a sense of transcendence. Some interpreters see the wisdom of past sages and the goal of sagehood as elements of transcendence. A full treatment of transcendence in the world's religions would also have to show when and how the transcendent is immanent within this world.

Transcendence can be thought of as helpful, useless, or dangerous. In one's personal life transcendence might be thought of as a helpful source of safety, power, or joy that goes beyond the merely finite resources of this world. However, as removed and distant, transcendence might be seen as irrelevant to this life. It might also be felt as dangerously oppressive, squelching the joys of life in the name of a fossilized tradition. In social and political affairs transcendence can also be thought of in these three ways. As blessing one's nation or cause it is helpful. As an impossible ideal it may be seen as irrelevant and thus needing to be separated from the affairs of the everyday world. It might also be seen as giving sanction to tyranny and the violence of hate groups. The Ku Klux Klan, for example, has always been a religious group. For various liberation movements the transcendent element in religion provides a fulcrum to challenge the status quo. Another debate concerns whether the transcendence of God alienates us from the significance of the natural world and thus increases the environmental crisis, or whether transcendence can challenge consumerism, habitat destruction, population explosion, and the depletion and poisoning of resources.

Recently a movement that could be called religious naturalism has gained momentum. This approach sees the divine as totally immanent (inherent) in all or part of the world. Typically in this view the divine or sacred is the aspect of the world that leads to the increase of value or the flourishing of creatures, instead of a special being called "God." This movement had its origins in Baruch Spinoza in the seventeenth century; its twentieth-century advocates include the British Samuel Alexander, George Burman Foster, Edward Scribner Ames, Henry Nelson Wieman, and later Bernard Loomer of Chicago, Ralph Wendell Burhoe, and Mordecai Kaplan, the founder of Reconstructionist Judaism. Recent proponents include Charley Hardwick, Henry Levinson, Robert Mesle, Wes Robbins, Marvin Shaw, and Jerome Stone. Biologist Ursula Goodenough's feelings of mystery, wonder, and awe over the "infinite and infinitesimal" are close to this. Religious naturalists disagree as to whether the divine is all or only part of this world and also whether it is a process, network, or plurality.

See also CREATIONISM; DIVINITY; GOD; HINDUISM; JUDAISM; NATURE RELIGION; NEOPAGANISM; NIRVĀNA; PANTHEISM; PROCESS THEOLOGY; RELIGIOUS EXPERIENCE; TAOISM; THEISM; THEODICY.

BIBLIOGRAPHY

Goldsmith, Emanuel, and Mel Scult. *Dynamic Judaism: The Essential Writings of Mordecai Kaplan.* 1985.

Hardwick, Charley. *Events of Grace: Naturalism, Existentialism, and Theology.* 1996.

Levinson, Henry S. "Naturalism." In *Blackwell's Companion to American Thought;* edited by Richard Wrightman Fox and James T. Kloppenberg. 1995.

Stone, Jerome A. *The Minimalist Vision of Transcendence: A Naturalist Philosophy of Religion.* 1992.

Jerome A. Stone

Transcendental Meditation

Popularly known as Transcendental Meditation (TM) and officially called the World Plan Executive Council, this neo-Hindu meditative practice eschews classification as a religious group by drawing attention to its scientific basis, the Science of Creative Intelligence (SCI). Research on TM reveals that its meditative technique brings about a relaxed state of mind, which has been verified using scientific methodology, and

hence the practice yields benefits that are not necessarily religious. However, TM is unequivocally based in classical Hindu religious traditions and espouses a religious message that is outlined in the 1962 text *The Divine Plan: Enjoy Your Own Inner Divine Nature,* published by the Spiritual Regeneration Movement. In 1978 critics who opposed the teaching of TM in public school districts of New Jersey won their case in U.S. District Court in Newark, New Jersey. The court ruled that TM was based on religious principles and therefore should be banned from the public schools. TM is seminal among the Hindu and Buddhist teachings that came to the United States after World War II.

Maharishi Mahesh Yogi (1911–), the principal exponent of TM, comes from Uttar-Kashi in the Himalayan region of India. He learned TM during thirteen years of rigorous study with Guru Dev in India. Before beginning his disciplined meditation practice, he had earned a B.S. in physics at Allahabad University in India. Arriving in the United States on his first world tour in 1959, Maharishi initiated the growth of his movement during the 1960s. His plan was to bring the Age of Enlightenment by disseminating the meditative practices among new members. His World Plan, announced in 1972, inaugurated this mission to spread the Science of Creative Intelligence around the world. Although the meditative technique gained fame in the 1960s when some well-known entertainers such as the Beatles, Mia Farrow, and Jane Fonda practiced it, membership has decreased dramatically since the late 1970s. However, there are still numerous TM centers throughout the United States and Europe, and the international headquarters is in Switzerland. While Maharishi has no legal affiliation with the World Plan Executive Council, his teaching inspires several contemporary institutes and agendas. Located in Fairfield, Iowa, Maharishi International University offers courses from a TM perspective and awards both bachelor's and master's degrees. Adjacent to the university is the Maharishi Center for Ayur-Veda. The Natural Law Party, which the council sponsors, supported a U.S. presidential candidate several years ago, and the party is now active in the United States and Europe.

TM practice has its roots in the Indian traditions of Yoga, and the specific variety of Yoga that Maharishi teaches is a simple technique of sound meditation (mantra-yoga) that uses a mantra, a terse sound, the repetition of which is the vehicle to purify one's awareness. The meditator begins to practice after receiving his or her private mantra during an initiation ceremony that includes acknowledgment of Hindu deities and a lineage of gurus. The goal of the practice is to calm the fluctuations of the mind through concentration on the sacred mantra. Meditating from one-half

Maharishi Mahesh Yogi seated on a couch in September 1967. (Credit: Nordisk Pressefoto/ Archive Photos.)

hour to an hour every day not only promises to bring tranquillity of mind but also promotes increased productivity, creativity, and general well-being. More specifically, widespread research studies at universities worldwide have documented the positive role of TM practice in reducing alcohol and drug abuse and raising intelligence quotients.

Maharishi's book *The Science of Being and Art of Living* outlines the cosmology of TM that undergirds the meditative practice. According to him, "the unbounded field of the Being ranges from the unmanifested, absolute, eternal state to the gross, relative, ever changing states of phenomenal life" (Mahesh Yogi 1963, p. 31). The practice of TM "brings the life to a state of eternal freedom, supplementing it with unlimited creative energy and harmonizing the abstract absolute values of divine Being with the concrete physical material values of day-to-day human life" (p. 81). The goal is God-realization.

Although membership statistics for the World Plan Executive Council are not known, the council reports that more than a million people have taken basic TM courses in the United States alone. TM peaked in 1976, when it initiated the most people, and thereafter it began to decline rapidly. Currently, active meditators number in the tens of thousands.

See also GURU; HINDUISM; MEDITATION; PRACTICE; YOGA.

BIBLIOGRAPHY

Bainbridge, William Sims, and Daniel H. Jackson, "The Rise and Decline of Transcendental Meditation." In *The Social Impact of New Religious Movements,* edited by B. Wilson. 1981.

Campbell, A. *The Mechanics of Enlightenment: An Examination of the Teaching of Maharishi Mahesh Yogi.* 1977.

Emery, C. Eugene. "Maharishi Followers Try Presidential Run." *Skeptical Inquirer* 17 (1993): 122–123.

Mahesh Yogi, Maharishi. *The Divine Plan: Enjoy Your Own Inner Divine Nature.* 1962.

Mahesh Yogi, Maharishi. *Life Supported by Natural Law.* 1986.

Mahesh Yogi, Maharishi. *The Science of Being and Art of Living.* 1963.

Mahesh Yogi, Maharishi. *The Treasury and the Market.* 1961.

Melton, J. Gordon. *Encyclopedic Handbook of Cults in America.* 1986.

Melton, J. Gordon. "World Plan Executive Council— U.S." In *Encyclopedia of American Religions,* 5th ed. 1996.

Patton, John E. *The Case Against TM in the Schools.* 1976.

Marcy Braverman

Transnational Religion

The world of the late twentieth century has grown smaller. The garments we wear are manufactured globally from cotton grown in Peru and cloth made in India, which in turn is sewn together in the Dominican Republic. They are marketed according to tariffs set by international political institutions. Has religion also "gone global"?

In some sense, religion is the oldest of global institutions. Religious diasporas began when the Jews left Canaan. The conquerors and missionaries who disseminated Catholicism throughout the world created a lasting global religious empire. But what is different about today?

One thing is the way in which people move. While most earlier migrants cut off their ties to the countries they came from, contemporary migrants often remain connected to their countries of origin at the same time that they are being integrated into the countries that receive them. Many earn their livelihood across borders, sustain at least partial long-term membership in two polities, and enact their social and emotional lives transnationally. Their ability to live lives that cross borders changes religious practices as well. A transnational religious relationship emerges that transforms religious life in both settings.

The terms "transnational" and "global" are often used interchangeably, but they are not the same thing. As Michael Kearney wrote in *The Annual Review of Anthropology* (1995), while global processes are not linked to specific national territories, transnational processes are anchored in but transcend one or more nation-states. Transnational religious relationships form at multiple levels. That is, migration may give rise to strong connections between parishes or chapters of the same organization in the respective sending and receiving country. Transnational ties also emerge when the national leadership of comparable denominations in the sending and receiving country enters into formal cooperative agreements in response to the increasing numbers of members these denominations share.

When large numbers from a small Dominican village settled in Boston, Massachusetts, but still remained strongly connected to their sending community, the relations between individual priests, parishes, and archdioceses, which evolved at multiple levels of the Catholic church hierarchy, created a transnational religious organization. Religious life in Boston and in the Dominican Republic was reciprocally changed or affected as a result. The social remittances migrants sent back to the island brought Dominican religious practices closer to those in the United States. Subsequent émigrés continued to infuse fresh "Dominicanness" into the Boston church, though it was a "Dominicanness" that was increasingly Anglicized in tone. In this way, transnational ties reinforced religious pluralism at the same time that they limit its scope.

Migrations involving greater numbers who are more loosely connected to one another may produce transnational religious fields characterized by weaker, more informal ties. Migration, however, is just one catalyst for the emergence of these transnational connections. Missionaries, tourists, and members of religious movements continue to disseminate religious ideas around the globe. Some researchers predict that this spread and thickening of religious structures and movements across borders will create a transnational civil society that challenges nation-states and security interests as we know them.

See also CYBER RELIGION; GLOBALIZATION; SYNCRETISM.

BIBLIOGRAPHY

Beyer, Peter. 1994. *Religion and Globalization* 1994.

Levitt, Peggy. "Local-Level Global Religion: The Case of U.S.-Dominican Migration." *Journal for the Scientific Study of Religion* 3 (1998): 74–89.

Rudolph, Susanne Hoeber, and James Piscatori, eds. *Transnational Religion and Fading States*. 1997.

Peggy Levitt

Trinity

Throughout Christian history various schools of thought have wrestled with the difficulty of explaining how belief in Father, Son, and Holy Spirit (or Holy Ghost, in the wording of the King James version of the Bible) as three divine persons could be consistent with strict monotheism. The word "trinity," derived from the Greek *trinus,* which means simply "threefold" or "triad," is not found in the Bible. Many argue, however, that the idea can be inferred from scriptural passages, and in addition, Trinitarian references appear as early as the second century in creeds, doxologies, and confessions of faith. Theologians try to think through the issue, but most say that the concept is essentially a mystery—that is, something not discovered or cogently demonstrated by unaided human reason. Such an idea was revealed, and even though it is above reason in origin, it is not contrary to reason when people reflect on their beliefs.

Most Trinitarian discussions are Christological, centering on some aspect of the nature and work of Jesus Christ. As various thinkers tried to retain belief in the exclusively monotheistic God of Israel and yet exalt Christ as Messiah, they put forth various theories. When a majority of church officials endorsed a viewpoint, it was held to be "orthodox," but when they rejected others, those unacceptable alternatives were labeled as "heresy." Christological controversies were particularly noticeable in the early centuries of Christian development. In all their complex variation, discussions revolved around two basic questions: Was Jesus so divine as to be equal to God? If Jesus was fully God, had he ever been completely human, too?

Some thinkers in early Christianity felt that deifying Jesus would compromise the monotheistic strictures inherited from Judaism. Consequently they adopted various theories that held Jesus to be the Messiah but not one to endanger belief in only one deity. The most sophisticated version of this approach, early in the fourth century, was called Arianism. Such thinking acknowledged Jesus to be a supernatural savior whose nature was higher than even that of the angels. But he was not completely the same as God. Since only

God was preexistent, they held that Jesus had been created, an entity superior to all other creatures but still a made thing who was secondary in origin and capacity. Arians revered Jesus in their hope for salvation, but they refused to invalidate God's exclusive place by equating Jesus' existence with it. Their opponents insisted that the two references were interchangeable and did not compromise monotheistic loyalty.

Debates yielded no resolution of these perspectives, and ideological strife sometimes spilled over into social unrest as well. Eventually the Roman emperor Constantine I tried to end factionalism by calling the church's bishops together at Nicea in 325 and urging them to determine a single theory for everyone. The resulting Nicene Creed rejected Arianism in favor of a more inclusive Trinitarian view. The preponderant opinion at Nicaea held Jesus to be not a creature but the only-begotten Son of God, light derived from light, true God in himself and the same as the true God from whom he came. Using a significant theological term, the council declared Jesus to be "of one being" with the Father, sharing the same essential nature while manifesting a separate personage in the created world. After 325, then, orthodox theologians accepted the formula of the Trinity, the Godhead as one substance that disclosed itself in three distinct forms. The Nicene Creed has never fully explained what the Trinity actually is, but it shows where alternative formulations are inadequate.

The Holy Spirit usually receives less attention than the Father and the Son in most Trinitarian thinking. But a controversy involving the third person of the Trinity came to a head in the eleventh century. The Nicene formula originally stated that the Holy Spirit (in some translations referred to as the "Holy Ghost") emanated from the Father; Greek or Eastern churches maintained that wording through all the centuries. But sometime during the eighth century, Latin or Western churches began to say that the Holy Spirit emanated from both the Father "and the Son." Arguments over that additional phrase, "Filioque," were symbolic of many other tensions that existed between Greek and Latin ecclesiastical authorities. These differences split the churches into Roman Catholic and Eastern Orthodox segments in 1054. Western churches still recite versions of the Nicene Creed, which says that the Holy Spirit "proceeds from the Father and the Son" in its Trinitarian formulation.

The vote at Nicea rejected Arianism but did not end it. There have been thinkers in every age who have perceived God as a single unit and have placed the Messiah figure in a subordinate, though still important, position. Such ideas found some backing in sixteenth-century Hungary and Poland. But modern

A mural, protraying the Father, the Son, and the Holy Spirit, on display in Las Trampas, New Mexico. (Credit: CORBIS/Craig Aurness.)

emphases on the unity of God became strongest in England and America. Beginning with anti-Trinitarian writings in the seventeenth century, Unitarian convictions appealed to a growing number of English Christians. In 1774 those believers formed a separate denomination, relying on the leadership of such clergy as Joseph Priestley.

Priestley immigrated to the United States in 1794, but the roots of American Unitarianism lie elsewhere. Liberal thinkers in New England Congregationalism such as Jonathan Mayhew and Charles Chauncy had already begun developing a perspective that stressed moral goodness and improvement rather than human depravity and divine rescue. In the early nineteenth century William Ellery Channing furthered this more humane, optimistic viewpoint through his pulpit eloquence and social polish.

Ideas and emphases such as these resulted in the formation of the American Unitarian Association in 1825. Denominational adherents were inclined to pursue individual virtue and greater social justice, but their opponents insisted on saying that their chief feature was denial of the Trinity. While the label remains in force, Unitarians have rarely made much of anti-Trinitarian convictions. Most of them refer to Jesus as simply a moral exemplar, and this modest role calls for nothing more than a human figure. With concepts about salvation wherein Jesus is expected to give encouragement, not supernatural grace, the idea of a Trinity is more subordinated than openly denied. This denomination has continued to flourish in contemporary America.

See also CREEDS; DIVINITY; EASTERN ORTHODOXY; FAITH; GOD; HERESY; MAINLINE PROTESTANTISM; NAMES AND NAMING; ROMAN CATHOLICISM; THEISM; UNITARIAN UNIVERSALIST CHURCHES.

BIBLIOGRAPHY

Allen, Joseph H. *Unitarianism and the Reformation.* 1986.

Gunlon, Colin E. *The Promise of Trinitarian Theology.* 1997.

Kuklick, Bruce, ed. *The Unitarian Controversy, 1819–1823.* 1987.

Torrance, Thomas F. *The Christian Doctrine of God: One Being in Three Persons.* 1996.

Henry Warner Bowden

Triple Goddess

The modern Wiccan movement is centered upon the worship of the Goddess, popularly seen against the male patriarchal images of God that have been dominant in Christianity. As Wiccans have developed their theology, the idea of the Triple Goddess as Maiden, Mother, and Crone, often symbolized by the different phases of the moon, has become a popular expression of their understanding of the deity.

Wicca is generally traced to the writings and organizational activity of Gerald B. Gardner (1884–1964), who created a new polytheistic religion based on the worship of the Goddess, the most prominent deity, generally understood as either a young maiden or the Mother; and of her consort, the horned God. These images dominated the movement and the early theoreticians, most of whom were male. They supported the idea of Witchcraft as a polytheistic fertility religion and suggested an underlying celebration of sexuality. However, by the 1970s a number of female leaders, most with a strong feminist consciousness, had arisen to positions of prominence, began to explore the idea of Wicca as Goddess religion, and sought insights from such varied perspectives as theology, anthropology/archaeology, psychology, and history. A spectrum of belief emerged within the movement that at one end continued the Gardnerian emphasis on the God and Goddess (though the God has a slightly subordinate role) and on the other developed a singular focus on the Goddess.

Underlying Goddess worship was an assumption that statements about the divine and images of the divine directly reflected understandings of human social roles. Female witches sought images of the divine that were supportive of liberation and self-sufficiency throughout the life cycle and that looked to the divine as a reflection of human life and aspirations. The Goddess satisfies those areas of life always considered feminine while at the same time opening space for women to assume traditional male roles.

Having discovered the multitude of Goddesses represented in both ancient and contemporary religious systems, they also debated the nature of their polytheism. Was there one Goddess who was manifested in different aspects/personas, or several goddesses who appeared under different names in different cultures? While most Goddess-worshipers appear to move toward a monotheistic belief, the idea of a Triple Goddess, suggested by such ideas as the Three Mothers in Celtic mythology or Bhavani (known as the Triple Universe in Indian mythology), was compatible with both polytheistic and monothistic interpretations of the Goddess.

Essentially, the idea of the Triple Goddess suggests the three dominant stages of female life as the Maiden, just coming into womanhood in the years immediately after puberty; the Mother, the nurturing, caring, and sexually fertile woman; and the Crone, the postmenopausal elder who embodies the wisdom of the community. The Maiden is the adventurous youth who leaps over obstacles, the fresh mind with a new perspective, and the sexually vital object of young men's desire. The mother is the woman in full adulthood who gives life, nurtures it, and molds it. She is powerful and protective of her own. The crone is the experienced wise woman, full of love tempered by understanding.

Among the most popular triads used within the Wiccan movement is that of Persephone (maiden), Demeter (Mother), and Hecate (Crone), but rituals and music move broadly across world mythology to call the names of different deities. Several volumes catalog the Goddess's manifestations worldwide. As the idea of the Triple Goddess has spread through the very decentralized Wiccan movement, it has provided comfortable roles for the various female members, each of whom may choose a particular Goddess with whom to interact at any given period of her life.

See also DIVINITY; FEMINIST SPIRITUALITY; FEMINIST THEOLOGY; GOD; GODDESS; NEOPAGANISM; NEW RELIGIOUS MOVEMENTS; WICCA; WOMANIST THEOLOGY.

BIBLIOGRAPHY

Crowley, Vivianne. *Wicca: The Old Religion in the New Age.* 1989.

Eller, Cynthia. *Living in the Lap of the Goddess: The Feminist Spirituality Movement in America.* 1993.

Farrar, Janet, and Stewart Farrar. *The Witches' Goddess: The Feminine Principle of Divinity.* 1987.

J. Gordon Melton

True Love Waits

The True Love Waits campaign is an interdenominational program that promotes premarital sexual abstinence. Founded in 1992 by the Southern Baptist Sunday School Board, the campaign has the cooperation of more than twenty-seven other Protestant Christian evangelical, fundamentalist, pentecostal, and holiness groups as well as the National Federation for Catholic Youth Ministry.

The primary goal of the campaign is to have young people commit to and sign the following pledge: "Believing that true love waits, I make a commitment to God, myself, my family, my friends, my future mate, and my future children to be sexually abstinent from this day until the day I enter a biblical marriage relationship."

More than a million young people in the United States, mostly preteens, but also high school and college students, are thought to have signed the pledge. In July 1994 a total of 210,000 signed cards were exhibited on the Mall in Washington, D.C.; in March 1996 a total of 340,000 cards from fifty states and seventy-six countries were displayed at a True Love Waits convention-rally in Atlanta, Georgia. Additional rallies have been held in Buenos Aires, Argentina; Ottawa, Canada; and Kampala, Uganda. The journal *The American Enterprise* has estimated that 450,000 cards were signed in 1997 and another 700,000 in 1998. This includes 500,000 cards signed by college and university students, who have formed True Love Waits clubs on university campuses across the United States; recently, a new organization called CrossSeekers has been established to serve college-age and twenty-something unmarrieds.

True Love Wait's target membership seems to be not American teenagers in general, but rather "churched" teenagers already within the conservative Protestant or conservative Catholic fold. Survey research has shown that sexual activity among "churched" youth increased from the 1960s to the 1980s, and then soared to a peak in 1987. Since 1987, the proportion of sexually active "churched" youth has declined; however, the young people reported that they postponed sex not because of a moral or religious belief, but for other reasons. The True Love Waits campaign concentrates on chastity in the individual as a means of cultivating increased commitment and solidarity within churches and religious communities. Another aim—manifested through the public display of signed pledge cards—is to demonstrate the strength and integrity of Christian youth.

Organizationally, the True Love Waits campaign is nondenominational: It seeks to supplement existing denominational teen ministry programs. Indeed, the campaign planning kit contains suggestions for incorporating into the formal liturgy a ritual for taking the sexual purity vows, and for reaffirming those vows regularly. In addition, the Baptist Sunday School Board has developed various tools that youth ministers and group leaders can use: commitment cards, a True Love Waits handbook, books and magazines on related subjects, a tract for youth evangelism, banners and posters, a retreat manual, a New International Version "True Love Waits Bible" with appropriate articles, and even a specially written musical.

True Love Waits has developed a powerful iconographic and artifactual tradition. "TLW" logos may be photocopied or made into stickers and buttons; moreover, group leaders and individuals can order T-shirts, caps, "commitment rings," compact discs and cassettes (featuring, among others, Grammy Award winners Amy Grant, DC Talk, and Petra, as well as Steven Curtis Chapman, Newsboys, and Audio Adrenaline), mugs and plates, and, as in the secular fashion industry, "True Love Waits Active Wear," including T-shirts and sweatshirts. The "commitment ring" is intended to be given to the young man or woman on the occasion of his or her abstinence pledge. One order form suggests that "the ring be worn until marriage and given to the marriage partner on the wedding night as [a] gift of purity."

One of the implicit messages of the True Love Waits campaign is that sex is more pleasurable if each partner abstains until marriage. The True Love Waits campaign argues that the spiritual and physical pleasures of sex are rooted in chastity and abstinence. Conversely, premarital promiscuity is said to rob young people of true sexual pleasure, through sexually transmitted diseases, pregnancy, and the social stigma associated with sexual impurity.

The True Love Waits campaign does not exclude teenagers who are already sexually active, but rather specifically targets these teenagers by emphasizing chastity rather than virginity. The campaign creates a category of "secondary virginity" that allows—indeed, welcomes—young people who have been sexually active to alter their behavior. Focusing on "acquired" purity over "original" purity places the campaign firmly within a Protestant tradition that emphasizes conversion experience over inherited religious affiliation. A decision *not* to have sex, even if one has already been sexually active, becomes a sacred act. Conversely, admitting and repenting sexual impurity simply removes it from the divine tally sheet.

The True Love Waits campaign claims not to pursue any larger social or political goals; it has stayed out of the sex education controversy in public schools. It is nonpartisan—indeed, at Stanford University, the True Love Waits club's founding president was simultaneously the president of the campus College Democrats organization in 1995–1996. At the same time, however, the campaign does encourage its adherents to make their social home within the church community; in return, the church community provides social, material, and religious rewards for chastity and loyalty.

See also Baptist Tradition; Catholic Charismatic Renewal; Celibacy; Chastity; Evangelical Christianity; Fundamentalist Christianity; Pentecostal and Charismatic Christianity.

BIBLIOGRAPHY

"Growing Respect for Saving Sex." *The American Enterprise* 9, no. 1 (1998): 53.

Hill, Kathie, and Travis Cottrell. *Waiters: A Youth Musical About Waiting on the Lord.* Libretto and cassette. 1994.

Hunter, James Davison. *Evangelicalism: The Coming Generation.* 1983.

"The Land Where Religion Is Hip." *The American Enterprise* 9, no. 2 (1998): 48–51.

Landres, J. Shawn. "Just Say Wait: A First Look at the True Love Waits Campaign." In *The Power of Gender in Religion,* edited by Georgie Ann Weatherby and Susan A. Farrell. 1996.

Landres, J. Shawn. "When the Medium *Isn't* the Message: The *True Love Waits* Campaign." *Religion and Education* (Spring 1996): 25–33.

McDowell, Josh, and Bob Hostetler. *Right from Wrong.* 1994.

"Sexual Backlash." *The American Enterprise* 9, no. 4 (1998): 11.

True Love Waits: A Fact Sheet. 1994.

True Love Waits Church Worship Ideas. 1994.

Willis, Nancye. "Sexual Purity Pledges Catch World Interest." *Baptist Press* (July 30, 1994).

J. Shawn Landres

Twelve-Step Programs

The twentieth-century boom of twelve-step programs can be traced back to 1935, the year in which Alcoholics Anonymous (AA) was formed by Bill Wilson and Robert Holbrook Smith. Both men, suffering from severe alcoholism, came under the influence of the independent evangelical Oxford Group, a religious movement that practiced strict moral standards, mutual confession among group members, and submission to God. In Akron, Ohio, the two men gathered together a small group of people seeking freedom from their addiction to alcohol, and AA groups similarly tied to the Oxford Group were shortly formed in several other cities as well. In 1938 Wilson and Smith published *Alcoholics Anonymous* and initiated an organization independent of the Oxford Group to gather dispersed local groups under one umbrella.

A substance-abuse counselor holds the hand of an alcoholic at a treatment center in Costa Mesa, California. (Credit: © Spencer Grant/Stock, Boston/PNI.)

The basic idea behind this formation was one that would similarly inspire a wide array of other self-help groups dealing with addiction, from Narcotics Anonymous (founded in 1953) and Overeaters Anonymous (founded in 1965) to Gamblers Anonymous (founded in 1970), Impotents Anonymous, and Sexaholics Anonymous: An addict cannot be cured by superficial, conventional treatment but can be cured only by means of a spiritual commitment to a set of specific practices within a group of empathic supporters.

These practices are based upon the "twelve steps" codified by AA. Emphasizing individual powerlessness over alcohol (or drugs, sex, food, etc.), the prescribed cure begins with acknowledging "a Power greater than ourselves" and surrendering to that Power for restoration to health. Evoking the process of Christian confession, the steps require the addicted to admit their wrongs to God, to themselves, and to others, by taking a "fearless moral inventory." They are then required to make amends to all whom they have injured and to remain alert against further wrongdoing in the future. The final step advocates spreading this message to other addicts and continuing to live out this transformation in all areas of life. National twelve-step groups are not affiliated with any particular sect, denomination, or political party and welcome participants across a broad spectrum of religious adherence and nonadherence. As of 1992 there were at least 130 national twelve-step organizations as well as numerous statewide and scattered local ones (Katz 1993, p. 11).

Twelve-step meetings often open with the "Serenity Prayer" and a formal explanation of the group and its goals. First-timers are invited to make their presence known, after which readings from twelve-step materials may be given and personal testimonies of trials and successes are relayed to the group. All members are encouraged to share strategies for overcoming addiction and to celebrate their abstinence, though meetings differ as to the amount of time devoted to each component of the meeting. A particularly wide spectrum as to spirituality is also evident, with some groups mentioning a Higher Power only in reference to the twelve steps, and other groups characterized by a rather more religious tone. The decentralization of twelve-step groups in general makes such diversity possible while encouraging potential participants to visit different groups until they find one compatible with their own beliefs and needs.

With roots in evangelical Christianity, twelve-step groups have moved far away from their religious heritage while retaining a vestige of spirituality that appeals to some even while estranging many others. While the vagueness of such groups' reference to a Higher Power has aimed at striking a compromise between the religious and the irreligious, conservative traditionalists and atheists alike often find such language more irritating than helpful. Still, the masses of people in attendance at twelve-step groups every week manage to incorporate this terminology into their private belief systems, finding the twelve-step model as a whole to be an important part of their own healing process.

See also DRUGS; GOD; PRACTICE; RITUAL; TESTIMONY.

BIBLIOGRAPHY

Alcoholics Anonymous: The Story of How Many Thousands of Men and Women Have Recovered from Alcoholism. 1938. Rev. ed., 1976.

Katz, Alfred H. *Self-Help in America: A Social Movement Perspective.* 1993.

Kurtz, Ernest. *Not-God: A History of Alcoholics Anonymous.* 1979.

Rice, John Steadman. *A Disease of One's Own: Psychotherapy, Addiction, and the Emergence of Co-Dependency.* 1995.

Woolverton, John F. "Evangelical Protestantism and Alcoholism 1933–1962: Episcopalian Samuel Shoemaker, the Oxford Group and Alcoholics Anonymous." *Historical Magazine of the Protestant Episcopal Church* 52, no. 1 (1983): 53–65.

R. Marie Griffith

U

Unidentified Flying Objects (UFOs)

In 1947 Kenneth Arnold, a pilot flying near Mount Rainier in the state of Washington, claimed to have seen some disks flying in formation in front of his airplane. These object were termed "flying saucers" by the press, and Arnold's sighting became the fountainhead of thousands of reports of strange aerial phenomena that have persisted to the present. Scientists attempting to understand the nature of these objects dubbed them "unidentified flying objects" or UFOs. Public interest was aroused by speculation that the UFOs were extraterrestrial craft. Consideration of UFOs peaked in the 1960s but was largely abandoned following a highly skeptical scientific report by Edward Condon in 1969, though a few dedicated scientists continue to work on the problem.

While researchers attempted to sort out the nature of UFOs (most of which were determined to be misidentified human-made objects such as balloons, unusual weather phenomena, or especially brilliant planets or stars), a few people, termed contactees, emerged claiming that the UFOs really were extraterrestrial in origin. Beginning with George Adamski in 1952, contactees such as George Van Tassel and George King asserted their authority because they claimed they had spoken to the crafts' owners, and a few claimed to have made trips on the saucers to their planet of origin. The initial message of the space brothers was said to be one of warning against atomic destruction and of the need for universal brotherhood. The seriousness of their claims was underscored when Gloria Lee, an early contactee and founder of the Cosmos Research Foundation, starved herself to death in Washington, D.C., while waiting for government officials to respond to her claims.

In the wake of the initial accounts of meeting the space brothers, the contactees created a new religious movement built around the continued channeled teachings they claimed to receive from extraterrestrials. Their expanded messages emphasized the need for spiritual unfolding that tended to follow the perspectives previously spread through Spiritualism or Theosophy, with the space brothers assuming the position previously held by the spirits and ascended masters.

Most contactee groups proved ephemeral, but several, such as the Aetherius Society, Unarius, and the George Adamski Foundation, all of which began in the 1950s, have continued, though never as very large organizations. They offered a metaphysical spirituality to a generation caught up in both the anxieties and aspirations of the new space age, but suffered as evidence from UFO sightings suggesting extraterrestrial origins proved unacceptable to the majority of the scientific community. Through the 1980s and 1990s the contactees were joined by a new group of people who claimed that they had been abducted by extraterrestrials and who offered a largely negative picture of the UFO occupants. The cause of the abductees was taken up by some in the older UFO research community, who were joined by a new set of colleagues from the mental health disciplines. Over time, as some abductees experienced multiple incidents, it was found that the sharp boundary between contactees and abductees tended to fade.

See also CHANNELING; EXTRATERRESTRIAL GUIDES; NEW RELIGIOUS MOVEMENTS; SPACE FLIGHT; SPIRITUALISM; THEOSOPHICAL SOCIETY.

BIBLIOGRAPHY

Clark, Jerome. *The UFO Encyclopedia: The Phenomenon from the Beginning.* 1998.
Steiger, Brad. *The Aquarian Revelations.* 1971.

J. Gordon Melton

Unification Church

The Unification Church, formally the Holy Spirit Association for the Unification of World Christianity, represents a blend of Christianity and Confucianism. The movement maintains an elaborate organizational structure and claims several hundred thousand members worldwide, but membership has declined since the 1970s. Full-time American membership, which peaked at five thousand to ten thousand, is currently in the range of one thousand to two thousand. At present, church growth is greatest in Latin America and Africa.

Sun Myung Moon: Founder of the Unification Church

The Unification Church was founded by Sun Myung Moon, born Yong Myung Moon in 1920, in what is now North Korea. His family converted to Presbyterianism when he was ten years old. At age sixteen he had a spiritual vision in which he was instructed to complete Jesus' unfinished mission of restoring God's kingdom on earth. By 1944 Moon began gathering disciples. His anticommunism and revisionist Christian theology resulted in his imprisonment on three occasions in the 1940s and 1950s. Following the Korean War he settled in Pusan, founded the Unification Church in 1954, and published his major theological treatise, *The Divine Principle* (1957). In the late 1950s he dispatched missionaries to Japan and the United States. In 1960 Moon was wedded, for the second time, to Hak Ja Han, who bore thirteen children over the next two decades. In 1971 Moon immigrated to America, which served as his primary residence until

Some of the 28,000 couples who participated in a marriage affirmation ceremony conducted by the Reverend and Mrs. Sun Myung Moon, founders of the Unification Church, at RFK Stadium in Washington, D.C., on Saturday, November 27, 1997. (Credit: AP/Wide World Photos.)

the mid-1990s, when he expressed disenchantment with American hedonism and began redirecting his movement's initiatives toward South America. He further announced that he had fulfilled the conditions requisite for the messianic role in the Restoration process (see below).

The Divine Principle

The core of Moon's theology, the Divine Principle, is the sequence of the Creation, Fall, and Restoration. God created the world to reflect his inner, loving nature; Adam and Eve were to share the joy of love and to form a perfect, God-centered family. However, Adam and Eve failed to realize God's purpose, as Eve was spiritually seduced by Satan and prematurely consummated a physical relationship with Adam. Sexual indiscretion thus constituted the Fall, the ultimate source of human sinfulness, and humanity thereby became rooted in a satanic lineage. Humans bear responsibility and must pay indemnity for their sins to earn the opportunity for Restoration. Jesus offered the most recent such opportunity. Although he was successful in creating the basis for spiritual Restoration (through acceptance of him as savior), he was crucified before achieving physical Restoration by establishing a new lineage of God-centered families. Moon represents the new messianic figure who can complete the Restoration process by bringing all relationships and institutions out of the satanic into the God-centered domain if humanity embraces his leadership.

Organization

Moon is a successful corporate executive with a network of enterprises in Korea, Japan, and North and South America. These corporations include industrial, food, fishing, newspaper publishing (most notably the *Washington Times*), consumer goods, and recreational enterprises. In the United States, corporations are organized through a holding company, Unification Church International, with profits redistributed to Moon's religious agenda. These projects and organizations include a broad range of political, economic, social, intellectual, and artistic initiatives that are all intended to link individuals and organizations to his messianic mission. The primary source of funding has been Japan; businesses elsewhere have had mixed economic fortunes. Recent organizational changes include the founding in Brazil of the New Hope communities, which Unificationists regard as the new Garden of Eden, and Moon's replacement of the Unification Church as the organizational vehicle for his mission with the Family Federation for World Peace and Unification, which sponsors lectures and programs supporting moral and family values.

The central project of Restoration is the creation of God-centered families; as the True Parents, Moon and his wife initiate this new spiritual lineage through the blessing (marriage) ritual. There have been a succession of blessings in mass ceremonies, generally held at outdoor stadiums and broadcast worldwide. The most recent such ceremony was held in 1998; it involved 30,000 couples on-site and 3.5 million overall (most were non-Unificationists renewing their marriage vows). During the 1970s and 1980s, Unificationist membership involved intense, full-time commitment, with married couples pursuing movement projects independently. More recently Moon has emphasized the home church, which encourages families to return to their former faiths to create bridges between Unificationism and other denominations.

Controversy

The Unification Church has been embroiled in controversy since its inception. Moon was imprisoned briefly in the United States on tax-evasion charges; the church became the most prominent target of the anticult movement during the 1970s for allegedly brainwashing adherents and was the target of federal and state legislative investigations; conservative Christian groups have continued to denounce Moon's theology and messianic claims; and the National Council of Churches has denied the church membership. Most recently, two daughters and a daughter-in-law have distanced themselves from Moon, and the daughter-in-law has offered public accounts of abusive family relationships within the church.

See also ANTI-CULT MOVEMENT; BRAINWASHING; CONFUCIANISM; CULT; CULT AWARENESS NETWORK; FINANCING RELIGION.

BIBLIOGRAPHY

Barker, Eileen. *The Making of a Moonie: Brainwashing or Choice?* 1984.

Bromley, David G., and Anson Shupe. *"Moonies" in America: Cult, Church, and Crusade.* 1979.

Lofland, John. *Doomsday Cult.* Enlarged ed. 1977.

David G. Bromley

Unitarian Universalist Churches

In 1961 the Universalist Church of America (UCA) and the American Unitarian Association (AUA) merged into the Unitarian Universalist Association (UUA). Many church members wanted to include

The Unity Temple, a Unitarian Universalist church in Oak Park, Illinois, a suburb west of Chicago, was designed by Frank Lloyd Wright. (Credit: CORBIS/Robert Holmes.)

"free" and "liberal" in the name of their new denomination, since both traditions had long cherished those adjectives. Neither group had required assent to any creeds, and both had a long tradition of liberalism in intellectual, social, and political matters. In the nineteenth century, both had strongly opposed slavery and had ordained women. Both denominations had welcomed the influence of sciences and encouraged toleration, not only among Christians but among the world's religions.

Each had emerged from opposition to New England Calvinism—Universalists rejecting the idea that God could predestine most humans to an eternal hell (i.e., salvation was instead held to be universal) and Unitarians rejecting the idea that human will was not free to practice virtue and thereby to deserve eternal reward (i.e., salvation by character). Unitarians were more elite and dominated Harvard for most of the nineteenth century. Universalists were more populist, and built Tufts, Allegheny, Lombard, and St. Lawrence for the less radical education of their youth.

The founding of the UCA was in 1790 and that of the AUA in 1825. Both were associations of local congregations with quite limited powers. These individual congregations could call, even ordain, their own ministers. Because they stressed freedom of religious conscience, democratic discussion and change became the order of the day, and tradition became a palette rather

than a carved stone. Only a few years after the UUA was founded, Ralph Waldo Emerson left to preach a Transcendentalism that moved well beyond even the relatively liberal Unitarian Christianity. Theodore Parker became Boston's most popular preacher and was shunned by his Unitarian colleagues for his religious and social radicalism. Hosea Ballou insisted that universal salvation took place here, not in some future place, thus radicalizing the earlier universalism of the UCA's founder, John Murray. A Free Religious Association was formed in 1867, bringing together dissidents within the two denominations as well as liberal Quakers, Ethical Culturists, and Reform Jews.

By that time, major seminaries were teaching a social gospel and considering the impact of evolution on the history of religions. The search was on for a historical Jesus who would be more of a model for living in this world while transforming it. Philosophies of idealism, which regarded mind as different from and superior to matter, were losing their appeal and were being replaced by naturalism, which regarded life and thinking as natural parts of this world. John Dewey illustrates this well.

World War I (1914–1918) shattered many dreams of a reasonable international order, and the world depression that shortly followed deepened the despair. In 1933 Dewey and a number of Unitarian and Universalist leaders signed a Humanist Manifesto that called for a "religious humanism" to replace outdated supernaturalism, relying on reasonable humans alone to create a better world. Such ideas were widely debated in American seminaries, colleges, and religious journals.

The Unitarian and Universalist movements had already experienced a general movement from a heretical Christianity to a liberal Protestantism to a more universal theism. Individual religious freedom meant that such adherents could still be found. The humanist stance, however, now seemed particularly appealing. A 1966 study through the National Opinion Research Center (Tapp, 1973) showed that humanism and naturalistic theism had become dominant. Smaller studies since then show that humanism in some form remains the stance of the vast majority of Unitarian Universalists (UUs).

American life has changed rapidly since the 1960s, and so has the UUA. During the civil rights struggle, half of the UU clergy went to Selma to march with the Rev. Dr. Martin Luther King, Jr. Annual General Assemblies committed major shares of endowment to black empowerment, but subsequent boards of trustees were unable to continue the commitment. The United States' involvement in Vietnam was opposed, early and strenuously. Gay rights took center stage early, with the UUA supporting gay and lesbian ministers. Same-sex unions were given approval. A sophisticated sexuality unit for religious education was created (and widely exported). An active feminist movement succeeded in reducing sexism. Gender-freeing of hymns and liturgies occurred with minimal ruffle. The UU Service Committee was a leader in opposing U.S. support for right-wing terror in El Salvador and Nicaragua. Such changes reflected the makeup of the UU laity—more members with advanced degrees and higher family-income levels and more urban residents than any other denomination. Despite (or perhaps because of) the absence of creed, every study has shown striking consensus on political and religious values among members.

More recently, broad American religious tendencies have affected the UUA. Pluralism, inclusiveness, and diversity have become slogans, not only in regard to race and ethnicity but to theology as well. Thus, such subgroups as pagans, Buddhists, and the Earth-centered are now being welcomed in this new version of spirituality. In past times, a kind of self-selection has preserved the high consensus, but the future is always open.

See also ETHICAL CULTURE; FREE WILL; HUMANISM; KING, MARTIN LUTHER, JR.; LESBIAN AND GAY RIGHTS MOVEMENT; NEW AGE SPIRITUALITY; ORDINATION OF WOMEN; RELIGIOUS EXPERIENCE.

BIBLIOGRAPHY

Bartlett, Laile. Bright Galaxy: Ten Years of Unitarian Fellowships. 1960.

Cassara, Ernest. Universalism in America: A Documentary History. 1971.

Olds, Mason. American Religious Humanism. Rev. ed. 1996.

Parke, David B. The Epic of Unitarianism. 1957.

Persons, Stow. Free Religion: An American Faith. 1947.

Robinson, David. The Unitarians and the Universalists. 1985.

Tapp, Robert. Religion Among the Unitarian Universalists: Converts in the Stepfathers' House. 1973.

Unitarian-Universalist Association. The Free Church in a Changing World. 1963.

Wilbur, Earl Morse. History of Unitarianism. 1945, 1952.

Wright, Conrad. A Stream of Light: A Sesquicentennial History of American Unitarianism. 1973.

Robert B. Tapp

United Church of Christ.

See Mainline Protestantism.

Unity

The Unity School of Christianity is in many respects a small mainstream Protestant religious denomination, but it also has strong affinities with the New Thought and New Age movements. Much of its activity is carried out through publications and the mail rather than primarily in church congregations. Worldwide, there are about 600 congregations with 70,000 members, but a considerably larger population is reached by the spiritual message communicated through literature, over radio, and now on the World Wide Web.

Unity emerged from the spiritual quest and ministry of Charles Fillmore and Myrtle Fillmore (Mary Caroline Page), who were influenced by Christian Science while they were living in Kansas City, Missouri. Like many founders of healing ministries, Myrtle suffered from chronic medical afflictions, which at one point were diagnosed as tuberculosis. In 1886, she and Charles attended a course on Christian Science, and in her desperation Myrtle focused upon these healing words: "I am a child of God and therefore I do not inherit sickness." She began studying the Gospels, sensing the presence of Christ and sharing the healing with her husband. The couple studied metaphysics, then were ordained in Christian Science. For a time, the Fillmores cooperated with Christian Science and the related New Thought Movement, but their ministry gradually established its independence from them, becoming incorporated in its present form in 1914.

In 1889, Charles founded *Modern Thought,* a periodical that was renamed *Christian Science Thought* in 1890 and took its current name, *Unity,* in 1891. Describing itself as "a spiritual resource for daily living," this inspirational monthly is widely read, even by many who may not accept Unity's metaphysical interpretations of the Bible. Standard columns in the paper at the present time include "The Spiritual Journey" ("A monthly thought for your daily walk along the path of spiritual enlightenment") and "Metaphysical Musings" ("An opportunity to explore the insights of metaphysics and the practical application of those insights in everyday life"). Readers in need of spiritual support are invited to accpt the free help of *Silent Unity,* a twenty-four-hour prayer ministry that claims to receive two million prayer requests annually.

Sociologically, it is important to recognize that Unity arose from a widespread cultural movement embedded in a social network, rather than being either the unique creation of the Fillmores or a schismatic splinter group from Mary Baker Eddy's Christian Science church. The first Christian Science course the Fillmores took was taught by Eugene B. Weeks, from an independent Christian Science school in Chicago, the Illinois Metaphysical College. The sister-in-law of Charles's business partner was Nona Brooks, who later founded the similar Divine Science Church. A chief contributor to *Unity* magazine in its early years was Annie Rix Militz, who had been a disciple of metaphysical teacher Emma Curtis Hopkins in San Francisco before meeting the Fillmores and who founded a long-lived New Thought group called the Home of Truth.

Also important to realize is the fact that Unity arose from an equal partnership between Myrtle and Charles. Popular notions about new religious movements tend to assume that each is the creation of a lone individual, and the tendency of many groups to revere a figurehead supports this misconception. In fact, it is quite common for movements to be created by a couple, and examples range from Seventh-day Adventism to the I Am movement. Myrtle's spiritual healing provided the link to divinity required by a new religious movement, and Charles's writings provided much of the theology.

Unity holds that proper metaphysical interpretation of the Bible can reveal valuable spiritual truths. For example, Adam represents the movement of mind in relation to the world, whereas Eve is the principle of love and feeling in individual consciousness. Jesus is considered to be the most important individual expression of the Christ idea, but Christ resides in all human beings who love truth, especially in their intelligence, life, love, substance, and strength. Humans are not really separate persons but factors in the cosmic mind. It is wrong to call Jehovah "the Lord," because he is not a being who rules the universe from outside but a divine mind that creates existence and can provide spiritual peace.

The Unity School of Christianity teaches that humans are spiritual beings who can establish right principles of thinking through the spoken words of prayer, denials, and affirmations—like the sentence quoted above that healed Myrtle Fillmore. Right thoughts influence feelings and deeds, thereby shaping the life of the individual. Thus the doctrines and practices of Unity see Christianity in a new light and apply its principles for the practical betterment of human lives.

See also CHRISTIAN SCIENCE; HEALING; NEW AGE SPIRITUALITY; NEW THOUGHT.

BIBLIOGRAPHY

Bach, Marcus. *The Unity Way.* 1982.
Braden, Charles Samuel. *These Also Believe.* 1949.
D'Andrade, Hugh. *Charles Fillmore.* 1975.
Fillmore, Charles. *Metaphysical Bible Dictionary.* 1995.
Simmons, John K. "The Forgotten Contribution of Annie Rix Militz to the Unity School of Christianity." *Nova Religio* 2, no. 1 (October 1998).
Witherspoon, Thomas E. *Myrtle Fillmore, Mother of Unity.* 1977.

William Sims Bainbridge

Upanishads

The Upanishads are a set of philosophical and didactic religious texts from India, the central lessons of which have been regarded by many as presenting some of the most fundamental elements of contemplative and mystical Indian religious sensibilities in general. The Sanskrit word *upaniṣad*—built on the root *ṣad* ("sit") with the prefixes *upa* and *ni* ("nearby")—is consistent with the traditional understanding that these texts originally were lessons given to students sitting at the feet of a learned master. The most influential of the Upanishads were composed in Sanskrit in both verse and prose form between the eighth and the second centuries B.C.E.; lesser-known works of this genre appear as late as the sixteenth century C.E. The major Upanishads have been translated into virtually all of the world's major languages and have become objects of study and sources of inspiration for people around the world.

European readers were introduced to these texts through the translation of fifty Upanishads into Latin by Anquetil Duperron in 1801–1802. They had considerable effect on such nineteenth-century philosophers as Arthur Schopenhauer, who maintained that the Upanishads were "the fruit of the most sublime human knowledge and wisdom." They also came to the attention of American philosophers and writers in the nineteenth century, primarily via various strands of the Idealist, Romantic, and Transcendentalist movements of Germany and England. (The opening lines of Ralph Waldo Emerson's 1857 poem "Brahma" closely paraphrase verses from the *Katha Upanishad*.) Interest in the Upanishads grew in the United States after such events as the visit by the Hindu philosopher-monk Swami Vivekananda, who was an influential participant in the World Parliament of Religions in Chicago in 1893, and by the subsequent founding in 1898 of the Vedanta Society, which was one of the first Hindu-based religious organizations to be established in the United States. Selections from the Upanishads now regularly appear in courses offered by American colleges and universities, and their teachings often guide the spiritual practices of contemporary individuals and groups in the United States influenced by classical Indian thought.

Teachings of the Upanishads

There are many Upanishads, and they all present their own sets of teachings. Nevertheless, there are some core themes that find expression in the Upanishads as a whole. The central lesson of the Upanishads centers on the notion that all of the many and various beings in the constantly changing world are infused with and inwardly supported by a single, subtle, pervasive, powerful, and abiding divine presence that stands as the ultimate and true reality. Because it is the ground of all being, the essence of the absolute abides hidden, as it were, within all beings. A related and key lesson, therefore, is that the subtle essence of the human being is identical to the essence of the single and eternal world soul.

The Upanishads refer to this ultimate reality by several terms. Earlier Upanishads tend to call it *brahman* (hence Emerson's poem "Brahma") or *atman*. Brahman applies more typically to the pervasive nature of the godhead (the word literally means "expansive, powerful, great"). Atman refers to the presence of the absolute at the deepest level of one's being (*atman* literally means "self"). The two terms often appear in translations as Brahman and Atman, capitalized to mark the ultimacy of the unitary world soul.

Some of the later Upanishads teach that this Brahman or Atman is actually God, who resides deep within the heart of all beings. These theistic Upanishads variously identify God as Shiva ("the benevolent one"), Vishnu ("the pervasive one"), or the universal Goddess, the latter known by a number of names.

No matter what it is called, the ultimate ground of all existence is said by the Upanishads to be unified and indivisible. It is the "inner guide," "hidden mover," and "finest essence" of all things. The *Chāndogya Upanishad* repeatedly proclaims *tat tvam asi*, "thou art that"—the "that" here referring to the world soul and the "thou" referring to one's truest self, the self that is Atman. Similarly, the *Chāndogya Upanishad* declares that "the whole world is Brahman," while the *Bṛhadāraṇyaka Upanishad* notes that "Truly, the Brahman is this Atman" and leads the seeker to realize "I am Brahman."

These four lessons—"thou art that," "the whole world is Brahman," "the Brahman is this Atman," and "I am Brahman"—form what tradition has come to call the *mahāvakyas*, the "great teachings" of the Upanishads. The *Katha Upanishad* notes that when one realizes the identity of inner self with the world soul, then one "is released from the jaws of death."

Upanishadic perspectives find succinct expression in these verses from the *Īśa Upanishad*:

[The divine Self] moves. It moves not.
It is far. It is near.
It is within all things,
    and yet it is outside all.
One who regards all beings
    as within the Self
and the Self as within all beings
    never turns away from him.
For one in whom all beings have become
    none other than the Self of the knower:
then what delusion, or what sorrow
    can possibly befall that one who sees the unity!

The Upanishads admit the difficulty of knowing an ultimate reality that is not defined or limited by time, space, and the particularities of personality. The *Katha Upanishad* describes the path leading to this knowledge as "like a razor's edge." (The British writer Somerset Maugham drew on this phrase for the title of his 1944 novel *The Razor's Edge*, about a doctor's spiritual search.) The Upanishads hold that this eternal, divine presence within can be known through attentive listening to teachings given by one who has fully realized the identity of Brahman and Atman; through sustained contemplation of the deeper, inner dimensions of one's life; and through the spiritual practice of meditation. That the reverential turn inward to find the divine presence within through meditation is an important and effective spiritual practice is represented in the *Śvetāśvatara Upanishad:*

> Those who were skilled in the practice of meditation
> saw the autonomous power of the divine,
> hidden within its own qualities. . . .
> The eternal one that rests in the Self should be known;
> for, truly, there is nothing higher than this to be known.
>   . . .
> Just as the form of fire is not visible when latent in its
>   source,
> but may be found over and over again by use of friction,
> so . . . by practicing meditation one may see the divine,
> hidden, as it were. . . .
> Holding one's body steady,
> and bringing the senses and the mind into the heart,
> one should practice meditation.

Upanishadic views in general recognize the value of the heart as the seat of the soul and abode of the divine presence that similarly dwells within all things, so it is to their hearts that the sages taught their disciples to turn. Indeed, to reach the true heart, and thus the divine self that dwells therein, is said to embrace all that exists. The *Chāndogya Upanishad* encourages seekers to remember:

> Truly, as far as the space of this [universe] extends,
> that far extends the space within the heart.
> Within it are held both heaven and earth,
> both fire and air, sun and moon, lightning and the stars.
> Whatever of him there is, and whatever there is not
> all of that is held within the heart.

See also BHAGAVAD-GĪTĀ; GOD; GODDESS; HINDUISM; MYSTICISM; VEDANTA SOCIETY; VEDAS.

BIBLIOGRAPHY

Hume, Robert E. *The Thirteen Principal Upanishads.* 2nd ed., rev. 1931.

Mascaró, Juan. *The Upanishads.* 1965.

Olivelle, Patrick. *Upanisads.* 1996.

Prabhavananda, Swami, and Frederick Manchester. *The Upanishads: Breath of the Eternal.* 1990.

Pye, Michael. "Upanishads." In *The Encyclopedia of Religion.* edited by Mircea Eliade. Vol. 15, pp. 147–152. 1987.

Radhakrishnan, S. *The Principal Upanishads.* Repr. ed. 1978.

William K. Mahony

V

Vatican

The Vatican is the organizational center of the transnational Roman Catholic Church and is the official residence of the pope and the various congregations and committees of the Roman Curia who are responsible for the theological and administrative governance of the church. Vatican City, where St. Peter's Basilica is located, is an independent, sovereign state surrounded by Rome and has the pope as its monarchical head. The Vatican therefore is independently both a religious and a political locus of authority. Not only does it have national conferences of bishops overseeing its multiple religious and political interests in particular countries, but in addition, as a political/secular power, it also has papal nuncios or ambassadors posted in many countries, including the United States, with whom it has exchanged ambassadors since 1984. It is the Vatican, whether the pope himself and/or its various bureaucratic offices, that determines the official stance of the Catholic Church on the broad array of issues with which the contemporary church is engaged, including questions of doctrine and faith, church rules and procedures, interfaith dialogue, diplomatic initiatives, and public policy positions.

For Catholics, the Vatican (or "Rome") represents the pinnacle of hierarchical authority in the church and symbolizes the historical continuity of the popes as successors to the apostles and to Peter, the first bishop of Rome. Although many Catholics disagree with the stances taken by the Vatican on various doctrinal and political issues, they nonetheless value the

Vatican and the papacy as important public symbols of Catholic unity and of the church's universal presence. In recent decades, the many trips abroad undertaken by Pope John Paul II (elected in 1979), and the expansion of international communications technology (including the establishment of a Vatican website), have made the Vatican a more immediate, visible, accessible presence in people's lives.

Historically, the institutional identity developed by the church can be seen as an expansion of the power of the Vatican. From 1075, when Pope Gregory VII formulated a set of principles asserting the divine source, supremacy, and universality of papal authority, down through the Council of Trent (1545–1563), and to the formal institutionalization of papal infallibility at Vatican I (1869–1870), the church sought to consolidate its interpretive authority over religious and moral questions. Vatican II (1962–1965) affirmed a more collegial understanding of decision-making and of the exercise of authority in the church, giving greater recognition to the voices and experiences of bishops, priests, and laypeople. Nonetheless, the papacy of John Paul II has attempted to reassert the power of the Vatican over the daily lives of Catholics. The Vatican's strategy is mulifaceted. On the one hand, it has curtailed the autonomy of national conferences of Catholic bishops to issue pastoral letters discussing moral issues (e.g., homosexuality) or political questions, and reminded theologians of their subordination to church officials. It has also reaffirmed the sinfulness of nonmarital sexual relations, artificial contraception, and abortion, and has stressed

Native Americans attending ceremonies at St. Peter's Basilica, Vatican City, in January 1981, for the canonization of Kateri Tekakwitha, the first North American Indian to be canonized by the Roman Catholic Church.   (Credit: CORBIS/Vittoriano Rastelli.)

the obligation of Catholics to accept papal decisions pertaining to the church (e.g., the ban on women's ordination).

At the same time as the Vatican has become more assertive in defining the boundaries of Catholic identity (but not necessarily influencing Catholic behavior), it has also engaged in actions that have focused renewed attention on the church's geopolitical power. The Vatican has used church resources and the personal charisma and global popularity of Pope John Paul II to advance pro-democratic political movements, most notably in Poland and more recently in Cuba. Because of its unique status as a "universal" church, the Vatican is able to articulate a moral voice that transcends the national or sectoral interests of any one country. Therefore, its vision of the common

good, when applied to specific issues, frequently puts it at odds with national governments that otherwise would see it as an ally. Relations between the American government and the Vatican are a case in point. While the Vatican pushes for the expansion of democracy, it simultaneously challenges military and economic policies that demean the dignity of individuals and societies. Thus, for example, contrary to American foreign policy, the Vatican opposes economic sanctions against Cuba and Iraq, notwithstanding its opposition to the political repression in those countries. Equally contentious are the Vatican's active participation in debates over global population policy and its opposition to legislation initiatives it regards as encouraging abortion.

The moral ideology that underpins both the Vatican's political engagement and its articulation of Catholic identity can perhaps be understood best from the "culture of life" thesis explicated by John Paul II (1995). In essence, the church subscribes to a universal "ethic of care" that values the sanctity of all life (from conception to death) and thus rejects any form of social, economic, or cultural discrimination. This ethic underpins the Vatican's opposition to abortion, euthanasia, and the death penalty, and its advocacy of social welfare, health care, and economic policies that seek to limit the negative effects of socioeconomic inequality on people's lives. It is the multiplicity of strands within the church's "culture of life" ideology that allows conservative and liberal Catholics alike to remain loyal to Rome while disagreeing with different aspects of its ethical stance. Whereas many liberal American Catholics reject the Vatican's position on sexuality or abortion and applaud its stance on social justice, conservative Catholics may reject the Vatican's opposition to the death penalty while favoring its stance on sexuality.

Many Catholics see a tension between the Vatican's push for the recognition of human rights throughout the world and its affirmation of church policies that discriminate against specific groups (e.g., the ban on women priests). With the dawning of a new millennium, however, there are grounds for new faith in the church's commitment to continue the project of institutional renewal set in place at Vatican II. In anticipation of the twenty-first century, the Vatican has undertaken a program of institutional "examination of conscience." So far this has resulted in the pope's apologizing for anti-Semitism committed by Catholics, denouncing the church's condemnation of Galileo, and investigating abuses committed by church inquisitions. There is thus hope that the Vatican may also revise some of the doctrines that prevent it from being the inclusive, pluralistic church that is necessary if Catholics are to maintain the vibrancy of their communal tradition in the new global society.

See also PAPACY; ROMAN CATHOLICISM; ROME.

BIBLIOGRAPHY

Burns, Gene. *The Frontiers of Catholicism. The Politics of Ideology in a Liberal World.* 1992.

Dillon, Michele. *Catholic Identity: Balancing Reason, Faith, and Power.* 1999.

John Paul II. *Evangelium Vitae: The Gospel of Life.* 1995.

Reese, Thomas. *Inside the Vatican: The Politics and Organization of the Catholic Church.* 1996.

Michele Dillon

Vatican II

French president Charles de Gaulle (1890–1970), not known to shade his own importance, characterized the Second Vatican Council as the greatest event in the twentieth century. If hyperbolic, de Gaulle's appraisal dramatizes that the Council institutionalized religious priorities that, in the long run, can influence millions of consciences and, to varying degrees, penetrate, if not shape, all cultures.

Ecumenical councils are global assemblies of the "college" of bishops from every part of the world, called by and presided over by the reigning pope. Unexpectedly called by the newly elected 260th pope, John XXIII (1958–1963), seventy-seven years old and expected to be a "caretaker" rather than an innovator, the Second Vatican Council (October 11, 1962, to December 8, 1965) was the twenty-first and most "catholic" of all the councils, with, for example, 311 of its 2,625 bishops coming from Africa. (After John's death, Pope Paul VI completed the council.) The council's tone, characterized as "pastoral," was captured by its opening "Message to Humanity." In the difficult aftermath of adaptation and adjustment, this dialogic tone was later found naive by some, especially when in Western nations the council was followed by massive resignations of clergy and nuns, public dissent about requirements for ordination, declining rates of Mass attendance, and several schismatic groups disputing the council's liturgical reforms by claiming the sole validity of the Latin Mass they declared as an irreplaceable guarantor of Catholicism's aspiration to universality, unchanging truth, and powerful evocation of the transcendent.

An evenhanded reading of council documents shows both the council's inevitable compromises, resulting from different models of the church, and its prescient critical tone toward major world trends. Its document "The Church in The Modern World" con-

demns nuclear weapons and growing global inequalities. The council's deepening of Roman Catholicism's self-understanding as a universal world religion necessarily involved some jarring and still seminal theological growth in understanding Catholicism's relationships to other religions and to the state. Major documents (e.g., "The Declaration on Religious Liberty" and "The Declaration on the Relationship of the Church to Non-Christian Religions") committed Roman Catholicism to a global defense of human rights and to ecumenical and interfaith dialogue. These council teachings permanently challenge inevitable sociological tendencies toward any focus of Catholic concern on institutional enlargement.

At least in retrospect, it should come as no surprise that the post–Vatican II era has experienced internal controversies over the meaning and range of doctrinal development and the exercise of authority. Vatican I (1869–1870) had declared that the pope cannot err in defining matters of faith and morals, but left unresolved the teaching role of the bishops. In the post–Vatican II era the meanings of "collegiality" (the respective roles and jurisdictions among the papacy, bishops, and regional and national councils of bishops), as well as the council's reflections on moral conscience, are particularly contested. But Catholic memory recalls that serious conciliar reform always produces initial disorientation and internal conflict. Dispute and mixed interpretation have characterized American Catholics' response, given the highly individualistic religious climate of the United States in the years since the Council convened.

See also CHURCH; CHURCH AND STATE; ECUMENICAL MOVEMENT; HUMAN RIGHTS; PAPACY; RELIGIOUS STUDIES; ROMAN CATHOLICISM; VATICAN.

BIBLIOGRAPHY

Abbott, W. M., S.J. *The Documents of Vatican II.* 1966.

Alberigo, G., and J. A. Komanchak. *History of Vatican II.* Vols. 1 and 2. 1998.

Hastings, A. *Modern Catholicism: Vatican II and After.* 1991.

Stacpoole, A., O.S.B. *Vatican II Revisited.* 1986.

James R. Kelly

Vedanta Society

The first Vedanta society was established in New York City by Swami Vivekananda in 1894. In subsequent decades additional Vedanta societies were launched in San Francisco, Chicago, Boston, Los Angeles, Providence, Saint Louis, Seattle, and Portland, Oregon, among other cities. Established in the United States to support the work of the India-based Ramakrishna movement, these societies have played and continue to play a key role in the introduction of Hinduism in the West.

Historically, the Ramakrishna movement's success in establishing Vedanta societies in the United States marked a radical departure from traditional Hindu practice. Throughout most of its history, Hinduism has passed down its teachings from generation to generation, not through the promulgation of official creeds or the founding of organized societies, but by individual transmission from teacher to disciple. However, Swami Vivekananda accepted the need for organization to support his work, following his decision to remain in the United States to lecture after the 1893 Parliament of Religions. As a spiritual teacher and monk, he was quite relieved to turn over the scheduling of his lectures and the handling of travel arrangements and financial matters to the newly founded New York Vedanta Society. From the first, a policy was adopted of splitting the work of the Vedanta societies, with the Indian swamis given responsibility for the movement's spiritual teachings and the board of each Vedanta society assigned responsibility for finances and support activities.

Questions concerning the nature and extent of Indian authority over the American societies have at times arisen. Though each Vedanta society has tended to operate autonomously, the Ramakrishna Matha (monastery) and Mission, based in Calcutta, has always asserted the right to select the resident swamis and to oversee the spiritual teachings promulgated in American centers. In the 1990s the Indian headquarters moved to increase control over the American societies. On occasion, this move has led to dissent and even secession, as in the separation of the Boston Vedanta Society and its Los Angeles affiliate following the death of Swami Paramananda in 1940.

Typically, a Vedanta society fills several roles, providing a home for the resident swami as well as serving as a center of the Ramakrishna movement's religious activities. In larger centers, American devotees may live in the society quarters. Unlike other Hindu movements—such as the Self-Realization Fellowship and transcendental meditation, which have aggressively propagated their teachings through advertising and other channels—the Vedanta societies have consistently rejected such methods, preferring to promote their message through word-of-mouth reports and the sale of books. As the century ended, the societies increasingly interacted with outside religious groups, frequently participating in interreligious conferences. While the adoption of Sunday services, emphasis on

a broad philosophical message, and acceptance of organization suggest significant accommodations to the West, the Vedanta societies remain quite Indian in their continued reliance on Indian-born swamis and control from the Belur Matha in Calcutta.

See also HINDUISM; RAMAKRISHNA MOVEMENT; SELF-REALIZATION FELLOWSHIP; TRANSCENDENTAL MEDITATION.

BIBLIOGRAPHY

Jackson, Carl T. *Vedanta for the West: The Ramakrishna Movement in the United States.* 1994.

Kaushal, Radley Shyam. *The Philosophy of the Vedanta: A Modern Perspective.* 1994.

Carl T. Jackson

Vedas

The Vedas are the ancient sacred scripture of India, known as *sruti,* "that which is heard." Though "seen" rather than heard in the ecstatic visions of the early sages who first sang these hymns, they have been transmitted orally from teacher to student for thousands of years. With intensive complex techniques of memorization unparalleled anywhere, practitioners could memorize by heart thousands of lines of text. On the basis of archaeological evidence and interpretation of the texts, most scholars date the Vedas to approximately 1500 B.C.E. However it should be noted that an intense debate has raged for the last several years, with some partisans giving dates as early as 5000 or even 7000 B.C.E. In any case, traditional medieval Indian scholarship instituted an exegetical trend asserting the timelessness of the Vedas. These books are authorless (*apaurusheya*); they do not come from any human hand or mouth, but rather at the dawn of each new cycle of the world, they reappear as the primordial wisdom to be "heard."

There are four major books of the Vedas, the Rg Veda, with 1026 hymns, songs sung to the gods in the sacrifice; the Yajur Veda, which deals especially with the Vedic fire ritual; the Sāma Veda, consisting mostly of hymns taken from the Rig Veda, but elaborately sung to a scale of seven notes rather than the three notes used for other Vedic recitation; and the Atharva Veda, the Veda associated with the sorcerer Angiras, abounding in magic incantations for a host of mundane concerns, such as luring away the poison from a snakebite, warding away miscarriage, bewitching the boy next door to fall in love, reversing someone else's magic spell, and so on.

A gilded sculpture of the elephant-headed Hindu deity Ganeśa stands on the grounds of the Festival of India in Middlesex County, New Jersey, ca. 1996. (Credit: CORBIS/Kelly-Mooney Photography.)

Each of these four Vedas chronologically subdivides into four sections of three types. The Brahmana portions explain the ritual. The Aaranyaka portions are transitional texts of philosophical and mystical speculation; and the Upanishads, known as Vedanta, the end of the Vedas, both chronologically and teleologically, speak of secret mystical teachings—the oneness that pervades the whole and the secret parallels between the cosmos and the human body.

What role do the Vedas play in contemporary American culture? The first murmurings were heard in the wake of nineteenth-century American enthusiasm for the mysticism of the Upanishads, which filtered into American culture via the writings of authors like Walt Whitman and Ralph Waldo Emerson. For their American readers, these mystical teachings opened a world unseen, a mystic unity with all of life, a diffuse mysticism—the "oceanic feeling" that Freud found so distasteful. In fact, *Leaves of Grass*, with its

celebratory catalogue of life, in many ways echoes the Black Yajur Veda piece Camakam, extremely popular in India even today, where the poet sings a celebratory catalogue of nature and the human body, of leaves and streams, the rocky pathway and the easy one, the eddying whirlpool and the eye, speech, the ear, the mind—all embraced within himself. The metaphor underlying this diffuse mysticism is especially the image of dissolving, as in the Chandogya Upanishad (6.13.1–3), where salt dissolves in water to be everywhere present, on all sides, but nowhere discretely seen.

Eventually, and especially pronounced in the 1960s, this diffuse and transcendent mysticism solidified itself in American consciousness in the pervasive image of the meditating yogi, scarcely clad and complete with long beard and an otherworldly mysticism, challenging what was felt as the West's materialist obsession. Probably the best representative of this Vedantic mystic ascetic is Maharishi Mahesh Yogi, made famous by the Beatles. He founded a popular movement that swept across the nation in the early 1970s, and his Veda is the mystic counterpoint to the science of the modern Western world; his Maharishi Vedic University offers not only courses on management and the sciences, but also courses like Validation of Experiences of Higher States of Consciousness through the Vedic Literature and Modern Scientific Research. The Vedantic perspective here follows the exegesis of medieval schools like Shankara's Advaita Vedanta, where the world is illusory, a transient and incoherent toy that Maya, the inexpressible power of illusion, creates.

Salvation lies in transcendence of the vicissitudes of this impermanent world. This presentation of the Vedas is most prominent in America, found in institutions like the Vedanta society and the Ramakrishna Mission (despite the fact that its eponymous founder himself embraced a tantric this-worldly devotion to the goddess Kali), to Dayananda Saraswati in Pennsylvania, to the Rishikesh-based Shivananda and his disciples, Satchidananda, Vishnudevananda, and especially the late charismatic Chinmayananda, an ex-reporter who had a transformative experience after meeting his guru Shivananda, and who drew crowds of thousands of students to talks at universities across the United States—and also to lesser known teachers, like Acarya Peter, of German extraction, who teaches to a dedicated flock outside Washington, D.C. More recently, beginning in the later 1980s newer apostles of a Vedantic mysticism have begun to germinate in the American landscape, from the South Indian "hugging saint" Ammachi to a host of American-born teachers like Gangaji and Andrew Cohen, who, after "getting" the message of the *Chāndogya Upanishad,* the great statement "you are that!" (*Chāndogya* 6.5.1ff), returned from India to spread the message to wisdom-hungry America.

Whether a notion of the illusory maya of the world is really espoused by Vedic texts, and particularly by the circa-sixth-century Vedanta, is debatable. But it should be added that at least since the charismatic teacher of the eighth century C.E., Shankara, an asceticism stressing the illusoriness of the world has been a prominent indigenous interpretation of the late Vedic literature. We can also spy a Vedantic perspective on the world seeping into the New Age movement with writers like Ken Wilber embracing the timeless mysticism of Shankara's Upanishads as embodied in the twentieth century mystic Ramana Maharshi. The book he would take, if stranded on a desert island, would be *Talks with Ramana Maharshi* (*One Taste*, 1999).

The New Age has gravitated toward the Vedas in another way also, in a practical this-wordly say, via a growing interest in what is traditionally known as Vedanga, the "limbs of the Veda." This includes especially Ayurveda, an indigenous medical system of India especially using herbs in treatment; and in jyotisha, Vedic astrology. Both have become quite popular in New Age circles, and Ayurvedic books on healing, like those of Deepak Chopra, are beginning to edge into the mainstream.

Finally we need to consider the impact of the Vedas on a newer section of America's population. Beginning with the great "brain drain" in the mid-1960s, numbers of well-educated Indians began migrating to the United States, especially in the computer software industry. And these immigrants have imported their religious traditions by building temples (mathas) in pockets of the United States like the Venkateshara Temple in Pittsburgh and its satellite in Chicago and especially the Srngeri Matha in Pennsylvania, which incorporates the traditional Vedic recitation of its namesake in India. In many of these temples and especially those with South Indian affiliation, a traditional Vedic recitation is included as part of the liturgy. These are just a few notable examples of a burgeoning phenomenon in the United States, one that is beginning to be recognized as a part of the American religious landscape, as evidenced by the fact that President Bill Clinton recently attended the inauguration of a new South Indian temple to the god Murugan.

See also BHAGAVAD GĪTĀ; HINDUISM; MYSTICISM; NEW AGE SPIRITUALITY; RAMAKRISHNA MOVEMENT; RELIGIOUS EXPERIENCE; VEDANTA SOCIETY.

BIBLIOGRAPHY

Isherwood, Christopher, ed. *Vedanta for the Western World*. 1945.

Jamison, S. W. *Ravenous Hyenas and the Wounded Sun: Myth and Ritual in Ancient India*. 1991.

Olivelle, Patrick. *Upanishads*. 1996.

Staal, J. F. *Agni: The Vedic Fire Ritual of the Fire Altar*. 2 vols. 1983.

Loriliai Biernacki

Vegetarianism

For millennia, abstaining from animal flesh has been an aspect of a variety of religions. However, the word "vegetarianism"—to describe a self-conscious diet of grains, vegetables, fruits, nuts, and seeds, with or without eggs and dairy products—is only 150 years old. Since the 1960s, the substantial growth of vegetarianism has been related to the emergence of new religious movements or the discovery and reclamation of established religious practices that highlight vegetarianism. Traditionally, religious reasons for adopting vegetarianism include asceticism; belief in reincarnation; respect for all beings; a belief that meat-eating causes "heaviness" in the body, impeding one's spirituality; and an ethic of nonviolence.

The idea of *ahimsā* (nonviolence) influences the practice of vegetarianism in Jainism, Buddhism, and Hinduism. Only Jainism requires it as a practice, but it has been followed extensively by Buddhists and to a more limited degree by Hindus. Many Americans, influenced by the example of Mahatma Gandhi's life, embraced vegetarianism. Others, influenced by the music of the Beatles and George Harrison, gravitated to Hinduism and in its law of karma found a motivation for vegetarianism. Recent interest in Yoga has fostered vegetarianism as well. Besides serving vegetarian foods, Yoga centers may promote vegetarianism as essential to the practice of Yoga because texts such as Patanjali's *Yoga Sutras* recommend ahimsā.

Distinctly American religious groups took a different route to vegetarianism. For example, the Seventh-day Adventists were influenced by the nineteenth-century American health movement. When Ellen G. White revealed that she had received a divine message extolling vegetarianism, she set in motion the development not only of a religious tradition of abstinence (approximately 50 percent of current Seventh-day Adventists are vegetarian) but also vegetarian food industries, whose products—meat analogues—are now widely available. Other American influences on the growth of vegetarianism include the anti–Vietnam War movement of the 1960s (some antiwar activists began to regard eating meat as a form of carnage); Dick Gregory's activism (which incorporated vegetarianism into the civil rights movement's nonviolent

Dishes of vegetarian Indian food arranged on a table.   (Credit: © Felicia Martinez/PhotoEdit/PNI.)

ethics); the emergence of a feminist spirituality movement in the 1970s (featuring vegetarian and ecofeminist sensibility); a concern about world hunger (galvanized by Frances Moore Lappe's 1971 book *Diet for a Small Planet*); and the 1990s straight-edge music scene, which actively promotes veganism (a totally vegetarian diet). Each of these demonstrated the interweaving of the political and spiritual in fostering a new dietary ethic.

Finally, spiritually motivated vegetarianism has included revisiting established religions such as Christianity and Judaism and rediscovering their vegetarian elements. In the numerous books they have written on the topic since the 1960s, Jewish and Christian vegetarians argue that their traditions require abstention from meat, pointing to Genesis 1:29 and other biblical sources that show that vegetarianism is the ideal state.

American exposure to vegetarianism has often occurred through vegetarian restaurants run by religiously associated groups such as the International Society for Krishna Consciousness, Yogi Bhajau's Healthy-Happy-Holy (3HO) organization, Buddhist societies, Seventh-day Adventists, and other Christians (one restaurant was simply called Genesis 1:29), as well as "Buddha's Delight," a staple in Chinese restaurants. In addition, health concerns, environmental issues, the existence of "factory farms"—which have industrialized the rearing of animals for their flesh—and the 1987 book that highlighted these issues, John Robbins's *Diet for a New America,* have been credited with the growth in the number of vegetarians. During the 1990s, these reasons for vegetarianism have prompted reactions against many formal religions that are viewed as conservative and regressive about vegetarianism. Instead, for many individuals, vegetarianism and veganism may displace an established religion in that they feature their own forms of conversion, revealed experience, and mores.

See also BUDDHISM; ECOFEMINISM; ECOSPIRITUALITY; FOOD; HEALTH; HINDUISM; INTERNATIONAL SOCIETY FOR KRISHNA CONSCIOUSNESS; JAINISM; MACROBIOTICS; NEW RELIGIOUS MOVEMENTS; SEVENTH-DAY ADVENTISM; YOGA.

BIBLIOGRAPHY

Adams, Carol J. *The Sexual Politics of Meat: A Feminist-Vegetarian Critical Theory.* 1990.

Chapple, Christopher Key. *Nonviolence to Animals, Earth, and Self in Asian Traditions.* 1993.

Rowe, Martin, ed. *The Way of Compassion: Survival Strategies for a World in Crisis.* 1999.

Spencer, Colin. *The Heretic's Feast: A History of Vegetarianism.* 1996.

Walters, Kerry S., and Lisa Portmess, eds. *Religious Vegetarianism from the Buddha to the Dalai Lama.* 1999.

Carol J. Adams

Vestments.

See Clothing, Religious.

Via Crucis.

See Stations of the Cross.

Vineyard Christian Fellowship

The Association of Vineyard Churches, or Vineyard Christian Fellowship, is a young denomination with roots in the Jesus movement of the 1960s. Its theological roots are evangelical, stressing a personal relationship with Jesus. The Vineyard seeks to combine the practical aspects of Evangelicalism with the supernatural characteristics of Pentecostalism. The Vineyard's emphasis on the spiritual gifts of healing and prophecy may lead to the characterization of this church as a Pentecostal denomination. Where it differs from classical pentecostal denominations, however, is that the Vineyard does not place the same emphasis on baptism in the Holy Spirit as evidence of sanctification and on speaking in tongues as the initial evidence of that baptism. The characterization of the Vineyard as anti-establishment in policy, therapeutic in ministry, and highly individualistic make it one of the fastest-growing Protestant denominations in the U.S. and abroad.

The Vineyard was, and to some extent still is, symbolized by its first leader, the late John Wimber. Wimber was an aspiring musician in the early 1960s when he had a conversion experience. In 1974 Wimber and his wife, Carol, became active members of a Friends (Quaker) church in Yorba Linda, California. The Wimbers and other future Vineyard pioneers met for Bible study and prayed for the sick. Sensing that their charismatic style of worship would not be accepted at the Friends church, the Wimbers left and joined Calvary Chapel.

Meanwhile, in 1974, a Jesus movement convert named Kenn Gulliksen started a church in West Los Angeles called the Vineyard; he "planted" seven more over the next eight years. In 1982 Wimber, then head of Calvary Chapel Yorba Linda, left the church following a disagreement over the overtly charismatic nature of worship at his church. Wimber joined Gulliksen's Vineyard, and in 1982 the Vineyard Christian Fellowship celebrated its first meeting. The growth of the Vineyard overwhelmed Gulliksen, who relinquished the leadership to Wimber.

In its short seventeen-year history, the Vineyard Christian Fellowship has experienced its share of controversies. The best-known occurred in 1994, when the Toronto Airport Vineyard church in Canada experienced charismatic manifestations as part of the "Toronto Blessing," with church attendants laughing and barking along with experiencing more traditional charismatic manifestations, such as prophetic utterances and healing. Worried Vineyard leaders did not view the animal-like manifestations as biblical. In 1996 the Toronto Airport Vineyard and the Association of Vineyard Churches split.

The Association of Vineyard Churches experienced perhaps its biggest loss in 1997 with the passing of its founder, Wimber. Plagued with serious health problems, Wimber stepped down as the senior pastor of the Anaheim Vineyard in 1995. In November 1997 Wimber died, leaving Todd Hunter as national director. The post-Wimber transition proceeds as the church continues growing, to more than six hundred churches worldwide.

See also DENOMINATION; EVANGELICAL CHRISTIANITY; HEALING; JESUS MOVEMENT; LITURGY AND WORSHIP; NEW RELIGIOUS MOVEMENTS; PENTECOSTAL AND CHARISMATIC CHRISTIANITY; TORONTO BLESSING.

BIBLIOGRAPHY

Miller, Donald E. *Reinventing American Protestantism: Christianity in the New Millennium.* 1997.

Wimber, John. *Power Evangelism.* 1986.

Arlene M. Sánchez Walsh

Virgin of Guadalupe

Devotion to the Virgin of Guadalupe among Mexican-American Roman Catholics in the United States has its origin in a legendary apparition at Tepeyac, a hill northwest of Mexico City that had been sacred to the Aztec goddess Tonantsi. According to pious tradition, on December 9, 1531, a poor Indian named Juan Diego was on his way to Mass when he encountered a

A procession of believers, carrying a banner honoring the Virgin of Guadalupe, heads toward a shrine in Watsonville, California, on June 17, 1999. (Credit: AP/Wide World Photos.)

beautiful woman who identified herself as the Virgin Mary. She instructed him to go to the Franciscan bishop of Mexico City, Juan de Zumárraga, and tell him that she wanted a church built for her there. After several audiences with Juan Diego, the bishop told him to ask the Virgin for a sign, and so three days after her first appearance, the Virgin filled Juan Diego's *tilma* (cape) with out-of-season Castilian roses. When the Indian opened his cape in the presence of the bishop, the roses tumbled out and miraculously imprinted on the tilma was the image now known as Our Lady of Guadalupe, a "dark Virgin" understood to have the complexion of the Indians to whom she had come. The

tilma is preserved in a basilica built especially for it at the foot of Tepeyac, and some ten million pilgrims come annually to Mexico City to view it.

In the ensuing centuries, Our Lady of Guadalupe became a symbol of Mexican culture. Her image often graced the banners of those struggling for Mexican independence, and she has been understood by many devotees to side with oppressed and poor people. Mexican immigrants to the United States brought with them their devotion to her—privately and affectionately called La Morenita (Little Darkling)—and have helped to perpetuate her identification with the downtrodden. In the 1960s, for example, Mexican-American farmworkers in the southwestern United States placed her image on their placards when they marched for economic rights. Because the symbolism of her belt is understood to mean that she is pregnant, Our Lady of Guadalupe has become a powerful emblem for many Roman Catholics opposed to abortion, and her image is often prominently displayed in antiabortion demonstrations. Despite her presumed identification with the oppressed, some recent writers, theologians, and artists have observed that the history of her devotion is more complicated and that her devotees also include conquerors and members of the elite. They have noted, for example, the connection between Our Lady of Guadalupe and the machismo of Mexican culture and have criticized devotion to her as contributing to and perpetuating the oppression of women. Others have found her connection with the ancient Aztec goddesses to be empowering and venerate her as a powerful Mother goddess. The essays collected in *Goddess of the Americas: Writings on the Virgin of Guadalupe* (1996) indicate the range of devotional attitudes toward Our Lady of Guadalupe among late-twentieth-century Roman Catholics. The feast of Our Lady of Guadalupe is celebrated on December 12.

See also MARIAN DEVOTIONS; MARY; PATRON SAINTS AND PATRON-SAINT FEASTS; PILGRIMAGE; RELIC.

BIBLIOGRAPHY

Castillo, Ana, ed. *Goddess of the Americas: Writings on the Virgin of Guadalupe.* 1996.
Lafaye, Jacques. *Quetzalcóatl and Guadalupe.* 1976.
Rodriguez, Jeanette. *Our Lady of Guadalupe: Faith and Empowerment Among Mexican-American Women.* 1994.
Wolf, Eric R. "The Virgin of Guadalupe: A Mexican National Symbol." In *Reader in Comparative Religion: An Anthropological Approach,* edited by William A. Lessa and Evon Z. Vogt. 1968.

Sandra L. Zimdars-Swartz

Visionary

"Visionary" is a term used in a broad as well as a narrow sense. In its broader reference it may mean a leader who has ideals of the future that reach beyond what the ordinary person can imagine. For example, Martin Luther King, Jr., might be called a "visionary" because he held forth an ideal of an interracial community that transcended the boundaries of ethnicity, race, and class. This is a special example because, in his most famous speech, King spoke as if he had indeed seen a "vision" when he said, "I have been to the mountaintop and I have seen the Promised Land" of interracial harmony. Whether he had indeed "seen" such a vision, or whether he was speaking only metaphorically, is not clear; normally such comments are taken in a nonliteral sense. Thus it is common to speak of a "visionary" leader if the person is highly idealistic, "visionary" art or poetry if the artist uses unusual and vivid imagery, and even "visionary" corporate structure if the overall purpose takes priority over practical logistics.

However, in the narrower meaning of the term "visionary," King's statement would be taken literally. "I have seen" would mean that the individual had experienced a visual image of what he was about to describe. The visionary in this sense is a person who, usually in an altered state of consciousness, has images that are believed to provide information beyond what is available to the senses. Such images are not accessible to others at the same place and time. They are usually described as being highly condensed and vivid, often described as beautiful and awesome, yet to the person experiencing them they are clearly packed with meaning.

Visionaries of this sort are attested to at least as far back as biblical times in the West. The Bible reports that Moses was shown a vision of how the desert tabernacle should be built; and other prophetic writings, such as Isaiah and Ezekiel, report that the prophet saw visions along with verbal messages from God. In Eastern traditions it appears that visions were sometimes translated into art; the famous Tibetan *thangkas* are probably based on visions that occurred during meditative trances.

From an exterior point of view, visions may appear to be like hallucinations; thus the psychiatrist Carl Jung found structural and imagistic similarities between what schizophrenics saw and the visionary art of Eastern traditions that he was studying. However, visionaries experience their visions as given with a meaning. Sometimes the visionary interprets the images later, when not actually experiencing the vision; sometimes the interpretation is said to be conveyed along with the vision. In some cases, visions are combined with elaborate verbal explanation known as "channeling." In this experience some agency, claimed to be beyond the personality of the individual visionary, states the meaning of the vision. In this way, visions are similar to certain dream experiences, in which the dreamer feels certain that the dream has a meaning even though it is not immediately apparent. However, visionaries usually can elucidate a meaning for their experiences.

Visions may serve as inspiration on an individual's personal path, as was the case with many medieval mystics. A visionary may also draw larger conclusions from his or her visions. For example, Ellen G. White, cofounder of the Seventh-day Adventists, claimed that she received information in a trance state that she said told her about events in the heavenly realms. White was a follower of William Miller, who had predicted the end of the world in 1843 or 1844. When the promised end failed to materialize, White claimed to have "seen" a transformation that occurred, not on Earth, but in the heavenly realms, in which the curtain of the heavenly tabernacle was torn. From this she concluded that indeed an event had taken place that was changing the direction of the world, even though it was not visible on Earth. Other visionaries who head religious groups may receive images as instructions. One woman reported seeing a finger pointing on a map, guiding her to the location where she should reestablish her religious movement.

Another common form of vision is that reported by certain individuals after the death of a loved one, either a family member or a close friend, when the deceased is seen in a waking vision. The person experiencing this is not normally considered a visionary, however, unless this experience inaugurates a series of subsequent experiences of similar type.

In recent times, New Age teachers have cultivated visions for a variety of purposes. Many examples could be given, but these will indicate the range: Michael Katz, a visionary in Portland, Oregon, practiced meditations during which he received elaborate and colorful visions together with an understanding of how gemstones could be used for healing. Psychologist Judith Orloff has held that visionary capacities can be cultivated along with other psychic abilities and that they are therapeutic in their effects. Carolyn Myss, an intuitive diagnostician who felt she was able to "see" a person's disease, believes that visions are among a variety of intuitive capacities that can appear in individuals. Others have argued, however, that visions taken alone, outside the discipline of a spiritual path, may be manifestations of mental illness.

Most common in New Age culture is the association of vision and visionaries with unusual capabilities in dreaming. For example, Connie Kaplan, a visionary in Santa Monica, California, had reportedly for many years experienced uncommonly complex and vivid dreams. After attending a Native American sun dance ritual, she had her first waking vision. Other waking visions followed, including angels, people who taught her, and colors with special meanings, through which she was able to help individuals understand their deeper purpose in life. Many individuals associated with Native American traditions have incorporated Native American ideas about visions, visionaries, and dreaming into their New Age teachings.

See also CHANNELING; DREAMS; MEDITATION; MYSTICISM; NATIVE AMERICAN RELIGIONS; NEW AGE SPIRI-TUALITY; PARANORMAL; PSYCHIC; SPIRITUALITY; SUN DANCE; VISION QUEST; VISUALIZATION.

BIBLIOGRAPHY

Kaplan, Connie Cockrell. *A Woman's Book of Dreams: Dreaming as a Spiritual Practice.* 1999.

Katz, Michael. *Gemisphere Luminary.* 1994.

Moody, Raymond, M.D., and Paul Perry. *Reunions: Visionary Encounters with Departed Loved Ones.* 1994.

Orloff, Judith. *Second Sight.* 1996.

Tamar Frankiel

Vision Quest

The term "vision quest" has typically been used to describe a Plains Indian ritual. Among Native American tribes of the Plains culture area, an adolescent boy's (and sometimes a girl's) initiation involved going into the wilderness alone, and fasting and praying for a few days until a specific kind of dream or (waking) vision occurred. In a typical quest, the seeker would pray to the Creator and invoke the forces of the cosmos—the "brothers" and "sisters" who are the forces of nature and the denizens of animal and plant worlds. Often, with fasting and prayer, the person's senses would become very acute. Then he or she would receive, in a dream or a waking state, a visit from a figure, either animal, human, or spirit, who would offer the adolescent teachings and give a symbol that would serve as an amulet for assistance in waking life. After the vision, the boy or girl would return home and report the dream to a shaman or elder. Assuming that the quest was certified as successful, the figure who appeared in the dream would henceforth be regarded as the young person's spiritual ally, similar to the idea of a guardian angel in Western religions. The symbol—such as a type of bird's feather or a musical instrument—would be worn or carried by the person on all significant occasions.

Recent scholarship has demonstrated that the initiatory quest at adolescence was only one of many forms of vision quest. Spontaneous and voluntary vision quests were also quite common. In a time of distress or crisis, an individual might undertake a fast with the intent of becoming receptive to a vision. Women often received spontaneous visions in times of emotional tension—for example, during times of grief. Certainly, the vision quest was not confined to neophytes but was used by experienced elders as well. Someone more experienced might supervise an individual's quest, but it was not uncommon for the individual to plan, initiate, complete and interpret a vision quest on his or her own.

In addition, more structured forms of vision quest were available, involving many individuals at once. These occurred particularly in ritual preparations for a communal hunt, and in the great sun dance ritual practiced near midsummer by nearly all the peoples of the Plains culture area.

Whatever the circumstances in which the individual sought a vision, the main criterion was that he or she should be able to demonstrate, after receiving a vision, a "gift of power." As indicated above, this would commonly be symbolized by an object offered to the person by the spirit ally, which represented a transfer of power from a more powerful being (the animal or guardian) to the individual in need. Frequently the vision would be acted out by other members of the tribe as a ritual, which would extend and share the power with others.

The imagery of the vision is comparable to, though often far more vivid and complete than, what a person might experience in a dream. Indeed, dreaming is regarded among many North American peoples as a variant form of vision. In contrast to the assumptions of most Western epistemologies, Native American peoples who use vision assume that the world in which we live is only one aspect of a vast cosmic order. Ordinary life is but one slice of an "implicate order," to use physicist David Bohm's term, which we do not ordinarily experience. That larger order is better understood through vision, for it is "enfolded" into the images and events of vision. The beings that one may encounter in a vision—the eagle or the "buffalo woman," for example—represent a concentration of power in one part of the entire cosmos, as a funnel, so to speak, through which larger powers are channeled. Thus, concludes scholar Lee Irwin, vision provides "direct experience of the enfolded order" through encounters with those beings.

Other North American tribes, from the Great Basin area and eastward, also possessed the ritual of a vision quest but did not necessarily require it as part of an adolescent rite of passage. The concept of receiving important symbols and information about allies in dreams or visions was quite widespread beyond the Plains area. In some tribes, shamans used techniques similar to those of the vision quest, although they may not have been commonly used by the rest of the tribe.

In contemporary American culture, some New Age teachers have incorporated the vision quest into a path of self-inquiry and spiritual growth. Teachers of Native American and non-Native American backgrounds have attempted to outline the steps of such a quest. Usually the advice includes some form of isolation from ordinary routines and familiar physical surroundings; fasting (either complete abstinence

from food and water, or at least abstinence from food, for one to four days); and meditation or prayer. The resultant vision, if any, frequently comes in a dream. This is most often interpreted as information about the self and one's path in life. Unlike many Native American visions, it is rarely regarded as a message for the larger collective—one's family, community, or humanity as a whole. The vision quest, as adopted by New Age advocates, has thus become part of a battery of techniques designed to expand consciousness beyond the ordinary, linear method of processing information, and to afford a wider conceptual framework in which to understand one's personal life.

See also Dreams; Fasting; Native American Religions; Nature Religion; New Age Spirituality; Paranormal; Prayer; Psychic; Rites of Passage; Ritual; Shamanism; Spirituality; Sun Dance; Visionary; Visualization.

Bibliography

Dugan, Kathleen. *The Vision Quest of the Plains Indians: Its Spiritual Significance.* 1985.
Foster, Steven, and Meredith Little. *The Book of the Vision Quest: Personal Transformation in the Wilderness.* 1992.
Irwin, Lee. *The Dream Seekers: Native American Visionary Traditions of the Great Plains.* 1994.
Medicine Eagle, Brooke. *Buffalo Woman Comes Singing: The Spirit Song of a Rainbow Medicine Woman.* 1991.

Tamar Frankiel

Visualization

Visualization is the process of holding a mental image (of God, the self, a symbol, a place, or an event) to obtain physical or spiritual transformation (focus of mind, healing, enlightenment, unity with God). In contemporary American religion, visualization is primarily associated with New Age religion and with religious healing. Yet visualization has long been used as a meditative technique in both Eastern and Western religions.

Although the origins of visualization are unclear, it is most widely used in religions that conceive of the divine as immanent in this world and its imagery and that use meditation to become one with or to acquire the powers of that divinity. Many Eastern religions, including those practiced in the United States, fall into this category. Taoists, for example, believe that the human body is a microcosm of the universe and each organ possesses an energy represented by a divinity. By visualizing that deity, the meditator accesses its corresponding energy and thus preserves chi (vital energy), which in turn promotes health and even immortality.

Hindus practice visualization to achieve unity with the divine. Krishna devotees visualize their lord as a lover as they dance and chant his name. Devotees of Shiva visualize his divine consort, Shakti, as a spiral of energy within the body. The practice of kundalini Yoga involves visualizing that energy rising from the base of the spine to the top of the head to unify the meditator's body with that of God. Tantrists visualize a yantra (a geometric diagram that represents an abstract form of a deity) to focus the mind and become one with God.

Although early Buddhist philosophy was nontheistic, seeking to empty the mind of all images, visualization was used as a meditative technique to reduce desires and facilitate concentration. Theravāda Buddhists visualized decaying bodies in a cemetery to help shed desires of the flesh. Later Buddhist schools developed rich pantheons of celestial bodhisattvas and restored visualization as a means of spiritual transformation. Vajrayāna (tantric) Buddhists visualize or elaborate mandalas (visual images of bodhisattvas) or imagine the whole world as filled with Buddhas, not only to assist concentration but also to actualize the Buddha within themselves.

By contrast, when the divine is conceived of as transcendent, as it is in Western religions, reflection on images becomes idolatrous, and locating the divine within may be perceived as heresy. Even within the monotheistic traditions, however, visualization is practiced by mystical sects as a means of achieving ecstatic union with God.

Jewish mystics such the Hasidim or Kabbalists visualize the divine as Shekinah (God's bride) or use various combinations of Hebrew letters that symbolize the divine name. Christian mystics such as Teresa of Avila visualized the union of bride and bridegroom as a representation of the marriage between her soul and Christ. Contemporary Christians may visualize themselves meeting Christ, the Virgin, or other saints, or being bathed in heavenly light. Even in Islam, whose orthodox teaching is most adamant about rejecting imagery, Sufi mystics visualize saints and sacred words to realize oneness with Allah.

American adherents of mysticism and of Eastern religions have long used visualization, but the minority status of these traditions meant that the practice remained obscure. It was the New Age movement that propelled visualization into mainstream attention. This type of visualization uses different images—of the self rather than God—for a different purpose: healing and self-fulfillment rather than union with God.

The shift toward New Age visualization began in the nineteenth century with the metaphysical movement (Christian Science, Unity), which argued that since we are all perfect reflections of divine mind, illness is an error in thought that can be overcome by visualizing oneself as healthy. Beginning with writers such as Norman Vincent Peale and continuing to more recent authors such as Shakti Gawain, the positive-thinking movement has expanded the desired results of visualization to include emotional satisfaction, creative expression, and financial success. The notion that "you can create your own reality" has also been boosted by scientific research suggesting that visualization could improve athletic performance and recovery from psychological or even physical illness. The counterculture's interest in mysticism and in Eastern religions, as well as subsequent research on the use of meditation to reduce stress, attracted media attention to visualization as a technique of healing and resulted in a host of popular books on the subject. Although the effectiveness of visualization to achieve health is disputed, the technique is now used by a variety of religious groups, including conservative Christians who otherwise reject New Age teachings.

See also CHRISTIAN SCIENCE; HASIDIM; HEALING; KABBALAH; MEDITATION; NEW AGE SPIRITUALITY; PEALE, NORMAN VINCENT; TANTRA; TAOISM; UNITY; YOGA.

BIBLIOGRAPHY

Braden, Charles. *Spirits in Rebellion: The Rise and Development of New Thought.* 1963.

Ellwood, Robert, and Harry Partin. *Religious and Spiritual Groups in Modern America.* 1988.

Gawain, Shakti. *Creative Visualization.* 1979.

McGuire, Meredith. *Ritual Healing in Suburban America.* 1988.

Melton, J. Gordon, Jerome Clark, and Aidan Kelly. *New Age Almanac.* 1991.

Simonton, O. Carl, Carl Simonton, Stephanie Matthews, and James Creighton. *Getting Well Again.* 1978.

Winters, L., and D. Reisberg. "Mental Practice or Mental Preparation: Why Does Imagined Practice Help?" *Journal of Human Movement Studies* 15 (1988): 279–290.

Christel Manning

Vodun (Voodoo)

The transatlantic slave trade removed Africans from their lands, families, and cultures. On the island of Haiti, the Fon people from Dahomey (Benin), and also the Yorubas, Kongos, and others, combined their African beliefs with Catholic lithographs, rites, and practices into a coherent whole. Slaves joined these various religious elements to create a belief system

A Vodun priestess heats the tip of a spear in candlelight, at a ceremony in New Orleans, ca. 1991. (Credit: CORBIS/Philip Gould.)

and worldview that constitute the core of Haitian vodou. The term most commonly used to refer to the religion, "Vodou," derives from the Fon word for "spirit" or "God." More accurate spellings are "Vodoun" or "Vodun." The term "Voodoo," an invention of the West, evokes malevolent notions that are not part of the religion. Vodun practitioners were forced to hide their religious practices and endured long periods of open persecutions and ostracism. Vodunists have finally begun to practice their religion openly since the 1987 Haitian Constitution recognized Vodun as a national religion. The majority of Haitians, who are also Catholic, do not see a contradiction in practicing both religions. Vodun today is practiced not only in Haiti but in Benin, the Dominican Republic, and various Haitian immigrant communities in the United States. Vodun is a comprehensive belief system and aesthetics that provides coherence within both the visible world and the realm of the invisible. It harmonizes the sacred and the profane, the material and the spiritual, and the world of the living with that of

the departed, the ancestors, and the lwa, or spirits. The Vodou ethos or worldview constitutes the basis of the moral system, which regulates behavior, social interactions, and communal duties. Vodun shares a common ethical denominator with other world religions—a strong sense of justice and service, respect for elders, beneficence, forbearance, and humanism. The notion of the unity of all forces of nature is central to Vodun. The connection between the living and the spirits, the Earth, the land, and various bodies of water is important in that all work together to seek balance and to restore harmony and rhythm.

The lwa preside over specific aspects of life and serve as intermediaries between the humans and the absolute supreme being—God, the Gran Met. Some of the most important lwa are Atibon Legba, Marasa Dosou Dosa, Danbala, and Ayida Wedo. Azaka Mede, Ogou Feray, Agwe Tawoyo, Ezili Freda Daome, Lasirenn and Labalenn, and Gede Nimbo; all of these belong to the gentler Rada rite tradition passed down from West Africa. Other important lwa include Met Kalfou, Simbi Andezo, Ezili Danto, and Bawon Samdi, who come from the more intense Petwo rite tradition, which originated in the New World.

During Vodou ceremonies, the lwa possess, or "mount," the devotees to communicate with the living and to answer questions. They deal with the human and spiritual conflicts, antagonisms, oppositions, and lack of harmony that are the source of moral ills and societal imbalance. They intervene in human affairs as they guide, chastise, and praise. They assist with healing and open channels to facilitate the continous flow of energy. With imbalance, things do not flow; they are spoken of as being "tied" or "blocked," which goes against Vodun's dynamic, fluid, and ever-evolving philosophy. Vodun is a very practical religion that is primarily about sustaining life in the community. Its influences range from individual spiritual healing to the survival of the group and communal sustenance. It is grounded in the family and the community and underlies systems of traditional medicine, justice, art, music, education, and cooperative economics. Vodun is not only a belief system and worldview; it is also a way of life and a mode of survival. Thus, for its adherents in the United States, Haiti, and elsewhere, Vodun is present in all aspects of life.

See also AFRICAN-AMERICAN RELIGIONS; AFRO-CUBAN RELIGIONS; ANIMAL SACRIFICE; NATURE RELIGION; SANTERÍA; SPIRIT GUIDES.

BIBLIOGRAPHY

Brown, Karen McCarthy. *Mama Lola: A Voodoo Priestess in Brooklyn.* 1992.

Murphy, Joseph M. *Working the Spirit: Ceremonies of the African Diaspora.* 1994.

Claudine Michel

W

War Memorials

Perhaps more than any other human endeavor, war engenders the passionate commitment to permanently emplace the nature of heroism, the meaning of martial sacrifice, and the ideal of patriotism on the American landscape and in the national consciousness. The term *war memorial* traditionally engenders images of heroic monuments: the Minuteman at Concord Bridge, dedicated on July 4, 1837, the majestic Robert E. Lee monument at Gettysburg, or any one of the thousands of Civil War monuments erected during the feverish memorial activity of the late nineteenth and early twentieth centuries in both the North and South. Or one thinks of the Marine Corps Memorial in northern Virginia, with the iconic image of battle-tested Marines straining to raise the flag on Mount Surabachi. All such monuments are war memorials, but the memorial vocabulary of Americans at war finds expression in many forms besides monuments.

Memorial Day itself, born in reaction to the massive casualties of the Civil War, is part of the American patriotic calendar, a day that seeks to respond to the personal and cultural question regarding the meaning of martial sacrifice. In the realms of art, literature, music, and film, there is a rich history of the struggle to represent war. There are, for example, over one thousand paintings of "Custer's Last Stand," many of them images that, for a considerable time, cemented in culture the heroic image of General George Armstrong Custer and the Christ-like sacrifice of the Seventh Cavalry on the banks of the Little Bighorn in June 1876. Edward Zwick's celebrated 1989 film,

Glory, is a memorial testimony to the Fifty-Fourth Massachusetts Volunteers, made up of black troops and white officers. *Glory* follows the Fifty-Fourth from their formation through their heroic but unsuccessful assault on Fort Wagner, near Charleston, in July 1863. It spurred the formation of black Civil War reenactors, some of them descendants of men who fought with the Fifty-Fourth, and it sought to restore to public consciousness the contributions of black troops to the northern war effort, contributions forgotten almost immediately after the war, when black Americans as history makers were written out of the nation's story.

Relics of war—flags, bullets, swords, uniforms, guns, and cannon, for example—are often treated as sacred artifacts, transformed by their participation in the battles through which the nation took shape. Certainly one of the nation's most sacred artifacts is the USS *Arizona,* sunk during the Japanese attack on Pearl Harbor, December 7, 1941. It is a tomb and a historic site, the center of memory of the Pacific War in American culture.

There are also war memorials that speak not to the drama of war but to the impact of war. The National Museum of American History's exhibition Toward a More Perfect Union, for example, told the story of the internment of Americans of Japanese ancestry during World War II, and the National Park Service has welcomed an internment site, permanently emplacing an uncomfortable memory in our historic consciousness. There are also indigestible memories of the impact of war. The fierce controversy surrounding the ill-fated *Enola Gay* exhibition at the National Air and Space Museum in 1995 demonstrated how a

A soldier guards the Tomb of the Unknown Soldiers in Arlington National Cemetary in Washington, D.C. (Credit: CORBIS/George Lepp.)

museum exhibition can engender controversy when the orthodox, redemptive story of the dropping of the atomic bomb is challenged.

Conspicuous by their presence on the landscape are American battlefields, often the subjects of contestation, as Americans argue passionately over the meaning of these places. Is the Washita the site of a battle or a massacre? How should Americans share the means of memorial production at the Little Bighorn, which is no longer a shrine to Custer and the Seventh Cavalry, but a place where different American stories are told side by side? Should the Angle at Gettysburg be the focus of anniversary ceremonies, or does that particular power point emphasize too much the glory of battle and ignore President Abraham Lincoln's enduring challenge enunciated in the Gettysburg Address?

Martial memorial space extends to American military cemeteries overseas, many of them constructed by the American Battle Monuments Commission founded in 1923, in the midst of controversy about bringing American war dead home to be buried. Many of these have become pilgrimage sites for veterans, their families, and other Americans who, in the age-old manner of pilgrims, wish to make a physical and spiritual journey to a place of power.

A number of significant war memorials have been created in the last two decades of the twentieth-century, a period of intense memorialization. The U.S. Holocaust Museum, which opened in 1993, not only tells the story of the rise of National Socialism and the destruction of Jews and many others, it also portrays the reaction of American GI's to the concentration camps on the western front. It tells a controversial story of the United States as "complicit bystander" to the Holocaust. This significant memory of World War II, told adjacent to the memorial center of the nation, the Mall in Washington, D.C., will soon be augmented by the first national memorial to World War II, scheduled to open on the Mall in the early twenty-first century.

Perhaps the most significant war memorial of the recent past is the Vietnam Veterans Memorial, erected on the Washington Mall in 1982. For some veterans it represents a "black gash of shame." For others, it is a neutral monument that seeks to heal the bitter cultural divisions brought about by the war. Others think that it forgot as much as it remembered and that it transformed Americans into victims of, rather than participants in or co-perpetrators of, the war. Soon those who came transformed the monument into a "people's memorial," taking rubbings of the names on the wall and leaving thousands of items behind, many of which now make up a memorial archive of material culture. And while it is a memorial distinctly different in style from traditional monuments of war, it is a memorial that has provided a site of reconciliation, refuge, and solace for others.

See also HOLOCAUST; JOURNEYS AND JOURNEYING; PILGRIMAGE.

BIBLIOGRAPHY

Hass, Kristin. *Carried to the Wall: American Memory and the Vietnam Veterans Memorial.* 1998.

Marling, Karal Ann, and John Wetenhall. *Iwo Jima: Monuments, Memories, and the American Hero.* 1991.

Linenthal, Edward T. *Sacred Ground: Americans and Their Battlefields.* 2nd ed. 1993.

Piehler, G. Kurt. *Remembering War the American Way.* 1995.

Edward T. Linenthal

Warrior

Down through the ages religion played an important part in warfare: in delineating the conduct of warriors, the role of the warrior, and the justifications for war. The interaction of religion and the state, particularly in this area, has been fraught with contradictions and paradoxes. The same religions often both legitimate and condemn warfare. Legitimation may take the form of casting a war as an epic struggle between good and evil and in assigning prestige to those members of society performing deeds of valor and bravery. Condemnation of violence and the advocacy of pacifism find prominent places in major religious traditions.

Historically, an ambivalence existed within cultures and religions regarding both warfare and warriorship. Many religions elevated the role of warrior. Viking culture and religion elevated heroic death. Death in battle or childbirth, both viewed as areas that added to the life and welfare of the community, guaranteed one a place in either Valhalla, Odin's feast hall for the slain, or Sessrumnir, Freya's feast hall. In the Middle Ages, Christianity lauded the chivalrous Christian knight, combining an idealized view of the warrior with the role of Christian. Although *jihad,* or holy war, does not necessarily refer to warfare, many Muslims view those who die a warrior's death while engaged in *jihad* as especially blessed. Even Buddhism, which traditionally teaches the ideal of *ahimsa,* or nonharm, at times advocated the path of the sacred warrior. For instance, Zen appealed to the samurai class in Japan.

In the United States today the connection between religion and warfare does not possess the clear-cut connections that often existed in the past. However, the warrior tradition remains, alive and well, within the new religions existing under the umbrella of Paganism, or Neopaganism. Like other religions, the relationship between Neopaganism and the role of warrior remains ambivalent. Many witches take the Wiccan motto "An it harm none, do what you will" as a pacifist manifesto. Other groups, such as the Asatru, who seek to follow Viking traditions as faithfully as possible, combine warriorship and leading a moral life. The constants between the various groups with regard to this issue lie in two areas: a romanticization of the past and an insistence that morality remains a matter of individual consideration and decision.

Within Neopaganism warrior lodges and warrior paths exist that draw from a variety of sources: Norse tradition, the eastern idea of *shambhala,* legends of King Arthur and chivalrous knights, dungeons and dragons, fantasy novels, and the Klingon culture of *Star Trek.* People drawn to the warrior path tend to come from two groups: those who serve, or served, in the military or police, and those whose idea of what it means to be a warrior comes from fantasy, science fiction, myth, or role-playing games. Whether one comes from a warrior background or whether one has fallen in love with the ideal of warrior, both types of warrior tend to emphasize valor and honor. Neopagans consider these virtues among the ancient ideals of warriorship.

See also NEOPAGANISM; PACIFISM; STAR TREK; WICCA.

BIBLIOGRAPHY

Fields, Rick, ed. *The Awakened Warrior: Living with Courage, Compassion and Discipline.* 1994.
Harrow, Judy. "Initiation by Ordeal: Military Service as a Passage into Adulthood." In *Modern Rites of Passage,* Vol. 2 of *Witchcraft Today,* edited by Charles S. Clifton. 1993.

Nancy Ramsey

Watchtower Society.

See Jehovah's Witnesses.

Way International, The

The Way International, Inc., is a sectarian Christian movement founded by Victor Paul Wierwille (1916–1985). Wierwille received an M.Th. in 1941 from Princeton Theological Seminary. In 1942 he was ordained as a minister in the Evangelical and Reformed Church and established a radio ministry, Vesper Chimes, which evolved into The Way International in 1974. Wierwille engaged in intensive biblical study through the 1940s. His spiritual investigation and experiences led in 1953 to the Power for Abundant Living classes, the central religious forum of The Way. By 1957 he severed his denominational affiliation to lead his organization until his retirement in 1983.

The Way's theology is rooted in dispensationalism, a doctrine that diminishes the importance of Scripture written prior to Pentecost. The ultradispensationalism espoused by The Way adds an eighth dispensational period to the seven traditionally designated and elevates the primacy of Paul's later epistles. Other tenets that separate The Way from much of mainstream Christian doctrine include rejection of Jesus' divinity, the personality of the Holy Spirit, and Trinitarianism; belief in receiving the Holy Spirit through its nine manifestations, most notably speaking in tongues; and acceptance of Aramaic rather than Greek as the original New Testament language.

In 1957 Wierwille headquartered his organization in New Knoxville, Ohio. Over the next two decades the church established a number of other organizations to further its mission, including The Way College in Emporia, Kansas, as educational auspices; The Way Corps to train church leaders; the Word Over the World Ambassador program to disseminate the church's message; *The Way Magazine* as its organizational voice; Way Productions to support biblically consistent artistic projects; and annual Rock of Ages Festivals to promote church solidarity. Organizational control is highly centralized through a three-person board of trustees. Wierwille remained church president until 1983, when he was succeeded by the current president, Craig Martindale. The Way is organized on a tree model, with international headquarters (root), regional organizations (limbs), municipal organizations (branches), local fellowship groups (twigs), and individual members (leaves) as the elements. The Way grew rapidly beginning in the late 1960s, drawing on the pool of converts to the Jesus Movement. Peak membership is uncertain, since the church is organized into informal fellowship groups rather than formal congregations. One indicator is estimated attendance at annual festivals, which increased from one thousand in 1969 to seventeen thousand by 1983.

The Way has encountered a variety of conflicts both internally and externally. During the 1980s, organizational conflict led to the exit of several leaders, a membership decline, and the formation of schismatic groups. Upon his appointment as president, Craig Martindale began purging leaders and members perceived as disloyal. Membership plummeted to a small fraction of its peak size, and the organization became reclusive. Protest continues through an oppositional magazine, *No Way Out*. The church also encountered substantial external opposition during the 1980s. It became a primary target of anti-cult opposition and deprogramming, based on allegations of brainwashing and tendencies toward violence, and of Christian groups on theological grounds. Amid these controversies, the IRS launched an investigation; tax exemption of The Way was withdrawn in 1985 but reinstated by a U.S. Supreme Court ruling in 1990.

See also ANTI-CULT MOVEMENT; BRAINWASHING; DISPENSATIONALISM; GLOSSOLALIA; JESUS MOVEMENT.

BIBLIOGRAPHY

Juedes, John P., and Douglas V. Morton. *After from Vesper Chimes to The Way International.* 1983.

Wierwille, Victor Paul. *Power for Abundant Living.* 1971.

David G. Bromley

Way of the Cross.

See Stations of the Cross.

Whitehead, Alfred North.

See Process Theology.

Wicca

Wicca is a contemporary nature-based religion that most practitioners believe is a reconstruction of the practices of pre-Christian tribal Europe. Its public appearance coincides with the repeal of the anti-Witchcraft law in Britain in the early 1950s and the publication there of Gerald Gardner's *Witchcraft Today*. Whether Gardner simply passed on what he had been taught in secret, as he claimed, creatively contributed to the development of an existing practice, or invented the religion has been and continues to be a matter of debate. However, most Wiccans today are more interested in the efficacy of the spiritual practice than in its origins.

In 1962 Raymond and Rosemary Buckland immigrated to the United States and began teaching about Wicca. The religion's appeal to members of the anti-authoritarian counterculture was strong, and Wiccan covens, groups usually numbering from three to thirteen, began spreading across the country. The first Wiccan church to be granted federal tax-exempt status as a religious entity was in Missouri in 1965. Within a fairly short time, different Wiccan sects or traditions appeared, and, as the religion continued to grow, it began to gain adherents in mainstream society. By 1978 the U.S. Army's handbook for chaplains contained a section on Wicca, and by 1993 Wicca had been institutionalized to the extent that several Wiccan groups were among the sponsors of and participants at the World Parliament of Religions.

Many Wiccans prefer the label of witch and refer to their religion as Witchcraft or simply the Craft, in part to honor those people persecuted during the witch-hunts of history. Practitioners believe that these people were their spiritual ancestors. Others find the words "witch" and "Witchcraft" too confrontational, and there is a growing trend to embrace instead the

Members of Wicca, dressed in robes, hold hands to form a ceremonial circle. (Credit: © Charles Gupton/Stock, Boston/PNI.)

word "Wicca," the Old English term for a male who practices Witchcraft. It is important to note that, despite misconceptions, Wicca has nothing to do with Satanism, which Wiccans argue borrows from and is a reversal of Jewish and Christian beliefs. Wiccans do not believe in the existence of the Devil or any similar entity.

Wiccans hold divinity to be immanent in nature, and they celebrate, honor, and/or worship the Divine as the Goddess in her triple aspects of Maiden, Mother, and Crone, also represented by the phases of the moon. Many traditions also honor her male consort, often referred to as the Horned God of the Forest or Lord of the Dance. Goddesses and gods from different cultures and religions may be invoked as well and used as a focus for personal or group "work."

This work is usually done within "sacred space," which is created by "casting a circle," invoking the energies of the four cardinal points of the compass and the elements of air, fire, water, and earth that these represent, and then envisioning a surrounding circle of energy. Magical work or "spellcasting" is based on the belief in immanence and loosely corresponds with the argument in quantum physics that, on a subatomic level, everything is interconnected. Wiccans believe that if energy is drawn up from the earth into their bodies and manipulated correctly, it can be sent out into the world and affect matter for a desired goal. This is achieved through the focus of attention or "will" during altered states of consciousness that are achieved through the use of ritual tools, meditation, dance, chant, drumming, and other means. Magic, sometimes spelled "magick" to distinguish it from sleight of hand, can be done for something mundane and tangible, such as a pay raise, or for something less concrete, such as healing the earth.

There is no sacred, authoritative text that is accepted by all Wiccan traditions, although several have a *Book of Shadows,* which originated with Gardner and which has been added to in various ways. The Wiccan Rede is the closest thing to a universal religious law. Its wording varies slightly in different traditions but says basically, "As long as it harms none, do what you will." As everything is interconnected, magic done for negative purposes is believed to come back to the one who performed it and to be three times stronger than it was when sent out.

Wiccans can be solitary practitioners or members of an autonomous coven, usually led by a high priestess, with or without a high priest. Some traditions, however, are egalitarian and have shared leadership. Eight major religious holidays or sabbats are celebrated as a way of attuning to the seasonal changes in nature. Their dates coincide with the spring and fall equinoxes; summer and winter solstices; and "cross-quarter days," the midpoint between solstice and equinox. Wiccans in the United States tend to be white, educated, and largely middle class, with females outnumbering males. Because of the tremendous cross-fertilization that occurs at festivals and the influence of the women's movement on mainstream society, American Wicca is generally more feminist than its foreign counterparts.

See also BELONGING, RELIGIOUS; DIVINITY; GODDESS; MAGIC; NEOPAGANISM; NEW RELIGIOUS MOVEMENTS; PRIESTESS; QUANTUM PHYSICS; RELIGIOUS COMMUNITIES; RITUAL; TRIPLE GODDESS.

BIBLIOGRAPHY

Adler, Margot. *Drawing Down the Moon,* 2nd ed. 1979, 1986.

Berger, Helen. *A Community of Witches.* 1998.

Lozano, Wendy G., and Tanice G. Foltz. "Into the Darkness: An Ethnographic Study of Witchcraft and Death." *Qualitative Sociology* 13, no. 3 (1990): 211–235.

Starhawk. *The Spiral Dance.* 1979.

Wendy Griffin

Witchcraft.

See Wicca.

Williamson, Marianne

(1952–), lecturer, author, activist.

Marianne Williamson is a New Age lecturer and author in the fields of spirituality and politics and a humanitarian activist. She was born in Houston, Texas, to a middle-class Conservative Jewish family. In high school she studied drama and then attended Pomona College in Claremont, California, for two years. From 1972 to 1978, Williamson traveled, experimented with drugs, developed her interests in spiritualism, metaphysics, and Eastern philosophies and meditation practices, attended twelve-step programs, and worked as a cabaret singer in nightclubs. In 1978 she began studying the "channeled" document *A Course in Miracles* (Foundation for Inner Peace, 1975) and from 1979 to 1982 ran a New Age bookstore in Houston. After recovering from a nervous breakdown during this period, she moved to Los Angeles in 1983 and began lecturing on the *Course* at the Philosophical Research Society and other venues, as well as counseling persons with AIDS. In 1986 she added a monthly lecture in New York City and from 1987 to 1989 founded the Los Angeles and Manhattan Centers for Living and Project Angel Food, organizations providing services to people with life-threatening illnesses. Williamson's first book, *A Return to Love: Reflections on the Principles of "A Course in Miracles"* (1992), promoted by media celebrities such as Oprah Winfrey, met with popular acclaim. Following *A Return to Love,* she published *A Woman's Worth* (1993), *Illuminata: A Return to Prayer* (1994), *Emma and Mommy Talk to God* (1996), *Illuminated Prayers* (1997), and *The Healing of America* (1997) and produced numerous lecture audiocassettes. She also led spiritual pilgrimages to various sites around the world, spoke with political and religious leaders such as Hillary Rodham Clinton and the Dalai Lama, and by 1999 had founded the Global Renaissance Alliance, a political and spiritual organization.

Williamson's use of *A Course in Miracles* as the foundation of her teaching and social activism locates her within the eclectic sphere of the New Age movement.

The New Age emphasizes personal spirituality over institutionalized religion, but Williamson has combined its psychotherapeutic individualism with a focus on humanitarian service. Williamson's interpretation of the *Course* teaches the illusoriness of the material world and the ultimate reality only of "love," which is God, an energy that pervades the universe and connects all things. Through "surrendering" the ego to God in prayer and meditation, an individual is able to change his or her perception and experience of the world. As thinking shifts—termed a "miracle"—a person moves from feelings of separatedness and fear to those of connectedness and love and is empowered to "heal" oneself and others, emotionally and physically. For Williamson, who teaches personal responsibility for one's experiences and actions, the realization of God's love generates nonviolent activism to promote the creation of an "enlightened society," that is, one committed to spiritual values and social justice. Williamson's self-identification as a baby boomer who thoroughly embraced the revolutionary culture of the late 1960s and early 1970s and her energetic dissemination of the principles of New Age spirituality have elicited the following of many spiritual seekers of her generation. Believing that many Americans in the late 1990s have become disillusioned with materialistic culture, inept government, and problematic social issues such as crime, public education, and welfare, she has adopted a millennialist vision of America as a nation in crisis. Arguing that the United States is in the midst of a turbulent transition that will inevitably result in the transformation or disintegration of the nation. *The Healing of America* uses *Course* principles to call people to prayer vigils and political activism in grassroots "citizen circles." In 1999 the Global Renaissance Alliance reported that there were circles in Canada, the Netherlands, and Austria, as well as in thirty-four states in the United States, with California (thirteen circles) and Florida (fourteen circles) representing the most activity.

See also DALAI LAMA; GENERATION X; HEALTH; MEDITATION; MIRACLES; NEW AGE SPIRITUALITY; SPIRITUALITY; TWELVE-STEP PROGRAMS.

BIBLIOGRAPHY

Oumano, Elena. *Marianne Williamson: Her Life, Her Message, Her Miracles.* 1992.

Williamson, Marianne. *The Healing of America.* 1997.

Williamson, Marianne. *Illuminata: A Return to Prayer.* 1994.

Williamson, Marianne. *A Return to Love: Reflections on the Principles of "A Course in Miracles."* 1992.

Martha Finch-Jewell

Wisdom Literature

Wisdom, the timeless, intellectual, and reflective tradition of antiquity, the forerunner of ancient Greek and modern philosophy, is the quest of the ancients to understand the most common and fundamental truths of the nature and limits of the human condition. As a tradition, wisdom sought coherency in places where traditional religion failed to provide answers. Deriving from ancient and diverse sources, this wisdom tradition and the literature it produced originated and flourished in royal courts of the great river valleys of the ancient world—the Nile in North Africa and the Tigris-Euphrates in Mesopotamia. In Egypt, "wisdom" was most often associated with the goddess Ma'at and was associated with such concepts and principles as "truth," "justice," and "order." Wisdom thought in both of these ancient cultures most often took the literary form of instructions, the more practical form of wisdom, or of laments, a more reflective or skeptical form of wisdom.

Generally, instruction texts, like the Egyptian *Instruction of Prince Hardjedef* (ca. 2450 B.C.E.) or the Mesopotamian *Instructions of Suruppak* (ca. 2400 B.C.E.), were educational tools that socialized young persons by giving pragmatic counsel. This advice covered a wide range of matters from how to find inner peace, to how to behave in the royal courts, to how to manage one's money, one's emotions, and even one's love affairs. While the instruction texts generally supported the status quo, other wisdom literature was far more pessimistic in nature and clearly disdained and even challenged traditional modes of thinking. This was the more reflective dimension of wisdom. *The Eloquent Peasant,* a dialogue between a peasant and an official of the royal court that recounts the injustices experienced by the peasant, and *The Dispute Between a Man and His Ba* are examples of this more skeptical wisdom.

In ancient societies, a class of sages produced and canonized wisdom thought. These were often officials sanctioned by the ruling authorities. State scribes kept records, counseled kings, trained future bureaucrats, and produced a type of "cosmopolitan training literature." Since they were the educated elite, they wielded a great deal of influence on the shaping of the politics, theology, and ideology of their societies. Although wisdom as it has been preserved is a highly stylized literature stemming from an urban, royal courtly setting, many of the themes typical of this official scribal production probably originated generations earlier as the folk sayings and anecdotes of clans in rural villages.

Wisdom thought also had an international-universal character and circulated far beyond its countries of origin. Because it was not tied to the views of a particular group, community, national history, or religion, it quickly adapted to other parts of the Near East.

Wisdom in the Bible

The proverbs, laments, instructions, and dialogues, the four literary forms in which wisdom thinking was passed down in ancient Israel, are a late heir to this long literary and intellectual tradition. Israel's intellectual literature, like that of its Egyptian and Mesopotamian predecessors, has an international aura. Israelite wisdom transcends the preoccupations of national religion such as ritualistic purity, worship, sacrifice, and covenants. Other than King Solomon, there is no mention of Israel's national heroes as personifying what it means to be wise. No appeal is made to Israel's deity. Also noticeably absent is any mention of the Israelites' chosen status. Confined mainly to the books of Proverbs, Job, and Ecclesiastes, Israel's wisdom literature is concerned with apprehending the social, natural, and moral order.

Where traditional Israelite religion focused on groups and emphasized Yahweh's revelation in a shared national history, Israelite wisdom sought the revelation of God in nature and in individual reflection. The sages were interested in the person as a human being and in those qualities, struggles, and concerns essential to the universal human condition. There is no emphasis on the notion of God intervening in history to move a particular people to a telos, or ultimate end (*heilsgeschichte*). Israelite wisdom literature is synchronic; it is less concerned with nonrepeatable saving events and more concerned with the common thread underlying recurring human experiences.

From the age of the monarchy (ca. 1000 B.C.E.) to the Persian period (539–333 B.C.E.), when canonization of the literature took place, Israelite wisdom survived and even thrived as an alternative to the prevailing religious traditions. Legends attribute much of the wisdom material to King Solomon, who reputedly uttered three thousand proverbs and one thousand and five songs (I Kings 4:32). However, wisdom as an alternative tradition comes in a variety of forms in the Old Testament. In addition to those mentioned above, one finds scattered patches throughout the canon—e.g., riddles (Judges 14:14), fables (Judges 9:8–15), and stories about diviners (Numbers 22–24).

Studies of the books of Job, Proverbs, and Ecclesiastes have revealed two extremes to Israelite wisdom thinking: the skeptical (e.g., Ecclesiastes and Job), which takes nothing at face value, and the pragmatic (e.g., Proverbs), which is pedagogical. Everyday instructional, practical knowledge concerning wealth and poverty, love, and behavior proper to one's social position is the focus of the book of Proverbs. It advocates industriousness, frugality, and temperance as the core of what it means to be wise. At the same time, sloth and overindulgence are equated with folly in Proverbs. Ecclesiastes and Job, on the other hand, question these values, arguing that just rewards do not always accrue either to good or to immoral people. The literature in these two books, more skeptical and reflective in tone, explores the limits of practical counsel and questions the validity of conventional thinking about divine retribution. Ultimately, the wisdom literature of the Hebrew Bible represents the intellectual tradition of ancient Israel. It is the record of a civilization's attempt to reflect upon, to philosophize about, and to appreciate the joys, sorrows, fears, and struggles of daily life and of the human experience. Israelite wisdom, then, in its international character and reflective quality is ageless, admonishing subsequent generations about the universal nature of all human life. As the sage of the book of Deuteronomy puts it, "The secrets belong to the Lord our God, but the revealed things belong to us and to our children forever . . ." (Deuteronomy 29:29).

Wisdom in the United States

While ancient wisdom emerged out of civilizations that no longer exist and was transmitted from generation to generation in ways for which we cannot always fully account, many of the insights about human existence captured by ancient sages continue to resonate in our contemporary society. Human beings still seek practical knowledge in order to negotiate the ethical, spiritual, economic, and environmental realities of their lives. Wisdom literature concerns itself with instruction and reflection on the basic orderliness of the world and how to cope when that order fails or seems to fail. The abiding interest of Americans in practical knowledge is nowhere better attested to than by the glut of books published over the past thirty years focusing on recovering deeply integral elements of our humanity that people think have been lost. The feeling among some is that the industrialization initiated during previous centuries and technology in this century have robbed societies of some basic values and insights. Questions like "What does it mean to be human?" or "Why is there evil?" or "What is my relationship to the environment?" or (more personally) "Who am I?" have been examined from both theistic and nontheistic points of view and have spawned best-selling books. A yearning for practical wisdom in particular is evident in the number of self-help books and the enormous proliferation of "little instruction" books containing proverbial aphorisms that have cropped up in recent times.

Not surprisingly, books about ancient mythology have been at the top of best-seller lists for some time. Authors have tried cataloguing the ancient teachings on life, death, love, and faith found in these myths. Whether such books have been written to reacquaint readers with the mythopoetic dimension of human existence, reminding them of the genius of stories in transmitting ancient wisdom, or reasserting values shared allegedly by all human beings, the popularity of books like Joseph Campbell's *The Power of Myth*, Mircea Eliade's *The Sacred and the Profane*, or Clarissa P. Estes's *Women Who Run with the Wolves* are indicative of the continuing spiritually and intellectually restive nature of North Americans.

The United States is a nation of seekers, and for as long as that description remains accurate, a yearning for wisdom as timeless knowledge about human existence will be with us. The questions, precepts, dilemmas, and skepticism embodied in wisdom teachings reflect the enduring and recurrent nature of the human predicament. As the writer of Ecclesiastes asserts, "There is nothing new under the sun."

See also BIBLE; CAMPBELL, JOSEPH; ELIADE, MIRCEA; MYTH.

BIBLIOGRAPHY

Bergant, Dianne. *Israel's Wisdom Literature: A Liberation-Critical Reading of the Old Testament.* 1997.

Brown, William E. *Character in Crisis: A Fresh Approach to the Wisdom Literature of the Old Testament.* 1996.

Crenshaw, James L. *Old Testament Wisdom: An Introduction.* 1981.

Morgan, Donn F. "Searching for Biblical Wisdom: Recent Studies and Their Pertinence for Contemporary Ministry." *Sewanee Theological Review* (1994).

Herbert Marbury
Renita Weems

Womanist Theology

Emerging in the mid-1980s, womanist theology is the work of African-American women theologians, church historians, ethicists, sociologists of religion, and biblical scholars. The term was coined by Alice Walker, who offered a definition of the word in her 1984 book *In Search of Our Mothers' Gardens.* Walker described a womanist as a "Black feminist or feminist of color" who is bold and assertive, relishes African-American culture, and is committed to the flourishing of the entire African-American community. Womanists explore the Christian faith in view of the unique experience and contributions of African-American women. Their focus is both historical and contemporary. It therefore gives voice to the particular concerns of African-American women, celebrates their strength and creativity, and is a form of resistance to the oppression they have suffered. Their goals include developing and transmitting insights that will lead to justice, revising theological doctrines so as to make them more inclusive, and, ultimately, making connections with other groups.

Womanists believe that traditional theology has not taken account of their experience. They have turned to black and feminist theologies in an effort to rectify this situation. Yet womanists have felt obliged to move beyond both, viewing them as wanting in significant ways. They object to the sexism of black male theology and the black church, as well as the racism of feminist theology. They stress what they call the multidimensional oppression of African-American women, who have been the victims of racism, sexism, and classism. Although they distinguish their movement from feminist and black theologies, womanists are not separatists. In fact, they see in their movement the possibility of reaching out to other communities. With all African Americans they share the reality of racism. Sexism gives them a point of contact with other women. Moreover, the poverty experienced by African-American women binds them to all poor people.

The sources used by womanists include the Bible, the thought and lives of historic African-American women, slave narratives, and African-American women's literature. Biblical scholars attempt to reinterpret biblical texts from their unique perspective, pointing to the need for different strategies of interpretation. In so doing, they focus on women of color in the Bible. Figures such as Hagar, the queen of Sheba, Mary, and others are explored to understand the ways in which they had been portrayed in the Bible, how they dealt with their situations, and how these texts have been interpreted. These scholars' primary interest in the life of Jesus centers on his identification with and concern for the poor. Church historians and ethicists seek to uncover the contributions of African-American women of the past. They ask how these women functioned within the church and within the African-American community. Sojourner Truth, Anna Julia Cooper, Jarena Lee, and Ida B. Wells-Barnett are among the women who have been of particular interest. In addition, the historians and ethicists have explored how the African-American church women have influenced the black community through their collection activities in the black church during slavery, the women's club movement, women's missionary societies, and political organizations. In addition, ethicists attempt to specify the values and virtues that can be used by contemporary African Americans to improve conditions.

Theologians have sought to reconstruct Christian doctrines, especially the doctrine of God and Christology. Like black, feminist, and liberation theologians, womanist theologians see in the Exodus evidence that God is particularly concerned with the poor and the oppressed. They stress this less than their black male counterparts, however, focusing on survival in addition to the theme of liberation. This notion of God's concern for the oppressed enables womanists to counteract the negative images of African Americans portrayed by the larger society. In thinking about the life and the work of Christ, they tend to stress his historic importance to the African-American church, especially women, and his ministry to and solidarity with outcasts. Jesus is therefore understood as a political messiah who suffers with and liberates African Americans.

Drawing on the example of historical figures and black women writers, ethicists attempt to uncover the values that have sustained the African-American community in the past, as well as those values that are needed today. They point to the fact that African-American women have embodied a communal ethic that has sought the survival of the whole community. To nurture the black community, African-American women have formed strong, supportive, nurturing relationships among themselves. These scholars have looked to the black women's literary tradition to understand the nature of these networks. Ethicists and theologians have found the works of novelists Toni Morrison, Alice Walker, Zora Neale Hurston, and Margaret Walker, among others, especially fruitful.

In the late 1980s there was a debate in the field about the advisability of adopting the secular term "womanist," particularly in view of Walker's endorsement of lesbianism in her definition. Despite this controversy, the term has gained widespread acceptance among most scholars. More recently, some womanists have debated whether womanist and Afrocentric thought are compatible. Some, pointing to the sexism of Afrocentric thought, have averred that womanists cannot embrace it. Others, however, believe them to be compatible, suggesting that womanism is inherently Afrocentric.

See also AFRICAN-AMERICAN RELIGIONS; BIBLE; FEMINIST SPIRITUALITY; FEMINIST THEOLOGY; MARY; RELIGIOUS STUDIES.

BIBLIOGRAPHY

Cannon, Katie G. *Black Womanist Ethics.* 1988.

Douglas, Kelly Brown. *The Black Christ.* 1994.

Gilkes, Cheryl Townsend. "The Role of Women in the Sanctified Church." *Journal of Religious Thought* 43 (Spring–Summer 1986): 24–41.

Grant, Jacquelyn. *White Women's Christ and Black Women's Jesus.* 1989.

Higginbotham, Evelyn Brooks. *Righteous Discontent.* 1994.

Riggs, Marcia Y. *Awake, Arise and Act.* 1994.

Townes, Emilie M., ed. *A Troubling in My Soul.* 1993.

Williams, Delores S. *Sisters in the Wilderness.* 1993.

C. Jarrett Gray, Jr.

Women's Aglow Fellowship International

Women's Aglow Fellowship International (hereafter "Aglow") is an interdenominational organization of Christian women centered on prayer and evangelization. Aglow was founded in 1967 as the Full Gospel Women's Fellowship, established in Seattle, Washington, by four women whose husbands were active leaders in the Full Gospel Businessmen's Fellowship. Both groups were outgrowths of healing and charismatic movements within Protestant and Catholic churches, and they correspondingly emphasized practices and doctrines such as spirit baptism, glossolalia, prophecy, and healing prayer. After starting a highly successful quarterly magazine in 1969, spurring rapid growth of the organization throughout North America and eventually much of the world, the nonprofit women's group incorporated under its new name in 1972. Throughout its history Aglow has been held together by local worship meetings and Bible studies as well as by larger (regional, national, and even international) retreats and conferences.

Most of Aglow's American constituents in the early days were white, middle-class homemakers, and the group's published literature—a significant collection of books, audiotapes, Bible studies, and magazine issues—strongly emphasized women's domestic roles as wives and mothers. Authors frequently criticized the Women's Liberation Movement for dismantling traditional gender hierarchies and scorning the notion that women's highest vocation is in the home. Aglow writers were committed to a worldview in which women ought to be "in submission" not only to God but also to earthly male authories such as their husbands and pastors. Aglow staff member Eadie Goodboy, in her Bible study *God's Daughter* (1974), affirmed that Christian women must reject the "role-reversal so common in society today" so as to find "service and creativity in our God-ordained roles" as wives, mothers, and homemakers.

This message extolling wifely submission and domesticity fit well with the "family values" campaigns increasingly waged during the 1970s, supported by President Ronald Reagan in the 1980s, and visible in such arenas as Anita Bryant's public war against homosexuality, Jerry Falwell's powerful Moral Majority, Beverly LaHaye's Concerned Women for America, Phyllis Schlafly's battle against the Equal Rights Amendment (ERA), and James Dobson's Focus on the Family empire. Unlike these leaders and organizations, however, Aglow was not a political organization and refrained from issuing public statements on issues such as abortion and the ERA. Nonetheless, the group experienced substantial growth during the formative years of the Christian Religious Right, and many of its members, aging along with the organization, have also been part of that movement as well.

At the same time, Aglow took an increasingly therapeutic turn during the mid-to-late 1980s, as meetings came to feel as much like recovery groups as worship meetings. Just as subjects like physical and sexual abuse and addiction received growing attention in American popular culture, so, too, such topics rose to the fore in Aglow meetings and published literature. Images of squeaky-clean families glued together by joyously submissive supermoms were replaced by dark tales of incest-ridden childhoods, alcoholic parents, and unfaithful husbands. No longer were women expected to submit cheerfully to such indignities but were urged to seek psychiatric help and, if necessary, divorce as well. Jesus, always a savior and friend to Aglow women, was increasingly imagined as a replacement father for women whose own fathers had abandoned them and as a replacement husband for divorced, widowed, or unhappily married women. Along with Bible studies, worship services, retreats, and conferences, Aglow established official support groups for women in need, promoted as Christ-centered alternatives to secular twelve-step groups such as Alcoholics Anonymous.

During the 1990s Aglow has been more successful at attracting middle-class women of color as the national leadership in Seattle has focused energy on racial reconciliation. References to homemakers have also sharply declined, as demographic shifts among their membership have made visible increasing numbers of single mothers and working women. Still, drawing in new members has proven very difficult: Unlike the early years, Aglow's potential members in the United States now have many other options, as evangelicals, inspired by the men's group Promise Keepers, have forged parallel women's groups such as Chosen Women, Promise Reapers, Praise Keepers, and Women of Faith. These newer fellowships are theologically looser than Aglow and draw a younger clientele, in part because they are not burdened by the language of wifely submission with which Aglow still contends. In recognition of Aglow's diminished appeal among younger American women, the organization's energies have shifted balance, global evangelization taking precedence over local growth. The story of Aglow's future almost certainly lies in Africa, Asia, and Latin America more than North America; but whether this global growth portends further imperialistic expansion of American Christianity or the genuine internationalization of Aglow itself remains, for now, an open question.

See also Dobson, James; Falwell, Jerry; Focus on the Family; Moral Majority; Promise Keepers; Religious Right.

Bibliography

Griffith, R. Marie. *God's Daughters: Evangelical Women and the Power of Submission.* 1997.
Setta, Susan M. "Healing in Suburbia: The Women's Aglow Fellowship." *Journal of Religious Studies* 12(2) (1986):46–56

R. Marie Griffith

Women's Studies

In the United States women's studies became a distinct scholarly discipline as an outgrowth of the "second wave" of feminism in the 1960s. While women and issues of sex and gender had been the subject of research and theory prior to that time, women's studies developed as a uniquely interdisciplinary and feminist endeavor. Early proponents of women's studies saw the establishment of their field as inextricably related to a larger movement for feminist social transformation. Like that of ethnic studies programs originating at the same time, the very existence of women's studies as a field challenged the self-declared objectivity and scholarly disinterest of academic institutions that had failed to perceive the significance of women, people of color, the working class, and other marginalized groups within American society. The essential feminist insight that "the personal is political" called for study of the status of women as the result of institutionalized forms of oppression. It also led to research and teaching methods that emphasized learning in interaction between individual subjectivity and the object of theory or study. Thus, from the outset, women's studies programs and scholars sought to redefine the very nature of scholarship.

Since the late 1960s women's studies research, courses, and programs have developed an extensive body of scholarly work in the humanities and sciences. As a part of a new, interdisciplinary field with activist roots, women's studies scholars have always had diverse and, at times, conflicting understandings of the nature and purpose of their discipline. From the start, there have been those who perceive separate women's studies programs as segregating and further devaluing the significance of feminist scholarship, rather than creating a demand for an integrated curriculum in all areas of study. Defenders of women's studies as an independent field argue that it gives feminist scholars greater support and academic freedom and also creates connections among numerous disciplines that enhance feminist scholarship. The enormous growth in the literature on women, sex, and gender has, in some ways, resolved the dispute. As the research has become more specialized and sophisticated, it has increasingly addressed an audience within its own specific field. On a purely practical level, the sheer volume of work in women's studies has made it impossible for any individual scholar to remain current in the discipline as a whole.

Another controversy has been the issue of essentialism: whether there actually is a distinct (essential) female nature or experience that can be the focus of discrete study. As working-class and ethnic-, racial-, and sexual-minority women developed their own scholarship, they critiqued the feminist research that had assumed a middle-class, Christian, white, and heterosexual perspective as normative. Their work challenged the notion that there could be any singular, universal voice or theory concerning sex and gender. Earlier feminist theorists had perceived the importance of distinguishing biologically determined sex (female or male) from socially constructed gender (feminine or masculine). The growing body of research on women as well as the influence of deconstructionism, a movement that challenged the idea that there are any fixed meanings or identities, led women's studies scholars to question even these categories and explore instead their fluidity and indeterminate nature. One response to this debate has been a growing emphasis on gender or gender studies rather than an exclusive focus on women.

The relationship between women's studies and religious studies has changed dramatically over the course of the past three decades. Like the feminist movement in general, early women's studies programs were at best indifferent and frequently hostile to religious traditions perceived as inherently and irrevocably patriarchal. This antagonism extended to feminist scholars of religion, especially those working within institutional religious frameworks. Even in the absence of overt antipathy, religious studies were generally excluded from the disciplines considered essential to women's studies programs.

During the late 1970s and early 1980s a number of factors began to change this situation. Allowing appropriate visibility to feminist scholars from racial and ethnic minority communities involved an acknowledgment of the continued significance of religion within those cultures. Feminist scholars in fields such as comparative literature, history, and sociology began to research topics in religion, conveying the importance that spirituality and ritual play in the lives of the vast majority of the world's women. A growing number of scholars in religion had experience in feminist activism, scholarship in other disciplines, or both and initiated ties with women's studies programs.

Nevertheless, there has continued to be an unequal relationship between the disciplines. To the extent that women's studies scholars perceive the study of religion as doctrinal, they fail to inform themselves of the larger theoretical issues raised in the field, such as feminist hermeneutics (theory of interpretation), epistemology (theory of knowledge), and historiography. In contrast, feminist scholarship in religion incorporates a wide range of feminist sources in other fields.

During the 1980s women's studies in religion became increasingly institutionalized and visible as a distinct area of scholarship. The American Academy of Religion, the professional organization of scholars in religion, established a Women in Religion section. Seminaries and university religious studies departments developed their own women's studies courses and programs. Fellowships, visiting scholar positions, endowed lectures, and a few endowed professorships in women's studies in religion have continued to be created.

See also ECOFEMINISM; FEMINIST SPIRITUALITY; FEMINIST THEOLOGY; GENDER ROLES; INCLUSIVE LANGUAGE; ORDINATION OF WOMEN; RELIGIOUS STUDIES; WOMANIST THEOLOGY.

BIBLIOGRAPHY

Farnham, Christie, ed. *The Impact of Feminist Research in the Academy.* 1987.

Gunew, Sneja, ed. *A Reader in Feminist Knowledge.* 1991.

Humm, Maggie, ed. *Feminisms: A Reader.* 1992.

Stanley, Liz, ed. *Knowing Feminisms: On Academic Borders, Territories and Tribes.* 1997.

Drorah Setel

Word of Faith Movement

The Word of Faith movement is an independent, Charismatic Christian network of churches and ministries, loosely bound by a basic doctrine, the Faith Message. Generally speaking, according to their understanding of the Bible, which they see as God's legal contract, the born-again Christian is guaranteed certain rights and privileges. Leaders teach that it is God's will for Christians to be prosperous, successful, and in perfect health in this present life. The Faith Message also teaches that faith, and certain other aspects of spirituality, must be properly applied according to immutable laws for believers to live a victorious Christian life. Central to the doctrine is positive confession—the practice of thinking and speaking only affirmatively to achieve a desired end. In addition, the movement is also charismatic in its beliefs and practices, insisting on the personal and corporate experience of the gifts of the Spirit as normative. Among these gifts is glossolalia, or speaking in tongues.

The original author of the precepts informing today's Word of Faith Movement was a little-known independent evangelist, Essek William (E. W.) Kenyon (1867–1948). Impassioned debate continues within the Christian community concerning the extent to which Kenyon was influenced by and incorporated elements of New Thought metaphysics into his theology, thus giving it so-called cultic roots. Based on the belief that this is the case, some have called the Faith Message heresy and "a different gospel" from what can be considered orthodox. Pastor and evangelist Kenneth Erwin Hagin, Sr. (1917–), commonly considered the leader of the contemporary Word of Faith Movement, has written numerous books that expand on Kenyon's work.

A pivotal figure in the formation of today's movement, Hagin established and incorporated the Kenneth Hagin Evangelistic Association in 1963. Through his books and tapes, his radio and television broadcasts, and the Rhema Bible Training Center (1974), in Broken Arrow, Oklahoma, he helped expand the audience for these teachings. Hagin's efforts facilitated the transformation of the Faith Message into the ideological basis of an international movement as well as producing a second generation of Faith teachers. Since the first graduating class (1974–1975), the Rhema Bible Training Center has sent more than 16,500 new Faith Movement ministers out to establish new ministries throughout the world. Hagin's magazine *The Word of Faith* reports a monthly circulation of 540,000.

In contrast to a denomination with a formalized institutional structure that maintains authority over its membership, voluntary organizations are the norm within the Word of Faith Movement. The International Convention of Faith Ministries (ICFM), founded in 1979, provides an organizational link among member ministries by offering opportunities for networking, fellowship, and support among ministers. The ICFM also holds a yearly convention at which member ministries come together for revivals, seminars, and other church-related activities. The Trinity Broadcast Network (TBN), self-described as the largest Christian television network in the world, is another major medium for disseminating this doctrine. The TBN has affiliates throughout North and South America and in a number of countries overseas.

Today's most prominent Word of Faith Movement ministers include Kenneth and Gloria Copeland (Fort Worth); Dr. Frederick K. C. Price (Los Angeles); Marilyn Hickey (Denver); and Dr. David Yonggi Cho (Seoul, Korea), whose church is reportedly the largest in the world, with over 750,000 members.

See also BORN AGAIN CHRISTIANS; CHARISMATIC MOVEMENT; EVANGELICAL CHRISTIANITY; GLOSSOLALIA; JOURNALISM, RELIGIOUS; NEW THOUGHT; PROSPERITY THEOLOGY; PUBLISHING, RELIGIOUS; TELEVANGELISM.

BIBLIOGRAPHY

Gossett, Don, and E. W. Kenyon. *The Power of Your Words: Walking with God by Agreeing with Him.* 1998.

Hagin, Kenneth E., Sr. *Classic Sermons.* 1993.

Hanegraaf, Hank. *Christianity in Crisis.* 1997.

Kenyon, E. W. *The Father and His Family: The Story of Man's Redemption.* 1998.

MacIntyre, Joe R. *E. W. Kenyon and His Message of Faith: The True Story.* 1997.

McConnell, Dan R. *A Different Gospel: Biblical and Historical Insights into the Word of Faith Movement.* 1995.

Simmons, Dale H. *E. W. Kenyon and the Postbellum Pursuit of Peace, Power, and Plenty.* 1997.

Milmon F. Harrison

Work

Religion and work are intertwined in complex ways. Sometimes religious beliefs and teachings give rise to cultural norms; sometimes religious and social standards are mutually supportive; and sometimes religion challenges prevalent views and practices. Three characteristics surrounding labor in the United States demonstrate how religion motivates, upholds, and confronts the world of work; they are the work ethic, the gender division of labor, and the right to work and workers' rights.

Work Ethic

Religious beliefs and teachings motivate individuals' labor and also sustain society's views toward work. Max Weber, a German social scientist, described how religion was an incentive for work. He noted that in northern Europe, prior to the Industrial Revolution, a set of ideas with Lutheran and Calvinist origins was prevalent; he termed it the "Protestant ethic." The ethic connected labor in this world to salvation in the next. It inspired people to work hard and long, to limit consumption of material goods, to save money, and to reinvest profits into business enterprises. It disposed workers to meet the production needs of fledgling industries, and it furthered the pursuit of wealth in commercial enterprises. Ultimately it contributed to the Industrial Revolution and to the growth of capitalism as an economic formula that stressed productivity and prosperity. In the United States the ethic was sometimes called the "Puritan ethic" in recognition of one religious group that brought it to the colonies.

Over time, the religious ethic converted into a secular one: working hard, remaining disciplined, seeking success, and cultivating profit became cultural norms. The ethic permeated individuals' lives and became so prevalent that the term "workaholic" was coined for individuals who manifest an extreme work ethic. Religious leaders, while encouraging work, also warn about sacrificing family for career. (See Salkin, 1994.) They exemplify how religion plays a dual social role, both upholding and confronting existing beliefs and norms.

The work ethic was reflected in the creed of commerce stressing acquisition and prosperity, which spread globally from Western Europe and the United States. Devoid of religious association, norms developed that promote acquiring profits, accumulating material goods and wealth, demonstrating disciplined effort, and making prudent expenditures. Business enterprises routinely appealed to "the bottom line" of profit, even when defending policies, practices, and procedures that negatively affected the employment and conditions of workers.

Further, the work ethic was manifest in U.S. policy. The cultural link between market forces and individuals' labor was reflected in income redistribution policies based on the premise that the market takes care of people's needs. Individuals' supplementary benefits are tied to their means, and decisions about welfare distribution are based on how much income individuals have and on whether they are "deserving"—that is, medically unable to work or, at least, trying to find a job. Often those without jobs and/or receiving welfare benefits are stigmatized. In contrast, many other industrialized societies distribute minimum benefits based on citizenship or on some other criterion not related to job-holding. (For further elaboration see Esping-Anderson, 1990.) In sum, the centrality of a "work ethic" is clear in the commerce and policies of the United States as well as in the motivations of individual workers.

Gender Division of Labor

Religious beliefs and teachings are tied in with the way work is divided by gender in the United States. Sometimes religious groups explicitly educate about gender roles and work; however, there is wide variability in teachings among and within groups. (See Demmit, 1992 and Ellison and Bartkowski, 1997.) More often, long-standing cultural norms implicitly reflect religious and other influences and shape labor in two ways. First, they affect individuals' occupational preferences and their actual selection of jobs. An emphasis on women's procreative, nurturing, and sustaining family roles legitimizes women's gravitating toward specific kinds of jobs and sanctions how men and women treat and value work inside and outside the home. Some want women to work at home; some think that women's work away from home should be in jobs, such as volunteering and doing part-time work, that do not interfere with family responsibilities. Others prefer jobs that socialize, nurture, or otherwise mirror women's roles in kinship groups, such as teaching, nursing, and service work. Often these jobs, as well as volunteer work, are named "good works."

Second, an emphasis on women's work as secondary or supportive to men's affects the groupings of workers available for employment, the apportioning of jobs by gender, the ranks in which women labor, and the type of rewards they get. Women are found in "pink-collar" occupations (i.e., occupations that are mostly filled by women, such as nurse, beautician, elementary-school teacher) and clustered at lower ranks (e.g., sales). Women are overly represented in part-time jobs and in the secondary labor market, which includes jobs that provide minimal benefits to workers in terms of income, job security, and chances to advance. And women in full-time employment earn about three-fourths of men's income. Certainly religion is not wholly accountable for the apportionment of the labor market in the United States, but affinities are apparent between religious beliefs and teachings and gendered occupational patterns and job choices.

The Right to Work and Workers' Rights

Religious groups often articulate the right of individuals to provide for themselves and their families as well as their duty to do so. They emphasize that self-reliance contributes to personal dignity and self-respect. (See Maxwell 1998.) Some church groups (e.g., the Mormons) make available employment rehabilitation and placement services. They maintain employment centers and enterprises that hire members. In so doing, religious groups support existing cultural norms about the value of work and individuals' right to it.

Some religious groups stress the rights of laborers and thus confront existing social norms. For example, churches in the South articulated the rights of African Americans to work and to have equal opportunities for employment during the civil rights movement of the 1960s. The Roman Catholic Church in its teachings articulates the rights of workers: the priority of labor over capital, the importance of participation in decision-making, the need for just wages and decent working conditions, and the prerogative to unionize. (See National Conference of Catholic Bishops 1986.) At times such teachings are explicitly involved in labor conflicts, even within church organizations. For example, in 1998 Catholic Healthcare West, the second-largest hospital network in California, faced unionization demands from ten thousand workers in ten hospitals in Los Angeles and Sacramento, who called attention to religious principles about their rights to join workers' associations. Indeed, issues surrounding the right to work and the rights of workers manifest how religion both accommodates to and comes into conflict with the culture and realities surrounding work in the United States.

Conclusion

In the 1950s, Gerhard Lenski studied the connection between individuals' occupational mobility and their religious denominations. The Protestant-Catholic differences found then had vanished by the 1970s. Nonetheless, the term Lenski coined, the "religious factor," captures a persistent feature of the culture and practice of work in the United States. The norms, values, beliefs, teachings, and practices of religion both sustain and confront the work world and labor within it. Put simply, a "religious factor" permeates work and vice versa.

See also CIVIL RELIGION; GENDER ROLES; SOCIOLOGY OF RELIGION; SPIRITUALITY.

BIBLIOGRAPHY

Demmit, K. "Loosening the Ties That Bind: The Accommodation of Dual-Earner Families in a Conservative Protestant Church." *Review of Religious Research* 34 (1992): 3–19.

Ellison, C. G., and J. P. Bartkowski. "Conservative Protestantism and the Household Division of Labor." Paper presented at the Association for the Sociology of Religion Meetings, Toronto. 1997.

Esping-Anderson, Gösta. *The Three Worlds of Welfare Capitalism.* 1990.

Greeley, Andrew. *The American Catholic: A Social Portrait.* 1977.

Lenski, Gerhard. *The Religious Factor: A Sociological Study of Religion's Impact on Politics, Economics, and Family Life.* 1963.

Maxwell, Neal A. "Put Your Shoulder to the Wheel." *Ensign* 28, no. 5 (1998): 45.

National Conference of Catholic Bishops. "Economic Justice for All: Pastoral Letter on Catholic Social Teaching and the U.S. Economy." 1986.

Salkin, Jeffrey. *Being God's Partner: How to Find the Hidden Link Between Spirituality and Work.* 1994.

Weber, Max. *The Protestant Ethic and the Spirit of Capitalism.* 1930.

Katherine Meyer

World Council of Churches

Throughout 1998 the World Council of Churches (WCC) celebrated its fiftieth anniversary, culminating in a service of recommitment by member churches to the ecumenical movement at its eighth World Assembly, in Harare, Zimbabwe. As a hopeful effort in the aftermath of World War II, Christian leaders from around the world brought together two strains of ecumenism at Amsterdam in 1948. The actual birth of the ecumenical movement, however, is generally dated from a meeting of missionary societies in 1910 at Edinburgh, Scotland. In Lausanne, in 1927, the Faith and Order Commission was formed; the Life and Work Commission began in Stockholm in 1925. Both of these commissions were united in Amsterdam to form the World Council of Churches, to which the International Missionary Council was added in 1961.

When founded, the WCC had 147 member churches, mostly Anglican and Protestant from North America and Western Europe. Gradually churches from all parts of the world have joined—332 Protestant, Anglican, and Orthodox churches, totaling roughly 500 million Christians by 1998. Although it cooperates on several key issues, the Roman Catholic Church is not a member. In their pursuit of Christian unity, WCC member churches, confessing the Lord Jesus Christ as God and Savior, have been moving toward an essential identity as a "fellowship of churches" rather than as an agency conducting programs and activities apart from its members. They also have become more conscious of the WCC as one part of a many-centered network of ecumenical partners that includes a wide variety of ecumenical bodies, churches not affiliated with the WCC (the Roman Catholic Church and Pentecostal and Evangelical bodies especially), and less formal organizations and groups.

Throughout its more than fifty years the WCC has undergone various restructurings. It has entered another as it tries to integrate its work in four basic areas under one administrative whole:

1. Selected issue and theme priorities (including the historic groupings of Faith and Order; Mission and Evangelism; Justice, Peace, and Creation; and Education and Ecumenical Formation).
2. Ecumenical, regional, interreligious, and international relations.
3. Communication, public information, publications, and documents.
4. Finances, personnel, house services, and computer and technology services.

Participation in the WCC has always been strenuous for its member churches. The issues of faith and order often took priority in the early years of its formation and were marked by dominant European scholarship. After World War II, much work was done immediately to provide aid to refugees and displaced persons and to serve in the rebuilding of communities torn apart during the war. The 1966 Geneva conference "Church and Society" brought many more participants from the Third World, who have continued to press for WCC priorities toward systemic change and justice issues, especially for the poor, ethnic/racial groups, and women. The WCC's Program to Combat Racism has been one of its most controversial efforts, because it attempted to alleviate suffering in areas of Africa, especially where conflict between political groups was occurring. The WCC has been at the forefront of concern for the degradation of the environment and has significantly tied this concern to justice and peace in its 1990 world convocation "Justice, Peace, and the Integrity of Creation" in Seoul, South Korea. It has also championed the dignity of women through the "Ecumenical Decade of Churches in Solidarity with Women" program.

Approximately every seven or eight years the WCC holds its World Assembly, which is the highest decision-making body. Past World Assemblies have been held, each with a central theme, in the United States (1954), India (1961), Sweden (1968), Kenya (1975), Canada (1983), and Australia (1991). The theme at the 1998 Harare, Zimbabwe, Assembly was "Turn to God—Rejoice in Hope." At this eighth World Assembly the delegates considered a major policy document titled "Towards a Common Understanding and Vision of the World Council of Churches," which was intended as a point of reference and charter for the future.

Between assemblies, a 156-member Central Committee, elected by the World Assembly, meets annually to monitor and develop policies set by the Assembly. There is a general secretary of the WCC, who since January 1993 has been Rev. Dr. Konrad Raiser, a member of the Evangelical Church in Germany. He meets semiannually with the Central Committee's Executive Committee, including its several presidents and officers.

The Administrative Center of the WCC is in Geneva, at 150 route de Ferney, P.O. Box 2100, 1211 Geneva 2, Switzerland. A modest U.S. WCC office is at 475 Riverside Drive, Room 915, New York, NY 10115.

See also ECUMENICAL MOVEMENT; NATIONAL COUNCIL OF THE CHURCHES OF CHRIST IN THE U.S.A.

BIBLIOGRAPHY

Nicholas Lossky et al., eds., *Dictionary of the Ecumenical Movement*, pp. 1080–1100. 1991.
World Council of Churches Yearbook 1998 and selected brochures from Geneva and U.S. offices.

Peggy L. Shriver

Worship.

See Liturgy and Worship.

Y

Yarmulke.

See Kippah.

Yi Jing.

See I Ching.

Yoga

There is no practice associated with Hinduism better known to Americans than yoga, and perhaps no other single term has a greater range of spiritual and secular connotations to those who practice it. The term "yoga" refers variously to an ancient philosophical tradition of orthodox Hinduism, to a number of mental, physical, and spiritual disciplines practiced widely in South Asian religious traditions, and to a range of different practices valued in modern life for their promotion of health and well-being.

Yoga was developed in India in ancient times by religious seekers (yogis) as a spiritual discipline. The etymology of the term derives from the Sanskrit verb *yuj,* meaning literally to "yoke" or "harness," and in this sense yoga is the harnessing of mental, physical and spiritual potential. Although its precise dating and origins are unclear, the theoretical and practical foundations of yoga were systematized in the *Yoga-sūtra* of Patañjali, which many scholars place in the second or third century C.E. This text forms the nor-

mative core of classical yoga, one of the six philosophical systems of orthodox Hinduism. The aim of classical yoga is to realize the absolute distinctness of spirit and matter, and thereby to bring about liberation and peace from the domination that the material world exerts over the immaterial spirit. The *Yoga-sūtra* describes eight steps of practices that cultivate mental tranquility, beginning with the observance of moral principles and culminating in a state of spiritual freedom.

In a more general sense, the term "yoga" is used in South Asia to refer to meditative and religious disciplines practiced not only by Hindus, but also by Jains and Buddhists. Yoga meditation also provided the roots from which forms of Buddhist meditation such as Zen and Vipassana developed and spread across Asia. It was within the Hindu tradition, however, that yoga was most elaborated and developed as a central form of religious practice.

Hindu authorities recognize several different types of yoga. In some contexts, yoga means discipline or religious path and suggests a plurality of different conceptions of the religious life. One important schema, articulated in the *Bhagavad Gītā,* describes three types of yoga to be followed according to an individual's inclination and abilities: *jñana yoga,* the discipline of wisdom; *karma yoga,* the discipline of works; and *bhakti yoga,* the discipline of devotion to God. All of these disciplines are aimed at the goal of liberation from the ignorance and limitations of the human condition.

In addition to this threefold schema, other traditions of yoga have developed through the ages. *Haṭha*

A woman demonstrates the half-spinal twist, a yoga position.   (Credit: CORBIS/Tony Arruza.)

yoga, the yoga of physical exertion, may be the yoga most familiar to Americans. It involves disciplining and controlling the body through assuming rigorous physical postures, regulating the breath, and cleansing the body by various purifying techniques. *Rāja yoga,* "royal yoga," refers to the meditative yoga articulated in the classical system of Patañjali. *Kuṇḍalinī yoga,* the yoga of serpent power, is a type of esoteric or tantric yoga that involves envisioning the divine energy that lies in a potential but unrealized state at the base of the spinal column, like a coiled serpent. The awakening of this energy and its movement up to the top of the head produces enlightenment. None of these varieties of yoga need preclude the others; *hatha yoga* is sometimes conceived to be a preparatory discipline for *rāja yoga,* and some modern teachers have combined different aspects of some or all of these yogas to form syntheses, as in the case of *integral yoga.*

Yoga has been known and practiced in the United States for more than a century. It entered America's literary imagination through Trancendentalist Henry David Thoreau's writings, in which he described himself striving to practice "the yoga" and claimed that at "rare intervals, even I am a yogi." However, a more substantial introduction of yoga to America came with the arrival of Swami Vivekananda from India for the 1893 World's Parliament of Religions in Chicago. Swami Vivekananda represented Hinduism at the Parliament with great flair and charisma, and went on to found the Vedanta Society in New York in 1894 to promote the teachings of Vedanta philosophy and yoga.

Although the Vedanta Society attracted a small following of Americans, it was not until the arrival of Paramahamsa Yogananda and the publication of his *Autobiography of a Yogi* (1946) that yoga began to become familiar to mainstream America. His organization, the Self-Realization Fellowship, attracted a considerable number of Americans to yoga and the teachings of Hinduism. Yogananda taught *kriyā yoga,* a form of *rāja yoga* that incorporates concepts and exercises drawing from *kuṇḍalinī yoga.* Other charismatic Indian teachers have introduced yoga to America, such as the disciples of Sri Aurobindo Ghose (1872–1950) of India, who established international associations and ashrams in the United States to teach his style of yoga. In addition, Sri Swami Satchidananda, a disciple of Swami Sivananda Saraswati, founded Integral Yoga International, an organization with centers across North America promoting yoga and a life of nonviolence, purity, and nonattachment.

The repeal of the Asian Exclusion Act in 1965 brought about the emergence of a vibrant Indian-American community, which has expanded and altered the nature and presence of Hinduism and yoga in America. Temples, ashrams, and summer camps offer yoga classes and retreats, and many Indian-Americans view yoga as a vital aspect of Indian culture and heritage.

Since the 1960s *hatha yoga,* the yoga of breathing and postures, has become popular as a form of exercise to promote health, strength, and relaxation, and is often entirely disassociated from its spiritual and religious moorings. While yoga was traditionally undertaken as a means for transcending secular and worldly existence, it has in modern times become a method for people not to free themselves from the human condition, but to find well-being, longevity, and tranquility within it. Its influence has grown steadily in the last several decades, such that yoga classes are now a staple in many fitness and wellness centers. Yoga has also been adopted by the New Age movement among seekers of holistic health practices and eastern wisdom.

Teachers of yoga within Hindu communities as well as New Age and secular yoga organizations often emphasize the scientific nature of yoga. For many Hindus, yoga is a meeting place where science and religion come together, and they view yoga as demonstrating universal and scientific truths of Hinduism. Many non-Hindus regard yoga as a means to inner peace and stress relief, with results that can be scientifically verified. In both cases, the distinctly modern regard for science combines with ancient spiritual teachings to form creative and adaptive responses to the needs and challenges of contemporary American life.

See also Bhagavad Gītā; Buddhism; Enlightenment; Hinduism; Jainism; New Age Spirituality; Self-Realization Fellowship; Vedanta Society; Zen.

Bibliography

Some of the best sources for further reading on yoga in contemporary America are periodicals, in particular *Hinduism Today* and *Yoga Journal.*

Eliade, Mircea. *Yoga: Immortality and Freedom.* 1973.

Feuerstein, Georg. *Encyclopedic Dictionary of Yoga.* 1990.

Iyengar, B. K. S. *Light on Yoga.* 1966.

Stoler Miller, Barbara. *Yoga: Discipline of Freedom.* 1996.

Maria Hibbets

Yogi, Maharishi Machesh.

See Transcendental Meditation.

Young Life

Today an international, evangelical Protestant organization whose mission is evangelizing high school students, Young Life was founded by a former Presbyterian minister turned youth evangelist named Jim Rayburn (1909–1970). Like similar organizations, the story of Young Life is the story of an evangelist who devised a new strategy for reaching potential converts, whose strategy in turn became the basis for a large organization that has outlived not only its founder but also the novelty of its founder's strategy (compare, e.g., Dwight L. Moody, Charles Finney, earlier evangelists). While Young Life is by no means faltering, as its 1,837 full-time staff and 9,430 volunteers in 1997 demonstrate, it has lost the innovative edge it once had and has grown consumed with its own preservation. Thus current staff spend much energy maintaining their aging programs and raising funds, with little time left for youth evangelization.

Jim Rayburn was a student at Dallas Theological Seminary in 1938 when the senior minister supervising his field placement challenged him to view the local, unchurched high school students as his ministry focus. After a failed attempt to reach these students through an after-school book club, Rayburn devised a strategy that combined socializing with high school students at popular sites such as sports games, pep rallies, or soda fountains, with an evening meeting at a student's home that featured up-tempo songs, com-

edy skits, silly contests, and a very brief gospel sermon. This successful strategy, which offered to a newly emerging American teen culture a midweek outing with their friends and a lively seminary student, spawned similar groups across the region and later across the country. Rayburn's approach, subsequently labeled "relationship evangelism," emphasized the building of relationships first between Young Life leaders and high school students, and evangelizing later. Rayburn often said that Young Life leaders must "earn the right to be heard," and that earning that right must involve fun, for it was "a sin to bore a kid."

Upon graduation, Rayburn rejected positions at several churches, and in the tradition of American voluntarism founded the "Young Life Campaign" in 1942—a nonprofit organization whose mission was nationwide implementation of Rayburn's youth evangelism strategies. In 1946 Rayburn instigated the purchase of Young Life's first camp, against the Young Life board of trustees' recommendation, and made camping an additional component in his strategy for evangelization. Today Young Life is best known among evangelical organizations for its camping program, as its methods of relationship evangelism have long been co-opted by churches and other evangelical organizations. Its midweek evening meetings, now called clubs, convene in suburban communities across the United States, though their Rayburn-era format strikes observers as increasingly anachronistic. While a small proportion of Young Life staff work in cities, their programs are generally small and succeed by ignoring Young Life's dominant programming and collaborating extensively with other community organizations and local churches. Absent another Jim Rayburn at the helm, Young Life shall likely continue exactly as it has out of sheer organizational persistence, irrespective of its relevance to future generations of American youth.

See also Campus Crusade for Christ; Conversion; Evangelical Christianity; Practice; Proselytizing; Psychology of Religion; Youth for Christ.

Bibliography

Borgman, Dean. "A History of American Youth Ministry." In *The Complete Book of Youth Ministry,* edited by Warren S. Benson and Mark H. Senter III. 1987.

Caillet, Emile. *Young Life.* 1956.

Meredith, Char. *It's a Sin to Bore a Kid: The Story of Young Life.* 1978.

Rayburn, Jim, III. *Dance, Children, Dance.* 1984.

Shelley, Bruce. "The Rise of Evangelical Youth Movements." *Fides et Historia,* no. 1 (1986): 47–63.

Timothy T. Clydesdale

Youth for Christ

Youth for Christ (YFC) is a nondenominational evangelistic youth organization. The Youth for Christ movement grew out of fundamentalist dissatisfaction with the perceived liberalism of organizations such as the YMCA. The movement's precise origins are unclear; however, the New York Christian Youth Center rallies begun in 1932 by Lloyd Bryant of Manhattan's Calvary Baptist Church constituted an early and influential example of a Youth for Christ–style program. Unrelated but comparable efforts were in evidence in Washington, D.C., Philadelphia, Indianapolis, Detroit, St. Louis, Minneapolis and other northern cities in the 1930s and early 1940s, while similar interchurch cooperative youth rallies appeared in the South among the Southern Baptists.

With the coming of World War II the movement picked up considerable momentum. While the various Youth for Christ efforts remained unconnected, its regional manifestations shared a number of important features. Most local rallies revolved around dynamic, young preachers impatient with the methods of traditional revivalism and aware of the tastes and expectations of the developing youth culture around them. Flashy dressers who wore styles favored by teens, they ran tight, well-rehearsed programs and often patterned their speaking styles after well-known radio personalities. Programs were designed to emphasize audience participation and featured humor and skits. Music was key to the emerging Youth for Christ style, with an emphasis on lively gospel songs for congregational-style singing and instrumentation and with vocal arrangements for special music that closely paralleled the era's popular Big Band styles.

Among the most successful of the Youth for Christ organizations was Chicagoland Youth for Christ, begun in early 1944 by Torrey Johnson, pastor of Chicago's Midwest Bible Church. Deluged with inquiries after a fall rally at Chicago Stadium drew a crowd of twenty-eight thousand and nationwide publicity, Johnson and his brother-in-law, evangelist Robert "Bob" C. Cook, dashed off a quick how-to book and took the lead in organizing a temporary Youth for Christ office in Chicago. A subsequent program on Memorial Day 1945 attracted seventy-five thousand to Chicago's Soldier Field, stimulating a renewed outpouring of press attention, including an endorsement from newspaper publishing magnate William Randolph Hearst. With this momentum, forty-two delegates from around the country officially organized Youth for Christ at a July 1945 meeting in Winona Lake, Indiana. Johnson was elected its first president, and a young pastor from Western Springs, Illinois—Billy Graham—was hired as YFC's first full-time field representative.

With a new institutional framework, YFC experienced tremendous growth during the next few years. In 1946 it was estimated that there were nine hundred separate YFC rallies scattered across North America, with regular attendance of more than one million. Additionally, YFC teams began extensive work among U.S. servicemen overseas and established a number of YFC branches in other countries.

YFC's growth was not without controversy, however. Many mainline Protestant critics denounced the movement as frivolous, while some conservatives frowned on its incorporation of worldly entertainment values. But in the face of growing juvenile delinquency and the specter of the Communist threat, many church leaders and a number of civic leaders and journalists were happy to back any movement that seemed to reaffirm religion and traditional American values.

In 1948, the same year that Billy Graham enlisted several YFC colleagues for an independent evangelistic team, Bob Cook replaced Johnson as YFC president. Under Cook, the organization's methods and focus gradually evolved as YFC concentrated in the 1950s and 1960s on the nation's growing suburbs, a change symbolized by the 1953 move of its headquarters from Chicago to nearby Wheaton, Illinois. Rallies gradually receded in importance, and the establishment of high school–based Bible clubs replaced work among servicemen. By 1960 there were nearly 2,700 YFC-sponsored Bible clubs in the United States and Canada. During the same period summer camping programs were expanded and Bible quiz teams became a YFC rage, leading to spirited local, regional, and national competitions.

Since the 1960s, the high school Bible club (renamed Campus Life in the early 1960s), controlled through local and regional YFC chapters, has remained the organization's basic strategy. However, since the mid-1960s there has been a conscious effort to keep YFC from being too narrowly identified with white, middle-class youth, and as a result it has—with uneven results—continually sought to extend its work among minorities and economically disadvantaged youth. YFC's organizational peak came in the early and mid-1970s (resulting from the convergence of "baby boom" demographics and the Jesus People Movement) but was followed by steady decline and attendant financial problems during the 1980s. In a move to stabilize its operation, it sold off its long-running magazine, *Campus Life,* in 1982 and in another cost-cutting effort moved its offices to Denver in 1991. As of 1998 YFC had 127 foreign branches, as well as 224 local chapters in the United States, overseeing more than 2,300 programs in schools, neighborhoods, and juvenile facilities across the country.

See also EVANGELICAL CHRISTIANITY; GRAHAM, BILLY; INTERVARSITY CHRISTIAN FELLOWSHIP; JESUS MOVEMENT; JOURNALISM, RELIGIOUS; MUSIC; PUBLISHING, RELIGIOUS; TELEVANGELISM.

BIBLIOGRAPHY

Carpenter, Joel A. *Revive Us Again: The Reawakening of American Fundamentalism.* 1997.

Hefley, James C. *God Goes to High School.* 1970.

Johnson, Torrey, and Robert Cook. *Reaching Youth for Christ.* 1944.

Larson, Mel. *Young Man on Fire: The Story of Torrey Johnson and Youth for Christ.* 1945.

Shelley, Bruce L. "The Rise of Evangelical Youth Movements." *Fides et Historia* 18 (1986): 47–63.

Youth for Christ records, Collection 48, Archives of the Billy Graham Center, Wheaton College, Wheaton, Ill.

Larry Eskridge

Z

Zen

The Sanskrit word *dhyana* (generally referring to an emptying or stilling form of meditation) was transliterated into Chinese as *chan-na* and abbreviated to *chan; zen* is the Japanese pronunciation of the Chinese character *chan*. *Dhyana, chan,* and *zen*, however, need to be considered separately. As an Indian word, *dhyana* refers to a meditation practice, not a sect of Buddhism. The practice of dhyana in America may or may not have any connection with the Chinese or Japanese sects known as Chan and Zen. Conversely, the American assimilation of Asian cultural elements associated with Chan and Zen may have nothing to do with any systematic meditation practice. Furthermore, despite the scholarly use of the terms *chan* and *zen* as if they were interchangeable, Chan and Zen in America need to be considered as distinct because China and Japan have distinct positions in American culture. Because of differences in the political histories of China and Japan in the last two hundred years, Zen has been much better known in America than Chan, and even Chan has been seen through the lens of Japanese sectarian scholarship. Chan is sometimes described as Chinese Zen, whereas historically it would be slightly more accurate to say that Zen is Japanese Chan.

Dhyana has been practiced at least since the beginning of Buddhism in India, and some monks were famous for their meditation skills, but the term identified no particular group. Buddhist ideas and practices began filtering into China in the first century C.E., but the "Chan lineage" emerged as a sectarian category much later. Efforts to date the birth of Chan

have produced widely varying answers, ranging from the fifth to the thirteenth centuries C.E., depending on what is meant by "Chan." Its mythical lineage identifies the obscure figure of Bodhidharma as bringing Chan to China in the fifth century, but the full articulation of Chan was a very gradual process. Most scholars locate the birth of the Chan lineage in debates during the eighth century C.E., followed by significant elaboration and the creation of lineage records in the tenth and eleventh centuries. In China, Chan became more or less identified with mainstream monastic Buddhism, but Zen in Japan became a sect among sects, continuing to compete with other monastic forms of Buddhism, such as Shingon and Tendai. Actually, two main subsects developed within Zen itself: Rinzai and Soto, dating from the thirteenth century.

Because of severe anti-Buddhist persecution in the early Meiji period (1868–1872) in Japan, and as a response to westernization, Japanese Buddhist leaders made efforts to redefine Buddhism as scientific and modern (in more or less Western terms). Because of the prestige of Western recognition, Zen leaders were much more oriented toward missionary work than were their Chinese counterparts. The contours of this newly redefined Zen owe much to the increasing nationalism and militarization of Japan from the late nineteenth century through to 1945. Zen in Japan was redefined as useful to the imperialist ideology, and identical to Japanese identity itself. This "Japanese exceptionalism" was the background to the early dissemination of Zen in America, starting with the Japanese delegation to the 1893 World's Parliament of Reli-

Musician Leonard Cohen meditating at the Mount Baldy Zen Center in California, November 10, 1995.   (Credit: CORBIS/Neal Preston.)

gions in Chicago, through the teaching and writing of D. T. Suzuki (1870–1966) and others. Suzuki, for example, claimed late in his life that he had never met a single Caucasian American who truly understood Zen. Even Westerners who had some inkling, such as Henry David Thoreau, had glimpsed only a reflection of Asian wisdom. These rather provocative claims are understandable when one sees that for a whole generation of Japanese Zen scholars, Zen was inseparable from Japaneseness. Furthermore, Japanese Zen leaders promoted the widespread perception of the association (or even identity) of Zen and the elite arts, especially calligraphy, martial arts, painting, landscaping, and poetry, arts that were by no means monopolized by Zen monks in Asia.

In the mid-nineteenth century Chinese immigrants to California established temples, usually blending Chan Buddhist elements with popular religion, Taoism, and Confucianism. Chinese communities in California have supported a number of Chan monasteries, such as the City of Ten Thousand Buddhas (Wan Fo Cheng) founded by Hsan-Hua (1918–1995), and the Hsi-lai Temple led by Hsing-Yun. Japanese immigration, around the turn of the century, introduced other sectarian forms of Buddhism. The Pure Land sect Jodo Shinshu was especially active, establishing the Buddhist Church of America in 1899. Though

Zen is the best known, there have certainly been many other forms of Buddhism in America. Zen in America has been marked by a tension (sometimes fruitful) between Japanese traditional orthodoxy and American nativization.

The 1893 World's Parliament of Religions was a pivotal event in connecting Japanese Zen monks (such as the Rinzai monk Shaku Soen, who made later visits as well) with American Transcendentalists and Theosophists. Paul Carus attended the Parliament and became instrumental in keeping open lines of communication between Zen and American culture. Other Japanese Zen teachers, disciples of Shaku Soen, arrived in America: Daisetsu Teitaro (D. T.) Suzuki in 1899, Shaku Sokatsu in 1906, and Senzaki Nyogen in 1905. A number of meditation halls were founded in California in the 1920s and after. In 1931, one of Shaku Sokatsu's disciples, Sasaki Shigetsu (also known as Sokei-an) founded the Buddhist Society of America in New York. D. T. Suzuki (1870–1966) worked at Paul Carus's Open Court Publishing Company from 1897 to 1909. He visited again in the 1930s and 1950s. One of Suzuki's enduring legacies is the widespread assertion that Zen in not a "religion." He steadfastly refused to reduce Zen to any particular form, organization, historical movement, or set of dogmas. Rather, Zen was the indefinable quality of enlightened experience itself, the pure basis of all other religions.

World War II undoubtedly stifled the development of Zen in America, with Japan a military enemy and Japanese-Americans subjected to discrimination and forced confinement in internment camps. However, in the 1950s Zen (and in particular D. T. Suzuki's work) enjoyed a revived interest and numerous Zen centers were established. These Zen centers were headed by Japanese Zen monks, but in the 1970s a generation of white American monks received full initiation and leadership, including Richard Baker, Philip Kapleau, and Robert Aitken.

Soto Zen developed in America after World War II, with, for example, the founding of the Chicago Buddhist Temple by Soyu Matsuoka Roshi, and the founding of the San Francisco Zen Center in 1961 by Shunryu Suzuki Roshi. Shunryu Suzuki Roshi had arrived in America in 1959. After his death the Zen Center was administered by his successor, Richard Baker. Attached to this center are the Zen Mountain Center (Tassajara) and the farm Green Gulch. Another Caucasian Zen leader was Jiyu Kennett, who founded the Mount Shasta Zen monastery in 1969.

A form of Zen that claimed to embrace both Rinzai and Soto was founded in Japan by Sogaku Harada. Taizan Maezumi Roshi established the Zen Center of Los Angeles in 1956. Another disciple, Hakuun Yasutani Roshi, visited in 1962 to promote his master's version of Zen. An American-born disciple, Philip Kapleau, founded the Zen Meditation Center in Rochester, New York, after thirteen years of training in Japan. Kapleau's best-known book, *The Three Pillars of Zen* (1966), remains popular and authoritative, though his willingness to nativize Zen in America led to a break with Harada.

Popular awareness of Buddhism after World War II benefited from the development of Asian studies and Buddhist studies programs in universities nationwide, and from the popularization of some elements of Buddhism by the "Beat generation." The literary work of Jack Kerouac, Allen Ginsberg, Gary Snyder, and others produced a Buddhism that was aesthetic, experiential, ecstatic, and philosophically antinomian. It was also largely their own invention.

Picked up later by the counterculture and various consciousness-expanding movements in the 1960s, and still perennially popular, this romantic "Beat Zen" had little to do with Zen in Japan. Whereas Zen in Japan emphasized monasticism, American Zen remains predominantly lay-oriented. Whereas Zen monks in Asia do not necessarily meditate on any regular basis, American Zen has emphasized meditation as the sine qua non of legitimate Buddhism. A whole series of stereotypes of Zen and Zen monks have been thoroughly deconstructed by scholars such as Bernard Faure and Robert Buswell, Jr., and serious practitioners today are usually realistic about Asian Zen mythology and its American twists. Still, in popular usage the word *Zen* can still mean almost anything: a carefree sentiment, an experience of intense focus, a label for Chinese landscape painting, empty-headedness, or a brand name on T-shirts and tea. The popular imagination of Zen owes much to the best-selling book by Robert Pirsig, *Zen and the Art of Motorcycle Maintenance,* and the works of Alan Watts (e.g., *The Way of Zen*). Given the individualistic voluntarism of the American Zen community, it is impossible to number American Zen Buddhists with any precision. American Zen Buddhists of non-Asian ancestry tend to be white, middle-class, urban, and often well-educated, though not necessarily: Zen meditation has become popular, for example, in prisons as well.

See also BUDDHA; BUDDHISM; CHINESE-AMERICAN RELIGIONS; JAPANESE-AMERICAN RELIGIONS.

BIBLIOGRAPHY

Buswell, Robert E., Jr. *The Zen Monastic Experience.* 1992.

Chadwick, David. *Crooked Cucumber: The Life and Zen Teaching of Shunryu Suzuki.* 1999.

Faure, Bernard. *The Rhetoric of Immediacy: A Cultural Critique of Chan/Zen Buddhism.* 1991.

Fields, Rick. *How the Swans Came to the Lake: A Narrative History of Buddhism in America.* 1992.

Kapleau, Philip. *The Three Pillars of Zen: Teaching, Practice, and Enlightenment.* 1966.

Pirsig, Robert M. *Zen and the Art of Motorcycle Maintenance: An Inquiry into Values.* 1974.

Suzuki, Daisetz T. *Zen and Japanese Culture.* 1959.

Watts, Alan. *The Way of Zen.* 1957.

Eric Reinders

Zionism

Zionism, the Jews' movement of national liberation, holds that the Jews constitute "a people, one people." Founded in 1897 by Theodor Herzl (1860–1904) to establish a Jewish state, Zionism created the State of Israel in 1948. The Zionist movement therefore identified the Jews as a political, not solely a religious, group, and maintained that the Jews' problem was a political one. They held that anti-Semitism was deeply embedded in Europe and that the Jews had to evacuate Europe to save their own lives. Building a Jewish state in Palestine formed the principal goal of political Zionism, which achieved success in 1948. Zionist thought extended to political questions on the definition of the Jewish people and the description and meaning of the history of the Jewish people. Zionism formed one of the principal sources for the definition of Jewish thought and scholarship in the first half of the twentieth century.

The Zionist Definition of "Israel," Worldview, Way of Life

First of all, Zionism defined its theory of "Israel" as a people, one people, in a secular sense. In Judaism, "Israel" had meant the people of God, brought together at Sinai to receive the Torah. Zionism therefore represented a considerable revision in the received definition of who and what the Jews were, now no longer just a religious community but also an ethnic or national entity. Zionism shaped a worldview that composed of the diverse histories of Jews a single, unitary history of the Jewish people, seen as a nation. That history led from the land of Israel through exile back to the land of Israel. Again, this recapitulation of the biblical narrative derived not from a religious but from a nationalist perspective. The way of life of Zionism, in place of the religious way of life of prayer, practice of the Commandments, and study of the Torah, for the elitist or activist Zionist required political action. That meant participation in meetings, organizing within the local community, and attendance at national and international conferences. Later, as settlement in the land itself became possible, Zionism defined as the most noble way of living immigration to the land, and, for the socialist wing of Zionism, building a collective community (kibbutz). So Zionism presented a complete and fully articulated Judaism, and, in its day, one of the most powerful and effective of them all.

Four main streams of Zionist theory flowed abundantly and side by side in the formative decades, expressed in cultural, political, socialist, and religious Zionist organizations.

Cultural Zionism

The cultural stream, represented by Ahad HaAm, laid stress on Zion as a spiritual and cultural center, to unite all parts of the Jewish people. Ahad HaAm laid emphasis on spiritual preparation, ideological and cultural activities, and the long-term intellectual issues of persuading the Jews of the Zionist premises. The revival of the Hebrew language as a living tongue represented the greatest achievement of cultural Zionism.

Political Zionism

From the beginning, Zionism maintained that the Jews should engage in practical activity, seeking recognition from the nations of the Jews' own nationality, too. This political Zionism sought further to provide for the emigration of the masses of their nation from Eastern Europe, then entering a protracted state of political disintegration and already long suffering from economic dislocation, to the land of Israel—or somewhere, anywhere. Herzl in particular placed the requirement for legal recognition of a Jewish state over the location of the state, and, in doing so, set forth the policy that the practical salvation of the Jews through political means would form the definition of Zionism. Herzl stressed that the Jewish state would come into existence in the forum of international politics. The instruments of state—a political forum, a bank, a mode of national allegiance, a press, a central body, and a leader—came into being in the aftermath of the first Zionist congress, in Basel. Herzl spent the rest of his life after 1897—less than a decade—seeking an international charter and recognition of the Jews' state.

Socialist Zionism

A third stream of Zionism derived from socialism and expressed a Zionist vision of socialism or a socialist vision of Zionism. The Jewish state was to be socialist, as, indeed, it was for its first three decades. Socialist Zionism in its earlier theoretical formulation (before its near-total bureaucratization) emphasized that a proletarian Zionism would define the arena for the class struggle within the Jewish people to be realized.

Religious Zionism

While many Orthodox Jews rejected Zionism because they believed only God would bring holy Israel back to the land of Israel at the end of days, some took a different view. Mizrachi (coined from the Hebrew words *merkaz ruhani,* spiritual center), founded in 1902, took the slogan "The Land of Israel for the People of Israel according to the Torah of Israel." Mizrachi Zionism propagated the ideal of a Jewish national renaissance among Orthodox Jews and formed the federation of religious Zionists within world Zionism.

The Zionist Success

Zionism became a mass movement in World War I. On November 2, 1917, the British government issued the Balfour Declaration, declaring that it favored the establishment in Palestine of a Jewish national home, provided that the civil and religious rights of others not be impaired. In the rising nationalism of European peoples and the breakup of the multiethnic empires such as Russia, Austria-Hungary, and Germany into nation-states such as Poland, Czechoslovakia, Lithuania, Latvia, and Estonia, the Jews of Central and

Eastern Europe saw in Zionism a counterpart of Jewish nationalism. In the aftermath of the Holocaust, most Jews worldwide favored the establishment of a Jewish state in Palestine. Led by David Ben-Gurion and in accord with U.N. decision of November 1947, the State of Israel was declared on May 15, 1948.

Zionism in the United States

In the United States, until the massacre of the Jews of Europe between 1933 and 1945 and the founding of the State of Israel in 1948, Zionism remained very much a minority movement in Jewry. Jewish socialism and Yiddishism, in the new nations of Eastern Europe, and the New Deal in American Democratic politics attracted a far larger part of Jewry, and the former, though not the latter, formed a competing Judaic system in particular. Reform Judaism rejected the definition of the Jews as a political entity and insisted that they formed a religious community. Before 1948 the Jewish population of the land of Israel/Palestine had scarcely reached half a million, a small portion of the Jews of the world. In the United States and in Western Europe Zionist sentiment did not predominate, even though a certain romantic appeal attached to the pioneers in the land. Down, indeed, to 1967, Zionism constituted one choice among many for Jews throughout the world. When the State of Israel regained access to Jewish holy places closed off from Jewish access from 1948 through 1967, many thought that Zionism had finally reached its goal: the reunification of Jerusalem as the capital of the Jewish State of Israel.

Zionism and Israelism as American Judaism

Since, at the present time, Jewry nearly unanimously attaches to the State of Israel the status of the Jewish state; affirms that the Jews form a people, one people; concedes all of the principal propositions of Zionism; and places the achievement of the Zionist program as the highest priority for Jewry throughout the world, we may say that today, but not a great many days before, Zionism forms a system bearing self-evident truth for vast numbers of Jews. But because post-1948 Zionism in the State of Israel defined "being a Zionist" as settling in the State of Israel or planning to do so, American Jewry has had to reframe its pro-Israel attitudes and activities into a different pattern from the normative Israeli-Zionist one. It has emphasized political activism in the support of Israeli causes, frequent trips to the State of Israel, learning modern Hebrew, and other activities connected with the culture and life of the Jewish state.

See also ANTI-SEMITISM; BELONGING, RELIGIOUS; HOLOCAUST; HOLY LAND; JEWISH IDENTITY; JEWISH RENEWAL; JUDAISM; RELIGIOUS COMMUNITIES; RELIGIOUS PERSECUTION.

BIBLIOGRAPHY

Avineri, Shlomo. *The Making of Modern Zionism: Intellectual Origins of the Jewish State.* 1981.

Cohen, Naomi. *American Jews and the Zionist Idea.*

Elon, Amos. *Herzl.* 1975, repr. 1986.

Halkin, Hillel. *Letters to an American Jewish Friend: A Zionist's Polemic.* 1977.

Jacob Neusner

INDEX

Page numbers in **boldface** indicate article titles.
Page numbers in *italics* indicate illustrations.

congregations, 515
deacon, 178
as denomination, 183–184
European persecution of, 248
evangelical, 237
first African-American congregation, 6
fundamentalist, 250, 251, 270, 271, 272, 455
hell and, 299
heresy and, 301
liturgy and worship, 395
ordination, 503
ordination of women, 52, 53, 178, 504
Religious Right and, 604
schism, 409
seeker churches, 659
in southern states, 687, 688
True Love Waits founding, 749
See also Brethren; Southern Baptist Convention
Baraitha, 581
Barbara, Santa, 9
Bare-Faced Messiah, The (Miller), 648
Baring-Gould, Sabine, 464
Bar mitzvah and bat mitzvah, 53–54, 61, 256, 372, 612, 613
Barna, George, 127
Barrett, Leonard, 714
Barth, Karl, 243, 398, 495, 729
Barthes, Roland, 606
Bartholomew I, Patriarch, 207
Base communities, 54–55
Basham, Don, 186, 244
Basic Lecture Series, 679
Basic Types of Pastoral Counseling (Clinebell), 519
Basil, Saint, 22, 153, 208
Bates, Joseph, 666
Bat mitzvah. See Bar mitzvah and bat mitzvah
Battin, Margaret Pabst, 235
Battle Creek (Mich.) sanitarium, 667
Bauer, Gary, 117, 605
Baum, L. Frank, 274
Bawa Muhaiyadeen, 55–56, 706
Bayh, Birch, 604
B.C. (Before Christ), 92
B.C.E. (Before the Christian Era), 92
Beachy Amish, 19
Bean, Carl, 390
Beatification. See Sainthood
Beatles, 59, 303, 744, 765, 766
Beat movement, 202, 279, 434, 469, 799
Beauvoir, Simone de, 243
Bebbington, David, 237
Beccaria, Cesare, 95
Becker, Ernest, 180
Beecher, Henry Ward, 546
Beethoven, Ludwig van, 243, 466
Begin, Menachem, 29, 371
Be Here Now (Dass), 303
Bel Air Presbyterian Church (Calif.), 109
Bell, Catherine, 73, 397
Bell, John, 13, 575
Bellah, Robert, 133, 327, 473, 606, 681
Bellevue Baptist Church (Memphis, Tenn.), 547
Belonging, religious, 56–58
ashram, 36–37

communes, 143–144
congregation, 149–150
cults, 161–164, 165
faith and, 247–250
future of religion, 273–274
stable U.S. levels, 656
See also Jewish identity
Beltane, 103, 630
Belur Matha (Calcutta), 584, 764
Benedict, David, 32
Benedict, Saint, 153, 595
Benedict, Dirk, 404
Benedictines, 394, 542, 595–596, 608
Benedictine Sisters of Perpetual Adoration, 595
Bene Israel Congregation (Cincinnati), 582
Bengal, 329, 330
Ben-Gurion, David, 801
Benjamine, Elbert, 38
Bennett, Dennis, 109, 531
Bennett, James Gordon, 354
Bennett, John, 703
Bennett, John C., 301
Bennett, William, 268
Ben Sira, 446, 645, 646, 684
Benson, Ezra Taft, 76
Bentougong, 114
Berg, David Brandt ("Mo"), 143, 251, 344
Berger, Peter, 123, 473, 681
Berlin, Irving, 120
Berlioz, Hector, 466
Bernadette, Saint, 524
Bernard of Clairvaux, 413
Bernstein, Leonard, 466
Berrigan, Daniel, 100, 301, 508
Berrigan, Philip, 508
Berry, Thomas, 156, 157, 213
Bertolucci, John, 99
Bethel Bible College (Topeka), 280
Beth Elohim Congregation (Charleston), 582
Bethlehem, 311, 539, 540
Bethlehem's Octave, 385
Bethune, Ade, 100
Beyond God the Father (Daly), 257
Beyond the Body (Blackmore), 599
Bezalel, 440
Bhagavad Gītā, 58–59, 287, 302, 373
on dharma, 188
on reincarnation, 591
on three thpes of yoga, 791
Bhagavad Gītā, As It Is, The (Prabhupada), 59
Bhajan, Yogi, 678, 767
Bhakti, 58, 791
Bhaktipada, Swami, 330
Bhaktivedanta, A. C., 221
Bhardwaj, S. M., 535
Bhavani, 748
Bias-free language. See Inclusive language
Bible, 60–62
as allegorical, 471
as androcentric, 257
apocalypse and, 29–30, 447–448
archetype and, 33
authority of, 448
blasphemy and, 71
born again Christians and, 76

capital punishment and, 97, 98
clergy and, 139
creationism and, 155–156
demons and devils mentioned in, 185, 241
demythologization of, 471–472
dispensational premillennialist interpretation, 549
Doubleday's Anchor Bible, 567
dreams and, 199
evangelical primacy of, 237
feminist preaching and, 548
feminist questioning of, 275, 522
first five books. See Torah
food symbolism in, 263
heaven and, 297
hell and, 299
"Higher Criticism" and, 394
human rights and, 233
inclusive language translations, 328–329
inerrancy of, 51, 61, 155, 156, 270, 299, 342, 401, 451, 561, 688
kingdom of God and, 227, 228–229
kosher regulations, 378
Lent and, 389
liberation theology and, 394
Luther and, 248, 399
marriage and, 418
miracles and, 451, 452
Mormons and, 75, 129
Nation of Islam and, 68, 478
Navigators and, 485
new religious movements and, 493
New Revised Standard Version, 477
patriarchy legitimization by, 328, 521
preaching commentary on, 449, 546, 657
Presbyterian reliance on, 549, 660
Qur'an compared with, 580
rabbinic midrash, 446
Rastafari interpretation, 587
Reconstructionist Christianity and, 589
salvation and, 637
school readings rulings, 267, 272, 544, 545
spirituals and, 700
on suffering, 241–242, 704, 731
as ultimate authority, 237
vernacular, 60, 61
Wisdom literature, 781–782
womanist theology and, 783
Word of Faith Movement, 786
See also Hebrew Bible; Old Testament; Torah; specific books
Bible and I Ching Relationships (McCaffree), 322
Bible Belt, 271
Bible Institute of Los Angeles, 485
Bible Presbyterian Church, 162
Bible Presbyterian Synod, 271
Bible Tract Society. See Jehovah's Witnesses
Biblical BluePrint Series, The (North ed.), 589
Biktashev, Val, 260
Bilalian News, The (newspaper), 462
Bill of Rights, 233, 266, 361, 407

American movements, 173, 302, 317, 407, 491, 536, 598, 717
animal rights and, 22
Buddha and, 85–86
celibacy, 100, 669
chanting, 107
Chinese-American, 113, 114–115, *114*
cremation, 159
death and, 178
deep ecology movement and, 182
definition, 734
dharma, 58, 85, 88, 90, 187–188, 591, 736
enlightenment quest, 221, 222–223, 357–358, 576, 734
euthanasia and, 236
gay and lesbian participation, 390, 392
gender roles, *276*, 277
home shrines, 428
Japanese-American, 339, 340, 421
Jewish Renewal and, 351
karma concept, 373
Korean-American, 376–377
mantra recitation, 412
meditation, 89, 317, 420–421, 428, 433, 435
meditative visualization, 773
monasteries, 595, 734, 735
New Age blends of, 59, 81, 537
nirvāna, 495–497
as patriarchal, 522
quantum physics comparison, 576
reincarnation, 591–592
relic veneration, 592–593
salvation conception, 637, 638
Soka Gakkai, 682–683
spiritual journey, 357–358
tantra, 716, 717
temples, 115, 536, 725, 726
Theosophy and, 732
vegetarianism, 766
World Parliament of Religions, 279
yoga, 791
See also Tibetan Buddhism
Buddhist Churches of America, 87, 798
Buddhist Mission of North America, 87
Buddhist Society of America, 798
Building design. *See* Architecture
Bulimia, 265
Bultmann, Rudolf, 243, 471
Burhoe, Ralph Wendell, 744
Burleigh, Celia, 504
Burners-Lee, Tim, 168
Burning Hell, The (film), 299
Burr and Burton Seminary, *664*
Burroughs, Edgar Rice, 689
Burroughs, William, 202
Bush, George, 267, 604
Buswell, Robert, Jr., 799
Buttrick, David, 547
Byodo-In (Oahu, Hawaii), *725*
Byron, Lord, 281

C

C&E (consciousness and energy), 585
Cabrini, Saint Frances Xavier, 524, 622, 636

Caesar, Julius, 91
Caesaro-papism, 124
Cahensly, Peter Paul, 622
Caitanya, 470
Calendars, **91–92**
   Advent, 4
   Celtic holy days, 103
   Chanukah, 91, 107
   Chinese festivals, 114
   Easter, 205
   Eastern Orthodox feasts, 208
   Epiphany, 223–225
   Jaina holidays, 339
   Jewish High Holy Days, 346–347
   Latino traditional cycles, 384
   Lent observance, 389, 390
   mestizo celebrations, 443
   Passover, 516
   Shavuot, 673
   Wheel of the Year, 629–630
   Wiccan, 629–630, 779
   winter solstice festivals, 91, 119
   See also Liturgy and worship
Caliphs, 333
Callahan, Kennon, 127
Calligraphy, 580
Calvary Baptist Church (N.Y.C.), 794
Calvary Chapel, **92–93**, 110, 344, *437*, 531
Calvary Chapel Yorba Linda, 768
Calvert, Cecil, 621
Calvin, John, 22, 145, 394, 413, 549
Calvinism
   altar and, 16
   Baptist tradition and, 32, 33, 50, 52
   condemnation of Christmas festivals, 119
   predestination doctrine, 270, 560, 561
   Reconstructionist, 588
   revival movements, 237
   salvation, 152, 562, 637
   Unitarian-Universalist opposing views, 756
   See also Puritanism
Camakam, 765
Cameron, Julia, 577
Camilista groups, 393
Campaign for a Peace Tax Fund, 508
Campbell, Joseph, **93–94**, 359, 472, 473, 577, 782
   and rites of passage, 611, 612, 613, 614
Camp Meeting Hour, The (radio program), 709
Campolo, Tony, 77
Campus Crusade for Christ, **94–95**, 239, 330, 377, 485
   Expo '72, 344
   Fasting and Prayer event, 254
   Moral Rearmament as model, 456
Campus Life, 794, 795
Camus, Albert, 243
Canaanite Temple, 497
Candlemas, 384, 629
Cannibalism, 23, 387
Canonization. *See* Sainthood
Cantombié, 24, 641
Cantors, 364, 711
Cantwell v. *Connecticut* (1940), 125, 126
Capadocian Fathers, 158

Capitalism, 220–221
   Prosperity Theology and, 528, 529, 561–562
   Reconstructionist Christian, 589
   theism and, 730
   work ethic and, 787
Capital punishment, **95–98**, 221, 460, 696
   Moral Majority support for, 604
   pacifist action groups against, *84*, 508
   theistic assumptions, 730
   value of life and, 235, 762
Capra, Fritjof, 452
Cardiac Celts, 103
Carismatico Católico Latino-Americano, 98–99
Caritas (charity), 397
Carlebach, Shlomo, 370
Carlson, Carole C., 448
Carmelites, 423, 608
Carnegie, Andrew, 561
Carrasco, David, 672
Carroll, John, 423
Carter, Jimmy, 495, 688
   as born again Christian, 52, 76, 152
   defeat by Reagan, 267
   evangelical Christian support for, 454
   human rights emphasis, 234
Carus, Paul, 719, 798
Carvalho, Emanuel Nunes, 582
Casey, Solanus, 636
Casimir, Saint, 523
Cassian, John, 104
Cassock, 140, 141
Castaneda, Carlos, 577, 673
Castro, Fidel, 9
Cataphatic meditation, 433
Catechism, 61
Catechism of the Catholic Church (1992), 110, 416
Cathedral of St. John the Divine (N.Y.C.), 156–157, *225*, 619
Catholic Alliance, 117
Catholic Charismatic Renewal, **98–99**, 215, 245, 280, 531
   faith healing, 186, 294
   Holy Spirit and, 691
   mysticism, 470
   new praise songs, 465
   paranormal events, 515
   religious experience, 598
   spiritual warfare and, 186–187
Catholic Healthcare West, 788
Catholicism. *See* Roman Catholicism
Catholic Sociological Society, 681
Catholics United for the Faith, 622
Catholic Worker, **99–100**, 622
Catholic Worker (newspaper), 99–100
Cattell, Raymond, 565
Cave paintings, 612
Cayce, Edgar, 515, 563, 697, 742
CBN (Christian Broadcasting Network), 604, 618, 723
C.E. (Common Era), 92
Cecilia, Saint, 523
Celebi, Celaleddin, 435
Celestial Kingdom (Mormon), 457
Celestine Prophecy, The (Redfield), 470
Celibacy, **100–102**, 173, 569
   chastity vs., 110

communion, 144–146
conservative. See Fundamentalist
    Christianity
conversion, 151–152
creationism, 155–156
creed, 157–158
cremation, 158, 159
cross as symbol, 529
divinity, 191
divorce and, 193–194
dowsing and, 199
early glossolalia, 280
early links with Rome, 624–625
eschatology, 228–229
evil and, 240–242
exorcism, 244–245
faith, 247–248
faith healing, 292–293
feminist spirituality, 256
global adherents, 279
healing practices, 292, 293
hell and, 299–300
heresy and, 71–72, 95, 300–301
Holocaust's significance to, 308, 309–
    310
Holy Spirit's function in, 691–692
human rights and, 233
inclusive language, 328–329
indigenous theologies, 453
Jewish bilateral discussions, 217
Jews for Jesus, 351–352
journeys and, 357
liturgy and worship, 394–396
Marian devotions, 412–414
matriarchal sects, 431
millennialism, 447–448
miracles, 451
missionary movements, 452–454
Moral Rearmament, 455–456
Nation of Islam and, 480, 497
Native American Church and, 480
ordination, 503–504
popular, 537
prayer, 542–543
priesthood, 552–554
process theology, 557
proselytizing origins in, 559
rapture concept, 586
salvation, 637–638
Second Coming, 651–653
slavery justification, 5
spirit possession, 694
spirituality concept, 698
suffering, 241–242, 704
temptation, 727–728
theodicy, 731
Torah and, 739
transcendence, 743
Trinity, 746–748
vestments, 140–141
womanist theology, 782–783
Women's Aglow Fellowship
    International, 783–784
See also Evangelical Christianity;
    Fundamentalist Christianity; Judeo-
    Christian tradition; specific branches,
    denominations, and sects
Christianity Today (journal), 97, 142, 239,
    286, 567

Christian Knights of the KKK, 381
Christian Methodist Episcopal Church, 7,
    443, 445
Christian music industry, 344
Christian Nurses' Fellowship, 330
Christian perfection, 305, 306
Christian political realism, 495
Christian Reconstructionism. See
    Reconstructionist Christianity
Christian Right. See Religious Right
Christian Science, 117–119, 274, 494
    Divine Truth and, 509
    goodness as more real than evil, 240,
        295, 494
    health beliefs, 118, 119, 292, 294–295,
        494
    as matriarchal, 431, 432
    Mother-Father God image, 284, 669
    as New Thought movement, 494, 509
    pilgrimage holy site, 536
    Spirit and, 692
    Unity and, 757, 758
    visualization and, 773
Christian Science Monitor (newspaper), 117
Christian Science Theological Seminary,
    494
Christian Science Thought (periodical), 758
Christian socialism, 495
Christian Voice, 455, 604
Christian World Liberation Front, 344
Christ Is the Answer, 344
Christman, Bruce, 593
Christmas, 56, 119–121, 342
    Advent and, 4
    calendar date, 91
    Chanukah and, 91, 108, 120
    civil displays, 40, 121, 730
    Epiphany and, 119, 223
    Latino traditions, 385, 539–540
    winter solstice correspondence, 91,
        119, 629
Christmas Carol, A (Dickens), 120, 121
Christmas tree, 120, 120
Christocentric Liberalism, 408
Christology
    Coptic Orthodox Church, 153
    creed of Chalcedon, 158
    humanity and historicity emphasis,
        284
    Trinitarian, 746
Christopher, Saint, 524, 594
Ch'uan, 18
Chuang Tzu, 358, 717
Church, 121–124
    altar placement in, 16–17
    arson and bombings, 634
    attendance, 41–42
    denominations, 123, 162
    financing methods, 260–262
    Generation X programs, 278
    heresy, 300–301
    megachurch, 436–437
    Mennonite, 439
    parish, 515–516
    postdenominational, 540
    as religious community, 596
    in United States, 122–123
    Weber's model, 121–122, 183, 655
    See also Denomination; Sect

Church, Frank, 604
Church and state, 124–127
    academic religious studies, 607
    atheism and, 40
    blasphemy and, 72
    born again Christians and, 152
    Christian Coalition and, 116–117
    Christian Science childhood deaths
        controversy, 118–119
    Christmas display suits and, 121, 730
    civil religion and, 125, 126, 133, 730
    conscientious objection and, 150–151,
        507–508
    creationism-antievolution laws, 155,
        156
    culture wars, 165–166
    disestablishment of all churches, 260
    European state-established church, 122
    evangelical politicization, 239
    fundamentalist politicization, 272
    Jewish law vs. secular separation of,
        349–350
    kippah-wearing controversy, 376
    Mormon polygamy, 125, 128
    Native American Church, 481
    new religious movements and, 491
    Niebuhr's views on, 495
    papacy and, 511–513
    political party moral agendas, 268
    prayer in school and, 543, 544–545
    public prayer and, 543
    Puritanism and, 237
    religious freedom and, 126, 266–268,
        599–600
    religious journalism and, 354, 355
    religious officiants of marriages, 417
    Religious Right agenda on, 603
    Roman Catholicism and, 512–513, 544,
        762
    secularization and, 656–657
    Seventh-Day Adventist issues, 667
    televangelism and, 267
    U.S. constitutional separation, 122–123
    See also Bioethics; Freedom of religion
Church Arson Prevention Act of 1996,
    634
Church buildings. See Architecture
Church Dogmatics (Barth), 398
Churches of Christ, 145, 237
Church for the Fellowship of All Peoples
    (San Francisco), 733
Church growth movement, 127
"Church in The Modern World, The"
    (Vatican II), 763
Church of All Worlds, 192
Church of Christ (Scientist). See Christian
    Science
Church of Christ Uniting, 217
Church of England. See Anglicanism
Church of God (Black Jews), 7
Church of God (Cleveland, Tenn.), 530
Church of God in Christ, 7, 238, 306,
    344, 530, 531
Church of Israel, 708
Church of Jesus Christ of Latter-day
    Saints, 128–131
    angelic visitations, 452, 514
    Bible and, 60
    birth control and, 66

Cyber religion, **167–169**, 272, 298, 588
"Cyberspace," coining of term, 168

D

Dahomey traditions, 8
Daimon, 185
Dalai Lama, 85, *86*, **171–172**, *172*, 221, 611, *675*, 736, 737
Dallas Theological Seminary, 189, 793
Daly, Mary, 257, 284, 303, 476
Damascus Christian Church, 627
Damnation. *See* Hell
Dance, **172–175**
    African, 5, 8
    drumming and, 204
    evangelical Christian bans, 728
    Native American, 465, 481, 482, 483
    New Age sacred, 489
    quinceañara celebration, 578
    rave, 588
    revival, 740
    spirit possession, 694
    Sufi ecstatic, 537
    Sun Dance, 661, 706–708, 772
    trance, 742
Dance therapy, 174
Daniel, Book of, 228, 299, 447, 548, 652, 666, 699
Daniel, Brother, 348
Daniell, A. G., 667
Dante, 21, 299, 620
Darby, John Nelson, 188–189, 549, 586, 652
Dare to Discipline (Dobson), 196
Darrow, Clarence, 12, 155
Darshans (spiritual programs), 437–438
Darwin, Charles, 12, 155, 452, 729
Dasgupta, Surendranath, 217
Dass, Ram, 303, 509, 577, 716
David, King, 552
Davidson, Israel, 646
Davies, Samuel, 237
Davis, Addie, 52, 504
Davis, Andrew Jackson, 693, 695, 697, 706
Davis, Avram, 434
Da'wa, **175–176**
Day, Dorothy, 100, 622, 636
Dayananda Saraswati, 765
Day of Atonement. *See* Yom Kippur
Day of the Dead, 92, **176–177**, 443
Days of Awe. *See* Jewish High Holy Days
DC Talk (music group), 749
Deacon, **177–178**
    Coptic, 153
    Episcopal Church, 226, 227
    historical background, 137, 138, 503
    priesthood and, 552
    vestments, 141
Deadly Deception, The (Shaw and McKenney), 268
Death and dying, **178–181**
    abortion and, 1–3
    afterlife conceptions, 11, 21, 296–297, 299–300
    cremation, 158–159
    Day of the Dead ritual, 92, 176–177, 443

Holocaust and, 308
Jewish memorial service, 346
Jewish mourning ritual, 674
journey symbolism, 357, 358
Latino traditions, 176–177, 386
near death experiences, 485–486
New Age spirituality and, 490
Tibetan Buddhism and, 358
visions and, 771
See also Bioethics; Euthanasia and assisted suicide; Reincarnation
Death of God, 40, **181–182**, 243, 729
Death penalty. *See* Capital punishment
"Declaration Against Speciesism." *See* Animal rights
Declaration of Independence, U.S. (1776), 233, 317
"Declaration of Religious Freedom" (Vatican II), 450, 513, 560, 763
Declaration Towards a Global Ethic, 239
Deconstructionism, 232, 258, 785
Dederich, Charles, 713
Deep ecology, **182–183**, 213, 484; *See also* Ecofeminism
Deep Ecology (Sessions and Devall), 182
Deere, Phillip, 483
Defender of the Bond, 417
De Gaulle, Charles, 763
De Groot, J. J. M., 260
DeHoyos, Art, 268
Deism, 282, 315, 484, 743
Delille, Henriette, 636
Deliverance. *See* Exorcism
Deloria, Ella Cara, 707
Deloria, Vine, 536
Dema deities, 741
Dement, William, 200
Demeter, 748
Democracy, 318, 512, 589
Democratic Party, 337–338, 512, 604
Democritus, 315
Demons. *See* Devils, demons, and spirits
Denial of Death, The (Becker), 180
Denomination, **183–185**
    Appalachian religions, 32
    congregations, 149
    decline of, 239, 723
    divisions over faith, 248–240
    examples, 162
    financing differences, 261
    former cults as, 163, 164
    gender role regulation, 275–276
    intradition proselytization, 560
    Methodist, 443, 445
    new evangelical, 344–345
    new fundamentalist, 271
    new nineteenth-century, 274
    pacifist, 507, 525–527
    Pentacostal, 530, 532
    postdenominational churches, 540
    Presbyterian, 550–551
    Protestant diversity, 408
    as religious community, 596
    as replacement for term "church," 123, 162
    sect development into, 655
    worship music controversy, 464–465
Denver, John, 404
Denver March Powwow, 467

Depression (economic). *See* Great Depression
Depression (emotional), 295
Deprogramming. *See* Anti cult movement; Brainwashing
Derrida, Jacques, 232
Descartes, René, 451, 452
Desecration, 633–634
Desert fathers, 104, 436
Destiny of the Mother Church, The (Knapp), 118
Determinism, 269, 270, 575
Deuteronomy, Book of, 194, 195, 388, 589
Devall, Bill, 182
Devayana, 591
Devils, demons, and spirits, **185–187**, 387
    evil and, 241
    exorcism, 186, 243–245
    hell and, 299
    paranormal beliefs in, 513, 514
    possession by, 694
    shamanism and, 671
    See also Satan; Satanists
Devotionalism, 414
Dewey, John, 231, 316, 527, 756
Dharma, 58, 85, 88, 90, **187–188**, 591, 736
Dharma Bums, The (Kerouac), 434, 469
Dhyana, 797
Dialogue preaching, 547–548
Dianetics, 640, 648–649, 650, 689
Dianic Witchcraft, 285
Dick, Philip K., 281
Dickens, Charles, 120, 121
Dick-Read, Grantly, 65
Didymus School, 153
Diego, Juan, 443, 768–769
Dietary practices. *See* Food
Diet for a New America (Robbins), 767
Diet for a Small Planet (Moore), 767
Dietrich, John, 315
Digambara, 339
Dignity, 233–234, 391
Dilloggún, 641
Dilthey, Wilhelm, 605
Di Mambro, Joseph, 683–684, 690
Diocese
    Episcopal Church, 226
    Roman Catholic, 515, 553, 554
Discipleship Journal, 485
Disciples of Christ, 407, 409
    communion belief, 145
    evangelical elements, 237
    ordination of women, 504
    People's Temple and, 533
    stewardship financing, 261
Disease. *See* Healing; Health
Dispensationalism, **188–189**
    free will and, 269–270
    Holy Land and, 311
    premillennial, 447–448, 549, 586, 589, 652–653
    survivalism and, 708
    Way International, 777–778
Disraeli, Benjamin, 318
Divination, 501, 610
    African-American, 8

Evangelical United Brethren Church, 443–444, 445
Evangelist, The (magazine), 709
Evangelium Vitae (1995), 221, 235
Evans, Warren Felt, 118
Eve, 189, 191, 241, 413, 420, 521, 589, 755
Evidences from Scripture and History of the Second Coming of Christ About the Year 1843, and of His Personal Reign of a Thousand Years (Miller), 5
Evil, **240–242**
  Christianity and, 731
  Christian Science dismissal of, 240, 295, 494
  hell and, 241, 299
  Holocaust and, 309, 729
  Islam and, 732
  Judaism and, 731
  patron saint protection from, 523
  process theology and, 556–557
  suffering and, 704
  theism and, 729
  theodicy and, 731–732
  See also Satanists
Evil spirits. *See* Devils, demons, and spirits
Evolutionism, 25, 729
  creationism vs., 155, 156
  evil and, 241
  fundamentalist countermovements, 272
  totemism and, 741
Excommunication, Mormon, 130
Execution. *See* Capital punishment
Exegesis, of Qur'an, 579–580
Existentialism, 40, **242–243**, 269, 270, 279
"Existentialist Aspects of Modern Art" (Tillich), 243
Existential psychology, 243
Exit counseling. *See* Anti-cult movement
Exman, Eugene, 36
Exodus, 140, 388, 440
  Passover celebration of, 516, 517
  salvation theme, 637, 638
  Shavuot and, 673
  womanist theology and, 783
Exorcism, 186, 187, **243–245**, 694
Exorcist, The (Blatty), 244
Exorcist, The (film), 186
Explanatory Notes Upon the New Testament (Wesley), 444
Expository preaching, 547
Expressive individualism, 317
Extrasensory perception, 562
Extraterrestrial cults. *See* Unidentified flying objects
Extraterrestrial guides, **245–246**, 297, 298, 689, 690, 697, 753
Ezekiel, 652, 770

F

Fabré-Palaprat, Bernard-Raymond, 683
Faces of Buddhism, The (Prebish and Tanaka, eds.), 88–90
Fackenheim, Emil, 309
Factor analysis, 564

Faith, **247–250**
  clerical child abuse and, 112
  Holocaust and, 209
  martyrs and, 522
  sainthood and, 522–524
  salvation by, 296
  snake-handling as test of, 679
  suffering and, 704
  testimony of, 728
  Tillich's redefinition of, 249
Faith and Order Commission, 477, 789
Faith healing, 292, 293, 294–295, 451
  Catholic Charismatic Renewal, 186
  Christian Science, 118, 119, 292, 294–295
  by Jesus, 292, 294
  People's Temple, 533
  preaching and, 547
Faith keepers (Native American women), 430
Faith Message, 786
Faith Temple, 391
Falun Dafa, 114
Falun Gong, 114
Falwell, Jerry, 77, 239, **250–251**, 267, 311, 366, 454–455, 604, 605, 619, 709, 784
  anti-Semitism and, 29
  Baptist affiliation, 52
  dispensationalism, 189
  televangelism, 722, 723
Familiaris Consortio (pastoral letter), 416
Families 2000, 117
Family, The, **251–252**, 397
  commune, 143
  as cult movement, 27, 162–163, 344
  "flirty fishing" practice, 251, 277
"Family, The: A Proclamation to the World" (Mormon statement), 129
Family Channel, 618
Family Federation for World Peace and Unification, 755
Family group conferencing, 555, 556
Family life
  bar mitzvah and bat mitzvah significance, 53–54
  birth control and, 276, 670
  Christian Coalition view of, 116
  Focus on the Family program, 262–263
  food and mealtime, 264
  gender roles and, 276
  home schooling, 312–314
  Jewish marriage and, 419, 427
  matriarchal power, 429–430, 521
  Mormon emphasis, 129–130, 194
  Orthodox Judaism and, 276
  Passover seder, 516–517
  Religious Right agenda on, 603
  reunions, 609
  Unification Church, 755
Family planning. *See* Birth control
Family Research Council, 117, 196
Family values rhetoric, 185, 193, 196, 366, 603, 605, 784
Family Worship Center (Baton Rouge), 709
Famine, 265
Fanaticism, 493

Fard, W. D., 7, 13, 68, **252**, 253, 460, 461, 478–479
Farley, Margaret, 397–398
Farmer, Paula, 220
Farndu, Mort, *219*
Farr, Florence, 159
Farrakhan, Louis, **253–254**
  anti-Semitism and, 28, 253
  Muhammad (Elijah) and, 461, 463
  Muhammad (Warwith Deen) reconciliation, 463
  Nation of Islam and, 8, 14, 70, 333, 461, 479–480
Farrow, Mia, 744
Fasching, Darrell J., 310
Fasting, **254–255**
  Advent, 4
  Baha'i and, 45
  Islam and, 15, 254, 331, 579
  Jainism and, 339
  Judaism and, 54, 254, 346, 363
  Latino tradition and, 384
  Lenten, 389–390
  Nation of Islam and, 479
  as purification, 569
  vision quest, 482, 693, 707, 771, 772
Fatalism, 30, 32
Father Divine, 7, **255–256**, 533
Fatherhood of God, 157, 158
Father's Blessing. *See* Toronto Blessing
Fatima shrine (Portugal), 414, 535
Faulkner, William, 62
Faure, Bernard, 799
Feast of Lights (Theophany), 223
Feast of Weeks. *See* Shavuot
Federal Council of Churches, 409, 477, 722
Federation of Jaina Associations in North America, 339
Federation of Reconstructionist Congregations and Havurot, 364
Fellowship of Christian Socialists, 495
Fellowship of Intentional Communities, 596
Fellowship of Reconciliation, 495, 508
Female figurines, 521
Feminism
  abortion arguments, 2–3
  on abuse of power, 112
  Baha'i and, 45
  body and, 73, 173, 699
  dogmatism and, 197
  gender role changes and, 275–276
  inclusive language and, 328, 669
  Las Hermanas and, 383–384
  love as self-sacrifice critique, 398
  marriage and divorce, 193
  masculine spirituality and, 427
  Mormon movement, 130
  Muslim, 276
  nineteenth-century, 275, 695, 696
  nonpatriarchal God and, 192
  on pregnancy and menstruation pollution, 568
  process theology and, 557
  Quaker participants, 573
  reaction against Promise Keepers, 559
  religious and secular relationship, 275
  Spiritualism and, 695, 696

mainline Protestantism and, 407
as missionizing aid, 454
new religious movements and, 491
peyote use and, 126, 481, 600
prayer in school rulings, 544–545
Religious Freedom Restoration Act of
1993, 600
religious persecution and, 601–602
religious pluralism and, 408
sacrilege and, 633, 634
school issues, 126, 155, 156, 545
Seventh-Day Adventist issues, 667
toleration laws, 266
Vatican II statement, 413
Freedoms Foundation, 366
Free love, 143
Free-market economy, 561–562
Freemasonry, **268**, 653, 654, 683
nature religion and, 484
Noble Drew Ali and, 497
occult elements, 500
pentagram symbol and, 529
Rosicrucians and, 626, 627
Free Methodist Church, 305, 443
Free Religious Association, 756
Free the Children of God, 165–165
Freethinkers, 315
Free will, **268–270**
Arminian Baptists and, 50, 52
to choose between good and evil, 240–
241
God's power vs., 731
predestination vs., 561
quantum physics and, 575
Unitarian Universalist emphasis, 756
Free Will Baptists, 32
French Revolution, 512, 626
Freud, Sigmund, 93, 229, 473, 518, 565,
729, 765
dream analysis, 200
on totemism, 741
unconscious, 243, 606
Freudian Myth of the Birth of the Hero
(Rank), 93
Friedland, Israel, 646
Friends Committee on National
Legislation, 507, 525
Friends General Conference, 525
Friendship Press, 477
Friends Upper Meeting, 525
Fromm, Erich, 527, 565
Fruit of Islam, 68
Fry, Franklin Clark, 400
Frymer-Kensky, Tikva, 65
Fuller, Charles E., 485
Fuller Theological Seminary, 127, 238,
540
Full Gospel Businessmen's Fellowship
International, 109, 531, 784
Full Gospel Business Men's Voice
(magazine), 109
Full Gospel Women's Fellowship. *See*
Women's Aglow Fellowship
International
Functionalism, 471
Fundamentalism Project, 422
Fundamentalist Christianity, **270–273**
abortion and, 3, 671
apocalyptic, 272, 447–448

astrology and, 39
Baptist tradition and, 51
biblical inerrancy belief, 61, 155, 270
Christian Coalition, 116–117
culture wars, 166, 271–272
dispensationalism, 188, 189
dogmatism, 197, 546–547
evangelical postfundamentalists, 238–
239
faith and, 249
first generation of, 270
five fundamental teachings, 270
Freemasonry criticism by, 268
healing practices, 292
Holy Land and, 311
home schooling, 312–314
Identity Christianity, 324
Jehovah's Witnesses and, 342
mainline Protestantism vs., 408
millennialism, 447–448
missionary movements, 454
Moral Majority, 250, 251, 267, 455
patriarchal religion and, 521, 522
Pentecostals compared with, 530, 619
political involvement, 267, 271–272,
603–605
preaching emphasis, 546–547
premillennial dispensationalism, 447–
448, 586, 589
rapture concept, 586
as reactive movement, 272
Reconstructionist, 588–589
rejection of Pentecostals by, 530
Religious Right, 603–605
schisms within, 271
Seventh-Day Adventists and, 667
strength in South, 270–271, 687, 688–
689
survivalism and, 708
televangelism, 250–251, 267, 721–723
theism, 730
True Love Waits movement, 749–750
Fundamentals, The (twelve-volume series),
271, 549
Funeral
afterlife and, 11
cost of, 180
gay and lesbian, 390
Satanic, 387
Furfey, Paul Hanly, 100
Furman v. Georgia (1972), 96
Future of religion, **273–274**
patriarchy and, 521–522

G

Gabriel, Angel, 413, 578
Gaia hypothesis, 213
Gaillot, Jacques, 169
Galactic Federation, 246
Galileo, 762
Gallicans, 512
Gamblers Anonymous, 751
Ganden Palace Victory Government
(Tibet), 736
Gandhi, Mohandas, 59, 171, 182, 188,
373, 374, 495, 508, *508*, 733, 766
Gandhi, Virchand Raghavji, 338

Ganeśa, 765
Gangaji, 765
Ganges, 357
García, Robert, 154
Garden Grove Community Church
(Calif.), 547, 646–647
Garden of Eden, 241
Gardner, Gerald, 103, 487, 748, 778, 779
Gardner, Martin, 452
Garrison, William Lloyd, 573
Garvey, Marcus, 69, 410, 461, 497, 587
Garvey Movement, 478
Gaskin, Ina May, 65
Gates, Bill, 728
Gathering of the Nations Powwow, 467
Gawain, Shakti, 773
Gay American Indians, 392
Gayman, Dan, 708
Gay rights. *See* Lesbian and gay rights
movement
Gébelin, Antoine Count de, 720
Geertz, Clifford, 607, 681
Geller, Larry, 220
Geller, Uri, 562
Gelupka Buddhism, 172
Gemara, 581, 715, 731
Gender roles, 73, **275–277**
Afro-Cuban religions, 10
bar mitzvah and bat mitzvah, 53–54
biological vs. social determination of,
785
Buddhism amd, 89, 90
divine sexual imagery and, 669
division of labor, 788
divorce and, 193, 194
evangelical changing views of, 263, 276
family reunion, 609
female nineteenth-century preachers,
546
Focus on the Family, 263
Hinduism and, 277, 431
inclusive language and, 327–329, 364,
365
Islam and, 276–277, 459
Jehovah's Witnesses and, 342
Jewish divorce, 194
Jewish marriage, 419, 568
kippah wearing, 375–376
marriage and, 193, 194
masculine spirituality, 426–428
matriarchal core, 429–430
Methodism and, 445
modes of religious participation, 429–
430
Mormon changes, 457
Nation of Islam and, 68, 479
new religious movements and, 493
official religious vs. secularized
operative norms, 275, 276
ordination of women, 275–276, 503,
504–505
orthodox Judaism approaches, 365,
711
pastoral counseling and, 519
patriarchy and, 275, 276, 277, 431,
521–522
pollution and purification rites, 568
priestesses and, 551, 552
Promise Keepers and, 557, 558, 559

Hierophany, 610
Higgins, John, 344
Higher education. *See* Seminaries;
    Universities
Higher Institute of Coptic Studies, 153
High Holy Days. *See* Jewish High Holy
    Days
Hijra. See Hegira
Hilary of Poitiers, 155
Hildegard of Bingen, 156
Hill, E. V., 547
Hill, Steve, 83
Hiltner, Seward, 518
Himes, Joshua, 5
Hīnayāna Buddhism, 85
Hinckley, Gordon B., 75, 457
Hinds, Robert, 587
Hinduism, 45, 56, 81, **302–305**, 373
    afterlife and, 10, 178
    American membership increases, 656
    American movements, 303, 329–330,
        407, 491, 584–585, 662–663, 759,
        763–764, 792
    animal rights and, 22
    apocalypticism and, 29
    ashram, 36–37, 190, 583
    avatar, 42–43, 437–438
    Bhagavad Gītā, 58–59
    celibacy, 100, 669
    chakra, 105
    chanting, 107
    cremation, 159
    death, 178
    dharma, 187, 188
    enlightenment, 221–222
    euthanasia and assisted suicide
        outlook, 236
    female fasting, 254
    feminist goddess worship, 277, 431,
        669
    Four States of Life, 612
    gay and lesbian participation, 390
    gender roles, 277, 431
    guru, 287
    Jaina shared worship space, 338
    journeys and, 357
    mantra recitation, 412
    meditation, 433, 459–460
    mysticism and, 469
    New Age ideas and, 466
    New Thought movement and, 494
    pantheism and, 509
    pantheons of deities, 510
    as patriarchal, 277, 522
    pilgrimage sites, 536, 676
    Ramakrishna movement, 584–585
    reincarnation, 591
    salvation conception, 637, 638
    Self-Realization Fellowship, 662–663
    sexual imagery, 669
    spirits, 186
    tantra, 716–717
    temples, 304, 536, 725–726
    Theosophy and, 732
    transcendence and, 743
    Transcendental Meditation and, 744–
        748
    Upanishads, 758–759
    Vedanta Society, 763–764

Vedas, 764–766
vegetarianism, 766
visualization, 773
World Parliament of Religions
    representation, 279, 759
yoga, 303, 466, 791–793
Hinduism Today (newspaper), 37
Hindu Students Council, 305
Hinn, Benny, 451, 547
Hip-hop music, 467
Hippies. *See* Counterculture
Hispanic American Bible School
    (N.Y.C.), 154
Hispanics. *See* Latino traditions
His Place coffee house (Los Angeles),
    344
Historical Atlas of World Mythology
    (Campbell), 94
History of Religious Ideas, A (Eliade), 607
Hitler, Adolf, 241
Hobbes, Thomas, 318
Hodel, Don, 117
Hodge, Charles, 409
Hoff, Benjamin, 718
Hoge, Dean, 127
Hohokam culture, 471
Holiday Inn (film), 121
Holiness Church of California, 306
Holiness Movement, 239, **305–306**
    African-American, 7
    Appalachian, 32–33
    glossolalia, 515
    Holy Spirit and, 691
    Latin American, 279
    Methodist theological heritage, 444
    offshoots, 306
    Salvation Army, 638–639
    snake-handling, 679–680
    See also Pentecostal and Charismatic
        Christianity
Holistic health, **306–308**
    alternative medicine and, 18–19, 293–
        294, 295–296
    New Age spirituality and, 488–491
    yoga and, 792
Holistic Health Handbook, The, 308
Holly, 119
Hollywood First Presbyterian Church
    (Calif.), 109
Hollywood Free Paper, The (newspaper),
    344
Holmes, Ernest S., 494
Holocaust, **308–310**
    abortion and, 3
    anti-Semitism and, 28, 601–602
    "death of God" and, 181
    evil and, 241, 309, 729
    Hasidic survivors, 289
    and hell as earthly dimension, 300
    human rights and, 233
    Jewish identity and, 348
    salvation conceptions, 637
    Six-Day War symbolism and, 308
    theism and, 729
    Yom Hashoah commemoration, 441
    Zionism and, 801
Holocaust Museum, U.S., 776
Holonomics (*I Ching* hexagrams), 322
Holy Ark, 346, 711

Holy Bible. *See* Bible
Holy Book of Women's Mysteries, The
    (Budapest), 285
Holy cards, 413
Holy Communion. *See* Communion
Holy Eucharist. *See* Communion
Holy Ghost. *See* Holy Spirit
Holy Koran of the Moorish Science Temple
    (Noble Drew Ali), 13, 497
Holy Land, **310–312**
    Hasidim and, 289–290
    Judaism and, 360
    pilgrimages to, 311, 535
    spiritual journeys and, 356–357
    Zionism and, 799–800
    See also Israel, State of; Jerusalem
Holy Mother (Sarada Devi), 584
Holy Order of MANS, 163, 493
Holy Orders. *See* Ordination
Holy Rollers, 271
Holy Saturday, 389, 632
Holy Spirit
    Appalachian Holiness religions and, 32
    born again evangelism and, 76
    Charismatic Movement, 98, 108, 109,
        110, 215, 465
    Christian theology and, 691–692, 747
    credal articles, 158
    divinity and, 191
    emotional states and, 215
    faith healing and, 292
    gifts of, 280
    papal infallibility and, 512
    Pentecostal emphasis on, 238, 271,
        280, 503, 530, 617
    Presbyterian emphasis on, 550
    revelation and, 610
    Sophia-Wisdom and, 684–685
    Word of Faith Movement and, 786
    See also Baptism in the Holy Spirit;
        Glossolalia; Trinity
Holy Thursday. *See* Maundy Thursday
Holy unction, 208
Holy war. *See* Jihad
Holy Week, 205, 390
Holy Wine Ceremony, 191
Holy Years, 625
Homage to the Devil (Martin), 244
Homans, George, 318
Home of Truth, 758
Homeopathy, 8, 17, 293, 295
Homer, 471
Home schooling, **312–314**
Homosexuality
    culture wars and, 165, 185
    Episcopal Church and, 226
    fundamentalist condemnation of, 342
    inclusion in faith communities, 670–
        671
    Islam and, 670
    as Nazi victims, 241
    Roman Catholicism and, 110, 633, 670
    sexual abuse of children mistakenly
        identified with, 112
    See also Lesbian and gay rights
        movement
Honesty, 391
Hood, Ralph, 197
Hoover, Herbert, 239, 512

Catholic Charismatic Renewal, 109
Catholic Worker, 99–100
cyberspace, 168–169
evangelical, 142, 286, 709
evangelical fundamentalist, 239
Focus on the Family, 262, 263
fundamentalist, 271
hymnal, 464, 467
InterVarsity Press, 330–331
Jaina, 339
Jesus Movement, 344
Jewish Renewal, 351, 363
Nation of Islam, 461
Navigators, 485
Niebuhr, Reinhold, 495
Peale, Norman Vincent, 528
Pentecostal, 531
Promise Keepers, 559
rapture concept, 586
Reconstructionist Christian, 589
Seventh-Day Adventist, 667, 668
sociology journals, 681
Spiritualist, 696
Sufi, 56, 705
Puebla Document (1978), 537
Puerto Rico
    Catholic Charismatic Revival, 98, 99
    first U.S. Roman Catholic diocese,
        620–621
    Marian shrine, 414, 425
    patron saint, 523
    Rosseau, Leoncia Rosado, 627–628
    santos, 642
    spiritualism, 245
Punishment. *See* Capital punishment;
    Evil; Sin; Suffering
Punjab, 667–668
Pure Land Buddhism, 87, 89, 115, 172,
    223, 340, 341, 497, 798
    mantra, 412
Pure Monday, 389
Pure white light. *See* Kundalini
Purgation, 569
Purgatory, 296, 414, 620
Purification, 30, **568–569**
    afterlife, 10
    mikveh, 111, 447
    sweat lodge, 710
Purim, 161
Puritanism
    apocalypticism, 30
    Baptist dissenter, 50
    condemnation of Christmas festivals,
        119
    congregations, 149
    conservatism, 602
    Easter and, 205
    establishment in Massachusetts, 266,
        407
    European persecution of, 248
    evangelical similarities and differences,
        237
    faith and, 248
    hell concept, 299
    infant baptism, 47
    liturgy and worship, 394
    masculine spirituality, 426
    New England seen as promised land,
        310

and new kingdom of God, 228
preaching as central to, 546
predestination doctrine precluding
    proselytization, 560
Prosperity Theology, 561
Quakerism vs., 571
Quaker persecution by, 47, 600–601
Salem witch trials, 300, 301
salvation, 637
utopian "city on a hill,"143, 228
wealth as sign of divine election,
    213
wilderness concept, 476
See also Calvinism; Congregationalism
Puritan work ethic. *See* Work ethic
Purity and Danger (Douglas), 73
Pursel, Jach (Lazaris), 106, 387
Puruṣa, 221–222
Pynchon, Thomas, 281
Pyramid, 34
Pythagoras, 465–466, 592, 732

Q

Qabalistic sign, 529
Qazwini, al-, 21
Qi. See Ch'i
Qigong, 114
Quadragesima, 389
Quadragesimo Anno (1931), 220
Quakers, **571–574**
    blasphemy charges against, 72
    capital punishment opposition, 98
    degrees of pacifism, 525
    gay and lesbian acceptance by, 391–
        392
    as historic peace church, 507, 525
    liberation theology and, 393
    marriage and, 417
    mysticism, 598
    pacifism, 150, 507, 515, 525, 526,
        571–573
    persecution of, 47, 571–572, 600–601
    rejection of ordination, 139, 503
    sacrament nonrecognition by, 631
    salvation, 637
    Sanctuary Movement, 640
    as sect, 183, 655
Quantum healing, 490, **574**
Quantum Healing (Chopra), 574
Quantum mechanics, 575, 690
Quantum physics, 322, 451, 574, **575–**
    576, 779
Quayle, Dan, 604
Queen of the Heaven, 113, 114
Queer studies, 258
Quest, **576–577**
    gender roles, 699
    as journey, 356
    mystical, 470
    New Age spirituality, 598
    as rave culture element, 588
    See also Vision quest
Quest generation, 491
Quietism, 399, 509
Quimby, Phineas P., 117–118, 563
Quinceañera, La, 386, **577–578**
Quinley, Harold E., 602

Quorum of the Twelve Apostles
    (Mormon), 130
Qur'an, 192, **578–580**
    Allah and, 13–15
    on bearing witness, 175
    discipline of, 332, 333
    on infidelity and apostasy, 71
    interpretation of, 579–580
    jihad references, 352
    on Ka'bah, 432
    as Muhammad's revelations, 331, 452,
        610
    mullah study of, 463
    Nation of Islam and, 68, *69*, 478
    polygamy provision, 276–277
    published as Holy Koran (1928), 7
    recitation vocalization, 107
    on spirits, 537
    structure and themes, 578–579
    on suffering, 704, 731–732
    women's rights under, 318
Quraysh, 331, 432, 578
Qusayy, 432
Qutb, Sayyid, 468

R

Rabbi Isaac Elhanan Theological
    Seminary, 583
Rabbinate, **581–583**
    circumcision regulation, 132
    Conservative, 646
    gender roles and, 275, 364
    Hasidic, 289, 290, 365, 712
    as Judaism's basis, 360
    marriage encouragement, 449
    as marriage officiants, 418, *419*
    midrash study, 446–447
    ordination, 503, 504
    ordination of women, 364, 503, 505,
        583
    Orthodox, 712
    Reform, 362, 364
    Talmud study, 715
    Torah study, 739
    vestment, 140
Rabbinical Assembly (of Conservative
    Rabbis), 363
Rabbinical Council of America, 583
Rabbinical Council of the Union of
    Jewish Congregations in America,
    362
Racial segregation, 135–136, 685
Racism and religion
    African-American preaching against,
        547
    anthropology of religion and, 26
    apocalypticism, 30
    arson of African-American churches,
        634
    Baha'i condemnation of, 45
    dogmatism and, 197
    Falwell sermon, 250
    Farrakhan statement, 253
    Father Divine's interracial movement,
        255–256
    Identity Christianity and, 324
    Kahane beliefs, 370–371